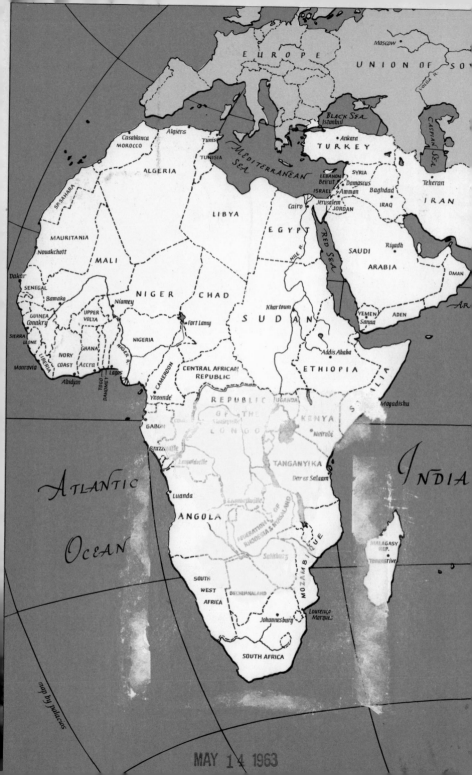

CIALIST   REPUBLICS

MONGOLIA

AMUR R.

N.KOREA
Peking   Pyongyang
Seoul
S.KOREA

JAPAN
Tokyo

C H I N A

YELLOW R.

YANGTZE R.

KASHMIR
Srinagar
Rawalpindi
N

New Delhi
HIMALAYAS   BRAHMAPUTRA
NEPAL
Katmandu   BHUTAN
GANGES R.   E.PAK.
Calcutta   Dacca
BURMA

MEKONG R.

Taipei
TAIWAN

PACIFIC

CHINA SEA

OCEAN

I N D I A

Bombay

BAY OF
BENGAL

Rangoon

THAILAND

Bangkok

CAMBODIA

Phnom Penh

N.VIETNAM
Hanoi
LAOS
Vientiane

S.VIETNAM
Saigon

Manila

PHILIPPINE
REPUBLIC

CEYLON
Colombo

Kuala Lumpur
MALAYA
Singapore

SUMATRA

BRUNEI
NORTH
BORNEO
SARAWAK

BORNEO

EQUATOR

OCEAN

INDONESIA

Djakarta
JAVA   BALI

WEST
NEW
GUINEA

A U S T R A L I A

SUBVERSION
OF THE INNOCENTS

BOOKS BY *Dan Kurzman*

KISHI AND JAPAN

SUBVERSION OF THE INNOCENTS

SUBVERSION
of the
INNOCENTS

Patterns of Communist Penetration in Africa, the Middle East, and Asia

DAN KURZMAN

RANDOM HOUSE

NEW YORK

Grateful acknowledgment is made to the following:

Stanford University Press for permission to quote from *The Philippine Answer to Communism,* by Alvin H. Scaff. © 1955 by the Board of Trustees of the Leland Stanford Junior University.

The Daily Telegraph and Morning Post (London) for permission to quote from "Moscow Trained Me for Revolt in Africa" by Anthony G. Okotcha, *Sunday Telegraph,* July 16, 1961.

Time magazine for quotations from the issues of August 30, 1954; February 16 and April 13, 1959; December 8, 1961.

Smith Keynes & Marshall for permission to quote from *The Philosophy of the Revolution* by Gamal Abdel Nasser (1959).

St Martin's Press, Inc., for permission to quote from *The Dragon's Seed* by Norman S. Elegant (1959).

Frederick A. Praeger, Inc., for permission to quote from *The Soviet Union and the Middle East* by Walter Z. Laquer (1959).

The *Washington Post* for permission to quote from an article by J. R. Wiggins (March, 1960).

Asian Survey for permission to quote from an article by Dr. Guy J. Pauker (March, 1961).

The New York Times for permission to quote from an article by B. Kalb (October 29, 1960) and an article by Robert Trumbull (January 20, 1962). Copyright by *The New York Times.*

The New York Times Magazine for permission to quote from "The Koran vs. *Das Kapital*" by Richard P. Hunt (May 10, 1959). Copyright by *The New York Times.*

Taplinger Publishing Company, Inc., for permission to quote from *The People Win Through* by U Nu (1957).

The HRAF Press for permission to quote from *Cambodia* by David J. Steinberg (1959).

Atheneum Publishers for permission to quote from *Stanley's Way* by Thomas L. Sterling (1961).

The *American Universities Field Staff Reports Service* for permission to quote from "From Jail to Jail: The Saga of Tan Malaka" by Willard A. Hanna (April 6, 1959).

The University of Chicago Press for permission to quote from "The Labor Movement of Ghana: A Study in Political Unionism" by Lester N. Trachtman, in *Economic Development and Cultural Change* (January, 1962). © 1962, by the University of Chicago.

Leon Dennen for permission to quote from *Trouble Zone* by Leon Dennen. Ziff-Davis Publishing Company (1945).

Duell, Sloan & Pearce, Inc., for permission to quote from *The Khrushchev Pattern* by Frank Gibney (1960).

Charles Scribner's Sons for permission to quote from *The Yennen Way* by Eudocio Ravines (1951).

Joel M. Halpern for use of his Laos project papers (1961).

The RAND Corporation for permission to quote from *Communist Strategy in Laos* by Abraham Meyer Halpern and H. B. Fredman (1960) and *Government, Politics and Social Structure of Laos* (1961) by Joel M. Halpern.

FOR *Chen*

AUTHOR'S NOTE

The purpose of this book is to illuminate communist methods of infiltration and subversion in the Afro-Asian world, and to appraise their success against the historical and cultural backgrounds of the various countries and regions treated. The situation in almost every nation in Africa, the Middle East, and Asia is considered in some degree, with separate chapters devoted to more important states where the communist problem is serious or of an unusual nature. Japan is the only country dealt with at length that cannot be considered underdeveloped, at least in the industrial sense. Its inclusion was motivated by the fact that significant sectors of the Japanese economy and social structure are still underdeveloped, or feudalistic, and also because Japan is, of course, one of the key nations in Asia.

While based primarily on recent research, this book is the product of some fifteen years of study, news reporting, and personal observation in more than sixty countries of the Afro-Asian world, as well as in the Soviet Union and Europe. It is a reflection of impressions and information gleaned from hundreds of books, magazines, newspapers, pamphlets, and diplomatic and intelligence files. It is also a distillation of thousands of conversations with prime ministers, taxi drivers, emperors, witch-doctors, peasants, students, professors, ambassadors, workers, businessmen, presidents, and fellow news correspondents.

I am deeply indebted to the late Edward Holten-Schmidt for his wise counsel on the handling of this book. I am also grateful to

Editor J. R. Wiggins and Managing Editor Alfred Friendly of
the *Washington Post* for waiting several months for my journalistic
services so that I could complete this work. My brother Cal helped
me greatly, in particular by providing me with his scholarly writings
on India. Igor Oganesoff, *Wall Street Journal* Asian correspondent,
offered invaluable information and advice regarding the Asian portion of the book. I was proud to have Executive Editor Albert
Erskine of Random House as my editor and Ruth Aley as my
agent.

Others whom I wish to thank for donating their talents and aid
include: Donald Klein, China expert for the Asian Foundation;
Richard P. Hunt, *New York Times* Middle East and African ex-
pert; Robert Trumbull, *New York Times* Southeast Asian correspondent; Minako Shimizu Kusaka, Pan-Asia News Agency; Abe
Rosenthal, *New York Times* Asian correspondent; Robert (Pep-
per) Martin, *U.S. News & World Report* Asian correspondent;
Murray Fromson, Columbia Broadcasting System correspondent;
George Natanson, *Los Angeles Times* correspondent; David E.
Reed, *Reader's Digest* expert on Africa and the Middle East; Ar-
nold Beichman, *Christian Science Monitor* labor correspondent;
Leon Dennen, News Enterprise Association authority on communist affairs; Sid Goldberg, Editor of the North American Newspaper
Alliance; John Denson, Editor of the *New York Herald Tribune*
(whose opinions on underdeveloped countries I found extremely
stimulating); Stanley Carter, *New York Daily News* (ex-Associated
Press correspondent in the Middle East); Joseph Ranft and other
officials of Radio Free Europe; Helen Zotos, free-lance writer; and
Miss In Chen, Singapore newspaper publisher and one of Asia's
foremost novelists.

I am grateful also to the many other persons not listed here who
have so generously contributed, directly or indirectly, to the realization of this book.

DAN KURZMAN
Washington, D.C.,
November 27, 1962

CONTENTS

Part III ASIA

SUBVERSION
OF THE INNOCENTS

I

THE ART OF DECEIT

Each day at dawn, the peasant emerges from his mud-walled, thatch-roofed, windowless hut and savors the cool morning air so refreshingly free of the stale dust that perpetually circulates inside the fragile structure. Dressed in torn, dirty trousers and shirt, or sometimes just shorts, he shuffles into the surrounding corn, wheat, and rice fields where he works for about twelve hours, earning from twelve to fifteen cents by day's end. His wife and children help him pull a plow or plant seeds, for every hand is needed if he is to earn even that much. He has often dreamed of sending his children to school, so that they might learn to read and write like the children of his wealthy landlord or his foreign master. But this dream seems beyond realization. He is hardly able to make ends meet as it is, particularly with the constant illnesses that so often incapacitate members of his family. It's either an eye disease, or an intestinal infection, or malaria. Always something. And there is no hospital nearby, not even a doctor for miles around.

This peasant lives in Ethiopia. He also lives in Egypt, in Indonesia, in the Congo, and in Afghanistan. In fact, everywhere in the vast, simmering, impoverished, underdeveloped world. He is the symbol of the lowly and the exploited. Until recently he passively accepted his underprivileged lot. After all, his father and his grand-father and his great-grandfather had lived in the same manner and worked the same fields and experienced the same grinding poverty and diseases and dust-saturated darkness. Was it not the natural way of life of people like himself—humble people born in a mud hut with a thatched roof and no windows?

Since World War II, however, this question is seldom asked. Instead, the humble people are demanding to know how long it will be before they have a better way of life, and can live in a house with wooden floors and a tile roof. The people of the underdeveloped regions have awakened after centuries of colonial sleep. Each day that passes brings new awareness that they have every right to share in the good life—and that they have the potential power to assert this right.

The two giant blocs of East and West are also aware of this power. Western nations like France, Great Britain, Belgium, and the Netherlands have either been forced out of their colonial territories or have voluntarily departed, bowing to the inevitable. At the same time, East and West are now engaged in a furious competition for the support of the underdeveloped nations. For these nations, while militarily weak, hold the political balance of power in a world precariously divided between the free and the enslaved. Nor are the underdeveloped countries themselves blind to the attractions they offer. Like a desirable woman wooed ardently by two suitors, many have assumed an irritating noncommittal, or neutralist, attitude, playing one off against the other and accepting tokens of affection, in the form of economic aid, without discrimination.

A few vital statistics offer a clue to the secret of this charm. The free areas of Asia, Africa, the Middle East, and Latin America together comprise more than one-third of the earth's surface and contain the bulk of the world's natural wealth, including most of its oil, rubber, tin, iron ore, copper, cobalt, gold, diamonds, cotton, coffee, tea, and rice. In strategic terms, these regions flank the vital international gateways of Suez and Panama, rim the southern edge of the Mediterranean Sea, and overlook large sectors of the Atlantic and Pacific Oceans.

The communists, who paid relatively little attention to the underdeveloped nations until after World War II, have made tremendous strides in the last fifteen years along the path of subversion. The most important, of course, was the communist subjugation of China in 1948. Although the only other underdeveloped lands to have fallen through revolution have been North Vietnam, in 1954, and Cuba, in 1959, the Red record of infiltration has been impressive. In Asia, communist Pathet Lao forces hold a dominating position in Laos and control a large part of South Vietnam. Communists in Indonesia, numbering a million and a half, are playing a significant role in the operation of President Sukarno's "guided democracy." The Indian state of Kerala actually voted into office a communist government in 1958—the first major territory ever to go communist by legal means.

In the Middle East, Syria in 1955 and Iraq in 1959 appeared to have one foot in the communist camp, and today the United Arab Republic is to a large degree economically dependent on the Soviet Union. In Africa, Guinea has adopted many aspects of communist administration, while Ghana is a consistent apologist for communist foreign policy. The Reds nearly won a foothold in 1960 in the formerly Belgian-controlled Congo under the short-lived, ill-starred regime of Patrice Lumumba, who opened the doors wide to communist technicians and propagandists. And in British Kenya, which will soon receive its independence, students are being smuggled out of the territory to attend schools in communist-bloc nations.

Significantly, most of this communist progress has been registered since the death of Joseph Stalin in 1953, which was followed by a vital Red policy switch in the underdeveloped countries, the last of a number made by Russia under communist rule. According to the international political climate, Stalin practiced either the "left strategy" or the "right strategy." The former is a sectarian policy which calls for the communist party in each country to isolate itself from noncommunist nationalist groups, referred to by the Reds as the "national bourgeoisie," and fight them as "lackeys" of the imperialist powers. Normally, this was the line Stalin took. However, he switched to the "right strategy," or co-operation through popular fronts with the national bourgeoisie, in periods of grave common danger, such as before and during World War II, when the Soviet Union was threatened by Nazi Germany.

Shortly after the war, when nations newly independent or struggling to attain independence were floundering in a vacuum of political and economic confusion, Stalin reverted to the "left strategy." Miscalculating that these countries were ripe for the picking, he ordered the communist parties of South Asia to revolt against their respective governments, including some led by Marxist-influenced but noncommunist nationalist movements. Red revolts thereupon broke out in all South Asian nations where communist forces were given the slightest chance of success—in Malaya, Burma, Indonesia, Indochina, and the Philippines. The Indian communists were too weak and divided to rebel on a national basis, but resorted to local violence; and Moscow described the neutralist government of Prime Minister Jawaharlal Nehru as a "lackey of British and American imperialism." President Sukarno of Indonesia, a good friend of the communists today, was lumped together with the "Nehrus, Jinnahs, Luang Pibul Songgrams, Quirinos, Rhees, and other feeble-minded bourgeoisie of the East," who were told to leave the "struggle against imperialism" to the revolutionary workers.

This Stalinist hard line, which did not take into consideration the particular conditions existing in each country, failed miserably. Only in Vietnam did the communist forces prevail, and then only because they had managed to win control of the nationalist movement before orders for violent revolt were issued. In Burma, Malaya, and the Philippines, Red guerrilla forces were crushed, though in each case after years of costly and hazardous jungle-combing for individual terrorists, a few of whom are still holding out. In Indonesia, the revolt ended quickly in what appeared to be the obliteration of the party, although in recent years the Reds have made an astounding comeback.

Stalin's abortive all-out attack on Southeast Asia represented a final monument to his disastrous postwar international record. It was made only after his strategy of direct proletarian action in Western Europe—strikes, riots, demonstrations—had failed to unseat a single "bourgeois" government, in embarrassing defiance of the Marxist axiom that highly industrialized, and not underdeveloped, countries were the most susceptible to communist conquest; that, in fact, a nation had to pass through the capitalist stage before it could proceed to socialism. Both Marx and Engels had predicted the independence of all colonies one day, but they had been convinced that the Western proletariat, after taking over their own countries from the capitalists, would lead the colonies to freedom, and presumably through a capitalist phase of development within a world already under communist domination. Colonial liberation was thus to be the final stage in the emancipation of mankind.

True, Stalin succeeded after World War II in developing mass communist parties in war-ravished France and Italy, with each boasting the support of about one-third of the national electorate. But, owing in no small measure to American Marshall Plan economic aid to these countries, party strength froze at this level. And though Stalin gained control of Eastern Europe, he did so only with the use of Soviet troops who had occupied this area during the war.

Yet, from Stalin's point of view, his failures were apparently not very important in the broad context of history. He gambled on a quick killing when the odds seemed favorable—and lost. Actually, all he—and Soviet Russia—lost was a little prestige, and that was all part of the game. The big losers were the local communist parties, and they were expendable. For history had shown that the local party, however beaten, suppressed, or humiliated, always managed to come back. Such cynical reasoning was underscored by the fact that neither the Soviet Union nor Red China furnished the rebels in the various countries with quantities of arms that might have turned the tide of battle.

If Stalin's calculations were proved wrong, those of Communist Chinese leader Mao Tse-tung were proved correct—one of the root reasons why Peking feels so little sense of obligation to Moscow today. When Stalin switched to his "left strategy," he advised Mao, who was still struggling for control of China, to fight Chiang Kai-shek along sectarian lines. Mao apparently indicated that he would but, in fact, did not do so. His theory was that he could beat Chiang only if he could swing most of the people behind him, and he wasn't interested in the political orientation of his supporters as long as they followed him. Ideological indoctrination would come later, when the country was safely in his hands. He therefore continued to practice a refined Chinese variant of the "right strategy," known as the Yenan Way, which he had first conceived in the 1930's in his isolated North Chinese stronghold in Yenan. It was the way that led to Peking. And as the Russian Revolution of 1917 became the model for revolution in modern industrialized countries, so has the Yenan Way become the pattern for Red rebellion and infiltration in most of the underdeveloped world.

The Yenan Way is the ultimate in the communist tactic of deception. It is the art of disguising communism in the mask of a legitimate national movement, such as anti-imperialism or agrarian reform, to win over workers, peasants, lower- and middle-class citizens, the intelligentsia, and even businessmen if they are opposed to foreign imperialists.

In many underdeveloped areas, especially in Africa, which is in a particularly primitive social and economic state, communist propaganda almost ignores Marxist doctrine. But even in the more sophisticated regions, doctrinal discussion is markedly subordinated to tirades against "Western imperialism," demands for reform that seem as reasonable or moderate as those asked by liberals and democratic socialists, and even promises to the local bourgeoisie that the communists would not dream of hurting their interests. Thus, Dipa Nusantara Aidit, Secretary-General of the Indonesian Communist Party, said in a typical party-line speech:

> The Indonesian Communist Party doesn't demand the seizure of lands belonging to landlords and the division of those lands among the peasants. The policy of the party with regard to land is the reduction of rent . . . In the present stage of development at least the communists don't regard nationalist capitalists as a danger. We not only do not oppose them, we even join with them in demanding that the government protect their economic interests . . . (so that they may) compete with foreign capitalists . . . Indonesia's poverty has not been caused by national capitalism, but rather by the lack of national capital and abundance of foreign capital . . .

Such ideological gobbledegook is fed to the underdeveloped countries day and night not only in local communists' speeches and periodicals, but also in a flow of radio rhetoric from Moscow and Peking made palatable with occasional interludes of local traditional music, and in a flood of propaganda literature, much of it smuggled into a country by diplomats or trade envoys. Moreover, as part of an intensive Russian and Chinese cultural offensive, expertly produced movies are shown in these countries. They seldom lecture, but through various subtle means make the point that life under communism is all sweetness and light, as contrasted to the misery suffered under capitalism. One Chinese movie, for example, never once mentioned the United States by name, but simply showed a character with pointedly greedy traits counting American dollars. Other cultural imports, from gymnastics to proletarian art, also create the image of a communist world that is really not too different from the capitalist one, except that the common people have greater opportunity for happiness. Needless to say, in underdeveloped countries that have diplomatic relations with the Soviet Union or Communist China, subversion is invariably directed by the diplomatic mission.

The central purpose of the Yenan Way is actually not so much to gain mass support as to win over influential noncommunist "friends," particularly in the political field, who can open channels for infiltration in the highest councils of the nation. Such friends are obtained by any means that will work—lies, flattery, threats, blackmail, bribery, or outright purchase.

In *The Yenan Way* by Eudocio Ravines, the author, a former Peruvian communist leader who has since turned against the Reds, recounts how Mao advised him in 1934 on the fine points of the Yenan philosophy. "The greatest talent in this work, comrade," Mao said,

is never to be associated with failure. Never to defend the weak even when he is right. Never to attack the pillager of the treasury if he is the owner of a great fortress. He might crush you and there's no use being a martyr. Our experience, the experience of the Yenan Way, is this: people like doctors, generals, dentists, town mayors, and lawyers who aren't rich, do not love power for itself; much less for the good they can do with it. They want it for the wealth it can bring. They achieve power and then they begin to call out like Napoleon for money, money, and again money. Get this through your head, comrade. If we help these people, if we are a ladder for them because it suits us well, then it would be absurd for us to stay their hands, sew up their pockets, or check their greed. If we did this, they would turn against us and try to crush us. That happened with Chiang in 1927—we tried to play the moralist and he hurled all his power against us.

Let them get rich today. Very soon we can expropriate everything. The more help they get from us in their pillage, the more positions they will let us take and occupy; they will help us to capture them and even to extend them. Of course, there are two important things to remember. Never participate in any fraud or plundering, which is more difficult than you might think; and carry out your collaboration without the people's knowledge, without leaving any proof of it for your enemies to find. This delights your robber friends, of course. For your integrity leaves more for them to divide among a larger number of fellow rogues.

Here are two things. The first is that this tiny man, this non-communist who, thanks to our arrangements, is chosen selectman or municipal councilor, will find the way easier when the party wants to elect a deputy or capture the mayoralty. Then the public won't elect the radical, but the communist. The end remains the same; the means change according to our power. This method seems slower, but it is actually quicker and surer.

Now for the second. Any person who receives our support and does not fulfill his part of the bargain must become the target for frontal attack of pitiless ferocity. It is enough to make an example of one; once they see that we can bar the path to a man, that we have the power to destroy him utterly, the rest will be afraid not to play our game. We communists have never given this fear enough weight. I don't know why. The ambitious petit bourgeois taken with the fever of greed feels real anguish when we strike him hard. He must be really destroyed with every arm at hand, be left a wretched tatter at the end.

When the Latin American communist agreed that the party must win "friends, sympathizers, and servants . . . at any price,"

Mao beamed: "That, especially that—servants. People who serve us through greed, through fear, inferiority, vengeance, what have you, but who serve us. Serve the party, serve the designs of the Comintern, serve the cause of the revolution. Congratulations . . . you have caught the very essence of the Yenan Way."

Other communist leaders have also caught the essence of the Yenan Way. The two underdeveloped territories, in addition to China, that have come under communist domination through revolution since the war—North Vietnam and Cuba—both reached their political destination via the Yenan Way. In Vietnam the communist leader, Ho Chi Minh, rallied the majority of peasants around him strictly with slogans vilifying the French occupier and with hardly a mention of Marxism—until, of course, the bamboo curtain crashed down. And in Cuba, Fidel Castro, while conducting his revolt against the regime of Fulgencid Batista, was pictured as a genuine nationalist and true democrat even by journalists reporting for right-wing American newspapers. Both Ho and Castro followed the footsteps of Mao with almost fanatical precision—and achieved the same goal. Similar tactics are being employed by communist parties throughout the underdeveloped world and are proving successful in varying degrees in almost every case, though up to now not decisively so.

That Russia has adopted some of the principles of the Yenan Way, which Stalin once opposed, was formally indicated in the draft program of the Soviet Communist Party presented to its Twenty-second Congress in October 1961, which many experts consider the most important policy document issued by the Soviet Union in twenty years. "The Communist Party of the Soviet Union," the draft read, "considers fraternal alliance with the peoples who have thrown off colonial or semicolonial tyranny to be a cornerstone of its international policy. This alliance is based on the common vital interests of world socialism and the world national-liberation movement. The CPSU regards it as its internationalist duty to assist the peoples who have set out to win and strengthen their national independence, all peoples who are fighting for the complete abolition of the colonial system."

But the program makes clear that the Soviet Union has no intention of maintaining the communist "fraternal alliance" with noncommunist nationalist forces, or national bourgeoisie, any longer than is necessary. "The national bourgeoisie is dual in character," the draft reads. "In modern conditions the national bourgeoisie in those colonial, one-time colonial and dependent countries where it is not connected with the imperialist circles is objectively interested in accomplishing the basic tasks of an anti-imperialist and anti-feudal revolution. Its progressive role and its ability to participate in the solution of pressing national problems are, therefore, not yet spent. But as the contradictions between the working people and the propertied classes grow and the class struggle inside the country becomes more aggravated, the national bourgeoisie shows an increasing inclination to compromise with imperialism and domestic reaction."

Therefore, the document concludes, "the development of the countries which have won their freedom may be a complex multi-stage process." In other words, the communists, at the opportune moment, must stab their noncommunist allies in the back, as Mao, Ho Chi Minh, and Fidel Castro have done. That is the Yenan Way.

Although the communists started concentrating on the subversion of the underdeveloped world only after the war, when they found the road to power blocked in the West, they had by no means ignored this world in previous years. Awareness of the possibilities of socialist revolution in the colonial or "semicolonial" areas at an earlier stage than Marx and Engels had foreseen dates back to the first years of the twentieth century, with the Japanese victory over Russia in 1904, the Persian revolution of 1908, the creation of a Chinese Republic by Sun Yat-sen in 1911, and the Mexican revolution of 1912.

In these first nationalist victories, the Reds saw a double opportunity for infiltration. The revolutionary leaders, westernized to varying degrees, would be attracted by the dynamics and militancy of communism, which promised crash industrialization of their countries and an end to dependence on the imperial powers. And the peasant masses, whose nationalism was then based primarily not, as today, on a passion for political and economic independence, but on a desire to rekindle the precolonial values of their traditional religions—Islam in Indonesia and the Middle East, Buddhism in Burma, a mixture of Buddhism and Confucianism in Indochina —might be drawn, it was reasoned, to a new faith that at once rejected Western values and offered new ones as rigid and inspiring as those they sought to resurrect: Marxism.

Lenin, in particular, saw great potential significance in the awakening of many colonial areas, and some of his writings prophetically indicated it could mean the start of a new era in world history. "Russia," he wrote, "belongs not only to Europe but also to Asia." According to Lenin's theory of imperialism, the industrial West has been able to delay its inevitable collapse by extending its exploitation from its own working class to colonial and dependent peoples to provide markets for its factories and raw materials and food for its urban centers. The disintegration of the "colonial system" would, accordingly, aggravate the "general crisis of capitalism" and weaken the West through a loss of markets, sources of raw materials, and military bases located in these regions.

Lenin shaped future communist policy toward the colonial and semicolonial world at the second Communist International (Comintern) Congress, held in Petrograd (now Leningrad) and Moscow in 1920, at which representatives of many colonial countries were present. The world balance of power, Lenin said, had shifted to the United States, which "has become so rich that it can buy everything, but there is nothing for it to buy and it has no way of selling." The time was ripe for world revolution. And this could be carried out most effectively through a "revolutionary union of progressive countries with . . . the revolutionary masses of the oppressed in all colonies and all Oriental states; and it depends on us to see that this union is strengthened." The war had "dragged these colonial countries from their isolation, recruited soldiers there . . . and taught them how to use firearms."

Apparently modifying orthodox Marxist doctrine, Lenin maintained that it is possible for a country to pass directly from the stage of feudalism or semifeudalism to communism without going through the capitalist stage—if the proletariat of the most developed capitalist nations, after taking power at home, comes to their aid. As for the lack of a proletariat in the colonial areas, "the struggle of agricultural laborers against landlord exploitation is the basis on which you can build an organization of toilers, even in backward countries." Lenin added emphatically, signaling the start of a campaign of subversion that today threatens the whole underdeveloped world, "In such countries it is quite possible to establish Soviet power."

With Lenin laying down the party line, the second Comintern Congress decided that all communist parties must support revolutionary liberation movements in the "oppressed" countries, even though led by "bourgeois-democratic" elements. The Soviet newspaper *Izvestia* joyfully summarized the results of the second Comintern Congress: "A new world is awakening to life and to struggle —the world of the oppressed nationalities which has been comprehended by us, though not quite correctly under the name of the East. For here are found not only the peoples of Asia, but also those of Africa and America . . . when the news of the decisions of the second Comintern Congress reaches the hundreds of millions of Indians, Chinese, Negroes, Malayans, and other oppressed peoples, it will be happy tidings for them and also the call for a new and greater struggle against the capital that exploits them . . . the fact that the Communist International was the first openly to raise the banner of the struggle and to call to this banner all the oppressed peoples and the organized proletariat, will stand to its eternal credit."

Certainly the decisions of the congress accelerated greatly the nationalist trend among the colonial peoples that had become apparent in the first decade of this century. As *Izvestia* said, this was the first time the "banner of the struggle" for national liberation had been raised outside the colonized areas, however nefarious the aims of the banner-wavers. Communist policy, or propaganda, added an incalculable impetus to anti-imperialist movements whose leaders had previously lacked full confidence that they could ever really loosen the grip of the mighty colonial powers on their lands and economies. The Reds gained an initial psychological advantage which the Western powers have never been able to overcome completely.

Exploiting this advantage, Mikhail Pavlovich, the Soviet Union's first genuine expert on the colonial areas, established an All-Union Association of Orientalists in 1921, uniting all scholars in Russia who were specially interested in the East. This was the first effort to study the problems of colonialism and imperialism systematically. In *The Soviet Union and the Middle East,* Walter Z. Laqueur writes of this group:

> "Even if their knowledge of the East was recently acquired and deficient, their mastery of Oriental languages imperfect, their ideas derived far too often from secondhand material, the achievements of the Pavlovich school were important. Their discussions were pertinent, their publications lively. They had excellent training in the interpretation of socio-economic developments and a more acute understanding of political trends than the West."

The decision to support liberation movements even if led by national bourgeois elements should not be confused with the Yenan Way that was adopted later. Lenin, supported by other Red leaders made it clear that the communists, far from disguising themselves as simple nationalists, had to identify themselves as "true communists" with a view toward "grouping together various elements of future proletarian parties . . . and educating them [to fight] bourgeois-democratic tendencies within their respective nationalities. The Communist International must be ready to establish temporary relationships and even alliances with bourgeois democracy of the colonies and backward countries. It must not, however, amalgamate with it. It must retain the independent character of the proletarian movement, even though this movement be in the embryonic stage . . ."

In 1927, however, Chiang Kai-shek threw his Chinese communist allies out of China's governing Kuomintang Party, delivering to the international communist movement its first severe defeat in the underdeveloped world. As a result, the Reds decided that it was senseless trying to co-operate with anticommunist nationalist groups. Stalin thus instituted the "left strategy," which, like his post-World War II policy, meant a strict class approach requiring, quite unrealistically, the establishment of proletariat-based parties, despite the lack of industrial areas where workers could be recruited. These parties were to oppose, in some cases with violence, all noncommunist movements, including those of leftist tendency.

This policy failed no less completely than did its postwar counterpart. It was only in 1934, when Moscow suddenly called for a new world-wide popular front program to meet the growing Nazi threat, that the communists started making headway again in the colonial regions. The popular front technique, however, was now sharply modified from what it had been up to 1927. The Yenan Way was born.

Since Soviet Premier Nikita Khrushchev has adopted many aspects of the Yenan Way as his own, there is considerable competition between Moscow and Peking for influence in these countries. From an over-all view, Peking appears to be keeping in stride with Moscow—one reason, no doubt, why Moscow is dispensing greater quantities of economic aid to those areas than ever before. Russia knows that Red China, which itself has been greatly dependent on Soviet aid, cannot compete in this respect.

Most underdeveloped states more closely identify their immediate economic problems with those of agrarian Red China than with those of industrialized Russia, for, like China, they are saddled with a massive peasant class living largely on a subsistence level. Many are waiting to see how Peking goes about solving its own peasant problem, and keeping an eye on its effort to lift itself to an industrial level in the minimum possible time—something which every underdeveloped state wants to do. The Soviet Union is too advanced industrially to serve as a model at this time. Moreover, China, unlike the Soviet Union, enjoys the advantage of being a nonwhite country, an important factor in countries where the white man, regardless of nationality, is regarded as the symbol of colonial exploitation.

But while Red China is easier to understand, the Soviet Union is more popular in some regions, particularly in free Asia and the Middle East, illuminating the discrepancy between the Russian and Chinese concepts of the Yenan Way, or "right strategy." Mao makes a distinction between national bourgeoisie who are willing to give support to communist causes and those who are not. He became convinced in 1927, when Chiang Kai-shek threw the communists out of his government and tried to crush them, that it does not pay to deal with actively anticommunist nationalists. It was only worth doing business with those who *served* communism, wittingly or unwittingly. Mao has gone out of his way to make friends in Africa with the leftist governments of Guinea and Ghana, as well as newly independent Algeria, which are relatively tolerant toward the far left even though not communist themselves. He has also aided leftist oppositionist groups in Africa, such as the guerrilla rebels in Cameroon and opportunistic politicians in Kenya and Somalia. But Mao has made fewer friends in the Middle East and free Asia, partly, at least, because most influential people in these areas make unreliable servants, even though they may be neutralist on the international plane. Fear almost exclusively has kept most Asians "friendly."

Peking has bitterly described as "imperialist puppets" such stolid neutralists as Egypt's Gamal Abdel Nasser and India's Nehru, whose jails have often contained substantial numbers of local communists. To Mao, such men are undependable hypocrites who cannot be expected to repay favors rendered them. And as both Nasser and Nehru are highly popular nationalists in their respective countries, the former being a dictator in addition, there is virtually no effective nationalist opposition for the Chinese to support as in Africa.

Another probable factor shaping China's attitude toward nationalist governments is economic in character. Peking has suffered considerably from Khrushchev's policy of doling out aid almost indiscriminately to non-communist Afro-Asian countries. For there is little Soviet money left over for China after those nations receive their share, though Mao desperately needs economic assistance. Chinese resentment of the recipients—as well as of the donor—may thus have resulted. In the case of India, at least, Peking may figure that it can sow discord between Moscow and New Delhi by forcing Khrushchev to choose between Mao and Nehru and, in the process, to reconsider Russian aid policy.

Mao's policy is not inflexible. For tactical considerations, he is willing to trade with Nasser; he even granted aid to a medieval king like the late Imam of Yemen. With Soviet Russia deeply committed economically in the Middle East, Red China feels that it must at least make its presence felt. Peking also finds it momentarily expedient to be kind to Burma and Cambodia, both of which are led by firmly anticommunist but neutralist governments, in order to keep them out of the Western camp until their turn comes for obliteration in accordance with the "falling domino" theory so applicable in Southeast Asia. Mao is shrewd enough to realize that whereas a bitterly anti-West nationalist like Nasser and a dedicated "doctrinaire" neutralist like Nehru—who lead countries that do not easily lend themselves to effective subversion or guerrilla activity—are not likely to ask the Western bloc for troops, whatever the communist provocation, small nations such as Burma and Cambodia might well seek such military assistance if they were overly frightened by communist tactics.

Khrushchev, on the other hand, has repudiated Stalin's "left strategy" to a far greater degree. He makes little distinction between members of the national bourgeoisie. He is just as ready to deal with Nasser or Nehru as with the ideologically more acceptable Kwame Nkrumah of Ghana, however many communists they may throw into jail. He reasons that at worst such anticommunist leaders will remain out of the Western Cold War camp, and at best, large-scale economic and cultural infiltration will eventually open the way to communism. The good will generated, Khrushchev calculates, will last a great deal longer than ephemeral leaders like Nasser and Nehru.

Mao's selective attitude toward the national bourgeoisie in the underdeveloped countries is one of the chief sources of friction that today divide Moscow and Peking. *Rude Pravo,* the official newspaper of the Czechoslovak Communist Party, which is often used to express Soviet bloc policy, said in March 1962, in obvious reference to Red China, that the "dogmatic sectarian" view of the colonial struggle was a dangerous threat to the final victory of "socialism." Communist parties, the newspaper said, "decisively" opposed those who maintain that an anti-imperialist policy must be conducted without compromise—by "fighting the national bourgeoisie," and thereby stimulating the "imperialist" powers to act. The people who take this line, said *Rude Pravo,* wished to speed up the struggle in the underdeveloped countries without taking into account the balance of forces within these countries. This, it concluded, was dangerous because it led to adventurism and isolation from the masses.

The extent to which Khrushchev has reversed Stalinist policy is evident in this argument, which, ironically, is the same one that led Mao to disregard Stalin's "sectarian" view.

Russia's desire to win the friendship of all nationalists is, at the same time, fueled by Red China's spreading influence in the underdeveloped world. If Khrushchev is determined that the neutralists shall not join the Western camp, he must find distasteful the possibility that once these countries are in the communist fold—an inevitable development by Marxist reckoning—they will look to Peking rather than to Moscow for guidance.

The Soviet Union today is, in fact, threatened with reduced support from both the neutralist and satellite countries as the result of two momentous Soviet setbacks that occurred simultaneously in late 1962—in Cuba and in India.

Khrushchev lost considerable prestige among the neutralists on a number of counts. By sending nuclear rockets to Cuba, especially after denying that he was doing so, he placed in question the sincerity of his perpetual cries for disarmament and peace. Furthermore, neutralists learned from the fate of Premier Fidel Castro, who was not consulted about the Soviet surrender, the risk involved in cuddling too close to the communist bloc. "The fact that Castro was humiliated by Moscow when that served its purpose," a Ghanaian observer commented to me over tea in the luxurious Delegates' Lounge at the United Nations during the crisis, "proves that it doesn't pay for a small country to digress from true neutralism."

The even greater humiliation suffered by Khrushchev at the hands of the Americans undoubtedly had a significant psychological effect on the Afro-Asians, who appreciate power, even though this effect may have been offset somewhat by the realization that Moscow, by not challenging the blockade, perhaps saved the world from nuclear war. This retreat was, in fact, viewed all the more sympathetically since it was taken despite the risk of losing communist-bloc support to the more militant Chinese, who almost openly described Khrushchev as a traitor to the Red cause for his "cowardice."

The Soviet Premier's Afro-Asian friendship campaign ran into much greater trouble when he found himself agonizingly caught in the middle as Mao's armies stormed into India in a full-scale attack. Unable to support openly a "bourgeois" state against a communist regime without committing an ideological heresy and risking loss of his hold on the communist world—especially after the humiliation to which he subjected Castro—Khrushchev, by remaining on the fence, was forced to sacrifice a substantial measure of the trust he had so painstakingly built up in the underdeveloped nations. "What the Indian crisis has shown," an official of a North African country observed to me, "is that Russia is a prisoner of its ideological commitments and that, whatever policy it might wish to pursue, it can only pursue it insofar as it does not conflict with world communist interests. We can therefore have only limited trust in the Soviet Union."

Communist China, of course, lost far greater sympathy than the Soviet Union for its overt aggression against India. Nevertheless, its voluntary cease-fire—however temporary—after a month of fighting appeased the shock of many neutralists, perhaps reflecting the reason behind the Chinese offer. "China, in the end, may actually profit in a propaganda sense from its policy in India, at least among the Asians," an African United Nations delegate told me. "On the one hand, it will have shown the neutralist world that it doesn't pay to defy Peking's demands. And on the other, it will have indicated that it can be quite reasonable." In other words, China committed just enough aggression to assure the co-operation of fear-ridden neighbors, but not enough to chase them into the Western camp as the only alternative to being devoured.

However that may be, China has not put all, or most, of its eggs in the "good will" basket as has the Soviet Union, and therefore is not as concerned about losing "friends." Actually, its loss of good will has been balanced to a large extent by the dictates of fear among the Asians, who may be more than ever prone to express affection for the dragon that threatens them in the hope of staying alive. Offering a smaller degree of compensation in Africa and the Middle East is the persistent image of Red China as an underdeveloped nation daringly, if sometimes overzealously, experimenting with answers to problems that are familiar to all Afro-Asian countries.

Thus, while Peking's loss was a calculated one, based on possible future gains, Moscow's setback was hardly intentional. Russia, furthermore, suffered a double-edged defeat. Khrushchev's "soft" version of the Yenan Way was dealt a severe blow by the Indian crisis, and his spectacular venture into Maoist-Stalinist pastures in Cuba met with total failure.

Khrushchev will continue trying to curb Mao's influence abroad, but he must make concessions, as in the Indian crisis, or risk a full-fledged split in the communist world that could do irreparable harm to the communist cause in general. This consideration has constituted an important element in Moscow's "tough" Cold War line in the last few years. Khrushchev today says, as he has said for several years, that he wants "peaceful coexistence" with the West. But in previous years he defined this term as meaning "friendly cultural and ideological competition" between the two power blocs, which he apparently believes the communists would win and thereby communize the world without the need for a major war. The militancy of international communism showed signs of weakening.

Red China, however, holds a different view of "coexistence." It is often pictured in the West as flatly opposing this concept and actually courting war with the West. And Moscow's thinly veiled criticism of Peking has not served to dispel this frightening interpretation of Chinese aims. But Peking itself denies this is its view, and many Western experts, particularly in Britain, also dispute it. According to an article published in March 1962 in *Hung Chi,* the Chinese Communist Party journal on Marxist theory, Peking opposes only "unconditional" peaceful coexistence. Peaceful coexistence is indispensable as long as countries with different social systems exist, the article said. But not to limit its application meant "constant adaptation, constant compromise, constant concessions toward imperialism." Experts who accept this evaluation of Red Chinese policy do not deny that Mao believes in the Marxist-Leninist theory that war is inevitable, but maintain that he is convinced that the capitalist powers, not the communist countries, will eventually launch a war in a desperate, last-ditch struggle to prevent communism from taking over the world by peaceful means. Khrushchev, on the contrary, thinks that communism will advance so swiftly in the coming years that the West will desist from fighting in the knowledge that to fight would mean its inevitable destruction, and that, in any case, a major war is unthinkable in the nuclear age.

At a world conference of communist parties in Moscow in December 1960, a formula of compromise between these two interpretations of peaceful coexistence was reached. Peking agreed to drop its contentions that war is inevitable, but in return Moscow agreed to redefine "peaceful coexistence." This concept was not to signify "friendly competition," but, according to the conference manifesto, "a policy of mobilizing the masses and launching vigorous action against the enemies of peace. [It] does not imply renunciation of the class struggle . . . On the contrary, it implies intensification of the struggle of the working class, of all the communist parties, for the triumph of socialist ideas."

"Peaceful coexistence" was no longer to mean a relaxation of the Cold War, but rather its intensification; and class struggle would presumably be promoted in all noncommunist countries, including the underdeveloped ones. The Red Chinese view prevailed, except where the inevitability of "hot" war was concerned. Peking was promised a return to the unrelenting violence and threats of violence characteristic of the Stalin era. Certainly Moscow's belligerent moves in Berlin and Cuba and its unilateral abrogation of the Big Power ban on nuclear testing have been in line with Red Chinese demands, although factors other than Chinese pressure have undoubtedly contributed to Khrushchev's switch in tactics. He may have judged that America's Western European allies would not support a United States decision to stand up to Soviet threats for fear of war. He might have felt that by conjuring up a "foreign threat" and increasing international tensions, he would take the minds of the Soviet people off food and consumer item shortages that he has not been able to reconcile with recent promises of plenty.

Even more important, Khrushchev has apparently been under strong pressure from Maoist-Stalinist forces in the Kremlin itself—in particular, it is believed, Defense Minister Marshal Rodion Malinovsky—to stand up more forcefully to the West. One theory prevalent in East European official circles is that Khrushchev, to prove to his Kremlin foes that "peaceful coexistence" is the only alternative to an all-destructive nuclear war or abject surrender to the West, deliberately fomented the Cuban crisis, calculating that the United States would react violently to the presence of missile bases in Cuba, and that Russia would have no choice but to retreat. Despite the humiliation involved, the story goes, Khrushchev felt that such a venture was necessary to consolidate his "moderate" position.

The validity of this theory is questionable. The desire to overcome America's superior intercontinental nuclear missile power through the installation in Cuba of medium-range rockets that could not reach the United States from Russia appears to have been one factor in the Soviet venture. The Kremlin might also have viewed the missile bases as a potential bargaining wedge for forcing the evacuation of strategically located American bases (just before Khrushchev agreed to dismantle the Russian bases, the United States had flatly rejected a proposal calling for the abandonment of its base in Turkey). And no doubt the preservation of Cuba as a center of Latin American communist agitation was at least a secondary Russian consideration. Nevertheless, Khrushchev may well have figured that even if he were forced to dismantle the Cuban bases, he would still profit; for the "hard line" advocates in the Kremlin would probably be easier to handle after they experienced the dangers involved in excessive provocation of the United States.

Furthermore, the situation would offer a valuable barometer reading as to how far international communism can push its policies without undue risk.

In any event, the 1960 compromise on "coexistence" may in the end mean very little. Since it was reached, relations between the two communist countries have seriously deteriorated, and the possibility of a complete split between them cannot be discounted. If a break does occur, each side would presumably be free to pursue its own tactics. But this might not work to the West's advantage, however appealing a crack in the monolithic communist structure may initially appear. Even if Russia reverted to the "peaceful competition" theory that led to Khrushchev's "good-will" trip to the United States in 1959, world tension might increase. For Red China, liberated from Moscow's moderating influence, might well intensify its violent activities in Asia, increasing the pressure on Taiwan (Formosa) and perhaps moving more boldly in Laos. The Soviet Union itself might have to display more hostility, rather than less, toward the West, in order to prove to the communist parties around the globe, for whose loyalty Moscow and Peking are competing, that Russia has not forgotten their ultimate mission— control of the world.

However bitter relations between Moscow and Peking may be, Khrushchev has learned one thing from Mao. The carrot may be useful in wooing the underdeveloped, newly independent nations, but the stick can be an excellent complement. Or, putting it another way, the fantasy of a bargain-basement paradise joined to the realism of naked terror apparently constitutes an effective safeguard against neutralist defection to the West, while permitting the communists to pursue whatever foreign policy lines they might consider expedient.

The conference of nonaligned states held in September 1961 in Belgrade offered considerable evidence of the validity of this theory. With an obvious contempt for the neutralists, almost all of them underdeveloped countries, Khrushchev announced that he would break the nuclear testing ban on the very eve of the Belgrade meeting, and then proceeded to explode bombs even while the speakers preached peace. He could not have hoped for a more favorable reaction. The United Arab Republic's Nasser mildly scolded Russia, and India's Nehru said he deplored all nuclear testing. But at least in public, all of the other neutralist leaders remained silent about Russia's action, and the final communiqué of the conference also ignored it. Most speakers urged the West to accept Soviet demands for the official division of Germany and recognition of the communist East German regime. Yet, certainly a great cry of moral indignation would have been heard around the world had the United States been the first to violate the ban.

This rather startling reaction on the part of most underdeveloped nations mirrored some hard truths about the East-West competition for their support. In the economic sphere, the United States handed out about $30 billion in aid, including some military assistance, from 1954 through 1962, with the immediate aim of alleviating hunger and poverty and the long-range purpose of building up the economies of the recipient nations to permit them to resist communist pressures. In the same period the communist bloc dispensed $7.8 billion in grants and credits, including $2.7 billion in arms and involving the dispatch of more than six thousand technicians to twenty Afro-Asian countries, in order to awaken their political consciousness, make them dependent economically, and hence politically, on the Reds, and shrink the West's world market. But despite the greater generosity and nobler motives of the United States, communist aid has in many respects had greater political and psychological impact than American aid.

The bloc's advantage lies in a number of factors. First, it normally offers more attractive terms than the United States. While American aid has usually been offered either in the form of loans carrying interest rates of 4½ percent, or higher, or as outright gifts which the recipient takes, but with wounded pride, the bloc gives loans carrying only 2½ percent interest or less, and confines its gift-giving to small, inexpensive, showpiece projects, such as a hospital or a model farm "thrown in" as part of a larger deal. The Reds thus make repayment of loans relatively easy and at the same time reap considerable good will from their "token" gifts.

Second, United States experts, considering aid from a long-term economic standpoint, favor a balanced growth between the various sectors of the national economy and often oppose immediate heavy industrialization in underdeveloped countries, advising agricultural development instead. But the Reds have played on the wishful desire of these countries to become great industrial nations overnight. The West, they say, wants to keep them in colonial subjugation, at least economically, by preventing their industrialization. They should, with communist aid, of course, concentrate on the construction of industrial enterprises—enterprises which, the Reds fail to mention, make excellent propaganda and produce more workers to serve their cause. Of the 350 or so communist projects undertaken up to 1961, about half involve industrial development—mine exploitation, steel mills, electric power stations, chemical plants, oil refineries, machinery plants. Other projects, including highways, railroads, ports, hospitals, football stadiums, schools, and research institutes, are equally eye-catching.

Third, whereas United States officials may have to do considerable consulting with various sectors of the government before aid is granted and dispatched, communist governments, not being responsible to their people for their political or economic policies, can send aid without delay and at any expense, if this is considered politically profitable. Russia exports many items in quantity that are very scarce at home. One-third of the 125,000 automobiles produced in the USSR each year goes abroad, though many Soviet citizens may have to wait years to buy a car. The same is true of tractors, trucks, petroleum, timber, silk fabrics, television sets, refrigerators, and many other articles. Furthermore, the Reds make no effort to see that their aid is not wasted through inefficiency or corruption, as the United States does to some extent. Since this aid is offered for political rather than economic reasons, they don't particularly care if much of it ends up in private Swiss bank accounts.

In the field of civil rights, the United States boasts of its democratic system as contrasted to Soviet dictatorship. But this democracy looks pretty diluted to the nonwhite underdeveloped nations when they hear of the racial discrimination against Negroes in the United States. And they become actively belligerent when they learn that their own diplomats have a hard time finding appropriate housing in Washington. They are, on the other hand, impressed by Russian claims that all Soviet citizens, regardless of color or creed, are treated as equals, though some learn the falsity of this propaganda when they visit the Soviet Union.

Also, political democracy has little meaning in most underdeveloped countries. Only a few practice it, and then usually as a result of special circumstances. The Republic of the Philippines is one such country, but the United States has been training it in democratic procedure since the turn of the century. Even so, Philippine democracy almost broke down after the war and was saved only because of the political genius of one man—President Ramón Magsaysay. India, too, practices democracy, owing to the unusually large, fine elite fostered by the British, and again to the extraordinary ability and popularity of an individual—Nehru, of course. When Nehru goes, there is considerable question whether Indian democracy, under tremendous strain even now, can long survive. Burma has tried democracy on and off, and certainly favors that kind of government; but it has had to revert to authoritarianism after each democratic experience to save the country from political and economic chaos.

Most Afro-Asian nations are led by dictatorial elite groups, as are the communist states, and therefore find nothing shocking about Red dictatorship. This may be disappointing to Westerners, but in the context of Afro-Asian development Western-style democracy may indeed be unworkable, at least in its full sense. Democracy literally means "rule of the people." But it is hard to see how progress toward the twentieth century can be registered if decisions are, in large measure, left up to people still living in medieval times, or even the stone age. An American observer in Ghana said of the squelching of opposition there: "As an American, I deplore this. Yet, if I were a Ghanaian leader, I might follow a similar policy. As funny as this may seem, in these countries you've got to rule with an authoritative hand if you're to make any progress toward the conditions that make democracy possible."

As for living standards, the United States loudly maintains that a free-enterprise, capitalistic system has produced affluence in this country and has therefore proved its worth. But the primitive new nations look upon the American experience as something entirely divorced from their own and which took place over a long period in another outdated era. Exploitation of our prosperity, far from inspiring them to follow the path we have followed, arouses jealousy and envy among the have-nots. But Russia is another matter, for here is a country that forty years ago was underdeveloped itself, yet is today one of the world's two great powers. Living standards may not be as high as in the United States; but then, it is argued, the United States had a tremendous head start.

The question of colonialism also provides the Soviets with an important advantage. For although the United States points to its own breakaway from imperial control in 1776 and its enlightened attitude toward its former colony of the Philippines, it is still identified with "imperialism" and "capitalist selfishness." Most Afro-Asian states, faced with vast social welfare problems such as widespread disease, illiteracy, and hunger, understandably favor some kind of socialistic system, particularly as colonialism produced few domestic capitalists. They view even the small number there are with distaste, and sometimes hatred. Since many of these capitalists feel little sense of responsibility to the state or the people— usually managing, through well-placed bribes and financial manipulation, to avoid paying more than token taxes—there is some justification for this resentment. In many countries detested alien residents control the economy—Chinese in Southeast Asia, Indians and Greeks in Black Africa. And Afro-Asians, as well as Latin Americans, think of "capitalistic exploitation" as the chief motivating power behind colonialism. For all these reasons, they tend to distrust the policies of the leading capitalist nation—a distrust, of course, nurtured by communist propaganda.

Equally important, the United States, which must rely on its allies for support in the Cold War, has felt it necessary to back, or at least not to oppose, many of the colonial policies of these countries. The Kennedy Administration has begun to reverse the United States attitude, voting in the United Nations, for example, to censure Portugal for its policies in Angola. But psychologically, Soviet Russia and Red China, despite their own brutally imperialistic policies in such places as Hungary and Tibet, are still making mileage out of their anticolonial propaganda; for most underdeveloped countries have known Western imperialism intimately, while they are far less acquainted with the distant communist brand, though the Chinese invasion of India has helped to awaken them.

These are some of the barriers which the West must hurdle in the struggle for the hearts and minds of the underdeveloped peoples.

Part 1

AFRICA

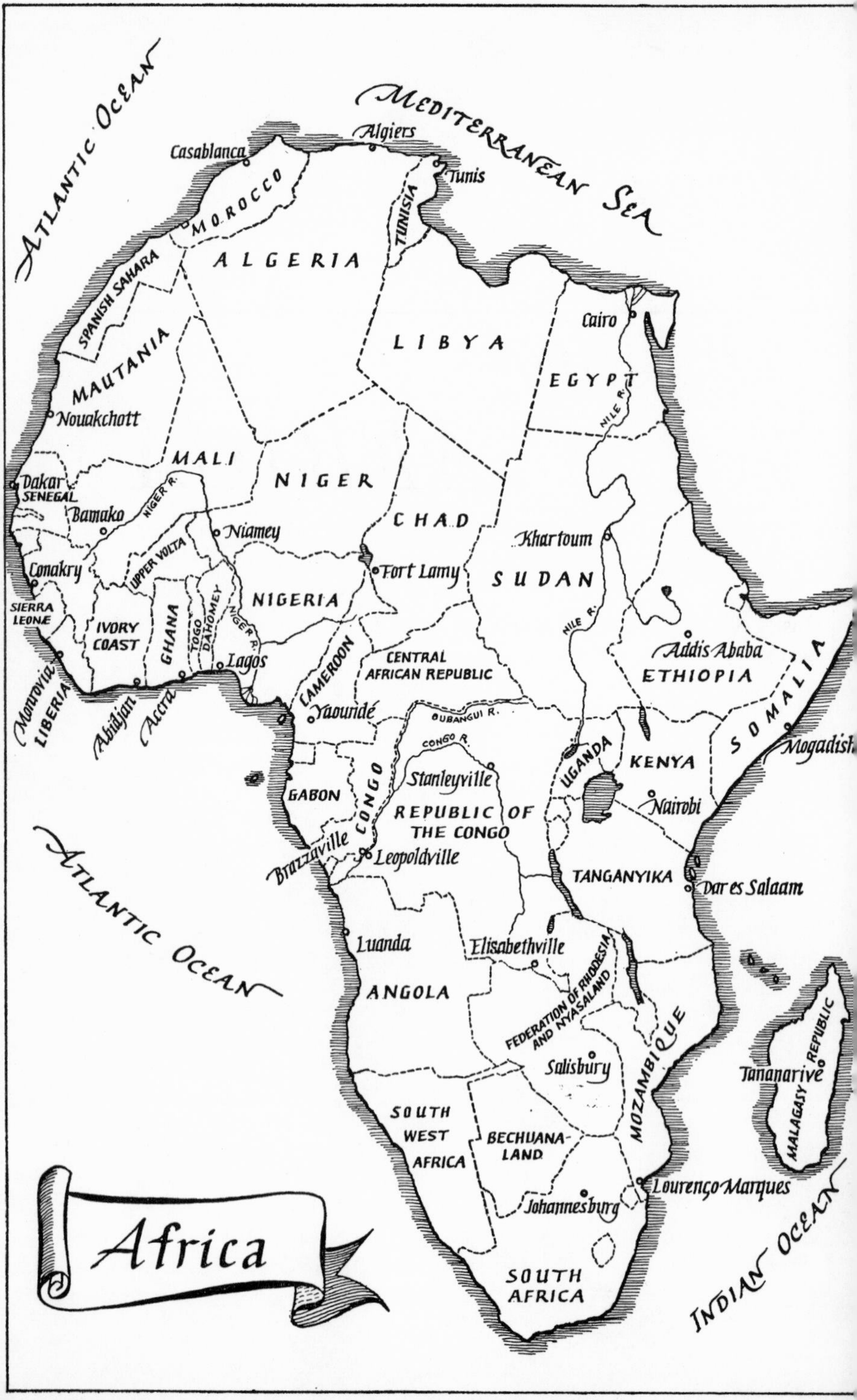
Africa
Atlantic Ocean
Mediterranean Sea
Atlantic Ocean
Indian Ocean
Casablanca
Algiers
Tunis
Morocco
Tunisia
Algeria
Spanish Sahara
Mautania
Libya
Cairo
Egypt
Nile R.
Nouakchott
Mali
Niger
Dakar
Senegal
Bamako
Niger R.
Niamey
Chad
Khartoum
Upper Volta
Conakry
Fort Lamy
Sudan
Nigeria
Sierra Leone
Ivory Coast
Ghana
Togo
Dahomey
Niger R.
Lagos
Nile R.
Addis Ababa
Ethiopia
Central African Republic
Cameroon
Monrovia
Liberia
Abidjan
Accra
Yaoundé
Ubangui R.
Somalia
Congo R.
Uganda
Kenya
Mogadish
Gabon
Congo
Stanleyville
Republic of the Congo
Nairobi
Brazzaville
Leopoldville
Tanganyika
Dar es Salaam
Luanda
Elisabethville
Federation of Rhodesia and Nyasaland
Angola
Mozambique
Salisbury
Tananarive
Malagasy Republic
South West Africa
Bechuana-land
Lourenço Marques
Johannesburg
South Africa

II

RED SHADOWS AT SUNRISE

Just a few years ago, the Soviet Union and Communist China were to most Africans, if they had heard of these countries at all, vague geographical entities as distant from them as the moon. But today, as numerous states, some with one foot in the stone age, emerge from a colonialism that has both exploited them and expedited their advancement, the shadows of the two Red giants and their satellites fall ponderously over the continent.

No African nation has yet succumbed to communism. The great majority of countries, more than twenty, belong to a group of states called the Monrovia bloc, which, though officially neutralist, leans toward the West. And even the rival Casablanca bloc—which consists of six radically nationalist nations that tend to be more willing to do business with the East, and in some cases to favor certain aspects of Marxism—discourages or suppresses domestic communism.

Even so, this ideology, starting in Africa from zero less than a decade ago, is gradually making its influence felt there. By 1961 the communist bloc had filled more than fifty diplomatic posts in Africa. Russia had diplomatic relations with thirteen nations, and Communist China with six. Even North Vietnam and Mongolia were represented in two. Communist broadcasts in English, French, Portuguese, Swahili, Arabic, and Amharic (Ethiopian), intended mainly or partly for Africa, totaled three hundred and eighty hours a week.

African newspapers were publishing communist-distributed propaganda. About twenty communist correspondents were stationed
in eight African countries. Some twelve hundred African students
were studying at communist-bloc universities, many of them
on scholarships granted by the communist World Federation of
Democratic Youth (WFDY), which has almost fifty African
affiliates. Communist sympathizers were infiltrating African trade
unions. Communist film festivals had been held in several African
nations. Communist cultural and athletic groups had swarmed
through the continent. In 1960 alone, no less than five hundred
diplomatic, economic, labor, and cultural delegations traveled between Africa and the communist world.

Communist credits and grants, moreover, amounted to about
$300 million (excluding Egypt) by 1961, while the number of
technicians accompanying this aid reached to nearly one thousand.
This aid is not much less than that granted by the West, a remarkable fact considering Africa's historical ties with the West. True,
much of it has been offered so far only on paper, and almost all
must be repaid, while Western aid figures indicate funds actually
provided, most of which do not have to be repaid. From the propaganda point of view, however, the communists have profited handsomely from their display of "generosity."

But though this record of recent Red infiltration in the politically virgin lands of Africa is impressive, the threat has been, up to
now, more in the nature of a cautious warning than an emergency
alarm. For if the communists have made many friends in Africa
in the last several years, few such friendships are rooted in ideological soil. Unlike the situation in most countries of Asia and Latin
America, there are very few hard-core communists among the
Africans, and no leftist leaders comparable to North Vietnam's
Ho Chi Minh or Cuba's Fidel Castro. The communist nations, at
least the Soviet Union and its satellites, have woven some of their
closest ties with military dictators, traditional monarchs, and backward tribal chieftains who could hardly be expected to encourage
the spread of communism in their countries.

Soft-pedaling Marxism, the Reds have largely concentrated on
exploiting Africa's anticolonial bitterness—racial prejudice in the
United States is one favorite theme—and trying to show that
African and communist interests are identical. They feel that
only by denying Africa to the West and thus creating a political
and economic vacuum on that continent can they attack with a
full-scale ideological broadside. Their objective is to fill the vacuum
and mold to their will the politically immature minds of the Afri-

can millions stirring from a slumber of thousands of years. And Africa's effort to condense all these years into an overnight meta- morphosis has understandably had results conducive to communist penetration. While the dynamism of communist industrialization attracts many African leaders, anticolonial rioting, intertribal mas- sacres, and economic chaos have given the Reds ample opportunity for infiltration.

Aside from colonial exploitation, probably the main ingredient in the communist-supported nationalist explosion has been the deep loneliness and dissatisfaction of the small but growing edu- cated and semi-educated groups that find themselves caught in a vice between two seemingly irreconcilable worlds. Youths, some of whose parents roam the forests stark naked except for cow dung smeared over their bodies to keep the mosquitoes away, have grown shameful of their heritage, yet lack any real understanding of Western materialistic and spiritual values. As they rush head- long into the white man's world, moving from their tribal areas into the towns to get jobs in mushrooming factories, they find they are rootless and deprived of the total security offered by tribal life, with its devotion to family interdependence and its lack of economic competition. The widespread psychological maladjustment that has resulted has to a large degree sparked such violent nationalist manifestations as the Mau Mau and the Congo riots, as well as attacks on Christian missionaries. Thus, independence means to politically conscious Africans not only an end to exploitation, but an opportunity to work out their own destiny, to wed Western concepts, including elements of Marxism, to indigenous cultural and spiritual values—explaining, for example, Kwame Nkrumah's effort to rule modern Ghana in the manner of a tribal chieftain.

The task of joining the two worlds has been, and will continue to be, arduous and frustrating. The traditional family system whereby all members of the family, including the most distant cousins, must help each other, with the richer members obligated to support the poorer, cannot easily be adapted to the modern urban setting. Nor can the extension of this family system to the supernatural—con- stant homage is paid to the ancestors, sometimes in the form of blood feuds with rival tribes or murder campaigns against the white man—be completely stamped out by a Christianity that even most African converts accept doubtfully and superficially. Yet, it is not impossible that some of the traditional values can be used to enrich family life in the new cities, and to render Christianity more mean- ingful in African terms through continued respect for the ancestors, respect, of course, shorn of voodoo worship.

I nearly fell victim to a chilling demonstration of the modern African's profound sense of insecurity when I visited a market-place in Kampala, the capital of Uganda, shortly before the country received independence from Britain. I put my camera to my eye to take pictures of nothing more subversive than Uganda women dressed in their traditional bustled Mother Hubbard dresses buying bananas, when I was suddenly surrounded by at least one hundred angry, fist-shaking youths. They screamed that I wanted to photograph their poverty simply to show the world that they were not ready for self-government. Violence was averted only when I gave them the role of film in my camera. This is the kind of anti-Western emotionalism that the communists hope will permit them to expand their own influence in Africa.

In their drive for influence, the Soviet Union and Communist China are competing not only with the West but with each other. Many observers think the Chinese may be the more popular, partly because they are not white. In the Congolese city of Stanleyville, when it was under the control of bitterly anti-American Lumumbists in early 1961, a Russian Tass correspondent told me: "I nearly got beat up today because some soldiers thought I was an American. Our politics may differ, but we're both in the same boat. We've both got white skin." Furthermore, fewer than twenty percent of the Africans have embraced Christianity, which is often regarded as the "religion of the colonialists," whereas more than forty percent adhere to the Eastern faith of Islam, and the remainder are largely pagans. Hence psychologically they feel more sympathetic to an Asian power like Red China.

Many Africans are also impressed by Red China's demonstration of an active interest in Africa only a few years after coming to power, as compared to Soviet Russia's delay of almost forty years. Peking established a Chinese-African Friendship Association in 1960, and is now planning an Institute of African Affairs, although, Africans point out appreciatively, Red China is plagued by domestic troubles far more demanding than those of Russia.

Red China's all-out effort to outshine Russia in Africa can be seen in its stepped-up radio propaganda. In 1961 the Chinese did more broadcasting to the African continent in English than did the Soviet Union, though the latter was ahead in total broadcasts. In addition, Peking broadcasts in Cantonese to the overseas Chinese in the Union of South Africa, the Malagasy Republic, and other regions.

In trade and aid Red China cannot compete with wealthier

Russia, but the help it does give is designed to produce maximum practical and propaganda results. Peking does not believe that Soviet aid policies are helping to foster communist ends. Moscow is granting large-scale assistance to almost any African government that will accept it, on the theory that the recipient nation would be obligated to maintain a neutralist, if not an anti-West, position. But the Russians have offered only limited aid to opposition groups in rebellion against established governments, even if these groups are leftist in character, preferring to extend their influence indirectly through politicians in power, whatever their ideological views. Unless the rebel opposition has extensive popular backing and is reliably communist in orientation—conditions that are not easily fulfilled in primitive Africa—Russia views the granting of significant aid to rebel groups as a dissipation of its funds and political opportunity.

Red China, conversely, thinks that it is the assistance given anticommunist governments that goes down the drain, for the recipients will never serve the Red cause, however much help they get. But aid that goes to dissident communists or groups tolerant of communism, it is convinced, serves a useful purpose if only to keep local wars going, stir up political hatreds, and create chaos, the kind of atmosphere necessary for the incubation of communism.

One difficulty Peking has met, however, has been Nationalist China's considerable foothold in Africa. It maintains embassies in sixteen African states, mainly the former French colonies, has sent agricultural missions to the two Congos, Gabon, Chad, and Dahomey, and has been negotiating an economic agreement with the Malagasy Republic.

For all the progress the communist bloc has made in recent years, the Reds have also found their strategy frustrated in other respects. The tone of anti-West propaganda is too consistently extreme for the liberated African countries, most of which wish to retain cultural and economic ties with their former colonial masters despite searing memories of their rule. The desire of most Africans to maintain a neutral position in the Cold War, at least on the surface, has worked to the disadvantage of the communist bloc no less than to that of the West. The Soviets, for example, found few African supporters when they started pouring supplies and technicians into the Congo under Premier Patrice Lumumba's rule, and even fewer African backers when they demanded the withdrawal of United Nations forces from the Congo, the resignation of the late United Nations Secretary-General Dag Hammarskjöld, and the decentralization of United Nations authority—measures calculated to ease the way for communist infiltration into Africa and other areas.

Finally, the nationalist fires that the Reds themselves are feeding serve, ironically, as a barrier to the spread of bloc influence. After winning their freedom from one form of colonialism, the new African states are wary about their relations with all big powers. They are prepared to borrow from the communist East as they are borrowing from the capitalist West, with most, in fact, strongly inclined toward socialism as well as toward authoritarianism. But they are not prepared to subscribe unconditionally to any alien philosophy, particularly one that requires obedience to a foreign power; and communism is clearly seen as such a philosophy.

The communists themselves are well aware of this obstacle. The *African Communist,* a periodical published by South African communists in London, said of African leaders:

> They are apt to be guided not by the interest of the masses but by their own special minority class interests. Often they are parochial, chauvinistic, tribalistic, and lacking broad vision. They are usually opportunistic, tend to compromise with the colonialists for small gains at the sacrifice of principle because they fear the revolutionary activities of the masses of workers and rural people.

A related difficulty encountered by the communists is the lack of highly trained communist elites in Africa to organize and direct Red policy and propaganda, a situation that has resulted in large measure from Russia's indifference to Africa up to a few years ago. Moscow devoted most of its attention to the subversion of Europe and Asia, considering Africa too distant from the communist nerve centers and too closely controlled by the colonial powers to warrant an important effort at infiltration. Furthermore, there were very few Africans who were sufficiently educated before the war to be able to grasp the complex Marxist philosophy, and the intellectuals who did emerge were too nationalistic to accept the role of Soviet puppet. Nor was Stalin prepared to co-operate with the national bourgeoisie.

The Soviet Union, at the same time, viewed Africa less as a geographical entity than as part of a larger racial problem. The Russians, completely miscalculating the African psychology, thought the Africans were aware of themselves only as members of the Negro race, not as members of any particular national group. In supporting the idea of a world Negro movement, the Comintern set up several Negro commissions in the 1920's and 1930's, but no Black Africans were included in them. One commission appointed in 1928 embraced thirty-two Negroes, including five from the United States, but the only African representative was a white from South Africa, and he was thrown out of the party for white chauvinism.

The Red International of Labor Unions, or Profintern, also had a special Negro commission, but it too failed to make inroads in Africa when its plan to send American and South African communists into tropical Africa was frustrated by the colonial powers. In 1930 several representatives from the British colonies of the Gold Coast, Gambia, and Sierra Leone attended a Profintern-sponsored Congress of Negro Workers in Hamburg, Germany, and the French communists organized a Negro League in the major ports of France. But in general, the communist influence seeping into Africa, particularly south of the Sahara, was insignificant.

Even after the war, in 1947, one of the top Soviet leaders, Andrei Zhdanov, told the inaugural session of the Cominform that Africa was simply part of "the rear of the capitalist system." In other words, Moscow had no immediate intention of supporting the middle-class nationalist leaders who wanted simply to establish capitalist states of their own. And as there were no communist parties as such in Black Africa to lead anticolonial rebellions, the Kremlin made no effort to stir up revolts after the war as it did in Asia, where well-disciplined parties were available.

But after Stalin's death, Africa soon felt the effect of the "right strategy" instituted by his successors, whereby the formerly "reactionary" national bourgeoisie suddenly became "progressive." In 1955 Professor I. I. Potekhin, the top Soviet Africanist, conceded, despite communist dogma to the contrary, that the African colonies would probably receive independence by nonrevolutionary methods. African participation in the governments of the Gold Coast, Nigeria, and the Sudan, he said, represented important "concessions by the colonialists." The colonial powers, he maintained, hoped to use the African middle class as a stabilizing element, but would fail because the national bourgeoisie were violently anti-imperialist. He tipped the Soviet hand. Moscow would exploit a sentiment common to communist and nationalist alike—hostility toward the Western ruling class.

Russia's new interest in Africa was evidenced in a program to train increasing numbers of African experts. Prior to this time, there existed only two small concentrations of Africanists in the Soviet Union. One opened in 1945 as a Department for African

Studies under the Institute of Ethnography in Leningrad, and the other was created in 1950 as a similar department under the Institute of Orientology. In 1958, however, a more important center of scholars was founded at the Moscow Institute of World Economics and International Relations, and in 1960 the Institute of Africa was formed under the direction of Professor Potekhin. It includes about fifty of Russia's top experts on Africa, whose mission is to turn out the most knowledgeable group of African specialists in the world.

This Institute is feverishly studying Africa's revolutionary potential and training small cadres in the "right strategy" as applicable to Africa through its four departments: African history, African languages, African art, literature, and culture, and current events, which deals in particular with the breakup of colonialism in Africa. The best students are given the job of teaching future diplomats and technicians the finer points of subversion at Moscow and Leningrad Universities. A Soviet Society for Friendship with the African Peoples was established in Moscow in 1959 and has been developing ties with various African groups, mainly in the scientific, cultural, literary, and artistic spheres, also under Professor Potekhin's leadership.

But though the "right strategy" opened the African door to communist-bloc influence, the Reds have found the going relatively rough in Africa. The difficulties facing the communists—as well as the potential threat the Reds represent—are evident in their effort to build up the kind of elite parties they need if they are ever to subvert Africa by indoctrinating hard-core African cadres.

The communists are counting on some of the African students studying in Red countries to become their trusted agents. Their trouble has not been in getting students to accept scholarships. On the contrary, far more students have applied to go to bloc schools than can be accommodated, and many, though they may be disillusioned after getting their wish, would prefer to study in the communist countries rather than in the United States.

This is due less to leftist leanings than to the bloc policy of guaranteeing all basic living and study expenses. In the United States, many African students, including those with scholarships, find themselves stranded without sufficient funds even to eat properly. According to a State Department report prepared for President Kennedy in October 1961, an untold number of African students in American colleges need a minimum of $500,000 in emergency assistance. The State Department does not have the money, the report said, and in any case the funds should be raised by private foundations and corporations and distributed through a central clearing house. But private spokesmen, especially representatives of the African-American Student Foundation, say that only a government-financed crash program can handle the emergency—which the Foundation helped to create by airlifting many students from Kenya to the United States without making sure they had adequate financial resources. Meanwhile, in the midst of this buck-passing between the government and private institutions, the unfortunate Africans, some of whom have threatened suicide rather than return home without a degree, are beginning to wonder about the value of individual freedom—freedom, it would appear, to starve.

This situation has contrasted sharply in the eyes of many young Africans with the highly organized system of dealing with foreign students in the communist bloc. They were particularly delighted by the establishment of Moscow's Friendship University—renamed Patrice Lumumba University after the Congolese leader's death—which is devoted entirely to students from underdeveloped countries. On opening day in October 1960, Khrushchev, at a gala welcoming ceremony, deeply impressed the students when he promised: "The Soviet Union has one aim, to help other countries train highly qualified people. Certainly we shall not impose our views or ideology upon any of the students. If you want to know my views, I'm a communist, and I think Marxism-Leninism the most progressive ideology. If some of you decide it suits you, too, we won't be offended. But we shall not be disappointed if you don't."

But the students got their first inkling of the true purpose of the university when they were given dormitory accommodations three to a room—including one Russian "student" in each. The Russians were supposed to help them learn the Russian language, but it soon became clear that their main function was, and is, to indoctrinate the visitors, if in a gradual and very subtle manner. Classroom teachers have displayed far less subtlety. An African medical student who had argued with his teacher complained that he was curtly told: "It's our job to indoctrinate you, especially you Africans." When the African said that this was not why he had come to Moscow, the teacher replied: "I know, but I have no choice but to do my job as I've been ordered."

A Nigerian student, Anthony G. Okotcha, whose wife is a sister of Dr. Nnamdi Azikiwe ("Zik"), Governor-General of Nigeria, fell prey to Red indoctrination methods. Explaining to the London *Sunday Telegraph* how this happened, Okotcha said of one of his professors:

He went on to expound Marxist-Leninist philosophy and launch a vitriolic attack on Christianity. He declared that our duty in Africa was to learn how to organize a popular front and drive the plundering imperialists into the ocean. The professor went on in this way for fully three hours. In spite of his poor English and rather comical gestures, he succeeded in impressing many of our fellow students, who told me afterwards that they felt ashamed of their Western democratic background. I felt unhappy, particularly because of his attack on Christianity . . . [But] how quickly the professors . . . can transform a rational being!

To be frank, within eight weeks of our arrival in Moscow my wife and I were ready to declare an all-out war on Western democracy. We had learned the Marxist-Leninist fundamentals by heart. We had learned to hate what Russians hated and to love what they loved . . . I watched . . . 200 students being shown how to dynamite a bridge, a railway train, a house and many other objectives. The classes were shown how to throw a hand grenade into a crowd, how to kill a man quickly with a dagger, and how to make surprise attacks at night . . . One army officer impressed on me that, when all other possibilities failed, the workers of oppressed countries must resort to arms. If the Soviet government, with unbounded generosity, was in a position to supply arms, the leaders of the rebellion must be able to use them properly.

Okotcha then described a "witch-doctors'" class that was conducted exclusively for African students. "As you know," he quoted the professor as saying,

in certain underdeveloped parts of Africa the people are highly superstitious, and it is only by playing on their superstition that they can be won over for political ends. Hence the need to adopt a system similar to that which sparked off the Mau Mau rebellion in Kenya. One witch-doctor operating among primitive people can do more than a dozen political lecturers. He can move the masses in any way he chooses. Well, then, supposing he is a communist?

The professor placed a skull on the table, and it appeared to say in a voice produced by radio microphone:

I am your ancestor speaking. I command you to go tonight, kill the British Governor and bring his head and hands to me. If you fail, I will cast evil spells on you and your family . . . I am the spirit of God. I command you to burn that Englishman's house and rape his wife and daughter. If you don't, you and all your family will be under the earth within seven days . . . I am Shango from the deep waters. I will fetch you if you refuse to join the Communist Party and do whatever its leader tells you . . . [He] then taught us how to simulate spirit rappings, cause a phantom to appear in a cloud of smoke, produce weird sounds in boxes, make a skeleton walk into dark rooms, haunt the houses of enemies, and pretend that we were possessed by spirits.

Okotcha was eventually sent on a spy mission to London, where he met other Nigerian communist students. "They told me," he related,

> that with the assistance of the Soviet Union, it was only a question of time before Nigeria would become a communist state. They expected great things of my wife and myself. My wife, being a sister of the Governor-General, would be able to infiltrate into government circles and learn some of their secrets. Meanwhile, it would be for me to coach selected members of the communist movements in the witch-doctor technique. These gentlemen then produced their political blueprint in the form of a typed booklet. As I read it I was amazed to find that their plans included assassinations, terrorism, arson, intimidation and all imaginable social unrest.

Bitterly disillusioned, Okotcha defected from the communist movement. He was not alone among African students in Moscow, who, even though not indoctrinated, felt sympathetic toward communism, but have since learned their lesson. In a letter sent to the United Nations and all African governments in the name of the Executive Committee of the African Students Union in Moscow, three African students protested the "deceits, the threats, the pressures, the brutality and the discrimination with which the Soviet administrators and strategists have so often handled African and other foreign students in the USSR." One African student, they wrote, protested in vain when he found that a picture he had taken in a boxer's pose was being used for anti-West propaganda purposes, with chains drawn on the wrists.

The very principle of Patrice Lumumba University was condemned by the letter-writing students:

> The height of discrimination was reached when the Soviet authorities announced their Friendship University plans. To build a separate university for Africans, Asians and Latin Americans is an insult to these people. It violates the traditional concept of a university as an open institution for learning, irrespective of race, religion or origin. We see this not only as an attempt to segregate these students and offer them lower standards of education, but as an endeavor to insulate Soviet people from contact with foreigners. We see in this proposal a propaganda stunt which ignores the opinion of African leaders.

Even if only a handful of African students are indoctrinated at communist institutions, the Red threat in the future will be considerable. Nevertheless, it appears that the great majority of students who had looked upon the communist nations with friendly eyes have become as disillusioned as Okotcha after experiencing communism at first hand.

African resistance to international communism is most directly mirrored in the fact that only seven communist parties exist on the continent. And of these, four are in Moslem North Africa and one consists almost entirely of whites.

THE MALAGASY REPUBLIC

The Communist Party of the Malagasy Republic, formerly French-controlled Madagascar, an island off the southeast coast of Africa, is Titoist in orientation. More influential in that country is the communist-infected Congress for the Independence of Madagascar (AKFM), the government's main opposition. This party, which, curiously, is led by a Catholic priest, the Rev. Richard Andriamanjato, is made up largely of Merina people whose ancestors dominated most of the island in the nineteenth century but who have been largely excluded from national politics in recent years. In 1959 the AKFM won a majority of seats in the municipal council of Tananarive, the national capital, and nearly took control of the city government. It also won majorities in Diégo Suarez, the site of a French naval base, and in Antsirabé, and showed important strength in several provincial capitals. Communists and fellow travelers in Malagasy published or edited seven daily or weekly newspapers in 1961.

THE SUDAN

The Sudan, which, in the Moslem north, is more Middle Eastern than African in cultural orientation, has the only other all-black Communist Party in Africa. Although the party has never been legal, it enjoyed considerable freedom before a military regime under the rule of the pro-West General Ibrahim Abboud came to power in 1958 and banned all political parties, promising "to overcome and completely wipe out communism in the Sudan." The party, originally called the Sudan Movement for National Liberation, is an offshoot of the Egyptian communist movement. Sudanese students set up the first communist cells in Cairo during

World War II when the Sudan was jointly controlled by Britain and Egypt.

After the war, the party won control of the Sudan's powerful Railway Workers Union, and founded the Sudanese Workers Federation of Trade Unions, which fostered strike after strike. The party also organized many peasants in the north, following the techniques of the Chinese communists. It has made little headway, however, in the pagan south, one of the most primitive areas remaining in Africa. In the sweltering jungle town of Juba, the southern capital, I found myself in a grocery store one day with two other customers: a fashionably dressed English lady of colonial heritage and a completely undressed African man—except for a necklace of red beads around the waist—who had walked to town from his village about one hundred miles away. There was little doubt that the man was utterly unaware of such machine-age concepts as communism.

Today, it is estimated that the underground party has less than three hundred hard-core members and under two thousand adherents, many of them university students in the national capital of Khartum. But despite their suppression, the Reds have continued to circulate newspapers and leaflets, while front organizations have probably retained their organizational structure. The Soviet Union is playing the same game with General Abboud as it is with Egypt's Gamal Abdel Nasser, in the hope of paving the way for future Red infiltration. In 1961 Moscow granted the Sudan $20 million in credits to finance development projects, and, together with East Germany, Czechoslovakia, and other bloc states, awarded about one hundred and seventy-five scholarships to Sudanese students in 1959-60.

THE UNION OF SOUTH AFRICA

The Communist Party of the Union of South Africa has from one thousand to two thousand members and supporters, mostly whites, though also embracing some Africans and Indians. Founded in 1921, the party went underground in 1950 with the promulgation of the Suppression of Communism Act by the white government. The party has exploited to the hilt government suppression of the nonwhite majority. As a result, the communists have easily infiltrated such African trade unions as exist and all important nonwhite political organizations, though most of them have been declared illegal.

Surprisingly, the government permits publication of such communist organs as *New Age,* a weekly newspaper which noncommunist African nationalists have more or less accepted as their mouthpiece; *Liberation,* a monthly journal aimed at left-wing intellectuals; and *Fighting Talk,* a bi-monthly periodical for veterans. The Reds oppose resort to violence, paradoxically enough, calculating that such tactics can only lead to greater government suppression of communism. Moreover, the white communists fear that antigovernment violence produces a reaction against all whites as such, communist or not, threatening their own, as well as the government's, position. "We're not communists," one African nationalist leader told me in Johannesburg, "but we'll gladly accept anyone's help. Do you honestly feel that we could be any worse off under communism than we are now? That would be impossible. The incredible thing is that despite the fact that we are treated like dogs, so few of us feel that communism is the only answer to our misery."

LIBYA AND TUNISIA

The Communist Parties of North Africa are so far among the weakest in the world, partly because of rigid government suppression, partly because of the strong Moslem influence among the workers and peasants. Party members in that area are almost exclusively intellectuals. The illegal Communist Party of Libya has about two hundred members, who work closely with the Soviet Embassy established in that country in 1956. In Tunisia, membership is estimated at two hundred and fifty to five hundred with an additional one thousand to two thousand supporters. The party, legal in that country, drew only about 3,400 votes in the 1959 elections but was influential in forcing France to grant independence to Tunisia in 1956. While reporting the anti-French riots that started the nationalist ball rolling in 1952, I found that communist propaganda had incited native mobs to attack European sections of Tunisian cities, although in several cities noncommunist nationalist leaders had tried to prevent the outbreak of open violence.

Also, the communists were responsible for publication of the most violent anti-French pamphlets, forcing the nationalists' hand in pressing for independence regardless of risk. After President Habib Bourguiba, who leans toward the West, took over the leadership of independent Tunisia, the Reds went into eclipse. But they grew in popularity following promises by Moscow in 1961 to "aid" Tunisia in its struggle to throw out French troops still occupying a base in Bizerte.

MOROCCO

The Communist Party of formerly French and Spanish Morocco
is about the same size as its Tunisian counterpart. But it is probably more dangerous, even though illegal, because it has enjoyed
greater success infiltrating noncommunist organizations such as
the National Union of Popular Forces, one of the nation's most
powerful political parties, and the Union Marocaine du Travail,
the largest labor federation. "The task of tasks," Communist Secretary-General Ali Yata has said, "is the formation of a national
alliance"—dominated, of course, by the Reds. Morocco, following
Egypt's lead, began to warm up to the Soviet Union in 1960, permitting a communist newspaper to be published for several months,
obtaining a Russian shipment of sixteen MIG aircraft, and welcoming Russian support for its claims on the new state of Mauritania. It also accepted technical aid in tea cultivation from Red
China.

But by mid-1961, the climate had begun to change. The Soviet
publication *Trud* said in July of that year that the situation of the
Moroccan workers "has noticeably deteriorated since independence." And Morocco began edging toward the West, asking the
United States, which has promised to evacuate three air and naval
bases it now operates in Morocco by 1963, for aircraft. One reason
for this apparently was that the MIG's were in too poor a condition to be used. At any rate, a cooling off between Morocco and
the Soviet Union has been evident, even though Morocco purchased Soviet arms in early 1962 when United States arms aid
proved "too little and too slow." Relations with Peking have also
faltered, with the return of the tea technicians to China after their
failure in experimentation with tea growing. Further, trade between
the two countries, started in 1959, has been steadily dropping.

ALGERIA

Algeria, which was granted independence by the French in July
1962, has the largest and best-organized Communist Party in
Africa, comprising an estimated five thousand to ten thousand
members. The party would probably be even stronger today if it
had not followed Stalin's "left strategy" in the early 1950's. In
1951 it won almost ten percent of the vote in a national election.
As a result of this success, the party was allowed to join a newly
organized Algerian Front for the Defense and the Respect of

Freedom, the nucleus of what was later to become the National Liberation Front (FLN), the nationalist organization that fought its French masters so bitterly in a seven-year war that cost 250,000 lives and $20 billion. "Algerians are all united against the French," a nationalist official told me in a small coffee shop deep in the maze of Algiers' Casbah. "And we're not interested in anybody's politics."

The Reds thus had a wonderful opportunity to infiltrate the early leadership of the nationalist movement and perhaps take it over. But in line with Stalinist policy, the party maintained itself as a unit and actually tried to discourage the struggle for independence, fearful that a nationalist government would be more difficult to overthrow than the French regime. A related reason lay in the large French element in the party; Frenchmen, Communist or otherwise, were not likely to be leaders in a nationalist government. Indeed, the "Frenchness" of the party helped to explain its lack of popularity.

It was thus not surprising when the communists denounced the nationalist revolution as "adventurism" and urged that it be converted into a proletarian revolution. The nationalists thereupon refused to have anything to do with the communists. Ironically, the French outlawed the party in 1955, offering the excuse that it was aiding the nationalist rebellion.

By this time, Stalin's successors were switching to the "right strategy," and ordering Reds everywhere to ally themselves with nationalist movements. In Algeria this movement, which the Kremlin had judged would never get anywhere against the French, was growing stronger all the time. The newly illegalized Communist Party formed a military organization of its own, called the Liberation Fighters, hoping to persuade the nationalists to accept communist aid again in the form of this ready-made military unit. But the nationalists, remembering how the Reds had previously deceived them, rejected the offer. In fact, they demanded that the communist unit be disbanded or be considered as hostile. Left without choice, the communists dissolved the organization. In return, they were permitted to join the FLN as individuals and in groups, provided they took orders from the nationalist command only.

Communists were thus absorbed into the FLN, but have been looked upon with considerable antipathy by the nationalists. Their effectiveness during the civil war was reduced still further by the capture and imprisonment of many of their leaders. In 1960 Ahmed Akkache, Secretary-General of the Algerian Communist

Party, was sentenced by the French to twenty years' imprisonment, and five other top Reds received shorter terms. One of them was Henri Alleg, who had edited the party newspaper *Alger Républicain* before it was banned several years ago, and who, while awaiting trial, wrote a sensational book, *The Question,* which described tortures he had allegedly suffered at the hands of French paratroopers. Following independence, Alleg resumed editing *Alger Républicain,* and immediately started complaining about censorship and calling for an alliance of "progressive" forces.

Ahmed Ben Bella, the "strongman" Premier of the Algerian government, is devotedly socialistic and has exhibited demagogic and extreme nationalistic tendencies akin to those of Egyptian President Nasser, who has greatly influenced him. Yet, even in his struggle for power with more moderate Algerian nationalist leaders in 1962, he did not appear to represent any direct ideological danger, though he is trying to set his country along the Nasserite path of nationalization, Cold War neutralism and economic cooperation with the communist nations.

A soldier in the Free French forces during World War II, Ben Bella left the army when peace came, embittered by the discrimination against Moslems he had encountered. He eventually joined the FLN and rose quickly to a position of leadership. But in 1956 he and four other rebel leaders were captured when a French fighter plane forced down a Moroccan airliner in which they were traveling. Ben Bella, a ruggedly good-looking bachelor of considerable charm, spent the next six years in French prisons, emerging as a martyr with Algerian independence.

As head of the post-rebellion FLN, a monolithic political party, Ben Bella, in one of his first moves after independence, prohibited communists from running candidates for a new National Assembly. He then warned the Reds to submerge themselves in the Front and forbade them to hold a scheduled press conference intended to answer the demand. He also supressed a local party organ, *Liberty,* and finally outlawed the party itself after one of its leaders complained in a communist publication that "a single party created by those at the top is not viable." A government spokesman stated succinctly, reflecting for the first time Ben Bella's awareness of the international communist danger: "We want no parties in Algeria that are run from abroad."

Ben Bella visited Cuba in October 1962 after a trip to the United States and received a tremendous welcome from the Castro government, which he, in turn, delighted with the words: "Algeria is with Cuba." He also supported Cuba's demand that the United States evacuate Guantanamo Naval Base. But, according to the Algerian leader, his backing was not for communism but for Cuban independence and some aspects of Castroite reform.

If Ben Bella himself may be a Nasser-style nationalist at worst, it is less clear what some of the people around him stand for. Defense Minister Colonel Houari Boumedienne, who controls the army, is believed to be considerably to the left of the Premier and an ardent admirer of Mao Tse-tung.

Algeria's multiple economic problems, meanwhile, are not likely to hinder communist propaganda efforts. The peasants cannot, in most cases, eke out more than a subsistence living from the sparsely cultivated land, yet lack the numbers and the skill to provide a base for extensive industrialization. About 400,000 unemployed have emigrated to France where they live in slum areas while sending home $25 million in factory wages each year. Aggravating this situation was the mass flight of Europeans—700,000 of the original 1,000,000—to France. They took with them about $800 million in capital and left the country desperately short of trained technicians. To lure back some capital, Ben Bella has had to promise to limit his nationalization program.

However that may be, it is likely that the Algerian leaders will maintain friendly relations with the communist bloc, where about two hundred and twenty-five Algerian students were studying in 1961. Up to now, the country appears to be oriented more toward Peking than toward Moscow. The Soviet Union granted considerable aid to the Algerian rebels, sending shiploads of arms, as well as food and factory and agricultural machinery for use in training Algerian refugees living in Tunisia "for production work." And it recognized the Algerian Provisional Government within twenty-four hours after the announcement of a cease-fire agreement with France. But in general, Moscow discouraged a full-fledged war against France, hoping thereby to keep French President De Gaulle from co-operating closely with the United States and Britain and to prevent a possible internationalization of the Algerian conflict that could lead to world war.

Red China, however, offered the Algerians tons of arms and other aid—though there is no evidence that much of it arrived—together with advice that they should prosecute the war vigorously without regard to the risks. "The Russians cautioned us about harsh initiatives [in North Africa] which might create an explosive situation," an FLN representative said in a confidential memorandum on his return from a trip to Moscow and Peking. "The Chinese did not . . . Undoubtedly the Chinese would be ready to consider the possibility of the extension of the conflict and its internationalization." Mao obviously saw an opportunity for communists to make hay in a Spanish-type civil war. But as far as the Algerians were concerned, it was Peking that supported their cause with the greatest vigor—a psychological factor that could have unfortunate consequences in the future.

In addition to the handful of communist parties in Africa, small Marxist intellectual groups have sprung up, mainly in formerly French and British West Africa, where Africans are more developed than elsewhere south of the Sahara. These groups may eventually become the nucleus of communist parties, though most are handicapped by the absence so far of any proletarian or peasant support. Their importance to the communist bloc was reflected in the world-wide communist program formulated in December 1960 at a Moscow meeting of eighty-one communist parties: "Like-minded Marxists are rallying in the countries which have shaken off colonial tyranny and taken the path of independent development." This statement obviously referred to countries in which no communist parties had yet been formed—meaning, for the most part, the new African states.

SENEGAL, TOGO, DAHOMEY, AND GABON

In the former French colonies, many of these Marxist groups have been recruited from the leftist Paris-based Federation of Black African Students in France, which is strongly influenced by the French Communist Party. One of these groups is the Parti Africain de l'Indépendance (PAI), which was founded in 1952 in Dakar but was banned by Senegal authorities when it led election-day riots in 1957. Larger and more dangerous is the Parti du Regroupement Africain, usually called PRA-Senegal. This was established in 1958 to oppose the De Gaulle constitution, which provided for continued ties between France and its territories. But despite this double threat to its power, the moderately socialist pro-French government of President Léopold Senghor, one of Africa's outstanding intellectuals, has the support at present of the great majority of Senegalese.

Another extreme West African group is the Parti de la Révolution Socialiste du Benin, an organization of Togo and Dahomey far leftists, who issued a communiqué when the party was formed in 1959 supporting Marxist-Leninism and the establishment of a Socialist United States of Africa. The Parti de l'Unité Gabonaise is a mildly Marxist group in Gabon, mainly backed by a Gabonese student organization in Paris called the Mouvement Gabonaise d'Action Populaire.

CAMEROON

The most menacing Red-oriented group in the former French territories is the small but violent illegal branch of the Cameroon's Union des Populations du Cameroun (UPC). The UPC started out as a radical nationalist party in banana-rich Cameroon and was banned by the French in 1955. It eventually split into two factions, with one returning to legal political activity to form the main noncommunist opposition in parliament, and the other going into exile and supporting guerrilla and terrorist activity against the French and their allies with communist-bloc aid. When Cameroon received independence in 1960, however, the illegal UPC could no longer pose effectively as a nationalist organ, but continued its violence as an ideological group, hoping to overthrow the moderate nationalist government by force.

Peking's influence on the terrorists is far greater than that of Moscow, which supposedly advised them that violence would get them nowhere and that they should try to take over the government through legal means. The late terrorist leader, Dr. Felix Roland Moumié, who was mysteriously poisoned in Geneva in 1960, is believed to have been criticized by Khrushchev for "infantile extremism." But Mao Tse-tung encouraged him to intensify his terrorist tactics, giving him a copy of his book on partisan warfare with the dedication: "Here you'll find out what is going to happen in Cameroon." In 1959 one of Moumié's lieutenants told me in a jungle village in the then British-controlled Southern Cameroons, which had since voted to unite with strife-torn Cameroon: "The Chinese had the right answer. They fought for power and they won. We'll do the same thing—whether we must fight the French or the indigenous reactionaries."

And the terrorists—some of whom, French and British officials claim, have been trained in China—are doing just this. French-led armed convoys—the newly independent Cameroon government has asked French troops to remain—keep the main communications routes open, and an all-night curfew is enforced in towns and villages. But such measures have not prevented guerrillas, often doped and branded on the chest with five cuts to make them "bullet-proof," from quietly chopping up men, women, and children with their machetes.

Nevertheless, such violence has greatly diminished since 1961 as the result of military vigilance. There is still some danger, however, that terrorism will spread to the hitherto calm Southern Cameroons, which has chosen to join the former French territory. Moscow may be right in considering the terrorist effort a lost cause, in view of the small popular backing it enjoys; but the guerrillas, shielded by dense jungle, could probably keep the infant nation in turmoil indefinitely. Moreover, the terrorists enjoy the support of the influential leftist trade union, the Confédération Générale Kamerounaise du Travail, one of the few African labor organizations still maintaining affiliation with the communist-led World Federation of Trade Unions. This union, however, is only one of several labor organizations in Cameroon.

It is not really clear whether the outlawed UPC, however much aid it may be receiving from the communist bloc, is communist in the orthodox sense. The party program says that "the aim of our revolution is not to oppose capitalism, but imperialism and its allies." Also, the use of the slogan, "All Africans are brothers," is seen by many observers as a denial of the need for class struggle. But the decision of the group to use China as a model for its revolt has led other experts to speculate that it would also pattern its political and ideological policies after those of Peking if it came to power.

The Marxist influence is even less notable in the former British colonies than in the French, due to the feeble propaganda machinery of the British Communist Party as compared to that of the much stronger French Communist Party; and also to the British policy of running each of its territories as a separate and almost isolated unit in contrast with the French tendency to centralize colonial administration, and thus permit a greater flow of alien ideas.

NIGERIA

Communism is particularly weak in the most important former British territory, Nigeria, which, with over forty million people, is the most populous nation in Africa, and comprises an area larger than France and Italy combined. Small competing Marxist groups constantly appear and disappear, unable to establish themselves firmly. In 1961 three groups existed, one of which is a political front for the procommunist Nigerian Trade Union Congress. The latter is, however, completely overshadowed in importance by the similarly named noncommunist Trade Union Congress of Nigeria.

The main activity of the various leftist groups so far has been to pass around among themselves communist literature which, though banned by the government, manages to trickle into the country— chiefly, it seems, from Red China rather than from the Soviet Union. But on a number of occasions they have made their voices heard. They are believed to have led an anti-American riot that broke out in the Nigerian capital of Lagos shortly after the assassination of Congolese Premier Lumumba. More than a dozen establishments were attacked, with the main targets apparently the American Embassy and the Bank of America. Members of these Marxist groups were also primarily responsible, it is thought, for trying to discredit the American Peace Corps through publication of the contents of a post card sent by a member of the corps, Marjorie Michelmore, to a friend in the United States describing her shock at Nigeria's poverty and primitiveness. The furor that resulted from communist-inspired cries of "neo-colonialism" forced Miss Michelmore to leave the country.

Often the communists are supported—particularly among the students—by radical nationalists of the stripe of Ghana's Nkrumah. Curiously, whereas most Ghanaian students appear to be protesting Nkrumah's curb on democratic liberties and his close relations with the communist bloc, many Nigerian students criticize their moderate, democratic, subtly pro-West government and seem to prefer the radical militancy of the Ghanaian leader—a commentary on the divergent and confused states of mind of many African intellectuals, who are not sure what they want but want something different from what they have.

The cynical attitude of Nigerian students is reflected in their sometimes cool relationship with American instructors at the University of Nigeria at Nsukka, in the country's Eastern Region, one of four new Nigerian universities. (A fifth, University College, has been operating for years in Ibadan under the auspices of the University of London.) Americans at Nsukka, who compose more than a third of the faculty, include the acting director and fifteen Michigan State University professors. In addition, thirty Peace Corps members teach there. Some students maintain that the American professors have been rushing them through courses without adequate preparation or books. Others resent what they consider the patronizing attitude of teachers who wear native Nigerian robes, even at functions where the Nigerians themselves show up in Western clothes.

In recognition of student sensitivity to any suggestion of "neo-colonialism," the Nigerian government, to balance the American influence at the institution, has employed a Marxist theoretician, Dr. Karl Markov of East Germany's University of Leipzig, as chairman of the history department, and two young professors from the same school—an American and a Nigerian—as his assistants. Thus, American aid can sometimes produce a counterreaction unfavorable to the West, though ultimately the West is likely to benefit from this aid.

Flurries of anti-Americanism have not been representative of the attitude of most Nigerians, who regard the United States as a friend. Nor, for that matter, can one hear much criticism among Nigerians of their former British masters, who performed one of their finest colonial jobs in developing the nation and preparing it for self-government. It is now the function of procommunists to tear down this good will, as evidenced by the blueprint for Nigeria's takeover that Nigerian students in Moscow are being trained to implement.

The Nigerian government of Prime Minister Alhaji Sir Abubakar Tafawa Balewa, however, is one of the most stable, mature, and reasonable in Africa, though it had to clamp military rule on western Nigeria in mid-1962 when political chaos threatened to produce violence. Despite the regime's pro-West leanings, for the record it is neutralist; it virtually has to be in order to avoid being called a Western puppet by such bitterly anticolonial countries as Ghana and Guinea. For one thing, to balance its economic ties with the West to some degree, Nigeria is negotiating trade and cultural agreements with the Soviet Union. But as a luxuriously robed Nigerian official frankly told me as we strolled through the bustling market quarter of Lagos past booths offering such diverse exotic items as multicolored silk cloth and dead rats and herbs guaranteed to chase away evil spirits: "Nigeria is a large and rich country. It is only a matter of time until it develops into a powerful nation with a high standard of living. Because we are so full of confidence, and because we haven't an inferiority complex like some smaller, less richly endowed nations have, we do not make a fetish of nationalism and anticolonialism, though we are as opposed to colonialism as anybody. And we don't feel we have to make an alliance with communism to prove we are nationalistic and anticolonial. We want to be friends with everybody, of course, but it is obvious to us which side in the Cold War best represents human freedom and dignity."

KENYA

A more threatened area may prove to be the East African territory of Kenya, which may be granted independence in 1963. Kenya is far less developed politically and economically than any of the other West African states. Moreover, it has a problem that none of the latter has: a large white settlement. Thus, when independence comes, anything might happen in this land which bred the Mau Mau. And the communist bloc is ready to take advantage of any channel of infiltration that may develop, as was the case in the Congo, although the Congolese were considerably less prepared for independence.

Whether the communists gain a foothold in Kenya will depend on a number of factors. One is what kind of man Kenya's nationalist leader, Jomo Kenyatta, turns out to be. Kenyatta is probably the most controversial personality in Africa. Most Africans in Kenya virtually worship him as the George Washington of their country. Most whites in Kenya fear and distrust him. He was released from prison and exile in a remote area of Kenya in 1961 after serving part of a seven-year term for allegedly "managing" the Mau Mau that had killed and maimed dozens of whites and thousands of Africans between 1952 and 1956 in the first significant nationalist uprising in Black Africa. A "leader of darkness and death" was the description given him by Kenya Governor Sir Patrick Renison only about a year before his release. "He is a communist, another Castro," a white settler told me in the attractive Europeanized capital of Nairobi, though Kenyatta vehemently denies he is one.

Kenyatta is a unique product of African nationalism. He was probably the first important nationalist leader in Africa, but the kind of nationalism he originally supported had little to do with modern African aspirations. The son of a witch doctor, he was essentially a tribalist, and his main political aim was to strengthen and protect the interests of his Kikuyu tribe, the largest in Kenya. A bearded man with piercing eyes and a devastating talent for oratory, Kenyatta took over the Kikuyu Central Association in the 1920's and began organizing it into a Western-style political party. In 1929 he went to London to demand better conditions for the Kikuyus, protesting in particular the "theft" of their land by white settlers, a clearly justifiable grievance.

Coolly received, Kenyatta made a splendid object of communist affection. The Communist League Against Imperialism fawned upon him while he was in London, and Soviet officials received him with open arms during a trip to Moscow in 1929. In 1932 he returned to Moscow, then studied anthropology at the University of London, sharing an apartment with Paul Robeson, the American Negro singer who has long been associated with communist causes. He is also said to have joined the British Communist Party—another allegation he has stoutly denied.

Kenyatta's writings would appear to make his protestations believable. They project him as a curious, frightening combination of Western intellectual and African witch doctor who yearns for a return to black-magic traditionalism—in any event, hardly the ideal Marxist-Leninist. He dedicated his mystical 1938 book, *Facing Mt. Kenya,* which Marx and Lenin would have read with shock and disgust, to the Kikuyu clans "and all the dispossessed youth of Africa: for perpetuation of communion with ancestral spirits through the fight for African freedom and in the firm faith that the dead, the living and the unborn will unite to rebuild the destroyed shrines." He demanded the rebirth of tribal ideals, bitterly attacking missionaries, for example, for trying to discourage the cruel ceremonial Kikuyu practice of female circumcision, the removal of the clitoris and part of the vulva.

In any event, it is far from clear that he was a communist, or even that he led the Mau Mau. Many observers claim that the British did not give him a fair trial. It is no less uncertain what his political philosophy is today, or whether he retains the forcefulness to impose it, despite his call for a democratic neutralist government that would respect white rights. Since he regained his freedom he has displayed far less capacity for leadership than had been expected.

When I arrived in Kenya for a visit late in 1958, Kenyatta's name was taboo. The British never mentioned him except in obscene terms, and Africans never mentioned him at all, at least not in public, fearing they would be suspected of pro-Mau Mau sentiments and detained by the police or, if they were politicians, possibly banished from the political scene. But before the end of my visit, one politician named Oginga Odinga stood up in the British-led Legislative Council, Kenya's parliament, and shocked the colony with the flat statement that "Kenyatta is the real leader of the African people" and should be freed immediately. Within a few months, almost every African politician in Kenya was similarly demanding his release. Kenyatta suddenly became a far more powerful symbol of Kenyan nationalism than he had been before his imprisonment. The national cry reached a crescendo when Odinga outdid himself by suggesting that Kenyatta was a god.

Many people, including some of his own colleagues, laugh Odinga off as a rather comic figure unburdened by an overload of intellect. But the communist bloc views him more seriously. He is probably the top Sino-Soviet agent in Kenya, and is quite open about it. A member of the Luo tribe, second in size only to the Kikuyus in Kenya, he is, ironically, one of Africa's pioneer capitalists, having founded the prosperous Luo Thrift and Trading Corporation. He entered politics after the war, and his crude but folksy demagoguery lifted him to the top political rank. But he never quite felt that he was appreciated by many of his fellow politicians, who sometimes snickered when he showed up at parliamentary meetings in feathered headdress and monkey-skin robe. Nor did he feel the United States realized how important he was. "I cannot forget," he told me with an agonized expression on his small, round face, "that your country refused to give me one of those State Department-sponsored trips to America, though it did not turn down other politicians."

There were people, he eventually discovered, who did appreciate his importance—the communists. In 1960 he visited and was given the red-carpet treatment in the Soviet Union, Communist China, Czechoslovakia, and East Germany. He returned to Kenya with a strong procommunist outlook, though denying that he was a communist. He also returned with about $30,000 presented to him for use in financing the dispatch of about one hundred African students to communist-bloc schools. He informed me in Nairobi in mid-1961 that twenty students had so far been sent to communist countries, casually confirming that they had to be smuggled out of the colony through underground means (via Uganda and Egypt), because of the refusal of the British to let them go.

Odinga said he had been particularly impressed by Red China. "Their communal agricultural system," he glowed, "is more or less like our own traditional system. We have always believed that the land belongs to the community and that the individual farmer is just a tenant." He added, picking at one of the colored plumes in his headdress, "We must face the fact that the world is heading toward socialism. Though I'm a capitalist myself, I would gladly sell my business to a co-operative. As for political freedom, did you know that China has nine different parties?" he asked, referring to closely regulated puppet allies of the Communist Party allowed to exist in China. "Why, I felt freer in China than in any country I have ever been."

Odinga's bitterest enemy is brilliant young Tom Mboya, a labor leader and politician who, while finding it politically necessary to support Kenyatta, may be the strongest man in Kenya today. Mboya, a handsome man with deceptively sleepy eyes and an arrogant manner, has many ties with American organizations, particularly with the AFL-CIO, and is known for his pro-United States tendencies. He considers Odinga, with his communist affiliations, a danger to Kenya, while Odinga never fails to remind the public that Mboya—who assured me, no doubt for political reasons, that he "couldn't be more neutralist"—is a friend of the "American imperialists." Their rivalry is intensified by the fact that both men are Luos.

If Odinga hopes to turn Kenya into a communist state, he might find conditions favorable when the colony receives its independence. For it could turn into another Congo. The threat of violence has, as in that country, two edges: intertribal and anti-white. And, as the Mau Mau episode showed, Kenyan tribes, or at least the dominant Kikuyus, can be second to none in terms of savagery. This savagery could be directed toward the whites as soon as British troops left. Though the Mau Mau itself has long since been crushed, a weaker successor organization, called the Kenya Land Freedom Army, has been operating in Kenya, if without serious consequences so far. Its estimated two thousand members are believed to have taken secret oaths to strike at the white man and all who oppose the organization, but it is not clear whether these oaths have yet called for murder, as did the Mau Mau oaths, which were administered amid obscene sexual rites. Perhaps ominously, neither Kenyatta nor Odinga has condemned the new movement. Nor is it certain that Kenyatta, for all his prestige, would be able to control it even if he wanted to. A captured official of the secret society arrogantly told the police: "If Kenyatta gets in our way, we shall cut him down like anyone else."

As for tribal rivalry, few countries in Africa are plagued as seriously with this problem as the Kenyans. Kenyatta himself, though he is now trying to play the role of the true, nonsectarian nationalist, can hardly have abandoned completely the narrow, fanatical tribal pride he exhibited in *Facing Mt. Kenya.* This attitude is reflected in Kenyan politics. Two large parties have formed an uneasy coalition. One is the Kenya African National Union, known as Kanu, of which Kenyatta is president, and the other, the Kenya African Democratic Union, referred to as Kadu. A two-party system may be desirable in a more developed society, but in a politically immature country like Kenya it means pitting two tribal groups against each other, each more concerned with its particular tribal interests than with the nation as a whole. Thus, Kanu, the stronger party, largely represents the Kikuyu, Luo, and Wakamba tribes, the three largest and most advanced in Kenya; while Kadu constitutes a defensive group of the remaining tribes, which intensely fear the domination of the bigger ones. The two parties have agreed to a compromise constitution giving the smaller tribes a certain amount of autonomy—the larger tribes favor a strong central government—but this accord may well disintegrate when Kenya becomes independent.

The Somalis of the north demand that the territory they inhabit come under the control of neighboring Somalia. Other small tribes insist they will never take orders from the Kikuyus. "If the Kikuyus and their friends try to run our lives, we will kill them all," a handsome but fierce-looking nomadic Masai tribesman with streaks of paint on his cheeks, a glittering spear in his hand, and a brown cloth cape wrapped around his otherwise naked body told me in the transient south Kenyan village, or *manyatta,* where he lived, protected from wild animals by a fence of thorns. The forty thousand Masais, he said, were satisfied with their traditional pastoral life. They liked living in windowless huts made of sun-baked cow dung, and they needed little nourishment besides cow's milk and blood—drained from the living creature in small quantities, like water drawn from a faucet. And no college-bred Kikuyu was going to make them change their ways.

The communists are thus looking forward to a new opportunity to establish a foothold in Africa in the midst of chaos. Much will depend not only on the intentions of Jomo Kenyatta, but also on how much influence such intelligent, mature politicians as Tom Mboya—who has authoritarian leanings, but would probably be a benevolent, Western-oriented dictator at worst—can exert in the service of calm and unity in a nation without a history of either.

Another determining factor could be the success of plans to form an East African federation that would unite Kenya with two other British-tutored territories: Tanganyika, which became independent in 1961, and Uganda, freed in 1962. The moderate leadership in these areas, where there has been no known communist activity, could constitute a significant stabilizing element in such a federation. Julius Nyerere, who resigned the premiership of Tanganyika in early 1962, probably because some of his colleagues considered him too moderate, apparently proved so indispensable to stable, public-supported rule that he was chosen President of the republic the following December. And certainly this slim, youthful man with lively eyes and an infectious smile is one of the wisest leaders in Africa.

"There is no room in Africa for political extremism or racialism," he told me, exhibiting a warmth and humility seldom found in African leaders. "Blacks and whites must live together in peace, each helping the other. Of course, I hate colonialism. But at the same time, I am grateful for the civilization that the British have brought us."

THE RHODESIAS AND NYASALAND

One British territory which has so far yielded little evidence of communist infiltration but which is particularly ripe for Red penetration is the Federation of Rhodesia and Nyasaland, in south-central Africa. Composed of three distinct areas—Northern and Southern Rhodesia and Nyasaland—the Federation is confronted with a white-settler problem far more difficult than that which has plagued Kenya. For while the proportion of Africans to Europeans in Kenya is over one hundred to one, it is twelve to one in Southern Rhodesia, and thirty-one to one in Northern Rhodesia, though three hundred to one in Nyasaland.

With an Algeria-like racial and political explosion threatening, the British in 1960 set Nyasaland on the way to independence by letting nationalist leader Hastings K. Banda virtually control the government under a British governor. In 1962 they gave Africans in copper-rich Northern Rhodesia increased voting rights, thus permitting the establishment of a Negro-run regional government by the end of the year. Southern Rhodesia, which enjoys a greater measure of self-government than its sister territories, is, however, solidly controlled by Europeans who vow to maintain their authority, although the local government has agreed to end racial discrimination in public places. (In a recent interracial beauty contest to choose Miss Rhodesian Federation, only one out of forty entrants was white.) At any rate, the Africans are not satisfied with the "crumbs" thrown to them and demand full political and social equality with whites; while the whites, particularly in Southern Rhodesia, are determined to hold the racial line, and turn their country into another bloody Algeria, or possibly join the Union of South Africa, if necessary.

Among the "moderate" white supremacists is Federation Prime Minister Sir Roy Welensky, who has the grin, gait, and bulging build of a department-store Santa Claus. But Sir Roy does not intend to play Santa Claus to the Africans. "What you Americans don't seem to realize," he said to me in his modest home in Salisbury, the clean, modern capital of Southern Rhodesia, "is that, quite unlike South Africa, we are moving in the direction of political and social equality between African and European."

In a sense, this was true, even before the British stepped in to impose reforms. Sir Roy's policy has been to move forward —but at an almost imperceptible pace. He has thus hoped to keep his promise of advancement to the Africans, at least technically, and to keep his white followers happy as well. The Prime Minister justified the snail-like tread of reform with the argument that "economic advancement must precede political advancement. Once we close the gap economically, political progress will come automatically. Political rights must be earned." Take, for example, the one African lawyer in Southern Rhodesia. Had not the Southern Rhodesian parliament passed a special bill exempting him from a law prohibiting Africans from occupying homes or offices in white areas?

Sir Roy says the African leaders are extremists. And some are. Several Southern Rhodesian nationalist chiefs I met could only spout the need for violence. But I also met a more moderate nationalist who said, while conducting me on an automobile tour of Salisbury, that he deplored violence. "Of course, the extremists have much power now. And as the people become more desperate, our leaders will become even more extreme. I'm hated now by some of my own people because of my moderate views."

He stopped the car in front of two vacant telephone booths, one marked, "For Europeans Only," and the other, "For Africans Only," and without hesitation entered the one intended for white use and made a telephone call. On returning to the car, he said, "The way to win our struggle is through passive resistance, but Welensky is pushing the moderates to the wall. Soon the extremists will listen to the communists. And that's when the trouble here will really start."

Shortly after this talk, my moderate friend was thrown into jail for passively resisting racial discrimination.

SOMALIA

Northeast of Kenya, straddling the horn of East Africa, is another country that has been zeroed in for communist infiltration—Somalia. An Italian colony before the war, it was occupied by the British in the early postwar years, became a United Nations trust territory under Italian tutelage in 1950, and was granted independence in 1960. Somalia's principal asset, it would seem, is its lovely women, whose small, sensitive features reflect the Somalis' Hamitic, rather than Negroid, origin. Although Somalia is a staunchly Moslem nation, the women do not wear veils as their counterparts in many other Moslem countries do to shield themselves from the gaze of men. In Somalia, premarital virginity is protected through another method, a process called infibulation: the sewing together—in childhood—of the vaginal lips with thread that is only broken on a girl's wedding day. Tall and slender in their brightly hued *futas,* long, flowing sarong-like garments, they glide by like swans in peacock's clothing. So delicately appealing are their faces, beaming with a touch of the Madonna lent by their long shawls worn loosely around the head, that many might be taken for Hollywood film stars smeared with grease paint.

But aside from this feminine wealth, Somalia is a poor country indeed. It is an arid, rocky, desert land. Just to stay alive requires more sustaining power that its nationalist will and meager resources alone can provide. Somalia is destined to depend indefinitely on large-scale outside aid. And because of its strategic location, this poverty has automatically made it a prime pawn on the Afro-Middle East Cold War chessboard. The new republic, a triangular peninsula made up of pre-independence Somalia and the former British Somaliland, juts into the Arabian Sea, with the Gulf of Aden on one side and the Indian Ocean on the other. Just north of the once British-controlled zone lies tiny French Somaliland, which voted in 1958 to remain under French rule but may well unite with Somalia eventually. Standing at the entrance to the Red Sea, it is a trade crossroads of the world. Whoever has the support of Somalia in the future could control this vital crossroads. If the communists won out, they would also have an invaluable springboard for penetration into Kenya to the south and Ethiopia to the west.

The government of Premier Abdirashid Ali Shermarke, though neutralist in the Cold War, has little regard for communism, and there are only a handful of communists in the country. Nevertheless, a Communist Party was established in 1956 under the Italian administration and enjoyed a brief existence of three months before being suppressed. The Reds also organized a teachers' union, Somalia's first trade union, though this, too, was soon outlawed by the Italians. Communists have since infiltrated other infant unions. The Italian Communist Party is believed to be behind most of the communist activity in this country.

With the local communists too feeble to work through, Moscow and Peking are both using other channels of infiltration. The pattern of their respective approaches approximates that in many other Afro-Asian countries. The Russians are trying to woo the legal noncommunist government, offering only token aid and encouragement to opposition forces, while the Chinese are helping only these latter forces in the hope of creating a chaotic, revolutionary atmosphere conducive to communist gain.

The Soviet Union, in 1961, granted loans to Somalia totaling $50 million, one of the largest aid programs per capita that the Soviets have given any country—amounting, in view of Somalia's small two million population, to about $25 for each Somali. One long-term loan of almost $45 million will be used for industrial and agricultural development, and a second five-year trade credit of about $5 million will permit the purchase of Soviet goods above the value of Somali sales to Russia. Moscow promised, in addition, to construct gratis two hospitals, a high school, a radio station, and a printing plant. It will also send teams of physicians and teachers to train Somalis and will receive Somali doctors in Soviet schools. A cultural agreement calls for exchanges in the areas of science, education, literature, health, art, and sports.

Red China is employing stealthier means of infiltration. It has concentrated on winning friends among extreme Somali nationalists. One of Peking's best friends is Hagi Mohammed Hussein, president of the Greater Somalia League, the largest opposition party. Hussein, a protégé of UAR President Nasser, broadcast the latter's pan-Islamic philosophy to his homeland from Cairo for four years. Shortly after he returned to the sleepy little oasis of Mogadishu, Somalia's Italian-style capital, I met two of Hussein's lieutenants in the outdoor café of Hotel Croce del Sud, a mass of white masonry stretched around a huge court. "We don't like communism," one of them said, "but we hate American imperialism. And we must see to it that you Americans do not get a foothold here." After Hussein visited Peking in 1960, his party's propaganda began to parallel that of the communists so closely that some party colleagues protested that he was abandoning Islam for communism.

But finally all sides agreed that the party dissension had resulted from the machinations of "American imperialism."

Peking at first tried to do business with Mohammed Harbi Farah, head of the National Pan-Somali Movement, the outlawed French Somali counterpart of Hussein's party. Harbi demanded that the French get out of its Somali territory and permit it to join Somalia. A fanatical nationalist whom officials in the French Somali Capital of Djibuti colorfully described to me as a "power-hungry criminal," Harbi was invited to Peking early in 1960 and given an estimated $4.2 million, deposited in a Swiss bank. With part of the money, he purchased a shipload of arms, which was to land in Berbera on the northern Somalia coast and unload its cargo secretly, due to the Somalia government's determination to stay clear of the Cold War.

But Harbi, who was to have arranged for the smuggling of the arms, was killed in a plane crash several days before the scheduled arrival of the ship. When the vessel arrived, ostensibly with a load of cement, and was not met by Harbi, the Egyptian skipper, fearing a trap, apparently dumped the arms overboard. Even so, the skipper was suspected of smuggling by the Somalia authorities. He was put on trial, found guilty, and heavily fined. Since then, several crates of arms have been washed ashore, arms that might have created the chaos on which the communists thrive.

They could have been used against several targets, all for basically the same reason. The fanatical nationalists want to establish by force if necessary a rigidly Moslem Greater Somalia that would embrace the Republic of Somalia, French Somaliland, and the Somali-inhabited territories of northern Kenya and Ethiopia. About 630,000 Somalis live outside the boundaries of the new republic. The nationalists might have employed their Chinese arms to "liberate" these Somalis, and perhaps also to overthrow the moderate Somalia government itself, which the extremists despise for insisting that only peaceful means be used to achieve Somali unity. Shortly before Somalia received independence, President Aden Abdullah Osman, a slender, quiet man of gentle demeanor, told me in Mogadishu: "Of course, we're for a Greater Somalia. But we can wait. Resort to bloodshed would be foolish." Osman has recently indicated that one possible peaceful solution would be for Somalia to join an East and Central African federation embracing, among other states, all the countries in which Somalis live.

At any rate, the Chinese arms would most likely have been used first against the Ethiopians, the traditional enemy of the

Somalis. In 1960, after members of the Somali Esa tribe in the Ethiopian province of Ogaden had killed a few Ethiopian soldiers, the Ethiopians massacred more than one hundred men, women, and children. The Esas, under Harbi's influence, retaliated by attacking the highly strategic railroad running between the Ethiopian capital of Addis Ababa and the French Somali capital of Djibuti, derailing and plundering a train and killing several people. The Ethiopians then wiped out a whole Somali village of two hundred and fifty people. A Harbi associate, Ahmed Goumane, is believed to have promised Ethiopian Somalis after this disaster that they would soon have Chinese arms with which to strike back, probably at the strategic railroad again. As a passenger on this desert railroad some time ago, I was jokingly told by the Ethiopian conductor that I should sleep soundly, for then I would never know what hit me if the Somalis attacked. I didn't realize at the time that it might be a Chinese bullet.

In the face of the concentrated Sino-Soviet offensive in Somalia, the United States is probably doing less than it could. A United States Information Service is functioning quite successfully. One student told me that Somalis considered it the cultural center of the country. But despite the impossibility of Somalia's getting along without substantial outside economic aid, the United States has offered the country little help—$4.5 million in 1961, somewhat more in 1962—compared to what it is giving to less needy and less strategic nations, thus permitting the communist bloc to dominate the Somali economy by default. Reflecting this indifference was the United States Commerce Department's incomprehensible refusal to participate in a Somali International Trade Fair in September 1961, though Embassy officials in Mogadishu pleaded that, in view of communist-bloc participation, the United States should take part even if it gained no profit from a trade standpoint. President Osman, at the opening ceremonies, expressed disappointment that the United States and other countries had not seen fit to play a role at the fair, then visited the impressive Russian and Bulgarian exhibits.

ETHIOPIA

Neighboring Ethiopia, too, enjoys little immunity from the communist-bloc influence. Actually, this country, which is the only nation in Africa besides Liberia that has never been colonized, was regarded as the center of communist infiltration activities for Black Africa before 1959. It had the only Soviet embassy in

Africa, the only known communist technicians—all at a Soviet hospital in Addis Ababa—and the only Red information center. Today propaganda is still disseminated through the hospital and the center. The hospital, a holdover from the Czarist era, offers fewer modern facilities than American clinics that have been established in the last few years, but is more popular, perhaps because of its long past. The information center, housed in an ugly, red-painted, barnlike structure and poorly equipped with books, is, similarly, more popular than the United States Information Service, which offers greater elegance and more reading matter. The American center caters mainly to intellectuals, while its Russian counterpart draws the common people with such easy-to-swallow propaganda as free movies about the joys of life in the Soviet Union. One Saturday afternoon, I saw hundreds of people, many of them barefoot illiterates, lined up around the block waiting for the next film showing.

But Moscow scored its biggest propaganda gain in 1959 when Emperor Haile Selassie visited Moscow. In Leningrad the Emperor found on display in the Museum of Anthropology and Ethnography pictures of himself and his father, as well as Ethiopian newspapers and an Ethiopian Bible. It is reported that the Russians even brought up the possibility of a merger between the Ethiopian Coptic Christian Church and the Russian Orthodox Church, which was first suggested in Czarist days. Russian clergymen soon flew to Addis Ababa to meet with officials of the Ethiopian Church, while Russian icons and a great bell were sent to St. George's Cathedral in the Ethiopian capital.

Most important of all, Haile Selassie returned home with a $100-million aid program, almost equaling the amount of aid the United States had granted Ethiopia in a decade. Part of this Russian assistance is being used to establish a Soviet-staffed technical school in Addis Ababa, which, after the third year, will turn out one hundred Ethiopian technicians a year, and probably some good communists as well. Another share of the aid will go to build a 500,000-ton-capacity oil refinery at the Red Sea port of Assab, which will meet all of the nation's own oil needs and leave a considerable quantity for export. In addition, over a score of Ethiopians were studying in communist-bloc schools in 1961.

The Soviet Union, true to its policy in Africa, is not trying to intrigue against the ruling power, but hopes to win over the people eventually through the indoctrination of students and outward manifestations of friendship for the country as a whole. It is willing to deal even with a "reactionary" Emperor, believing that when he disappears from the scene it will be in a good position to exploit the chaos that might result. Haile Selassie, who was openly pro-West before he went to Moscow, would like to see Ethiopia become a leading power in Africa but knows this would be impossible unless he, like most other African leaders, assumes a neutralist stance, agreeing to do business with the communists as well as with the Free World. Ethiopia has traditionally considered itself part of the Middle East—the Emperor, according to folklore, is a direct descendant of King Solomon and the Queen of Sheba— but as one of the Sovereign's advisers explained, "The Emperor now sees that Ethiopia, long a small fish in the Middle Eastern pond, can be a big fish in the African pond."

This attitude is reflected in the role he wants to play as mediator between the radical pan-Africanist Casablanca bloc and the more moderate Monrovia group of African states. At a meeting of the latter nations in Lagos in January 1962, he said with imperial aloofness: "Ethiopia considers herself a member of one group only—the African group." The country's swerve toward neutralism is also no doubt due to the Emperor's calculation that the United States will increase its own aid to keep the nation friendly. He made it clear to me in an interview that he was unhappy about the amount of assistance granted by Washington.

An interview with the Emperor suggests a factor that is favoring the cultivation of communism: the nation's lingering medievalism. On entering the Imperial Palace grounds in Addis Ababa, I found myself face to face with a live, full-grown male lion, a symbolic Conquering Lion of Judah, as the Emperor is traditionally known, perfectly at liberty except for a thin leash held loosely by his keeper. Before I could scream, the animal arrogantly nudged against me. "Don't worry," the keeper said, "he likes people."

That's what worried me.

Once past the beast, I entered the palace and was led into a darkly ornate audience room about half the size of a football field. A bearded, shaggy-maned little man with the face of a Biblical sage stood waiting at the far end of the room. Ramrod stiff in his beribboned tan military uniform, the Emperor returned each of my labored bows, executed on the march, with a brief nod. When I reached him we shook hands, and I sat down on a plush chair, about five yards from his, almost too fatigued from my trials to conduct the interview. When the audience was over, I got up, and started the long trek to the door, walking backwards and bowing simultaneously. I nearly bowed out of an open window.

Such archaic protocol may not be significant in itself, but it is symptomatic of the difficulty Ethiopia is experiencing in trying to throw off the chains of feudalism. Perhaps the worst manifestation of this difficulty is the problem of land. It is estimated that the Coptic Church, to which most Ethiopians belong, and the absentee landlord group of the nobility own about one-third each of the cultivated land in the country, making most peasants tenant farmers. Such remnants of feudalism constitute one of the main causes of the poverty gripping Ethiopia—poverty that has produced an army of beggars, including many blind old men who are led through narrow, twisting streets in search of alms by hungry children as raggedly dressed as themselves. Nor are the people unaware of the better life that should be theirs. When I tried to take pictures of some pitiful shacks housing poor families in one town, I was detained by a local policeman, who warned me that I could snap only "nice buildings." "These people have pride," he said.

Ethiopia is beset by other awesome problems, some the product of nature, and some, of man. I discovered a few of them during a three-day, one-thousand-mile trip on a native bus that wound its way from Asmara, capital of the northern province of Eritrea, to Addis Ababa through some of the world's most magnificently picturesque highland. As the ancient vehicle chugged along, jammed with men garbed in white cotton robes and women wearing multibraided hairdos that had been soaked in melted butter to remove the kinks, a kind of horizontal rain began to sweep by—a locust storm. Swarms of locusts gradually filled the air on all sides. They flew low, forming a solid blanket of tiny glittering stars as millions of transparent wings flashed under the sun. Above this droning, irrepressible army dramatically glided another hungry echelon of life—a huge brigade of hawks. They circled around, swallowing juicy locusts; while the insects, settling across the landscape, swallowed almost everything else in sight, including the thatch on native houses.

Next came an attack by human beings. Bandits, called *shiftas,* began shooting at the bus. Several passengers reached for rifles they carried with them. I reached for the floor. The shooting finally stopped, and several minutes later, groups of people from a nearby village walked past the bus singing. Each group carried two bamboo poles, from which were suspended, like captured animals, the bound, blood-soaked bodies of the *shiftas,* their

heads crushed in and their intestines bulging out. When one of
the group saw me with a camera, its members posed smilingly, as
if at a grotesque picnic. They were proud of having caught the
bandits. Several other outlaws who were taken alive were to be
hanged in public the following day to discourage other members of
their profession.

Later, the bus passed through a thatched village which might
have been dangerous had this been spring. For that was the mat-
ing season in this region, a time when the ardent husband-to-be
traditionally woos his beloved with a rather odd gift—the repro-
ductive organs of a man he has murdered, which the lucky girl is
supposed to wear at her wedding as costume jewelry.

Still, it is significant that banditry and barbarism in Ethiopia
have been reduced to isolated incidents, partly due to prompt police action, partly to the increasing maturity of the people. Hardly
thirty years ago medievalism existed in Ethiopia, completely undiluted by modern civilization. But under the leadership of Haile
Selassie, who has adroitly wedded the liberal leanings of a modern
constitutional monarch to the absolute authority and gaudy trap-
pings of an ancient Oriental potentate, the nation has been moving
steadily forward, even if slowed down by evils still not rooted out.

Moreover, this progress has been registered, until very recently,
largely without Western guidance. A vast mountain fortress, Ethiopia was able, up to the Italian occupation in the 1930's, to keep
out all foreign intruders. When Haile Selassie took over control of
the country by a *coup d'état* in 1917, he found himself ruler of a
nation composed of many squabbling, disunified feudal kingdoms,
some of which refused to accept his rule. Since then he has, through
force and persuasion, united the country to a large degree, and virtually dragged it into the modern era. He has filled the role that
colonial occupiers have assumed in most other underdeveloped
areas—but without the money and experience of these Western
nations.

In his modernization effort the Emperor has enjoyed one advantage over the colonial powers. He has not been handicapped by
motives of self-interest. On the contrary, his forceful personality
has given this effort a vital sense of urgency that fairly makes the
invigorating mountain air vibrate in many areas—particularly in
Addis Ababa, where streamlined university and office buildings
are swiftly converting a shantytown into a leading African cultural
and business metropolis.

While the Emperor is not ignoring agricultural and industrial
development—witness the Russian and American aid programs—

education is the keystone of his plan for progress. Only a small percentage of children can go to school today because of the lack of classroom space and qualified teachers, but enrollment is swiftly increasing. The day I visited the Sovereign at his palace, scores of noisy children arrived on buses from an outlying desert area of Ethiopia and were put up in special dormitories on the palace grounds, where they would live while going to school in Addis Ababa. Many of the youngsters, used to sleeping on dirty mats, were almost uncomfortable between the crisp, clean sheets of their new beds.

The Emperor is giving top government positions to young men who have returned from universities abroad, hoping to create a cadre that will be able to lead the nation toward democracy. "I feel toward democracy as if it were my son," he told me. "I'm gradually helping to nurture and develop it. My ultimate goal is a completely democratic constitutional monarchy modeled on the British form of government." The Emperor, in striving for this goal, has voluntarily given the nation a parliament, though with limited powers. Much of the difficulty in distributing power in Ethiopia lies not in his autocratic ways but in the undeveloped sense of responsibility of most government officials, who are still too used to taking orders.

But for all Haile Selassie's efforts to modernize and democratize his country, many Ethiopians, in particular the very intellectuals he sent abroad to study means of speeding up the process, are dissatisfied with the Emperor's progress. They are reluctant to make compromises with such reactionary forces as the Coptic Church and the nobility. The Emperor, however, wants to avoid bloodshed, which he is convinced would result from any revolutionary reform program. Reaction, he thinks, must be dealt with through persuasion and patience, not through violence; and he points to the headway already made to show that this can be done.

But many of his young subjects are not oblivious to the fact that the communist nations have with considerable success used force to destroy entrenched interests. Feudalism has disappeared from those countries, and industry has mushroomed with incredible speed. Some of those who were impressed by these feats were among the rebels who tried to overthrow Haile Selassie and replace him with his son in late 1960. They are not communists, but with sufficient indoctrination they could be in the future—a possibility that Moscow hopes to foster. Even if the Emperor is not overthrown, he is approaching seventy and cannot remain in power too much longer. When he leaves the scene, there will be a power vacuum, for his imperial heir, Crown Prince Asfa Wasan, lacks a strong personality. And then the warm feeling now being generated in Ethiopia toward its communist benefactors could handsomely pay off.

It is clear that few African countries are isolated from communist ideas today. But it is no less clear that the doctrinaire communism of the Sino-Soviet bloc has so far made insignificant headway in Africa. What happens when African Marxists actually take over a government? Three countries can provide at least a tentative answer—Ghana, Guinea, and Mali. All of them are led by men who consider themselves Marxists to some degree. The communists have perhaps best summed up the answer. The *African Communist* said of such African left-wing intellectuals: "They have been the founders of our national liberation movement and have carried the spark of enlightenment and rebellion from one end of Africa to another." But their value as "proletarian" leaders, the publication continues, is limited. "In conditions of modern society, the intellectuals vacillate between one camp and another, are always swinging helplessly between the oppressors and the oppressed . . . We must remember that it (the intelligentsia) as a group is inherently unstable and unfit for leadership." In other words, African leftists in power can hardly be depended upon to carry the ball for communism.

Unable to infiltrate effectively into the ruling nationalist parties of Ghana, Guinea, and Mali, or to generate popular rebellions against them, Moscow is apparently trying to integrate these parties gradually into a political community with the world's communist parties and front groups to soften them up for future penetration. In response to a Soviet invitation, the three parties sent delegates to the Twenty-second Congress of the Soviet Communist Party in autumn, 1961—the only parties not directly identified as "Marxist-Leninist" to do so.

MALI

In September 1962 a Soviet delegation reciprocally attended a congress of the Sudanese Union, Mali's ruling party. A message to the congress printed on the front page of *Pravda* read: "Dear Comrades: We are sincerely glad that party relations have been established in the last few years between the Sudanese Union and the Soviet Communist Party and we hope that these relations will steadily grow and strengthen."

The communist bloc is only too well aware, however, that its ties with the radical nationalist states of Africa are economically and politically inspired rather than ideologically anchored, and that, therefore, the status of these ties is entirely dependent on opportunistic African whims. Actually, the Mali government of President Modibo Keita would have been considered hopelessly reactionary in the Stalin era. Despite Keita's mildly Marxist outlook and his neutralist Cold War stand, he has few good words to say about communists, maintaining that his regime will "build a dam against them." His moderate view toward the West—for an Afro-Asian leftist—was underscored when he visited the United States in the autumn of 1961 following the Belgrade conference of neutralist nations and said after a meeting with President Kennedy that world crises could be settled if Khrushchev showed the same spirit of good will that Kennedy exhibited.

But Keita, a tall, amiable man with authoritarian leanings, whose ancestry reportedly can be traced back to the Keita dynasty that founded the Mali Empire and ruled it during the thirteenth and fourteenth centuries, has displayed no timidity about accepting aid from either power bloc. This is partly because of his neutralist policy, but also because Mali, the former West African colony of French Sudan, is in near-desperate economic straits. When the French Sudan was granted autonomy in 1958, it joined its wealthier neighbor, Senegal, in the Mali Federation. But two years later, with France offering full independence to its Black African colonies, the Senegalese, fearful of Sudanese domination, broke away from the Federation and cut off the Sudan's access to Senegal's port of Dakar, the Sudanese lifeline. Retaining the name Mali, the small, isolated state looked in all directions for aid.

Keita, an African representative in the French parliament in the colonial era, obtained substantial credits from Western Europe and $2.5 million in American assistance. He also signed a barter arrangement with Communist China under which Chinese machinery and building supplies are being exchanged for Mali's farm products and handicrafts. In early 1961 the Soviet Union, which is far more enthusiastic than Red China about helping noncommunist leaders who are not actively serving the communist cause, offered $44 million in long-term credits. They will be used for preliminary work on a railway line to Conakry, Guinea, that will give Mali an outlet to the sea; improvement of navigation on the Niger River; establishment of a technical training center; exploitation of largely unexplored iron, gold, and phosphate deposits; and construction of a football stadium in the Mali capital of Bamako.

With colonialism swiftly dying in Africa, this continent of new nations has polarized to a considerable extent into the fiery, ultra-nationalist Casablanca bloc, whose leaders tend toward opportunism and leftism and dream of establishing a united Africa in the near future, and the moderately nationalist Monrovia bloc led by practical men who suspect the "union now" advocates of imperialistic motives and think more in terms of building up areas they now control. The radical group, named for the Moroccan city where it was formed, consists of Ghana, Guinea, Morocco, the United Arab Republic, Mali, and the newly independent state of Algeria. The more moderate Monrovia bloc, also named for the site of its first meeting (Monrovia, Liberia), is supported by over twenty states, including Nigeria, Liberia, Somalia, and most of the former French African territories.

The Casablanca powers, particularly Ghana, make a fetish of the need for pan-African unity that would lead to the establishment of a United States of Africa. Yet Ghana, Guinea, and Mali, despite their own union on paper, have so far been unable to implement their intentions even to the smallest degree. This radical bloc, during the Congo crisis, fanatically supported Patrice Lumumba because he indicated he would ally the Congo with it. And as it is generally more emotional in its anticolonialism than the other states, and therefore more suspicious of the West, it has been willing to snuggle up to the communist world, even while rejecting communism.

The Monrovia nations, by contrast, are wary of political mergers, at least in the foreseeable future, because they regard those most interested in unity as power-hungry and demagogic, and because they are too concerned with building themselves up to drain off national energy in trying to make unworkable schemes work. The Nigerian leaders, for example, have all they can do to unify their own sprawling nation of diverse regions and peoples. The Monrovia group is trying to foster co-operation among African states in economic and other fields which might eventually lead toward political unity. They plan to lower trade barriers, merge airlines and shipping companies, link telephone and telecommunications systems, standardize road networks, and in other ways extend areas of collaboration.

This practical approach to unity reflects the moderation of the leaders of this group, particularly such men as Nigerian Prime Minister Sir Abubakar Tafawa Balewa, Liberian President William Tubman, and Ivory Coast President Felix Houphouët-Boigny, whose wealthy country dominates most of former French Africa. "I'd like to see a united Africa as much as anyone," President Tubman, casually dressed in a sport shirt and smoking a huge cigar, said in his office in Monrovia. "But we've got to use common sense. Unity must come gradually, from the inside. It cannot be imposed."

At an African "summit" meeting in Lagos in early 1962, which only the leaders of the Monrovia bloc agreed to attend, although the Casablanca powers had also been invited, Governor-General Azikiwe of Nigeria cited "one basic difference of an ideological nature" between the Casablanca and Monrovia groups. "It is the conspicuous absence of a specific declaration on the part of the Casablanca states of their inflexible belief in the fundamental principles enunciated at Monrovia [in May 1961] regarding the inalienable right of African states, as at present constituted, to legal equality, irrespective of their area and population; the right of African states to self-determination; the right of African states to safety from interference in their internal affairs through subversive activities engineered by supposedly friendly states; the right of African states to be secure in the inviolability of their territories from external aggression."

Not all the Monrovia states, even if they made such declarations, are living in peace and harmony with each other. Senegal hopes, like Guinea, to grab Portuguese Guinea some day, and also claims the British colony of Gambia. Somalia wants Ethiopian territory inhabited by Somalis. Other bickerings and jealousies, too, will make even simple co-operation among these countries in the economic and communications field difficult. But it goes without saying that the relative level-headedness of the Monrovia bloc has made its leaders the least susceptible to the influence of the communist world, which invariably scores its greatest successes among emotionally inclined men of unrestrained ambition, who, like the Reds themselves, are willing to deal with the devil for their own ends, sometimes to the ultimate detriment of their countries.

The communist bloc is actually in no hurry to see a united Africa, for at present the moderates by far outnumber the leftists and opportunistic radicals and would probably have the principal say in a federal government. It would go only as far as approving the establishment of regional federations in strongly leftist infiltrated areas—it favors a tightly federated Congo, for example —where communism would have an opportunity to make inroads into the central government of each. But if its friends in Africa want a united continent, the communist world is only too ready to give lip service to this ideal, knowing full well that it cannot in the near future be achieved.

Up to now, the Red bloc has had reason indeed to doubt the general popularity of leftist or opportunistic anti-Westernism in Africa, as represented by the Casablanca group. The reason is perhaps best reflected in the sharp setback suffered by Nkrumah and his allies in their trade-union policies. This setback was particularly galling to the communist bloc in view of its desire to develop a procommunist proletariat in Africa to replace "unreliable" intellectuals as an ideological spearhead—though almost all leaders of Africa's embryonic labor unions today are intellectuals rather than workers who have risen through the ranks. The Reds originally had hoped that their puppet World Federation of Trade Unions (WFTU) would extend its influence in Africa. In 1959 this organization began to run a series of four-week courses in Budapest for African trade-union "militants," attracting about thirty trade-union leaders from ten African countries to its first course.

But even the Casablanca nations wanted nothing to do with the WFTU. At about the time the Budapest courses were starting, they began a campaign for the establishment of an all-African trade-union federation completely free of world labor ties. Russia was actually not too disappointed, for as very few African unions belong to the WFTU, this campaign was aimed primarily at the dissolution of African bonds with the democratic American-backed International Confederation of Free Trade Unions (ICFTU), which is much stronger in Africa, embracing twenty-two African labor affiliates and operating a training college in Uganda. Ostensibly, the reason for this campaign was to affirm African neutralism and keep all African nations out of the Cold War. But the underlying motive was probably to make it easier for the Casablanca powers to exert pressure in favor of pan-Africanism in other African territories through trade unions dominated by them.

In early 1961 this group called an organizing convention for a new All-African Trade Union Federation (AATUF), to which almost all African unions sent representatives. The Casablanca bloc demanded that all unions secede from international labor organizations. With the convention ending on a controversial note, John K. Tettagah, secretary of the Ghana Trade Union Congress and a Ghana cabinet member, declared "total war" on African unions that chose to stay in the ICFTU, drawing the praise and approval of the communist bloc. The moderate unions took up the challenge. They held an African trade-union conference in Dakar, Senegal, in early 1962 which organized a Pan-African Labor Federation that specifically accorded its forty-one founding unions the right to belong to any international organization of their choice. (Twenty-three are affiliated to the ICFTU, twelve to the Christian Trade Union International, and six are independent.) And while "Afro-socialism," rather than "capitalism, of which colonialism is one of the most inhuman forms," was called for, "communist and all kinds of dictatorship" were sharply rejected.

The usually neutralist-sounding African unionists surprised even themselves when they enthusiastically applauded one Congolese speaker, Alphonse R. Kithima, Secretary-General of the Confederation of Free Trade Unions of the Congo, when he warned that "a new imperialist wave was preparing to fall" on Africa. "This new imperialism," he said, "spoke of freedom and the brotherhood of nations but behind it lay the workers massacred in the streets of East Berlin for demanding bread and justice, the Korean peasants dead in the field over which a ruthless war of conquest had just passed, the workmen and students of Budapest crushed by foreign tanks for having dared to proclaim their country's right to independence and the government of its choice."

Drawing further cheers was a statement by Lawrence L. Borha, Secretary-General of the Trade Union Congress of Nigeria, that the new organization "will not seek to exploit honest trade unionists in the cause of expansionist policies of certain governments and it will not require anyone to act as a rubber stamp nor will it declare total war on those with whom it may have differences."

The great majority of African states, as reflected in their labor unions, which the Casablanca bloc and its communist supporters had most counted on for an extension of their respective interests, had dramatically demonstrated that they would neither cut ties with the West nor exhibit tolerance toward communism. The few countries that would opportunistically co-operate with the communists appeared to be isolated, while the communists themselves could realistically conclude that, for all the progress they have made in the last few years, they still have a long distance to go before they have a real foothold in Africa.

III

GUINEA:

SNOWPLOWS AND

CHRYSANTHEMUM WATER

"We've come here to help the people of Guinea build up their new country. The leaders here are very progressive and they realize that our aid has no strings attached. They know we are their friends."

A young Bulgarian diplomat offered this comment in a talk we had in the plush lobby of the Hotel de France, the finest—and only first-class—hotel in Conakry, the sleepy, primitively dignified capital of Guinea. The communist bloc has done its best to promote this image of "big brotherliness" in the eyes of the Guineans and, at least on the surface, with considerable success. Dynamic, youthful President Sékou Touré, with communist economic aid and political advice, has, since his country was granted independence by the French in 1958, converted Guinea into a state almost indistinguishable, in terms of organization if not of ideology, from any communist-bloc member.

But the Soviet Union apparently outsmarted itself in late 1961, shattering the "big brother" illusion, and possibly losing whatever chance it had to push Guinea over the line into the communist camp in the foreseeable future. Khrushchev is perfectly willing to deal with all Afro-Asian governments, whatever their politics are, and in most cases to reduce subversion to a level that will not disturb the noncommunist leaders in power. Unlike Mao, he seldom tries to instigate violence and demonstrations in these countries, hoping to keep them neutralist and to soften them up until they are ready to drop, almost of their own weight, into the Red basket. He probably calculated that Guinea had reached that stage of ripeness.

Guinea's leftist Teachers' Union, which had been infiltrated by many student agents returning from Moscow, went on strike in November 1961, setting off riots and an attempted march by students, armed with Molotov cocktails, on Touré's home. The police put down the demonstrations, and at least fifteen persons were tried and sentenced to death. "The embassy of a socialist country," Touré stormed, had inspired "a Machiavellian plan to take power in Guinea . . . based on racism, corruption, and falsified Marxist theories." Then the President, making it clear what socialist country he was referring to, told Soviet Ambassador Danil S. Solod to get out of Guinea.

Moscow, desperately trying to regain its toehold in Guinea, sent its top troubleshooter, First Deputy Premier Anastas Mikoyan, to the country on a "good-will" trip. Touré, who had conspicuously remained away from the airport welcoming ceremonies, icily told Mikoyan that Guinea "refuses to be drawn into choosing sides in a power struggle between world blocs." And though the Soviet leader offered, and Touré accepted, a new Soviet loan, relations between the two countries have been distinctly cool ever since. During the Russian-sparked Cuban crisis in late 1962, the Guinean leader, on a visit to the United Nations, ignored Cuban President Osvaldo Dorticos. He also refused to let the Russians use Conakry's new jet landing strip to service Cuba-bound aircraft, though Soviet technicians had built it.

Khrushchev might have sized up Touré more deftly before he tried to engineer his overthrow, as claimed by the Guinean chief. Touré, perhaps more than any other new African leader, is the embodiment of his country. There are other strong men in Africa, of course, such as Ghana's Kwame Nkrumah and the Ivory Coast's Felix Houphouët-Boigny, but none has managed to stamp his personality so completely on a nation as has Touré. When all other French territories in Black Africa voted in a French-sponsored referendum in 1958 to accept autonomous status within the French Community, Guinea, under Touré's sway, voted almost unanimously for full independence. While most African leaders find it extremely difficult, if not impossible, to unify their tribally and politically divided nations, Touré, a good-looking, broad-shouldered man in his late thirties, is the idol of almost all his 2,500,000 subjects; and the few who oppose him are utterly powerless because of the tight weblike nature of his political organization, the only one in the country. Touré has managed in large degree to weld Guinea's tribes into a national unit that thinks like a nation and looks upon its leader with the awe and reverence once reserved for individual tribal chiefs.

Evidence of this awe and reverence is not hard to find. Wherever Touré goes in his country he is greeted as a near god. At political rallies held in wind-blown fields, he is an imposing figure as he cries, "Vive l'indépendance!" the signal for the crowd to shout back hysterically, "Vive l'indépendance! Vive l'Afrique!" While native xylophones echo through the jungle, limber Guinean dancers wearing brightly colored turbans and little else shake and stomp as if bewitched, and African minstrels, or *griots*, dressed in leather capes decorated with pieces of mirror, strum away madly on their one-string gourd guitars. True, much of this tempestuous greeting is carefully organized by Touré's party cadres, but there is no mistaking the spontaneity of the emotionalism aroused by Touré's magnetic presence.

In a sense, Touré views the birth of independent Guinea as symbolic of the reawakening of the great Mali Empire that in medieval days embraced Guinea and much of the remaining area. Eventually it was incorporated into the French West Africa that today consists of many small fledgling nations. He sees Guinea as the potential leader of a new and expanded Western African empire, including Ghana and Mali, with which it has already agreed to unite, at least on paper, though it is not clear how he expects to persuade Ghana to relinquish its own claims to African leadership.

Touré is an expert on the history of the Mali Empire, and if anyone suggests that Africa has never tasted glory, he will point to the golden era of Mansa (Sultan) Musa six hundred years ago. Musa once made a pilgrimage to Mecca, accompanied by sixty thousand men and twelve tons of gold carried on the humps of eighty camels. He converted the jungle town of Timbuktu into a center of trade and learning. And he presented his wife with a swimming pool in the desert filled with water carried in skin bags by slaves who marched great distances.

But Touré is proudest of all when he speaks of Almamy Samory Touré, his grandfather, who, in the late 1800's, voluntarily substituted for his mother as the slave of an enemy tribe and eventually took over the leadership of the tribe. He bitterly fought French advances into West Africa until he was captured in 1898 to become a martyr of Guinea.

Sékou Touré himself is one of seven children of a poverty-stricken peasant. He had to leave school to work at an early age, but through self-study qualified as a French colonial treasury clerk, quitting eventually to take over leadership of the Guinea branch of France's communist-controlled Confédération Générale du Travail (CGT). His communist friends saw in this silver-tongued young African leader a promising vehicle for Marxist penetration of Africa and sent him on trips to Warsaw and Prague. He became fascinated with the dynamics of Marxist political organization and the humanism of some aspects of Marxist theory; but, the Reds were to learn later, only to the extent that what he learned could be wedded to traditional African values.

Touré joined the Rassemblement Démocratique Africain (RDA), a leftist-oriented front of several French West African political parties, and quickly worked his way up from assemblyman in Guinea's legislative assembly to mayor of Conakry. He finally became a deputy in the French Assembly in Paris, where he astounded his French colleagues with his aggressive nationalist demagogy. Touré took over Guinea's RDA and rebuilt it according to Marxist organizational principles. His answer to French accusations that he was becoming a Red puppet was to establish a new independent labor union completely free from the direction of the French CGT, a powerful blow to the communists in Paris who had considered him their creation. This action appeared to confirm the suspicions of European communists that Africa was not yet ripe for the introduction of orthodox communism, and they wisely agreed to co-operate with Touré largely on his own Afro-communist terms.

As a result, the communist bloc today all but controls Guinea economically. The nation's foreign trade, which under the French was over eighty percent with the West, is now about eighty percent with the communist bloc. As compared to American aid of little more than one million dollars in the first three years of independence, the Reds contributed more than one hundred million dollars, including almost sixty million dollars by Russia for twelve years at two percent interest, twenty-five million dollars by Red China for twenty years without interest, and ten million dollars by Czechoslovakia for ten years at two and one-half percent interest. With most trade conducted on a barter basis, the Guineans have mortgaged an estimated sixty percent of their coffee, banana, and palm nut exports—their principal products—to the communist bloc.

Characteristically, most of the communist aid is going for proj-

ects designed to impress or "educate" the people. The air strip at
Conakry has been lengthened to three kilometers to take jets, including the Czech-piloted Russian Ilyushins that are the pride of
Guinea's national airline. The road to the airport is being converted
into a four-lane modern highway. Russian Moskvitch taxis, Czech
Skoda trucks and sedans, long black Chinese Red Flag passenger
cars with wrap-around windshields, and Hungarian buses jammed
with barefooted, colorfully saronged Guineans race through the
streets of the main towns, ignoring traffic policemen embellished
with Budapest-made flat-top caps. In military parades, Guinea's
two thousand soldiers, wearing Russian helmets, march with Czech
rifles alongside Soviet artillery, armored cars, and trucks. NAFAYA,
a department store on the Avenue de la République, Conakry's
Champs-Élysées, is amply supplied with Polish canned fish, Czech
toys and distilled dry gin, and even Russian champagne, though
France, Guinea's former master, produces the world's finest champagne. Other communist-manufactured items include textiles, flash-
lights, bicycles, hardware, and household wares. East German
Radegerger beer is sold in bars and restaurants with French names
like Chez Maître Diop and Le Royal St. Germain; and Chinese
products, everything from agricultural machinery to Double Happiness cigarettes and bottled chrysanthemum water, have been on
exhibit in an exhibition hall designed like a pagoda.

Conakry's only bookstore, whose owner usually greets customers with a cheery, "So happy to see you, Comrade," features the
collected works of Lenin, speeches by Khrushchev and Mao, the
latest revised edition of the *History of the Communist Party of the
Soviet Union,* and anti-Western pamphlets of every variety. The
education of the masses will be further facilitated by the construction of an East German printing plant that will publish Conakry's
first daily newspaper as well as literature for distribution throughout Africa. At this writing, Guinea has only a daily mimeographed
government propaganda bulletin—plus "foreign news" sheets distributed by the Soviet, Red Chinese, and East German news
agencies. The Russians are building a radio transmitter far more
powerful than is necessary for Guinea alone, and reclaiming swamp-
land in Conakry for use as the site of a permanent Soviet exhibition hall. And in the schools, teachers from the communist bloc
offer instruction hardly of a nature to endear the West to their
pupils. At the same time, more than three hundred and sixty
students were studying in Moscow, Warsaw, Peking, and Prague
in 1961. True, a few hundred are also enrolled in French universities, but the United States took less than ten in 1960.

Soviet aid still to come includes a shoe factory, a sports arena seating twenty-five thousand, a railroad connecting Guinea and Mali, three modern hotels, and a new building for parliament. The Russians may also build a $300,000,000 dam on the Kondouré River to provide power for processing Guinea's rich bauxite deposits, a project that would be about three-fourths the size of the mammoth Aswan Dam the Soviet Union is constructing in Egypt. The cheap power produced by such a dam, the Guineans believe, would go far in permitting the development of an industrialized society.

Helping in the distribution and utilization of all this aid are over five hundred advisers and technicians—Russians, Czechs, Poles, Hungarians, Bulgarians, East Germans, Red Chinese, and French communists—who occupy most of the lobby space at the Hotel de France at night, and a good many government offices during the day. Touré's chief press officer is a French communist, and almost every ministry or department has a communist adviser. For example, the Poles advise the department of mines, and the Czechs, the police department. Czech doctors and midwives operate clinics in the bush, and Czech teachers have conducted classes in Marxism for students from all over Africa. About one hundred and fifty Red Chinese are teaching Guinean peasants how to increase their rice yields.

So grateful has Guinea been for East Germany's help that it extended diplomatic recognition to that communist satellite in early 1960, the first noncommunist country to do so. This decision set a possible precedent for the emerging independent nations of Africa, where West Germany had hoped to play an important role as a source of economic aid.

Though Soviet Russia and its satellites have so far granted the most aid to Guinea, Communist China appears to be the most popular of the Red states. Guinea, like many underdeveloped nations, is better able to identify its own economic problems with those of agrarian China than with those of industrialized Russia, while friction arising from antiwhite feeling and the Soviet plot does not arise in the case of China. Peking fired its first big propaganda guns in Guinea in May 1960, when it presented the nation with a gift of ten thousand tons of rice, a staple food in Guinea. A few weeks later came a cultural pact under which, among other things, Guinean teachers and students were to study in China. In September 1960 Sékou Touré visited Peking and came away with a $25,000,000 interest-free loan and a treaty of friendship and trade calling for the exchange of almost five million dollars' worth of goods annually. In return for Guinean coffee, rubber, industrial diamonds, and other raw materials, China offered to provide such prestige items as agricultural machinery and implements, building materials, medicines, textiles, and, most important of all as far as the Chinese are concerned, "educational and cultural supplies."

The Chinese loan was granted "without any conditions or privileges attached," with Guinea simply obliged to repay it after ten years in ten yearly installments. Peking, moreover, agreed not only to send technicians to teach Guineans how to use their new agricultural machinery, but to pay their traveling expenses and keep their living standards at a level not exceeding "that of personnel of the same rank in the Republic of Guinea"—a blunt effort to nullify any good will that might result from the work of Western technicians, who usually take their living standards with them to underdeveloped nations.

Hardly was the ink dry on the aid agreement when Red China started reaping propaganda profits. In a joint communiqué, Touré and Liu Shao-chi, chairman of the Red Chinese Republic, jointly announced that "at present, all threats and obstacles to world peace come from the side of imperialism." After Liu condemned the United States as the greatest imperialist of all at a state banquet, Touré, while not mentioning the United States by name, demanded that "ideological, economic, and cultural imperialism be brought to an end." And he added, "Even though many slanders have been directed against your people, whom the imperialists wish to isolate from African political consciousness, we can assure you that the Africans know where the truth lies . . . They know also the lesson they can draw from your history—to unite more effectively in the anti-imperialist struggle." Commenting on the results of the Touré visit, the Peking *People's Daily* glowed, "It is a momentous event not only in the history of Chinese-Guinean relations but also in the history of relations between China and Africa."

Not only were the Guinean leaders "neutralist" until recently on the side of the East, but they appear only too willing to organize their state along tightly controlled communist lines. After Guinea withdrew from the franc zone in 1960 and printed its own francs, the government's Bureau Politique, or Politbureau, established a state trading agency to regulate and determine the flow of foreign trade as well as the sale and distribution of goods internally. Foreign banks must deposit fifty percent of their accounts in the government National Bank, a requirement that has forced four out of five such banks that were doing business in Guinea to leave the country. Most big industries have been nationalized, and many

French businessmen have been forced to close their white-walled shops—attested by the shuttered ghost-town atmosphere in many parts of Conakry and other towns.

The rural areas, too, have taken on a communist look. In almost any other country in Africa, little activity can be seen in the villages. Men sit outside their mud huts or in the shade of trees talking or sleeping, while the women prepare the meals and sometimes work in the fields. This is also still true to a large extent in Guinea, but a change is in the air, partly as a result of Red Chinese influence. Under a "human investment" program that is expected to pay for one-fifth of Guinea's development budget, seventy percent of the population will have to "volunteer" twenty days' service a year in Chinese-style labor brigades. This program is spreading, particularly in the villages, where some ninety percent of the population lives, even though regimentation is still extremely loose. In one village I visited, almost everyone—men, women, and children—was busy clearing several acres of bushland, either carrying foliage or swinging machete knives, for the planting of banana trees. The women, dressed in soiled sarongs—they have been forced to cover their breasts under the new modern order—took only a few hours off to fix communal meals.

This village would eventually be converted into a modern collective farming community, the village head, a bearded man wearing a white turban and robes, told me proudly. This wouldn't be too different, he explained, from the traditional way of life. The land was owned by the village in any case, with the individual peasant working a specified plot which he could put to use for his own purposes. Most peasants, satisfied to live on a subsistence level, had made little effort to grow more corn, potatoes, rice, or manioc than was necessary for their own consumption. But now everybody would work for the village as a whole. New farming methods would be introduced and there would be tractors and other agricultural machinery to share. Everybody would have to work harder, the chief said with an expression that appeared to question whether this was necessarily good, but they would become prosperous. At least that was what the yellow-faced strangers who had visited the village to teach them new methods of growing rice had told him.

Soon, President Touré promised his people, "you will no longer be able to see a single young Guinean girl, torso naked, carrying two bananas on a platter, going out to engage in prostitution. We have our will, our arms and legs, and we know how to work."

To make sure that everybody who doesn't know will soon learn,

Touré has used communist-inspired methods to organize his country into one of the tightest political units outside the Sino-Soviet bloc. His success would be remarkable in any country. In Africa, with its divisive tribal influences and lack of modern political know-how—factors that have torn the Congo apart and have kept even militant Ghana in a state of political chaos—it is little less than incredible.

"The Democratic Party of Guinea, guardian of the peoples' will," reads Guinea's government bulletin every day, "shall lead the nation in honor and dignity toward progress, justice, and solidarity." The Democratic Party (PDG), which has grown out of the old RDA, is indeed leading the nation. Not only is it Guinea's sole party but, through an intricate cell system, it reaches down to the lowliest of Guinea's four thousand villages, touching and directing the life of every Guinean citizen every day. "Down with Individualism!" and "Death to Opportunism!" cry slogans on the wall of PDG headquarters in the town of Labé.

The party, of which Touré is Secretary-General, even sees to it that every last person in a particular village or town stands by to cheer when a visiting dignitary, particularly Touré, who travels in a white Cadillac with a motorcycle escort, is scheduled to pass through. A cobbler I met in one town told me that he had waited in a crowd for four hours to "spontaneously" greet a minister, then finally had given up and returned to his shop to work. A member of the party's militant youth branch came by and told him he would be fined two weeks' earnings if he didn't return to the crowd. He returned.

Touré claims that his system is a "true democracy," much as the "People's Democracies" say they are democratic. In Guinea's case, at least, there is an element of truth in this claim if it is judged by African standards, which are rooted in iron tribal authoritarianism. The four thousand village party cells, or local committees, are elected by universal suffrage and in turn elect one committee for every six hundred men, women, and children. "The election of women, *griots,* and former slaves," Touré said, "is the mark of a veritable prize of political conscience, a spiritual revolution." If the people wish to modify party policy, he pointed out, they can do so in the local and regional committees—within the party, of course. And in fact, the one major organizational difference between the PDG and the communist party in Red-controlled countries is that every citizen is automatically a member of the PDG, while the communist party is an elite group above the masses.

While this mass participation in government is something new for Africa, it is hardly democracy as the concept is understood in the West. As in the communist countries, the local cells invariably approve the opinions of the seventeen-man Politbureau that runs the party—and nation.

The kind of pressure Touré can exert toward this end was reflected in the fate of more than twenty Africans and a few French, Swiss, and Lebanese who were charged with treason in April 1960 for allegedly plotting to overthrow the government with guns smuggled in from Senegal. After a mock trial that saw the defendants deprived of defense counsel and even of the right to testify, most were given the death sentence. Coincidentally, a few died of "natural causes" during the trial.

Touré's political astuteness even extended to using the French for his own ends. In fact, it was they who—unintentionally—paved the way for the establishment of Touré's dictatorial one-party system. When France, in 1957, under a *Loi-cadre,* granted Guineans the right to choose their own leader as vice-president of the Executive Council, but under a French governor, Touré, now in a position of power, called together the French *commandants de cercle,* or regional commissioners. He sympathetically asked them their opinions about the tribal chiefs with whom they were working. They were inefficient, lazy, corrupt, he was told. They were robbing the government of more than one million dollars a year, but, the commandants said, there wasn't much that could be done about it. After all, it was all part of the African tribal tradition. Touré, however, did do something about it. Using the French charges as a lever, he simply abolished chieftain authority, enraging the chiefs, who suddenly found themselves out of job and loot, as well as the French, who had been perfectly willing to accept the shortcomings of the chieftain system as long as it offered them an instrument for controlling the country. Touré was thus free to create his own instrument of control—a communist-style party. So confident did he now become that he went to Paris and demanded that the French turn over complete power to him. "We are not here to be told what the law is," he said arrogantly. "We are here to make the law."

Despite the sovietized appearance of Guinea's economic and political system, the government adamantly denies that it is communist or even sympathetic toward communism. If certain people wished to found a Guinean Communist Party, Touré warned in 1960, the PDG would vigorously oppose them. "Communism," he said, "is not the way for Africa." And certainly, he added, Guinea would never submerge its newly won independence in any international system, communist or otherwise. He conceded only that "we have adopted Marxism to the extent that it is valid for Africa." A high Guinean official explained to me in Conakry: "People who think that we are communists mistake the form for the substance. We have borrowed the organizational techniques of Marxism, it is true. And why not? These techniques will help us lift the nation out of its backward state much faster than your kind of democratic methods. We can't wait one hundred years to modernize ourselves. We need mass organization—down to the village level—so that even the most backward people will feel the modern influence immediately. And it just so happens that Marxism offers us a ready-made system to apply for this purpose. But organization is not ideology. We have borrowed little of Marxist ideology."

How does the Guinea government feel it differs ideologically from the communists? For one thing, it does not believe in the theory of class warfare. "We have substituted the anticolonial struggle for the class struggle," Touré has said, adding that there is no class structure in Guinea, where almost the entire population lives on a uniform subsistence level, and that the family and village community, rather than proletarianism, is the fundamental basis of Guinean society. A second ideological difference, according to Touré, is that Guineans not only reject the atheistic dialectical materialism of communism but are deeply religious people, most Guineans being Moslems. Touré, who has himself made a pilgrimage to Mecca, declares forcefully, "We believe in God. So how can we be communists?"

The reason why he is accepting so much aid from the communist bloc, he points out, is that the Reds offered him almost unlimited assistance without any strings attached at the very moment the West turned its back on Guinea. That moment occurred in September 1958 when France, under President Charles de Gaulle, held a referendum offering its overseas territories the choice of integration in France, autonomy within the French Community, or complete independence. Guinea was among the colonies of French West Africa participating in this referendum, which was also conducted in the West African colonies of Senegal, Mauritania, Upper Volta, Niger, Sudan, Dahomey, and the Ivory Coast, as well as in Gabon, Chad, Ubangi-Shari, and the Middle Congo, the regions of French Equatorial Africa. Guinea alone, among all these Black African colonies—which together extended from Dakar at the westernmost edge of Africa southward in an enormous arc to the banks of the Congo River, comprising an area almost as large as the United States—chose full freedom. And it did so with a 95.4 percent vote—an overwhelming tribute to Touré's unique political organization. This decision, which was eventually to force the French to grant complete independence to the other Black African states as well, compounded the bitterness between Touré and De Gaulle that had flowed from a meeting in Conakry prior to the referendum. "We prefer poverty in liberty to riches in slavery," Touré had shouted. De Gaulle, after the ballots were counted, decided to give him just that.

He immediately cut off all aid to Guinea and ordered French civil servants there to return home within two months. Touré fumed, "Too long. Get them out in eight days." The French complied, leaving government departments in utter chaos and spitefully taking with them everything, including, in at least one case, the kitchen sink. They took the law books, bringing French justice to a halt. They took all movable broadcasting equipment, and Radio Conakry went off the air. They took medical supplies, telephones, stationery, even electric wiring. They stripped policemen of their uniforms. At the governor's palace, workmen sweated carrying furniture in and out, as Frenchmen and Guineans argued over which pieces belonged to whom. By the time the French had gone, Touré, who moved into the palace, found himself living in a half-empty building without even a telephone or a sheet of official writing paper with which to conduct business.

But Touré did not bow in defeat as the French had hoped he would. On the contrary, with bursting drive he began building a new government structure with the aid of his old supporters— trade unionists, teachers, students, and minor bureaucrats—who suddenly found themselves occupying ministerial and other high administrative offices. And he also had the help of some sympathetic Frenchmen who remained—mainly communists. Meanwhile, the United States, which wanted to please its French friends, made little effort to compensate for French indiscretion. Thus, by the time the United States opened an embassy in Conakry, Guinea had reached bananas-for-arms and other trade agreements with East Germany, Czechoslovakia, and Poland; and the Bulgarian ambassador, the first to arrive, was looked upon as an old Guinean hand.

"We'll trade with or accept aid from anybody," a Guinean official told me in early 1959. "Can we help it if the United States is rather slow in offering help? Or if we're a bit distrustful of all Western nations after what France did to us? The British left Ghana in a healthy condition, and continued to aid the country

after they left. The British were fond of Ghana. Go to the Lido
night club in Accra and you'll see British men dancing the High-
Life with Ghanaian girls. You won't find that here. There never
was the same relationship. They left us high and dry. And you
Americans did not come rushing to our aid. Now if you'll excuse
me, I've got a lot of work to do. Unfortunately, I have to do my
own secretarial work. No more French secretaries."

The segregation issue in the United States has not helped to
brighten the Guinean view of America. When a group of American
white and Negro students visited Guinea in late 1960, virtually
the only questions they were asked concerned the treatment of
Negroes in the United States. One Guinean believed the friendly
relations between the two racial elements in the group was an act
performed for the Guineans' benefit. Others were afraid to apply
for scholarships in the United States, because, they thought, whites
might attack them, though Touré himself, after returning from a
trip to the United States in 1960, during which he visited the
South, reported that the situation of the Negroes was better than
he had imagined.

Not all the Guinean leaders share Touré's relatively liberal
and independent view of America and Marxism. For example, his
militant half-brother Ismael, Minister of Public Works and a member of the Politbureau, is considered far more procommunist in the
ideological sense and strongly anti-Western. Nevertheless, over the
protests of such extremists, Touré has indicated that he wishes to
improve relations with the West, particularly with the United
States. The occasion for Touré's gradual effort to warm up to the
United States was the change of American administrations. Touré
was impressed with President Kennedy's apparent sympathy with
African nationalist aspirations, as reflected in American support
of a United Nations censure motion against Portuguese policy in its
African colonies. The American posture looked all the better following Guinea's disillusionment with Moscow.

At the same time, Touré would like to balance the communist-
bloc influence to some extent with Western assistance and
innovations, not only in keeping with his at least nominally neutralist Cold War policy, but because he realizes that the communist
"ideology" may seep into the Guinean way of life if Red propaganda is not countered. Many Guinean officials openly complain
about the fact that communist diplomats have been distributing
propaganda material throughout the country.

Touré has tried to offset Guinea's preponderant dependence on
communist aid to some degree by forming economic unions with

its African neighbors, Mali and Upper Volta, but these efforts have failed. He has also signed trade and aid pacts, providing, among other things, for a $28,000,000 Guinean loan, with Ghana's Nkrumah, but they, too, have foundered. Ghana, with a disintegrating economy of its own, has hardly been capable of shoring up someone else's economy.

Moreover, Touré is not unaware, especially since the Teacher's Union riots, that the communist bloc, while trying to buy his country lock, stock, and barrel, hardly looks upon him as a true and lasting friend. In April 1960 the *African Communist,* a clandestine periodical of the illegal Soviet-controlled South African Communist Party published in London, maintained that Touré's party contains little more than a "proletarian kernel." There is danger, according to the publication, in the "swollen-headedness of the leaders as the result of imperialist flattery and respect shown, and homage paid to, Guinea by the great powers of America, Europe, and Asia." The return of Guinea to capitalism, the paper said, could not be ruled out unless a strong communist party emerged, though, it was implied, this country still looked like the best current channel for communist penetration in Africa.

But not only ideological differences stand in the way of a complete understanding between Guinea and the communist bloc. The very factor that appears to threaten Guinea's independence most—large-scale economic aid—has led to a certain amount of disappointment with the Reds, particularly the European communists. For the communist aid program has in many cases proved a failure.

The man in the street is not impressed with Red "progress" when he finds that Polish Black Cat matches won't light because they haven't been treated for tropical humidity. Nor when he discovers that the Russians have so overtreated their sugar for humidity that it won't dissolve in coffee. Shoes and electric irons don't last long, movie projectors burn out quickly, and there is always something wrong with the typewriters. Perhaps the most disillusioned Guineans of all are the taxi drivers who have been stranded in the bush outside Conakry because their Soviet Moskvitch or Czech Skoda vehicles, with their thin axles and small engines, cannot take the steamy climate and rugged roads.

Plenty of criticism of the bloc's supply system can be heard, too. Along the road leading to Conakry airport, Guineans gaze at huge crates stacked up for weeks at a time—in one case, containing ten thousand toilet bowls without seats, water tanks, or fittings. One shipment was said to contain one million screwdrivers

—a screwdriver for every three Guineans. Many people were recently puzzled to see two snowplows on the docks, in view of the fact that Guinea wilts under a blazing tropical sun all year. A Soviet factory had apparently been given an order to ship to Guinea a complete road-making unit, which included snowplows. Furthermore, few residents of Conakry have credited the communists with good sense on the many occasions when whole shiploads of bananas have been left to rot on the docks for lack of space on Soviet vessels. As for the banana producers, they not only lose bananas they might have sold elsewhere, but in most cases must replace the rotting shipments. Some of this bungling may well be due to Guinean inefficiency when orders are being placed and shipping arrangements made. And certainly Guinean maintenance work on machinery is not of the highest caliber. But as far as most Guineans are concerned, the communists alone are at fault.

This irritation has been intensified by the ill-concealed contempt for Guinean inefficiency exhibited by some communist technicians, and by the impatience of many Guineans, for their part, with advisers who cannot speak French—meaning about three out of four. One of the worst blows of all to communist prestige was the arrest in September 1961 of eighteen Soviet mining technicians for stealing diamonds from Guinean mines. The diamonds, it is reported, were smuggled out of the country in parcels of coffee beans sent to Eastern European addresses. "The technicians were showing Guineans how to mine diamonds with one hand and taking the gems with the other," an American official pointed out.

Added to this measure of disenchantment with the communists have been the difficulties of making some aspects of Touré's Marxist program work. The "human investment" plan, for example, has not been paying off as expected. The great majority of Guineans, like most Africans, are simply unused to working hard under the relentless sun when they really have all they need without working—enough food to eat and a thatched roof over their heads. Only with education will they come to realize that life offers more to those willing to expend energy. Right now, there are no Joneses to keep up with, and they would rather save themselves for the sinuous, tiring tribal dances they like to do in their spare time. Nor have the nationalized foreign trade agencies proved a devastating success, as attested by the weakening Guinean franc, shops that can offer little more than the cheap products arriving from the communist bloc, and new regulations permitting private traders to handle some goods from abroad.

Whatever theories Touré may espouse, there is an indelible streak of realism running through him. Addressing the United Nations General Assembly in late 1960, he appeared to line up with the communist bloc when he warned the new African states that though they might have won political independence, they were in danger of being "asphyxiated economically" by their former colonial masters. "As long as Africa remains an economic appendage of the metropolitan powers," he said, "true emancipation will never be won." But hardly had the echo of Khrushchev's shoe pounding on his desk died down, when Touré accused the communists of "cluttering up" the colonial question with propaganda and "trying to feed the fires of discontent and disturbance." What was needed, he said, was "an atmosphere of understanding and collaboration."

Even while Touré warned of the Western economic grip, he was supporting one of the biggest and newest Western capitalistic enterprises in Africa, and the most modern alumina-producing firm in the world—the Compagnie Fria. A few years ago, the bauxite-rich area occupied by Fria—alumina is made from bauxite —about one hundred miles north of Conakry, was dismal bush-land. Today, as you drive along the rough red-clay road leading to it, occasionally paralleling a new single-track railroad that conveniently connects Fria with the port of Conakry, you see at the end of a paved approach, rising out of the wilderness on a hill, this great monument to Western free enterprise.

The Compagnie Fria is an international consortium embracing the American Olin Mathieson Chemical Corporation, which has a 48.5 percent interest, the French Compagnie Pechiney-Ugine, which controls the company board, the British Aluminium Company, Ltd., a Swiss concern, and a West German firm. It has a production capacity of 480,000 metric tons of alumina a year, which could be tripled with minor design alterations. About twelve hundred people are employed here, eight hundred Guineans and four hundred Europeans. Though there has been some speculation that this company would soon be nationalized, the owners only agreed to pour in the enormous capital required after they were assured this would not be the case.

But this example of "understanding and collaboration" between Guinea and the West was almost unique until the beginning of 1961. Touré's friendlier attitude was first manifested, in fact, on New Year's Day, 1961, when two U. S. Navy destroyers were permitted to spend the holiday in Conakry. They had earlier been denied permission to anchor there. Minister of State Abdour

Aumani Diallo, who is considered one of the most leftist members of the Politbureau, and Mrs. Camara Lofo, leader of the Guinean women, even returned the Navy's courtesy calls—passing communist ships in the harbor to do so—although Guineans usually refuse to visit foreign vessels in port.

At the same time, customs officials, who used to examine every item of American luggage—it took me an hour to complete customs formalities in 1959—now usually let Americans pass through without trouble. Western journalists also find ministers and other officials easier to see. R. Sargent Shriver, United States Peace Corps Director, was given red-carpet treatment by Touré during a trip to Guinea in 1961. An air-conditioned United States Information Service library, situated in the shade of green mango trees that line the Avenue de la République, is permitted to compete freely with communist-bloc propaganda agencies and has proved extremely popular. USIS broadcasts of English courses over Radio Guinea have produced bagfuls of letters expressing gratitude from French-speaking listeners—even in neighboring Senegal and Sierra Leone. The U. S. Agency for International Development (AID), for its part, has purchased the services of a private firm, English Language Services, Inc., of Washington, D. C., which is teaching English to Guinean teachers, more than one hundred of whom, having graduated, are now instructing primary school children. With the United States offering about one hundred and fifty scholarships, English is becoming more popular than ever. Touré has proclaimed it the nation's second language, after French.

American economic aid has also begun to flow into Guinea under a 1962 agreement providing for the expenditure of more than $20 million on food imports, education projects, and vocational training. The local currency earned by the government from the sale of the food will, in turn, be used to finance development projects.

Guinea has also improved relations with France. The two countries signed a new cultural agreement, and when former French Premier Pierre Mendès-France attended a conference of the PDG in 1961, he was given a tremendous ovation. More remarkable was the red-carpet welcome given pro-French President Houphouët-Boigny of the Ivory Coast in late 1962; Touré used to call him a "colonialist stooge."

But despite the Guinean government's evident determination to edge toward the west, in Touré's view, United States aid methods are "not adapted to the means and conditions of underdevelopment existing in all of Africa." He and other Guinean officials point out, for example, that in late 1960 about forty students selected for scholarships in the United States were stranded in Conakry for weeks without funds before formalities were completed and they could leave for New York. By contrast, students assigned to communist countries who were summoned to Conakry from the interior at the same time were flown out immediately. The United States, it was implied, was guilty of either inefficiency or "bad faith."

American officials conceded that the delay was due in part to cumbersome visa regulations, which required the students to fill out forms, obtain three letters of reference, take medical tests and shots, and be x-rayed. However, Guinean authorities themselves could not be absolved from blame, the Americans said, as they had brought the students to Conakry without paving the way for their speedy departure. The communist nations are only too glad to accept students, regardless of their qualifications, for the purpose of their scholarships is not to educate but to indoctrinate. The Guineans expected the United States to be as "liberal" in its attitude. The American Embassy was unable to learn even the names of the students for days, much less know anything about their qualifications for higher learning. And when interviews were held, it was discovered that many were unqualified to enter institutions to which they had been assigned, lacking even a knowledge of English. The African-American Institute, a nonprofit private organization, then arranged for the students to enter a vocational training center in Chicago where they could be taught in French. "How do you like that?" one Guinean official, unoriented on America's educational system, exclaimed. "After all that trouble, they are sent to a private institution."

The Guineans are also disturbed by the fact that three out of twenty American teachers brought to Guinea in late 1960 by the African-American Institute broke their two-year contract with the Guinean government and left the country after a few months. "The Americans missed their refrigerators, their television, their Broadway shows," a Guinean official commented acidly. "Life here was too hard for them."

Sharp conflict has characterized negotiations between the Guinean government and the United States over the terms of technical assistance. These terms, based on agreements made with European allies after World War II, are the same for every beneficiary country, and little resistance has been met, even from Ghana. But Guinea, one of the most sensitive of the new nations, considers these terms an infringement on its sovereignty. After all, the government says, the communist countries don't apply "strings" to their aid.

One resented "string" is the "no duplication" requirement, which prohibits the use of United States funds on projects partially financed by other countries. In other words, Washington does not want to share in the financing of projects with the communist bloc. "It is for us to decide how to use the aid," say the Guineans. Guinea is equally unenthusiastic about the requirement that a permanent aid mission be set up with full diplomatic privileges. One such privilege would be the importation of food and household effects duty-free. Yet, the Guineans point out, even American embassy personnel, other than the ambassador, are not given this right. Another privilege would be diplomatic immunity from arrest, which, say the Guineans, is reserved only for diplomats and not for technicians.

In September 1960 Guinea finally permitted the establishment of a permanent United States Operations Mission in Conakry, though it is not clear whether the other American requirements have been met. In any event, to some extent communist aid is still appreciated more because of the complete lack of conditions—at least, visible ones—attached to it. "Why must you Americans haggle over administrative details?" a Guinean official asked me. "Such small-mindedness takes away from the warmth generated by your aid—and needlessly. You should try to understand the African mind better."

The delicate nature of relations between Guinea and the United States was still further underscored in November 1961, when American sailors who had received permission to visit Conakry were asked to leave on the second day by Touré's brother, Ismael, because their "attitude disgusted the people of Conakry. They walked in the capital as if it were a conquered country. A peaceful citizen received a stab wound. They took photos where it was not allowed. They organized fetes in order to mock the people."

Still, despite considerable obstacles that stand in the way of a close relationship between the United States and Guinea, the chances are fairly good that relations will continue to improve. It is possible that the domination of the Guinean economy by the communist bloc, even if the United States does make some inroads into it, could eventually snuff out Guinean independence. But this isn't very likely in the near future. The bloc also has a substantial hold on the Egyptian economy, but Nasser's jails are still crammed with domestic communists. And if the Reds were to start using their economic advantage for political ends, Touré knows that he always has a safety valve in accelerated business with the West.

The communist nations will almost certainly continue to concentrate on nonideological propaganda in Guinea, as well as in the rest of Africa, in view of the lack of militant political sophisticates in the area at this stage of its development. As the article in the *African Communist* indicated, the Reds are not overly confident about the politics or friendship of the Touré government, an attitude no doubt hardened by the failure of the Red-led teachers' strike. In the long run, they probably feel, with considerable reason, they are likely to make greater progress subverting semicapitalist states like India, Fabian socialist countries like Burma, or "guided democracies" like Indonesia, where true, elite, reliable communist parties have an opportunity to feed on chaos and exploitation.

Touré's party, potently combining indigenous nationalism and pseudo communism, and offering much the same promises as orthodox communism, may constitute a bulwark against the alien ideological doctrines of the latter for a long while to come, perhaps indefinitely. A communist party would have little appeal in competition with the PDG—if indeed it were permitted to exist. Moscow and Peking may therefore have a more difficult time absorbing Guinea into their bloc than many other countries with governments less oriented toward Marxism.

I V

GHANA:

GILDING THE GOD

As President Kwame Nkrumah of Ghana was about to board a plane at Moscow airport during a ten-week tour of the communist bloc in the summer of 1961, he told the crowd seeing him off that the successes achieved by Russia in "such a short time" proved what could be done by a "united and loyal people. This is a lesson for us which I will take home with me."

It is not yet clear how much of what Nkrumah learned will ultimately be put into practice in Ghana, a former British West African colony, but there is little doubt that he was impressed by the lesson. In his effort to mold a "united and loyal people" of his own, he has resorted to political suppression and economic totalitarianism in drastic measure. This trend, from the viewpoint of Western interests, might not in itself be foreboding in view of the need for some kind of authoritarianism in most primitive lands suddenly burdened with the responsibilities of independence. What is disturbing is that many of the screws being applied are coming right out of the communist storehouse. Ghana, moreover, has recently taken to rubber-stamping most communist foreign policies, from Berlin to NATO.

Yet it would be a mistake for the West to write Ghana off as a lost cause. The country is oriented somewhat to the right of Guinea, which has a more thoroughly Marxist-style government and party apparatus, and is far more dependent on the communist bloc economically. "It is inconceivable," a Ghanaian official told me, "that Ghana will ever go communist. If it did, there would probably be a counterrevolution here." And Nkrumah himself said in early 1961, "We are anticolonialists and we shall always remain so until all the colonialists are gone. How could my country be a satellite of any country when we believe that? It is very unfair— to be accused of being communist on the basis of anticolonialism. I think anticolonialism was invented in the United States."

The absence of a communist party in Ghana appears to confirm the lack of a strong Moscow-oriented ideological flavor in Ghanaian leftism, no less than in the Guinean brand—even though many of Ghana's leaders seem to be attracted to certain aspects of Marxism and the seeming efficiency and dynamism of communist organization. Ghana is, in fact, one of the few independent Black African states with no known communist-front organizations. The communist World Federation of Democratic Youth (WFDY) has listed among its affiliates Ghana's Maabang Youth Association, Takoradi Youth Organization, and Wassa Youth Association; but relations with the WFDY, if they exist, are believed to be on a personal rather than an organizational basis. And while Ghana, despite its professed neutralism, supports most communist Cold War policies, this tendency stems not from a desire for the spread of communism, but from a common immediate interest having nothing to do with that creed. Both Ghana and the Red bloc hope to further their own respective imperial ambitions in Africa through the use of anticolonial (e.g., anti-West) slogans.

However that may be, Ghana's doors are still wide open to the West, economically and culturally, and most of its aid, including an enormous sum for a Volta River development project, is being provided by the United States and Britain. Furthermore, the people of Ghana, despite their bitterly anticolonial attitude, retain a warm feeling for the British, as demonstrated by the remarkable display of affection shown Queen Elizabeth II when she visited Ghana in November 1961, a fact that their leaders cannot ignore.

Ghana's attitude toward its former British master contrasts sharply with the hostile feeling of Guinea toward the French. Both sentiments were shaped at birth. The French left their colony with great bitterness, cutting off all aid, after it voted in 1958 for complete independence rather than for internal autonomy within a Paris-led French Community, which was the choice of all other French territories. The British, on the contrary, voluntarily granted full independence to Ghana, which became, in 1957, the first Black African colony to be freed, and they have continued to help Ghana ever since.

Still, if Britain set off the independence vogue in Black Africa with the liberation of the Gold Coast, as the colonial territory was called, its decision was to a large extent shaped by the unrelenting anticolonial pressure exerted by Nkrumah, whose quick mind, flamboyant personality, and spell-binding tongue paved the way to nationalist leadership while he was still a youth. Born in the mud-hut village of Nkroful in 1909 on a Saturday—his name means "Saturday's Child" in his tribal language—he completed school at a Roman Catholic mission, enrolled in the colony's Achimota College, then, with money provided by a diamond-prospecting uncle, went to the United States to study at Pennsylvania's Negro Lincoln University, waiting on tables to supplement his funds. After graduating, he lectured on philosophy at Lincoln for a while, then earned his master's degree in anthropology at the University of Pennsylvania. In his autobiography, he admits to having toyed with communism during his student days in the United States, though only as a means of studying Marxist political organization.

After ten years in the United States, he enrolled in the London School of Economics, where he further developed his leftist tendencies. "I felt that the Communist Party in England," he wrote, "was fortunate in having among its leaders personalities such as Emil Burns, Palme Dutt, and Harry Pollitt." When the British found an unsigned Communist Party card in his possession, he explained that he used it to gain admission to party meetings so that he could "learn their techniques."

Later, he wrote, though he was not a communist, the British and his own colleagues in the United Gold Coast Convention (UGCC), a gradualist independence party which he helped lead, accused him of being a Red, partly because he used the word "comrade" when he addressed people in letters—a word still used by the Ghana Trade Union Congress. He left the UGCC in 1949 to form an organization of his own, the People's Convention Party. Although he was jailed by the British for fourteen months for sedition shortly afterwards, his party was in firm control of Ghana on independence day in 1957, and has ruled ever since.

Nkrumah, a rather homely man with large soulful eyes, a high receding forehead, and a flat nose, is, like many educated Africans, a complex, often tormented figure unsure of the world to which he really belongs. He is torn between Western culture and African tradition, a struggle that is compounded by the conflicting

Western concepts of Christianity and Marxism. Desperately trying to reconcile these competing influences, he calls himself a "Christian Marxian socialist," and mixes the Bible and Marx with African voodoo. Often, small leather bags, or *jujus,* are attached to the arm of his chair in his office to keep evil spirits away.

Nkrumah recognizes the value of superstition in maintaining control over his people, who are impressed with great chiefs wielding mysterious divine powers. A larger-than-life statue of Nkrumah stands impressively in front of Parliament House in the teeming, semimodern capital of Accra. The head is tilted boldly upward, one arm is upraised in a "follow me" gesture, and the clothes are those of a workman, although Nkrumah, since independence at least, has almost never been seen in anything but a natty Western suit or, on special occasions, in one of his elegant three-hundred-dollar tribal robes of multicolored kente cloth, which he drapes over his shoulder like a Roman toga. Inscribed on one side of the base of the statue are the words: "Seek ye first the political kingdom and all other things shall be added unto it."

There are a considerable number of Ghanaians today, however, who would like to subtract a few things from Ghana's political kingdom—mainly Nkrumah—as suggested by a bomb blast that blew the feet off his statue shortly before Queen Elizabeth's visit. For the President, who started out at the helm of a relatively democratic government—he was Prime Minister until a new republican constitution was put into effect in July 1960—today heads a totalitarian state controlled as tightly as the existence of an implacable opposition will permit. Ghanaians, under this "democratic centralist" system, are expected to regard him not only as their country's founder and president, but as a Messiah endowed with the near supernatural powers of the great tribal chiefs of old. He is usually referred to by his followers and the controlled press as Osagyefo, meaning the Redeemer. So as not to overuse this lofty title, newspapers call him by other titles, too:

Ahuna Bo Birim—He Whose Presence Electrifies.
Atenka Suro—He Whose Fame Is Dreaded Far and Wide.
Bre Nsem Ase—He Who Is Able to Manage Unmanageable Events.
Kasapreko—He Who Speaks Once and for All.
Katamanto—He Who Never Breaks an Oath.
Oyeadieyie—Renewer of All Things.

Local newspaper writers are prone to use even Biblical language when describing their leader. "I pondered," one writer said, "the mystery of volcanic dynamism which inhabits your Great Mind and erupts so often in utterances of . . . matchless radiance. In the name of the Seventy-seven Deities that guard the Destiny of Ghana, I invoke on your High Dedication the blessings of Longer Life, so that you can fulfill your Messianic mission of a Prosperous Ghana among the coming of a Peaceful United States of Continental Africa."

For those who prefer their propaganda in simpler terms, a large neon sign designating "Kwame Nkrumah Circle" in Accra flashes on and off in three colors.

It is illegal for any Ghanaian even to hint that Nkrumah is not infallible. A Criminal Code Amendment bill states that "any person who does an act with intent to insult or bring the President of the Republic of Ghana into hatred, contempt, or ridicule is punished by a fine not exceeding five hundred pounds or to imprisonment for a term not exceeding three years or to both." Nor can any distinction be made between Nkrumah as head of state and Nkrumah as head of government. "We cannot differentiate between these two offices," said Kofi Baako, leader of the House. The law applies to Ghanaians anywhere in the world and is retroactive to the date of independence.

When I asked one British businessman in Accra how far to the left he thought Nkrumah was leaning, he replied, "Well, he's certainly not a communist. Russia would never have him. Look how much trouble Khrushchev has had trying to tear down Stalin for his 'cult of personality.' Imagine what he'd have to go through with this African Jesus Christ."

And Osagyefo apparently does not rate himself as a much lesser figure. He once told his colleagues: "I am like the man who walked into Jerusalem two thousand years ago and got the people to follow him." Yet, unlike that man, Nkrumah seldom walks among his people today, for he doesn't want to meet the same end. He travels in a bullet-proof Rolls Royce with a heavily armed police escort—that is, when he dares to leave his headquarters in Flagstaff House, occasions that are never announced in advance. For while the majority of Ghanaians, even though harried by his iron rule, probably still support him for his past glory, there are many "atheists"—those who do not believe in the Renewer of All Things, who wish the real Nkrumah had been standing on the pedestal before Parliament House when the bomb went off. And their numbers have increased as the result of a measure passed by his puppet parliament proclaiming him president for life.

To deal with the unbelievers, a Criminal Procedure Amendment bill has been promulgated setting up a new high court composed of three judges appointed by the executive branch for the trial of persons accused of treason, sedition, rioting, unlawful assembly, or other such crimes. A majority decision only is necessary for conviction, and if there is a minority opinion, it is not revealed. Those found guilty are given sentences ranging from long prison terms to death, and no appeal is possible. This law supplements a previous Preventive Detention Act passed in 1958 which permits the government to imprison persons without trial up to five years, with further extensions obtainable, on suspicion of intending acts injurious to the state. About three hundred and fifty political enemies of Nkrumah are believed behind bars under this law, which Nkrumah has promised to amend, so that detainees can be held without trial for twenty years if rearrested after being released.

One village *mallam,* or Moslem religious teacher, was jailed for these official reasons: "a. . . . you have been concerned in incidents of violence and gangsterism; b. . . . your detention is necessary in order to prevent you from acting in the future in a manner prejudicial to the security of the state." What was the *mallam's* crime? He performed the wedding of his daughter, when this function, according to the state, was within the province of another *mallam.* Not without significance, the imprisoned teacher belonged to the opposition United Party.

Nkrumah's principal enemies are members of the United Party, a loose coalition of conservative and traditionalist regional groups, which received over a third of the votes in the nation's last national parliamentary election in 1956, shortly before independence. This party still exists, but it enjoys only a nominal life, for most of its leaders are either in jail or in exile, and those who are not know they will be if they take their opposition functions too seriously.

The basic conflict between the United Party and Nkrumah's People's Convention Party is their divergent view on the structure of the state. The President has established a unitary state under what amounts to his absolute control, whereas the United Party wants a federated state that would grant a large degree of autonomy to provinces formed along tribal lines. Fundamentally, the dispute is similar to the one in the Congo in which Moise Tshombe's Katanga has demanded autonomy as opposed to the central government's view that it be controlled from Leopoldville. Nkrumah's preoccupation with his own problem of national unity is one reason why he so violently opposes Tshombe's contentions. While Ghana's constitution guarantees the principle of chieftaincy, the chiefs have been deprived of all but symbolic authority, and unco-operative ones have been dethroned.

Nkrumah's main regret is that he did not follow the example of Guinea's Sékou Touré, who squashed the power of the tribal chiefs while his country was still under colonial control. Touré, however, never had to deal with a tribe as powerful as the Ashantis in Ghana, whose leaders are the mainstay of the United Party and have proved virtually impossible to pacify, despite every attempt at suppression. The party is not permitted to use loudspeakers on campaign vans, making it difficult for candidates to hold political rallies. Opposition newspapers are censored, mail is opened, phones are tapped. Then there is always the threat of jail. Sometimes, government and opposition forces terrorize each other, usually committing arson. Scores of "plots" against Nkrumah's life have been "uncovered," though such revelations have never been accompanied with proof.

Leader of the United Party is Dr. Kofi Abrefa Busia, an Oxford-trained sociology professor of mild, scholarly appearance, who is in exile. "I have always believed Africans can develop as free societies," he said. "Ghana, which entered the world so full of hope and with such good will, has failed. The people of Ghana are less free than they ever were under colonial rule. . . . It has to be realized that black men are now fleeing from oppression by black men and adding to the world refugee problem." About four thousand Ghanaians have fled suppression in Ghana and are now living in neighboring Togo.

The President, spurred on by leftist advisers, is determined to eliminate political opposition, even though his Convention People's Party already is an all-powerful political instrument. As the party-operated Trades Union Congress organ, *Labour,* points out, "the party's supremacy is unquestionable. Its decisions of democratic centralism are binding on every individual no matter what. All instructions go out from the central committee to ministers, to constituencies and wards, to the workers in the Trades Union Congress and farmers under the United Ghana Farmers Council and co-operatives who form the main stream of the party, to schools and homes. Nothing . . . is too small to escape its house-to-house attention." Moreover, all party members must attend Marxist classes, which are held in even the smallest factories and workshops, under a study program supervised by the party's "ideological secretary."

But Nkrumah and his advisers are not satisfied. They want to establish communist-style cells in every sector of Ghanaian life not yet reached, and they have drawn up a plan to do it. Young People's Leagues would be set up with branches in all secondary schools and colleges. Branches of the Ghana Young Pioneers, a uniformed party-controlled organization of teen-agers, would be introduced in all primary schools. Church congregations would contain party cells. Ghanaian interpretations of Marxism would even be taught in the classroom. A new education act is expected to be put into effect giving the state control over all education, including what goes into textbooks and how teachers should teach. To make the point that Nkrumah's program must be the root of all thought, Osagyefo appointed himself chancellor of the University of Ghana. Even Sékou Touré was taken aback, refusing to attend his installation. "Whoever heard of a politician and head of state taking over the whole direction of a country's higher education so blatantly?" he remarked to a visitor. "It's too obvious."

Nkrumah could live to rue such "obvious" actions. For popular discontent with government policy exists not only within the United Party, but is also spreading among people who had always accepted Osagyefo as a man who could do no wrong. The first rumblings on a significant scale were heard in mid-1961 when, to make up a deficit of about eighty-seven million dollars, he introduced an austerity budget that has staggered the population. The budget called for an increase in import duties up to one hundred percent, causing an estimated twenty percent rise in living costs. It raised taxes on liquor, tobacco, and gasoline and on urban property, and tightened tax collection procedures. It doubled the price of automobiles through increased purchase taxes. It froze wages to put the brakes on inflation. It instituted a compulsory savings scheme under which people had to invest between five and ten percent of their incomes in government bonds.

Ghanaians began to ask why such harsh measures were necessary when the economy is growing at a highly satisfactory rate of eight percent a year. Many wonder if the heavy expenditure on so-called "prestige items" is practical under present conditions— the Western and Soviet aircraft used by Ghana Airways, Accra's new Black Star Square built simply for reviews and parades, a powerful radio to beam Ghanaian propaganda throughout Africa, a pan-African news agency. Should not the reality of Ghana be served before the dream of a United Africa?

In recognition of the rumblings, the government has gone all-out in a budget sales campaign. Top officials speak at rallies, loudspeaker trucks shout explanations of the need for sacrifice. Special movies are shown offering further reasons for this need. But the most dramatic effort of all to ease public discontent is reflected in Nkrumah's demand that all ministers and other government officials set an example of austerity living themselves. Speaking in a dawn broadcast "in accordance with the cherished customs of our fathers whereby advice is sought and given at early dawn," Nkrumah condemned corruption and warned that members of his party must not use their "party membership or official position for personal gain or for the amassing of wealth." He announced a ban on unauthorized foreign travel by high officials, and asked them to give up all private commercial interests and properties in excess of two cars, two houses limited in total value to $56,000, and $1,400 worth of real estate. It is not clear whether Nkrumah, who lives more splendidly than most of his colleagues, has responded to his own call.

In any event, this sweetening of the pill has not been enough for many people. The austerity measures soon resulted in a dockyard and transport strike of three thousand workers at Sekondi-Takoradi which Nkrumah ruthlessly crushed, issuing warrants for the arrest of fifty "enemies of the state," including United Party leaders, Dr. Joseph Danquah, one of the founders of independent Ghana, and Joseph Appiah, a lawyer and son-in-law of Sir Stafford Cripps, the late British Finance Minister. The government, with its usual subtlety, let the public know what it thought of strikers in a notice asking all Ghanaians to be on the lookout for Obetsebi Lamptey, one of the leaders who had escaped the police net. He is, according to the notice, a "criminal, scoundrel, assassin, coward, nincompoop, swindler, and desperate political lunatic. Bloodthirsty, obdurate fiend, heartless looking, addicted to the opium of tribalism, vain, boasting, and often suffering from fits of mad yelling and screaming and using his fists on innocent people."

It is probably not coincidental that Ghana's swing to the left has paralleled the implementation of the austerity program. Nkrumah was apparently convinced that nobody knew better how to make the public suffer and like it than experts with a far-leftist outlook, particularly those who had helped him draw up the program. He therefore reshuffled his cabinet in late 1961, ousting six ministers and bringing in several more of these experts. Godfrey Bing, a former leftist member of the British parliament and the last remaining Briton in an important official position, lost his job as Attorney General, but was appointed a presidential adviser, a job that may be even more influential. His advice soon resulted in the hiring by the University of Ghana of Allen Nunn May, the British atomic physicist who had spied for the Soviet Union, to teach physics, and of a Polish professor to head the economics faculty. Bing's transfer was apparently necessary in view of a decision by the government to dismiss British officers who had led Ghana's army for the announced purpose of giving all important state jobs to native Ghanaians.

Krobo Edusei, known as "Crowbar" because of his toughness, was selected as Minister of Light and Heavy Industries. He was reputed to be one of the most rabid of Nkrumah's leftist followers, having traveled extensively in Eastern Europe and Soviet Russia where he studied communist methods of industrialization. He returned to Soviet Europe on his first ministerial mission and obtained trade agreements with the Soviet Union and other communist countries. He arranged also for industrial experts from Poland, Czechoslovakia, and other Red nations to help Ghana establish state consumer industries.

But if Edusei appeared to be a dedicated leftist, he obviously had capitalistic leanings. This was first brought to the public's attention through a whim of his wife, Mary, in early 1962. Vacationing in London in a sixty-dollar-a-day hotel suite, she became entranced by an eight-thousand-dollar gold-plated bed she saw in a department-store display window and purchased it. When the news got back to Ghana, Ghanaian women, many of whom sleep on straw mats, were enraged by this extravagance. After all, wasn't Minister Edusei always talking about socialism and the redistribution of wealth? Sensing political repercussions, Edusei telephoned his wife and ordered her to return the bed. But after some hesitation, she refused. "Mary want this bed," she told a reporter, "and nothing in world can make Mary change mind." Edusei personally flew to London to make it clear to his wife that his political future was at stake. But it was too late. Nkrumah, under public pressure, dismissed him from office. Mary's indiscretion had spotlighted the fact that Edusei had amassed a fortune of about $1.4 million while in office plus five luxurious homes, suggesting a capitalistic attitude that threatened to send him to prison. Fortunately for him, Nkrumah, plagued by a dearth of ministers whose loyalty he can be sure of, brought him back into the cabinet several months later.

In August 1962 Nkrumah jailed two other ministers and the executive secretary of his party for alleged involvement in an abortive bomb plot against him.

Working closely with Nkrumah's leftist government are the

Trade Union Congress (TUC) and Martin Appiah-Danquah, chief of the United Ghana Farmers Councils. Both organizations are state-operated. Lester N. Trachtman of the United States Department of Labor wrote in the January 1962 issue of *Economic Development and Cultural Change* that while it would be a "misguided oversimplification" to describe the TUC as a communist-type organization,

> "it is difficult to avoid noting the similarities in [its] policies . . . with those of the unions in a communist society. There is the familiar call for obedience to a supreme party leadership which will direct all important popular organizations in the endeavor to achieve a socialist state. Party members are to serve as the well-organized elite responsible for seeing that party policies are implemented. The resultant disciplined organization will control and direct the union movement, as well as other groups, for the movement is expected to act as a transmission belt of official policies as far as that is possible or practical in an economy that is just beginning to industrialize."

Probably the principal target of Nkrumah's cabinet turnover was outgoing Finance Minister Koula Agbeli Gbedemah, one of the President's closest collaborators since independence and among the most pro-Western of the Ghanaian leaders. Gbedemah, who was ousted from office ostensibly for extravagant living and outside business dealings in conflict with his job, is actually quite conservative. He wanted to reduce government expenditures rather than increase taxes. "The President and I don't always agree on policy," Gbedemah told me in his Accra office while he was still minister. "But that is natural. We always come to some agreement based on what is best for the country, and I'm sure we always will." He spoke like a man struggling to believe his own words.

The ouster of leaders like Gbedemah and their replacement by young radical nationalists suggest that Nkrumah may not be in full control of his government. Previously, he was able to pull all the strings by playing off one group of advisers against the other. Some observers think that he may now have to listen almost exclusively to his far leftist associates in view of the fact that he has broken with all other groups. These are the associates who have been pressing him to tighten the government dictatorship through one-party rule, squeeze the nation economically, improve relations with the communist bloc, and attack the West in the press— all this to be facilitated through the virtual deification of Nkrumah himself on the theory that few people would question the wisdom of a saint.

The rising power of this militant group, whose political machinery Russia no doubt believes true communists will one day take over, also points up Ghana's drift toward socialization. Actually, most new Afro-Asian nations are building some form of socialist society, and this is almost a necessity in countries where there are few or no indigenous capitalists. But the new Ghana government apparently intends to pattern the nation's economy to a large degree on the totalitarian Soviet model.

The Soviets, through their Economic Mission in Accra, have already granted Ghana a low-interest loan of fifty million dollars to defray Russian expenses under a technical co-operation agreement, and have agreed to increase their purchases of cocoa, the nation's principal crop, to sixty thousand tons a year over a five-year period. Ghana, for its part, is importing from the communist bloc machinery, transport equipment, rolled steel, petroleum products, and building materials. Between one hundred and two hundred communist technicians have been sent to Ghana, and more, including civil servants, are expected to come. Russian crews operate and maintain Ghana Airways' eight Ilyushin jet planes. Russian architects and engineers are drawing up blueprints for residential quarters in Ghanaian cities, building houses in Tema, Ghana's new port, and establishing factories outside Accra for the construction of cheap, precast homes. Russian prospectors are searching for minerals. A permanent Russian trade exhibition occupies the ground floor of the quasi-governmental Cocoa Marketing Board Building in the capital.

I was unable to get a room in one leading Accra hotel because several communist economic and cultural delegations had arrived simultaneously and occupied all the available space. In Accra bookstalls that once sold Western publications only, you can now buy copies of the magazines *Soviet Life* and *Soviet Woman,* or Major Yuri A. Gagarin's book *Soviet Man in Space.* Turn on the radio, and you get Radio Moscow or Radio Peking. Russian automobiles are on sale.

Many Ghanaians are learning the "advantages" of communist life at first hand. Over seventy military cadets are now receiving three years' training in the Soviet Union, and more than three hundred are to follow. Twenty-seven Ghanaian Young Pioneers are also in Russia learning youth organization, while other Ghanaian students are studying at Moscow's Friendship University and the Soviet School of Aviation. The Soviet Academy of Sciences

106 /

AFRICA

has offered to train Ghanaian scientists and co-ordinate Ghana's scientific research program. Soccer players are learning the finer points of the game in Prague. Ghanaian delegations stream in and out of the communist nations. A delegation from the Ghana Transport and Telecommunications Workers Unions was the guest of the Soviet Workers Oil and Chemical Industry Union, while a group of Ghana war veterans were hosted by the Soviet War Veterans Committee. Ghanaian editors have toured the *Pravda* and *Izvestia* newspaper plants.

Since mid-1961, when Nkrumah visited Peking on his tour of the communist world, Red China, no less than the Soviet Union, has been bent on making its influence felt in Ghana. Nkrumah left Red China with the promise of a twenty-million-dollar loan without interest over a period of six years. Under the loan agreement, Peking will also supply technical assistance and complete sets of "equipment, machinery and materials, technical and other goods." During Nkrumah's stay in China, the Communist Chinese Embassy in Accra widely advertised in Ghanaian newspapers Radio Peking's special coverage of the tour in English, French, and Arabic on its regular daily African transmissions.

Simultaneously, Peking opened a huge, well-attended economic exhibition which—streaming red banners announced—was intended to cement Afro-Asian solidarity and spur the joint fight against colonialism and imperialism. So as not to leave the main colonial offender unidentified, English translations of Mao's speeches were on display over such headings as "Drive United States Imperialism Out of Asia" and "Oppose United States Occupation of Taiwan." There was also an enormous photograph of a mass rally held in Peking to protest the assassination of Congolese Premier Patrice Lumumba, as well as a Chinese translation of Nkrumah's autobiography.

Ghanaian visitors, however, were more impressed with an exhibit of tractors, drills, lathes, spinning machines, printing presses, and models of hydroelectric schemes. And they lingered even longer around displays of such diverse export consumer items as phonograph records, canned goods, toys, Chinese dolls, and musical instruments.

But even while these products generated an image of a peace-loving communist world, large shipments of arms were flowing into Ghana from that same world, intended, it is believed, for use in other African territories. The Ghanaian forces have been well equipped by the British and could probably obtain more arms from Britain if that country were satisfied they were needed for internal use. The arms, it was speculated, would find their way to the Angola rebels who are fighting their Portuguese colonial masters.

In helping Ghana to involve itself in the affairs of other African states, the communists well realize they are playing their ace card in winning the government's sympathies. For Nkrumah is Africa's chief exponent of a federated continent, or if that is impossible for the moment, a united Africa south of the Sahara, or at the least, for a starter, a united West Africa—with Nkrumah, of course, running the works on all these levels. For the leader of a nation with only about seven million people, Osagyefo's Pan-African appeals have made no small impression in Africa. More than any other individual, he has created a feeling among many Africans that, whatever political, tribal, historical, and economic differences may divide them, they are all part of the same African family. When Nkrumah made a visit in 1959 to Cameroon, another West African territory, I saw huge, shouting, cheering, weeping crowds greet him wherever he went, many of them carrying banners with slogans like, "Welcome to Kwame Nkrumah, the Leader of All Africans." He was not simply a distinguished visitor from a foreign country; he was the symbol of the coming African millennium.

But while the dream of a great united Africa that might some day become one of the world's most powerful states, if not the most powerful, is likely to linger on, the man who conceived it has already faded in importance on a continental scale. Nkrumah's influence was at a peak in the first years following Ghana's achievement of independence. For Ghana had broken the colonial ice, and opened the doors to a national freedom that had seemed impossibly out of reach until then. Nkrumah, whose small country would probably be just another minor African state had it not been the first Black African colony to win independence, became the spokesman of all Africans surging relentlessly toward the same goal, and the atmosphere was ripe for spreading the dream of African unity.

But as country after country achieved independence, Ghana no longer loomed so brightly as the great beacon of freedom in Africa. Today, while many Africans still have a special regard for the country that originally led the way, they can hardly imagine Nkrumah as the leader of all Africa. Indeed, many dismiss him as simply an egoistic upstart. "It's interesting," a Nigerian official, whose country has more than five times the population of Ghana, told me in Lagos, "that Nkrumah should fancy himself as the

head of a united Africa. The leaders of our provinces rule more
people than he does."

Furthermore, few Africans are impressed with the example
Ghana has set in uniting—on paper—with Guinea and Mali.
Guinea's Touré also considers himself something of a Messiah,
and wants to take no orders from Nkrumah or anyone else. The
three countries cannot even unite economically, for Guinea's
francs are worthless outside that country, while Ghana's pounds
are at par with sterling, that nation being a member of the
British Commonwealth. Nor are the three countries bound by a
common culture. On the tribal level there are no ties; on the national level, Guinea and Mali are at least superficially imbued
with French culture, Ghana with British culture. Officials from
the two French-speaking countries cannot even converse with
their Ghanaian counterparts without an interpreter.

But Ghana's prestige in Africa has suffered most from its naked
efforts to interfere in the internal affairs of other African states—
efforts undertaken with the full support of the communist bloc.
The governments of Togo and the Ivory Coast, which flank
Ghana, have bitterly castigated Nkrumah for trying to unite under his control the Ewe tribe on the two sides of both Ghanaian
borders, and also for harboring political exiles from these countries. The Cameroon government has criticized Nkrumah, as well
as Nasser, for housing the headquarters of an outlawed com-
munist-infiltrated Cameroon terrorist organization, the Union des
Populations Camerounaises.

Nkrumah interfered most blatantly of all in the Congo, in-
triguing against all Congolese who were opposed to ex-Premier
Lumumba and to his successor, Antoine Gizenga, including the
regime of Congolese President Kasavubu and that of Katanga
President Tshombe. The belief that Kasavubu, and particularly
Tshombe, may have been guided by colonial hands might have
been a secondary reason for Ghana's involvement in the Congo
situation. "It would be a mistake," Nkrumah told his parliament
in August 1960, "to look upon the Congo as a case apart or to
suppose that the basic conditions which have produced the present
situation in the Congo do not in fact exist in one form or another
throughout the whole continent of Africa. The problem of Africa
is essentially bound up everywhere with a struggle between a ruling
minority and the underprivileged and economically exploited majority . . . it is therefore no solution to the African problem for a
colonial power to hand over authority to a small clique of African

politicians who are not generally representative of the people from whom they have sprung."

But the basic reason for Nkrumah's intense interest in the Congo lay in the hope that a unified Congo under Lumumba, and, after his assassination, under Gizenga, both of whom were supposedly "representative of the people," would join a Ghana-controlled African federation. The extent to which Nkrumah tried to manipulate Lumumba was revealed in a letter that he wrote to him and which fell into the hands of Kasavubu's supporters shortly after the Congo attained independence from Belgium in 1960. The letter advised "Dear Patrice" not to try to oust Kasavubu "now" but to deal with him later, and to take advantage of the United Nations' facilities and help rather than expel it from the Congo. The Congolese Premier was urged to work with "your closest enemies" without giving up his principles, to consolidate his hold on his power and be "cool as a cucumber." Describing himself as an expert at handling the "colonialists," Nkrumah grandly concluded, "Whenever in doubt, consult me." The political demise of the Lumumba-Gizenga forces, ending his chances for controlling them, was a bitter blow to the Ghanaian leader.

The communist powers are far too realistic to believe that Nkrumah has any chance of succeeding in his furious endeavor to unify Africa, even in a loose federation—the Ghanaian leader's minimum goal. Nor would they like to see a united Africa any more than they would welcome a united Arab world, considering that Africa today contains hardly a handful of hard-core communists. Moscow-Peking tactics are designed, instead, to foster conditions for the establishment of communist bases in Africa from which the rest of the continent could be gradually subverted.

But the Reds are only too willing to support Ghanaian efforts to win control of Africa, with both money and arms, as long as they can do so without giving the impression to other African countries with no love for Nkrumah that they really favor Ghana as continental leader. Not only has this policy led to closer relations with Ghana, but the Ghanaians are spreading just the kind of propaganda the communists want spread. To further the cause of African unity, Ghana constantly harps on the anticolonial theme, which parallels the anti-West diatribes put out by Moscow and Peking. And now that old-fashioned colonialism is swiftly disappearing from Africa, Ghana is using another theme dear to the heart of the Reds—neo-colonialism.

"The colonial powers," Ghana's Foreign Minister Ako Adjei told the United Nations in late 1961, "realize that the time has come for them to concede independence to the African people. However, they try to use every device to deprive the new African states of the real substance and meaning of their national independence . . . by such devices as military pacts, economic and cultural agreements, and the granting of scientific and technical assistance" —the very charges the communists have been making for years.

Yet, incredibly, even as Ghana warned other newly liberated countries against the dangers of "neo-colonialism," Nkrumah was urging the United States to please finance his country's mammoth Volta River dam project at Akosombo, about eighty miles northeast of Accra. This scheme is dear to the heart of Nkrumah, who views it as the ultimate answer to Ghana's economic troubles. When completed, it will generate 768,000 kilowatts, or more than twenty times the total electric power produced in Ghana today. A huge aluminum smelter, which will be built and partly financed by the Volta Aluminum Company, an American concern of which Kaiser Aluminum Company is the principal stockholder, will use most of the power. In addition, the construction of an electric grid serving all major localities in southern Ghana is expected to give rise to a complex of new small industries. The dam will create a lake 250 miles long with a shoreline of 4,500 miles, the third largest man-made lake in the world. It will not only irrigate a tremendous area but will provide cheap water transport through a large part of the country and permit the establishment of a fresh-water fishing industry.

In mid-1961 Washington had indicated it would grant Ghana a $133-million loan, more than a third of the total cost of the project, the rest to be provided by the World Bank, Britain, and the Ghanaian government, with Russia contributing technical aid in carrying out survey work and building a power dam. But following Nkrumah's tour of the communist world, which resulted in his support of Soviet foreign policy right down the line, United States officials had second thoughts about coming to his aid. This might have given Nkrumah a fine opportunity to "reject" United States help on the grounds that political strings were attached, and to appeal to the Soviet Union to take over the whole project. Instead, Nkrumah wrote two conciliatory notes to President Kennedy indicating he would appreciate United States participation, whereupon a special mission was sent to Ghana to make recommendations. With the Soviet Union presumably standing by ready to step in with a dramatic offer as it did in Egypt when the United States refused to build the Aswan Dam, Washington finally approved the project. Perhaps the most valid reason for doing so was not the likelihood of a Soviet move, but Ghana's obvious desire to have the United States do the main job—a strong indication that Nkrumah, despite the lessons he has learned from the communists, is wary of becoming economically dependent on them.

Indeed, for a man in mortal fear of capitalistic "neo-colonialism," Nkrumah has sold a considerable portion of his soul to the devil. About ninety percent of Ghana's imports are in the hands of Western businessmen, and private capital, much of it from the West, has provided the bulk of investment in industry, probably exceeding in amount the capital in the public sector of the economy. On one occasion Nkrumah alarmed foreign investors with a remark that with "collective ownership and the means of production and distribution in the hands of the people, our dear country will soon say good-bye to the exploitation of man by man." With this public pronouncement off his chest, he called in representatives of eighteen foreign companies to reassure them that Ghana did not intend to nationalize private enterprises. He actually stood for four streams of development, his aides added: co-operatives, government-owned industry, private industry, and a mixed sector.

Nor did the visit of Queen Elizabeth to Ghana offer any indication that Nkrumah is about to turn into another Fidel Castro, despite government accusations that British businessmen and diplomats are backing the "treasonable activities" of the opposition. Nkrumah accompanied the Queen on a tour of the country, trying to bask in the reflections of her glory. And glory there was. Huge crowds turned out to welcome the Sovereign, crying, "Long live our Queen," and "Our Queen is a beautiful," though the government had instructed the people to call her "Queen Elizabeth of England," since Ghana, while a member of the British Commonwealth, is a republic owing no allegiance to her. Accra's *Evening News* described the Queen as the "world's greatest Socialist monarch in history" and the "most modest and lovable of sovereigns."

The greeting given the Queen confirmed the durability of the influence of British culture on Ghana. There is still a reverence in that country for things British. At my hotel in Accra, the bellboy entered my room every day at four o'clock sharp, smiling over a tray of tea and crumpets. A Ghana military band, resplendent in bright-red tunics and braided caps, played British and American tunes on a bandstand outside the hotel. At the popular outdoor Lido Cabaret, pretty Ghanaian girls were not at all surprised when I invited them to dance; many Englishmen frequented the club, and some, I noted, could do the Ghanaian "High-Life," a shuffling, rhythmic step, with as much grace as any African. In parliament, though Nkrumah is crushing all political opposition, the forms of British democratic precedure are still observed. The chamber rings with such cries as "hear, hear," and occasionally an oppositionist will even be given the opportunity to criticize the government mildly, though never Nkrumah personally. Judges take pride in their curly white wigs and black robes, even as they maintain that Britain's habeas corpus does not apply in independent Ghana.

"British culture and philosophy have been retained in Ghana more in form than in substance," a British diplomat told me. "But it may nevertheless be sufficient to stand in the way of communist culture, which is entirely alien to these people. If we have not been able to instill our ideas in the Ghanaians any more than we have, whatever communist influence is introduced is likely to be even thinner in substance. One thick overlay of foreign culture is enough for them. They're now thinking in terms of building a new uniquely African way of life, perhaps including elements of communism, but not enough to turn Ghana into a communist country."

V

ANGOLA:

OVERHEAD,

THE SCAVENGERS

In March 1961 one of the most savage and uninhibited rebellions in recent times broke out in the Portuguese colony of Angola. One needs a strong stomach to listen to some of the tales told by Portuguese who have survived rebel attacks. An elderly man I met in the northern fighting zone described how some forty Africans attacked him and his eighteen-year-old son with long murderous machete knives. "I got away," he said, "but they caught my son. From a distance I saw them cut off his arms and his legs while he was still alive. And all the while he screamed and wept."

The Portuguese, many of them half-crazed by such slaughter, have, for their part, killed thousands of Africans in retaliation, sometimes decapitating the bodies and displaying the heads on sticks. Sitting in the rear cockpit of a diving Portuguese T-6 fighter-bomber as it fired rockets into rebel strongholds, I saw countless villages that had been burned to the ground either by napalm attacks from the air or by ground troops.

The Portuguese charge that the rebellion, which continues to simmer, is largely communist-inspired. There is little evidence to back up this allegation, but certainly it is possible, if not likely, that communists are involved in this magnificent opportunity for exploiting chaos. The Reds themselves claim such involvement in their propaganda. According to the Soviet publication, *Interna-*

tional Affairs, an underground Communist Party of Angola was organized in October 1955. This appears to have been confirmed by Mario de Andrade, now second in command of one of the two competing rebel groups, the Popular Movement for the Liberation of Angola, though he refers only to the establishment of a "Marxist group." "In October 1955," he stated in a Portuguese-language broadcast on Radio Prague in February 1961, "a Marxist group was founded in the strictest secrecy. Its young leaders did not have enough political experience in view of the difficult conditions in which Africans live in Portuguese colonies. Nevertheless, the group achieved remarkable success in disseminating Marxist ideas among the people. In 1956 the United Struggle of Angolan Africans was formed. Its program was very similar to that of the Angola Marxists . . ."

International Affairs explains that in 1956 the Communist Party (or "Marxist group") joined with the United Struggle of Angolan Africans to form the Popular Movement for the Liberation of Angola (MPLA). The initial activities of this all-embracing organization, the Moscow weekly *New Times* said, were confined to the "distribution of leaflets, manifestoes, action programs, and appeals for the intensification of the anticolonial struggle." Then, on Easter Sunday, 1959, the Portuguese police went into action, arresting over one hundred and fifty Africans suspected of membership in the Communist Party or associated nationalist organizations in the beautiful seaside capital of Luanda, and many others elsewhere in the colony. The period of pamphleteering had largely come to an end, but the seeds of armed revolution had been planted. Shortly after the Easter arrests, the MPLA established its headquarters in Conakry, the capital of leftist Guinea, where the organization is believed to have received training from communist-bloc advisers in that country.

Meanwhile, another independent nationalist group, the Union of the People of Angola (UPA), based itself in the Congo capital of Leopoldville as soon as the Congo, which shares Angola's northern border, received independence from the Belgians in June 1960. Organized in 1954 as the Union of the People of Northern Angola, it dropped the word "Northern" in 1958 to give the group a national character, then changed its name again in 1962 to the National Front for the Liberation of Angola (FLNA). This organization has done most, if not all, of the fighting.

One month after the uprising started, leaders of the two rebel groups, as well as representatives of other Portuguese nationalist movements from Mozambique, in southeast Africa, and Portuguese Guinea, in northwest Africa, met in Casablanca, according to *New Times,* to co-ordinate plans for revolts in all the Portuguese African territories. But no co-ordination, even between the Angolan groups, was achieved. The Popular Movement, which has moved its headquarters from Guinea to Leopoldville, keeps in close touch with the radical nationalist Casablanca bloc of African nations, while the National Front appears to lean toward the relatively conservative Monrovia bloc with its close Western ties. In the bitter competition for control of the rebel movement, Holden Roberto, leader and founder of the National Front, announced in April 1962 the formation of an Angolan government-in-exile. The Popular Movement violently reacted with the charge that Roberto was a "traitor" to the cause of unity who had "massacred" eight thousand rebel guerrillas and other Angolan natives in "fratricidal" clashes.

Relations between the two groups, however, improved in the summer of 1962 with the reappearance of Agostinbo Neto, chief of the Popular Movement, who escaped from Portugal after more than two years of imprisonment in the Cape Verde Islands and house arrest in Lisbon. Neto immediately held discussions with National Front officials regarding the possibilities of union. At least on the surface, the two organizations have considerable in common. They both demand independence and promise social reform and political democracy under a multi-party system. But the radical leftist tendencies of the Popular Movement are evident, though it is not clear just how radical it is. Its leadership may simply be non-communist Marxist like Guinea's Touré or Ghana's Nkrumah, or it could have Castroite ideas.

On the other hand, Roberto's leanings appear to be toward the moderate side, as evidenced by his attraction to the Monrovia bloc, although the Portuguese claim that he, as well as Neto and De Andrade, are communists. The Portuguese submitted to the United Nations a photostat copy of what they claimed was a circular letter bearing Roberto's signature and the stamp of his organization that is supposed to show that he is a Red. Written in French and addressed to "Dear Congolese Compatriots," the letter, which most observers scoff at as a fraud, reads:

> You must spend much money for support of our illustrious friend Patrice Lumumba whom the tribalists would like to choke. We delivered to Mr. Lumumba five million francs which will permit him, without doubt, to obtain the necessary means to conquer and liberate Angola. In a few words here is our plan for the future. Sékou Touré must reign over North Africa, Comrade

Nkrumah over the central part, and your servant Holden Roberto over the south. We hope that our most distinguished comrade, The Devil, strictly between us, will help us to realize our destiny. Besides, the future is being forged. Don't believe the story-tellers; communism is not a bad thing. During our stay in Moscow we had the opportunity to see many magnificent things that the Westerners will never have . . . Money, money, and more money. First Lumumba, then ourselves. Comrade Devil is standing by, watching vigilantly.

The Portuguese also submitted a document to the United Nations dated December 3, 1960, which was supposed to have been found in the possession of a captured terrorist: "Long live UPA—Long live Nikita—Long live Angola . . . Prepare your arms . . . We are going to open fire . . . We have no fear, Russia will give us weapons and Lumumba will help the UPA. Let us kill the whites . . . Lumumba has given authorization. Long live UPA. Long live Khrushchev . . . Long live Angola." Even if this document is legitimate, it appears to hail Khrushchev more for his expected generosity in the dispensation of arms than for his communism.

Another letter submitted to the United Nations and dated October 26, 1960, is addressed by "L'Alliance des Bakongo," or Abako, the party of Congolese President Kasavubu, to the youth group of the organization: "We call your attention to the fact that we are in possession of concrete evidence proving that UPA is procommunist. For this reason we invite you to boycott UPA in Leopoldville and in the lower Congo. To close UPA offices wherever they are to be found, and in case of resistance, the young people should be encouraged to take measures to achieve this result . . ." Yet, the UPA offices have never been closed, while Abako arms have been found in possession of the rebels fighting in Angola.

Whatever the degree of communist involvement in the Angolan revolt, if there has been any, no communist guns have been discovered. Still, it is not impossible that arms, and even men, have been, or will be, smuggled ashore somewhere along Angola's long southwest African coastline. (Presumably, Congolese authorities would not permit such arms to be sent via the Congo.) At the peak of the rebellion, Portuguese officials told me that a fleet of Soviet trawlers with African crew members were "fishing" off the coast and might have been engaged in such operations. Polish ships unloading iron ore in Angolan ports also could have participated.

Polish exiles in London maintain that about fifty Poles returning to Poland from Brazil, where they learned to speak Portuguese fluently, will be sent, some of them disguised as "diplomats," to the Congo, from which they will infiltrate into Angola and serve as instructors and officers with the rebels, though it is not made clear which group of rebels. According to this unconfirmed information, the idea came from Major Mieczyslaw Lepecki, an adjutant to the late prewar Polish leader Marshal Pilsudski. Lepecki recently visited Brazil, ostensibly to put his plan into motion. Lieutenant General Wojciech Jaruzelski, chief of the Central Political Board of the Polish Armed Forces, will also allegedly play a leading role in this plan.

The utter fanaticism of the rebel leaders has made Portuguese intelligence work extremely difficult, as the most any captured leader says is: "My duty is to kill whites. Now you may kill me." Roberto's officers were indoctrinated with nationalist fervor in the Congo even before that country became independent. People from scattered villages were selected from thousands of Angolans who, when the Belgians were in power, migrated to the Congo to work part of the year for the relatively high wages offered there. With independence, Kasavubu, a member of the Bakongo tribe like most northern Angolans, did nothing to discourage such underground activities. Spurred by the Congo's success in achieving freedom, trainees went back to their Angolan villages to organize, with the aid of village chiefs, a mass-murder campaign against the whites. Roberto opened a full-fledged guerrilla training camp in the Congo in mid-1962.

The sadistic bitterness of the rebels which the communists are trying to exploit reflects the deep sense of frustration and urgency among the four and a half million Angolans who for nearly five centuries have suffered oppression and degradation under Portuguese colonial rule. The Portuguese now hope to pacify the Africans with long-overdue reforms. They thing that by belatedly appeasing the Africans they can maintain their rule over them. But this desperate gesture to save an empire, without which Portugal would be reduced to the status of an insignificant Iberian enclave, may have come too late. The Angolans want independence and nothing less.

The Angolans are, as the present savagery suggests, even more obsessed than most Africans about escaping the colonial grasp. Whereas the British, French, and Belgian colonialists, from the beginning of their rule, had in most cases promised their subject peoples eventual independence, the Portuguese have irrationally maintained that their colonies would forever be Portuguese ter-

ritory, thereby inviting irrational defiance. Compounding this un-
reasonableness, the Portuguese, unlike the other colonialists, gave
little thought, until recently, to the need for reform as a political
safety valve.

All but a handful of Africans in Angola were, before the new
reforms were instituted, deprived of the civil rights granted the
whites, few as even these rights may be under the totalitarian
Portuguese regime. Education, as in Portugal itself, has been deliberately neglected—only about two percent of the Africans are
literate—on the grounds that thinking people tend to become
subversive. Few medical facilities are available for Africans. Economic policies grossly discriminate against the blacks. And, worst
of all, force has been an integral feature of the government's approach to the colonial problem.

It is not without significance that the first African attacks were
made in early 1961 against the jails in Luanda, which are jammed
with Africans picked up by the dreaded secret police, an organization responsible only to Premier Antonio de Oliveira Salazar himself. Ironically, this Portuguese Gestapo, which was only imported
from the mother country to forestall a possible rebellion after the
Congo became independent, may have triggered the recent uprising with its brutal methods of "interrogation." Portuguese forced-
labor policies, too, no doubt constituted an important factor in the
revolt. Every African man must work at least six months each
year, a requirement that has upset the life of the African masses
far more profoundly than any policy ever instituted by the other
colonial powers, whose effective control has seldom reached down
to the bush African living, often quite happily, on a subsistence
level.

The rebellion that has been fanned by such oppression could
produce another world crisis of Congo proportions. Already the
United Nations has passed resolutions, supported by both Russia
and the United States, censuring Portugal for its colonial policies.
Washington's decision indicates its willingness to disturb the unity
of the North Atlantic Treaty Organization, of which Portugal is a
member, in order to win the sympathy of the newly independent
African states. Russia, of course, has a stake in the spread of
chaos.

If Portugal persists in its refusal even to consider black independence, rebel activity, though it may be halted temporarily,
may never be entirely crushed. And if Portugal does grant independence, the ensuing chaos that would probably result, even
if the United Nations should offer guidance to a free Angola, would

make the Congo look like a model of national orderliness. Not only is there virtually no educated elite, but there are not even important tribal leaders comparable to the Congo's Joseph Kasavubu or Moise Tshombe, who are at least able to keep order to some degree within their own regions. For the Portuguese long ago broke up large tribal organizations to discourage African political activity.

Even Holden Roberto, a reputedly ideological moderate, has proved himself to be an utterly ruthless extremist in tactical terms, who will employ any means to achieve his ends. Deceptively professorial and dignified in appearance, particularly when he wears eyeglasses, Roberto, who moved from his native northern Angola to Leopoldville in childhood, later serving as a Congo civil servant and as a clerk for a Belgian firm while preparing his revolution, has explained: "I am a revolutionary because a Christian who remains silent before a crime becomes a participant in that crime." In breaking his silence before the Portuguese colonial crime, he has himself committed a grave crime—ordering the calculated slaughter and mutilation of whites and non-co-operative blacks in Angola. It is not unlikely that he, and probably his enemies too, would use similar tactics against all political and tribal opposition within an independent state.

The searing hostility of such men toward the Portuguese, however, is at least understandable. I did not meet a single Portuguese in Angola who even suggested the possibility of African independence. "We just need a little time," the editor of a leading Portuguese newspaper in Luanda said. "Just enough to bring this bloodshed to an end and start our reform program rolling."

But the rebels, whom the Portuguese have not yet been able to crush entirely, despite bombing and strafing attacks and the burning of rebel-held territory, show no sign of yielding to the "temptation" of the Portuguese reform bait. Thousands of activists supported by tens of thousands of sympathizers have been fighting for independence with fanatical zeal, and—even more upsetting to the Portuguese—with considerable guerrilla prowess. While participating in one rocket attack on rebel objectives, I saw below me an example of their skill. A long Portuguese convoy was held up on the single north-south road running from Luanda to the Congo border by a system of roadblocks that even had the frustrated Portuguese marveling. So many trees lay across the road that from the air it looked almost like a railroad track.

Even southern Angola, where there has been no fighting yet, has been haunted by fear. In Nova Lisboa and Sa Da Bandeira, two of the leading southern cities, few people until recently could be seen on the streets during the day and almost none ventured outdoors at night. Some whites barred their windows and women carried pistols in their handbags and lived in hotels when their husbands were away for fear of being attacked by their own African servants. In some villages the Portuguese, hoping to find safety in numbers, brought their mattresses to neighbors' homes or slept together in large warehouses. Feeding the panic were constant rumors of African murder plots. One persistent rumor in Nova Lisboa while I was there was that one hundred and fifty African terrorists armed with machetes were captured in a Catholic Church while going over final details of a planned massacre.

The southern blacks, for their part, have expected every knock on the door to mean arrest and brutalization by the secret police, which has rounded up thousands of suspects, particularly among the educated Africans. Some have disappeared and are believed to have been sent to the notorious cocoa plantations of São Tomé and Principe, island colonies in the Gulf of Guinea, which are known for their near-concentration camp conditions. The secret police is little impressed by the argument that its tactics, which failed so miserably in the north, could foster rather than deter the spread of black terroism. Nevertheless, there is an evident danger that the southern tribes, traditionally hostile to the rebel Bakongo tribesmen, could eventually be provoked into making common cause with them.

The need for social, economic, and political reform is recognized by most Portuguese in Angola, who particularly want increased autonomy for the colony, which is now under the direct control of the Overseas Ministry in Lisbon. This recognition is linked in large degree to the opposition to Salazar's dictatorial regime, though most people keep their sentiments to themselves for fear of disappearing, courtesy of the secret police. Many hope the pressure of the rebellion will result in Salazar's overthrow. Several dared to tell me frankly that they agreed with the sixty-eight Portuguese intellectuals in Lisbon who in mid-1961 petitioned Salazar for reforms. And one newspaper editor openly deplored the censorship that has effectively muzzled the Portuguese as well as the foreign press. But more often this opposition is expressed in subtler terms. A Portuguese taxi driver in Luanda remarked with a sardonic grin: "Everybody here loves Salazar. I don't believe the story that the reason he hasn't visited Angola in all the thirty-three years he's been in office is that he is afraid to leave Portugal."

Surprisingly, the most liberal element among the 250,000 Portuguese in Angola seems to be the military, particularly those officers recently arrived. The dispatch by the Portuguese government of more than 20,000 soldiers could have ironic consequences indeed for the government. Many soldiers are discovering for the first time some of the factors that led to the revolt. "Now that we are suddenly asked to risk our lives to save Angola," one officer said, "we have started asking ourselves how this catastrophe happened. The problem here is not basically military but economic and social. It's made to order for the communists. And I don't think we are going to leave until it is solved." This new awareness by many military elements could crystallize into pressure for genuine reform, if by no means for African independence; for it is clear that the army and air force will in the future have a louder voice than ever before in determining the future of Angola.

Yet the military, which appears to have far greater understanding of the African position than have the civilians in either Portugal or Angola, have been engaged in the extermination of many of these Africans. Although it is impossible to gauge accurately the number of rebel dead, certainly many thousands have been killed. (About 1,500 whites and loyal Africans have died.) Yet, despite many accounts to the contrary, indiscriminate killing on the part of the military has been kept to a minimum. Armed civilians have probably been responsible for most atrocities committed against the Africans. In Luanda, maddened armed civilians went amuck in the African quarter in the spring of 1961, killing more than thirty innocent blacks before the military clamped a temporary curfew on the area. However unjustified such indiscriminate murder may be, it is no less understandable than black atrocities committed against the Portuguese. After seeing their own or their neighbors' families chopped into bits, the Portuguese civilians are lusting for revenge.

The military are less emotionally involved in the war, for their families have not been endangered. They think not in terms of revenge but of bringing order, and eventually reform, to Angola. The army has burned down many villages, and the air force has bombed and strafed others. But an effort has been made to discriminate between rebel and "peaceful" villages, and since few Africans would disobey the advice of the village chief, a community is almost always wholly rebel or wholly peaceful. Few people are in their thatched huts when they are set afire, for most Africans in northern Angola remain hiding in the bush during the day. When the Portuguese attack suspected villages at night they kill most of the men, but, except in individual cases, do not harm the women and children.

I flew over many areas in which some villages had been destroyed and others were untouched. Of three villages situated near the Portuguese town of Mucaba, which for a while was under constant attack by the rebels, only one was burned. In the other two only individual houses were in ashes. "We burn down villages," a Portuguese officer told me, "only when we are convinced most or all of the men have attacked Portuguese. If we can pin the guilty parties down to particular houses by interrogating informers, we destroy only those houses. Some women and children unfortunately are killed in these attacks as they are in any war, particularly when they are used as shields by the rebels. But we don't deliberately kill the innocent with the guilty. After all we've got to live peacefully with those people one day."

This officer put his finger on a dilemma facing many Portuguese in Angola, particularly the military. It seems quite evident to them that the uprising, which is already fairly general in the north, must be completely stamped out before African hatred for the Portuguese spreads and hardens to the point where "peaceful co-existence" becomes impossible. And to do this, ruthless means are believed required. But there is deep concern, not without justification, lest these means achieve the very results they are trying to avoid. Wishfully, the Portuguese are hoping that reform will cushion the horns of this dilemma.

"Peaceful coexistence" has a special meaning for the Portuguese. They have long prided themselves on their "multiracial" policies. The wife of a high Portuguese administrator told me, "I wouldn't care if my son married an African girl—as long as she was cultured and they didn't live abroad where they would suffer social indignities." Certainly not every Portuguese in Angola is as liberal-minded as this woman. But until the rebellion broke out there was relatively little racial friction in the colony.

True, most Africans are living under abysmal conditions, finding it difficult, if not impossible, to rise under the burden of a double handicap. The Portuguese ruling class tries to keep them a politically impotent source of cheap labor, while the lower-class Portuguese want to keep them out of employment categories they now dominate. Even so, the Africans are not exploited much more than the poor Portuguese themselves, many of whom live in African quarters in African-style mud houses. Discrimination against the blacks in Angola, unlike that in most African colonies, is basically economic and political rather than racial. In short, there is a kind of democracy in poverty here.

Antonio Monica is a typical lower-class Portuguese immigrant. He lives with his wife Maria and five children on the outskirts of Nova Lisboa in southern Angola surrounded by African homes. He purchased his house from an African when he arrived here several years ago from Portugal, where he had been unable to find a job. It can be distinguished from neighboring African residences only by improvements he has made. He has painted the brown abode walls white, replaced the thatched roof with tile, and cemented the dirt floor. The interior, however, looks no different from the inside of any African house. One of the two rooms contains only a table and chairs, and the other, two springless beds for the whole family. The letters "DDT" are stenciled on the front wall, indicating the house has been sprayed by government "delousers."

As a part-time plasterer, Antonio earns only one dollar a day—about twice the pay of an African day laborer. He grows corn and cabbage on his two acres of land to keep the food bills down. Like most African children, his offspring go without shoes and the younger ones don't even wear pants or underclothing. They play with the African children, and those of school age go to the same school with them. One of Antonio's sons was born to an African mistress he had before he married Maria, but Maria is bringing up the child like her own.

Some Africans enjoy much higher living standards than Antonio's family. To a considerable extent, these few are accepted as social equals with the upper-class Portuguese, just as the poor Africans are so accepted by the lower-class whites. They were called *assimilados* until recent reforms abolished this patronizing and, in the view of many Africans, degrading, designation. Without a special friend or bribe-taking patron in a key administrative position, it was extremely difficult for an African to obtain an *assimilado* certificate declaring him "civilized" because he spoke Portuguese, lived in Western style, and ate with a knife and fork. Yet the forty-thousand-odd Africans who were given such a certificate could compete for political and economic status with the white man, send their children to Portuguese schools, and even marry into high white society. Therefore, when the Portuguese say they must end the rebellion quickly before it is too late, they mean before it is too late to prove that Portuguese policy is, despite the cries of outrage from the United Nations, rooted in moral principle. Multiracialism is the one argument they have, or that they think they have, to meet the world's anti-colonial campaign.

To stress this moral factor, the Portuguese hope to project their reforms within the framework of an old Portuguese dream—a Lusitanian world community. Ideally, this concept calls for a binding spiritual unity of all Portuguese-speaking territories, including Brazil. No hope is now held out for Brazil's co-operation, but the Portuguese are likely to do their best to cultivate the idea in Angola and the other Portuguese colonies. And they won't be deterred by the damage already done to this project by the uprising, or by the fall of Goa to India. They are determined to prove that, despite these setbacks, Salazar was prophetic when he told the Portuguese national assembly in November 1960 that "here and overseas, on national or foreign territory, the Portuguese, whatever his color or race, sharply feels [the unity of the Portuguese nation]."

Before the rebellion, this "unity" propaganda was intended mainly for white consumption. The poverty-stricken Portuguese at home were to subordinate their worries to pride in empire, and those in the colonies were to be reassured that Portugal had not abandoned them. These will continue to be important considerations, but the primary purpose of the community concept in the future will be to give Portugal's subject peoples, especially the Angolans, a sense of true equality with whites as a substitute for black independence.

"We must instill in the African," a Portuguese official said, "the feeling that he belongs to the Portuguese world and that this world offers him the freedom he wants. The reason for the present trouble is that we haven't moved fast enough in the direction of an assimilated community, not only within Angola, but within the whole Portuguese empire."

Africans, it is reasoned, must be spiritually conditioned to "feel Portuguese." And the reforms that have been introduced in Angola, as well as in Mozambique and Portuguese Guinea, will be geared to hasten the conditioning process. All Portuguese Africans have been granted the same legal rights previously enjoyed only by whites and the *assimilados*—including the right, if they are able to read and write Portuguese and pay seven dollars a year in taxes, to vote and hold office. Educational facilities are likely to be increased. New health and housing projects are also contemplated.

But what is not clear is whether the worst evil of all can be eradicated in view of the dictatorial principles of the Portuguese government—the resort to force to achieve desired ends. Still, in the last few years, the Portuguese have modified their labor policies considerably, though certainly not sufficiently. In the embattled north, I visited with one hundred and twenty members of the Bailundo tribe who had come from southern Angola to engage in contract labor on a coffee plantation. I arrived shortly after six workers had been killed and mutilated by rebel marauders. The Bailundos, like other southern tribes, have little use for the rebellious Bakongolese. That is probably the main reason why the revolt hasn't spread southward and the contract workers haven't joined the rebellion.

But the loyalty of these laborers to the Portuguese reflects also the changing Portuguese attitude toward African labor. Mario, a thin twenty-one-year-old youth, was one of the workers I met. A professional Portuguese recruiter came to his village in the fall of 1960 and, with the co-operation of the village chief, asked for volunteers to work on a northern plantation, spelling out the conditions of work. Mario volunteered. A few years ago he would have been told to go—with no questions asked. For though under Portuguese law no one can be forcibly recruited for private contract labor, this law was largely ignored. Recruiters worked hand in hand with local administrators and tribal chiefs in obtaining plantation or construction labor by force, for which all concerned received a cut—so much per head.

Today many violations of the law still take place but the government has been cracking down. Administrators found to have profited from forced recruiting are being jailed. It is more difficult to control the pressures exerted by corrupt tribal chiefs whose subjects traditionally obey them, but even these pressures have been reduced.

However, Mario's decision wasn't entirely voluntary. He would have preferred to remain home lolling in the sun outside his thatched hut while his energetic wife sustained the family on manioc and vegetables she grew in the garden. He saw no good reason why he should have to exert himself unnecessarily, despite Portuguese propaganda efforts to glorify work as a sacred duty. But it wasn't easy to get a job in the semi-arid south, where there is a comparatively large reservoir of manpower, and in view of the regulation requiring him to work part of the month, it seemed logical, if not necessary, for him to take a job for a year in the coffee-rich north, which is short of plantation labor. He would be paid only seven dollars a month, but this would all be "gravy" for he would be provided with most of his needs, including a cement house, food, clothing, and medical care. Moreover, he could not be punished, as he could have been previously, for breaking his contract.

The Portuguese have instituted other improvements as well. They have broadened local home rule by permitting towns of five hundred population or over to set up municipal councils and elect officials. Moreover, they plan to break the semi-official cotton monopoly that has forced Africans to grow specified quantities of cotton and sell it at controlled prices.

Along with such reforms has come an intensified effort to develop the colony, a larger share of whose wealth may be used for the benefit of the people in the future. Until now, Angola has simply been considered a means of keeping Portugal itself from going hungry. The colony's coffee exports alone, totaling about fifty million dollars a year, more than make up for the deficit in Portugal's balance of payments with the United States. The colony is also a vastly profitable market for Portuguese goods, buying almost fifty percent of its imports from the mother country. Further, Angola is a pressure valve for some of Portugal's excess population—about two hundred thousand Portuguese now live in Angola —that has created an intolerable unemployment problem.

Considering Portugal's economic anemia and its traditional reluctance to permit foreign investment in its colonies, whose outdated policies it hasn't wanted disturbed by liberal outside influences, the Portuguese have done an excellent job, since about 1950, in developing Angola. Local industries producing tobacco, beer, cement, and other items have mushroomed. Hydroelectric and irrigation projects have been completed, and others are under construction. Port and transport facilities have been improved. Villages have sprouted into gracious modern towns. Recent construction in Luanda itself has all but transformed and enhanced the Latin splendor of this city. If the drain of the rebellion can be ended before Portuguese resources give out, development is likely to be accelerated. Portugal recently concluded an agreement with West German interests to aid in mineral development, and joined the International Monetary Fund and World Bank.

But there is reason to doubt that reforms and economic development can convince any substantial number of Africans that a Lusitanian community is the answer to their grievances. The greater autonomy the Portuguese now envisage for Angola is likely to benefit the Portuguese settlers more than the Africans. They, rather than Lisbon, would be able to make the major political and economic decisions. Even though in theory the blacks would have the same opportunity as the whites to reach the highest administrative posts, the whites would hardly permit the Africans to hold positions which would threaten their control of the government. In fact the settlers, who are even more reactionary than the Lisbon administration because of their interest in personal profit, might use their enhanced power to prevent the implementation of reforms.

Portugal even now faces a troubling dilemma. Government officials think educated Africans, particularly those trained in church and mission schools, are behind much of the terrorism. Yet these officials may have to risk creating new Frankensteins. For if they do not, assimilation is all but impossible inasmuch as education and Christianity are essential catalysts in the process. Nor is it clear that the Portuguese will be able to finance significant reform immediately, whatever their intentions. Even intentions are subject to the limitation imposed by conditions in Portugal itself, for it is hardly likely that the Portuguese would, or could, agree to reforms in a colony that exceeded in scope those instituted in the mother country. Meanwhile, the pressures of nationalism are bound to mount as an increasing number of African states win independence. But the most important barrier of all to realization of the Portuguese dream may be the harvest of hate produced by the brutality of the rebellion—a harvest that will inevitably feed the communist cause.

VI

THE CONGO:

WAYWARD APPRENTICES

In the spring of 1961, shortly after the assassination of Congolese Premier Patrice Lumumba, I visited Stanleyville, the stronghold of his leftist followers. In almost every talk I had with Lumumba's heirs, they volunteered an answer to the inevitable question even before I could ask it:

"No, we are not communists. We are Africans, and we want an African solution to our problems."

These words were probably spoken in sincerity. In the chaos that followed the end of Belgian rule in the summer of 1960, the Soviet influence crept in to a considerable extent. But if it is any consolation to the West, which has had its share of headaches in Africa, including the Congo, the communists have also had a painful experience in that infant nation.

After gaining a foothold in the Congo during Lumumba's regime, they were ignominiously thrown out of the country when his enemies came to power. And in late 1961 and early 1962, when it looked for a while as if the Lumumbists might make a comeback, that danger, too, fizzled out. Why has the communist bloc found the going in the Congo, perhaps the most invitingly anarchistic territory in the world since mid-1960, so rough?

First, the bloc has been unable to find any truly reliable puppets in the Congo. What ties some Congolese, including Lumumba, have had with it have been based mainly on political opportunism, not ideology, of which most Congo-brand leftists are singularly ignorant.

Second, these opportunists are not even good at making the most of opportunity. Almost no one has had a college education, and most have proved rather dull-witted.

This lack of adequate communist material has utterly frustrated bloc policy in the Congo. The Reds finally gave up on Antoine Gizenga, whom they had energetically supported as the successor to Lumumba, when it became clear that he was a weak, unpredictable man. The communists had lost the game, at least for the time being, when Lumumba met his death. For though Lumumba appears to have had no ideological inclinations at all, his lust for power, together with his powerful personality and superb talent for demagogy, made him a most usable instrument for communist ends, far more so than any less impressive Congolese who happened to be Marxist-oriented. When Belgium decided to grant freedom to the Congo, it backed Lumumba as the man to lead the new nation for precisely the same reasons the communists put their money on him later. If he could be manipulated, so could the country he led.

In January 1959, right after bloody riots in Leopoldville—the majestic, Europeanized Congo capital—had opened Belgian eyes for the first time to the inevitability and, indeed, imminence of Congolese independence, a Belgian administrator informed me: "There are only two important nationalist politicians in the Congo: Joseph Kasavubu (who led the Leopoldville riots) and a much more reasonable man named Patrice Lumumba."

As it turned out after independence, Kasavubu, who assumed the presidency, became identified with the moderate pro-West Congolese faction, and Lumumba, as Premier, proved, to the short-lived joy of the Red bloc, almost as immoderate as a politician could be. Still, considering the immature character of the Congolese political mind, the two men might have confirmed the original Belgian appraisal of them if the United States had supported Lumumba before he turned to the communists to help him stay in power. The Congo split up along cold war lines largely on the basis of the question: "What's in it for me?"

Before the 1959 riots, neither Lumumba nor Kasavubu, nor any other Congolese, had the least hope of obtaining independence in the foreseeable future. Until five years prior to independence, there had never even been a demand for freedom among the Africans. The reason, explained the Belgians proudly, was that the Congolese were happy under their enlightened rule. Most visiting journalists and other observers agreed. While the British and French colonies seethed with open discontent and political agitation, these visitors pointed out, the Congo was calm and prosperous. The Belgians, they concluded, had obviously applied the best formula for running a colony.

This conclusion seemed reasonable enough. No one denied that the Belgians did quite well for themselves in the Congo, one of the richest regions in the world. They profited handsomely from its huge deposits of cobalt, copper, industrial diamonds, zinc, manganese, cadmium, tin, and other minerals. They pocketed a fortune from the export of cotton, coffee, pyrethrum, precious woods, and palm oil products. But the Belgians, while making money themselves, did not neglect the Africans. In 1950, for example, the Belgians inaugurated a ten-year development aimed as much at improving living standards as at making a profit. Of nearly a billion dollars earmarked for the plan, about half was for the improvement of roads and communications, which, of course, would be of permanent benefit to the Africans, if also necessary for the expansion of Belgian business enterprises. The other half was reserved entirely for direct aid to the Congolese—schools, clinics, housing, the provision of drinking water, and other social projects.

Even in the midst of the Congo's post-independence anarchy, the results of such policies were evident. Traveling with a heavily armed jeep convoy of United Nations soldiers through the animal-infested jungles of Kivu Province in the eastern Congo, which is still a lawless region, I visited numerous isolated clinics. The Belgian doctors had all fled, but well-trained African male nurses were managing to keep the disease rate under control with the help of large supplies of Belgian medicines.

In the tree-shaded native quarter of Leopoldville, I found some of the most pleasant African homes I had visited in Africa. Typical is the house of Pierre Lubamba. He lives in a neat, two-room, concrete house, fitted out with linoleum, tables, and chairs. Two beds, one for his wife and himself, the other for their three small children, are set up at night. Mrs. Lubamba, an attractive woman in her multicolored, ankle-length sarong, cooks meals in a mud oven located in the court. By Western standards, of course, the Lubambas are hardly prosperous. But they are living on a higher level than most Africans in other colonies, though Lubamba, a bricklayer who once earned twenty-five dollars a month, including fringe benefits, has been unemployed since many Belgians were terrorized out of the Congo.

Living standards went up under the Belgians despite the tremendous problem posed by a mass migration from tribal areas to the cities by Congolese like Pierre Lubamba in search of the "luxuries" of urban life. By 1960 over a quarter of the natives had migrated. Leopoldville, which had an African population of about 4,000 in 1920, contained 300,000 in 1960.

As economic levels rose, social benefits increased. Although Lubamba himself is illiterate, his children probably will not be if the Congolese government follows the primary education policies that were instituted by the Belgians. A greater number of children have had the opportunity for education in the Congo than in most African colonies, largely in mission schools subsidized by the Belgian administration.

The Belgians were proud indeed of their work.

Then what went wrong? Why was the nationalist explosion in the Congo, when it came, so much greater than in the colonies with lower economic and social standards? The answer lay partly in a fundamental Belgian miscalculation. Extreme paternalism was the key to colonial efficiency and responsibility, the Belgians had thought. The Africans were like children and had to be treated as such—kindly and fairly, but with a firm hand. The answer was not, as the French—who had even permitted African leaders to participate in the French parliament—and British had decided, to train and civilize a small elite while largely neglecting the mass of Africans. On the contrary, the way to bring up a nation of children was to concentrate on civilizing the mass and discourage the development of an elite that, cultivated out of historical and psychological context, could only be superficial creatures of the twentieth century. Belgium's job, argued the colonialists, was to foster economic development of the colony's resources and people, not political development.

The Belgians saw in this philosophy of government two advantages. It was in the best interests of the great majority of Congolese, whose living standards would rise, if gradually, over many years. And it was also in the best interests of the Belgians, who would not, like the French and British, have to cope with halfbaked African nationalists who returned from European universities determined to bite the colonial hand that fed them. Primary schooling, yes. But the Congolese weren't ready for higher learning. It would only give them subversive ideas. Thus, few Africans were permitted to attend a European university or even to visit Europe, where, it was feared, they might make dangerous contacts. Though two universities were established in the Congo in the 1950's, the nation could boast of only a handful of college graduates when the Congo received its freedom.

As for political activity, political parties were forbidden until shortly before independence. Nor were Africans given any important administrative posts. But if political development was deliberately stunted, it was done so in a curiously "democratic" spirit. Neither white settler nor black native could play a role in governing the territory, thus guaranteeing, explained the Belgian government, that the two peoples could not exploit each other.

The Belgian formula seemed to work—until the 1959 riots revealed that a key psychological factor had been overlooked. Economic and social development within a political vacuum was possible only up to a point, for when living and educational standards reached a certain level, the birth of indigenous political ambitions was inevitable. The French and British had realized this and trained elites in their colonies that could eventually fulfill these ambitions with maximum efficiency, order, and—hopefully —loyalty to those who had prepared them for power. In most cases, the political agitation in these colonies, which the Belgians claimed could not develop in the Congo, served as a pressure valve when the nationalist surge proved irresistible and the territories were granted freedom. The French- and British-trained political leaders may be half-baked, but they are relatively stable men with considerable understanding of the meaning of the modern state and economy. There has been a minimum of bloodshed in those new countries, however misgoverned many of them may be.

The Congo, however, was another matter. Shocked into irrationality by the 1959 nationalist explosion, Belgium tragically compounded its original miscalculation by granting full independence to the Congo within a year and a half. Incredibly enough, a huge, disunited, tribalized nation with no trained political leaders or top administrators, no military officers, no doctors, engineers, lawyers, or other skilled technicians, and few college graduates in any field, suddenly found itself drifting on its own in the strategic heart of Africa. Inevitably, the country disintegrated into chaos and became a Cold War, and almost a hot war, battlefield.

The violence of the nation's birth, while attributable in large measure to the political immaturity of the Congolese, was also rooted in a genuine animosity among the people toward the Belgians. The French and British are sharply, sometimes bitterly, criticized in the territories they rule or have ruled. But in most cases, this criticism reflects only a superficial resentment, something like that of a teen-ager rebelling against the authority of parents while harboring considerable respect, and even affection, for them.

Ghanaian newspapers might violently accuse Britain of retaining colonial aspirations in Africa, but when Queen Elizabeth II visited that country late in 1961, she was received with all the warmth and reverence that might be expected of the British public itself. And though the newly independent French Congo is separated from its Belgian counterpart only by the width of the Congo River, the two Congos are worlds apart psychologically. The French find friendship in their former possession, the Belgians hostility in theirs, although living standards under the Belgians were substantially higher.

The reason for this resentment lies partly in the ban that the Belgians had imposed on political activity and preparation for self-government, particularly among chiefs and politicians who had been most directly affected. Many Congolese saw this ban not through nationalist eyes but in terms of inadequate protection against individual Belgian injustices. In 1959 several Belgian plantation owners bragged to me that they kept their black workers in line with whippings despite government regulations forbidding such punishment. "Who can we complain to when we're mistreated? one of the plantation workers asked me. "Most of the time the government doesn't listen to us, and when they do our white bosses are seldom punished."

Moreover, mistreatment did not always take a physical form. Sometimes the most searing pain was psychological. Africans were constantly ridiculed and called "stupid" and "lazy" to their faces. Many Belgians acted as if their employees had no personal pride, and often the employee himself, so used to this harsh relationship with his master, did not realize that he had any. But within him a deep, silent antagonism churned. When I asked one tempestuous Belgian why he had to shout orders at his houseboy and constantly remind him of his shortcomings, he replied: "You don't know what it's like trying to get these Africans to do anything. You need nerves of steel." If that is so, then it would seem that no white should be permitted to live among the Africans who does not possess that basic requisite for harmonious racial ties.

Nor were most Congolese impressed by the argument that they were living in greater comfort than Africans in neighboring colonies. Living standards are not of primary importance to them. Many do not see the great advantage of a concrete house over one made of mud. "If the average Congolese suddenly inherited a million dollars," a Belgian technician in Leopoldville said, "do you think he would spend it to improve his daily life? Not very likely. He would buy an expensive car and plenty of whiskey, but his mode of living still wouldn't change much. You've got to be educated to know how to use wealth."

Precisely because most Congolese are not, they had little appreciation for the economic advancement they enjoyed under the Belgians. But they were only too well aware of Belgian political suppression which, as their chiefs did not fail to point out, contrasted markedly with French and British policy in their colonies.

Anti-Belgian sentiment is rooted in another factor, too—Congo history. The extraordinary wealth of the Congo was first revealed to the world in the early 1870's, when Sir Henry M. Stanley, three years after his dramatic jungle meeting with Dr. Livingstone, explored the Congo basin. He reported that if a way were found to circumvent the rapids and falls at the lower end of the Congo River, this wealth could be easily exploited. King Leopold II of Belgium decided that these riches were just what he needed to finance his expensive playboy activities. Stanley, as his agent, returned to the Congo and established a number of settlements which, in 1884, were recognized by the United States and other powers as constituting an independent Congo Free State under Leopold's personal control.

In 1888 the King, with the support of Belgian financiers, embarked on a gigantic project to test Stanley's contentions—the construction of a two-hundred-and-sixty-mile railroad from the port of Matadi at the mouth of the Congo River to Stanley Pool, a point on the river just beyond the steep gorges and rapids that made entry from the sea impossible. Leopold basked in the anticipation of becoming one of the world's richest men. Construction of the railroad took eleven years—eleven years that the Congolese will never forget. Thousands of tribesmen were captured and forced to work under the most horrifying conditions. They died like flies from disease, overwork, brutal whippings, and shootings. Standard punishment for men, women, and children who did not work swiftly or efficiently enough was the severance of their hands. Tribes that resisted capture were massacred. As the railroad opened the way for the exploitation of rubber fields, thousands more were put to work under similar conditions, and new ghastly penalties were invoked. Some victims were forced to swallow raw rubber, which expanded in their stomachs, killing them slowly and painfully. Thomas Stirling, an American author, wrote in *Stanley's Way:*

Obviously the King was informed of the reports of atrocities . . . There is now incontestable evidence that organized atrocities occurred on a frightful scale for at least fifteen years, and one must conclude that the King deliberately, coldly, killed millions of people for his personal profit . . . Leopold is one of the greatest monsters to have lived.

France and Britain, jealous of Leopold's potential windfall, did their best to fan the international uproar, as word of atrocities leaked out to a shocked world. Finally, under pressure from his own ministers, the King, in 1908, agreed to turn over the territory to the Belgian government.

Belgian paternalistic policy toward the Africans started then, partly conditioned by a national conscience that agonized as the result of Leopold's cruel and selfish excesses. But the Congolese have never forgiven the Belgians for those excesses, even though they had been committed by a small unrepresentative group of sadistic men. Tales of Belgian atrocities have, in fact, been exaggerated over the years, if possible, as stories have been passed down from generation to generation and become part of the Congolese subconscious attitude toward the Belgians.

The first political demands made by the Congolese appeared in 1956 in a manifesto published in *Conscience Africaine,* a Catholic periodical in Leopoldville. Written by Joseph Ileo, who was later to replace Lumumba as Premier, the manifesto shockingly called for independence—within thirty years. The Abako, which members of the Bakongo tribe in the Leopoldville area had formed in 1950 under Joseph Kasavubu as a cultural, nonpolitical group, reacted with a demand for immediate independence that nobody, including the Abako, took seriously.

But while the Africans themselves did not yet realize their own strength, conditions were gradually coming to a boil. The Congolese were not unaware that the British had granted independence to Ghana in 1957, and that France's President Charles de Gaulle had offered the French African colonies the opportunity to choose independence in 1958. A depression that hit the Congo in 1958, resulting in fifty thousand unemployed in Leopoldville alone, did not ease the growing discontent with Belgian rule. The Belgians, finally realizing the necessity of developing an elite that could eventually share to a limited extent in the governing of the colony, established two local universities and gave both resident Belgians and Africans in 1957 a role in the administration of the larger municipalities. But it was too late. In January 1959 the storm broke.

Encouraged by the call of an all-African conference in Accra, Ghana, the month before for the granting of independence to all Africa, Kasavubu's Abako group went on an antiwhite rampage in Leopoldville. At the end of three days of rioting, more than seventy people, almost all Africans, were dead, dozens more were wounded, numerous stores had been looted, and some homes had been burnt down.

A shroud of bewilderment cloaked the sprawling, usually care-free city. "The awakening here has been brutal indeed," I wrote in a dispatch to the North American Newspaper Alliance a few days after the riots. "People who would have laughed a few weeks ago at the suggestion that the Congo might be independent within a decade are now wondering if Belgium can hold the line beyond 1960." A Belgian businessman agreed: "We'll be leaving here soon; there's no doubt about that. But if only we had shown our intentions a little earlier, it wouldn't look as if we were being kicked out."

Within a week after the riots, Belgian King Baudouin formally announced a plan for "eventual" self-rule in the Congo, starting with the election of local councils in March 1960. Political parties mushroomed in profusion, with almost every tribe converting itself into a "party," few understanding even the rudiments of modern political procedure. Two men emerged as possible national leaders.

One was Joseph Kasavubu, who had been jailed by the Belgians for allegedly fomenting the riots. His Abako group embraced only the Leopoldville area, but was one of the largest and probably the most active in the Congo, having set off the nationalist explosion. Actually, Kasavubu, a stout, tame-looking man, was mainly interested at the time in re-establishing the old Bakongo tribal kingdom that had vanished with the appearance of the Belgians. Though part of the Bakongo tribe was embraced by the French Congo and other remnants were living along the northern fringe of Portuguese Angola to the south, Kasavubu dreamed of a reunited kingdom comprising as many tribesmen as possible. His political ambitions were reinforced by a mystical religious philosophy called Kibangism. A quasi-Christian sect, Kibangism has preached hostility toward the Europeans ever since its founder, an African named Kibango, was converted into a prophet by his followers about forty years ago. Kasavubu's adherence to this faith was one reason why the Belgians feared him more than any other African leader.

The second African of political importance was Patrice Lumumba, a thin, goateed man, who headed the Congolese National

Movement (MNC). Centered in Stanleyville, the capital of Oriental Province and Lumumba's home, it was the only party with a national, nontribal program. The Belgians regarded Lumumba with contempt, and enjoyed pointing out that he had been jailed for embezzling $2,500 from the post office for which he worked, scoffing at Lumumba's explanation that he used the money "honestly"—for anti-Belgian nationalist purposes. Nevertheless, they preferred him to other politicians because he fanatically supported the establishment of a unitary, as opposed to a federal or confederal, state. The Belgian government was convinced that the Congo could only remain strong and prosperous if it were tightly united.

Moreover, the Belgians conceded, he was a man of considerable intelligence, unlike many of the other Congolese leaders who attained their positions through tribal heredity. Born in 1925, he had attended Belgian mission schools and graduated from high school as a brilliant but erratic student. He was dismissed from one institution for fighting with the teachers. He got himself a job in the Stanleyville post office, where he did his embezzling; after a short term in prison, he worked as a beer salesman, becoming the beer firm's commercial director in 1958. One year later he quit, after having amassed a fortune under questionable circumstances.

When the Congolese National Movement was established by leading African businessmen and community leaders in 1958, Lumumba was not bashful about his ambitions. As a committee head, he prepared a roster of officers with himself as president and gave it to the press. Members were shocked but they accepted the list intact. Several months later, however, his party split when many members became jealous of his growing power, but the Lumumbist wing that remained became stronger than ever. In October 1959 Lumumba made a speech in Stanleyville, demanding "total independence—now, now, now." A riot resulted, and the Belgians jailed him again.

But not for long. Belgium, under increasing nationalist pressure, called a Round-Table Conference of Belgians and Congolese in January 1960 to decide when and how independence should be granted. They needed Lumumba to support their concept of a unitary state, in view of the strong demands for a loose federal structure on the part of Moise Tshombe, leader of Katanga Province's Conakat Party, and Belgian business interests in that province. Lumumba went to the Brussels conference and won his point. A unitary independent state would come into being on June 30, 1960. The Belgians attempted to delay the date of independence, arguing that the Congo wasn't ready for freedom, but finally gave in. They feared widespread violence if they didn't. Some also reasoned that the Congolese would find themselves in such chaos after independence that they would be only too glad to let the Belgians run the state for them. Perhaps all was not lost yet, they daydreamed.

Parliamentary elections were held in May 1960 and Lumumba's party won the largest number of seats. The following month Lumumba was chosen Premier and Kasavubu, President, a largely figurehead post. On Independence Day, in the presence of King Baudouin, Lumumba offered a hint of what was in store for his Belgian "supporters." "Slavery was imposed on us by force," he said in a speech. "We have known ironies and insults; we remember the blows that we had to submit to morning, noon, and night because we were Negroes!"

The communists were delighted. The Congo was made to order for them. A government of political juveniles was coming to power, and its leader was a power-hungry opportunist who hated the West. They had only to bide their time, and then strike.

Much of the communist bloc's spadework was done by the Belgian Communist Party. Party sources claimed that a secret Congo Communist Party had been active in the territory since 1950, led by one Mwamba Mukanya, who was known to be affiliated with the French Communist Party in Brazzaville, capital of the French Congo, just across the Congo River. Though no evidence that such a party existed, or exists, has been found, a secret Belgian Communist Party report that Belgian sources claim is authentic was drawn up just prior to independence, outlining Red plans for the communization of the Congo. The report, which the party denies having prepared, called for:

Scrapping of agreements reached by Belgium and the United States for the shipment of raw materials to the latter.

Denial of Congolese co-operation with the North Atlantic Treaty Organization.

Banning of Western bases, such as those in Kamina and Kitona, in the Congo.

Refusal to sign a treaty of friendship and co-operation with Belgium.

Prevention of the Congo's integration into the European Common Market.

The report also supposedly demanded the orientation of the Congo's foreign trade toward the communist bloc and the creation of a "National Association of Foreign Trade":

a. through the elimination of monopolist or political opposition;

b. by utilizing means of increasing commerce greatly and rapidly with the socialist countries where the Congo will find partners who will act automatically and as a matter of principle on a basis of equality and mutual interest, and moreover, with the will to grant disinterested aid to the young Congolese state. Furthermore, the socialist countries have a rapidly expanding economy undisturbed by crises . . .

c. by lifting obstacles to Africa's interior trade;

d. by the orientation of imports . . .

We have already made contact with all leftist Congolese elements and the statutes of a large party are now being formulated. After June 30 (Independence Day), a congress will be organized and attended only by those persons who have so far indicated leftist tendencies. A common program will be drawn up . . . To facilitate this work and make the most contacts possible, we will . . . install organizational committees in all the provinces. Once the party is established, the leaders elected will choose two or three members to discuss with the socialist countries the aid they will give us to permit us to work.

In addition, said the report, cadres would be sent to bloc countries for training at a cost of 1.8 million francs a person, and a newspaper with a circulation of 30,000 would be established. The creation of a "new labor organization" was also envisaged.

Actually, a procommunist and Lumumbist labor union, the National Union of Congolese Workers, had already been founded in April 1959 by Antoine Tshimanga, a young man in his early twenties, who had close relations with the French Communist Party in Brazzaville and had been President of the leftist Congo Intellectual Youth Movement. But the union, which affiliated itself with the Guinea-sponsored General Union of Black African Workers and the communist World Federation of Trade Unions (WFTU) based in Prague, never got off the ground because of an internal conflict over the misuse of funds.

Valentin Mutombo, First Secretary-General, had returned from a month's trip to Communist China just before independence, apparently expecting to be the undisputed leader of the union. The secret report of the Belgian Communist Party is supposed to have said: "Everything will be done to assure that Comrade Mutombo will lead the new organization . . ." But two days after independence, the WFTU sent 200,000 Belgian francs to Tshimanga for the holding of a congress and the establishment of branch offices. Mutombo and his assistant, Secretary-General Leon Mukanda, accused him of using the money instead for his own needs, and the communist bloc had its first taste of Congolese dependability.

Nevertheless, Moscow and Peking had high hopes that Lumumba would serve them well. Russia had an excellent agent in Pierre Elengesa, who studied in Moscow in 1959-60, contributing commentaries to Radio Moscow and *Pravda,* and returned to the Congo right after independence with an elaborate Soviet proposition for aid and co-operation that gave the first real impetus to the Congo's leftward swing. The USSR was prepared, Elengesa told the government, to build industries in the Congo and to open factories with Soviet capital and technicians. Investment capital would not have to be paid back "in liquid," but through commercial accords under which Russia would receive Congolese goods. Interest on the capital would be only 2.5 percent a year. The Russian technicians would be paid by the USSR, would live in the Congo "without any luxuries at all," and would leave the country when Congolese technicians would be qualified to take over from them. In any event, Elengesa added, the Russians counseled the government to have nothing to do with the Common Market or NATO, for if it did, it would be "exposing the Congo to long-distance Soviet guns."

The impression this proposition made on the government was reflected in Elengesa's appointment as Special Counselor for the Government Presidency. But after Lumumba's fall, Elengesa met a grisly death. He was among a number of Lumumbists whom Kasavubu's soldiers arrested for their role in trying to force South Kasai back into the Congo through mass killing and brutality. They were turned over to the secessionist South Kasai government headed by Albert Kalonji, whose chiefs slowly cut them into bits —a finger here, an ear there—until they died.

Another influential leftist in the Lumumba government was Jacques Lumbala, State Secretary for the Presidency, who, in early 1960, attended Czech-conducted classes in Marxism-Leninism in Conakry, Guinea. Shortly after United Nations troops were sent to the Congo in July 1960 to maintain order, he declared: "The U.N. troops are incompetent. We will have to call on another force that hasn't imperial designs." He made it clear to reporters that he meant the Russians. Having led the bloody effort to end South Kasai's secession, he suffered the same end as Elengesa.

Ministers, too, figured among Lumumba's leftist aides. Pierre Mulele, Minister of National Education, who had also studied in the Czech classes in Conakry, was believed to be preparing Marxist courses for Congolese students. His chief assistant was a

Greek communist, Elie Bouras. Alphonse Nguvulu, Minister of Economic Affairs, had attended the Belgian Communist Party congress at Liège in April 1960, ostensibly as an observer. Shortly after independence, he shouted over Radio Leopoldville: "The white bosses are living off the sweat of the Congolese workers. In the future, for each drop of sweat we will exact a drop of blood from the whites."

Even more inflammatory was Anicet Kashamura, Minister of Information and Cultural Affairs, a classmate in Conakry of Lumbala and Mulele. Considered by many observers to be mentally ill, Kashamura was once even reprimanded by Lumumba for "distorting" the facts over the national radio which he controlled. Ironically, he had failed a radio announcer's test in 1958. As the representative of the African Regrouping Center, a small political party, at the Brussels Round-Table Conference that decided on the Congo's independence in early 1960, Kashamura had selected a former Belgian communist member of parliament named Terfve as his delegation's adviser. During the conference, he visited Prague for a short time. On another trip to Brussels shortly after becoming minister, he was welcomed at the airport by Terfve and had long talks with Albert De Coninck, National Secretary of the Belgian Communist Party, and Edgard Poncelet, National Secretary of the Belgian Communist Youth.

Another important leftist in the Lumumba government was Deputy Premier Antoine Gizenga. A homely, hard-eyed man who is reputed to be the best-dressed politician in the Congo, Gizenga is a sullen introvert whose name seldom made news while Lumumba ruled, despite his high position. Actually, he had never been a close collaborator of Lumumba before he entered the cabinet. He had, in fact, been president of a political organization, the African Solidarity Party, which had rivaled Lumumba's. Gizenga demonstrated his lack of popular appeal when he was decisively defeated in the race for the presidency of Leopoldville Province just before independence. But Lumumba selected him as his deputy to obtain the support of his party, and also because he didn't want a man in the position who could compete with him in terms of popularity.

Gizenga's religious training—he had studied in a mission school and a seminary, and worked as monitor at the Roman Catholic mission school in Leopoldville—had little effect on his politics. After making a brief appearance at the Round-Table Conference, he went to Prague and Moscow for about fifteen days. He then enrolled in the Czech-sponsored Marxist-Leninist course in Conakry, where apparently he was the only Congolese to remain for a full six months of indoctrination.

One of Gizenga's first acts as Deputy Premier was to tell a *Pravda* correspondent that the Congo would establish "friendly relations with the Soviet Union." Several days later he said in a radio broadcast: "It is with hatred that the King (of Belgium) proclaimed independence." He added that the Congo would "ask for Russian aid if necessary."

Perhaps the most important influence on Gizenga was in the shapely form of a mysterious, thirty-eight-year-old half-caste woman, Mme. Andrée Blouin, who might have been the Congo's strongest link with the communist world. Before independence, Mme. Blouin, who traveled on a Guinean passport, was an adviser to Gizenga's political party, and reportedly his mistress as well. The Belgians expelled her from the Congo in June 1960 for subversive activities, but she returned a few weeks later, after independence, and, on Gizenga's recommendation, became the Lumumba government's chief protocol officer. This job gave her tight control over the access of foreign diplomats to government officials. One diplomat who found all the doors open was Czech Ambassador Josef Virius, a close friend. "The West," Mme. Blouin once said, "tries to achieve its aims by ruse and corruption."

Lumumba's press officer, Serge Michel, a Frenchman, was a far leftist who had worked with the Algerian rebel movement against France. Many reporters observed that he often put interpretations on Lumumba's statements that went far beyond what the Premier had intended to say.

Felix Moumié, the exiled procommunist politician from Cameroon, was a Lumumba adviser. The instigator of the leftist terror that was plaguing his own country, he got Lumumba to establish youthful terrorist commando units who beat up political enemies.

The communist influence could be found outside labor and government as well. Leftist Alphonse Makwambala directed the Popular Youth. He had made trips to Moscow and Peking and was president of the Sino-Congolese Friendship Society. He brought back a message from Moscow to Congolese university students asking that they "work hand in hand with the USSR for the restoration of African liberties."

Reinforcing the propaganda of such procommunists were several "neutralist" states, particularly Ghana, Guinea, and the United Arab Republic—each for its own purposes. Each of them wanted to control Lumumba and thereby extend its influence into the heart of Africa.

With its agents, wittingly or not, in key positions and with circumstances ripe for chaos, the communist bloc did not have to wait long for a chance to move in. Trouble had long been brewing within the Force Publique, the Congolese army. This was led, even at the time of independence, by Belgian officers who had not yet trained Congolese to replace them. What good was independence, the African enlisted men reasoned, if they were still under Belgian orders? And communist agents did not fail to take advantage of this smoldering resentment. Leaflets, many of which are believed to have been sent from Antwerp by Belgian communists, flooded the army camps, urging mutiny. One typical leaflet read:

"The excuse offered for not making you officers is that you are incapable of commanding a platoon or company, while other people who, like you, were nothing yesterday, are now getting more important jobs. Dismiss your officers and take their place . . ." Another leaflet said: "The Belgian officers were yesterday at the service of colonialism; colonialism will enable them to retake what they have given you. Independence will be meaningless if the army is not commanded by Congolese exclusively."

Enlisted men began demanding that Congolese replace the Belgian officers. But before Lumumba could act on the matter, Africans mutinied on July 5 against their Belgian officers in Thysville, eighty-five miles from Leopoldville, and beat up and raped many Europeans. The powder keg exploded. As news of the revolt spread, so did the mutinies and the brutality, throwing Belgians into panic and resulting in a dramatic mass flight from the Congo. With most of the ten thousand Belgian technicians who were needed to run the country gone, transportation, communications, electric power, water systems, and other services came to an abrupt halt. With the disappearance of Belgian businessmen, shops and factories shut down and most urban Congolese found themselves without work.

The country was in anarchy only a few days after its birth, and the communists were delighted. It is believed they played an active if peripheral role in the actual mutinies. In Stanleyville, two Greek communists, Emmanuel Arghiri and Georges Yannakis, were arrested in this connection. And the newly established Czech consulate in Leopoldville is thought to have intervened when, on July 8, the Belgian government sent paratroopers into Katanga Province to protect its nationals. Shortly after a plane carrying a group of paratroopers from Kamina to Elisabethville took off, a consulate radio operator allegedly transmitted false orders to the pilots to return to their base.

On July 12 Provincial President Tshombe announced Katanga's secession from the Congo, an action which the central government took as confirmation of its suspicion that the landing of Belgian paratroopers in the Congo was aimed at the reconquest of the country. Kasavubu and Lumumba requested that the United Nations send military aid to throw the Belgians out, end Katanga's secession, and maintain order. The first United Nations troops arrived on July 15 but refused to force the Belgians out of the country or the Katangese into a united Congo again.

Enraged, Lumumba sent a telegram to Khrushchev the following day, July 16, saying: "It is possible that we will be forced to request the intervention of the Soviet Union if the Western camp does not end the aggression against the sovereignty of the Republic of the Congo." Khrushchev replied: "If the states which are directly engaged in imperialist aggression against the Congo Republic and those which are supporting it continue with their criminal actions, the USSR will not hesitate to take firm measures to end this aggression . . . The demand of the Soviet Union is simple: 'Hands off the Congo Republic.' "

With the Russians behind him, Lumumba, urged on by his leftist advisers, sent Dr. Ralph Bunche, United Nations Secretary-General Dag Hammarskjöld's assistant, an ultimatum: "If the United Nations has not expelled Belgian troops by Tuesday, July 19, the Congolese government will seek Russian help." On that day Lumumba warned, "If the Security Council which meets today in New York ignores the question of the imperialists, it will be perfectly justifiable for us to seek the aid of the Eastern bloc, whose sympathy we have had from the first." On the following day, with the United Nations having failed to act on his demand, Lumumba made good his threat. He called for Russian help.

The smell of world war spread as Soviet technicians, their bags loaded with propaganda literature, began to flow into the country. Bulgaria, Czechoslovakia, East Germany, and Albania also offered aid. In Peking, more than ten thousand persons gathered to "demonstrate the support of the Chinese people for the struggle of the Congolese people." Guest of honor was Theodore Bengila, Assistant Secretary-General of Gizenga's African Solidarity Party. In the Congo itself, Kashamura, Mme. Blouin, and other procommunists fanned the flames with inflammatory pro-Soviet and anti-Belgian radio commentaries.

"The Soviet Union," Kashamura said, "is better qualified than other countries to send a large number of well-trained engineers and other technical personnel to the Congo for their use in our country over a long period." Youth leaders Tshimanga and Makwambala cried in a joint communiqué: "We will force the government to request Soviet troops, to whom we shall all rally." And in the United States a spokesman solemnly warned: "We will do all that is necessary to prevent the entry of all military forces not requested by the United Nations."

Despite the danger involved, the Lumumbists plunged recklessly ahead, even as the Premier cried, "We are not communists, and never will be!" On August 15 Lumumba asked Soviet Ambassador Yakovlev, who had recently arrived, to forward a request to the Soviet Union "without delay" for troop transport planes with crews, trucks, arms, communications materials, and food for the troops. Moscow immediately promised to meet this request in full. It did so, and also concluded an accord with the Lumumba government whereby Soviet planes and crews would be used to transport Congolese soldiers to South Kasai to help put down the secessionist movement there.

On September 8 Gizenga sent a request to the Red Chinese government for "voluntary personnel," helicopters, artillery, armored cars, funds to "cover urgent expenses," and food. Four days later, the Communist Chinese Ambassador in Cairo, Chan Hiankang, wrote back: "The government of China and the Chinese people support the government of the Congo and the Congolese people against the military aggression and intervention launched by the imperialists led by the United States under the protection of the United Nations flag. The Chinese government strongly condemns the plots of the imperialists to replace the government of the Congo. In view of the Congo's geographic situation in relation to that of China, it is difficult for the latter to send military volunteers. However, the government of China is sending initial aid of a million pounds sterling which it is putting at the disposal of the Congolese government. As for the other aid requested by the Congolese government, in particular, means of transport, the government of China is now studying this problem."

Gizenga immediately expressed his gratitude in a letter to Premier Chou En-lai: "Your Excellency: In the name of the Congolese government . . . I have the honor to thank the Government of the People's Republic of China for having been kind enough to grant us aid . . . The Congolese government counts much on aid from your country as you would be able to count on support from ours. Our government is disposed to tighten the friendly relations and good will between our two countries. Your gesture in this tragic moment . . . is an indication of the sympathy and support of your country . . ."

By early September, seventeen twin-engine Ilyushins, about one hundred army trucks, and thirty jeeps from the communist bloc were in operation. Soviet and Czech technical and embassy officials (only Russia and Czechoslovakia of the bloc had established embassies) numbered four hundred and seventy, scattered in most parts of the country. A five-man good-will mission from Communist China had arrived. Small East German and North Vietnam missions had been set up. No communist troops had been dispatched, though it was later discovered that seven supposedly civilian automobile mechanics working in Camp Leopold II, Leopoldville's military compound, were actually Soviet officers in disguise.

Furthermore, the Soviet Embassy had distributed in Camp Leopold II and elsewhere thousands of propaganda leaflets, including one that proclaimed the words, "Hands off the Congo," under a photograph of Khrushchev. Under the auspices of the Soviet and Czech Embassies, dozens of young Congolese were sent to study in Moscow and Prague; while in Budapest, Congolese labor leaders were taking special courses.

The Soviet Embassy was also believed to have subsidized Congolese periodicals. One newspaper, *Emancipation,* published in a single issue a story on American monopolists, a report on the visit of a Congolese delegation to Moscow, an article on "peaceful coexistence" with the headline "Comrade Workers," a message from Khrushchev, a reproduction of an article from the Soviet journal, *Red Flag,* and a communiqué from the central committee of the Belgian Communist Party and the Belgian Federation of Socialist Students.

Less clear was the total sum of money contributed to the Lumumbists by the communist bloc. In addition to the million pounds sterling donated by Peking and the two hundred thousand Belgian francs dispatched by the WFTU to labor and youth leader Tshimanga, Moscow is believed to have sent at least thirty-seven million Belgian francs. One check is known to have amounted to twenty-seven million francs, while another donation amounted to another ten million francs. Of the latter sum, almost half was dispatched in the form of propaganda material, including twenty vehicles, pamphlets printed in Belgium, insignia, and photos. About seven hundred and twenty-five thousand francs are believed to have been deposited in Lumumba's accounts in Brussels,

Geneva, and Leopoldville. The remaining five million francs were supposedly delivered to him by Belgian communist agents.

As collaboration with the communist countries tightened and undisciplined Congolese troops massacred anti-Lumumbists, particularly in South Kasai, President Kasavubu dramatically dismissed Lumumba as Premier and appointed Joseph Ileo, a moderate but weak man, to replace him. It is not clear what motivated Kasavubu most: the peril facing the nation or that facing himself. Kasavubu and Lumumba had long been violent political rivals, and the stronger the leftists in the government became, the stronger Lumumba would be. Already the Lumumbists were preparing a constitution which would provide for popular election of the president rather than for his selection by parliament, a measure that seriously threatened Kasavubu's power.

General Victor Lundula, a moderate-minded man of considerable character who backed Lumumba largely because he, like the Premier, wanted a tight, unitary Congo and because he was grateful to him for his promotion from sergeant to Congolese Army Commander, later told me in Stanleyville: "Kasavubu blames Lumumba for having accepted Russian aid, but the fact is that he himself approved the deal. He backed out when he saw the opportunity to get rid of a political enemy and receive support from the West."

In any event, Lumumba reacted to Kasavubu's action by, in turn, dismissing Kasavubu as President. The Congolese parliament then canceled both dismissals. Out of this deepening anarchy stepped Colonel Joseph Mobutu, a former journalist, who had joined the army as an officer only after independence and had just been chosen by Kasavubu to replace Lundula as Army Commander. He tried to settle matters by suspending everyone concerned—Kasavubu (who approved the arrangement), Lumumba, and Ileo. Declaring himself head of a "caretaker government" with the aid of a commission of fifteen young college graduates, he immediately halted the leftward trend. All communist-bloc representatives in the Congo were thrown out, and Lumumba and a number of his leftist colleagues were put under house arrest, guarded by United Nations troops. The West drew a sigh of relief. The communist threat in the Congo had ended as abruptly and shockingly as it had begun, and the danger of a big-power war had receded—at least for the time being. It was the bloc's turn to ponder ruefully the unpredictability of Congolese politics.

But if the communist advance had been halted, Mobutu found no easy time ending the anarchy or subduing leftist efforts to get back in the saddle again. This was partly due to the pro-Lumumbist attitude of United Nations forces on the spot, which strongly influenced the United Nations leadership in New York. Ghanaian troops guarding Lumumba would not permit Mobutu to arrest him. The chief representative of the United Nations in the Congo, Rajeshwar Dayal, an Indian, sharply criticized Mobutu and his army for violence and for permitting many Belgians to return to the Congo. He asked that his soldiers be disarmed, all Belgians be expelled, and, by implication, that Lumumba be returned to power—measures that were strongly supported by the Soviet Union, and as strongly opposed by the United States. Finally Mobutu, in frustration, gave power back to Kasavubu and Ileo, though retaining considerable influence as Army Commander.

Lumumba, meanwhile, escaped from detention in Leopoldville, was captured by Mobutu's men, escaped again, and was captured a second time. To make sure that he wouldn't get away again, the central government turned him over to the Katanga authorities, who despised him for trying to force Katanga into a unitary state under his control. In December 1960 the Katanga government announced that he had been killed by "villagers" while trying to escape. In all likelihood, he was deliberately assassinated.

The West trembled in anticipation of the bloody consequences that seemed inevitable. Both the communists and some neutralists did their best to fulfill expectations by making Lumumba a nationalist martyr. Anti-American riots broke out throughout the communist and neutralist world. The United Arab Republic dedicated a stamp to him. Russia named a street in Kiev and a school for students from underdeveloped countries after him. Only in the Congo itself did the people take Lumumba's death more or less in stride. He had been extremely popular in most parts of the country, but he was dead. He no longer wielded, or could wield, practical power, and the Congolese respect, above all, power. A martyr? Perhaps to some degree. But any living leader could hold greater sway over the people than any dead one. Therein lay the weakness of the leftist Lumumbist forces in the Congo who tried to continue to profit from his name.

Lumumba's mantle fell to Antoine Gizenga who, in October 1960, after Mobutu's takeover, had taken refuge with other leading Lumumbists in Stanleyville, where the Premier's following was the strongest in the country. In December, before Lumumba's death, he declared that in the absence of the Premier he, as Deputy Premier, now headed the "only legal government" in the Congo, which, he said, would henceforth be run from Stanleyville. This

government, supported by the part of the Congolese army loyal to
General Lundula, was soon recognized by members of the Sino-
Soviet bloc, Yugoslavia, the United Arab Republic, Ghana, Guinea,
Mali, and Morocco. Gizenga proclaimed himself Premier on the
announcement of Lumumba's murder.

At first the communist empire was not overly disturbed by this
development, despite its great show of grief. On the one hand, it
thought it could still use Lumumba's name as a leftist rallying cry;
on the other, it saw in Gizenga a man far more ideologically inclined toward communism than the opportunistic Lumumba. The
communists promised him all kinds of aid.

Gizenga ruled by terror and violence, which was only held in
check at all by General Lundula, who exerted every effort toward
maintaining discipline. After Lumumba's death was announced
and violence against the few whites remaining in Stanleyville was
expected, Lundula pleaded with his men: "Leave the Europeans
alone. Let us show them—and the whole world—that we are more
intelligent than those who have committed this crime." As a result,
a planned murder spree was called off.

But Lumumbist youth groups, including a strong army youth
movement under District Commissar Bernard Salumu, roamed the
streets of Stanleyville and other parts of Oriental Province, beating up planters, missionaries, and people suspected of anti-
Lumumbist sentiments. On Christmas Day, 1960, terror spread to
Kivu Province, the easternmost section of the Congo, which had
been about the only peaceful area in the country up to then. Kashamura, accompanied by Gizengist troops, suddenly turned up
in the picturesque provincial capital of Bukavu, kidnapped the
whole regional government, and took over control of Kivu, although United Nations chief Dayal had learned in advance of his
intentions. "We have no right to interfere," he was quoted as saying. Thus Kivu, once a holiday wonderland, with its huge Lake
Kivu, purple volcanoes, and pygmy forests, was turned into an
inferno of anarchy and brutality, as Kashamura "nationalized"
Belgian-owned commercial establishments, troops attacked whites,
and doctors, engineers, and other indispensable technicians fled
for their lives.

By early February 1961, with all economic life in Kivu at a
standstill and utter chaos reigning, even Gizenga grew alarmed.
He accused Kashamura of preparing a secession of his own, with
himself as head of an independent Kivu, and dispatched his Interior Minister, Christophe Gbenye, to bring him back to Stanleyville. After a comic-opera series of events which saw both Kasha-

mura and Gbenye captured and freed several times by each other's troops, Kashamura was finally returned to Stanleyville and placed under arrest.

But anarchy continued to reign in Kivu. Entering Bukavu with false papers in the spring of 1961, I found a dead, decaying city. Although the troops had been pacified, hundreds of civilian bandits robbed, harassed, and attacked the two hundred-odd whites—out of five thousand—who remained. Some threatened whites had to live with United Nations troops in the area until they could be smuggled out of the country. One Swiss big-game hunter returned with two live gorillas to find that bandits had slashed his wife's face with a knife while he was gone. Bands of youths wandered aimlessly in the street, reflecting the almost total unemployment. Almost all stores were closed. The Belgian Sabena Airlines couldn't spare enough gasoline to have me driven to the airport.

Lumumbist violence was even more widespread in the tortured town of Kindu, in northern Kindu Province. Behind a wall of fear, hate, and suspicion, I found in progress a grotesque contest of will and stamina—with human lives the table stakes. Every day, two or three officers of the United Nations Malayan Special Force sat across the table from local officials and bargained patiently, hour after hour, for the freedom of about fifty white refugees, including several American missionaries, who had fled there from outlying areas after being tortured, raped, and beaten by Lumumbists. While the haggling went on, refugees were held like prisoners in the Hotel Relais, which had once served vacationing Belgians. The town, an attractive, Europeanized urban center with broad tree-lined streets, was simmering with tension. Sandbags were piled in front of the Leopold II Hotel on the road to the airport and Malayan soldiers quartered there manned machine guns that pointed in all directions. Several months later, thirteen Italian United Nations flyers were chopped to bits in Kindu by Gizengist troops.

In another Kivu jungle town, Kasongo, I made the acquaintance of a gang of Lumumbist "leopard men"—youths who wore strips of leopard skin around their heads and arms, and for months had terrorized northwest Kivu with their bows and poisoned arrows. Fortunately, they were being held by United Nations troops in the area when I met them. The "leopard man" chief invited me to dinner in the mess hall, but though I happily learned that I was not to be on the menu, I declined anyway. The "leopard men," who had beaten up and terrorized many white missionaries, reminded me of an African version of New York's dead-end gangs, with the bow and arrow replacing the switchblade as the symbol of social defiance.

On a trip through northern Kivu with United Nations troops, I found the way dotted with ghost villages where hardly a shop was open. In the town of Butembo, we discovered, hardly a single white had escaped the wrath of Stanleyville soldiers sent there. "On Christmas Day, they came into my hotel and beat me with fists and rifle butts," Belgian hotel owner André Van Neevel said. "And when my Congolese wife tried to help me, they beat her, too. Then they went after the others in the hotel." When the whites began fleeing with the help of United Nations troops, civilian hoodlums destroyed almost all European homes, tearing them down brick by brick.

Still, some whites stuck it out. Dr. Karl Becker of the Oicha Mission, an American from Boyertown, Pennsylvania, remained throughout the violence. On one occasion, after being warned to flee to Uganda by American officials, he drove to the border with his wife and assistants—only to return when local officials followed and refused to let the doctor go. "We need you," they said. So he returned to his mission where hundreds of shouting, weeping Congolese surrounded his rickety, mud-spattered car in a wild explosion of joy. But Becker is no ordinary missionary. "He is a greater man than Dr. Schweitzer," one Belgian told me. "He is a saint— even if he is an American and a Protestant." Now in his late sixties, Dr. Becker, a tall, modest man, has been performing medical miracles in the Congo since 1929. Today he operates a hospital and one of the world's largest leper colonies. The legend of Dr. Becker has brought patients from hundreds of miles around. Some of them come in canoes, others on foot. Even witch doctors have come— and have publicly burned their feathers and other black magic paraphernalia after experiencing the magic of Dr. Becker. The four-year-old son of one of Dr. Becker's assistants, Dr. Herbert Atkinson of Philadelphia, summed up the mission's attitude when he excitedly shouted to his mother as a Congolese soldier approached: "Quick, Mommy, tell him about God before he shoots us."

By the spring of 1961 the communist bloc had begun to have doubts about the ability of Gizenga to serve their purposes as effectively as Lumumba had done. There was nothing wrong with a little terror, but quite obviously the Gizengists, after having initially encouraged violence against whites and suspected anti-Lumumbists, found themselves helpless to control the anarchistic monster they had helped to create—as supporters as well as enemies fell victim to it. Mass unemployment and the halt of most economic activity had sent living standards down to the subsistence level. Tens of thousands of urban dwellers returned to the villages from which they had originally come, living in mud huts with their relatives and eating only what they grew themselves.

The situation was aggravated, moreover, by a Congo River blockade imposed by the Leopoldville regime, and by the refusal of Western-oriented Sudan, to the north of the Congo, to permit the shipment of goods over its territory from Cairo. Thus, not only food and other necessities, but the arms promised by the communists and African neutralists, could not be delivered to isolated Stanleyville.

At the same time, hope diminished among the people that Gizenga ever would be able to unify the country, by force or otherwise, and this seemed to be a requisite for economic recovery in the Lumumbist-dominated areas. Both the Kasavubu regime in Leopoldville and the Tshombe regime in Katanga were strongly entrenched in power, and the areas under their authority were far better off economically than that run by Stanleyville.

Nor did Gizenga have the personality or dynamism to sustain the will of the people to hold out indefinitely if necessary. He was a recluse. He seldom spoke to, or mixed with, the people, who backed him solely because of his Lumumbist political inheritance. And he didn't even have the advantage of being a native of the area he controlled.

Most disturbing of all to the communist nations, Gizenga exhibited less warmth toward them than they had expected—partly because of his frustration at their inability to make good most of their aid promises, and partly because he was not as ideologically oriented as they had hoped. True, communist diplomats and advisers had his ear. Also, Stanleyville's only radio station and its only newspaper, *Uhuru,* reviled the United States, the United Nations, and the Leopoldville government—in line with communist policy. Both organs were controlled by a man they could deal with —Antoine Mandungo, who had visited Prague and Moscow, as well as neutralist Cairo. At times there were more than thirty bloc journalists in Stanleyville simultaneously, while it was difficult, even dangerous, for Western correspondents to visit the city.

Nevertheless, a Russian Tass correspondent dejectedly told me in Stanleyville during Gizenga's reign that he had to fly to Rome to cable his stories, for only two of twelve dispatches he had sent from the Lumumbist stronghold had reached Moscow. On the other hand, an American diplomat who had previously been thrown out of the city as a "spy," returned for a visit and was guest of honor at a party thrown for him by Gizenga himself. On various occasions, the regime ousted journalists from Stanleyville without distinguishing between communist and Western newsmen. Gizenga was obviously a weak, mixed-up, unreliable man, the bloc concluded, but it was stuck with him.

Finally, in August 1961, the Leopoldville regime decided to take a calculated gamble. Previously, it had demanded that the Gizengists recognize it unconditionally as the legitimate government. Stanleyville had always replied that it would agree to unity only if parliament, which had been dismissed by Mobutu at the same time he overthrew Lumumba, was recalled and decided who should run a united government. As the Lumumbists were believed to hold a majority in parliament, the Kasavubu regime was reluctant to agree for fear of a Gizengist victory. But now with the Gizenga government demoralized and in desperate economic straits, Leopoldville announced it would call a meeting of parliament.

After some hedging, the Gizengists agreed to participate, believing they had a good chance to head the new government that would be chosen. In any event, many of Gizenga's colleagues, particularly the nonleftists, no longer saw any political capital in continuing to live off the dead Lumumba's disintegrating influence. They were ready to switch to the other, stronger side if necessary. Also, the leftists, with the apparent support of Red-bloc diplomats, saw an opportunity to revitalize their movement. If Gizenga won uncontested control of the central government, the Congo would again be on the way toward communism. If he lost, he and other top leftists would still have to be given influential positions in the combined government, and could eventually achieve control anyway through infiltration and subversion.

So parliament met in a tense atmosphere, though Gizenga himself was absent, and chose Cyrille Adoula as Premier. The selection of Adoula was a turning point in the short history of the Congo Republic. For he was one of the few Congolese leaders with the necessary requisites for relatively stable leadership: superior intelligence, personal dynamism and courage, and a devotion to reason rather than emotionalism.

"There is no room for extremism in the Congo," he said in a long interview in his modest office in Leopoldville before he took over as Premier. "There's no room for communism or for antiwhite outbreaks. We want true independence and friendship with all nations. That is the only way our young nation can grow. We must crush those who think otherwise."

Originally a "capitalist" official in the Belgian Central Bank of the Congo, he switched to trade unionism in 1955 and became a leader of the moderately socialistic General Federation of Congo Workers. He helped Lumumba found the National Congolese Movement in 1958, but split with him a year later, accusing him of serving "his personal ambitions." After independence, he sharply criticized some of Lumumba's anti-Belgian actions and denounced Kashamura for spreading racial hatred over the radio. Eventually, he was selected to head the Ministries of Interior and National Defense in Premier Ileo's Leopoldville government.

As soon as he acceded to the premiership, Adoula, in an effort to patch over past quarrels, offered Gizenga the post of Vice-Premier. Gizenga, faced with the fact that his own parliamentary delegates had approved Adoula's selection, reluctantly agreed to go to Leopoldville and accept the job.

The communists were bitterly disappointed. They had lost a magnificent chance to control Congo policy again, and only by a few votes. Even harder to take was the fact that the Lumumbists might have won the day if only Gizenga had attended the parliamentary meeting personally and rallied his forces instead of sulking in fear in his heavily guarded Stanleyville home. But now that the die was cast, opportunity still knocked. With Gizengists in important government positions, including the second highest post, the leftists could still influence policy and eventually determine it. The Soviet Union and the eight other countries that had recognized the Stanleyville regime moved their embassies to Leopoldville.

Inevitably the communist influence began to reassert itself. A communist-line newspaper, *Le Matin,* suddenly appeared. East Germans tried to talk Adoula into a deal whereby arms labeled as "machinery" would be imported. Ten percent of the sales proceeds would be placed in an anonymous Swiss account, which presumably would be used to finance leftist activity in the Congo. The East Germans also circulated propaganda leaflets.

The leftists made their biggest play in a bold effort to exert their influence in Katanga. They not only wanted to get their hands on its wealth, but to crush and take revenge on the Tshombe government which they held responsible for frustrating Lumumba's efforts to unify the nation under a leftist regime, and, in fact, for murdering him. Tshombe was nothing more than a creature of the Belgians who had no African following, they cried. But they knew better. He was a power in his own right. His own Lunda tribe of southern Katanga looked upon him almost as a god, while the political party he led, the Conakat, had, with its allies, come to power as the result of a popular provincial election held under the Belgians shortly before the Congo received independence. However, Tshombe's supporters won only by a small majority over the party of the rival Balubas, who, in their frustration, rebelled, if ineffectually, against his Lunda-led forces.

Tshombe was the eldest son of the richest Lunda, a merchant who owned village stores, a hotel, a sawmill, plantations, and a trucking company. After graduation from a Methodist teachers' college, Tshombe, then a playboy with a penchant for pretty girls and sporty American cars, ran the family interests for a while and even extended them. Finally, several bankruptcies sent him fleeing into the political arena, where he could capitalize more on his great personal charm. He was not politically handicapped by his marriage to the daughter of the top Lunda chieftain. Quickly working his way from Elisabethville city council to the provincial council, he helped to found the Conakat Party in 1959, made up mainly of members of the Lunda tribe. It was all for independence from the Belgians—Katangan independence. With most of the Congo's wealth located in Lunda country, the tribesmen, including Tshombe, saw little point in sharing the wealth with the rest of the country unnecessarily.

Thus, backed by the Belgian-operated Union Minière du Haut Katanga, Tshombe, at the 1961 Round-Table Conference in Brussels, advocated a loose confederal type of government. Nor would he accept defeat when Lumumba's concept of a unitary state, backed by the Belgian government, won out. If necessary, he told friends, Katanga would secede from the Congo. A few months later this is exactly what Katanga did.

Adoula, no less than the Gizengists, wanted to end the secession. He didn't particularly wish to get rid of the Tshombe government. He simply hoped to force it to accept Leopoldville's rule. But the leftists would have no truck with Tshombe, who would give them considerable trouble as a top central government leader, which he would automatically become if he ever did decide to return to the Leopoldville fold. Certainly he would do his best to prevent leftist infiltration in Katanga.

Adoula agreed to remove him. A Gizengist would be put at Katanga's helm. With relations between United Nations forces stationed in Katanga and the Katangan government conveniently deteriorating, the Premier and the United Nations mission plotted an attack on Katanga. Secretary-General Dag Hammarskjöld, persuaded by the mission that the United Nations forces had to attack Katanga in self-defense, approved the plan.

United Nations troops struck one dawn in September 1961, and captured the strategic post office in Elisabethville after a stiff fight. "The secession of Katanga has ended," announced Ireland's Dr. Conor Cruise O'Brien, who led the operation (and has since been named Vice-Chancellor of the University of Ghana by a grateful Nkrumah), as most United Nations members, including the United States, nodded their approval. Simultaneously, Davidson Bocheley stepped off a United Nations plane that brought him from Leopoldville and prepared to take over the province. Bocheley had been Minister of Agriculture and then State Commissar for Oriental Province in Gizenga's Stanleyville government. He was not entirely unknown to the United Nations. In its files was a report that accused him of leading much of the violence and terror that occurred in Oriental Province during Lumumba's heyday. His reasonableness was further indicated in a telegram he had sent Lumumba, denouncing the presence of "Belgian paratroopers" in United Nations ranks.

Bocheley, as he waited at Elisabethville airport for United Nations troops to mop up Katangese resistance, glowed with anticipation of the big moment in his life. So did the masters of the communist bloc. They couldn't lose. If Tshombe were in fact overthrown and a Gizengist were to replace him, the Congolese leftists would be in a powerful position. If by chance the United Nations operation failed, the bloc would still have come out ahead. For the tremendous loss in prestige suffered by the United Nations would fit in neatly with Soviet plans to reduce it to impotence so that the United States could no longer use it to frustrate Red ambitions. Moreover, the prestige of Adoula and other Congolese moderates would also suffer, to the benefit of the leftists, who could blame them as well as the United Nations for "softness" toward Katanga.

Many hours after Bocheley had slumped into his airport seat, he was still sitting, his dream of power gradually fading away. For the Katangese, led by Belgian officers and several hundred white mercenaries of various nationalities, had strongly rallied against the United Nations forces in various parts of Katanga. They were actually winning after several days of fighting when both sides agreed to negotiate a cease-fire. Dag Hammarskjöld himself, a confused and tragic figure who had been misled by his Tshombe-hating subordinates in the Congo both as to the strength of the Katangan forces and the need and justification for attacking, agreed to meet with the Katanga leader in North Rhodesia to formalize the United Nations failure in person. But almost as if providence had decided to save him the grief of this humiliating blow to the peaceful cause that was his life, he died in a jungle plane crash on his way there. An assistant signed a truce for him, and the communist bloc, if disappointed by this new failure to extend the influence of its protégés, could at least take satisfaction in the damage done to United Nations prestige and Hammarskjöld's timely disappearance from the scene.

But strangely, the leftists did not effectively exploit the demoralization that gripped Leopoldville for their own political advancement. Gizenga, instead of remaining in Leopoldville to exert the maximum of pressure on Adoula, and perhaps take his job as the disillusionment over Katanga deepened, returned to Stanleyville, apparently with a view toward setting up his own government again and seceding from the Congo.

The communist bloc was aghast. It couldn't quite follow his reasoning. If he had failed to make a go of his previous adventure in Stanleyville when he had communist and neutralist diplomatic support, the backing of a large segment of the Congo army, and an impressive legal claim to the premiership, how could he expect to succeed now when friendly countries had already switched their recognition to the Adoula government, when almost all of his former troops were under its control, and when most of his old political colleagues had no intention of following him again? Yet Gizenga broodingly promoted his own downfall at a moment when the central government was most susceptible to pressure and infiltration.

Hardly more than two months after the initial United Nations assault failed, the organization attacked once more, maintaining this time that a Katangan army defense blueprint that had fallen into its hands indicated that the Katangese had planned to attack its forces—an unsubstantiated pretext vaguely reminiscent of that used by many aggressors in history.

Largely as a result of reports by State Department Congo experts, who evaluated the situation more on the basis of misguided anti-colonial emotionalism and a desire to please the Afro-Asian bloc than on the facts, the United States backed this new action more ardently than the first one, despite the open opposition of its NATO partners, Britain and France. The United States was more certain that the United Nations forces, which were much stronger than previously, would win this time, and with the leftists in Leopoldville seemingly checked, no Davidson Bocheley would now be likely to take over a subdued Katanga. Equally important, United States officials were led to believe by Adoula that if the Katanga forces were beaten, he would be in a position to destroy Gizenga's power once and for all.

But not all Americans agreed with the official government view. Public opinion crystallized along paradoxical lines. Most liberals, who consider themselves the most zealous champions of the United Nations, became identified with the anti-Tshombe faction, rationalizing in many cases that even if the United Nations was wrong, the United States had to support its action simply because it was the United Nations. Most conservatives, particularly the radical right wing, which has little use for the "communist" United Nations, staunchly supported Tshombe and protested the United Nations move.

Yet the struggle between the Katanga and central Congo governments has been waged not on a basis of liberalism versus conservatism, but on the far less sophisticated level of economic, tribal, and personality conflicts having little or nothing to do with political theory—for all Tshombe's anticommunist outcries. Nor, from the point of view of the United Nations' future, did the American liberals and ultraconservatives choose sides in accordance with their respective professed interests. For win or lose militarily, the United Nations was setting a precedent that could only reduce its effectiveness as a moral force for peace.

The United Nations violated its own basic principles, taking it upon itself, whatever pretexts it offered to justify its action, to determine by force the political structure of a sovereign nation. A clearly aggressive venture, as attested by the fact that the United Nations forces struck first on two occasions, the attacks were all the more regrettable, morally and practically, in view of the organization's failure to explore fully, before they were launched—with the patience and diplomatic restraint intrinsically required of it— the possibility of peaceful negotiation between Katanga and the central government.

From the beginning, most United Nations officials in the Congo, apparently motivated by a misplaced idealism, exhibited an arrogance toward the Katanga government hardly becoming the peacemaker. Puffing slowly, deliberately, on his pipe with the air of a man basking in the radiance of a supreme truth, one United Nations representative in Elisabethville commented quietly in a pronounced Irish brogue shortly before the first United Nations attack: "We now have a chance to display the real power of the United Nations. We must first of all try to exert our moral authority.

But if it proves insufficient, we need not hesitate to impose a solution to the Congo problem by force, for we have the authority to do so."

This authority supposedly stemmed from a Security Council resolution urging the immediate withdrawal of foreign military and political personnel from the Congo and authorizing the use of force to prevent civil war. The Katanga government, United Nations officials charged, insisted on retaining white personnel and threatened to bring about civil war by refusing to end its secession. But the United Nations was not authorized to employ violence to enforce the resolution involving foreign personnel; and though such authorization was granted as an ultimate means of heading off civil war, Leopoldville, not Elisabethville, threatened to take the initiative in such a venture. In any event, enforcement of the resolution was not a genuine motive but an excuse for a United Nations military attempt to impose national unity on the Congo, though the United Nations had no authority to force the country or any part of it to accept any specific political structure.

The United Nations, in many respects, has performed well in the Congo. Its very presence has minimized violence and chaos. In anarchistic northern Kivu, I observed doctors of the World Health Organization treat patients in remote jungle clinics. In South Kasai, I accompanied United Nations missions delivering tons of food to refugee villages where thousands of Balubas, chased from their homes in neighboring provinces by rival tribesmen, had starved to death in 1960. And I saw in once-barren fields surrounding these villages new crops of potatoes, corn, and peanuts cultivated from seeds provided by the United Nations. But in Katanga, the United Nations has failed to discharge its obligations as an international peacemaker.

United Nations officials at first looked favorably on an agreement reached by Congo leaders in March 1961 in Tananarive, Malagasy Republic, providing for a loose confederation. The plan, skillfully proposed by Tshombe, was even approved by Kasavubu. But the United Nations and Kasavubu later realized that they had bought far less unity than they had bargained for. The president's power would be extremely limited, with even foreign policy subject to a provincial veto. When Tshombe tried to leave a subsequent meeting in Coquilhatville, central government troops abruptly ended the honeymoon, arresting him while United Nations forces silently—and approvingly—stood by.

United Nations representatives have justified such arrogance with the argument that Katanga is really little more than a Belgian colony, and that Tshombe is simply a Belgian agent. But this argument does not hold water. The Belgian government, unlike the Katangan leaders, has, in fact, preached Congo unity since pre-independence days, even though—after freedom was granted —it may have permitted the Katanga regime to hire Belgian military officers for a period to build up Tshombe's army.

A United Nations official told me on my arrival in Elisabethville that Tshombe and his colleagues would never dare to speak about or decide policy unless their white advisers were around. But when I visited the President at his official mansion, he curtly asked his advisers to leave so that we could speak alone. On another occasion, I overheard Vice-President Jean Kibwe refuse his adviser's advice that I be granted an interview, a response accentuated by the crash of the Vice-President's fist on his desk.

"We don't take orders from the Belgians," Interior Minister Godefroid Munongo, who wears dark glasses and has the rugged features of a prize fighter, assured me while his Belgian advisers sat nervously by. "They take orders from us. We hire them because they understand our language and people. It's convenient for us. When we don't need them any more, we'll tell them to leave."

Munongo is reputed for his anti-Belgian views, as was his grandfather M'Siri, a cruel and powerful tribal leader who was assassinated by an agent of Leopold for refusing to deal with the Belgians. One report has it that the Interior Minister, on a visit to an Elisabethville bar one evening, slapped a Belgian's face and shouted: "Don't think I've forgotten that you Belgians killed my grandfather!" But Munongo, like his fellow Katangan leaders, is realistic, recognizing the need for white co-operation as few other African nationalists do.

Nor have United Nations authorities correctly interpreted the relationship between the Katanga regime and the Union Minière du Haut Katanga, a partly Belgian-owned company—actually, British and other European financial participation is greater, though Belgians are in charge of operations. Contrary to the attitude of the Belgian government, this firm, which runs Katanga's enormously profitable copper and cobalt mines, vigorously opposes a tight Congo unity that would dilute its influence. Mine officials exude nothing but optimism about the future. In Kolwezi, the largest mining zone, they proudly showed me great terraced earthen basins grandly splashed green and blue-gray, signifying the presence of copper and cobalt. They took me on a tour of fully automated mineral plants under construction which, when completed, will have cost fifty million dollars. A lone Belgian technician, like a figure in a science fiction movie, pressed buttons and flashed red and green lights in an immaculate, multiwindowed control room. "We're not spending this kind of money because we expect to leave," a mine official told me.

But Union Minière, however suave and self-assured its front, is not quite that certain about the future. It needs the good will of the Katanga government more than that government requires the affection of the company. If Union Minière were forced to leave Katanga as the result of bitter relations with the governing authorities, it would stand to suffer fantastic losses, but the government could turn to other firms interested in operating the mines. The degree of influence Union Minière exerts on Tshombe is not the important question. What is significant is the magnitude of the pressure Tshombe, or for that matter, the central Congolese government, if it gains control of the mines, intends to exert on Union Minière for a greater share of the wealth. The company today nets from the mineral produce of the four mines in Kolwezi and other smaller ones in Elisabethville and Kambove about seventy million dollars annually after taxes. But the Katanga government reaps from taxes, royalties, and dividends—it owns seventeen percent of the stock—approximately sixty percent of the gross profits, representing some forty percent of Katanga's income. The Katangese, who want to develop their territory swiftly, and the Belgian businessmen, who wish to continue their profitable activities, are using each other for their own respective ends. But the Katanga leaders, aside from the fact that they are men of strong personality, are in the more advantageous position, and therefore would hardly accept the docile role of Belgian puppet.

The United Nations mission also miscalculated Katanga's military capability, particularly before the first attack. After white officers were ousted by their men throughout the Congo following independence, the Katanga provincial government, announcing its secession from the Congo, expelled all non-Katangese soldiers from the province. Then, retaining the services of some two hundred Belgian officers, the Tshombe regime began to build a strictly Katangan army of about eight thousand men. To guarantee its loyalty, military pay was raised to new levels. A private suddenly earned forty dollars a month plus allowances. Foreign mercenaries, hired as shock troops, were given from four hundred dollars to six hundred dollars a month plus expenses and ten dollars a day for combat duty. About one hundred Katangese were sent to European officer training schools. Military equipment flowed in from abroad. Army expenditures were so great that they exhausted

Katanga's foreign exchange despite the astronomical mine earnings.

A competent army by Western standards was not the result. However, training in months of fighting against the Baluba rebels hardened Tshombe's soldiers, while the leadership of European officers made the difference between an army and an armed mob. Not that it was always easy for the white officers to exert authority over their men, who insisted on negotiating military decisions with them in the spirit of labor-management relations. A young Belgian commander at one military post I visited ordered his company to raid and set afire a nearby rebel village, but his men would not obey, arguing that the assignment be reserved for the unit that was about to replace them. The raid was called off.

But the Katangese, as the United Nations discovered, do not always lack a will to fight. "This is a nasty little war," a Belgian officer sitting next to me on a troop train observed. "One minute everything's quiet and peaceful, and the next—zing—you're dodging bullets and poisoned arrows." Suddenly a "zing" split the air, and we were dodging bullets and poisoned arrows. I dived under the seat, finding myself face to face with the raised rump of the officer, who had also decided that discretion was the better part of valor. But the Katangan soldiers on the roof, though dangerously exposed to Baluba fire, sprayed guerrillas hiding in the tall grass, expressing disappointment later that the train had not moved more slowly to permit them to inflict greater losses on the enemy.

Shortly after we arrived at our destination, a small military post, the troops, it appeared, would have a second chance at the Balubas. Shots were heard in the distance as another train approached. Within minutes the whole company was mobilized and heading in trucks toward the scene of the new attack. A Belgian officer manning a machine gun in a jeep in which I hitched a ride said excitedly, "Now you'll see some fun." And he was right. Lying near the railroad tracks was a huge elephant—the target of Katangan soldiers on the train. "Better luck next time," the officer commented regretfully.

Under the Belgian Congo administration, Katanga, with only one-eighth of the colony's population, provided about one-third of its revenue. Tshombe told me that in a confederation of Congo states, Katanga would continue to contribute a percentage—to be negotiated—of its income to the rest of the country. "There is no reason why Katanga should necessarily be part of a tightly unified Congo," he said. "We have no cultural, linguistic, or historical ties with the other states, except the artificial ties imposed by the Belgians for their own administrative and economic purposes."

But it was clear that Tshombe, a realist, had never really expected Katanga to maintain completely independent status indefinitely. He needs friendly relations with the rest of the Congo for economic reasons; not only is the Congo a cheap source of agricultural produce, but as long as Katanga is at odds with the central government, it will have to continue to drain its treasury for military expenditures alone. Nor is Tshombe unaware that few if any countries would recognize his regime.

He has simply been holding out for the largest degree of provincial autonomy he can get. Even if he wanted to do otherwise, he could not. For it would be politically impossible for him to ignore the wishes of other more extreme leaders in Katanga, particularly Interior Minister Munongo, who may be the regime's real strong man. Munongo is believed to have engineered the assassination of Lumumba—some observers say against Tshombe's will—and he has probably been more responsible than anyone else for Katanga's anti-United Nations policies. One of the most chilling sounds I have ever heard was the scrape of thousands of machetes being sharpened on sidewalk curbs during a wild anti-United Nations demonstration in Elisabethville in May 1961. Munongo, who had distributed the weapons, characteristically explained to a Belgian associate: "You'd be surprised what a little violence can accomplish sometimes."

The United Nations, employing this same aggressive philosophy, managed, from the military point of view, to emerge from the second round of fighting in better shape than it had after the first round. After a bitter struggle, which probably resulted in the death of more noncombatant civilians than soldiers, its forces won control of Elisabethville. The fighting stopped when Tshombe agreed to hold talks with Adoula, but a verbal stalemate resulted. In December 1962, the United Nations, using as an excuse some armed provocations by undisciplined Katangan soldiers, launched a third attack, and apparently ended the secession at last. With Adoula tottering, Washington again approved the use of force for a politically expedient end, and a dubious one at that. The Congo's future depends on factors more complex than Adoula's fate.

Shortly after the second round, Adoula accused Gizenga of trying to start a secession movement of his own, and his soldiers put the leftist leader under house arrest. Gizenga's political downfall was apparently complete, at least for the time being. Only his own small African Solidarity Party supported him in parliament, and even the communist bloc had apparently abandoned him as too hopelessly weak a horse to continue placing bets on.

The United States government gloried in what appeared to be a diplomatic victory. Gizenga's political demise, it was said, confirmed the wisdom of American support for United Nations action in Katanga, which was described as necessary to permit Adoula to move against the leftist chief. But this reasoning is impaired by several factors. First, Gizenga was in sharp eclipse before the United Nations launched its second attack and would almost inevitably have suffered the fate of a has-been whether or not the attack had taken place.

Second, the United States was grossly indiscreet in backing a United Nations military effort that, even though launched in greater strength the second time, was a risky venture that jeopardized the already waning prestige of the organization. As things turned out, the United Nations had a hard enough time taking Elisabethville in the second attack, and the overwhelming third attack did not assure an end to violence in the Congo.

Third, whatever the immediate diplomatic advantages or disadvantages of the United Nations action, from the moral viewpoint it represented a tragic refutation of the concept of peaceful settlement of disputes that the organization is supposed to embody, giving respectability to the use of force to achieve foreign policy goals. It would be unrealistic to ignore the correlation between the Katanga adventure and such aggressive attitudes as that displayed by India when it seized Portuguese Goa by force.

Moreover, if the United Nations' effectiveness as a long-range instrument of peace was compromised by the Katanga episode, there is little assurance that the leftist menace will not re-emerge in the Congo whoever is premier. Many of Adoula's staunchest supporters and most trusted assistants were, after all, the staunch supporters and trusted assistants of Gizenga only a short while ago. Gizenga's replacement as Vice-Premier for several months was Christophe Gbenye, who, as Interior Minister in the Stanleyville regime, was a powerful figure in that government. "It's ridiculous to say we're communists," he had said in an interview in his Stanleyville office during Gizenga's heyday, not quite sure how I, as an American, had managed to enter his communist-backed, anti-American stronghold.

And Gbenye, who was ousted from Adoula's government in July 1962, is not a communist. He is anything that it is timely and profitable to be. Some Western diplomatic observers think that, with the political demise of Gizenga, he is now Moscow's man in the Congo—despite his ideological ignorance of Marx. Adoula, in fact, jailed him for a short time, apparently for dealing with the communist bloc. *Le Progres,* a new Leopoldville daily, published in November 1962 a photostat of a letter from Senator André Kiwiwa, Secretary-General of the Lumumba party, to Gbenya, another party leader, indicating that the organization received funds from foreign sources, presumably the bloc, via Cairo. Other letters hinted that Gizenga's African Solidarity Party also received foreign funds, and, not too oddly by Congolese standards, that both parties were getting, or trying to get, subsidies from Tshombe.

Like Gbenye, most politicians who backed Lumumba and Gizenga, including many who actively encouraged their dealings with the communist bloc, were probably never genuine leftists. They are simply political opportunists who were, and no doubt still are, ready to switch politics at the drop of an opportunity. Furthermore, the few legitimate procommunists in the Congo can be counted on, with the help of their bloc masters, to infiltrate in ever greater numbers into key positions in government and labor.

And, contrary to the logic of the United States State Department, they are likely to get a lot further in the long run within a tightly unified Congo, whatever the economic and administrative advantages of such unity, than they could under a loose federal or confederal system. The Gizenga Stanleyville regime controlled a large sector of the Congo with the full support of the communist and neutralist blocs, but nonetheless withered on the vine in its isolation. The leftists, after this experience, were for the most part only too glad to join forces with the Leopoldville regime, even in a subordinate capacity, and work for a national unity that would give them the opportunity to infiltrate the whole Congo instead of a small piece of it. No doubt they appreciate American efforts to help them achieve this end, even if the United States is motivated by contrary purposes.

But however discouraging the situation in the Congo may become, the United States can always take consolation in the fact that, as the communists themselves have so agonizingly learned, nothing is irreversible, or predictable, in the Congo.

Part 2

THE MIDDLE EAST

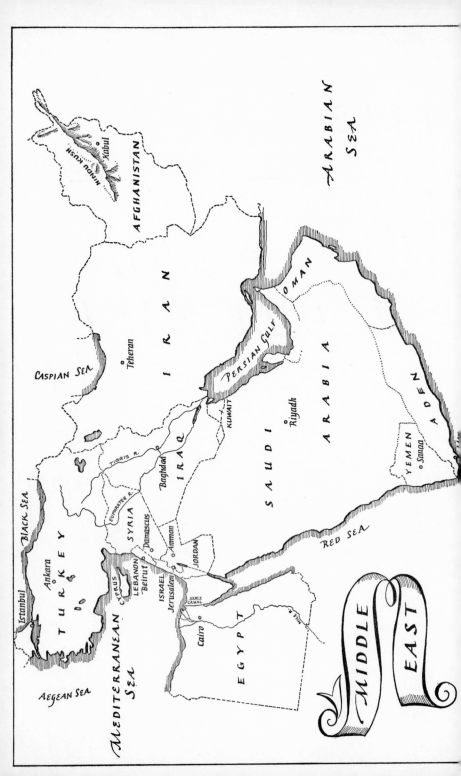

VII

A PLAGUE ON BOTH HOUSES

A stroll down the Street Which Is Called Straight in the bazaar quarter of Damascus, the ancient capital of Syria, is a stimulating adventure for eyes, ears, and nostrils. Here are teeming, chattering, laughing crowds of men dressed in white robes and *kafiyeh,* the traditional Arab towel-like headdress held in place by a black band, or *aghkal,* around the head; women wearing black robes and veils that leave only a pair of mysterious, alluring brown eyes exposed; and donkeys piled high with crates of exquisite wood mosaics and inlaid brass, or baskets of dates, candied fruits, mint leaves, and spices of every exotic scent.

As I made my way through this swarming conglomeration of people and animals, a merchant in one of the stalls lined up endlessly on either side of the narrow street called out to me over the din and confusion: "American come here. Nice brocade tablecloth cheap!" A fat, mustached man, who wore Western clothing and a tasseled *tarbouche* tipped to one side of his round head, managed to sell me a couple of tablecloths—cheap—after an hour of energetic bargaining. Between references to price, we discussed, as is the custom in this part of the world, where bargaining is a subtle, devious, and highly enjoyable battle of wits, other matters having nothing to do with the business at hand.

He was happy to see me, he said. The Syrian people liked Americans. I was tempted to believe him after having returned the smiles of scores of strangers and the cries of "hello" from innumerable barefoot, dirty-faced, raggedly clad, but happily giggling children. But it was hard for me to reconcile this warm, open friendliness, I told the merchant, with the vaunted anti-West bitterness of the Middle Eastern world that had produced bloody riots from Iran to Egypt.

"Yes," he replied in stuttering English, "it is very difficult understand. Also difficult for politicians understand. One day everybody friendly, everybody like leaders, have no enemies. Next day everybody hate somebody, ready kill him, especially Western peoples. I am Syrian, I am Arab. But I don't understand."

This semi-educated merchant pinpointed a factor that must be taken into account in any judgment of the Middle Eastern political mood. Today, the Middle East does not appear to be in any immediate danger of fatal communist penetration. This observation, however, should be tempered with caution, for political change in this area often comes in sudden, convulsive upheavals in which some of the world's most hospitable but explosively emotional people can be turned into irrational hate-filled mobs willing to follow the leader with the loudest voice, particularly if it nourishes their long-starved egos with nationalist slogans.

Such political explosions are usually far more unpredictable and spontaneous than those that have rocked Africa and Asia. Most African violence has either been well organized by tribal or nationalist leaders who can turn riots on and off like a faucet, as in Angola, or has simply represented individual banditry or tribal rivalry arising from a sudden disintegration of authority, as in the Congo. Asian violence has been even more meticulously organized by nationalist or communist demagogues. But little or no organization is required to set off a full-fledged holocaust in the Middle East. As the fat, friendly Syrian merchant said with unusual candor for an Arab, "If I stood up on a box right now and screamed you stole something from me and let's kill all Americans, I could start riot myself. Soon everybody forget who started it and why, but nobody could stop people fighting. And then poor nice Americans!"

Little wonder I bought the tablecloths!

The communists have often taken advantage of this mass emotional instability, of which Westerners and their supporters are usually the main victims. In the early 1950's, after flash-fire mob action had put Dr. Mohammed Mossadegh, a fanatically anti-West nationalist, in power in Iran, the communists tried to take over his movement and might have done so if they had been more expertly led and had not been hamstrung by Stalin's refusal to permit co-operation with national bourgeoisie who would not accept communist leadership. In 1952 Egyptian Reds tried but failed, partly for the same reasons, to win control of mobs who went on a rampage in Cairo in protest against British occupation of the Suez area. In 1958, with the Kremlin now encouraging communist co-operation with the national bourgeoisie, even in the capacity of followers, the Iraqi Reds actually did take over the nationalist movement for a while, and barely missed assuming power when many nationalists suddenly turned against them. Thus, if the Reds have managed to manipulate the hot Middle Eastern temperament to some degree, they have also been victimized by it.

A Western-garbed Iraqi businessman who sat next to me on a luxury bus that sped across the desert flatlands between Damascus and Baghdad, the Iraqi capital, explained—between sips of a Scotch and water served by a pretty Lebanese hostess—what made this temperament so easy to manipulate. "As you can see, I am fairly well off," he said, "but I am one of the few lucky Arabs to have been born into a wealthy family. Most of my people are jealous of me, even hate me, and I can't very well blame them, though I have never exploited them personally. If they hate me, you can imagine how they must feel toward those who are exploiting them, especially toward the Western colonialists who do not even belong here and are the friends of Israel. After so many centuries of subjugation and misery, they are ready to listen to anyone who promises to give them dignity and a better life, to help them leap over a gap of centuries overnight. And they are in no mood to ask for the person's credentials—as long as he is not a Westerner, of course. In their blind eagerness, they will even switch loyalties without notice, if some new leader offers bigger and better promises. True, this is essentially the same attitude you find in many other underdeveloped areas as well, but the Middle Easterners are especially proud, impetuous and hot-blooded."

In his *Philosophy of the Revolution*, Egypt's Nasser offers a similar but more complex explanation:

> Often, when I go back to turning the pages of our history, I feel sorrow tearing my soul as I consider the period when a tyrannical feudalism was formed, a feudalism which had no other object save sucking the blood of life out of our veins and sapping from these veins the remnants of any feeling of power and of dignity. It left in the depth of our souls an effect that we have to struggle long to overcome.
>
> European society passed through the stages of its evolution in an orderly manner. It crossed the bridge between the Renaissance

at the end of the Middle Ages and the nineteenth century step by step. The stages of this evolution systematically succeeded one another. In our case everything was sudden. European countries eyed us covetously and regarded us as a crossroad to their colonies in the East and the South. Torrents of ideas and opinions burst upon us which we were, at that stage of our evolution, incapable of assimilating. Our spirits were still in the thirteenth century, though the symptoms of the nineteenth and twentieth centuries infiltrated in their various aspects. Our minds were trying to catch up with the advancing caravan of humanity.

At one time I complained that the people did not know what they wanted. They were not unanimous in their choice of the way to take. I realized later that I demanded the impossible and that I took no account of the circumstances of our society. We live in a society that has not yet crystallized. It is still boiling over and restless. It has not yet calmed or settled down, so as to continue its gradual evolution parallel with other nations which preceded it along the road.

Just as China's proximity to free Asia gives Peking an edge in influence over Moscow in that area, so does Russia's nearness to the Middle East make Soviet influence dominant there. Nor do the histories of China and Russia, in terms of desired expansionism in their respective parts of the world, diverge greatly. In 1900 Czarist General Kuropatkin declared: "When we shall rule over the Bosporus [Turkey] and the entrance into the Mediterranean, we shall be able to tackle the Egyptian [Suez] question with energy . . . We will extend our tentacles toward the Bosporus, the Indian Ocean, and the Atlantic."

Soviet Russia has had to adjust this program for aggression in the Middle East to modern political realities, but in general it has followed Czarist policy—for ideological as well as strategic and economic reasons. Significantly, following discussions between Soviet Foreign Minister Molotov and Nazi German Foreign Minister von Ribbentrop that led to the Stalin-Hitler pact in August 1939, Baron Ernst von Weizsacker, Secretary of State in the German Foreign Office wrote in a memorandum: "The focal points in the territorial aspirations of the Soviet Union would presumably be centered south of the territory of the Soviet Union in the direction of the Indian Ocean." These aspirations were later incorporated in a secret protocol signed by Germany, Italy, Japan, and the Soviet Union.

It is understandable that the Russians should covet the strategic, wealthy Middle East, which embraces mainly Turkey, Iran, Israel, Afghanistan, West Pakistan, Cyprus, and the Arab states of Saudi

Arabia, Iraq, Syria, Jordan, Lebanon, Yemen, and Egypt United Arab Republic. The area is, literally, the crossroads of the world, bordering on three continents—Africa to the west, Europe to the north, and Asia to the east. Europe and Asia are linked by the waterway that extends from the eastern Mediterranean through the Suez Canal and the Red Sea to the Indian Ocean. The Middle East is also vastly rich, its barren deserts covering the world's largest oil deposits.

To establish its authority over this cherished region, the Kremlin originally planned, like its Czarist predecessors, to seek control first of the Balkans from the Adriatic to the Aegean, and thus convert the eastern Mediterranean into a Russian preserve. Meanwhile, Stalin hoped to build up communist parties in the Middle East which would be prepared to take over the area.

The first communist groups were formed in the early 1920's in Egypt, Turkey, and Palestine, but made little headway largely because of their disregard for local political, religious, and social institutions. In particular, they shocked the fervently Islamic masses with attacks on Islam. They also tried to create proletarian mass parties, though there were few workers to join them. In the mid-1930's the communists changed their tactics, pushing for popular fronts as did communist parties everywhere during this period when Russia sought all the friends it could win as the Nazi threat grew. Marxist propaganda was greatly reduced and all attacks on Islam ended.

Communism established its first tentative foothold in the Middle East during the war, when the Soviet Union emerged as one of the two great world powers. Industrial expansion produced a growing proletariat in the Middle East and an almost fanatical enthusiasm among intellectuals for economic revolution. After the war this receptive attitude toward communism was nourished by bitter anti-colonial hatred. The French and British were forced to evacuate most of their territories, and the Reds set up many communist-front organizations, while trying to take over the anti-imperialist front that had grown out of the prewar and wartime popular front.

After the war, too, Yugoslavia, which borders on the Adriatic, found itself in the communist camp. Greece was gravely threatened by a communist rebellion and, had it fallen, Russia might have attacked Turkey. Iran, a natural springboard into Turkey to the west and the Arab world to the southwest, was still occupied by Soviet troops that had entered the country during the war.

It looked as though Russia's traditional plan for moving into the Middle East might prove feasible at last.

But overnight, Soviet strategy collapsed as Yugoslavia's Marshal Tito rejected Soviet domination; the United States instituted the Truman Doctrine, under which Greece crushed the Reds with American aid and Turkey was promised aid if necessary; and Soviet troops evacuated Iran after the United Nations, backed by the United States, threatened to use force to get them out. Moreover, the communists in the Middle East failed to gain as much influence as had been hoped. In any event, they did not win control of the anticolonial forces.

Stalin temporarily abandoned his interest in the area, concentrating instead on an attempted conquest of Southeast Asia. There were strong communist parties in Southeast Asia that could put up a fierce fight against colonial and national bourgeois regimes. But the Middle Eastern communist parties were still weak. They were incapable of winning control of the nationalist movements either through infiltration and subversion, or through outright rebellion. And Stalin would not co-operate with the national bourgeoisie. "The principal orientation of our effort and activity," Khalid Bakdash, Syrian communist leader and the most eminent Red theoretician in the Middle East, said in 1951, "must be toward isolating the nationalist bourgeoisie and ending its influence among the people. For this bourgeoisie, no matter how much the names of its parties may vary, uses its influence to deceive the people and turn it away from the revolutionary struggle; it works also for an understanding with imperialism." In line with this policy, Russia violently denounced Gamal Abdel Nasser after he took control of Egypt in 1952 for his "unsympathetic" attitude toward communists.

But while rash Soviet propaganda did not set well with most Middle Easterners, who supported Nasserite nationalism, reaction was mild compared to that which greeted Western "imperialist" policy in the region, particularly the establishment in early 1955 of the Baghdad Pact, which was directed against Nasserite as well as communist expansionism. Not only did the Arabs consider the pact—which embraced Turkey, Iraq, Iran, Pakistan, Britain and, informally, the United States—an effort to pressure them into the Western Cold War camp, but a direct threat to their hero Nasser.

Soviet leaders, no less than Nasser and his followers, were greatly alarmed, viewing the alliance as a dagger pointed at the USSR's underbelly. But they also saw the pact as an opportunity for the Soviet Union—which had by now switched to a policy of wooing the national bourgeoisie—to make a dramatic re-entry into the Middle East. The situation in the Middle East, said *Izves-*

tia on April 17, 1955, had greatly deteriorated, and Russia would do everything to develop closer relations with the countries of that area. Simultaneously, Russia revived a magazine for Middle Eastern specialists *Sovietskoye Vostokovedenie,* that had not been published for eighteen years. New books and school courses on the area suddenly became available. The Kremlin then struck. It offered the same Nasser it had been denouncing a huge shipment of arms to balance the threat of the Baghdad Pact. Nasser accepted, and the Soviet Union, in one bound, had entrenched itself in the Middle East that had so long eluded Czars and communist dictators alike.

Since that time the communist bloc, mainly Soviet Russia, has poured over $2 billion into the Middle East, with almost half going to Egypt, mostly for its huge Aswam Dam project. In 1960 more than 1,300 students from the area were studying in bloc schools, and over 100 delegations had been exchanged. Communist propaganda broadcasts in nine regional languages totaled 440 hours a week. Over 275,000 copies of 68 communist books were distributed in six languages. Bloc cultural exhibitions numbered 35.

Despite accelerated Russian aid, the USSR's popularity in the Middle East has been going downhill in recent years, as the area has familiarized itself with Soviet tactics. When Soviet arms began flooding into Cairo, almost the whole Arab world proclaimed its "eternal gratitude." Russian popularity reached an emotional peak when Moscow diplomatically supported Nasser after Egypt was attacked in 1955 by France, Britain, and Israel, following its seizure of the Suez Canal. But Khrushchev's subsequent involvement in the communist effort to grab control of Iraq and the bitter public arguments with Nasser that resulted shook the Arab world; and Russia is now considered less a genuine friend than a counterforce to Western influence in the Middle East, a supporting diplomatic arm against Israel, and a source of considerable economic aid. And in pro-West Turkey and Iran, which border on Russia, the Soviet Union is both hated and feared.

Red China, which is recognized only by Egypt, Syria, Iraq, Yemen, and Israel, is liked even less by most Middle Eastern countries, having lost much prestige as the result of its repressive actions in Tibet and its naked aggression in India. Nor has Peking made great efforts to woo these nations, devoting most of its propaganda activities to Asia and Africa. For contrary to the situation in countries like Ghana, Guinea, and Indonesia, few regimes in the Middle East are tolerant toward domestic communism or even noncommunist Marxism, and most of them ruthlessly suppress such movements. Peking, except if there are overriding factors, does not believe in supporting actively anticommunist governments, even though they may be neutral in the Cold War. In the mid-1950's Mao warmed up to the United Arab Republic, as he did to India in that period of experimentation, but eventually turned against Nasser in favor of Iraq in 1958 when General Abdul Karim Kassim came to power and permitted communists to flourish. When Kassim eventually clamped down on the communists, his relations with Peking also began to cool. But Red Chinese policy has a certain flexibility in special cases.

YEMEN

Before medieval Yemen found itself in the throes of revolution in late 1962, Mao dealt with one of the most reactionary regimes in the world—one which mercilessly repressed the few Reds in that tiny country at the southwestern tip of Saudi Arabia. It is not clear at this writing what Yemen's future policy will be, for virtually since the death of Imam (King) Ahmad bin Yakya in September 1962 a civil war has raged between the forces of Imam Mohammed al-Badr, Ahmad's son, and those of General Abdullah Sallal. Sallal overthrew Badr several days after he succeeded to the throne and set up a republic. But Badr escaped from his besieged palace and made his way to Saudi Arabia, returning to lead a rebellion of several thousand Yemenite tribesmen against the republicans.

With Saudi Arabia and Jordan supporting Badr in a protective union of Middle Eastern monarchies, Egypt's Nasser, who was probably involved in Sallal's coup anyway, sent about 10,000 troops to Yemen in defense of the General's regime and spent some $20 million a week to supply it with Soviet jets, tanks, and other arms. Meanwhile, Sallal, with Nasser's support, proclaimed a new "Republic of the Arabian Peninsula," embracing almost forty kingdoms, sheikdoms, and sultanates near Aden, most of which are under British protection. He also threatened to invade Saudi Arabia; and indeed, the Egyptian navy and air force reportedly attacked Saudi territory.

Both sides claim they want reform in Yemen, which can boast only two high schools and three hospitals and has a one percent literacy rate and a sixty percent infant mortality rate. Badr, however, is probably thinking in terms of minor changes within the traditional system. For example, he has declared himself opposed to the unveiling of women. Sallal, on the other hand, appears to desire revolutionary reform on the Nasserite model. And his fervor has been nourished by ten years of imprisonment for plotting against the Ahmad regime, which he vowed to overthrow after training at a military academy in Iraq, where he had his first taste of twentieth-century life.

Sallal might be more immune to communist efforts at infiltration than Badr, for he is the pupil of Nasser, who has registered considerable success so far in taking Soviet handouts without permitting local Reds to establish a foothold in Egypt. Furthermore, by instituting large-scale reform, he will have taken the steam out of the social pressures that would inevitably feed the communist cause if the nation is not brought swiftly into the modern world from which it has been sealed off.

Conversely, Badr's limited reforms would probably be insufficient to satisfy the people, but enough to make them appreciate the utopia promised by communism. It is he who facilitated, as a prince, Yemen's first relations with Peking and also with Moscow. Mao granted relatively large amounts of economic and technical aid, complete with technicians, to Yemen, largely for a showcase highway from the Red Sea port of Hodeida to the capital of Sanaa, which a few months after completion was laced with cracks and potholes. Yemen's outdated regime posed no competitive threat to Peking, as Nasser, with his schemes of social reform, did. Sooner or later, Mao knew, there would be an explosion among the enchained people of Yemen, and when that time came, he wanted to have a foot in the door. And with considerable reason. Situated near the narrow gateway from the Red Sea to the Indian Ocean, Yemen is one of the most strategically important countries in the world. Catering to Yemen would be particularly wise, Mao no doubt felt, because of substantial efforts by Russia to extend its own influence there.

As an envoy of his autocratic father, Badr visited Moscow in 1957 and came away with promises of Soviet economic aid, as well as arms presumably for use in Yemen's border fight with the British over control of Britain's Aden protectorate on the Red Sea, which Yemen wishes to absorb. Russia completed its biggest project in early 1961—a port at the Red Sea town of Hodeida. More than 300 Soviet specialists worked at Hodeida for three years, equipping the port with modern docking and loading equipment, radio and electrical facilities, oil storage tanks, warehouses, cranes, and living quarters for the dock workers. The port, Soviet newspapers have said, is for the "freedom-loving people of Yemen," and would fulfill the Yemenite dream of overcoming their dependency upon British-controlled Aden.

When Sallal came to power, Russia was the first country to recognize his government. "Any act of aggression against Yemen," Khrushchev cabled, "will be considered an act of aggression against the Soviet Union."

Communist aid to Yemen, totaling more than $60 million from 1954 through 1960, has already yielded an important benefit to the Reds. In 1961 forty Yemenite students were enrolled in Russian, Czech, East German, and other bloc schools, giving the communists a golden opportunity to plant their first trained agents in secluded Yemen. Some of these students, however, as well as other Arab students, have complained about the conditions of study and life behind the Iron Curtain.

If it is difficult to predict whether Red China and Russia will be able to extend their toeholds in Yemen in the future, certainly they can be expected to take full advantage of the tragic confusion engulfing that unfortunate country—a confusion they had long known would come, offering new opportunities for subversive activity and infiltration.

The limited success of international communism in winning genuine, nonopportunistic Middle Eastern friends seems impressive compared to the generally feeble condition of local Reds, even though in some countries they have made important strides in recent years. Only in the tiny states of Israel and Cyprus is the true Communist Party legal, and even in Iraq, where the Reds were so powerful a few years ago, the government recognizes a rump Moscow-disowned Communist Party rather than the real one. It is estimated that all Middle Eastern communist parties together, legal and illegal, embrace little more than 15,000 members and followers.

The great majority of these communists are members of the intelligentsia, many of them frustrated students or college graduates who cannot find, or cannot expect to find, jobs commensurate with their education, often obtained only at great sacrifice and at the point of starvation. They want to revolutionize the society that has permitted such injustice, and they want to do it overnight —an achievement which only communism, they believe, can register. That communism suppresses individual liberty means even less to Middle Eastern than to Asian intellectuals. For in most Asian countries, elites have been exposed to Western philosophy since the last century under European colonial rule, while such exposure has been much more limited in the Middle East, most of which, until France and Britain moved in after World War I, was incorporated in the backward Turkish Ottoman Empire. Precisely for this same reason, not many liberal or democratic socialist parties existed in the region to which intellectuals can turn as an alternative to either communism or neo-feudalism.

Few workers, however, have been corralled. The small degree of industrialization in the Middle East has not yet produced a mass proletariat, while most governments brutally suppress communist tendencies in the budding trade unions. In Egypt workers have, to a great extent, been immunized against communist influence by the benefits and promised benefits of a militant Nasserite unionism. Communism has had an even harder time penetrating the Middle Eastern peasantry, which is traditionally loyal to either landlord or king, despite the fact that in most countries in the area the peasant earns little more than forty or fifty dollars a year and lives in a deplorable condition.

One obstacle to the development of communism in the Middle East has been Islam, which in varying degrees has a hold on most of the people of this region. The numerical insignificance of communists among them can be attributed in considerable degree to this hold. But to the extent that Islam, at least in its orthodox form, has lost its grip on the people, communism has made progress. An important reason why few peasants have proved easy targets for communism is that they cling to orthodoxy, in terms of both theology and practical custom, and still tend to be fatalistic and unreservedly obedient to powerful local priests, or *mullahs,* who often work closely with reactionary government authorities and feudal landlords. The Reds, though, have been making some headway among the workers, particularly in Iran and Iraq, as modern urban life and exposure to Western materialism gradually corrode their dependence on Islam as a guide for living.

The corrosion process, as might be expected, has made its greatest advance among the restless, embittered, Western-educated intellectuals and other members of the growing urban middle class, many of whom view orthodox Islam as a tool of the vested interests and an obstacle to social and economic progress. Hungry for new spiritual roots, some see in communism, or something akin to it, a substitute for their decaying faith—an ideology that can feed both the soul, the stomach, and, in supporting their anti-West attitudes, the ego. As far back as World War II, Leon Dennen, the noted foreign correspondent and authority on world communism, wrote in his book, *Trouble Zone:*

Every intellectual and middle-class Arab is compelled to live partly under Western influence; to speak Western languages and employ Western techniques. To bridge the gap between tradition and innovation, there is a search for a synthesis, a reconciliation of the Koran with Western and revolutionary ideas. Russia . . . seems outwardly to provide such a synthesis.

With the gradual disintegration of Islam as a pervasive answer to all problems, communism is pressing to replace its somewhat withering roots, or to enmesh itself with them. Many experts believe that Russia may provide a "synthesis" eventually. Charles Malik, a Christian Arab and former Lebanese Foreign Minister, once said: "I don't believe at all that Islam is a bulwark against communism any more than Greek Orthodoxy was in Russia. I don't believe it at all." A Syrian professor at the American University in Beirut, Lebanon, said to me in similar terms: "I know it is quite popular in the Arab world to say that communism can never get very far because the people are so staunchly Moslem. But why should Moslems be more immune to communism than, say, the Roman Catholics? Look how strong communism is in France and Italy, two Catholic countries. We haven't even got an administrative hierarchy like the Catholics to put pressure on believers not to follow communism. In fact, Moslem authorities are divided as to the compatibility of communism and Islam."

One Moslem authority who, at least a few years ago, found them compatible is the Mufti of Syria, Sheikh Abdul-Yusr Abdin. Among the many Moslem dignitaries given a conducted tour of Russia, the Mufti declared after returning from such a trip: "Forty million Moslems in the Soviet Union worship as they please. This is the greatest proof of the myth created by the imperialists about religious persecution there." As Richard P. Hunt of the *New York Times* wrote:

> From this statement, and from many others like it made by lesser lights, it is easy to see why there is confusion about communism in the minds of faithful Moslems. For the Koran, antedating Karl Marx as it does by 1200 years, contains no interdiction against communism as such. It calls upon all to believe that "there is no god but God, and Mohammed is His prophet." The believer must pray, fast, give alms and make a pilgrimage to Mecca. If the plain man of the Arab world is assured by his divines that these observances are permitted in the Soviet Union, it is not easy for him to see for himself just where communism and the Koran do conflict.

Many other Middle Eastern experts also believe that traditional Mohammedanism, rather than constituting a barrier to communism, fosters it. Both concepts, at least in theory, envisage a universal society founded on equality and social justice and produced by sudden, cataclysmic reform. Both faiths, too, in their orthodox form are often characterized by totalitarianism, missionary zeal, collectivism, fanaticism, economic statism, and intolerance of competitors.

The Soviet Union, which abortively began its campaign of subversion in the Middle East in the early 1920's with broadside condemnation of Islam, long ago realized that Islam should be used rather than condemned. Even before the war, Soviet experts began analyzing every verse and chapter in the Koran for possible use in supporting the compatibility of Marx and Mohammed, usually propagandizing such passages out of context. One verse, they delightedly found, says the hungry masses have the right to rise up against the rich and deprive them, by force if necessary, of the gold they have obtained through exploitation of the people. They also linked with communism a quotation from a Koranic chapter called *Zekat,* which orders the faithful to distribute each year some of their earnings among the poor. Still another useful passage says: "Take the hand of Islam as the true guide to social reform."

During the war, when Stalin wanted the support of the Moslem world, especially because of the considerable pro-Nazi sentiment among Arabs who thought Hitler would free them from French and British rule and help them prevent the Jews from taking over Palestine, the Soviet dictator opportunistically recognized his central Asian territories, where most of Russia's Moslems live, as "Moslem republics." And for the first time since the communist revolution he permitted, and even encouraged, Soviet Moslems to make pilgrimages to Mecca. The Soviet Union had the opportunity to appeal, through its Moslems, for *Jihad,* or Holy War, the fanatical battle cry that the Ottoman Turks had so successfully used against their enemies when they controlled most of the Middle East.

In June 1941 the Soviet Moslem chief, or Mufti, Abdurrahman Rasuleve, exhorted the Moslem world to "rise in defense of the fatherland against the enemy threatening destruction and misfortune to all Moslems, children, brothers and sisters of our religion. Organize religious services in houses of prayer and mosques and consecrate them to the victory of our army . . . Arise in defense of Islam. The Moslem people of the USSR will assist the Red Army wherever possible." Such appeals had a significant effect.

Egyptian moviegoers cheered whenever Stalin's picture was flashed on the screen, while young Arabs in Egypt, Syria, and Palestine organized societies of the Friends of the Soviet Union.

In 1944 the Kremlin set up near Tashkent a school of Islamic theology, or *medreseh,* where students from almost all the Middle Eastern Moslem countries, as well as Indonesia, have since followed up communist study in Moscow with postgraduate courses in how to sell communism by quoting the Koran. These students have had either to memorize the whole Koran or enough verses to earn the title of *hafiz,* a title of respect bestowed on those who know the Koran virtually by heart.

In the first phase of study at this institution, called the symbiosis of Marxism and Islam, students learn that the two faiths must initially collaborate in defeating their common enemy, the Western world. Only in the second phase, in which students are selected and trained for specific Moslem countries, is discussion permitted regarding the existence of God, or Allah, and the truth of the Islamic revelations as announced through the prophet Mohammed. The budding Red propagandist is now ready to learn how to expose, gradually and systematically, the "falsity" of the very concept of Allah.

Graduates from the Tashkent school are believed to be scattered in almost every Moslem state, and they don't need passports. Wearing turbans and carrying Korans, they are permitted to pass any Moslem frontier without the least trouble. They have infiltrated *medresehs,* Moslem monasteries, or *tekiyehs,* and Moslem political organizations. Furthermore, they are the best of all Moslem preachers. They speak with demagogic fervor and amaze their audiences with their knowledge of such varied subjects as current events, nuclear energy, and engineering. But they always return to the question of "social and economic justice," and without realizing it, listeners find themselves entranced with the doctrine of communism subtly and expertly disguised in Koranic language.

SAUDI ARABIA

Significantly, communism poses the least immediate danger, but may eventually explode with the greatest force, in the less developed and most traditionally Moslem areas of the Middle East where a middle class is virtually nonexistent and therefore intellectual thinking on social and economic problems is at a minimum. Yemen is one prime example. Saudi Arabia, also a relic of the

Middle Ages, is another. Though it is blessed with enormous oil wealth, most of the profits earned by King Ibn Saud, an absolute feudal monarch like the late Ahmad, are wasted on such luxuries as jewel-studded palaces and Cadillacs with special windows to permit the Sovereign's many wives and concubines to look out without anybody looking in. Slaves have been smuggled in from remote parts of Africa. Nobody complains, at least openly, for fear of losing his head or suffering some medieval torture. Isolated from the modern world, few Arabians have ever heard of communism, or could possibly understand it if they have, in view of the absence of secular education. The handful of communists there—primarily non-Saudi Arabs who engage in clandestine activity on a minor scale—are subject to ruthless punishment, as are all political oppositionists, if they are caught.

Relations between Saudi Arabia and the communist bloc were almost non-existent until September 1962, when two high Saudi officials visited the Soviet Union—apparently in a move to join in the old and highly lucrative Arab game of playing off East against West.

The East may profit to some degree from a revolutionary explosion in the country, as they might from the chaos in Yemen. And such an explosion is being carefully planned by Egypt's Nasser with his merciless attacks on Saud for his corruption and backwardness. The King has been so frightened that he sleeps in a different bedroom almost every night and uses Jordanian soldiers to guard him, distrusting his own. A number of his air force pilots have already defected to Egypt. Hoping to forestall revolution, Saud, in late 1962, abolished slavery and announced a program for free education and medical care. But such crumbs may only whet the appetite of his long exploited people.

If the most primitive states are the most resistant to immediate communist penetration, nations in the early stages of political, economic, and social development appear to be the most susceptible to Red subversion. For the masses have come to believe that they have been exploited by both the colonialists and their own feudal leaders, and have a right to a better life, yet are not politically mature enough to distinguish between communist promises and communist designs. This accounts for the Iraq communist scare in 1958, and explains why the situation in Iran today is so explosive. As for Egypt, which also falls into this category of states, only the competition of Nasser's "Arab socialism," the disunity of the Egyptian Communist Party, and governmental suppression have so far prevented Egyptian communists from achieving much success.

JORDAN

Jordan was seriously threatened by communism a few years ago, and this threat could snowball again should this small arid country be gripped again by one of its recurrent political crises. The Jordan Communist Party, which is outlawed, has only about two hundred members, but can boast of fifteen hundred to two thousand active supporters. The hard-core supporters are mainly Palestinians—students and members of the small intelligentsia, some Christians, and a small labor wing that had been developed in Palestine before the creation of Israel. The party also has important influence among other elements of the 800,000 Palestine Arabs, about half of whom are refugees from Israeli territory, who added their numbers to the country's original 450,000 inhabitants when the part of Palestine not incorporated into Israel was annexed by Jordan in 1949.

In addition to seething with hatred for the Israelis, most Palestinians, far more sophisticated and educated—as a result of their past association with the highly advanced Jews—than the original Jordanians, mainly Bedouins, despise their new compatriots. They belittle the "inferior" culture of the Bedouins and resent them for largely monopolizing key positions in the government, army, and police despite their smaller numbers. This disdain is projected in their unrelenting opposition to young King Hussein, whose principal support comes from the Bedouins. Their hostility is fed by bitterly anti-Hussein propaganda emanating from Nasser's Egypt, which accuses the King of kowtowing to the Western Powers—meaning that he refuses to kowtow to Nasserite pan-Arabism.

Palestinian communists started preparing for a Red takeover of Jordan shortly after Arab Palestine's integration into the country. They made no initial effort to obtain mass support but formed small, hard-core cadres among the embittered intelligentsia, and established cells in secondary schools. Party propaganda attacked Hussein's regime as feudalistic and demanded reforms—ignoring the fact that some reforms had already been instituted. The party cleverly maneuvered several political groups into the formation of a communist-dominated National Front called the Al Jabha al Wataniyya, which won the support of three members of parliament and even a feudal landowner, and published four weekly periodicals. Though the government refused to recognize the front, it won several seats in parliament in 1954. But government attempts to suppress its campaign activities produced student riots that resulted in the burning of the United States Information Service and the death of twelve people. As the riots spread under communist and Nasserite instigation, and the army reacted with harsh suppressive measures, many noncommunist opposition groups co-operated with the Reds.

The communists started concentrating on establishing cells in the British-officered Arab Legion, the Jordan army, and winning over noncommissioned officers in particular. By 1956 not only was the Communist Party, acting through the front, amply represented in parliament, but one of its members was a cabinet minister. The Reds now tried to win control of the pro-Nasser nationalist movement.

In January 1957, with a communist-nationalist coup in the making, King Hussein decided to act. His first step was to send a note to Prime Minister Sulaiman Nabulsi demanding that a new communist newspaper that had begun to appear, as well as eleven other Red-inspired publications, be immediately banned. When Nabulsi ignored the order, the King, influenced by the strength of the combined anti-Hussein forces, courageously played his ace. Though uncertain of the army's loyalty, he used the Premier's disobedience as a pretext for ousting the government, dissolving parliament, and purging the Arab Legion of procommunist and pro-Nasser officers. The coup worked, and Red leaders who had not escaped to Syria were rounded up and jailed. This success was due in considerable measure to a fatal communist error. By trying to grab control of the Nasserite movement, the Reds split the anti-Hussein forces, permitting the King's supporters to come out on top.

Since the coup, the struggle between nationalists and communists in Iraq and Nasser's strong condemnation of communism have intensified the rift between Jordanian nationalists and Reds. Periodic police roundups have kept the party on the defensive. And the possibility, if not the likelihood, that Israel, for security reasons, might seek to take over part of Jordan if an extremist government replaces Hussein's moderate regime has given both communists and Nasserites pause to consider the wisdom of a new move against the King. In any event, Moscow would probably find a communist Jordan, completely isolated from the Red heartland, of even less value at this time than a communist Iraq, which it did not seem to be anxious to set up even while the tide was running with the Reds in that country in 1958-59. But the Jordan communists could make a comeback at the propitious moment, for with unbounded hatred and dissatisfaction to exploit, they have the capacity for rapid regrowth—though this capacity may gradually diminish as the result of serious efforts by Hussein to institute social and economic reforms.

SYRIA

Syria, which shares Jordan's northern border, has been even more seriously threatened by the communists in recent years. Though they do not appear to constitute a danger at the moment, they probably have an even greater capacity for resurgence than their Jordanian counterparts. The Syrian Reds, who number about fifteen hundred, mainly intellectuals, share a single party with the communists of Lebanon. Almost since its creation in 1930, it has been the strongest and best organized of all Middle Eastern communist parties, long serving as a kind of mother organization for the others and their principal liaison link with Moscow. The most militant and most durable Red leaders in the region are Syrians who began their political careers in the early 1930's under French colonialism. The top party leader, Khalid Bakdash, a lawyer like more than half the members of the leadership echelon, is probably the most able, and certainly the best-trained and best-known of the Middle Eastern Reds.

Bakdash and some of his cronies, unlike most regional communist chiefs, have had years of intensive training in Moscow. When they first took over their party—Bakdash became Secretary-General in 1937—they had tough sledding due to Stalin's rigid requirements that the organization had to be proletarian in nature and that it propagandize against Islam. Things went better shortly before World War II, when the Kremlin switched to the popular front vogue—so much better that the French banned the party in 1939. A year later the Vichy regime came to power in France and its possessions. Bakdash was arrested, with more than a score of his colleagues, and given five years in prison. Liberated by the Allies, Bakdash, after the free French government granted Syria independence in 1945, began preparing for elections that were to be held two years later. He stunned observers by polling the largest communist vote in Middle Eastern history in Damascus, barely missing election to parliament.

The frightened Syrian leaders confirmed the illegality of the Communist Party in 1948, but an apparent tacit agreement with the government in the next few years permitted the Reds to operate without hindrance except when their propaganda attacked the regime with excessive violence. While there existed standing orders for Bakdash's arrest, he constantly—and openly—commuted between Syria and communist countries. One reason for this tolerance was Moscow's success in cultivating the friendship of the Syrian dictator, Colonel Adib Shishakli, a Nasser-style reformist. The fact that Nasser was jailing communists and being condemned as a "ruthless reactionary" during this same period, underscores the possibility that there was some kind of understanding between Russia and the Shishakli regime. The key to it perhaps resided in Syria's extreme bitterness toward Israel, which was—and probably still is—greater than that in any other Arab country. With the West usually supporting Israel, Shishakli looked toward Russia as an ally in the United Nations and other world councils.

When during an interview in Damascus in 1952 I asked Shishakli, a man of charm but of explosive temperament, about his attitude toward Russia, the muscles in his face grew taut, and he shouted: "I don't know about Russia, but I do know about the United States. It is helping Israel, our bitter enemy. How can we love a country that helps our enemy?"

With the overthrow of the Shishakli government in February 1954 by his enemies and the return to parliamentary government, the communists found themselves in an enviable position. Shishakli had banned all political parties but had permitted the communists to retain their cadres and continue with their activities even in conditions of illegality. When the government succeeding Shishakli lifted the ban, only the communists emerged into the open with their organization and program intact. In elections held in September 1954, Khalid Bakdash made up for his close defeat a few years earlier and became the first communist ever to win a seat in an Arab parliament, a victory that one Damascus newspaper described as "the most important event in the Middle East in the twentieth century." Communists also polled large votes in other cities such as Homs and Gezira, and were defeated in some places only because of the formation of noncommunist coalitions. Khaled al Azm, a fellow traveler, and many of his followers captured an important bloc of seats. The Reds also found a willing ally in a new Ba'ath Party, a vaguely socialist and violently anti-West organization which greatly influenced the army officer corps. Conservative politicians held a parliamentary majority, but they were all but silenced by the leftist minority backed by key elements in the army. The time was ripe for the Soviet Union, whose policy now called for Red co-operation with the national bourgeoisie, to move in at full speed.

Moscow launched the biggest cultural and economic offensives it had attempted to date. Delegations of students, doctors, scientists, farmers, and religious dignitaries swarmed in and out of both countries, and one group of Syrian Moslems returned from Moscow raving about the "spiritual freedom" in Russia. Soviet film festivals and commercial fairs drew huge Syrian crowds. Russian propaganda played up to nationalist sentiment, condemning Israeli "aggression," Western "imperialism," and Turkish "designs" on Syrian territory. Soviet arms started pouring in, reaching a peak flow during the Suez crisis in late 1956. Economic aid followed. Between 1954 and 1960 communist military aid amounted to about $130 million and economic assistance to $180 million, most of this granted by 1957.

In 1956 a communist-led national front emerged—a "union of all the forces of the country against imperialism, and for the co-operation of the Arab states in the field of economic development." Intellectual popular front organizations mushroomed, including students' and teachers' groups, a Lawyers' Association, and an Arab Writers' Congress. All three Syrian trade-union confederations fell under communist control. Reds had infiltrated the army, the police, and other political parties. Conservative and pro-West leaders, accused of trying to overthrow the government, were purged or imprisoned, though not a critical word could be spoken about the Soviet Union. In mid-1957 a Red coup looked near when the moderate Syrian army commander Tawfiq Nizam ad-Din was replaced by a communist sympathizer, Colonel Affif al Bizri, and the Syrian government, charging an American conspiracy to oust the government, threw four United States diplomats out of the country.

Syria had been pushed to the brink of communism. The economic factor could not have been strong, for Syria during this period was in the middle of its biggest postwar boom. Salaries were higher than in most Arab countries, and the peasants were far less in need of land reform. Opportunism on the part of many politicians was a more important reason. The influential communist sympathizer, Khaled al Azm, was a multimillionaire capitalist; but he wanted revenge on his political enemies who had kept him out of the presidency or premiership, and the financial advantages that came with a side job as representative of several Soviet economic agencies.

Intellectuals and army officers were deeply impressed with

Soviet industrial dynamism and fed up with the instability and inefficiency of the noncommunist political parties. The whole population felt a sense of satisfaction in defying the West that was aiding Israel and trying to maintain a colonial foothold in the Middle East, as "demonstrated" by the Suez invasion. Khalid Bakdash, who a few years before had described the nationalist movement as a "tool of the imperialists," now told parliament that Syria was and would remain "Arab nationalist and nothing else in addition." Even so fanatical a nationalist as Colonel Abdel Hamid Serraj, a ruthless intelligence officer who had helped to overthrow Shishakli and had become second in command to Colonel Affif al Bizri, though he was believed to be the real power in Syria, seemed to have swallowed this propaganda and thrown his weight behind the Reds. The least significant factor in Syria's leftward swing—the first time a nation had moved willingly, and in fact, with ardor, toward the Soviet orbit—was ideology.

Whatever the reasons, so swiftly did the communist influence grow that even Moscow became uneasy. It had wanted to infiltrate and influence Syria, yes, but to take over the country at this time was another thing. In winning Syria, it could lose the rest of the Middle East, which, in fright, might become hostile. And it could not help to prevent the overthrow of a communist government in the future in view of the lack of a land bridge between Syria and Russia. Therefore, the Kremlin counseled the Syrian communists, as it was to caution the Iraqi Reds a year or so later, to slow down their drive for power.

The Russians were not mistaken in their fear that haste would make political waste. For with Syria tottering on the edge of communism, some noncommunist collaborators with the Reds began to grow alarmed for the first time. It looked as though nothing could head off Syria's rush into the communist camp, including, ironically, Soviet advice to the local Reds—nothing, that is, except one desperate measure. With the support of the socialist Ba'ath Party, Colonel Serraj went to Cairo in October 1957 and had a secret talk with President Nasser. In February 1958 Egypt and Syria merged to form the United Arab Republic.

The communists were caught flatfooted. Overnight, all their gains vanished in a pan-Arab nationalist sea. The Syrians lost their enthusiasm for communism, which they had never embraced as an ideology anyway, with the same incredible speed with which they had welcomed it. The Communist Party itself was faced with obliteration, at least as a legal organization. For Nasser ordered the dissolution of all Syrian political parties, including the communists, in line with his policy in Egypt. No communist party had ever voluntarily dissolved itself, Bakdash brashly replied, and thereupon went underground. Within a year after the union, the UAR government claimed that every Communist Party member in Syria was either under arrest or being sought, and Bakdash was demanding from abroad the breakup of the UAR.

His wish was eventually granted. In September 1961 Syrian military officers who were resentful of the subordinate roles given them in the UAR army, supported by Syrian businessmen dissatisfied with Nasser's nationalization and other economic policies, revolted against Cairo's rule and split Syria off from the UAR. The Soviet Union immediately recognized its independence, and Bakdash called from exile in Moscow for the creation of a National Democratic Front. He also asked the new Syrian leaders to permit him to return to Syria, promising to put down "any reactionary or imperialist plot." But Syria had changed since it was last independent. Bakdash was told that he would be welcomed back—by policemen with an order for his arrest. Nasser's ban on communism remained in force.

The Red danger in Syria, however, has by no means been wiped out. For just as communism fed on political instability and ineffective rule in the past, it may well feed on it in the future. Only six months after the coup that regained for Syria its independence, other officers overthrew the conservative civilian government in power because it went too far in undoing some of Nasser's reforms, in particular, returning to dispossessed landlords land that had been distributed to the peasants. Syria would revert to Nasser's "Arab socialism," ordered the officers, but without Nasser. Not all officers agreed. Some, particularly in the northern town of Aleppo, wanted to join the UAR again, and tried to rebel against the others. This rebellion ended only after all parties decided to consider a closer relationship with Nasser. Instability once more has gripped Syria—to the communists' delight.

The Reds have also been cheered by the recent dispatch of a Syrian mission to Prague and Moscow to discuss aid for such development projects as railroads, oil prospecting, and construction of a fertilizer plant. Since the Syrian armed forces had been supplied when they were part of the UAR forces with communist equipment, the country is today dependent on the communist bloc for replacements and many kinds of training. More important, the Syrian Red movement, though outlawed, is still fairly well united and operating from Lebanon. And what was almost won once could possibly be won in a second try.

LEBANON

The most advanced countries in the Middle East may be the least likely to go communist in the long run, and certainly the least likely to be the victims of a Red coup or spontaneous uprising, despite their large middle and proletarian classes. This is due in part to their relative political maturity, which tends to make them shun extremism, but also to their special strategic, historical, and demographic circumstances.

In Lebanon, the most highly developed of the Arab states, the Communist Party, which Bakdash also heads, was, as in Syria, first outlawed in 1939 by the French mandatory regime. This proscription was confirmed by the Lebanese government in 1948. But the party is only technically illegal. Though under careful police surveillance, it is relatively free to operate. Nevertheless, it has managed to attract less than one thousand Lebanese, and has influence only among labor groups, Armenian minority elements, and some students, who use Beirut's American University as a rallying center.

Actually, it is not the principal function of the party to win over the Lebanese. Rather it is mainly concerned with maintaining Beirut as a liaison command post for the whole Middle East communist network—the city's traditional role. As far back as the 1930's the Communist Parties of Palestine, Egypt, and Iraq looked to Beirut party headquarters to settle internal quarrels. Though there was no effective contact between Beirut and Moscow from 1938 and 1944, the Lebanese capital became Russia's main channel for infiltration throughout the region in 1945. Today the party in Beirut, it is believed, has direct connections with a party high command for the Middle East in Milan, Italy, or Sofia, Bulgaria.

Lebanon makes an ideal regional headquarters for the Reds because the government is lax in regulating communist activity and traffic, and also because this little nation is easily accessible to Syria, Jordan, and other areas where communism is strictly suppressed. In addition, false passports are believed available for party travelers, as are facilities for the publication and distribution of Red propaganda, including a printing plant in Beirut—the an-Najah Press. Lebanon's importance as a communist center increased after Syria and Egypt formed the United Arab Republic and Nasser began suppressing the Syrian communists, for Beirut became headquarters for the Syrian as well as the Lebanese Reds.

But for all the Red activity in Lebanon, the Lebanese people themselves have not been attracted to the party. Local communists noisily tried to win friends between 1948 and 1952 with rallies, demonstrations, and leaflets, and were the most potent political force in Lebanon during that period, but this campaign soon wilted for lack of public interest and the Reds have been relatively quiet ever since. In early 1958 Bakdash returned to Beirut from Moscow with orders to launch a new militant campaign against the government of pro-Western Camille Chamoun. But the feebleness of pro-communist sentiment was reflected in this effort. Although many other Lebanese also wanted the ouster of Chamoun, who was, in fact, forced to resign after he had called in American troops to put down a Nasserite armed revolt against him, his noncommunist Lebanese opponents would not co-operate with the communists.

But the Reds are nevertheless actively propagandizing among the Lebanese. About a dozen communist and procommunist publications are freely distributed, including the daily *An-Nida,* with about 2,000 circulation, and the weekly *al-Akhbar,* which are the principal communist voices on the Arab Mediterranean. At least two Beirut bookstores serve as outlets for propaganda. More than half a dozen youth, labor, and cultural front organizations are also functioning.

The communist bloc is not ignoring Lebanon as a target for propaganda, either. The Soviet Embassy in Beirut publishes a regular Tass bulletin, though this material is used regularly only by the communist press, and also prints special releases and a weekly magazine, *Soviet News,* in Arabic. Lebanese television has been using increasing amounts of communist-bloc movies, with subtitles or lip synchronization in Arabic, French, or English. Russia has an agreement with a 500-seat theater in downtown Beirut to show Soviet films exclusively. A number of Lebanese students are studying in Czechoslovakia. In 1960 the bloc held three cultural exhibitions in Lebanon, while five delegations were exchanged with the USSR alone.

Occasionally, the Lebanese government has cracked down on communist propaganda activities, particularly as a result of Nasser's crusade against Arab communism. One communist newspaper was temporarily suspended, and a number of foreign Arab communists have been deported. In 1960, when the Soviet Embassy issued a special release quoting a *Pravda* article that implied criticism of the Lebanese government for permitting the United States Sixth Fleet to use Beirut harbor, the government informed the Soviet Ambassador that the distribution was considered an unfriendly gesture. A Soviet film about Russian astronaut Gagarin was banned by Lebanese censors in 1961 because of its heavy propaganda content. Soccer league authorities suspended the soccer team of the Racing Club of Beirut in 1960 for the remainder of the season following an unauthorized trip by the team to Communist China. But such minor control measures have not greatly disrupted communist efforts at subversion.

Curiously, the explanation for this laxness, as well as the explanation for the failure of the communists to make much headway in Lebanon despite these activities, stems largely from the same root. Lebanon, ancient home of the sea-faring Phoenicians, has a divided population, split almost evenly between Moslems and Christians, and the Christians are splintered into various sects and ethnic minorities. Though all the Moslems and most of the Christians are Arabs, the two religious groups feel little in common with each other. The Moslems seek close ties with the other Arab states, and most favor the pan-Arabism of Nasser. The Christians, mostly Maronites, who are far more educated and, in general, enjoy higher living standards than the Moslems, feel greater affinity for the West, and fear their eventual absorption into a pan-Arab Moslem world. Although internal politics played an important role, the question of whether Lebanon should tighten its ties with Nasser's United Arab Republic produced bitter fighting in 1958, which ended only with intervention of American troops. The Moslems wanted closer bonds with the UAR, and the Christians, led by President Chamoun, did not. When the conflict exploded into violence, Chamoun requested the landing of United States forces.

During the American occupation of Beirut, Pierre Gemayel, a tall, lean man with fiery eyes and deep lines in his face, who leads the fanatically Christian Falange Party that did much of the fighting against the Moslems, told me: "We want the American forces to stay until Nasser fully recognizes Lebanon as an independent state. Lebanon has a Western society. We must lean toward the West." Conversely, the Moslem rebel leader, pudgy Saleh Salem, whose followers specialized in exploding bombs in crowded streetcars, said in his headquarters deep in the barricaded, barbed-wire-enclosed Moslem quarter of Beirut that "Lebanon is part of the Arab world and we must not forget that"—a statement that was pointed up by the sight of Nasser's picture plastered all over the rebel-controlled area. Aging, heavy-set Sami Sohl, an anti-Nasser Moslem who was Prime Minister under Chamoun, ominously summed up the danger that threatened Lebanon when he said between nervous puffs on his long rubber-stemmed water pipe in the garden of his heavily guarded home: "Once the Americans leave, there could be a massacre involving the whole population. This isn't an empty warning. It could happen very easily."

But the American forces were withdrawn a few months after they had landed, and peace settled over Lebanon. General Fuad Chehab, a Christian, who had been commander of the Lebanese armed forces, took over the presidency, and terrorist Saleh Salem himself eventually became his premier. The new government settled communal differences by adopting a neutralist foreign policy, which would keep Lebanon out of any Western project, and by agreeing to steer equally clear of any pan-Arab movement. Every Lebanese breathed more easily, wondering how long Lebanon could walk its communal tightrope.

But the need to continue walking it has fostered the closest thing to Western democracy in the Arab world. The manner in which General Chehab rose to political power was a study in Arab political unorthodoxy. Military heads of state are, of course, no novelty in the Middle East, but usually they achieve their positions by a *coup d'état*. Chehab, in contrast, reached his by peaceful parliamentary means. Bitter though the civil conflict had been, the country in the end resorted to democratic methods in seeking to resolve it; and Chehab himself, more than anyone else, made the maintenance of democracy possible. When he headed the armed forces under Chamoun, many people criticized him for refusing to use the army to put down the Moslem revolt. But Chehab realized that if the army were ordered to take sides, it, like the country itself, would have split into two sectarian parts, and the "holy war" so feared by Sami Sohl might be set off.

He therefore kept the army out of the conflict, except for a display of power by tanks on the streets of Beirut as a symbolic reminder to both sides who had ultimate power, leaving it to terrorists and private political armies to fight it out on a minor scale. He also urged the American troops who had come at Chamoun's behest, despite the General's opposition, to limit their area of occupation to the beaches of Beirut and refrain from intervening in the struggle. About the only United States soldiers on duty in town were the military police who, with undue dedication, marched from whorehouse to whorehouse in the gaudy off-limits red-light district of Beirut, breaking into rooms and peeping under beds in search of G.I.'s who found the sinful temptations of this traditional Arab playground irresistible.

Violence continued even after the arrival of the United States forces, though it was clear that their very presence precluded the possibility of a decisive military victory by either side. On one occasion, I was about to deliver a radio broadcast to the United States from the Beirut telegraph office, when a bomb exploded in a washroom in the building, giving me a fresh lead for my story. Another time I got caught in the middle of an exchange of firing. To keep from getting hit, I had to dodge into doorways, one of which I shared with an attractive, olive-skinned girl who suggested that I sit out, or rather, lie out, the battle in the brothel upstairs. But aside from such sporadic violence, the nature of the civil war was very circumscribed as the result of Chehab's calculated aloofness. This permitted a relatively rapid return to peace and parliamentary rule —the only alternatives to catastrophe in a nation over which no single leader or group could possibly gain full control, as Chamoun, who had tended to assume too much authority, had sadly learned.

This pressure toward democracy does not, however, preclude the possibility of military rule imposed for nonsectarian purposes. In December 1961 the army angrily bared its teeth when a comic-opera revolt staged by the fanatical Greater Syria Party, which demands a union of Lebanon, Syria, and Iraq, caught army leaders with their pajamas on. Although the rebellion was crushed, the army was placed in a ridiculous light, making all Lebanese soldiers forget for the moment whether they were Christians or Moslems. Determined to regain face, the military went to extremes to catch the plotters, arresting more than four thousand persons on the flimsiest pretexts while the civilian government remained helpless to do anything about such excesses. But if a political or religious question had been at issue, threatening to split the army, it is unlikely that the military would have acted decisively.

This spirit of tolerance has benefited the communists no less than other political groups. Though most Moslems and Christians alike strongly oppose communism, they are reluctant to suppress it for fear of creating a disturbing precedent. If the government completely throttled communist activity, Falange or Nasserite activity could be the next target. Then the fuse to the Lebanese powder keg might start sputtering again. But though the Reds are largely free to carry on their subversive work, they have found the Lebanese among the hardest of all Middle Eastern peoples to subvert. For the very heterogeneous and mutually antagonistic nature of the population that has made their freedom possible has proved an obstacle to their success. The primary loyalty of the Lebanese is to his religious or ethnic group, not to any national political organization unrepresentative of that particular group's interest. Except for some trade unions in which religious and clan loyalties have become blurred, communism, a national and international movement, of course, has not yet been able to attract much public attention— although it did make headlines, if in a derogatory way, when Nasser condemned it as a treasonous doctrine.

ISRAEL

Communism is even more handicapped in Israel, which is by far the most advanced state—socially, politically, and economically— in the Middle East. A moderately socialist state with strong democratic roots, Israel has a legal Communist Party with three seats in the Knesset, or parliament, and about two thousand members, including twelve hundred Jews and eight hundred Arabs. It also has the extremely left-wing socialist Mapam Party which ranks as the fourth-largest party in the Knesset, but has no links with the communist bloc. Ten communist-front organizations freely operate and fifteen Red newspapers and periodicals pour out the party line.

But the Reds can make virtually no headway in view of their opposition to Zionism and popular Prime Minister David Ben-Gurion, and their support of Soviet and Arab policies. Unlike communists in most other countries, the Israeli Reds, to remain in harmony with Moscow, must fight rather than ride the nationalist tide. They must advocate, in fact, the destruction of Israel and its conversion into a biracial Arab-Jewish state, which would include the 900,000 Palestine Arab refugees who fled into neighboring Arab countries during the 1948 Arab-Jewish war that resulted in the creation of Israel. These refugees had been ordered to do so by Arab leaders with the promise that they would return when the Jews were driven into the sea—an event, of course, that did not materialize. The minimum communist demand, like that of the Arabs, is the acceptance of the original United Nations Palestine partition plan, under which the great Negev desert, incorporated into Israel as a result of the war, was to be part of the Arab sector of Palestine that, minus the Negev, was ultimately absorbed by Jordan.

Within the party itself, only a small, hard-core leadership, composed mainly of Jewish settlers who migrated to Palestine in the 1920's and 1930's, are ideological communists. Outside the party there are probably some doctrinaire Red agents who entered Israel with other refugees from the communist states of Bulgaria, Poland, and Rumania. Most Jewish party members are also immigrants from those three countries, as well as from Iraq, but have become "communists" mainly in protest against the difficulties they have encountered in their integration into the state, which has more than doubled its population since its creation as the result of unrestricted Jewish immigration. Many newcomers drop out of the party as their living conditions improve.

Arab communist strength is centered in Nazareth and represents, almost totally, a protest against the establishment of the state of Israel. Even this strength has diminished as a result of Nasser's condemnation of communism. As for the Mapam Party, it can be distinguished from the Communist Party mainly by its pro-Zionist attitude and its rejection of the use of force to attain power. If it ever came to power it might well establish a kind of national communism, but one which would be unaffiliated with, if not antagonistic to, the Sino-Soviet bloc.

The Israeli communists, ironically, were at the peak of their popularity when Israel was born, for despite their traditional anti-Zionist outlook, they supported the state's creation because Moscow at that time did so, if largely in the hope of getting British colonial troops out of Palestine. But once the British had departed, the Soviet mood changed. Not only was there no longer need to back Israel, but its establishment had given birth to "treasonable" agitation among the three million Jews in the Soviet Union for migration to the new state, a development that produced an anti-Semitic campaign, including accusations that several Jewish doctors had tried to poison Stalin. Also, it was time to start wooing the Arabs, who had been neglected since World War II, and the best way to do this was to turn on Israel. When the Israeli Reds slavishly followed this line, public regard for them quickly plummeted.

TURKEY

Turkey is another country that is more advanced politically, socially, and economically than most Middle Eastern states. But it is still an underdeveloped state, especially in the social sense, and the masses are dissatisfied with its present rate of progress. In particular the peasants, though enjoying living standards far higher than those of their brothers in Iran and the Arab states, are clamoring, with considerable justification, for land reform. But despite the discontent, communism can make virtually no headway in Turkey.

If Turkish awareness of the meaning of communism is a contributing factor to this failure, a more important element is Turkey's strategic position, which in turn has shaped a tempestuous historical relationship with Russia. Turkey straddles the Dardanelles and Bosporus Straits which connect the Black Sea with the Mediterranean. Russia, sharing a short strip of Turkey's eastern border and separated from Turkey's long northern frontier by the Black Sea, covets these straits, of course. From the seventeenth century to the end of World War I, when Turkey was the center of the great Ottoman Empire, the Turks fought Russia in thirteen major wars. Shortly after World War II the Soviet government, following in the path of its Czarist predecessors, also exerted pressure on Turkey to yield control of the straits as well as the Kars-Ardahan area of northeastern Turkey, but this effort was frustrated by stiff Turkish defiance backed by the United States. Russia, realizing that any new attempt to take over the straits could, if pressed, set off World War III, particularly in view of Turkey's membership in the North Atlantic Treaty Organization and the Central Treaty Organization, has since "admitted" that it made a mistake in pushing its demands, but this has not reduced Turkey's fear and hatred of its traditional enemy.

In Istanbul, a magnificent relic of the glorious Ottoman Empire, with its golden bulb-steepled mosques, its glittering imperial monuments, and its mysterious winding alleys, a young professor dressed in Western clothes like most urban Turks, observed: "Communism might have taken hold here if it had originated in the West. But it has been introduced by the Russians, and is therefore looked upon as simply a modern Russian instrument for achieving an old Russian goal."

The nation's Communist Party, founded in 1920 as the Angora Communist Party, was banned in 1922. Except for brief periods in 1946 and 1950, when it was permitted to operate openly, the party, as well as most other left-wing movements, has been suppressed. A clandestine party is estimated to embrace from 2,000 to 3,000 members, mostly urban intellectual and white-collar elements, but only 200 or 300 are believed hard-core members. The party was all but eliminated in 1953 when 131 of its members were convicted and jailed. The best-known Turkish communist leader is Nazim Hikmet, a poet who fled Turkey in 1951 and now broadcasts from the Soviet Union, but his influence is less political than literary. The main potential Red threat in Turkey comes from the Turkish Kurds in the eastern part of the country, who constitute about ten percent of the population and, like their brethren in Iran and Iraq, want to establish an independent Kurdistan—a project that Russia has long sponsored as a means of fostering chaos in the Western-influenced Middle Eastern heartland.

Mustafa Kemal, popularly known as Atatürk, who was the founder of modern Turkey, set the pattern for relations with the

Soviet Union during his rule from 1923 to 1938. Although he temporarily collaborated with the USSR and accepted Soviet aid in the
early stages of the Republic, he did not hesitate to suppress domestic communism. Successive governments have also tried to maintain
friendly relations with Russia, while seeking Western ties to balance Soviet pressures and keeping communism underground. Actually, Atatürk did more than suppress communists. He demolished
the appeal of their revolutionary platform by instituting a fantastic
revolution of his own that swept away medievalism, westernized
the country, even to the point of introducing the Latin alphabet,
built up industry, pushed through dozens of social and economic
reforms, and, most startling of all, considering that he was a dictator, cultivated a political opposition which, after his death, was
voted into power.

Recent events in Turkey have indicated that Atatürk's job is not
entirely done. Aside from the need for increased economic development and more agrarian reforms, democracy has taken a beating
on two accounts. On the one hand, the government of President
Bayar and Prime Minister Menderes, which ruled from 1950 to
1960, grew corrupt and repressive; on the other, it was ousted from
power not by the electorate but by a military junta that tried the
leaders as criminals and hanged some of them, including Menderes.
The junta has since permitted the political opposition to take over
the government but is closely supervising its direction. Nevertheless, the willingness of the militarists to step into the background
indicates the existence of at least the beginnings of a democratic
tradition—something rare in the Afro-Asian world, and a factor
that will not make it any easier for the communists to penetrate
Turkey.

CYPRUS

One relatively advanced Middle Eastern state, the island of Cyprus, is perhaps menaced more seriously than any country in the
area—and in a unique way. If communism takes over this east
Mediterranean island, its victory is likely to come through the
democratic process, for the Communist Party is believed to be supported by about thirty-five percent of the 600,000 Greeks and
Turks who make up the state's population, and this proportion,
observers say, is gradually increasing. Up to now, the only independent state to vote communism into power has been the tiny
European territory of San Marino.

At present the Communist Party of Cyprus, functioning under

the name of Reform Party of the Working People (AKEL), has five seats in the fifty-member unicameral legislature, and three seats in the Greek Communal Chamber (separate Communal Chambers are elected by Greek and Turkish Cypriots). Communist mayors run the leading towns of Famagusta and Limassol, the latter electing a communist vice-mayor as well, and a fellow traveler administers Larnaca.

The party itself has about 5,000 or 6,000 members, a very large number by Middle Eastern standards, but not indicative of the true influence of communism on the country. The communists operate youth, women's, and farmers' groups. Most important of all, they control the Pan-Cyprian Confederation of Labor (PEO), which has about 40,000 members, more than half the union membership on the island. In 1955 the British, who ran Cyprus before it became independent in 1960, banned AKEL and all its affiliate groups except PEO, and imprisoned many communist leaders. However, these Reds were eventually released, and the party was declared legal just prior to independence.

Support of communism is confined almost entirely to the Greek community, which comprises about eighty percent of the Cypriot population. Turks, who make up most of the Cypriot peasantry, are little attracted by the Red movement because of its domination by the Greeks and the traditional Turkish distrust of anything Russian in origin. Even so, the Reds are believed to be winning the support of some Turkish peasants.

The communist danger in Cyprus may eventually produce the West's most serious crisis in the Middle East. This highly strategic island controls the shipping lanes in the eastern Mediterranean and, though nominally neutralist, serves as a launching site for Western "fire brigade" forces needed to fulfill obligations of the North Atlantic Treaty Organization and the Central Treaty Organization. Britain maintains military bases and the United States has important psychological warfare installations on the islands. If the communists gain much more influence, and certainly if they win control of the government democratically, the pressure for Western military evacuation may be irresistible.

But even if the West could afford to give up the island as a defense bastion, a communist-controlled Cyprus might well become the scene of a war between Greece and Turkey, dangerously disrupting the eastern flank of NATO, to which both countries belong. Anticommunism is preached in unison by Greek and Turkish Ambassadors in Cyprus and the commanders of small military detachments of the two nations stationed here as well as by Greek Orthodox Archbishop Makarios, the bearded, black-robed President of Cyprus, and the island's Turkish leaders. If the Greek Reds took over the island, however, relations between Greece and Turkey, precarious even now, might well reach the breaking point. For Turkey, only forty miles north of Cyprus, is not likely to let this island fall into communist hands without a fight, because of security considerations and because it feels responsible for the protection of Cyprus' Turkish minority. Turkish intervention would almost certainly bring Greek troops in, not to protect the communists as such, but to defend Greeks against Turkish attacks.

The possibility of the Reds coming to power by democratic means is consistent with the strange, unorthodox development of the Cyprus Communist Party, which has fed on circumstances comparable to those existing in no other state. These circumstances were rooted in an old Greek dream—*enosis,* or union of Greece and Cyprus. Since the days of Ottoman rule, the Greek Cypriot community has been led by a so-called Ethnarchy, an elected ruling council of the Greek Orthodox Church, consisting of the Ethnarch, or Archbishop, and several bishops. The Ethnarchy began demanding *enosis* when the British first arrived on the island in 1878. After World War II, under Archbishop Makarios, who was to become Cyprus' first President, it sought to accomplish this end by every possible means, including terror spread by a secret organization called EOKA.

The British constituted one EOKA target. The Turkish community, which has always been loyal to Turkey and bitterly refused to be placed under Greece's rule, was another. The Turks struck back with terror of their own. "As a minority group, we are no longer safe living among the Greeks," the Turkish leader, Dr. Fazil Kutchuk, a physician who is today Vice-President of Cyprus under Makarios, said to me in 1958 in his office, which was eerily decorated with a large jar containing an almost full-grown fetus preserved in alcohol. "We will fight to the last man if Greece tries to take over this island. And Turkey will help us."

EOKA hit hardest of all at fellow Greeks who were willing to compromise on the question of *enosis.* "We shall brand [persons who co-operate with the British government] as traitors," cried Archbishop Makarios in a church sermon in 1955, "and we shall be unable to protect them from the people's rage." With almost every sermon pleading the cause of *enosis* rather than of God, with the cross held aloft in one hand and a gun in the other, few Greeks were prepared to follow the path of moderation—and death as traitors. But among these few were the communists, many of whom were tortured, and even killed, by the fanatical EOKA for favoring independence—which would give them a chance to take over the island—rather than union with anticommunist Greece. The reaction of the Communist Party was not to denounce EOKA but to plead: "Let's not hurt our cause by fighting among ourselves. After all, we're all Greeks fighting for basically the same thing—freedom from British imperialism." Furthermore, said the Reds, differences with the Turks should be settled by peaceful means. The communists, who normally act on the theory that chaos breeds communism, became known as the party of peace among the many silent moderates who were fed up with terror and bloodshed regardless of their political views.

By 1959 not only did the Communist Party have a large following, but miraculously Britain and the Greek and Turkish Cypriots, with the approval of Greece and Turkey, agreed to the establishment of an independent Cyprus, the solution desired by the Reds all along. This accord, which represented recognition by the Greeks that *enosis* could not possibly be achieved in the face of Turkish and British opposition, was not all that the communists had hoped for. Cyprus was to remain a Western military base, thus ruling out any immediate possibility of a Red takeover by force. But there was little the Western forces could do if the communists worked their way into the saddle through use of the West's own political system: something they could not have done if the island had merged with Greece, where the Reds are weaker.

The victory of communism is by no means certain. The anti-Red preachings of the Greek and Turkish Cypriot leaders may in the end have a decisive effect. The United States is also contributing substantially to the "stop-communism" movement with one of the least expensive—and most successful—aid programs it has introduced anywhere. In 1961 it delivered 40,000 tons of surplus wheat and 10,000 tons of barley to relieve Cypriot farmers from the results of a drought. The barley and 12,000 tons of wheat went to farmers who had lost their crops and the remaining 28,000 tons of wheat were sold to other Cypriots.

The $2 million earned from this sale was left in the villages to be used on community projects. Almost immediately more than 600 out of Cyprus' 800 villages went to work building schools, roads, retaining walls, sheep-dipping tanks, small dams, and other public works. Once these projects got underway, the villagers became so enthusiastic that they contributed funds of their own and volunteered free labor, while landowners did not charge for land required for many of these schemes. Remarkably, few people who are benefiting from the improvements fail to recognize that it was the United States that made them possible—as any American visitor to Cyprus soon learns.

But despite such hopeful signs, the communists have been making progress. They have profited from the country's economic anemia and accompanying unemployment, and also from a feeling of good will engendered by barter trade agreements reached with the Soviet Union, Bulgaria, Czechoslovakia, Hungary, and Poland.

New internal dissension is also helping the Reds. Sporadic Greek-Turkish riots reflect the disappointment of many members of both ethnic groups, particularly the Greeks, with many aspects of the independence agreement—an attitude that the communists have been adroitly exploiting in the service of ethnic friction. Cyprus, with its British bases, is still a Western colony, say the Reds. The Cypriots were tricked into believing that they were getting independence. This argument has fanned the anger of the Greeks, who still dream of *enosis,* and the fear of the Turks, who view with uneasiness the possibility that Western troops, whom they consider their protectors, may be pressured to leave the island. With *enosis* no longer an open issue, the Reds are no longer the peacemakers.

"There could be plenty of trouble in Cyprus in the future," a British reporter with long duty in the country observed. "Cyprus is a state, but not a nation. The people don't think of themselves as Cypriots, but as Greeks and Turks. There's no patriotism at all, nothing to weld the two peoples together. The situation contains the seeds of chaos, and the communists are doing their best to cultivate these seeds."

Since there is much greater anti-West feeling in the Middle East, at least in the heart of the region, the Arab world, than in either free Asia or Africa, Western military defenses in the area must necessarily be limited. In addition to United States bases in Iran and Turkey and British bases in Cyprus, a Central Treaty Organization, usually called CENTO, embracing Britain, Turkey, Iran, and Pakistan, with the United States informally but closely associated with it, has emerged from the residue of the earlier Baghdad Pact. This pact included Iraq before neutralist Abdul Karim Kassim ousted the pro-West Iraqi leaders in 1958 and withdrew his country from it. Like SEATO in Asia, CENTO is little more than a paper pact, though bilateral American agreements signed in 1959 with the three Middle Eastern members do give it some value as an instrument for co-ordination. CENTO committees set up to study methods of countering subversion in member countries, particularly Iran, may also be of some benefit.

Israel, though pro-West and possessing the best army, man for man, in the Middle East, cannot be included in defense plans without inflaming the whole Arab world. As for the Arabs, they want nothing to do with the Cold War—particularly partnership with the Western troops they have so recently managed to throw out. Their participation in an alliance would, in any case, be of doubtful value. Western short-sightedness in pouring guns into Iraq when it had a dismally unpopular pro-West government, only to find one day that the regime no longer existed and that the guns had fallen into anti-West hands, should serve as an example of how *not* to deal with the Middle East.

The Arab world is a power vacuum, yes, but if the West cannot fill it, there is no immediate indication that the communists will, especially in the light of Red experiences in Iraq, Syria, and Jordan. Whereas the Red nations were virtually unknown in the Middle East only a few years ago, they are much better known now; and fortunately for the West, they have made serious mistakes. The West is also likely to benefit from the world overproduction of oil, together with the discovery of important new fields. As Western reliance on Middle Eastern oil diminishes, so will Arab arrogance and bargaining power lessen.

It should not be forgotten that when the chips are down, somehow even the most unpredictable of the people in this region have so far proved predictable. Without knowing what they really want, as Nasser so frankly admits in his book, they want it to be of domestic origin. This characteristic is quite consistent with Western aims, but it is an intolerably frustrating barrier to communist designs—though a barrier that could be removed in the confusion of a mass fit of emotion.

VIII

EGYPT:

THE CAGE OF IRONY

The huge, magnificent face of the Sphinx hovered in the background as the camel lazily unfolded its spindly legs and stood up. Its burden, namely myself, was planted firmly upon its hump, which was decoratively covered with a yellow-fringed red blanket. My *dragoman,* or guide, a brown-skinned man who sported a large mustache and wore the nightgown-like robe and tasseled *tarbouche* of traditional Egypt, put the camera to his eye and was about to snap the shutter when suddenly he paused. He ran over to a vendor of soft drinks nearby and returned with a Coca-Cola.

"I take picture while you drinking Coca-Cola," the *dragoman* proposed quite seriously. "Then you don't look like British imperialist. You look like American imperialist instead."

This remark was intended to indicate that I wasn't really such a bad fellow after all. American imperialism wasn't nearly as abominable as British imperialism, which the Egyptians bitterly remember from the recent era of British rule. But the guide's words also reflected one reason why the Soviet Union has been able to gain a considerable foothold in Egypt in recent years, if strictly in the economic and cultural sphere. Its imperialism has been even less known to the Egyptians than that which is attributed to the United States.

Yet this very foothold has opened the eyes of Egyptian leaders to Moscow's true motives. As a result, the relationship between the

Soviet Union and Egypt today is a unique study in diplomatic irony. For Moscow, the irony lies in the fact that although it is more heavily committed economically in Egypt than in any other noncommunist nation, few states, certainly none that receive Soviet aid, are suppressing domestic communism more ruthlessly than the government of President Gamal Abdel Nasser. For Egypt, irony resides in its heavy economic dependence on a country that periodically refers to Nasser as a "fascist torturer." Despite the bitter disdain which the two governments harbor for each other, they find themselves trapped together in an economic cage forged from mutual opportunism that may prove to yield for both more liabilities than profits.

The profits, at least on the surface, have not been small for either party, from their respective points of view. Russia, by granting large-scale aid to Egypt, has opened the Arab world, which until recently was an exclusively Western preserve, to significant communist penetration for the first time. Egypt, by accepting this aid, has been able to strengthen its economy without having to depend on the hated West for help, to defy the West when it desired, as illustrated by its seizure of the internationalized Suez Canal, and to build up a relatively strong army, the key to prestige in the power-conscious Middle East. Soviet aid has, in short, permitted Nasser, who, as an Egyptian, is not a true ethnic Arab, to become one of the most heroic "Arab" figures in history and the driving force behind a pan-Arabism that is, however elusive, a regional rallying cry of tremendous emotional import.

But the liabilities of the tight economic alliance for each of the two countries are also great. If Russia decided, for political reasons, to cut off its assistance to Egypt, the Egyptians would be economically helpless—unless they agreed to swing full force toward the West. Even then, it would be difficult, if not impossible, for Egypt to disengage itself from the Soviet-bloc economy. Western engineers could hardly be expected to work satisfactorily with Russian equipment. Nor is it a simple matter to obtain spare parts for Soviet machinery in the West.

On the other hand, the Soviet Union finds itself knee-deep in economic undertakings—totaling almost one billion dollars from 1954 through 1960—in a country whose people it has not been able to influence greatly because of the violent anticommunist attitude and actions of its popular leader, when many Red nations, including Communist China, are far more drastically in need of such assistance. And it probably could not withdraw from its commitments if it chose to. For the whole Arab world, and in all likelihood most other underdeveloped regions, would immediately be wary of ties with Moscow. Furthermore, such action would amount to admission that Peking, which is opposed to granting aid to nations that persecute local communists, has been right all along—a concession that the Kremlin could ill afford to make at a moment when it is facing severe competition from Peking for leadership of the communist world.

The knowledge of Russia and Egypt that neither can easily withdraw from the economic alliance has led each to make the best of the situation. Flurries of mutual name-calling usually dissolve in statements of moderation holding that a difference in social systems should not be permitted to stand in the way of co-operation and friendship between the two countries. Actually, the firmness of the alliance has permitted the name-calling, for each side knows that the other, however angered, would not dare to cut the ties binding them.

The Soviet Union was not always willing to deal with Nasser. Following Nasser's overthrow of King Farouk in 1952, Stalin's government constantly denounced him for his anticommunist orientation and ordered the small Egyptian Communist Party to oppose him at every turn. The revolutionary government was accused of meting out "cruel punishment to the workers' movement," and even of betraying the nationalist movement in not pushing hard enough for control of the Suez Canal, which was still being operated by the British. Then, in 1954, as Nasser's relations with the West deteriorated and the post-Stalin leaders in Moscow called for communist co-operation with the national bourgeoisie regardless of its attitude toward communism, the Kremlin began to warm up to the Egyptian nationalist government. Egypt started importing large quantities of Soviet fuel and wheat and to trade with the Soviet satellites. The Egyptian public was treated to the first Soviet films and athletic exhibitions to be seen in the country.

These first modest communist efforts to improve relations with Egypt were the prelude to a dramatic Soviet psychological breakthrough in the Middle East. In May 1955, at a diplomatic reception in Cairo, a Soviet envoy let Nasser know what was really on Russia's mind.

"He led me into a corner," Nasser related later, "and asked me whether my government would be disposed to buy arms from the Soviet Union. In case of an affirmative reply he would inform Moscow . . . I replied, in the same tenor, that this suggestion appeared very interesting indeed, and that I was ready to enter negotiations in this spirit . . ."

Nasser was ready for a number of reasons:

An Israeli attack in the Gaza strip in February 1955 had exposed the feebleness of the Egyptian armed forces.

A dramatic move was necessary to bolster Nasser's prestige in other Arab countries and facilitate their unification under Egyptian leadership.

At the Afro-Asian Conference in Bandung, Indonesia, in early 1955, Nasser was influenced by the friendly attitude displayed by most participating nations toward the communist bloc, which was represented by Red China's Chou En-lai, as well as by his own highly favorable impressions of Chou.

Nasser's bitterness toward the West reached new intensity with the establishment of the Baghdad Pact against his strong opposition.

The West refused to sell Egypt substantial quantities of arms outside the pact for fear Nasser would use them to impose Egyptian rule on the whole Arab world.

Nasser needed to take the minds of the Egyptian people off his difficulties in implementing his economic and social reform program.

So in September 1955 a deal was struck, and Soviet-bloc arms began pouring into Egypt, feeding the long-starved egos of the Arabs, satisfying their desire to defy the West, and giving them a sense of power for the first time. "It's clear who our real friends are," beamed the Cairo press, even as Nasser assured the West that his neutralist policy had not changed. Khrushchev and company listened with glowing satisfaction as the whole Arab world showered Russia with expressions of "eternal gratitude." They had moved into the Middle East with an explosive momentum that threatened to overturn the Cold War balance of power.

Within three years, communist arms shipments to Egypt totaled over $300 million. They included several hundred MIG fighter aircraft and Il-28 medium jet bombers, hundreds of T-34 heavy tanks and self-propelled guns, and a number of late-model submarines, minesweepers, torpedo boats, and other naval craft. In return, Egypt mortgaged a large part of several cotton crops, though payment could be made over a period of seven to ten years at an interest rate of only two to three percent.

Russia followed up its arms shipments with massive economic aid and commercial trade. In 1956 the Soviet bloc did half of its Middle Eastern trade with Egypt alone. Russia agreed to build a nuclear laboratory in Cairo, as well as other industrial projects, and presented Egypt with a 700-million-ruble loan.

Despite all this communist aid, Nasser did not discourage offers of American assistance, though he charged that, unlike the Reds, the United States attached strings to its help. To balance communist aid, he wanted the West to finance and build a huge dam on the Nile River at Aswan in southern Egypt—which would be the world's biggest power, irrigation, and flood control project. But though United States and West German technicians had already drawn up an engineering blueprint of the dam, Secretary of State John Foster Dulles finally decided not to commit the United States to so expensive a scheme in a country that seemed to have one foot in the communist camp. He tartly notified Cairo that United States participation in the project was "not feasible in present circumstances." The British and the World Bank then took the same stand. Nasser was infuriated, not so much by the refusal itself— Russia had offered no aid either up to then—as by the tactless manner of the rejection. He had been made to appear as a beggar who had been casually spurned. The tremendous prestige he had gained throughout the Arab world as a result of the Russian arms deal, which meant to the Arabs primarily a slap in the West's face, was now gravely threatened by this humiliation at the hands of the West. In an emotional frenzy Nasser, in July 1956, nationalized the Suez Canal and announced that the revenues earned from tolls would be used to finance the building of the Aswan Dam.

This act gave Russia the opportunity to ingratiate itself still further with the Arabs. And when Britain, France, and Israel attacked Egypt shortly afterwards in an effort to take over the Canal (Israel was mainly interested in clearing Egyptian armed forces out of the Gaza strip, which it did), Moscow warned that it would send "volunteers" to fight the invading forces if the assault was not called off. Ironically, the United States, though it had provoked Nasser's seizure of the Canal in the first place, also opposed the invasion. This double-barreled pressure forced Britain and France to stop short of their main goal, but it was only the Russians who were credited by the Arabs with frustrating their attack. Khrushchev became even more eternally the Arabs' "true friend."

Communist embassy staffs in Cairo trebled within a year, and when Soviet pilots arrived to replace Western Suez Canal pilots who quit their jobs after nationalization, they were greeted with screaming, tearful embraces by welcoming Egyptians. The Kremlin even permitted several Soviet Moslem students to study at Cairo's Al Azhar University, the first time Soviet citizens were allowed to enroll in a foreign theological seminary.

Then, in 1958, Russia made a decision exceeding even the arms deal as a spectacular bid to win Arab trust and friendship. It agreed to build, and finance the greater part of, the $1.2 billion Aswan Dam project. The dam, Russia figured, would represent a permanent monument to Soviet technical skill and generosity in the Middle East and Africa.

"You Americans," an Egyptian official told me, "missed a rare opportunity when you refused to undertake the Aswan project. This will be more than a dam, more than a great technical achievement. It will be a lasting symbol of good will for all Afro-Asians to see, good will that will now be directed toward the Russians."

Whatever its political implications, the Aswan Dam, when completed (the target date is 1971), will be second only to the Pyramids as an engineering feat in the Middle East, and will constitute one of the technical masterpieces of our time. The dam, an enormous wall of earth and concrete 3.1 miles wide and 365 feet high, will contain a man-made lake 400 miles long that will irrigate two million acres of desert and provide 10 million kilowatts of power a year—five times the capacity of the Grand Coulee Dam—for a new industrial complex, the largest in the Middle East. The project is expected to increase Egypt's national income by one billion dollars annually.

About seventy Russian technicians and five thousand Egyptians have been working under a blazing sun since Nasser set off the first dynamite explosion in early 1960 amid the granite quarries that supplied the ancient Pharaohs with the rock they used for their enormous tombs in Luxor, north of Aswan. The Russians early impressed the Egyptians with their boasts that they could construct the dam cheaper and faster than prescribed by the original American and West German plans. New Soviet engineering techniques, say the Russians, will save almost $30 million and reduce construction time from six years to four and a half years in the building of an upstream cofferdam and its diversion canal.

Moreover, the tremendous challenge of Aswan, already one of Egypt's top tourist attractions, has forged a common bond of determination between the Russian engineers and the Egyptian workers, who drive to work in trucks marked "CCCP" (meaning "USSR" in Russian) and operate twenty-five-ton Soviet trucks moving on twelve wheels and enormous mechanical shovels with buckets that in a single bite can swallow eighty-eight feet of earth. The fact that the Russians live in small air-conditioned apartments in a settlement complete with their own clubhouse, while the Egyptians must crawl each night into shacks, tents, and caves does not appear to have produced any friction.

The Soviet-bloc economic offensive in Egypt has been complemented by an equally massive cultural offensive. Communist books and magazines can be obtained through at least two Cairo bookstores, and some periodicals are sold at newsstands and through subscriptions. The Dar ash-Sharq bookstore in Cairo has advertised fifteen percent discounts on purchases to persons subscribing to one of seventeen Soviet magazines. The Soviet, Red Chinese, Czech, Bulgarian, East German, and Hungarian news services all maintain staffs in Cairo, producing daily or weekly bulletins for the Egyptian press, much of which is used, though only the Soviet agency Tass is honored with attribution. The Soviet Union often purchases full-page advertisements in the semi-official Egyptian daily, *al-Jumhuriya,* to publicize Khrushchev's speeches and other special events. Red China has done the same to express solidarity with African causes. In addition, four communist embassies publish Arabic periodicals entitled *Bulgaria, New Hungary, Czechoslovakia, Soviet Magazine,* and *Ash-Sharq,* a Russian publication.

About three hundred Egyptian students are studying in Soviet-bloc countries, and Soviet and Czechoslovakian cultural centers are teaching the languages of the two countries in Cairo. The Soviet Union has also inaugurated a two-year course in Russian for graduates of Egyptian secondary schools, and has provided at least two instructors in Russian for Cairo's Higher Institute of Languages. Russia and the now split UAR exchanged about thirty cultural and technical delegations in 1960 under agreements covering broad fields of higher education, advanced technical training, and cultural and media activity.

Cairo, with its large bloc diplomatic missions, is the center for communist contact with Arab and African students, African exile groups, and the communist-backed Afro-Asian People's Solidarity Council. The International Confederation of Arab Trade Unions based here has often met with the communist-led World Federation of Trade Unions in conferences of the Trade Union Committee for Solidarity with Algeria.

Nasser himself has been a prime target of the Red cultural offensive. On a state visit to the Soviet Union, where he arrived aboard a special Soviet jetliner to be greeted by thousands of cheering Muscovites who showered flowers on him all along the route from the airport, the Egyptian leader was given to believe that almost every Russian spent his spare hours absorbing Arabic culture. He was shuttled from party to intimate party where Russian translations of Arabic, particularly Egyptian, literature were available for his proud perusal. He found some of his own speeches in books that were, he was told, regarded as "masterpieces." Soviet Moslems who had been to Mecca were paraded in to assure him that they are free to practice their religion. And then, inevitably, came a grand tour of Russian factories that produced everything from guns to agricultural machinery.

The red-carpet treatment reserved for Nasser, which hypocritically exceeded in fervor, flattery, and emotionalism the welcomes given most visiting communist dignitaries, reflected the studied Soviet approach toward nationalist leaders in the underdeveloped world, most of whom tend to be egocentric and highly impressionable. Whereas such leaders are greeted in the United States with no more, and no less, fanfare than the more sophisticated politicians of Western countries, they are made to feel in communist capitals as if only the Reds truly appreciate in their person the greatness, and even genius, of their people.

Yet for all the economic and cultural ties binding the Soviet bloc and Egypt, Nasser is utterly intolerant of domestic communists, about four hundred of whom were behind bars in mid-1962. The Egyptian Communist Party was founded in 1920 and joined the Comintern in 1922, but Egypt's British masters banned the party in 1924, and it has never enjoyed legality since. Until the end of World War II, the party consisted of less than one hundred members whose main activity was to meet in Marxist study circles. It became a minor political factor after the war when it devoted itself to agitating nationalist mobs against British troops who remained in the Suez Canal Zone under a postwar agreement with King Farouk's government, and by the early 1950's could boast of about seven thousand members.

In January 1952 the communists helped to provoke the Black Saturday anti-British riots during which wild mobs went on a rampage in Cairo, killing and mutilating Britons, and burning down Western-owned shops and even the historical Shepheard's Hotel. I arrived in Cairo the day after the riots, sorry to have missed the story, but grateful, too, for I had had a reservation at Shepheard's. Ernest Hill of the *Chicago Daily News,* who has since died, was in his room at this hotel at the time of attack. "My wife and I were taking a nap," he told me, "when suddenly we awoke and smelled smoke. We looked out of the window and saw that the building was on fire. And surrounding the hotel was a huge, screaming crowd armed with rocks, bottles, pipes, and knives. We had to decide quickly which way to die—in the fire or at the hands of the mob. We decided to take a chance on the mob, and dashed downstairs just before the building began to collapse. The mob started coming for us. I never saw people with such hate in their eyes. We thought we were doomed, when suddenly a beautiful Egyptian actress who had run down the stairs with us stood before the mob and told them in so many words that they should be ashamed of themselves. The crowd was stunned. This gave us time to dash to a taxi nearby and get away."

After the riots, an Egyptian official, pointing out of the window of his ministry at a city in ashes, acidly commented, "The communists are largely responsible for that." The Polish Embassy, it seems, had helped to instigate the violence in the hope of ousting Farouk and setting up a communist government. It ordered local communists to organize and harangue the mobs, which they did, in co-operation with the fanatically anti-Western Moslem Brotherhood and other ultranationalist elements. The mobs, significantly, first attacked Farouk's palace, and then, when held back by gunfire from the royal guards, embarked on their mission of murder and arson, which lasted throughout the day while policemen looked on. When the Polish plot was discovered, the Polish Ambassador was quietly hustled out of the country. But the Reds had done their work, though they had failed to oust the Farouk regime.

A few days after the troubles, I interviewed Haj Amin el Husseini, the former Grand Mufti of Jerusalem, who was the Arab world's most durable master of intrigue. He had been Hitler's agent in the Middle East during World War II, and had led the Palestine Arabs against the Jews after the war. He was also suspected of having engineered the assassination of Jordan's King Abdullah in 1951 for seeking peace with Israel, and now, as the chief spirit behind the Moslem Brotherhood, of being implicated in the Black Saturday orgy of destruction. In his large Cairo suburban home, which was surrounded by his own soldiers, Husseini, dressed in a long black robe and flaring white turban, denied involvement in the riots. Did he think the communists had been involved? He played with the fringe of his white beard, and his shrewd, narrow eyes smiled. He could only say, Husseini replied, that the Arabs would co-operate with anyone who would help them throw the British out of the Suez Canal Zone and the Jews out of Palestine.

The nationalists and communists had a common goal in the expulsion from Egypt of the last remnants of imperialism. But the nationalists were not all Husseinis. They also included many brooding army officers who had little use for the likes of the Grand

Mufti and the Moslem Brotherhood, whom they considered irresponsible emotionalists, and even less regard for the communists in view of their loyalty to a foreign power. They were disgusted by the riots, which resulted simply in the destruction of their own beautiful city without forcing the expulsion of a single British soldier, and saw them as symbolic of Egypt's decadence. They were fed up with their weak, corrupt government, by the disgraceful playboy antics of their king. They dreamed of Egypt's resurrection as the great nation it once was under the ancient Pharaohs. Little did I realize when I reported exclusively for the National Broadcasting Company in early 1952 that an army officer had been killed by royal guards after trying to assassinate Farouk that the would-be assassin was an agent of a young, conspiratorial colonel named Gamal Abdel Nasser, who was destined to be Egypt's modern Pharaoh.

When Nasser finally managed to overthrow Farouk a few months later—grandfatherly old General Mohammed Naguib, because of his rank and prestige, was projected for several months as the real leader of the coup before being deposed by Nasser—the communists could hardly have been struck a worse blow, despite their own desire for the king's ouster. For the Reds lost whatever control they had had over the nationalist movement. The new leaders not only refused to collaborate with them but arrested and persecuted them mercilessly. In 1954 many Reds were put on trial for subversive activities and given long prison sentences. The crackdown intensified when the government discovered that in addition to the Polish Embassy, other communist diplomatic missions were working with the domestic Reds. Nasser set up pseudo-communist cells to trap genuine Reds into them, and had government agents infiltrate real cells.

The communists had other troubles also. They had always been deeply split, and at times there were factions with a membership of one. Shortly after Nasser came to power, they polarized into three groups. A minor faction, mainly writers and journalists, supported the government in the hope of infiltrating it eventually. But two larger groups, the Democratic Movement for National Liberation (DMNL) and the smaller Egyptian Communist Party bitterly opposed the new regime in line with Stalin's thesis that the Reds must oppose all nationalist movements they cannot control. Within these various factions there were even exclusively Jewish, Armenian, and Greek cells, each with its own axe to grind. Thus, divided in their policies and immediate aims, the communists could offer little effectual resistance to government suppression.

The communist movement also suffered, and still does today, from the lack of true, convinced Reds. It consists mainly of fellow travelers who join and resign from their respective factions in accordance with their feelings on any particular issue. Most of those who call themselves communists are from the intelligentsia, with the universities harboring the most strongly organized cells. Few workers and fewer peasants have been attracted to the movement. As for labor, Nasser, taking a leaf out of the book of deposed Argentine President Juan Perón, has placed men faithful to him in key labor union positions, preventing the spread of communist influences. Most workers believe that Nasser is helping them, and pay little attention to communist propaganda that he has enslaved them. They became particularly distrustful of communism when the Reds, for purposes of expediency, allied themselves in 1953-54 with members of the corrupt Wafd Party that had led Egypt under King Farouk. On the other hand, Red headway among the peasants has been blocked by the latter's Moslem orthodoxy, their traditional acceptance of existing conditions, stemming in part from the fatalistic aspects of Islam, and their support of Nasser, who has given many of them land of their own.

But despite all these handicaps, the communists continued to make themselves heard from underground, even while their persecution reached a new peak in 1955 with the holding of mass trials of Reds and other politicians working against the Nasser government. Clandestine leaflets and publications denounced the regime for its "mistreatment of 26,000 political prisoners," which included, they charged, murder and torture to extract confessions. From his secret headquarters, Yussef Hilmi, Secretary-General of the communist Egyptian Partisans of Peace, bluntly called for the overthrow of the "illegal and criminal government." To take full advantage of Nasser's crackdown on noncommunist as well as communist political foes, particularly the intensely nationalist Moslem Brotherhood, the Reds wooed these other dissidents by deploring their plight no less fervently than their own.

That their hatred for the Nasser government ran deep was reflected in the refusal of most Reds to take their cue from the post-Stalin Kremlin leaders when Russia reached an arms agreement with Egypt. While Moscow began referring to Nasser as a "friend" and a "progressive," the bulk of domestic communists continued to heap scorn on him. In December 1955, three months after the arms deal was signed, a communist leaflet called the government a group of usurpers, liars, degenerates, and enemies of the workers and peasants, who had been duped with a fraudulent land reform program. Naked terror alone ruled, stated the pamphlet, and the Egyptian people were despised abroad for accepting it and could only rediscover dignity by overthrowing the government.

The Soviet Union was apparently unhappy about this dual communist attitude toward Nasser, for at least on one occasion the Soviet press denounced "so-called communists" and "provocateurs" in Egypt who opposed the Nasser regime. At any rate in early 1956, after constant soul-searching discussion among themselves, most Reds announced their support of Nasser, and some, by camouflaging their communist affiliations, managed to infiltrate into the government, particularly in the propaganda organs, as prescribed by the new Yenan Way adopted by Moscow. Yet some Reds still could not bring themselves to back a government that wanted to destroy them, and two new communist factions appeared to develop, one befriending and one opposing the Egyptian leadership. It is not impossible that this paradox was planned in the Kremlin to facilitate Nasser's downfall from both inside and outside the government—through infiltration by one group, open denunciation by the other—while permitting Moscow to pose as the supporter of only those communists willing to co-operate with Nasser.

This would at least be one way for the Soviet Union to handle the dilemma with which it is faced—how to remain on friendly terms with Nasser while simultaneously working for his overthrow. Nasser, for his part, has acted on the assumption that he can suppress communism and still retain Russian support, because the Soviet Union cannot pull out of Egypt without losing prestige in the whole underdeveloped world. So far, his reasoning has proved sound, with Khrushchev reacting to his anticommunist activities with little more than ferocious verbiage.

Nasser's first dispute with Moscow following the arms deal came after the Iraqi revolution of July 1958, in which Kassim ousted the pro-West government of King Faisal and Premier Nuri as-Said. With the encouragement of the Moscow-backed Iraqi communists, who gained tremendous influence in the postrevolutionary period, Kassim refused to join the United Arab Republic, exposing to Nasser for the first time the double-dealing nature of the Soviet Union. Furthermore, he became convinced that Russia hoped to get Syria to split away from the UAR through its support of an independent Iraq, which would provide a provocative example for the Syrians, many of whom already felt like second-class citizens under Egyptian rule.

The kinks in the Cairo-Moscow alliance first began to show in

December 1958 with the publication of an article by Khalid Bakdash in the Beirut communist weekly *Al-Akhbar* calling for the
establishment of "separate governments and parliaments" in the
two regions of the UAR. Nasser's Damascus press and radio, while
not implicating Russia itself, lashed back that the "left" might become more dangerous to the Arab cause than its "traditional enemies." Late in the same month Nasser, in a speech at Port Said,
raged, without mentioning Russia itself:

> The Communist Party in Syria . . . [agitated] against Arab
> Nationalism and against Arab Unity, for they were sure that Arab
> Nationalism will prevent opportunism. But they also were unable,
> they could not, Brethren, lift their heads before Arab Nationalism
> or face the sweeping tide of Arab Unity. Yes, Brethren, the Com-
> munist Party in Syria rose agitating against unity, against Arab
> Nationalism, but your power and the power of the Arab people in
> Syria made them shrink back into their holes and flee from the
> people's face.

Bakdash, who had returned from exile in Eastern Europe only
a few weeks before, was forced to flee again, Reds were arrested
in greater numbers than ever before, the government-controlled
press exploded a barrage of anticommunist comment, the few communist publications and publishing houses that still existed were
closed, and newsstand sales of communist material suspended.

The Cairo weekly newspaper *Akhbar al-Yom* castigated the
Iraqi communists who "did not know anything about the [Bagh-
dad] *coup d'état* until after the revolution, and who now brazenly
demand to inherit it and who try to destroy all anticommunist elements: the Arab nationalists should be crushed so that 2,000 Iraqi
communists shall have the chance to rule Iraq!"

Yet Nasser's awareness of the need to retain at least a minimum
of Soviet good will was indicated in another more conciliatory
article that appeared in the newspaper *Al-Ahram:*

> Communist activity in the Arab world has increased a little of
> late. In the past, communist organizations have stood by the na-
> tionalist forces in the bitter struggle against imperialism, pacts,
> imperialist collaborators, and feudalism. The struggle has ended or
> is about to end. What will be the attitude of the communists in the
> future? Will they be deflected from the clear nationalist line in
> order to raise red flags in the Middle East? Or will they keep their
> mouths shut?

Khrushchev, as might have been expected, didn't keep his
mouth shut. An *Izvestia* article accused *Akhbar al-Yom* of "false

reporting" and of slandering the USSR, though Nasser had not yet mentioned Russia by name in any of his blasts. Nevertheless, the Russian Premier, speaking before the Twenty-first Congress of the Soviet Communist Party in the midst of the controversy, declared, after describing Nasser's anticommunist moves as "reactionary" and "naïve," that differences on ideological questions should not hinder the development of friendly relations. He even praised Nasser as a nationalist leader. Russia, too, realized it was not practical to strain relations to the breaking point.

The crisis came to a head in March 1959, when communist-led Iraqi forces crushed a UAR-instigated revolt against Kassim at Mosul in northwestern Iraq. Nasser, frustrated and furious, then for the first time called the Arab communists "agents of a foreign power," obviously referring to the Soviet Union. UAR secret police began keeping watch on Soviet diplomats. UAR journalists stopped visiting the Soviet Embassy, and the exchange of intelligence information between the two countries halted. UAR censors held up Russian books and films, and several bookshops that had operated on Soviet subsidies suddenly went out of business. Most significantly of all, propaganda attacks against the West began to ease off.

Khrushchev's reaction: "Nasser is a hot-headed young man . . . using the language of the imperialists."

Though such bitter mutual recriminations might have produced a complete break in economic, and perhaps diplomatic, relations if they had taken place between either of the two nations and another country, they had little practical effect on the Moscow-Cairo alliance. Both sides had gambled that they could pursue policies inimical to the other without severing the economic ties binding them; and they both won. It was clear that they were stuck with each other for better or for worse.

Since then, relations between Moscow and Cairo have seesawed between better and worse. One severe crisis came in May 1961 when Khrushchev, irked by the continued persecution of UAR Reds and their purge from the government, the schools, and the press, asked a visiting UAR parliamentary delegation in Moscow, "If our people live under communism better than you, why should you declare yourself against communism? I warn you. History will teach you. Ideologies cannot be buried in prisons. Your people will ask you to step aside and demand that they handle their own affairs." Moscow newspapers then called Nasser "ungrateful," and charged that a Lebanese communist, Riad el Turk, had been tortured to death in prison. When the UAR produced a healthy Riad at a press conference, Moscow switched its attention to Farajallah el Helw, Secretary-General of the Lebanese Communist Party, who, it said, had been the victim of a "savage fascist crime, like the killing of Lumumba."

Al-Akhbar shot back that "Arab public opinion is not ready to take lessons on freedom from the organizers of the blood baths in Mosul and Kirkuk"—a reference to communist attacks on Nasserite nationalists in Iraq after Kassim came to power.

For once, Moscow didn't reply. It was little concerned with Nasser's opinion of the USSR, which had long been known, but it was shocked to learn that the rest of the Arab world, including even Iraq, stood by Nasser. Saudi Arabian Foreign Minister Ibrahim Sowail expressed the view of this whole area when he said, "We will not abide Soviet attacks on any Arab country, and least of all on the UAR, our biggest sister." Khrushchev thus learned the limitations to which he had to submit in his quarrel with Nasser if he didn't want to lose his whole enormous investment in the UAR. He could not come out openly with a plea for a communist Middle East.

He did find one way, however, to strike hard at Nasser without turning the entire Arab world against Russia. And that was by pressing for the "liberation" of Syria from the UAR, an idea not unpopular among many Syrians, nor for that matter, among anti-Nasserites in Iraq and other Arab countries. Russia had ample reason for wanting an independent Syria, aside from its desire to weaken Nasser's position in the Middle East and pave the way for his eventual overthrow. Khrushchev, while paying lip service to the concept of Arab unity in order to ingratiate himself with the Arabs, by no means favors such union, which would simply strengthen Arab nationalism at the expense of communism. It was all right, indeed necessary, to collaborate with the national bourgeoisie during the period of national liberation from colonialism and for a time afterwards to permit the communists to consolidate their position; but eventually the nationalists would have to be ousted. Konstantin Ivanov, a Soviet authority, wrote in the Moscow journal, *Mezhdunarodnaya Zhizn,* in 1958: "As Marxists we do not want to make a fetish of Arab unity, and do not want to close our eyes to the fact that it may be exploited temporarily to impede the progressive development of the Arab peoples"—that is, development toward communism.

In the Arab world, it would be easier for the Reds to take over each country individually in domino fashion than to try to swallow at once the whole area, particularly when there are anticommunists like Nasser and Saudi Arabia's feudalistic King Ibn Saud with whom to contend. Certainly an independent Syria would be easier to subvert than one attached to the UAR, especially as Syria had one of the largest and best-organized communist parties in the Middle East, and the only communist leader of stature—Khalid Bakdash—before that country came under the rule of Nasser.

Actually, the union of Egypt and Syria had been foisted on a reluctant Nasser in 1957 by the Syrian leaders themselves, who feared that their country, which had been deeply infiltrated by communists, could be saved from the Soviet grasp only by throwing itself under Nasser's wing. While the Egyptian chief had dreams of leading a united Arab state one day, he feared that, with Egypt barely launched on his economic and social reform program, premature unity might make its implementation more difficult. But once convinced of the wisdom of the move, he enthusiastically embraced Syria—viewing the merger as the nucleus of a united Arab world.

Almost from the beginning, Syrian army officers resented the secondary commands to which they were assigned by Egyptian superiors, while Syrian businessmen, who were used to operating freely, even smuggling when possible, became alarmed by Nasser's control and integration policies. Dissatisfaction reached a crisis point in 1961 when Nasser carried these policies to new extremes. The strongly nationalist Syrian army was horrified when Cairo abolished the regional cabinet in Damascus, ending Syrian autonomy completely. And the businessmen panicked with the extension of Egypt's trade and currency controls to Syria, the nationalization of most industrial and commercial enterprises in the UAR, and the imposition of a steeply graduated income tax.

With barracks battles between Egyptian and Syrian soldiers raging, Syrian capital clandestinely flowing out of the country, and the Syrian pound nose-diving in value, Moscow played its ace card to the hilt. The Kremlin-sponsored *World Marxist Review* carried an article in February 1961 by Khalid Bakdash, who wrote:

> The experience of the nearly three years that have passed since the formation of the UAR has taught the peasants and all Syrians that the union imposed on them has no sound basis, that the policy of the Cairo government is wreaking havoc with the slogan of Arab unity and Arab nationalism; this slogan is being utilized to push Egyptian nationalism, which is the embodiment of the expansionist and jingo features of the Egyptian big bourgeoisie. The way out of the present situation is through the creation of a front of the workers and peasants, the progressive national bour-

geoisie, youth, students, women—of all patriots and democrats—
for the purpose of waging a struggle for a radical revision of the
fundamental principles underlying the union, for liberation from
Egyptian colonialism, for a genuine policy of national liberation,
for peace and democracy.

Not satisfied with spurring revolution and implying that Nasser,
the once "great nationalist leader," is in fact a colonialist himself,
the *World Marxist Review* of August 1961 continued the attack:

> Communists and other democrats held in Syrian prisons, espe-
> cially those confined in the Mezze Fortress in Damascus, are again
> being subjected to torture more brutal than anything endured
> throughout their more than two years' imprisonment. Nasser's
> gendarmes are trying to force political prisoners to sign statements
> denouncing the Communist Party and declaring their loyalty to his
> regime. "The law will not help you," is the grim threat of the Nas-
> ser torturers, "no court will handle your case. Don't expect to be
> treated like other prisoners or that you will have the benefit of the
> law. Either you sign the statement or you die."
>
> Those who refuse to sign are savagely beaten, starved, and sub-
> jected to cruel torture: forced to stand on one leg with arms up-
> raised for six hours at a time, strung up by the legs for several
> hours and tortured with needles and electric shocks. This savagery
> against communists and other democrats in Syria is part of the
> campaign to crush the growing struggle against the UAR regime.
> Nasser's design is to intimidate his political opponents, isolate
> them, and prevent the communists from co-operating with the other
> democratic forces.

The month after this diatribe appeared, in late September 1961,
Syria, led by its soldiers and businessmen, broke away from the
UAR. Nasser tried to stop the revolt, but when two hundred of two
thousand paratroop commandos he sent to Syria were killed on
landing, and it became evident that the Egyptian army did not have
the amphibious capability to launch a successful invasion, he conceded defeat—a defeat which he acknowledged was an even
"greater disaster" than the attack on Suez had been.

Nasser's plans for heading a united Arab world had already
been dealt a severe blow by the refusal of Iraq, Jordan, and Saudi
Arabia to recognize him as the over-all Arab leader; by the ability
of Lebanon's Christian Arabs, who constitute about fifty percent
of the Lebanese population, to keep their country out of the UAR
orbit; and by the unwillingness even of Yemen, which had become
federated with the UAR shortly after Syria had united with Egypt,
to co-operate with Cairo until the 1962 Yemenite revolution.

To these many Middle Eastern failures had been added Nasser's inability to establish himself in Africa as the African leader he wants to be. North African states like Morocco, Tunisia, and Algeria, with their strong European cultural ties, feel little in common with Egypt, which is considered more closely associated with the distant Middle East, for all of a common Islamic bond. And the peoples of Black Africa, despite Nasser's radio propaganda about Cairo-inspired African unity, still regard him as a "white man." Thus, Syria appeared to sound the death knell for his dream of empire.

As if to rub salt in Nasser's Syrian wound, the overjoyed Soviet Union, as well as Czechoslovakia and Bulgaria, recognized the new Syrian Arab Republic within a few days after the break—before such action was taken by the United States and Britain.

The thinly veiled hostility between Cairo and Moscow has even affected work on the Aswan Dam. On one occasion Nasser refused to permit the Russians to establish training centers for Egyptian workers, fearing communist indoctrination, and Soviet engineers retaliated by virtually halting work for three months. Major articles appearing in *Pravda* and *Izvestia* have showered criticism on Cairo for alleged lack of co-operation at Aswan. They have protested mainly that the Cairo press has deliberately minimized the Soviet role in the project, and that guides do not even mention the presence of the Russians to foreign tourists. When a complaint was made to an Egyptian official, *Pravda* charged that the official answered, "And what is there to write? There are no results yet. When it is finished, we will write about it." It was ridiculous, replied the communist journals, to say there had been no progress yet. But if Russian complaints were intended as a threat that Moscow might just pull out of Aswan altogether, Cairo ignored it. For, right or wrong, Nasser is convinced that Khrushchev would no more do that than he himself would tell the Russians to leave.

Some Egyptians have struck back with a few complaints of their own. Many of the Soviet machines imported for the Aswan and other projects, they say, are inferior, obsolete copies of Western models purchased at thirty to forty percent over the world price. Russian kerosene has had to be refined again before it could be used. One shipment of Russian wheat was moldy and wormy and possibly poisonous, apparently as the result of a blunder by a Soviet bureaucrat who had ordered the wheat stacked in a warehouse ordinarily used for storing insecticides. Russia has resold to Eastern Europe for hard currency much of the cotton Egypt has shipped to that country in payment for Soviet aid. When Russia broke the nuclear test moratorium, Nasser was one of the few participants at the Belgrade conference of neutralists to condemn the action.

While Egypt's relations with Russia may be poor, yet buoyed up by mutual self-interest, its relations with Red China are much worse. After reaching a crescendo of warmth at the Bandung Conference, these relations soon began to deteriorate as Nasser filled his jails with communists. Peking, as the initiator of the Yenan Way, certainly wasn't against infiltrating nationalist governments such as Nasser's. But except for a few anticommunist countries like Cambodia which, virtually bordering on the communist empire, could be softened up for the kill with economic aid, or remote politically backward nations like Yemen, where communist technical magic could feed revolutionary discontent, Mao is opposed to helping out governments that persecute Reds.

Relations between Red China and the UAR began to cool perceptibly after the Iraqi revolution of July 1958, at about the same time the glow of Russian friendship started to wear off in Cairo. For Peking, like Moscow, threw its support to the Iraqi Reds in the struggle against the Nasserites, viewing Iraq's Kassim as the right kind of nationalist leader with whom to deal.

In the autumn of 1959 the roof blew when Khalid Bakdash visited Peking and, before an audience that included high Red Chinese officials, denounced Nasser and his regime for "pro-Western and imperialist" leanings. Radio Cairo stormed back that Peking was seeking communist domination in the Middle East, and Nasser asked the governments of twenty-five nations that had been represented at the Bandung Conference to recall their ambassadors in Peking in protest against recent Red Chinese "aggression" in Tibet, India, Laos, and the UAR. At the same time, orders went out to all UAR government officials at home and abroad to shun Chinese Embassy celebrations of the tenth anniversary of communist rule in China.

A violent protest to the Chinese Ambassador in Cairo, calling on Peking to explain its "vicious and unscrupulous" attack on Cairo, brought the half-apologetic response that the Red Chinese government regretted Bakdash's public assault, but that it was not responsible for the speech. Relations began to improve slightly, but have remained distinctly chilly, as was demonstrated when Nasser, more enthusiastically than any other neutralist leader, sought to line up support for India among the Afro-Asian nations when Mao's armies drove into India in late 1962.

Nasser's discovery that communist "friendship" is, to the Reds,

simply a means to an end, namely his political demise, has produced unmistakable signs that he is trying to decrease his economic
dependence on Moscow and move from Eastern-oriented "positive" neutralism toward genuine neutralism in the Cold War. One
of the most hopeful signs for the West was the withdrawal in
1959 of about 650 Egyptian and Syrian students, out of a total of
more than 1,000, from Soviet-bloc universities and the reassign-
ment of most of them to American, British, and Canadian institutions. About 200 have been added to the 700 students from the
now two independent Arab states already in the United States,
and a substantial number to the 600 already studying in Britain.
The twenty-odd students who have been transferred to Canada
are the first from those countries who have been sent to Canada at
the Egyptian government's expense. Nasser gave as the official government reasons for the switch the difficulty encountered by the
Arab students in learning Russian and the disparity between
Marxist and UAR economic theories and practices, but the basic
factor was undoubtedly his fear of communist indoctrination. Nasser early in 1960 flatly accused Bulgaria of trying to indoctrinate
UAR students, and castigated that country as well for "persecution" of its half-million Moslems.

Nasser is also moving closer to the West economically. Recently,
for example, he has favored Western firms in awarding contracts,
and about half the foreign aid he has been receiving has come
from the West. From 1959 to 1962, Washington furnished him
with more than $480 million in assistance, mostly in the form of
sales of surplus grains for Egyptian pounds, but also including
technical aid projects and fertilizer and diesel locomotive plants.
Perhaps the most important technical project is the Egyptian-
American Rural Improvement Service, which is reclaiming 26,000
acres of wasteland near Alexandria, where five thousand peasant
families are being resettled in new villages. Shortly after Syria's
breakaway, the United States moved in with an offer of $20 mil-
lion in foodstuffs to help offset Egypt's 1961 crop failures.

British and Dutch firms have also granted Nasser considerable
credit recently; and before the UAR split, the West Germans
signed an agreement for a $200,000,000 loan covering projects
in both Egypt and Syria. Significantly, a large part of this loan was
earmarked under the UAR government for the construction of a
gigantic Euphrates Dam in Syria, comparable to that at Aswan.
Other important signs that Nasser is trying to reduce his dependence on the communist bloc are his purchase of spare parts from
West Germany for his Russian industrial machinery and military

equipment, and a drop in the proportion of trade with the communist bloc from thirty-eight percent in the year starting June 1960 to twenty-seven percent in the following twelve months, as compared to a jump in trade with the West from thirty-eight percent to fifty-four percent in the same period.

Nasser, however, realizes that the advanced markets of the West offer him only limited possibilities of reducing his trade with the communist countries. Also, that the Arab world promises uncertain prospects, with Iraq and Syria hostile to Egypt, and Saudi Arabia, Yemen, and Kuwait increasingly wary of Nasser's socialist policies. Cairo, therefore, is going all out to mend fences in Black Africa, which is a huge potential market for Egyptian goods. Not only has Nasser tried to influence the Africans at neutralist conferences such as those held in 1960 and 1961 at Casablanca and Belgrade, but also through the medium of Islam, which is spreading swiftly in Black Africa, thanks in part to heavy African enrollment in Cairo's Al Azhar University and the conscientious work of religious attachés in Egyptian embassies.

Nasser's experience with the communist bloc has affected not only his economic policies but his cultural policies as well. Cultural relations with the Red states are still extensive, but they have been limited to some degree by official actions and by a slackening of interest in communist "culture" on the part of the Egyptian public. For one thing, almost all communist-front organizations are banned. A National Committee for the Partisans of Peace exists but has had to operate outside the country. Even Soviet, Red Chinese, and Polish Friendship Societies, while still permitted, have been strangely inactive since 1960. And despite extensive cultural agreements with the bloc for the exchange of radio and television program material, relatively little has been used in Egypt by either medium. From its inception in 1960, UAR television has relied primarily on material of Western origin.

Although the communist bloc is giving technical aid to Egypt's film industry, the Egyptian public is responding with increasingly less interest in films from bloc countries. A movie house in Cairo and another in Port Said stopped showing Soviet films because they failed to attract customers. Nor were films shown by the Soviet Union, Communist China, and North Korea at an Afro-Asian Film Festival in 1960 enthusiastically received. This has also been the case with several Soviet-sponsored film festivals.

Actually, Nasser is depending less on containment of communist propaganda activities and of lagging public interest in them to keep Egypt out of the communist camp than on a grandiose social and economic reform plan called "Arab socialism." This is the most important aspect of a recent reorientation of his tactics for achievement of his goals of glory and prosperity—a switch that has been accelerated by the disillusionment of the Syrian secession. Without giving up his efforts to use the West and Israel as scapegoats for his difficulties and failures, Nasser has embarked on a more positive road toward these goals. He appears to have concluded that only by appealing, through example as well as through Radio Cairo and other propaganda means, to the masses over the heads of their governments can he become the leader of the Arab and African worlds or even regain what prestige he held in these areas before disasters like Syria and Iraq. Arab socialism, Nasser hopes, will keep communism out of Egypt as well as strengthen his influence in the Afro-Arab world.

His new approach became clear when, after the Syrian secession, he no longer made any pretense about his true feelings toward medieval reactionaries like the Kings of Yemen and Saudi Arabia. Nasser had hoped that Yemen's federal ties with the UAR would produce reform in that feudal kingdom. But the late Imam wanted not reform but simply money from Nasser, refusing even to permit the UAR co-ordinating committee to convene in Yemen. When Nasser announced his Arab socialist plan, the Imam wrote a poem in classical Arabic that went:

> *The Koran says, do not nationalize*
> *other people's property.*
> *Let us return to Islamic laws and let us*
> *have union on our own terms.*

When Nasser got hold of this poem, he reacted by throwing Yemen out of the UAR, leaving Egypt as the only member of the "union."

Almost simultaneously, Nasser's relations with Saudi Arabia nearly reached the breaking point when he accused King Ibn Saud of having contributed $5.6 million to assist the Syrian breakaway. The Saudis claimed—like the Yemenites—that Arab socialism was contrary to the teachings of the Prophet Mohammed, and that the hour had come to strike down the UAR because "Cairo was faced with a serious financial crisis."

The Cairo newspaper, *Al-Ahram,* a Nasser mouthpiece, stormed back: "Our debts are contracted for development purposes while your debts are quite unjustifiable. The new sumptuous palaces, beautiful slaves, de luxe cars and night clubs may afford pleasure for a time, but they are a detriment to national life."

Nasser, in a speech, added: "If social justice is applied in Saudi Arabia, how can King Saud finance his harem and his slaves?"

Shortly afterward, in September 1962, Saud concluded an agreement with Jordan's King Hussein, another enemy of Nasser, calling for a merger of their armed forces and a co-ordination of their economies in a move toward Arab "unity" in competition with Nasserism. A few months later, Saudi Arabia broke diplomatic relations with Egypt as the two countries opposed each other in the Yemenite civil war.

The Egyptian leader's plan to go straight to the people with his condemnation of "reactionaries" and talk of reform has given Middle Eastern leaders cause for alarm. For though Nasser may be hated by most Arab leaders, largely because they are jealous of his power and fearful of revolution, he still has a strong hold on a large proportion of the common people in the Arab world. Even in Syria his influence was reflected in the coup in March 1962 by army officers who demanded that the Syrian government carry out many Arab socialist policies, and in the barely contained follow-up coup by other officers, who, apparently supported by many Syrians, demanded that Syria rejoin the UAR.

In fairness to Nasser, his interest in reform is not simply a matter of selling Nasser but of trying also to improve the impoverished condition of the Arab masses. Whatever his personal ambitions may be, he has idealistic tendencies, stemming from his boyhood days when, as a member of a middle-class village family, he developed a deep sympathy for the peasants and an intense hatred for the few wealthy landlords who ran Egypt. His many years of plotting against Farouk as an army officer represented in a sense a crusade for a better Egypt. It was when he discovered, soon after he came to power, that few Egyptians were interested in such a crusade, that he decided to concentrate on the Napoleonic aspects of his program as the easiest means of maintaining himself in power.

"I thought we were only the pioneers and commandos, that we would be in the front for a few hours and that we would soon be followed by the solid masses marching to the goal," he wrote in his book, *Philosophy of the Revolution.* Instead, the very people on whom he had relied to help him considered the revolution only as "a weapon for revenge and hatred. I felt my heart charged with sorrow and dripping with bitterness . . . The mission of the vanguard had not ended. In fact, it was just beginning."

When Nasser took over Egypt, most peasants, or fellahin, were the serfs of absentee landlords who used private armies to keep them working hard for annual earnings that amounted to about

$40 per capita. Illiteracy was almost total in the villages, and disease ravaged the countryside. In one mud hovel that I visited in 1952 I could hardly keep my eyes open for the cloud of flies that swirled through the interior. Today these conditions still exist to a considerable extent, but yearly peasant incomes are gradually rising, and clinics and hospitals are sharply cutting down on disease —a fact that, ironically, threatens the value of the Aswan dam. For with the death rate decreasing, and the population expected to rise by five million from 1960 to 1970, the one million acres of new farmland to be created by the dam are likely to be absorbed by this increase, leaving the average peasant little better off than he is now. The only answer is to move some of the fellahin into industry, not an easy or a popular thing to do.

But Nasser is hopeful that his Arab socialism will solve at least some of Egypt's vast social and economic problems. This plan has resulted in the almost complete nationalization of the Egyptian economy and will soon mean a thorough redistribution of the nation's wealth. These aims, of course, are also the aims of communism; but, says Nasser, his program, unlike that of the communists, is founded on "democratic" principles. With its full application, he adds, communism will lose whatever appeal it has had for the people.

Even so, Arab socialism is by no means mild medicine. Under decrees issued in 1961:

Landholdings previously limited to 200 acres have been reduced to 100 acres. The 300,000 acres that 5,200 landlords must give up will permit the distribution of five acres each to 60,000 families.

Ninety percent of the "organized sector of the economy"—all except retail outlets, artisans, and other small enterprises—have been put under government control, affecting about a third of the total economy, including seventy percent of industrial production. About 260 companies—banks, insurance companies, utilities, and other "essential" enterprises—have been fully nationalized, while other firms, particularly textile concerns, have had to give the government a fifty-percent interest. Government managers have been installed in ninety-one companies. A workers' representative sits on the board of directors of each firm, and twenty-five percent of company profits are going to the workers. No individual can own more than 10,000 Egyptian pounds' worth of stock.

New labor regulations include the reduction of the work week from 48 to 42 hours, and the abolition of the wide practice of Egyptians' holding two jobs simultaneously.

The most drastic decree of all has frozen the assets of all of

Egypt's most prominent families, about 600, involving a total of more than $1 billion in cash and real property. The government will decide how much each person may retain for personal use, with $14,000 a year the ceiling.

These revolutionary decrees, particularly the sequestration, have stunned Egypt's capitalist class, though each person deprived of land or of shares in an enterprise will presumably be compensated with fifteen-year government bonds bearing four percent interest. Business tycoons like Ahmed Abboud, whose wealth, earned in shipyards, sugar cane, and fertilizers, among other things, is estimated at $100 million, will find it difficult living on $14,000 yearly. And so will François Tagher, a Lebanese who came to Egypt in his youth and built up one of the largest textile businesses in the Middle East. No longer will he be able to afford having a single dish flown in from Maxim's in Paris for a dinner party, as he has done in the past. The Magaga family, which owned 50,000 acres worked by about 5,000 fellahin, will have to do with a small farm—for all their armed defiance several years ago when Nasser's first land reform measures were being applied. The head of the family is now in prison. The implementation of this far-reaching program has been speeded up since the Syrian secession, which Nasser blames on the greed of rich Syrian businessmen who saw what was coming. He is making sure that Egyptian businessmen are disarmed before they too have a chance to strike at him.

Is his Arab socialism genuine reform, or is it just another form of communism? Denying that it is communism, Nasser said the socialism he sought would do away with class differences, while nationalization converted "exploitative, capitalist ownership into public ownership." But he did not mean, he added, that every owner of capital was an exploiter. "Had we been against ownership, we would have resorted to confiscation, would not have handed out bonds which are worth a good deal of money, and would not have paid interest on them."

A Lebanese communist newspaper agreed that the plan was not communism, calling it "state capitalism" and blasting its provisions for some private ownership. Local capitalism had failed to achieve its major aims, the paper said, and so had turned to the state for help. The Cairo newspaper *Al-Akhbar* replied in the Reds' own idiom:

> The hostile attitude adopted by the communist lackeys toward our new socialist experiment is nothing new or unfamiliar. The communist agents have a long record of betraying the Arab cause

and of co-operating with imperialism against Arab nationalism
. . . They are poor slaves parroting views and words which are
not their own and which are fed to them to parrot . . . Our socialism believes that the true socialist evolution stems from the
nation as a whole and not from a single class . . . We believe that
class distinction and paradoxes should be dissolved without resorting to bloodbaths and concentration camps.

Lenin, said the writer, at first endorsed the principle of private
ownership, establishing the kulak class. "But later he annihilated
them by steel and fire and burned their farms and cattle."

Expanding on this theme of the superiority of "Arab socialism"
over communism, *Al-Ahram* explained that whereas communism
wants one class to put an end to all others "even by killing," Nasser
"advocates the dissolution of class distinction." Whereas communism holds that every owner is an exploiter "and hence must be
eliminated," Nasser believes in the liquidation of exploitation and
not the exploiter, and regards individual ownership as a right.
And whereas communism stands for confiscation, Nasser stands
for nationalization with compensation.

Actually, it is not clear yet whether those who have lost their
wealth will be fully compensated for their losses. But in any event
Nasser's socialism does not appear to be following any particular
ideological line. His concept seems aimed at splitting up Egypt's
wealth into small shares to be divided as equally as possible among
all the people, with only the government in control of the larger
means of production. Small shopkeepers will presumably be permitted to continue operations, while new peasant landholders will
presumably be their own bosses. As the communists themselves
point out, this is certainly contrary to the communist thesis that the
government should own all commercial enterprises and land and
that every individual must be an employee of the state.

Nasser's aversion to communism can be partly explained by the
fact that it is a foreign ideology, and he is too nationalistic to accept
any ready-made alien concept, particularly one whose sponsors
would like to impose it on his country, as on all others. His devotion
to Islam, in contrast to the apathy toward this traditional Arab religion displayed by many of his urban compatriots, is also an important factor. Nevertheless, the abruptness of his tactics and his
effort to revolutionize Egypt overnight are reminiscent of, if less
cruel than, communist methods. It is, in fact, highly likely that his
methods were influenced to a considerable degree by his good
friend, Marshal Tito of Yugoslavia, who has been following his
own, rather than a Moscow- or Peking-dictated, interpretation of

Marxism. But if both men are independent-minded, Nasser is no Tito. The Yugoslav dictator is a confirmed, if unorthodox Marxist, while Nasser is not an ideologist. It is, however, understandable that the dynamism of communist tactics has appealed to this Arab leader, who has always displayed a flare for the shocking, dramatic move.

In the case of Arab socialism, the move is at least in part intended to counter his defeats in Iraq and Syria and permit him to recoup the loss in prestige he suffered through them. To maintain his popular support in Egypt and to brighten his tarnished image elsewhere in the Afro-Arab world he wants to dominate, he has even proclaimed that free elections will be held—a function he did away with long ago. "The people themselves," he said, "must now lead the purging of the country and thrust their way, armed by nationalist faith, to the morrow they have been looking forward to." If he means what he says, this would represent a further distinction between Nasser's socialism and Khrushchev's communism. But so far he has not permitted the emergence of political parties other than his own monolithic National Union, although such permission is a prerequisite for genuinely free elections.

Nasser, who once looked almost exclusively to the communist world for the help he needs to achieve his domestic and external aims, realizes that he must also seek aid in the West. Yet it would be folly to expect him to move much closer toward the West than true neutralism in the Cold War. For as Nasser frankly told the editor of the London *Spectator,* "If I were to give up our neutralism, I should wake up in the morning as a general without an army." Nor has Nasser lost any of his distrust of the West or any of his confidence that he can still wring considerable aid out of Russia without having to make political concessions. Typically, he said in a speech in May 1960 at a cotton yarn factory built with Soviet assistance: "The UAR opposes and will continue to oppose communism as a social system, and on occasion clouds have shrouded Soviet-UAR relations. Yet Russia has never threatened to cut off aid or taunted the UAR about such aid. For this she has earned our eternal gratitude."

IX

IRAQ:

JUGGLING ACT

Within a year after the overthrow of the pro-West Iraqi monarchy in July 1958 by General Abdul Karim Kassim's nationalist followers, Iraq was virtually part of the communist bloc. The Reds had won control of all propaganda organs, schools, industrial and farm programs, welfare plans, and key posts in the military. No government action was taken without communist approval, nor were anticommunist groups permitted. General Kassim, who became Premier, was described as a "weak reed" who had become a Red puppet.

Nevertheless, Westerners who were ready to write Iraq off made several miscalculations. They underestimated the political tightrope artistry of Kassim and overestimated the shrewdness of the Iraqi communists. Most important of all, they failed to take into account the extraordinary fickleness of the Middle Eastern mob, a factor that was compounded by the failure of the communists to cultivate enough popular appeal among the masses, particularly the peasants, to make their advantages stick once the heat and emotionalism of the revolution began to cool. Actually, the Reds gradually lost much of the appeal they had with a stupid, ruthless, premature drive for power that cut them off from the nationalist movement they had for so long pretended to support. And the more isolated the communists became, the easier it was for Kassim, who had used the Reds to consolidate his rule after the revolution, to trim them down to size when he felt he no longer needed their active support.

The communists still had some influence in Iraq in late 1962. Several ministries, notably those of Guidance, Planning, Oil Affairs, Municipalities, and Education, were still heavily infiltrated at lower levels. And although hard-core communists were estimated to total no more than 500, Red supporters might have numbered as many as 10,000, a large figure as specific political groups go in the Arab world, even if fractional in terms of the over-all population. While relations between neutralist Iraq and the communist bloc were not nearly as warm as they were in the heyday of Iraqi communism, economic and cultural ties were nevertheless distressingly close. It is entirely possible that in another upheaval, perhaps resulting from the overthrow or assassination of Kassim, the local Reds could surge again into a position of leadership and, considering the unpredictability of Arab public opinion, even with something resembling mass support.

But in 1962 the communists were by no means in an advantageous position. About thirty communists had been condemned to death and ten others given life imprisonment for atrocities committed in 1959 rioting. Reds had been purged from important positions in the government, the military, most trade unions, and teacher-student organizations. Communist newspapers had been shut down. Showers of tomatoes and shouts of "hang him" often greeted communist leaders seen in public. And while Kassim had not destroyed the "official" Communist Party—a pseudo-communist party disowned by Moscow also exists—he had suppressed its activities, thereby cleverly rendering the organization ineffectual without provoking open opposition in view of the communist fear that some other leader might crush the party altogether.

Kassim's crackdown on the local Reds has not been ignored by Moscow, which sent several messages of protest in 1961. One, signed by the president of the Soviet Academy of Sciences, charged, "Iraqi patriots who staunchly fought for the independence of their country and defended the gains of the revolution of July 14 are being brutally victimized." Another message from the Central Council of Soviet Trade Unions asked Kassim to "take the necessary measures to release and discontinue the persecution of patriots, democrats, and trade-union leaders, and to restore trade-union rights and the freedom of the working people of Iraq." But significantly, these messages criticized "antidemocratic representatives" rather than Kassim himself, who the communist bloc no doubt feels may be the best Iraqi leader they can hope for at this time.

Certainly it must have considerable respect for him. Though a simple, unpretentious man, not very imaginative or widely read, this innocuous-looking, mustached military dictator with a shy, snaggle-toothed smile and feeble, high-pitched voice has proved to be far from a "weak reed." He possesses tremendous drive, born of a genuine will to help his people, and sometimes works up to twenty hours daily, cat-napping on a couch in his office. He has even refused to marry for fear that family responsibilities might prevent him from working as hard for the fulfillment of his—and his country's—destiny. Born into a lower-middle-class Baghdad family, Kassim graduated from the Royal Military College in 1934 and began planning a revolution almost immediately, recruiting younger officers and absorbing other conspiratorial groups as he was gradually promoted in rank.

This long period of secret plotting hardened his naturally suspicious nature to the point where he trusts no one—something the Reds found out just when they thought they had him eating out of their hands. Above all, he has a subtle native shrewdness that none of his enemies has been able to match, a characteristic most eloquently reflected in his defeat of the communists at their own game—using people for one's own ends. He utilized communist mass support during the first year after his revolution to counter powerful pan-Arab nationalist elements who wanted to unite with the beckoning United Arab Republic of President Gamal Abdel Nasser. With Nasserite strength shattered, he used the army to suppress the communists. Thus, the two greatest potential threats to his power have been significantly reduced—an incredible political feat whatever Kassim's ultimate fate may be.

But if the Iraqi Reds appeared to be on the decline in 1962, their history indicates that this trend could be reversed overnight. From its founding in the early 1930's to 1948, the official Communist Party—now called the People's Unity Party—was an insignificant organization incapable of identifying itself with national interests. Then, in 1949, four communist leaders were hanged for allegedly instigating riots, giving the party the martyrs it needed to win widespread sympathy. Intellectuals, particularly students, poured into the party, and cells soon sprang up in secondary schools as well as in the military academy. Demonstrations and riots against the government spread accordingly; but serious attempts to infiltrate the nationalist movement and the peasantry were made, as in most underdeveloped countries, only after Stalin's death.

Party members were told by their leaders in 1953 that they must support the establishment of a

> government within the framework of the existing system which is not based on totally smashing the enemy, but on forcing it to retreat; a government which makes a genuine stand against war plans and blocs and rearmament, abolishes the 1930 treaty [with Britain] and war bases in Iraq, works for the expulsion of the oil and other monopoly companies and guarantees democratic liberties for the people. Our party has made it clear that it supports such a government while it takes national and democratic steps, but will criticize it for any hesitancy or compromise, not for the sake of weakening it, but to strengthen it. The party does not stipulate its participation in such a government. It does fight to bring such a government to power through popular struggle led by a broad, united, militant national front.

Conditions for such a "popular struggle" could hardly have suited the communists more. The prerevolutionary government of King Faisal and Premier Nuri as-Said, a cunning politician for decades, was despised by the people. Middle-class ambitions were frustrated by a ruling-class monopoly of all good government jobs. Trade unions were banned. The press was controlled. A few hundred landlords, including some of the government leaders, owned over ninety percent of the land. True, the government devoted a large share of the $200 million in annual revenue drawn from the British-operated Iraq Petroleum Company to economic development. But while the landholders profited greatly from irrigation and other projects started under Nuri, without social and land reform little if any of the investment seeped down to the fellahin. One Iraqi peasant told me in 1952, "I wish the government would stop making more of the land good. It just makes more work for us because the landlord says we must plant crops on all this land. More work for the same money. Can't you American and British people stop helping Iraq so much?"

Nuri's pro-West political policies, moreover, hardly eased popular discontent, particularly with Nasser, a pan-Arab hero among the Iraqis before the revolution, laboring the point that the government was exploiting the country in league with the hated Western imperialists. As American arms poured into the country, the point was rendered all the more effective by the designation of Iraq as headquarters of the Middle East military alliance that became known as the Baghdad Pact. The people viewed this decision as a symbol of the contempt in which the government held them.

All these grievances produced just the atmosphere the communists needed to gain supporters. When the explosion came on July 14, 1958, they were ready to exploit the resultant chaos for their own ends.

Kassim struck swiftly in a dawn attack. His men captured the Baghdad radio station and shelled the royal palace, mowing down King Faisal and members of the royal household as they tried to flee. Nuri as-Said was killed as he attempted to escape veiled as a woman, and his body was dragged through the streets of Baghdad. The people of Iraq went wild with joy, and pictures of Kassim and Nasser soon plastered every wall. The forces of nationalism had been victorious. At this point the communists, merely part of the nationalist mob, were not in a commanding position. In fact, with Nasserism riding high, the communists, it appeared, might actually be squeezed out of any influential role in the determination of Iraqi policy—particularly if Iraq were to become associated with the United Arab Republic, as many observers predicted at the time. For Nasser, while tightening economic and cultural ties with Moscow as a matter of expediency, was completely intolerant of domestic communists.

"It would not at all surprise me if Iraq decided to join the UAR," a Nasserite leader in Lebanon, whose supporters were rebelling against the pro-West Lebanese government at the time of the Iraqi revolt, told me in the barricaded native quarter of Beirut shortly after American troops landed in that city, "and you Americans should be happy about that, because then Iraq will never go communist."

But the history of Iraqi politics offered considerable evidence that that country would be in no hurry to share its immense oil wealth with impoverished Egypt, especially in the light of the traditional rivalry between those two states for domination of the Arab world. In a dispatch to the *Washington Post* sent shortly after the Iraqi revolution, I wrote: "Nasser has gone far in his efforts to dominate the Arab world. But he has hit a dead end. And if Arab history is any indication, the main roadblock may still be Iraq, despite its supposedly pro-Nasser character. Iraq has been willing to talk friendship with Nasser, but not a greater UAR to which it would contribute its oil wealth . . ."

Indeed, it was not long before history repeated itself—seemingly for the benefit of the communists. Kassim's chief lieutenant, Colonel Abdul Salam Aref, who immediately after the revolt glowingly referred to himself as "Kassim's son," favored associating Iraq with the United Arab Republic, placing pan-Arab nationalism over the narrower concept of Iraqi nationalism. Kassim, however, saw the future in more practical terms. He was an Iraqi first. The two men fell out, and the communists were quick to seize the opportunity afforded by this split. Favoring Kassim's kind of nationalism because it could be more easily infiltrated, the Reds, with his approval, turned their street mobs against those supporting Aref and Nasser. Organized and disciplined—unlike the Nasserites—the communists seized control of the People's Resistance, a paramilitary force originally formed to help the Kassim government consolidate its power, and set up or consolidated their control over many front groups, including the Peasant Front, the Students' League, the Peace Partisans, the League for the Defense of Women's Rights, the Workers' Union and Liaison Committee, the Democratic Youth, and the unions of teachers, engineers, physicians, artists, and journalists. A number of Moslem preachers, some probably trained in Russia, supported the Red struggle for the "social ideals of Islam."

With the power of the Cairo-encouraged Nasserite mobs in check, Kassim decided to exile Aref to the post of Ambassador to West Germany. But when approached, Aref refused, pulling a pistol from his holster. Kassim grabbed his wrist and yelled, "What are you trying to do, Abdul Salam?" "I wanted to take my own life," Aref replied. "I forgive you for this, too," Kassim said. "But you have to leave. You are dividing the country. I want to keep you away from evil people." And so "Kassim's son" left Iraq—only to head for the UAR where he conspired with officials for the overthrow of his chief. Secretly returning to his country to arrange for a Nasserite uprising, he was arrested and eventually sentenced to death. Kassim's victory over the Nasserites was complete, and the communists swiftly consolidated their position. Anticommunists were ousted from all important government jobs or quit in protest against the growing Red threat.

The communists, it developed, had even infiltrated the top echelon of Nuri's pro-West regime. Thus, Colonel Wasfi Tahir, who had been Nuri's chief aide and had strangely continued on as Kassim's, turned out to be procommunist, and largely under his influence other extreme leftists were put in key government positions. His brother, Colonel Lutfi Tahir, a party member, was given supervision of the press, and Major Selim Fakhri, another pro-Red, became director of the government radio. Red-leaning Ghadban as-Said joined Kassim's staff as an aide, and a communist stepped in as Minister of Information. Even more important, with the purging of pan-Arabists from the military, procommunist Colonel Jalal al-

Awqati assumed command of the air force, and other extreme leftists took over the tank corps and military intelligence. A communist, Taha ash Shaikh Ahmad, became chief of the political police.

Nasserite and anticommunist resistance appeared to disintegrate
completely in March 1959, when a premature UAR-sponsored revolt led by Colonel Abdul Wahab Shawaf, commander of the gar-
rison at Mosul in northern Iraq, was crushed by the communist
People's Resistance and Red-dominated Kurds. The victors went
on a rampage of murder and vengeance. Throughout the country,
scores of political opponents were killed, and hundreds of other
anticommunists were jailed on Red orders. The government and
the army were systematically purged. Setting up their own "action
committees" in the ministries, the communists went through the
lists of employees, blackballing persons they even suspected of being opposed to them. Military officers who had once been discharged for communist activity were called back to duty. An extreme leftist, Ibrahim Kubba, took over the Economics Ministry.

But communist power was perhaps most effectively exerted
through the People's Court, which, under presiding Judge Colonel
Fadhil al Mahdawi, a procommunist demagogue and cousin of
Kassim's, offered television audiences a courtroom circus spectacle
reminiscent of the Stalin purge trials. Typical of the testimony was
this exchange:

Prosecutor: Colonel Aref went to Damascus and plotted with
Nasser to invite Kassim there so that Kassim might be assassinated
when he landed at the airport. (Horrified gasps from the audience.) But our leader knew of this plot and rejected the invitation, and will reject it forever. (Applause.)

Judge Mahdawi (interrupting): Yes, he will reject it, but when
the Syrian people are emancipated [from the UAR] we shall all be
there.

Audience: Kassim is a true leader! Long live, long live, long
live!

Prosecutor: The prosecution, in the name of liberty, requests
that the heads of the accused be cut off because of their co-
operation with Abdel Nasser, agent of American imperialism and
enemy of the democratic republic.

Mahdawi: Nasser is a villain, despot, a vile President, a Pharaoh
Ramses who could not break the will of the struggling Syrians. His
newspapers are all servants of Dulles.

Suddenly, a man in the balcony stood up and began reading a
poem: "Hail to thee, Kassim, our jewel, defender of democracy,
destroyer of our enemies!"

The accused were found guilty and shot.
"You may rave, al Mahdawi," Radio Cairo raged,

but the man whose place should be in dock has no right to sit in the judge's chair. The man who remained hiding in his house until 4:00 P.M. on July 14 [the day of the Baghdad revolution] has no right to try the heroes of July 14 . . . The man who was to be tried by a military tribunal on July 17 for stealing 50 coalbags from army stores has no right to place himself above army officers whose clean hands held guns to purge the country of corruption and graft . . .

The Iraqi government was now largely under the control of a coalition of procommunist colonels, fellow-traveling lawyers, and out-and-out Communist Party members. The colonels, as indicated above, were among Kassim's closest advisers and held sway over the communications media, the armed forces, and the courts. Emerging, like Kassim, from Iraq's discontented middle class, none understood, or in most cases, had even read, Marx or Lenin, but they were attracted—at least for the time being—to the propaganda concept of communism by a vague idealism stemming from bitter memories of ruling-class exploitation in the past, and even more strongly by the opportunities for personal advancement offered by this new and spreading doctrine. The fellow-traveling lawyers, led by Aziz Sharif and Tawfiq Munir—a third important leader, Kamil Kazani, was killed in the Mosul revolt—had supported communist causes since the end of World War II, but found it tactically expedient to remain outside the party. Thus, during periods when the party was illegal, they were able to set up other leftist parties to carry on the communist program above ground. Such parties were not necessary with the Communist Party in a favored position, but the lawyers were useful in establishing numerous front organizations such as the Peace Partisans' Movement, which Aziz Sharif headed, as a means of manipulating public opinion and the street mobs.

The Communist Party Politbureau itself consisted mainly, as it does today, of three groups: Reds imprisoned under the Nuri regime, such as Aziz al Haj and Mohammed Abu el Iss; those who had lived in Eastern Europe, where they were given intensive Marxist training; and those who had resided in Cairo, Damascus, or Paris. Abdul Kader Ismail is the leading representative of this last group, having lived in Egypt since 1947. Other top Politbureau leaders included, and still do, Professor Abdulla al Bustani of Baghdad Law School, one of the leading communist intellectuals, and Mohammed Hassan al Uwaidi, who is believed to be party secretary.

This ill-disciplined conglomeration of Reds and pro-Reds did not see eye to eye on how to proceed on the next step leading to full communist power, and their discord grew as conflicting advice came from Moscow and Peking, both of which flooded Iraq with propaganda in an apparently competitive effort to win Iraqi communist support. The Iraqi Reds who had been released from prison, the most vindictive and extreme communist group, tended to support the Peking thesis that called for intensified activist tactics to achieve the establishment of a People's Democracy as soon as possible, even if this meant the liquidation of a reluctant Kassim.

The groups that had been living in relative comfort outside Iraq for many years appeared to favor the more moderate and calculated approach advocated by Moscow. Khrushchev seems to have been in a dilemma from the first about proper Red policy in Iraq. There was considerable argument for seizing the country. A communist Iraq would open the whole Middle East to Soviet penetration. The coveted Persian Gulf would be secured. Turkey's eastern border could be subjected to pressure. With relations between Russia and Afghanistan tightening, Iran, hemmed in by those two countries and Iraq, could be isolated. The West could be deprived of Iraqi oil.

But Khrushchev decided as events drew to a head that these advantages would be outweighed by the disadvantages of abrupt action. The long-nurtured Soviet effort to identify communist interests with national movements throughout the underdeveloped world would have gone for nought, and many such movements might, in fear, rush into the Western camp. Nor would the West miss Iraqi oil, the loss of which could easily be compensated for through increased production in other oil-producing areas. And as the Soviet Union could not absorb Iraq's oil, since it exported its own, Iraq would be stuck without a market—hardly a situation conducive to order in that country or to procommunism in other countries which sell their oil to the West. Further, if a communist Iraqi government began to totter, Russia could not send troops to support it, for it had no land bridge across Iran, which separates the USSR from Iraq. Khrushchev also foresaw difficulties in an immediate overthrow of Kassim, in the event he refused to go all the way with the Reds, as seemed likely, after the communists had built him up as a great national hero.

The Russians, therefore, unlike the Red Chinese, made no appeal to the mobs, but operated strictly on a government-to-government basis, wanting nothing more for the moment than to retain a strong influence within a noncommunist government that could provide a springboard for a future coup when the time was ripe for one. They lauded the program of the new leaders, supplied equipment for the two Iraqi army divisions, and promised the government almost $140 million in aid over a seven-year period for the construction of metallurgical, engineering, and chemical plants, a woolen textile mill, a radio station, a cannery, irrigation structures, and factories that would produce shoes, glass, electric light bulbs, and clothing. Moscow also agreed to rebuild a railroad between Baghdad and the port of Basra.

Actually, the activist role of the communists at Mosul, while strengthening the Reds' tactical control of Iraq, also contained the seeds of their political decline. For the brutality and ruthlessness they displayed in smashing the Nasserite nationalists had a powerful psychological effect on the people. Such tactics could justifiably be used against Arab "traitors" like the followers of Nuri, but they were hardly justifiable in the public's eye against the nationalists, whether of the Nasser or the Kassim stripe. The reaction of one Iraqi youth who had favored the communists before Mosul was typical: "After the revolution I began supporting the communists because they seemed to be the truest Iraqi nationalists. And they kept talking about helping the poor people. I joined demonstrations whenever I was asked to. But at Mosul I saw what the communists were really like. I saw them enter my cousin's house just because he liked Nasser and tear his clothes off, and then drag him through the streets, and finally hang him. I despise the communists now. They fooled me once, but never again. I would like to kill them all."

But the moderates were unable to restrain the activists, and bitterness against communist tactics swiftly accumulated during a reign of Red terror after Mosul, finally culminating in an explosion at Kirkuk in northeastern Iraq in July 1959. The communists and the Kurds, the same combination that had put down the Mosul revolt, this time took the initiative, as urged by the Red Chinese, and attacked a community of anticommunist Turkomen, Iraqis of Turkish descent, to solidify the Red position in that area. This assault, which resulted in about eighty deaths, spelled the beginning of the end of the communist drive for power.

With anticommunist sentiment sharply on the rise throughout Iraq, the Reds swung toward Moscow's go-slow approach in a desperate move to save themselves. A humiliatingly self-critical report published by the Central Committee of the Iraqi Communist Party, and reprinted approvingly in *Pravda,* told the Iraqi communists that they must face the "necessity of a long coexistence" with the Iraqi nationalists under Kassim, and further announced that there would be a "gradual purge" from the party's ranks of harmful elements, including those who refused to relinquish their "opportunist" views. The purge, it was indicated, would extend to the leadership itself. By "opportunist" the order meant those members who wanted to take decisive steps without advance assurance of success.

> . . . The maximum solidarity of our Party with the leadership of government [said the report] played a basic role in protecting the Republic and promoting the gains of the revolution as well as consolidating the national regime and concentrating its leadership . . . However, this solidarity and the successive major victories which were its fruit caused our party to commit the error of underrating the role of other national political parties and of belittling the importance of co-operating with them in the field of defending the democratic gains and rights of the masses . . . Our demand to participate in the patriotic government was erroneous because it did not give consideration to the position and relationships of the national forces in the country, nor to the conditions of development of the revolution in relation to the Arab and international situation at the time . . .
>
> Moreover, the mass method which was taken as a means to express this demand for participating in the government was another factor which deepened the negative results in the situation. The press campaign, our overlooking or encouraging the penetration of this demand to the masses . . . as well as the wide educational campaign—all this exaggerated the strength of our Party and distorted its intentions in the view of the government, of considerable sectors of the Iraqi and Arab bourgeoisie, and of many moderate forces. As a result they became panicky at that demand . . . There is a clear difference in the application of the Party's policy by various Party organizations. Some have been reasonable and complied with the Party's policy—they bear no great responsibility for big mistakes pertaining to them; other organizations committed extremist "leftist" mistakes . . .

Communist mob activity suddenly slackened and the Reds began working to form a popular front parliament and eventually a cabinet, hoping to consolidate their hold on Iraq by legal means. At the same time, it was decided, in accordance with Moscow's wishes, to concentrate on using Iraq as a base for communist activities throughout the Middle East rather than on the immediate communization of Iraq itself. Most communist parties in the area moved their headquarters to towns in Iraq that offered easy access and communication with the countries they represented. The Iranian Tudeh Party was believed to be centered in Suleimaniya and Basra, the Turkish and Syrian parties in Mosul, and the Jordanian party in Kerbala and Najaf.

But the Reds had learned their lesson too late. As most Iraqis boiled with indignation at the Kirkuk massacre, Kassim decided it was time to go into his balancing act again. The communists had destroyed the effectiveness of the Nasserite nationalists, and could now be dispensed with themselves. Proclaiming his shock at Red lawlessness in Kirkuk, he ordered the army to disarm and disband the People's Resistance, the kernel of communist power. He dismissed Reds from the military and the government, and by mid-1961 only one of seven far-leftist ministers remained in office. He dissolved or purged many professional organizations, had anticommunist newspapers that had been previously banned attack the Communist Party, and "encouraged" military courts to pass severe sentences on Red terrorists, twenty-eight of whom were condemned to death and ten of whom received life imprisonment in 1960-61.

With the government no longer shielding the communists, anti-Reds began taking vengeance on them, beating them in bars and killing them in the street, sometimes while the police looked the other way. People began blaming the Reds for everything, including the failure of the Iraqi revolution to bring an improvement in living standards, the closing of factories for lack of imports, the constant labor strikes, the soaring inflation, the chaos of "land reform."

Simultaneously, Russian stock in Iraq plummeted. None of the major industrial projects that were to be undertaken by the Russians had got off the ground. Kassim himself told the Soviet Ambassador that his country was acting "in bad faith" and "tying political strings to loans." The Iraqis were further irritated by Russian contempt for the Iraqi dinar, which was valued at $2.80 by Kassim's government but at much less by the Soviets. "We are very poor cousins," one Iraqi diplomat commented acidly. Soviet technicians turned out to be not only inferior to the Westerners they had replaced, but, despite the lower wages paid them, more costly, for they could speak neither Arabic nor English and therefore had to have interpreters. Soviet goods also proved to be low in quality and high in price. Baghdad's taxi drivers refused to drive the Russian vehicles that were being imported, forcing the government to remove the ban that had been placed on American taxis after the revolution.

Another irritation was reflected in the remark of a shopkeeper in the teeming Baghdad bazaar. "The only thing cheap about Russian aid," he said, "is the character of the people giving it." This shopkeeper and many others haggled for hours with Russian men and women over American second-hand clothes that no Westerner would take if they were given away. When the Russians, who had to remit eighty percent of their wages home, visited a bar, a "spree" meant nursing a single bottle of beer all evening. They sometimes tried to show their generosity by dividing a cigarette or a soft drink with a startled Iraqi.

Communist influence reached rock bottom in early 1960 when the party was banned as a political organization. Even in this final humiliation of his former friends, Kassim proved clever. The Communist Party, like all other political parties in Iraq, submitted an application to the government for permission for legal status under a new law allowing the activity of approved parties and public organizations. The government returned the application with the request that the word "revolutionary" be deleted from the description of the party's character, and that the words "Marxist-Leninist," which also appeared in the description, be clarified. The party agreed to the deletion of the objectionable adjective and explained that Marx and Lenin were the authors of a "scientific analysis of economic problems" showing that each country should approach the goal of socialism according to its own characteristics.

The government was still dissatisfied. It rejected the application, explaining that another political group also calling itself the "Communist Party," had been approved as a legal organization and that, quite naturally, two parties with the same name could hardly be permitted. The approved party was a small, uninfluential dissident group under Daoud as-Sayegh, a leftist of independent mind who claimed he headed the true Communist Party despite the fact that Moscow disowned him. The legalization of his group was bitter medicine for the Reds. The *Iraqi Review,* a communist weekly supplement, wrote of Daoud:

> During the Second World War, when loyal and conscientious forces were devoting their energies to uniting in order to defeat the fascist aggressor, Daoud as-Sayegh was working to disrupt the unity of the labor and national movements. He was expelled from the Communist Party and concentrated on forming a dissident faction of opportunist and politically backward elements. In 1956

he applied for admission to the Communist Party. The party asked him to define his stand, to condemn his previous subversive activity, and to exercise self-criticism. He wrote a letter in which he criticized his part, admitted that he had engaged in opportunist factional activity running counter to Marxism-Leninism, and promised that he would work to re-educate himself under the leadership and guidance of the party . . .

During the latter half of 1959, when the national movement in our country was undergoing a crisis, when reactionary forces lifted their heads, and imperialist and reactionary propaganda both in and outside the country was attacking the Republic under the guise of "combating communism," Daoud as-Sayegh resumed his subversive activities. This compelled the party to expel him.

The party submitted another application under a different name, the People's Unity Party, but this too was rejected. The application of a third group of communists, calling itself the Republican Party, met with no greater success. Allied with the real communists, this group included Aziz Sharif, the Peace Partisans' chief, and other "independent lawyers," who had long specialized in front parties and organizations, as well as such important government figures as Abdul Fattah Ibrahim, Director of the Oil Refineries Administration, Dr. Sadik al-Atroushi, Director General of Education, and poet Mohammed Mahdid al-Jawahiri, editor of the leftist newspaper *Al Rai al-Aam*.

The People's Unity Party, though technically illegal, was nevertheless permitted to operate freely until November 1960, when the Reds organized a strike of tobacco workers in Baghdad to protest alleged government interference in trade-union elections. Since then, the party's activities have been suppressed, and anticommunist propaganda has been intensified by the government. The controlled press has constantly condemned Soviet press criticism of Iraq's internal policies, and offered detailed descriptions of communist infiltration of specific ministries and other government operations.

An even more revealing index of the communist decline has been the disintegration of Red influence within labor and other groups formerly dominated by the communists, despite Red protests—like that voiced following the tobacco union elections—that the government is guilty of stuffing organizational ballot boxes. Noncommunist electoral victories have ended communist control in almost all the major professional organizations, including the highly influential Iraqi Trade Union Federation and Iraqi Teachers Union.

When groups have not been able to be wrested from Red control by elections, competing organizations have been set up, or the Red-led groups have been banned. A noncommunist Union of Iraqi Authors and Writers was organized to compete with the communist Iraqi Writers Union, while the Iraqi Democratic Youth Federation, the Iraqi Peace Partisans, and several branches of the Iraqi Women's League and the General Union of Iraqi Students were ordered to disband. In other anticommunist moves, the government removed 72 nonpracticing leftist journalists from the rolls of the Iraqi Journalists Association immediately prior to its 1961 elections, and facilitated the establishment of a General Federation of Peasant Societies, using the same name as that of a banned communist group.

Moreover, circulation of communist literature has been largely suppressed. The magazine, *Soviet Union,* which hit a top circulation of 10,000 in 1959, was down to 1,000 copies in late 1960. The East German *Majalla,* the most popular communist publication in Iraq, maintained a circulation of 5,000 but may be banned shortly. Six of eleven communist or procommunist dailies, including the top-circulation official voice of the illegal orthodox party, and eight of seventeen other Red publications were already banned by mid-1961. The communist press has been excluded completely from three of Iraq's southern provinces by local authorities.

In a parallel purging process, all unlicensed libraries have been closed. Primary and secondary school history and geography books that had been adopted by procommunist elements in the Ministry of Education will be rewritten. All foreign publications intended for distribution in Iraq must be censored by a Foreign Office committee, a requirement that has curbed the activities of the large Tass staff, as well as information activity of all embassies.

The new anticommunist mood in Iraq has resulted in a corresponding improvement in the Iraqi attitude toward Westerners, who, in the year after the revolution, were taunted and spat at in the streets—that is, those who were not thrown out of the country altogether. West Germans, Austrians, and Swiss have resumed building bridges and ports, and British goods are again featured in shop windows. The Iraqis even smile at Westerners occasionally. Yet few people who know Iraq would venture to guess that this smile will not again turn into a hateful scowl at almost any time. For the communists, despite the severe beating they have taken in recent months, are by no means flat on their backs and can take considerable comfort in a number of factors that may help them in the future.

One is the ever-simmering Kurdish problem, which could within the next decade become the most explosive Cold War issue in the Middle East, possibly starting with Kassim's fall. With a history reaching back to Sumeria 4,500 years ago, the tough, warrior Kurds are an ultranationalistic people without a nation. They number, it is roughly estimated, eight and a half million, including four million in Turkey, two and a half million in Iran, one and a half million in Iraq, and half a million in Syria and the Soviet Union, living mainly in the mountains. The Kurds are particularly influential in Iraq, where they constitute about one-fifth of the population. In addition many Iraqis, including, it is believed, Kassim himself, have Kurdish blood.

The Kurds had their own independent state of Kurdistan until the early sixteenth century, after which this state became a vassal territory of the Ottoman Empire. Following World War I, the Kurds were promised independence by the victorious allies, and in 1920 the Treaty of Sèvres, which divided up the Ottoman Empire, called for a Kurdish state carved out of Turkey and Iraq. But the British had second thoughts about this promise, particularly as oil-rich Mosul and Kirkuk were to be in the new kingdom. They decided that these areas should be part of Iraq and that the Kurds should serve as a buffer between Turkey and Iraq. The Turks, under Atatürk, also denounced the Treaty of Sèvres. In 1923 the Treaty of Lausanne substituted for the project some vague reference to Kurdish minority rights. The Kurds, feeling themselves betrayed, have been in constant revolt ever since; and in their bitterness they have become violently anti-West, anti-Turk, anti-Iranian, and anti-Arab.

They have found only one "friend"—Russia. The aim of the Soviet Union, the Kremlin has long proclaimed, is the establishment of an independent Kurdistan, including the Soviet Kurds. In other words, a Soviet Kurdistan in the heart of the Middle East, or, at the least, constant turbulence and instability in Iraq and pro-West Turkey and Iran. The top Soviet agent in this project is the most powerful of the Kurdish leaders, Mullah Mustafa al-Barzani, a mysterious and romantic figure even in his stylish English-cut suits that contrast so sharply with the pantaloons and tasseled turbans that most Kurds wear. Mullah Mustafa dreams of becoming—with Soviet aid—another Saladin, the Kurdish hero who defeated the crusaders. Though wielding an enormous influence among most Kurds, Mustafa, a heavy-set man with thick, black, beetle brows, a large nose, and a mustache, is actually the chief of the Barzani tribe only, a fanatical and superstitious sect which believes he is immune to bullets. His supernatural reputation grew in 1930-31 when only the British Air Force saved Iraqi armies from destruction at his hands, and also during fierce fighting in 1941-42 and 1944-45.

In 1945 Mullah Mustafa and over 1,000 members of his tribe joined in a Soviet-sponsored revolt in the Iranian province of Azerbaijan, which was to become the kernel of a new Kurdistan. But when the revolt failed, Mustafa, exiled by the Iraq government, went to Russia and became a general in the Red Army. He spent most of the postwar years in Moscow and Prague, learning his Marx and planning for the day of his triumphant return. This day came following the Iraqi revolution in 1958. He was personally welcomed back by Kassim and put up in the luxurious house that had belonged to his hated enemy, Nuri as-Said.

With his communist friends virtually running Iraq, Mustafa was sure that Kurdish autonomy, at least within his country, was but a step away—a step toward an ultimately "independent" Kurdistan. While he waited, his men, who had been given arms by the Kassim government, helped the communists perpetrate the massacres at Mosul and Kirkuk, fearful that the Nasserites, if they got into power, would never listen to Kurdish demands. But he found the going tougher when he tried to consolidate his control over the various Kurdish tribes whom he expected to rule once autonomy was achieved. Far from being unified, the Kurds have always felt greater loyalty to family, village, clan, sheik, and tribe than to any nontribal leader claiming to represent the Kurds as a whole.

Refusing to accept Mustafa's rule, the Zibari and Baradost tribes began raiding the villages of Mustafa's followers. Mustafa then laid waste some twenty-five Kurdish villages before government troops finally intervened. When he resisted, the government, which had begun to turn against the communists and their supporters, sent aircraft against him and armed his enemies, who had for months protested the issuance of arms to Mustafa's tribe but not to them. Mustafa, now convinced that Kassim would never grant autonomy to the Kurds, particularly with him as the leader, fled to Russia again.

Meanwhile the Kurdish Democratic Party, which also claimed to represent all the Kurds, including those of Mustafa, began complaining to Kassim that the Kurds had not yet received any benefits from the revolution. It suggested that he could at least make a start by permitting the instruction of the Kurdish language in the schools and the publication of books in this language, there being only about 140 such books available in the libraries. But with the anticommunist phase of the revolution now going into high gear, Kassim was in no mood to listen to the Red-leaning Kurds, especially after Mustafa's brazen defiance of his authority. He promptly slapped Ibrahim Ahmed, Secretary-General of the Kurdish party, in jail on charges that the party newspaper he edited had tried to spread dissension by criticizing the government. Eventually released, Ahmed, encouraged by the communists, went right on criticizing the Kassim regime, though his party was banned.

Mullah Mustafa returned to Iraq, obviously with Soviet blessings, and in September 1961 led a full-scale Vietcong-style guerrilla revolt against the government in northern Iraq that Kassim claimed he crushed. But in March 1962 a new rebellion broke out on an even larger scale and reports leaking out of Iraq in the next several months indicated that casualties among Iraqi troops and civilians, many of whom were assassinated with razor-sharp Kurdish daggers called *khanjars,* numbered in the thousands. Hundreds of villages were destroyed by aerial bombardment, sacking, and burning. Mustafa, with most Kurds now behind him, demanded establishment of an "autonomous Kurdistan within the Iraqi Republic" and the withdrawal of Iraqi forces from the north. Mustafa also demanded, knowing the Premier could not accept such a condition, an end to "Kassim's incompetent dictatorship." Kassim immediately sent reinforcements to the north, but with only two days' supplies and ammunition for fear of a mutiny, since a fourth to a third of his army and police are composed of Kurds.

The Soviet genius for adapting its tactics to circumstances has been conspicuously evident in this situation. On the state level, Moscow has been pouring aid into Iraq and in other ways been trying to get Kassim to give his neutralism a pro-East slant once again. But on the party level, Kassim is condemned with increasing violence, especially in relation to the Kurdish problem, which, the Reds say, must be solved on Mustafa's terms. An article that appeared in the August 1962 issue of *Problems of Peace and Socialism,* an international communist periodical published in Prague, demanded that Kassim end military operations against the Kurds and said that the communists were organizing a mass movement in Baghdad and other Arab cities to obtain recognition of Kurdish rights. The article described the Kurdish Democratic Party, which Mullah Mustafa dominated after his civil war spread, as "a party of the national bourgeoisie and the small liberal landowners. It also includes part of the petty urban bourgeoisie and intelligentsia. It pursues an anti-imperialist policy."

But the article, interestingly enough, made no secret of some of the difficulties the Reds have encountered in trying to put a communist label on Kurdish nationalism. "As for the Kurdish bourgeois nationalists," it said,

> they have placed their narrow nationalist conceptions above the interests of the common struggle. This has frequently led them to adopt a course that weakens the common struggle and to advocate the liquidation of communist organization in Kurdistan . . . Thus, Kurdish bourgeois nationalism, despite its general democratic content, tends to result in erroneous sectarian methods of struggle at a time when unity should be enhanced and the national front strengthened.

Mustafa himself has denied that he is a communist and has even said, incredibly enough, that he would turn Iraq into a Western stronghold—if the United States furnished him with aid and helped him to overthrow Kassim. Otherwise, he has warned, he would have to depend on help from the Soviet Union, which, because of its friendliness toward Kassim on the state level, has been reluctant to supply Mustafa with more than unofficial encouragement. In any event, the Mullah has up to now done pretty well with Iraqi arms, bought, stolen, and captured. An Iraqi official told me in a masterpiece of understatement: "It's difficult to keep the Kurds in line. They're more dangerous than the Communist Party because they're more impatient for victory. But if we gave them autonomy, it's clear what the dangers would be to Iraq's unity and security."

If the Kurds may eventually give communism a new opportunity to come to the fore in Iraq, the communists are also likely to profit from Kassim's economic difficulties, though they themselves have been blamed for most of them. Aside from the Kurds, the Iraqis are anxiously waiting for the fulfillment of the revolution's promises, and they are growing impatient. If Kassim fails to deliver soon, they may, in desperation, begin to believe the current communist refrain that if only the Reds were given the free hand they had been denied even at the height of their power, every Iraqi would already be on the road to plenty.

Symbolizing Iraq's frozen revolution is the condition of an Iraqi Statue of Liberty, or more precisely, bas-relief, riveted to a huge concrete slab in the Bab el-Sharja in the center of Baghdad. Unlike the subdued version in New York harbor, the Iraqi Miss Liberty is almost beside herself with joy, with both arms held aloft in ecstatic glee, a torch of freedom grasped firmly in one clenched hand. Unfortunately, however, she has no feet. Workmen never got around to finishing the figure, which is supposed to represent the "meaning of the revolution," and for many Iraqis it's just as well. Because they're not quite sure that the revolution had a meaning. Certainly Kassim's intentions are good. He wants to keep his promise of giving higher living standards to all. But he has discovered that remaking a nation is a far more complex process than the mere elimination of a reactionary government.

About half of the more than $200 million in oil revenues filling the treasury each year is going for development, but in mid-1962 no big construction contracts had been signed since the revolution, and development may be restricted when contracts concluded by the previous government run out. Most administrators with a knowledge of contract negotiation were purged, while big foreign contractors are hesitant to make new deals in view of the apparent instability of the Kassim government. Even Iraqi officials are wary about making commitments that might politically benefit their enemies should they come to power. Yet a continuing diminution of industrial activity is also bound to have unfavorable political consequences, for it will mean increasing unemployment.

Land reform, the biggest and most spectacular of Kassim's announced revolutionary tasks, has so far proved a failure. Almost 900,000 acres of a total of 9,300,000 acres scheduled for distribution to landless peasants were distributed up to mid-1961. And the actual turnover of this land has been greeted in each case with wild celebration by the peasant beneficiaries. When Kassim personally distributed land titles to fifty peasants at the village of Abu Ghuraish near Baghdad in July 1961, they sang and danced and even tried to kiss his hand. (The embarrassed, rough-hewn Kassim backed away and patted the peasants on the shoulder.) The bearded elder of the village jumped up and down shouting, "Hoo, hoo, hoo," and his subjects, wearing white nightgown-like *galabias* and white *kafiyems* around their heads, chanted, "We have driven Abu Haji into the dark, dark sea." Abu Haji is the Iraqi nickname for the British, deriving from the name of a man who is supposed to have spied for the British in World War I.

But the happy new peasant landowners soon find themselves disillusioned. This disillusionment is mirrored in the fact that after the first confiscations of big estates, plus a drought, agricultural production nose-dived to a level about twenty-five percent of normal. It can also be seen in the expenditure of $45 million for wheat imports and the domestic consumption of the whole barley crop in 1960, though Iraq is normally an exporter of these items.

The reasons for this failure are complex. The government has not been able to set up co-operatives fast enough that would enable peasants to purchase seed, sell their produce, and learn how to irrigate their land. This problem has been intensified by the bitterness and ill grace of many dispossessed landlords who leave no seed or machinery at all behind for the new owners to use. Matters have not been helped any by the arbitrary division of land by government agricultural "experts" who sometimes cut peasants off without any irrigation water at all, while making available excess water to others. As a result of such difficulties, many peasants have cut back production or quit farming altogether, often heading penniless for Baghdad, where they settle in squalid mud *sarifa* huts within the glare of the city's bright lights.

As Kassim's economic burdens increase, so does his dependence on communist-bloc aid, which he is only too happy to accept despite his current anticommunist domestic policies. And the Russians and their satellites, for their part, are only too happy to oblige, even while condemning these policies. So upset was the Soviet Union about criticism of its aid program that it responded with a sensational burst of speed on several projects. In less than two months, thirty-two Russian technicians rushed through the construction of a $3.5 million radio station, second in power in the Middle East only to a Soviet-built station in Egypt. The USSR has also finished designing a steel works for Baghdad, has equipped two-thirds of the Iraqi army, and may take over oil prospecting in areas from which Kassim has excluded technicians of the Iraq Petroleum Company. A law passed in 1961 confines the IPC to sectors it is already exploiting. Unless it is rescinded the company may simply decide to get out of Iraq—Iraq needs a market more than the firm needs Iraq—and let it stew in its own oil.

Russia is also recovering its reputation among the Iraqi people as it becomes clear that the Iraqi government and not the USSR was responsible for most of the delay in launching the Soviet aid program. While the Soviet Union agreed to supply machinery, designs, and technicians, Iraq was supposed to furnish buildings, utilities, and roads. But Iraq hasn't been able to construct buildings swiftly enough. The fittings for five factories are believed rusting away awaiting the construction of plants. Meanwhile, Czechoslovakia has decided to grant Iraq about $33 million in credit for oil-refining and hydroelectric projects. Kassim has indicated he also wants private investment, but in partnership with the government. In any event, his economic plans call for major industries to be owned by the state.

The communist bloc is also trying to help Kassim out of his

agricultural dilemma. Russian experts have set up five Soviet-style experimental farms, with Iraq paying the bills and the Soviet Union furnishing some equipment on credit. The Ministry of Agriculture has decided to replace its hasty provisional land re- form program with a five-year plan designed with the aid of Polish and Czechoslovakian advisers. The United States is helping to train Iraqi agricultural technicians, but the communist-bloc in- fluence appears to be prevailing.

In the Cold War too, Iraq, while neutralist, leans toward the East. Foreign Minister Hashim Jawad, in a speech before the United Nations General Assembly in October 1961, took the So- viet-bloc view on the questions of Berlin, Germany in general, and the representation of Communist China in the United Na- tions, and credited Russia with having made a disarmament pro- posal that "has gained wide support and has had an impact upon world public opinion."

This pro-East attitude is to a large extent rooted in anti- British feelings, which were intensified when British troops moved into oil-rich Kuwait in June 1961 after Iraq indicated it would ab- sorb the territory. In any event, it is clear that Iraq is by no means in the Western camp. It is also clear that the possibility of an early comeback by the domestic communists cannot be dis- counted. There are still more Reds or pro-Reds with government jobs in Iraq than in any other country in the Middle East.

In 1962 Premier Kassim was far from being the great popular leader he had once been. During celebrations of the third an- niversary of the Iraqi revolution, crowds were small and un- responsive. Both the pan-Arab nationalists and the communists despise him for turning against them. The Kurds were in control of some parts of Iraq. The rest of the people, disillusioned with the revolution and impatient for reform, have lost their stomach for worn-out slogans and promises. Kassim has nevertheless managed to maintain himself in power through his highly successful balanc- ing act.

As he took up with the Reds once before when he needed them to offset the opposition of the Nasserites, so might he again find them a convenient tool should the Nasserites or some other group, possibly even the Kurds, seriously threaten his power—though Syria's breakaway from the UAR has reduced any new potential pan-Arabist danger. The Reds are undoubtedly ready and avail- able to help out again when the time comes. Meanwhile, they are leaving it to their communist friends in Moscow and elsewhere to soften the government up. If Kassim suddenly disappeared from the scene, things might even be easier. For the communists, as the only tightly organized political group in the country, would have as good a chance as anybody to fill the power vacuum. And next time they get their foot in the door, they are not likely to repeat the mistakes that led to their downfall when they had just about reached their goal.

X

IRAN:

A MATTER OF WAITING

In early 1961 Soviet Premier Khrushchev prophesied in a Moscow interview with American columnist Walter Lippmann that the Iranian people would soon revolt against Shah Reza Pahlevi, their pro-West ruler. "You will assert," he said, "that the Shah has been overthrown by the communists, and we shall be very glad to have it thought in the world that all the progressive people in Iran recognize that we are the leaders of the progress of mankind."

This prediction was based on far more than wishful thinking. To judge from conditions in Iran it may seem rather surprising that the lid hasn't blown before now. The communists could not ask for a situation—geographical, political, economic, and social—more suited to their ends. No country, it would appear, is riper for a communist takeover. Consider these factors:

Iran shares more than 1,000 miles of its northeast frontier with the Soviet Union and can easily be infiltrated by Red agents.

Iran, as a land bridge to the Middle East and to the warm waters of the Persian Gulf, is one of Russia's most coveted targets in the Afro-Asian world, as evidenced, for one thing, by the massive communist radio campaign in that country, probably the most intensive in the world.

The disparity in living standards between the few mink- and Cadillac-owning rich and the impoverished masses is one of the greatest in the world, with 1,000 landholding families possessing more than half of the arable land and wielding feudal power over eighty percent of the population.

Probably no ruling class in the world is more corrupt than that of Iran.

The misery of the masses is made all the more unbearable by the knowledge that Iran has vast oil wealth and receives vast additional funds from the United States that somehow never reach them.

The Iranian capital of Teheran offers a capsule picture of the fantastic gap in living standards between the ruling class and the ruled. From the plush Park Hotel, one looks down on streets bordered by open gutters, or *jubes,* in whose filthy waters raggedly dressed women, their babies tied to their backs with a sash, wash dishes, men urinate, and children bathe. The same gutters are also a common source of drinking water. Remarkably, disease is not widespread. "If a child lives past its fifth birthday," an Iranian student told me, "it is by then immune to most germs. Unfortunately, only about fifty percent live that long."

In Teheran's luxurious night clubs, men with Italian-made suits drink bottles of French champagne in the company of hostesses imported from Spain, while their wives are vacationing in Austria with money stashed away in Swiss banks. A few blocks distant, families huddle in mud huts warming themselves over an open fire and eating rice and onions. Outside shops displaying expensive imported wares, from emeralds to air conditioners, gaunt, unshaven, unemployed men sit on the sidewalk that is their bed at night and talk, watching with hateful eyes as women wearing fur coats and the latest Western hairdos emerge with ribboned packages under their arms.

Yet despite such ideal conditions for the growth of communism, the Iranian Communist Party, known as the Tudeh, or People's Party, is a relatively uninfluential force in Iran today, deriving most of its strength from the discontent of the growing but small urban middle class, particularly the intellectuals. Present active membership is estimated at only about 2,000, one reason being the party's vigorous suppression by security forces. Communism has been outlawed in Iran since 1931, though it was given the opportunity to function in the open under the guise of the Tudeh Party following a parliamentary amnesty to all political prisoners about a month after Soviet troops invaded Iran in 1941. Tudeh itself was outlawed in 1949, following charges that it was implicated in an attempted assassination of the Shah. Despite its illegality, it enjoyed

new life under the ultranationalist regime of Prime Minister Mohammed Mossadegh from 1951 to 1953, but since Mossadegh's
overthrow its activities have been effectively checked, particularly
as the result of the execution of twenty-six party leaders in 1954.
Its front organizations have been disbanded, and the army purged
—or so it is believed—of Red infiltrators.

Aside from the police factor, the Shah is the core of the communists' difficulty. He is the son of Reza Pahlevi, a six-foot-four-inch
army officer who overthrew the Qajar dynasty in 1921 and established himself first as Minister of War, then as Premier, and finally
as Shah. A tough, ill-tempered man who would beat his own ministers with a riding whip when they dared to argue with him, Reza
Shah became a kind of minor Atatürk, dragging his country into
the twentieth century despite the bitter opposition of the feudal
landlords and the *mullahs*. He ordered women to remove their
purdah veils, built the Trans-Iranian railway with its 4,100 bridges
and 54 miles of tunnel, and crushed tribal revolts—taking time
out, however, to amass a great personal fortune. The current Shah
inherited the throne when, in 1941, his father was exiled for co-
operating with the Nazis by the British, who had invaded Iran
jointly with the Russians.

The peasant masses, who constitute the greater part of the Iranian population, strongly support him, partly because it is tradition
to obey and respect the Shah, whoever he may be, partly because
they feel that he is at least trying to protect them against excessive
exploitation by their hated landlords. Despite their misery, the
peasants are proud of Iran's rich national heritage, and the Shah is
part of it. Shahs have been sitting on the Peacock Throne for 2,500
years, and the idea that this symbol of Persian greatness be abandoned, as the communists are urging, has little appeal. That would
be like disowning the past—a magnificent past of a people who can
trace their ancestry to Cyrus the Great, who unified the Medes and
the Persians in 550 B.C., to Darius the Great, who ruled an empire
extending from the Nile to the Indus, and to Xerxes, the great warrior whose armies reached the gates of Athens before perishing in
defeat at the Battle of Salamis; a past glorified in the poetry of
Omar Khayyám and extolled by the sculpted friezes of Persepolis
and the glazed mosques of Isfahan and Shiraz.

In the center of a small patch of wheat field near Abadan in
southern Iran, I asked a peasant for his opinion of the Shah. He
turned his stubbled, bony face toward his village, a complex of mud
huts nestled at the foot of a hill. "My people like the Shah," he said.

"The Shah is our leader. Our country is poor, but it is great. It is great because we have the Shah. And besides, he wants to help us. He wants to give us our own land."

And this is precisely the aim of the Shah, a kindly, intelligent man with a handsome, hawk-nosed face and a slim, straight, athletic build (he is a fine skier, tennis player, and sports-car racer). Having inherited from his industrious father 700 "crown villages," comprising an area totaling 600,000 acres, he has made numerous trips to various parts of the country since 1950, ceremonially parceling out pieces of his land and hoping that other landlords, most of whom receive high rents and personal services from the peasants, would follow his example. When they didn't, he decreed a new land reform law in early 1962 under which landlords must give up all their holdings to peasant tenants except for one village. Owners will be reimbursed by the state in ten yearly installments and the peasants, organized in co-operatives, will pay the government for their new properties over a period of fifteen years.

Though over one million acres of land were redistributed in less than a year, the battle is not yet won, for the landlords, mainly about 450 families, are struggling to sabotage the new law by instigating street riots, forging ballots in village elections, and falsifying land ownership records. One group of landlords even arranged the murder of a land reform agent, stirring the government to declare martial law in the area and a national day of mourning for the victim. Moreover, much state aid, which might not be available, will be needed to help the new owners manage their farms, to provide credits, and to supply tools, improved seeds, and fertilizers. But the peasants are impressed almost as much by the Shah's good intentions as by the better life that the law promises them.

They are also impressed by the advice of local *mullahs,* who strongly support the Shah as a barrier to communism. Most Iranian peasants are devout members of the highly disciplined Shiite sect of Islam and listen more carefully to their religious leaders than do the peasants in Arab countries, most of whom belong to the more loosely organized Sunni sect. Thus, propaganda disseminated in the villages vilifying the Shah has so far had little effect.

"The Tudeh Party, as usual, has miscalculated the situation," an Iranian politician told me. "If they were smart, they would stop trying to tear down the Shah, which is like trying to tear down God, and concentrate on the people's poverty."

The Tudeh is still suffering from miscalculations it has made in the past. In particular, it failed to exploit its opportunities in the chaotic era of Mossadegh, who nationalized Iran's oil industry with the help of his street mobs—it had been controlled by the British previously—and led his country to bankruptcy before finally being deposed by pro-Shah forces in 1953. Under the Stalinist influence, the party, though expanding its activities through a multitude of front organizations and infiltration of army officer ranks, made little effort to collaborate with Mossadegh's fanatically nationalist mobs, but simply tried to take them over as their own. In 1951, when Mossadegh first came to power, Moscow actually accused the Prime Minister of being a tool of American imperialism. Even toward the end of his regime, when it was conceded that he was not, after all, an imperialist agent, he was charged with "inconsistency" for not mobilizing the "popular democratic forces" in the "common struggle"—in other words, for not accepting communist control.

Mossadegh hardly considered communism the answer to Iranian ills. The son of a princess of the Qajar dynasty and of a politician who was Finance Minister for thirty years, he was—and still is—an extremely wealthy landowner who has always been far too nationalistic to concern himself with international ideologies. Ever since Britain and Persia signed a colonial-type treaty in 1919, Mossadegh, who first entered politics in 1906, has shouted from the halls of the Majlis, or parliament, of which he was a veteran member: Persia for the Persians. Nevertheless, his deep distrust of the West happened to parallel the Tudeh Party line, and for tactical purposes he might very well have welcomed the Tudeh into his National Front, a loose conglomeration of his followers, if it had not pressed for control. Instead, Mossadegh was hostile to the Reds and refused to give them the arms they demanded; though, in his desperate effort to survive, he did not reject their aid in street riots against the British and his domestic enemies.

Shortly before his fall, I visited Mossadegh at his Teheran home, where, from his bed—he was constantly ill, or imagined he was —he imperiously ruled the land, issuing orders that no Iranian politician would dare oppose for fear of retribution by his mobs. A monstrous-nosed, nervous man with the mannerisms of a frustrated old woman, he warmly grasped one of my hands in both of his in the traditional Persian handshake and had one of his aides kick his bedpan under the bed. He began speaking with great intensity. "You Americans say that I am dealing with the communists, but I am not. I don't like the communists. And if the British will stop trying to reassert their imperialism, and if the world will help us, I shall put through social and economic reforms that will prevent the communists from taking power. Already, under my regime, peasants have been given a share of farm profits for the first time.

But because of the British, and you Americans, too, we haven't got the money to carry this program further."

The Tudeh Party itself recognizes its error, and, in fact, never stops talking about it in its "self-criticism" sessions. The *World Marxist Review* quotes one Abdossamad Kambakhsh, who is identified as Secretary-General of the underground party—the real leaders are not definitely known—as saying:

> Our failure in 1953 was due chiefly to the absence of close co-operation between the Tudeh Party and the national bourgeoisie. The natural distrust with which the national bourgeoisie regarded the working-class party had been aggravated by the party's failure to understand the nature of the national bourgeoisie and its anti-imperialist potential, which had led to the party adopting the wrong tactics in relation to the Mossadegh government. The party has outlined a course of action aimed at rallying all the national forces in a united front against imperialism and domestic reaction. Unity in the party's ranks that had been shaken by defeat has been revived.

The Reds now see an opportunity to correct their mistake, for the National Front, which was disbanded with its leader's fall, was revived in July 1960. Unlike the previous one, which had no program or clear-cut organizational structure—actually it had split in the course of the struggle for nationalization of the oil industry, only the more radical section of the "national bourgeoisie" remaining in it—the new group has a charter, local organizations, congresses, a central council, and an executive bureau. It includes the Liberal Iran Party, the Pan-Iranian Party, a few merchant and artisan associations, and some student organizations. In general, its main support comes from the strongly nationalist urban middle class, embracing, among other groups, civil servants, teachers, truck drivers, technicians, and professional men—a highly discontented new class that has benefited enough from exploitation of Iran's natural wealth and from American aid to know that they would be benefiting much more if a large share of these riches were not going into ruling-class pockets. Some of these people, in their frustration with the existing order, have gone communist and probably form the backbone of the Tudeh Party today. But the great majority have not. They are simply nationalist, which automatically makes them distrustful of the West, including the United States, but by no means any more trustful of the communists, whom they view as opportunists. The Reds have nonetheless joined the Front in calling for Mossadegh's return to power and implementation of the organization's program: greater social

justice and more equal distribution of the nation's wealth, an end
to corruption, and transfer of government control to young, educated, honest men without traditional and entrenched vested interests.

One teacher with communist leanings, when asked if he did not
appreciate the fact that he was able to get an education only because of Iran's oil earnings and American aid, replied testily: "I
come from a peasant family, and our living standards have, it is
true, improved a little bit over the last fifteen years because of new
irrigation facilities constructed on our farm. But our landlord has
almost doubled his earnings since those improvements were made.
Do you think we should be satisfied?"

In February 1961 the Tudeh addressed an open letter to the National Front:

> Our victories and defeats in the past should be a lesson to us, and
> in the coming struggle we must be guided by past experience. Had
> a united front existed, had the Tudeh Party and the National
> Front acted together against our common enemies, Iranian reac-
> tion headed by the Shah and backed by the imperialists would not
> have been able to defeat us and drown our national movement in
> blood. Today, too, if we strengthen the alliance between the Tudeh
> Party and the National Front, if we create a united front of all
> patriotic and freedom-loving forces from all sections of the popu-
> lation, our success is assured and our country will be saved from
> the treacherous policy of the present regime.

One of the National Front leaders, Keshavarz Sadr, a former
Majlis deputy, replied indirectly, "We are not revolutionaries. We
are advocates of reform based on the declarations of the rights of
man and the Constitution." Another spokesman for the organization said, "As Moslems and believers in the Western style of parliamentary democracy, like Sweden or England, we must be anticommunists." Co-operation with the communists thus appears to
have been rejected.

Nevertheless, the Reds have been taking advantage of the
Front's activities. A state security official said in early 1961, "We
noticed that during the last years some old communists began
turning up at National Front meetings. In a demonstration, they
would be the ones to start circulating communist slogans through
the crowd." One of the biggest such demonstrations took place in
July 1961. While troops with fixed bayonets patrolled Teheran
behind tanks, extremists believed to be communists hurled rocks
at jeeps and passed out leaflets declaring: "The National Front is

victorious! Mossadegh is victorious! We condemn illegal acts of the government!" A number of communists were arrested.

The persistence of the Red propagandists is paying off to some degree. National Front officials make no secret of their desire for a neutralist foreign policy. Many oil workers in Abadan, where Iran's nationalized refinery is operated by an international consortium, including the United States and Britain, and textile workers in Isfahan, have been won over, though an American AFL-CIO labor representative is trying to help anticommunist workers in the Isfahan textile mills set up a democratic union. Tudeh members based in Iraq have succeeded in "brainwashing" some of the thousands of Iranians who make pilgrimages each year to Najab and Kerbala in south-central Iraq, where the main shrines of the Moslem Shiite sect are located. The Tudeh, however, has registered its best record neither among the workers nor among the peasants, but with the middle class, which hardly gives the party a mass character.

Strongly discouraged with the quality of Tudeh's leadership, the Russians have been doing their best to foment a revolution on their own. About 1,000 Soviet agents are attached to the Soviet Embassy in Teheran. The police have kept a close watch on them, particularly since a Tudeh conspiracy was uncovered in the army and air force in 1954, implicating Soviet Military Attaché General Rodionov and resulting in the arrest of several hundred officers. Previously a Tudeh leader had been arrested in the car of another Soviet diplomat. But the Russians in Iran are still among the most active in the world. A "reporter" for Tass News Agency, for example, took part in a bakers' union meeting in early 1961 and persuaded the bakers to go on strike. For the Iranian reading public, the USSR published almost 50,000 copies of fourteen books in Persian in 1960. The Iran-Soviet Cultural Relations Society in Teheran issues a monthly periodical called *Modern Message* (*Payam-e-Novin*) and Tass puts out a weekly and monthly edition of *News* (*Akhbar*). In addition, a Tudeh newspaper, *People* (*Mardom*), published behind the Iron Curtain, is clandestinely distributed in Iran.

But far more important, radio broadcasts to Iran from all communist sources in 1960 expanded from 76 hours a week to 96 hours, one of the sharpest increases anywhere in the world. The Soviet bloc relies mainly on three radio stations to disseminate its subversive ideas. One is Radio Moscow, which dwells mainly on themes concerning Iran-Soviet relations. Another is the National Voice of Iran (*Seda-ye-Melli-ye-Iran*), which pretends to broadcast from Iran itself, but which is known to be located in Baku in the Caucasus. It concentrates mainly on internal matters, significantly making a special effort to win over the reluctant peasants and tribesmen. "You are poor and hungry," one broadcast went. "You make the landlords rich with your toil and get nothing for it . . . you should take your revenge on these feudal lords." The value of such propaganda is usually invalidated by accompanying attacks on the Shah and his family.

A third station, the semiclandestine Iran's Messenger (*Peky-e-Iran*), was once operated by Iranian communist exiles in Leipzig, East Germany, but was recently moved to Bulgaria, where the signal to Iran is stronger. *Peyk-e* is directed largely toward Iran's political groups, identifying itself as the spokesman of the Tudeh Party. Its broadcasts also stress the importance of capturing the peasants. "The regime's crisis, which has already begun," one commentator declared, "should be intensified from all directions . . . Initially one must direct one's attention toward the villages . . . The town's masses must be directed toward a more serious struggle. The participation of the peasants and the people of the provinces in the struggle will expand."

All these stations, plus broadcasts from Communist China, which offered ten and a half hours of propaganda weekly in 1960 as compared to seven hours in 1959, constantly urge revolution against the Shah's regime. Just before the scheduled July 1961 demonstration of the National Front, Radio Moscow urged: "The present regime of Iran will fall in the very near future, despite efforts of the police and the security agency . . . July 21 is the day when the regime must fall. The people should rise against the regime on this day." On several occasions, commentators have contended that even the West is abandoning the Shah, reading excerpts from the American press out of context to "prove" their point. Propaganda also calls for the neutralization of Iran and friendship with the Soviet bloc. Iran is advised to break away from CENTO, expel its American advisers, reject American loans, discourage foreign imports, and join with other oil-producing countries to oppose imperialistic domination and exploitation. Refusal to follow such policies, Iran is warned, could mean interregional war and even the bombing of air bases in the country, whereas "neutralism" would guarantee the nation's safety.

The extraordinary intensity of Russia's propaganda campaign in Iran is rooted in some hard strategic facts. With Iran situated on the Soviet border, neutralism could mean a preliminary step toward full Soviet control of the country, with its Persian Gulf ports and Azerbaijan land bridge, which links the USSR with Iraq and the whole Middle East and Africa. Such a highway would facilitate the dispatch of Red Army troops overland to these vast areas. If Russia had possessed this bridge at the time of the communist-supported Iraqi revolution in 1958, it might have been able to assure Red control of that country.

Though Azerbaijan, which is wide open to Soviet infiltration, would appear to be easy pickings, the Reds in that region have never recovered from the effects of Russian brutality in 1941, when Soviet troops indiscriminately destroyed Persian villages during an invasion of the country launched jointly with the British. Nor from the demoralization of their defeat by Iranian government forces in 1947 following the withdrawal of Russian troops under pressure from the United Nations. The Red Army had left a puppet regime behind in the province, but it put up only token resistance to central government efforts to bring it back into the fold.

There is little likelihood that the Soviet Union would, in the near future, try to take over this area by force, even if Iran went neutralist; for such a move, in view of its strategic importance and American military commitment, would almost certainly spark World War III. But Moscow thinks it might be able to achieve the same end through manipulation of the Kurdish tribal minorities living in northwestern Iran, as it is manipulating the Kurds in Iraq. Moscow would no doubt be satisfied with the creation of a puppet Kurdistan in Iran alone, which would provide the land bridge it wants. Armed and unarmed Kurdish agitators trained in Russia are believed operating in this region, working with the Tudeh Party which, to facilitate subversion, recently united with the Soviet-controlled Azerbaijan Democratic Party.

It is precisely because of Russia's immediate designs on Iranian territory that Iran, unlike neighboring neutralist countries such as Afghanistan and Iraq, which are less endangered by the USSR's proximity, is maintaining a pro-West course, at least for the time being, despite a long history of neutralism before World War II. Iran first learned that it could not always play off one nation against the other when Britain and Russia invaded it in 1941, forcing the government to sign a Treaty of Alliance with them. After the war, Iran relied on Western, mainly United States, support against Soviet pressures to bring it under Russian domination. The United States started to provide military and gendarmerie missions in 1947, and, following the exposure of communist infiltration in the army, Iran joined the Baghdad Pact in 1955.

Russia has alternately used threat and kindliness in a futile effort to draw Iran into the neutralist ranks. A trade agreement signed in 1956 providing for the exchange of Iranian rice for Russian sugar was a prime example of its wooing tactics. When Iran, lacking modern granaries, delivered to the Soviet trade commission tons of rice mixed with the droppings of mice that inhabit Iranian barns, the Soviet trade representative in Iran, Peter Gordeytchik, made a historic political decision:

> . . . Rice with mouse-droppings is not suitable for consumption and according to the views of the Soviet Ministry of Health this kind of rice is even injurious to the health and hygiene of the Soviet people. Consequently the sale of rice which contains mouse-droppings is legally prohibited . . . Although the Ministry of Monopolies and Customs undertook by the agreement it signed to deliver rice without mouse-droppings, mouse-droppings were very much in evidence from the samples taken from the first consignment . . . In accordance with the agreement signed, we would be justified not to take delivery of the rice; but, since the governments of Iran and the Soviet Union desire to improve and expand the commercial relations of the two countries, we reported the situation to Moscow and requested permission, as an exception for this year alone, to take delivery of rice with mouse-droppings . . . Although the Soviet Union buys rice from three other countries, it never takes delivery of rice with mouse-droppings from any of them, and at present, Iran is the only country that will deliver rice with mouse-droppings . . . Soviet trade representatives at the port of Pahlevi have been instructed to take delivery of rice with only a minimum quantity of mouse-droppings, namely, not more than two mouse-droppings in each sack . . .

Soviet reasonableness in taking the rice, mouse-droppings and all, pleased the embarrassed Iranians but didn't change their politics. In February 1959, however, it looked as if they might. Fearing the threat of what appeared to be a communist-dominated government in Iraq, they began negotiating a nonaggression treaty with Russia. Soviet negotiators demanded that in return Iran should sign no pact with any other country permitting it to set up bases in Iran. The United States government, horrified by the possibility of a neutralist Iran, exerted pressure on the Shah to refuse the condition and promised more aid. The infuriated Russians were sent home empty-handed. In September 1960 Russia tried a new approach. It offered to grant economic aid to Iran if the government agreed in writing to deny the United States the use of bases for any possible attack on Russia. Iranian officials replied that Iran would accept this condition provided Moscow did not follow up with other demands, such as for the expulsion from Iran of United States military and technical advisory missions. This deal, too, fell through, but in September 1962 Iran agreed to a similar request from Moscow, apparently without conditions attached. Nevertheless, the government remains staunchly pro-West.

But keeping Iran this way has been costly to the United States, which has poured about $1 billion into Iran since 1950. Yet few Iranians think this aid has done much good. About half of it has gone for dams, roads, water facilities, and other projects of benefit to the people. But few people see these projects or note any increase in living standards flowing from them. They do see, however, the military installations, guns, and military advisory teams that have eaten up the remaining $500,000,000, as well as $200,000,000 out of the $275,000,000 Iran earns yearly in oil revenue. And to hungry people, these are fantastic sums to spend on armies.

In a sense they are right. Much of the American aid is going down the drain. Unlike the situation in some countries where United States contractors and technicians have sacrificed quality for economy, in Iran considerable funds are being squandered unnecessarily. Army camps are being built according to American specifications completely out of line with the traditions and requirements of the local military. Four showers for every 100 men are installed in each barracks—yet Iranian soldiers have never seen a shower before and usually steal the faucets and other bathroom equipment for sale in the bazaars at fat prices. Fully equipped mess halls, costing almost $100,000 each, have been built, only to be ignored by the soldiers, who are used to eating rice cooked over open fires out of doors. At Marand, fifty buildings have been constructed, including barracks, mess halls, bakeries, recreation halls, maintenance shops, sewage-disposal units, officers' quarters, laundries, warehouses, and motor-pool sheds—for soldiers who had previously lived under the most primitive, crowded conditions.

While millions of dollars are thus spent on what the Iranians consider military frivolities—the United States finally told Iran in 1962 that it should reduce the size of its military establishment—the masses continue to wallow in poverty, while the rich grow richer. "Where did they get their money?" the people ask, a sarcastic question that has recently become a bitter cliché in Iran. Where did General Haj Ali Kia, former chief of army intelligence, get his? By running an organization known only as K.O.K., which he set up with a budget of $1.5 million a month to compile confidential reports on the Shah's popularity—reports dreamed up by the General himself, the sole member of the K.O.K. And General Ahmed Ajodani, former director of Teheran's electrical system—where did his come from? He formed a "consulting firm" to supervise the wiring of a $2 million power plant. Oddly, the Shah, when he pulled the switch at an inaugural ceremony, electrocuted several swans in a nearby reservoir. And everybody knew about Ehsan Davaloo, Iran's "Caviar Queen" and intimate friend of Princess Ashraf, twin sister of the Shah, who bought a $450,000-a-year caviar concession by bribing officials. It was clear where some U.S. aid was going, too. At one American-built regimental camp, three 300-kilowatt Diesel generators imported from West Germany at a cost of $250,000 stopped providing light because money intended for the purchase of fuel disappeared.

In this atmosphere of poverty and corruption popular discontent rose to an explosive crescendo in May 1961, when 4,000 schoolteachers paraded to parliament to demand a pay raise. The police opened fire, killing one demonstrator and wounding several others. The next day 30,000 teachers and students demonstrated, shouting "savages" and "down with the government." And to their surprise, the Shah obliged them by dismissing the government and parliament, appointing the strike leader as Minister of Education, and promising to punish the policemen responsible for the casualties. He then pledged a social and economic revolution and selected Ali Amini, former Minister of Finance and Ambassador to Washington, to carry it through. Suddenly, instead of demonstrations there was dancing in the streets.

The Shah's choice of Amini to save Iran was perhaps a measure of his sincerity and selflessness. There has never been any love lost between the two men. Amini, a serious, gray-haired man with protruding eyes, is descended from the dynasty that the Shah's father overthrew in 1921, and has often criticized the Shah severely. He also served in the cabinet of Mossadegh, who, of course, was no friend of the Shah. Moreover, he is a millionaire landowner himself. Yet the Shah was convinced that he was a determined reformist and, putting aside his personal feelings, selected him to push through the reforms so vital to the preservation of Iran as an independent, noncommunist state.

Almost immediately Amini announced a land reform program, if without enforcement provisions. Farming methods and the tax-collecting system were to be improved. Prices were to be lowered and imports and exports brought into balance. Government agencies were to reduce expenditures, and corrupt officials were to be severely punished. To show he meant business, Amini forbade all Iranians except those with legitimate business excuses from traveling abroad, explaining, "Some ladies have been in the habit of going to Paris for hairdos." He slashed imports of "unnecessary luxuries" such as champagne and expensive automobiles to save $50 million and remove "the major cause of husband-wife disputes leading to the divorce court." About 500 government employees who held several lucrative jobs simultaneously have had to confine themselves to one. And more than thirty persons, including five army generals, two former ministers and former governors, majors and undersecretaries in ministries were arrested for corruption and graft.

But while such actions were dramatic, they barely scratched the surface of Iran's social and economic problems. Well-meaning and dynamic though he is, Amini found himself bucking a stone wall of opposition from the powerful vested interests and grappling with enormous political and technical difficulties. Bitterly, he resigned in July 1962, to be replaced by Assadolah Alam, a former cabinet minister of much less impressive personality. It remains to be seen whether the new land reform law, which does provide for enforcement, will produce the necessary results. But the previous program came to a virtual halt when peasants turned against the landlords and refused to pay rent, and landlords turned against the government, ceasing to supervise the farms. Nor are there enough engineers in Iran—less than one hundred are available—to do the surveying required for the redivision of land.

Rigid anti-inflationary measures, on the other hand, have meant a sharp reduction in investments and purchases, with a resultant increase in unemployment. All over Teheran, partially completed homes and office buildings attest to economic stagnation, while workers remain in their shacks on the outskirts of town, many of them listening to communist radio broadcasts that tell them how they can have a prosperous life. Corruption is still deeply rooted in the government. Arrests have been stopped, many Iranians claim, to keep charges from spreading to the royal court itself. Perhaps the most serious of the Shah's handicaps is that he has no real means of enforcing reform, for the top levels of the army are no less riddled with corruption than other governmental agencies, and no less feudal-minded than the landlords, whose sons are the leading army officers.

What Iran urgently needs is honest, strong, and even ruthless leadership that can enforce reform regardless of the difficulties. Even so forceful a man as Amini was not able to provide it. Perhaps some senior military figure comparable to Pakistan's General

Ayub Khan, who has performed a miracle cleanup job in his country, which was also steeped in corruption and anarchy a few years ago, can be found. Otherwise the pressures for revolution may very well get out of hand. And if an explosion comes, it is likely to be sparked by the radically nationalist middle class that lacks the peasants' devotion to tradition and covets the good jobs held by the corruption-ridden ruling class—in other words, the National Front followers of Mossadegh, and, in some cases, of the Tudeh Party that is still clinging to Mossadegh's coattails. This middle class, moreover, has an instrument of revolution— not only in street mobs, but in young army officers who find themselves frozen out of the top military positions by ruling-class members.

The danger of revolutionary violence was underscored by what appeared to be carefully arranged riots that broke out in Teheran in January 1962. Students set them off by stoning policemen and demanding that parliamentary elections be held, though these rioters were among those who had rejoiced when the Shah dismissed parliament in 1961 and promised to do by decree exactly what he is now trying to do—clean up corruption and institute reforms so that parliament, which has largely been controlled by the landlords and other vested interests, will have some democratic meaning. As the demonstrations spread, many students, as well as those held responsible for encouraging them to riot—National Front leaders, former members of parliament, businessmen, and a newspaperman—were arrested, and three daily newspapers were suspended.

But according to Amini, there was still another instigator—the Soviet Union. He maintained that several Soviet diplomats were seen in embassy cars among the rioters and demonstrators. "We want to have friendly relations with our northern neighbor, but inciting antigovernment riots by subversive elements is against friendly relations," he said, adding that the government had evidence that he was to be hanged if opposition elements had succeeded in overthrowing his government.

It is possible that a National Front surge to power, if it did not restore the irrational Mossadegh himself as the nation's leader— he is now under house arrest at his farm near Teheran—and was able to generate real reform, would not damage Western interests. Much would depend on whether the National Front successfully resisted communist infiltration. A nationalist government would almost certainly resort to neutralism, but this again would not necessarily militate against the West, considering that even today it is almost impossible to control Soviet infiltration from across the border, while American military concentrations in Iran tend to create anti-American feeling without, in all probability, affecting Russian military intentions in regard to Iran. The real deterrent to a Red Army invasion is the knowledge that aggression in this vitally strategic nation, whether it was pro-West or not, would almost certainly set off World War III. At the same time, the chances of keeping a reformed neutralist Iran out of communist hands would appear at least as good as the chances of keeping a precariously pro-West Iran, subject to revolutionary convulsions, on our side. Certainly the example of Iraq, which was an ally of the West until overthrown by a revolution that barely missed putting the Reds in power, must be kept in mind. Lest we place too much trust in the expensive military establishment we have built in Iran, it could, like the one we built in Iraq, be turned against us overnight.

Still, the danger that a revolution might bring into power an irresponsible nationalist government such as that which ruled the nation under Mossadegh several years ago is great. And in the chaos that would result, the communists would have another excellent opportunity to slither into power. But of course, even without revolution, the Reds will inevitably build up a popular following among the Iranian masses, however gradually, if genuine reform is not achieved.

XI

AFGHANISTAN:

THE LION AND THE LAMB

As the two-engined Soviet plane headed north from Kabul, Afghanistan, toward Tashkent in Soviet Central Asia, weaving through the snow-blanketed valleys of the great Hindu Kush mountain range that separates the two countries, I nervously clutched the arms of my chair for lack of a seat belt. The plane's wings seemed almost to brush the steeply sloping white walls on either side. Adding to the discomfort were the frightened cries of a small child who refused to let his mother put an oxygen mask on him, though all passengers were ordered to wear them by the Russian steward of the aging, unpressurized aircraft.

When we had crossed the mountains and removed our masks, the Turkish businessman sitting next to me, a stout, jolly man with a large mustache, said, "One minute in Afghanistan, the next in Russia. Yet I doubt if the Afghans realize the great danger that lies in close collaboration with the Russians." He paused for a moment. "Did you ever hear the story of the lion and the lamb? One day, it seems, an American senator visited the Moscow zoo and stopped at a cage in which a huge, growling lion sat side by side with a tiny little lamb. 'What do those words over the cage say?' the senator asked his interpreter-guide. 'They say Peaceful Coexistence is Possible,' replied the guide. The senator, in a startled voice, said, 'Well, this is really something. Perhaps peaceful coexistence is worth looking into after all. Tell me, how is it

possible for that ferocious lion and that helpless little lamb to co-
exist so peacefully?' 'Very simple,' answered the guide. 'They put
a new lamb in the cage every morning.' "

The Turk roared with laughter at his own joke until interrupted
by an Afghan sitting in the seat just in front of him. "I heard your
story," the Afghan said in an offended tone. "I must inform you
that Afghan lambs are famous throughout the world. Not only do
they offer fine wool, but they are extremely intelligent animals.
They know how to protect themselves from lions."

This man's words accurately reflected the proud, confident
attitude of most Afghans that they can snuggle up to the Russian
lion perched on their doorstep, which they are doing today in line
with their neutralist policies, without ending up in its stomach. This
is not a false sense of confidence, rooted, as in the case of many
neutralist countries, in fear. It is rooted primarily in the nation's
long history of independence. Though strategically bordered by
the Soviet Union on the north, Iran on the west, and Pakistan on
the east and south, this almost forgotten land link between East
and West and potential invasion route to India has managed to
maintain its territorial integrity throughout the centuries. Alexander the Great tried to subdue Afghanistan in the third century
B.C. but in the end failed. Genghis Khan in the thirteenth century
and Tamerlane in the fourteenth left the nation in ruins—catas-
trophes that were to freeze progress until today—but the people
remained unconquered. In the more recent colonial era Afghanistan, as a buffer between Russia and British India, skillfully played one off against the other. And when its independence
was occasionally threatened, mainly by the British, hordes of fierce
Afghan warriors guarding the fabled Khyber Pass that opens into
the plains of the Indian subcontinent made it clear that colo-
nization of their country would be costly indeed.

Afghanistan, for its part, paid a heavy price for independence,
particularly after the opening of sea routes to India rendered this
landlocked nation obsolete as an Asian crossroads. On the one
hand, fanatical Moslem leaders were able to keep out all modern
influences; and on the other, the country was deprived of the
economic and technical benefits reserved by the colonial powers
for areas under their control. As a result, Afghanistan is only today
beginning to drag itself out of the Middle Ages. But unlike ty-
rannically led medieval states such as Saudi Arabia, it is doing
so with a vengeance, hoping to condense six centuries into
a few decades. It dreams of a new golden age like that which it
enjoyed in ancient times when it was the principal center of Ori-

ental culture. And it is not particular who helps it to regain this lost glory. It is raking in record amounts of aid, on a per capita basis, from both Russia and the United States, complacent in the logic that a country that could resist Alexander the Great, Genghis Khan, Tamerlane, the Russian Czars, and the British imperialists would be able to handle any new potential aggressor.

In view of Russia's proximity, Soviet power is highly respected, while an ethnic relationship between some people in northern Afghanistan and Soviet Central Asia has facilitated mutual friendship. Still, there are probably not more than a handful of Reds and fellow travelers in the country today, and there is no Communist Party. Russia wants to impress the government with its respect for Afghan law, which bans all political parties; but more important, it realizes that the nation is simply too backward and too deeply steeped in theocracy at this stage to apply Marxism, or even understand it. The Afghan political and social structure is still tribalistic without even a top layer of Western-trained leadership as in the primitive states of Africa. Government decisions are made by a forward-looking royal family council, with King Mohammed Zahir Shah as its theoretical head, though the real ultimate responsibility rests with his cousin, suave, hard-faced Prime Minister Sardar Mohammed Daud. Such democratic forms as a parliament and cabinet exist, but in name only.

Authority on the village level today as in the past resides largely with reactionary *mullahs* who are convinced—quite correctly—that the modern education and political innovations being introduced into the country, which now has about a five-percent literacy rate, constitute a threat to their power. Under their influence most Afghans still live in the Middle Ages, slaves to the outdated practices of ultra-orthodox Islam. I learned something of their devoutness while traveling through southern Afghanistan in a lorry jammed with men dressed in knee-length shirts, loose cotton pantaloons, curly-toed slippers, or *babouches,* and broad colored turbans, and women draped in long black robes and hoods with netted eye-masks. The vehicle coughed and hissed to a halt every few hours so that the male passengers could climb out and pay their homage to Allah in the traditional way. On small prayer rugs, they knelt and bowed in the direction of Mecca at about ten-yard intervals along the lonely roadside—humble dots of men etched against an infinity of sky and desert, men fatalistic in their awe and satisfied with the stagnant feudal norms proclaimed as the will of God by their *mullahs.*

Another time, I boarded a dilapidated old mail bus jammed

with peasants and found myself the object of incredulous stares. "These people have never seen an American before," the driver told me in broken French. Nor were they very impressed by this initial contact when I sat down on a mail bag—there were no seats in the bus—next to a woman dressed in the traditional purdah. A tall, powerful Afghan with brown, hashish-stained teeth got up in another part of the bus and, pointing a homemade rifle at me, began shouting. "You're sitting next to his wife," the driver explained. "It's against Moslem custom. You'd better move—fast." "Tell him I'll exchange places with him," I replied. "Then he would surely shoot you," I was told. "An Afghan husband doesn't sit next to his wife in public." I finally managed to squeeze in between two other male passengers.

On still another occasion, a lorry carrying a young American woman writer and me had to go around one village in western Afghanistan because the local *mullah* would not permit a "female of naked face" to be seen in his bailiwick. Due to social pressures, Afghan women even in Kabul are reluctant to remove their veils, though many have done so recently with the encouragement of the government. When I first arrived in Afghanistan, I asked a British businessman if Afghan women were as attractive as they are supposed to be, and he replied testily: "Since I've been here, I managed to see on one occasion that part of the female anatomy utilized to nurse babies. Good heavens, man, you don't expect me to judge the beauty of Afghan womanhood on the basis of one solitary breast, do you?"

The first breath of twentieth-century civilization was felt in Afghanistan in the late 1920's and 1930's when, despite the resistance of the powerful *mullahs*, enlightened monarchs exchanged diplomatic missions with Western nations. Even so, this breath, until a few years ago, was contained, as if in a vacuum, in the Afghan capital of Kabul in the northeast corner of the country. Thus today, in this city of intrigue, where British and Czarist agents plotted fruitlessly for control of the country for more than a century, the conflict between medievalism and modernism constantly meets the eye. Windowless adobe shacks, shaded by stick-supported canopies of slender branches and dried foliage, stand in pitiful relief against a backdrop of large, well-constructed buildings. In the dirt-floored bazaars, blond Westerners mingle with olive-skinned natives. Long black Cadillacs bump along narrow, dusty lanes bordered by mud walls that hide beautiful green gardens built around cool, clear pools. Men dressed in slickly tailored modern suits walk side by side with men clad in traditional fashion, while their veiled wives, often wearing nylons and high heels under their robes, follow along on donkeys.

In the last decade Kandahar, an ancient town on the northern fringe of the great Helmand desert in southeastern Afghanistan, has also begun to exhibit a new look as the result of an American effort to develop and resettle this once lushly productive area. Kandahar, founded by Alexander the Great, is situated closer to a seaport (Karachi, Pakistan) than any other Afghan city, and has therefore always been in commercial contact with the outside world, which receives from this country some of the finest fruit and wool produced anywhere. Nevertheless, before World War II few Western eyes glimpsed its clean cobbled streets teeming with strollers, bicyclists, donkeys, camels, and bell-clanging *tongahs*, or horse-driven carriages, which at every intersection— to the utter frustration of Keystone-like traffic cops—meet in a great tangled confusion of squeaking wheels, rearing horses, and cursing drivers.

Nor did many machine-age visitors wander through the bustling, spice-scented bazaar where metalsmiths, working monkey-style with their nimble toes as well as their hands, carve strange Oriental trinkets out of copper, tin, and silver. Where cobblers fashion *babouches* from wrinkled leather brought by camel caravan via the Khyber Pass from Peshawar, Pakistan. Where merchants, between puffs on their long-stemmed, pottery-based *hookahs*, skillfully bargain with equally shrewd shoppers in a myriad of shops and stalls featuring finely spun rugs, bright-colored cloth, fruit of a dozen varieties, delicately embroidered skull caps around which turbans are wound, and hundreds of other items.

Modern influences are today perceptible in the more isolated areas as well, particularly with Russian and American technicians feverishly competing to make dents in the nation's hard medieval shell. When I arrived one night in the walled town of Herat in western Afghanistan, the art center of the East before the Mongols destroyed it, after hours of exhausting travel over desert trails designed for camel caravans, a sleepy, raggedly dressed boy emerged with an oil lamp to carry my baggage and led me into the lobby of a hotel resplendent with Persian rugs, plush draperies, finely carved, silk-upholstered furniture, and even a white-enameled grand piano. I slept in a beautifully furnished bedroom, almost not minding the used sheets and the lack of water in the modern plumbing.

The story behind this miniature Waldorf-Astoria amid the pompous ruins of a fourteenth-century wilderness is that the mayor

visited Europe shortly after World War II and decided that
what Herat needed most was an up-to-date hotel—just in case
stray adventurers like myself happened by. "We like to go out of
our way to be hospitable to visitors," the hotel manager explained
in masterly understatement. Then, to make sure that I didn't think
there was any Cold War significance in this hospitality, he added:
"We are also happy, of course, to have Russians stay here."

And there are plenty of them who do. Aware that the Afghan
masses are not yet ripe for communist-style leadership, the Soviet
Union is refraining from political subversion and is wooing the
country with economic and technical example almost exclusively
in an effort to create a receptive atmosphere for future application
of the Yenan Way. From 1954 to 1961 Russia invested about
$220 million in Afghan development and an additional $40 million for modernization of the Afghan armed forces, more money
than it has spent in any underdeveloped country other than India,
Indonesia, and Egypt. In addition, Czechoslovakia has contributed $5 million in aid. By comparison, American assistance over
the same period amounted to approximately $180 million, much
less than the Soviet total even though representing an impressive
$14 per Afghan. Russian technicians, furthermore, number some
2,000 as compared to about 350 Americans. And as if this quan-
titative edge in aid were not enough, in most cases Russian schemes
have had far more immediate impact than American projects, in
terms of both visual effect and efficiency.

The Soviet program includes such easy-to-see projects as the
paving of Kabul streets, the construction of a grain silo in Kabul
(as the tallest structure in the capital, observers point out, it can
easily be seen, but no one can see the American grain it contains),
a Kabul bakery that uses Russian trucks for delivery, oil storage
dumps, automotive machine shops, textile factories, an all-weather
landing strip for Kabul's civil airport, a huge dam and irrigation
project at Jalalabad on the Kabul River, which will be completed
in 1964, and another dam near Kabul to provide electricity for the
city, to be in operation shortly afterwards.

More ominous, and no doubt a factor in Russia's decision to
"plunge" so uninhibitedly in Afghanistan, are Soviet projects of
military value which Russia could use to facilitate an invasion of
Pakistan and India. Soviet engineers have been building a road
that will tunnel through the Hindu Kush mountains and connect
Kabul with the Russian border on the Oxus River, where the Russians are constructing an Afghan port. This road will shorten the
existing route by almost one hundred miles. The Soviets will also

build a southern road between Kandahar and the Soviet frontier, as well as a military airfield on this road, at Shindand. They have completed a military airfield near Kabul. In addition, Soviet aid has reorganized the Afghan army and air force and supplied a number of jet fighters, helicopters, tanks, artillery, and motor transport, as well as instructors and technicians, after the United States turned down an appeal for arms in deference to its ally, Pakistan, a bitter foe of Afghanistan.

The Russians have made some mistakes. Kabul's streets were paved so poorly that the Afghans have had to redo many of them. But, in general, the Afghans have been extremely impressed with Russian dispatch and efficiency—on some projects, such as Kabul Airport, the Russians work twenty-four hours a day—and also by the complete lack of strings, or at least visible ones, attached to Soviet aid.

Most American assistance so far has not gone for "impact" endeavors, but has been designed to help Afghanistan in the long pull. It is being used for help in forestry and soil conservation, in police organization, and in fiscal matters. United States technicians are organizing an educational system. About $15 million was devoted to school building and scholarships, and almost five hundred students were sent to American universities to study through 1961. But the impatient Afghans do not see any immediate returns from this kind of aid.

American technicians have been working on some projects comparable to those of the Russians: an international airport at Kandahar and provincial airstrips, all-weather roads between Kabul and Pakistan to the east and to the south via Kandahar, expansion of the Kabul University campus, the operation of a civil airline, and the Helmand River Valley development and resettlement scheme. But even these efforts have not greatly impressed Afghans familiar with Russian accomplishments. Though the United States so often points to the red tape and bureaucracy of a socialist system, it is the capitalist system that seems ponderous and inefficient to the Afghans. Work is constantly delayed owing to the tardy arrival of construction equipment, some of which turns out to be unsuitable when it does arrive. Technicians are sometimes not the best. Private bidding on construction contracts takes time, and congressional regulations must be followed. The Afghans are not satisfied with explanations that all equipment must be imported from thousands of miles away while the Soviet Union is next door, or that democratic processes, including those affecting aid, take longer than the processes of a totalitarian state. All this proves to many Afghans is that the Soviet system operates more satisfactorily.

The greatest disappointment so far to both Americans and Afghans has been the Helmand River Valley project, though this was to have been the most spectacular example of fruitful co-operation between the two countries. Begun in 1946, this scheme was the keystone of Afghan hopes for a quick economic leap into the twentieth century. It is intended to harness the turbulent Helmand River, which winds for eight hundred miles from the Hindu Kush Mountains through southern Afghanistan into Iran. Before the Mongols destroyed the ancient waterworks in the valley, this area was a fertile farming paradise on which the economic well-being of the whole country was based. Its reclamation was expected once again to mean national prosperity.

According to the original grandiose plan, by 1965 about 65,000 of the nation's two million nomads would be hitching plows to their camels and donkeys, and eventually to tractors, working 500,000 acres of newly irrigated farmland. The nation's hungry population would have abundant quantities of wheat, corn, and sugar to supplement their present meager, monotonous diet which consists largely of rice, lamb, and fruit. And the rhythmic grinding of factory machinery would resound incongruously through hundreds of crumbling mud and straw villages that would gradually develop into modern towns.

That is the dream, but it is far from realization. About $100 million was spent on the project up to 1961, half representing American aid (this includes $40 million in U. S. Export-Import Bank loans and $10 million from the International Co-operation Administration), and half Afghan financing, a tremendous burden for a country with an annual per capita income of only $40. But there has been relatively little to show for all this expenditure. By 1962 the U.S. firm, Morrison-Knudsen, had directed the construction of two earth-filled dams and the digging of 600 miles of irrigation canals, but only 170,000 acres had a firm water supply. Furthermore, fewer than 15,000 persons were resettled, only a third of them nomads, indicating a basic miscalculation of the willingness of these desert wanderers to stay in one place. In Nad-i-ali, the first entirely new farming area to be opened, the soil was found too salty for cultivation—after a new village was already half built. A hydroelectric power station with a 3,000-kilowatt capacity was completed in 1958, but has never been used. A water leak developed, which took two years to repair; and then, it was discovered, no qualified technicians were available to operate the station. Modern American agricultural machinery imported to grow wheat for United States technicians and their families has been rusting in idleness for years and is not suitable for use on the small Afghan plots. Many farmers, untrained in the use of the new irrigation facilities, have flooded their fields.

The project has produced some beneficial results. Model villages have been built in the Marja area, complete with schools, mosques, settlers, and large green fields. A model town with the only pure water supply in the country has been constructed at Lashkar Gah, headquarters of the Helmand Valley Authority. Moreover, workers paid fifty cents a day are digging ditches by hand in the Nad-i-ali area which, it is hoped, will drain off the salt and make the land cultivable after all, and conditions are expected to improve also as the result of extensive agricultural research being conducted at Marja by Afghan experts with United States technical aid. Many students are being sent to the United States for technical training that will permit them to replace American technicians eventually.

But this American project has not lived up to Afghan expectations, whereas most Russian schemes have. And this discrepancy in technical efficiency may be further underscored when Russian engineers start working on a comparable, though somewhat smaller, development project at Jalalabad on the Kabul River, which the USSR will help finance to the tune of $22 million. Afghan Foreign Minister Mohammed Naim has said that unless the American project could be completed soon, his people would have to conclude that they were getting no "reasonable return" from their investment. Such a conclusion drawn from the feverish competition between the United States and the Soviet Union could do irreparable damage to the American reputation in this highly strategic nation, as well as in the whole of Asia. Fortunately, the Helmand project was progressing relatively smoothly in 1962.

Americans in Afghanistan also appear to be doing little to win the hearts of the Afghans on the social plane. The Afghan people are among the warmest and most hospitable in the world. I discovered this almost from the first moment I entered the country overland from Iran. When the primitive bus in which I was riding reached the customs post, the customs chief, a fat man in bright-red Afghan pajamas, had someone carry my unopened bag to a nearby mud teahouse, where he kept me company over tea while all the other passengers had to unwrap their carpet-covered bundles for inspection. Such warmth typifies the Afghan attitude toward Americans, as well as toward most other foreigners. Unlike the people of most underdeveloped countries, who tend to associate all whites with colonial oppression, the Afghans, never having submitted to colonialism, have no such antiwhite complex. Proud almost to an extreme, they hardly know the meaning of discrimination based on race or nationality.

Some Americans, however, have taught them the meaning, particularly in Kandahar, where more than thirty Helmand technicians and their families live in attractive, garden-surrounded stone houses equipped with refrigerators, freezers, and modern furniture. They drive to work or to town in large American cars and throw parties at which the finest duty-free American liquor and delicacies are served. "This is like a little bit of America transplanted in Afghanistan," one American engineer told me. Unfortunately, few Afghans are invited to share in the enjoyment of this "little bit of America." They have found themselves unaccepted as equals even at project headquarters, where ugly little signs reading, "For Americans" or "For Afghans," tell native employees that they are not clean enough to use the same lavatory facilities as the Americans.

Soviet technicians also rarely mix socially with the Afghans, but they live unostentatiously in Afghan communities and buy their food and other necessities in the bazaar. The fact that they don't live much better in Russia is of little significance to the proud Afghans, who appreciate their "democratic ways."

Diplomatically, the Soviet Union has come out flatly in support of Afghanistan in its bitter conflict with Pakistan over "Pakhtoonistan," while the United States, desiring to remain friends with both countries, has remained noncommittal on this question. The Pakhtoonistan issue has plagued relations between Afghanistan and Pakistan since Pakistan became an independent state in 1947. The seed of this problem was planted in 1893, when a British official in India, Sir Mortimer Durand, visited Afghanistan and signed with King Amir Abdur Rahman an agreement fixing the Indian-Afghanistan boundary at the so-called Durand Line. This boundary cut across a mountainous territory inhabited by Pathan tribesmen, or Pakhtoons, leaving about five million on the Pakistan (then Indian) and three million on the Afghan side of the line. In a referendum conducted by the British in 1947 shortly before they withdrew from the subcontinent, almost all Pathans on the Indian side of the border voted to join Pakistan rather than India. But Afghanistan says that the referendum was worthless as the Pathans were not given the opportunity to express a preference for an independent state of Pakhtoonistan, which it obviously would like to control. Ever since, the Afghans have been charging that Pakistan is oppressing the Pathans, and Pakistan has been denying the charges, pointing out that its President, Ayub Khan, is himself a Pathan.

Actually, to avoid friction in its Pathan area, Pakistan has given it semi-autonomy, though it isn't clear whether this move has satisfied most of the Pakistani Pathans. In any event, these tough fighting tribesmen usually abide by their own rigid moral laws. I visited one Pathan village that specialized in manufacturing with the crudest tools rifles that could hardly be told apart from those produced in Western factories. In fact, the words, "Made in Birmingham (England)" were inscribed on each rifle because weapons to be sold in other villages would fetch a better price with that marking. The village chief, an old, turbaned man with a long curly white beard, explained that shooting was the penalty for serious breaches of Pathan law. Just the day before, he said, a man and a woman had been executed for refusing to swear on the Koran that they had not committed adultery. "Didn't they have a trial?" I asked. "Trial? What for?" he replied. "No Pathan would tell a lie with his hand on the Koran. If they had sworn they were innocent, we would have let them go."

As for the Pathans in Afghanistan, they are loyal to that country though there would probably be little resistance to joining a new independent state. Proud of their fighting ability, as are their Pakistani brothers, they often look with scorn on Afghans of other tribes. The driver of a lorry in which I hitched a ride in southern Afghanistan was a Pathan, complete with black mascara-like rings under his eyes and a full beard dyed carrot-red with the juice of a tropical plant, the traditional Pathan make-up. While driving through the desert one night, we came to a halt behind another truck stalled near the top of a ridge. We could have driven around the vehicle, but my Pathan driver would have none of it. He ordered the other driver to back his truck out of the way so we could pass. When he refused, the Pathan, with the help of passengers in our truck, started beating the other driver with sticks. Still the latter would not agree. Finally, the Pathan gave up and decided to drive around the stalled truck after all, but he cursed and bit his lips for the next hundred miles. His pride had been injured by defeat—about the worst thing that can happen to a Pathan.

Whatever the sentiments of the Pathans themselves about independence, Russia is all for it—because Afghanistan is, while Pakistan is allied with the West. According to the Pakistanis, Moscow encouraged an incident that took place in September

1960 in which about 50,000 Afghan tribesmen were supposedly sent by the Afghans to create trouble in Pakistan while the United Nations General Assembly was in session. The conflict came to a head in August 1961 when Pakistan asked the Afghans to close their consulates and trade agencies in Pakistan, accusing Afghan officials of subversive activities. This couldn't have pleased the Russians, nor alarmed the Americans, more. For though the Pakistani government promised that transit facilities for goods going from the port of Karachi to Afghanistan would not be impaired, Kabul threatened to import all items through Soviet trade channels, which it had been using until then as a secondary gateway to the outside world. If this threat had been carried out, the United States would have been placed in the ironic position of having to route its aid to Afghanistan through the Soviet Union as the only alternative to withdrawing from that country altogether. Finally, in January 1962 Afghan authorities permitted the entry of long-accumulated United States aid goods via Pakistan for a period of eight weeks. All additional aid, the Afghans said, would henceforth have to be sent through Iran. As a result, a new road connecting Afghanistan and Iran was built, opening in late 1962.

As the ties between Moscow and Kabul draw tighter, the communist bloc is expanding its propaganda network in Afghanistan. Broadcasts in the native languages of Tadzhik and Pushtu consume more than twenty-four hours a week, and, while no local communist newspaper is published, the government-controlled press frequently uses the news services of Tass and New China News Agency. Moreover, the Soviet Embassy issues a daily news bulletin, and four new Russian films per month are imported. All this propaganda, of course, gives the Cold War picture a pro-communist slant, but without dealing with Marxist ideology. It is therefore significant that in 1960 Russia published its first books in local Afghan dialects, opening the door to initial intellectual discussions of Marxism as a doctrine.

Further indications of the prevailing trend lie in a twenty-per-cent increase in delegation exchanges in 1960, including trips by Prime Minister Daud to Moscow and by Khrushchev and Red Chinese Foreign Minister Chen Yi to Kabul. The Soviet Premier's visit resulted in a cultural treaty and the Chinese Foreign Minister's, in a Treaty of Friendship and Nonaggression, plus a promise by King Zahir to visit Peking sometime in the future. In 1961, following the break with Pakistan, Afghan Foreign Minister Naim hurried to Moscow, presumably to discuss an increase of trade through the Soviet Union.

Afghanistan's boldness in curling up beside the Russian lion could prove dangerous. Economically it is already dependent to a considerable degree on the Soviet Union, making it subject to pressures the Russians may choose to exert. And with Pakistan its bitter enemy, it might conceivably jump into the lion's mouth with little prodding if this were the only alternative to humbling itself before the Pakistanis in order to avoid trade strangulation. The fact that Afghanistan has only a fifteen-day reserve of gasoline, which could perhaps be stretched to forty-five days if the military seized all stocks, points up Russia's advantageous position.

However, Afghan history suggests that the Russians may in the end find Afghanistan a difficult nut to crack. For no people are more independent or less open to communist influence, at least in their present stage of development, than the Afghans. Even while the government vows everlasting friendship with the communist bloc, it has rebuffed Soviet offers of aid in the educational field, which it has left entirely in American hands. The Soviet Embassy has not even been permitted to open a library in Kabul, although the United States maintains a 5,500-book library, as well as an auditorium where films, lectures, exhibitions, and concerts are presented, and a language center offering English courses to about one hundred students. It is significant, too, that the Afghans all but pleaded with the United States for military aid before seeking such assistance from the USSR, and that top government officials, who previously would have little to do with the press, have been making a special effort to impress on Western newsmen that Afghanistan, while accepting Russian aid, will never sell its soul to Moscow.

"If Russia wanted to use force," one Afghan diplomat commented, "quite obviously it could swallow up Afghanistan overnight. On the other hand, no one in my country believes in communism and we cannot be subverted. Therefore, what have we got to lose by accepting aid from Russia? Would we be in a safer position if we joined the Western bloc and did not accept Soviet aid? On the contrary, Russian aid, as well as American aid, will help lift us out of poverty and thereby further insulate us from the communist influence."

The shrewdness of the Russian lion should not be underestimated. But neither should the cleverness of the Afghan lamb.

Part 3

ASIA

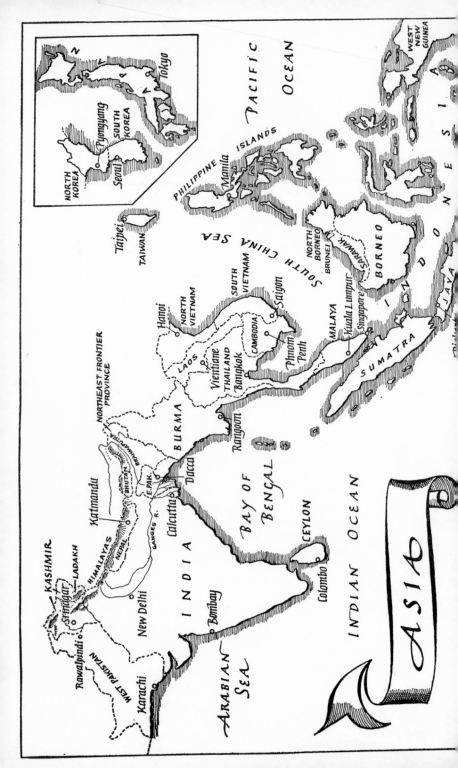

XII

STEEL MILLS AND
STEEL BULLETS

Noncommunist Asia is the most gravely menaced region in the underdeveloped world. The communists already control China, North Korea, and North Vietnam, which together encompass—excluding Soviet Siberia—forty-seven percent of Asia's population, fifty-four percent of its area, and thirty-five percent of its rice. Communists are now making a serious effort to win control of Laos and South Vietnam, and most other free Asian countries may fall, domino-style, if these two nations go. Mao's armies occupy Indian border areas.

Though Russia is strongly bidding for Asian support, Red China is the central factor in this threat. Like an enormous dragon, it lies heavily and hungrily along the noncommunist southern fringe of Asia, and within glowering distance of the necklace of islands, stretching from Japan in the north to Indonesia in the south, that roughly parallels the rugged contours of China's eastern seacoast. China was feared by its smaller neighbors long before the communists took over that country in 1948, for it has a notoriously aggressive history in Asia. During the T'ang dynasty, from 618 to 907 A.D., Russian Asia, Afghanistan, and the principalities of the Indian subcontinent all recognized Chinese authority. The Mongols further extended Chinese rule in the thirteenth century, barely failing to conquer the islands of Japan when a timely storm broke. Under the Mings in the fifteenth century, the Chinese invaded

Burma, Indochina, Thailand, Java, and Ceylon—bringing the Ceylonese king to China in chains—and forced even the Arab holy city of Mecca to pay tribute to them.

Chinese leaders, however, were never able to consolidate their hold on the territories they conquered, particularly in more recent times, having found it difficult enough trying to impose their authority on their own country, which was split into feudal principalities, each run by a war lord and his private army. Speaking more as a Chinese than as a communist, Mao said bitterly in the late 1930's, while he was still struggling to overthrow Chiang Kai-shek and seize power: "In defeating China in war, imperialist powers have taken away many Chinese dependent states and a part of her territories. Japan took Korea, Taiwan [Formosa] and the Ryukyu Islands, the Pescadores and Port Arthur. England seized Burma, Bhutan, Nepal, and Hong Kong. France occupied Annam [Vietnam], and even an insignificant country like Portugal took Macao."

With Mao's victory in China, the nation achieved unity and a national purpose for the first time under a centralized dictatorship that reached down to the lowliest peasant. As a result, China is in an infinitely better position to realize its dream of Asian conquest than it has been in the past. And it has more reason to do so. Conquest is no longer considered simply economically and politically desirable; it is essential for the spreading of Marxist-Leninist doctrine, assuming the aura of a holy crusade.

Red China also needs free Asia as a strategic bulwark against American military might. It needs free Asia's rubber, oil, and mineral riches, and most of all, living space for China's swelling population and food to prevent starvation. China's population, now over 600,000,000, may exceed a billion by 1980, yet in area the country is only two-thirds the size of the United States. Already, because of the shortage of cultivable land, and also because of catastrophic communal farming methods, poor economic planning, and natural disasters, the diet of the average Chinese has a calorie content far under what is considered the minimum for good health.

The government has moved several million people to thinly settled parts of Northwest China, Manchuria, and even distant Tibet, but studies have indicated there is little land not now under cultivation that can be turned into farmland in the future. Cambodia, Laos, North and South Vietnam, Thailand, Malaya, and Burma comprise an area of almost 800,000 square miles— more than a quarter of the size of China—yet have a population of only 80 million people and a rice surplus of some 3.5 million tons annually.

Red China's over-all strategy in Asia is tied to its population problem. Its most immediate objective appears to be control of the great river systems that flow through Southeast Asia. Their valleys offer the communists some of the richest ricelands in Asia, while the waterways themselves would provide them with a ready-made transportation network to facilitate their aggression. The Reds already control one of these systems—the Red River in North Vietnam. With the capture of Laos and South Vietnam, they would control the Mekong River, which runs along the Lao-Thai border, through Cambodia, and into South Vietnam. Thailand promises the communists the rich valleys of the Mae Nam River. Once Thailand was in their grasp the Reds would inevitably head southward down the Malayan Peninsula, where communists still holding out in the Malayan jungles after losing a twelve-year guerrilla war against the British are hopefully waiting for help from the north. With the rubber and tin of Malaya securely behind the Bamboo Curtain, the next goal would be the fabulously rich islands of Indonesia, which, in view of the massive strength of its Communist Party, could fall peacefully. Burma's turn would then come, and ultimately India's. The rest of free Asia, including Japan and the Philippines, finding themselves completely isolated, geographically and economically, from their neighbors, would then presumably drop into the Red net of their own weight.

If Red China's ambitions in southern and eastern Asia can be frustrated, it is possible that Peking will eventually be tempted, and economically pressed, to seek another outlet for expansion—Soviet Asia—thus making an all-out defensive stand in the non-communist areas all the more necessary. China, whatever its politics or ideology, has never forgotten that Czarist Russia swallowed up a large part of the Manchu empire in Central Asia and north of the Amur River. Before Russian-Chinese relations reached the present explosive stage, the two countries agreed to explore and develop jointly the resources of the Amur region. With little likelihood that this agreement will be implemented until relations between them improve, China may view ever more hungrily the rich fertile lands that lie just across its borders—lands, the Chinese feel, that should never have been taken from them in the first place. The time may still be distant when China will be strong enough to commit aggression against Soviet Russia; but if South Asia, with Western aid, can resist substantial communist penetration until this time comes, the inflation of the Chinese population may well burst over into Russian territory, resulting in a clash that could benefit the West.

Despite the obvious incentives for communist adventures in Asia, many people in the free Asian countries rejoiced when Mao Tse-tung first won control of China. They considered Chinese communism, as did most Chinese peasants themselves, little more than "agrarian reform" and a manifestation of Asian nationalism. Looked upon as an anti-imperialist liberator of his people, Mao was considered far less a threat to the independence of neighboring countries than any leader China had ever had. Chinese communism seemed to many noncommunist Asians the possible answer to Asia's critical need for political stability and economic development. But Peking, under Stalin's influence, almost immediately dissipated this good will by attacking India, Burma, Indonesia, and other "uncommitted" nations as "running dogs of the imperialist camp."

The Red Chinese regained some of this lost friendship early in the Korean War, when, contrary to Moscow's policy, they dropped this line, hoping to win Asian support in their struggle against the American-led United Nations forces. China signed an accord with India calling for "peaceful co-existence"; then in early 1955 at the historic Afro-Asian Conference held in Bandung, Indonesia, Premier Chou En-lai called for an expansion of the principles agreed upon between Peking and New Delhi throughout the Afro-Asian world.

The Kremlin, having by this time also switched to the "right strategy" in underdeveloped countries, suddenly converting "reactionaries" like India's Nehru and Indonesia's Sukarno into "progressive patriots," was not unaware of Red China's growing popularity in Asia, which threatened Russia's own influence in the region. The Russians made their first important bid to enhance their position in the face of the Chinese threat in late 1955, when Khrushchev and Bulganin toured India. Soviet economic aid then began to cascade into Asia, exceeding China's more limited generosity. But it was clear that Asians were more amiable toward Red China, because of both its proximity and its seemingly greater sincerity. It had manifested a friendly attitude toward the rest of Asia since the start of the Korean War—at a time when the Kremlin still supported communist rebellions against nationalist regimes.

Noncommunist Asia's honeymoon with Red China was first seriously disturbed when Chinese armies ruthlessly crushed Tibet and ended its traditional autonomous status, throwing out Indian diplomats and businessmen in the process, despite promises

China had given India that Tibetan autonomy and India's special position in Tibet would be respected. Then in 1959 Red Chinese soldiers began infiltrating border areas of India itself, as well as such Indian Himalayan protectorates as Bhutan and Sikkim. A terrifying chill gripped the nations of free Asia. China had deceived them. It had asked for "peaceful coexistence," but it practiced raw, unprovoked aggression.

The sudden shift in Peking policy simply meant that Mao was adjusting Chinese willingness to co-operate with the national bourgeoisie to meet the standards he had set for dealing with noncommunists in the late 1920's. He had collaborated once with Chiang Kai-shek who, in 1927, suddenly turned upon him and nearly destroyed the communist movement. Mao's principle after that experience was to do business only with noncommunists who he was certain would serve communism. India's Nehru had not passed the test. He had persecuted Indian communists, jailed them, called them "traitors." Nehru was not only a noncommunist but a bitter enemy of the communists; he could serve communism in no significant way. Also, it was not necessary to buy Nehru's Cold War neutralism. He was a neutralist by conviction, not by opportunity, and would remain one regardless of the attitude of the communist world toward him.

Peking's reasonableness toward noncommunist governments had also failed to yield ideological dividends in such countries as Thailand, Burma, and even Indonesia, where anticommunist influences were growing in strength, compensating for any gains local Reds might have made.

Asian trust in Red China turned to fear as Peking's aggressive, arrogant posture swept away illusions of a warm-hearted neighbor. To soften the reaction in free Asia to their actions in Tibet and India, the Chinese concluded an agreement with Burma that ended a traditional border dispute between the two countries. The nations of Asia, Mao wanted to show, could still do business with China. But Peking is not nearly as concerned as Moscow is about being liked in Asia. This is a secondary consideration to Mao, who has found that fear is often more effective than brotherly love in winning the support of weaker nations. While most free Asian nations have tended to be neutralist in the Cold War from the time they became independent, their wariness of dealing with the West has become more pronounced since Peking started baring its teeth. Cambodia, which leaned toward the West while China was playing the protective Big Brother, moved sharply toward genuine neutralism when the true image of Peking began to show through. Even strongly pro-West Thailand, before United States troops arrived in mid-1962, had begun to exhibit neutralist tendencies as the result of fear born of the deteriorating situation in neighboring Laos.

Mao's main interest, in any event, is to secure China's military position and to promote communist revolutions in Asia. He did not hesitate to grab Indian border areas that would give the Chinese a commanding military advantage in their long-term effort to win control of all Southeast Asia. Nor did he pass up the opportunity to profit from the revolt of neutralist Captain Kong Le against the rightist government in Laos, or to lend fuel to communist guerrilla action in South Vietnam.

Thus Mao has, to some degree, reverted to Stalin's policy of fomenting communist rebellions in Asia, whether against Western colonialist or noncommunist nationalist governments. But Mao's program is far more discreet and clever. Whereas Stalin ordered almost all communist parties in Asia to revolt simultaneously, regardless of strength or local conditions, Mao is taking into consideration both strength and conditions. He moved against Laos only when an opportunity presented itself that offered the communists the maximum possibility of success. He stepped up the guerrilla campaign in South Vietnam only when Red control of parts of Laos simplified the problem of guerrilla and supply movement into South Vietnam, and when the West was embroiled in a war threat over Berlin. He has refrained from encouraging premature revolutionary activity in most other Asian countries that might easily be crushed.

In particular, China wants no more full-scale guerrilla wars in countries like Malaya, where Red jungle forces were defeated in recent years, until such nations border on communist-controlled areas that can provide guerrillas with a rear base sanctuary from which to launch their attacks. North Vietnam, of course, provides that sanctuary for communists fighting in Laos and South Vietnam. Mao, it should be noted, is letting the North Vietnamese rather than his own Chinese troops fight in both countries, and he might well intend to have them, because of their efficiency and high degree of indoctrination, lead revolts in other Southeast Asian nations as well. North Vietnamese President Ho Chi Minh, a very ambitious man himself, may be scheduled to exercise considerable control over all Southeast Asia as Red China's top agent. At any rate, Peking wants to swallow its victims in an orderly, systematic way as foolproof as that which won China for Mao.

Russia is less confident that China's plan for constant, accelerated revolutionary upheavals in countries under the rule of the national bourgeoisie will prove profitable in the long run. It fears that such activity will eventually create a situation in which the Western and communist worlds will find themselves inexorably spiraling into World War III. With the United States committed to keep South Vietnam out of communist hands at any cost, Moscow and Peking may yet have to make a choice between giving up their full-scale guerrilla struggle in that country or sending in their own troops. While China might prefer the latter course if necessary, provided internal economic conditions made it possible for it to engage directly in war, Russia would be hesitant to approve an expansion of the conflict.

True, Russia helped to unleash the crisis in Laos by air-lifting arms and supplies to the Lao rebels, but it started doing so when the possibility of an international war breaking out was almost nil in view of the approach of American presidential elections—a time when United States politicians speak peace, not war. It is possible that Russia's decision was also motivated by pressure from Peking or by the fear that if it did not involve itself to some extent in Mao's blueprint for conquest, China itself would intervene more openly in Laos, sparking a larger war and perhaps reducing Soviet influence in Asia. Moscow feels that it is dangerous and unnecessary, except in special cases, to force violent revolutions in countries which could lead to a world war, when the communist end can be achieved peacefully through gradual and persistent infiltration and subversion of national bourgeois regimes; and even subversion, it appears to believe, should be kept to a minimum in order to win the confidence of these governments. Significantly, while helping the Lao rebels, Russia, unlike Red China, supported efforts to bring an early end to hostilities in Laos. Communization may take longer through peaceful means, but such means involve little risk of a catastrophe that could sweep away all that the communists have gained.

A complete split between Russia and Red China could possibly prove more a detriment than a blessing to the West. For however ragged relations between the two countries may be at present, each is careful not to antagonize the other to the point where an irreparable break will become necessary. The Soviet Union is still, to some degree, able to hold the reins on the wild-eyed ideologists in Peking. But if such a break should come, Russia would no longer constitute a restraining influence on Red China, which might push ahead with its program for aggression in Asia without regard to the danger of world war. In such a case, the USSR, forced into ruthless competition with China for the loyalty of satellite communists, may find it necessary to take greater gambles itself with the peace of the world.

In Asian countries not yet ripe for all-out guerrilla rebellion Red China is confining its activities to infiltration and subversion —with the accent, unlike Russia's, on subversion. Though it is less popular than Russia, which is generally regarded as a sensibly moderate communist nation, it is able to wield a formidable influence simply because it is feared—feared both by national governments and by the communist parties that are supposed to infiltrate them. These parties find themselves facing a cruel dilemma. The majority of Reds would probably prefer to pay primary homage to Russia, which is, after all, the father of communism and is able to provide them with far greater funds than impoverished, half-starved Red China. But they are somewhat disturbed by Khrushchev's tendency to ignore them as a consequence of his efforts to woo national bourgeois governments. Nor do they feel they can afford to antagonize Peking, which is in constant contact with them and which, they feel, is likely to win control of all Asia in the future.

So most communist parties pay lip service to Peking's policies, but without criticizing the Soviet Union. Asian communist leaders have been careful not to support Moscow's bitter campaign to discredit Albania, which leans heavily toward the Red Chinese ideological view. Even the Indian Communist Party criticized China only with great reluctance—and then under the irresistible pressure of public opinion—for invading Indian territory.

Red China is recruiting many of its most ardent supporters with generous scholarships granted to Southeast Asian students. Almost 50,000 young men and women are believed enrolled in communist schools in Yünnan Province, many of them members of respected village families who are expected to return home as agents for Peking. Mao hopes eventually to indoctrinate in these schools at least one youth from every sizable village in Southeast Asia. As in Russia, many of these students become disillusioned with the harsh and regimented life in China and leave antagonistic toward communism. But indoctrination is cleverly handled: students are permitted to take any courses they desire in addition to a subtle political course—and some fall into the psychological trap, a sufficient percentage, in any event, to cause concern for the future.

Peking has another potential instrument of infiltration and subversion in almost all Southeast Asian countries—thirteen million overseas Chinese, or *Hua-Chiao,* as China refers to them. Most of these Chinese are apolitical and are trying to avoid serving Peking's ends. They are concerned far more with their own personal problems, mainly how to increase their wealth and avoid the lash of racial discrimination in their respective countries of residence, than with the ideological status of China. Nevertheless, these Chinese are very pragmatic and invariably bend with the political wind. If they should feel that Peking will inevitably devour their country of residence, their "loyalty" is likely to go to Peking. Though they make up only eight percent of the total Southeast Asian population, they control the commerce of most of these countries and could bring their economies to a halt, creating political chaos in the process, if they so desired. And such a desire is amenable to cultivation in direct proportion to the Peking threat.

In some cases, the *Hua-Chiao* represent a more direct menace. The Malayan communist guerrilla army that fought the British for a dozen years after World War II was composed almost entirely of Chinese, as are the communist gangs that have terrorized Singapore in recent years. Through propaganda, pressure, and outright threats, Peking has managed to win at least the ostensible support of many *Hua-Chiao,* including a large number who were once strong supporters of Chiang Kai-shek.

Mao's propaganda is mainly designed to remind the race-conscious overseas Chinese of their glorious heritage, and to convince them that China, the fountainhead of this heritage, has at last become one of the most respected and powerful nations in the world. Chinese newspapers praise Red Chinese policies either directly or indirectly, depending on the political orientation of the country of publication. Subsidized merchants sell cheaply or even give away literature about life in China. Children's books telling of the magical wonders being performed in China are particularly popular. Almost all literature that is not communist-inspired is condemned by communist publications and organizations as a product of the West's "yellow," or decadent, culture. Communist Chinese movies offering subtly procommunist, anti-American themes are assured of outlets in Southeast Asia in view of the fact that almost all theaters in the region are owned by local Chinese, who are often guaranteed a profit for showing communist films. Peking-influenced Chinese drama groups portray the happy life of the Chinese peasant today as compared to the misery he suffered in precommunist days.

The *Hua-Chiao,* clinging to cultural roots that offer them both a feeling of superiority and their only real sense of security, look and listen avidly, despite their indifference toward politics and ideology. They are all the more disposed to identify themselves as Chinese, rather than as nationals of their country of residence, because of the persecution to which they are subjected by governments that resent them for their wealth, their aloofness, and their lack of patriotism, even while rendering their assimilation impossible.

As most overseas Chinese glow with the same racial pride and dignity felt by most Jews because of the creation of Israel, it has been relatively simple for Peking to trap them into serving Communist China, if not into conversion to communism. "Overseas Chinese," explained the Hong Kong communist newspaper *Ta Kung Pao,* "must do as directed principally because the motherland is trying to strengthen her friendly ties with other countries . . . Overseas Chinese must voluntarily act as a bridge of friendship and mutual understanding between people of the motherland and people of their countries of domicile." This was an oblique way of telling the *Hua-Chiao* that they were expected to work in the interests of China if for no other reason than that they were Chinese.

Some overseas Chinese have not had to be pressured to serve Peking, for they are ideologically as well as culturally oriented toward China, or at any rate are prepared to give the "great experiment" now in progress there a chance to prove itself. This is particularly true of students, many of whom attend Red-supervised Chinese-language schools in their countries of residence, or are among the approximately five hundred students a month who stream into Red China to pursue high school and advanced studies at institutions giving them priority in admission. A special overseas Chinese high school has been built in Toishan at a cost of $20,000, while in Chimei, near the port of Amoy, a middle school has been converted into an exclusively *Hua-Chiao* school which offers, in addition to indoctrination, allowances for books, clothing, and medical treatment. A large number of overseas Chinese also attend Amoy University.

Other *Hua-Chiao,* though not ideologically attracted to Peking, voluntarily back its policies because they are already convinced that Peking will win control of all Southeast Asia in the near future, and they want the favors they think will be bestowed on early supporters in the conquered areas. Almost no overseas Chinese believe that Chiang Kai-shek's regime will ever regain power, and there is little disposition to endanger one's future by placing money on a sure loser.

Many Chinese businessmen fall into this opportunistic category. Yet their heads would probably be among the first to roll if Red China took over their adopted countries, regardless of their contribution to the cause. Perhaps the most important of them is Lee Kong-chian, whose Singapore-based Lee Rubber Company has been an instrument of Red subversion throughout Southeast Asia. Agents of this firm, one of the largest rubber-exporting companies in the world, with plantations and sawmills in Malaya and offices elsewhere, travel from country to country loaded down with propaganda literature, communist directives, and funds for subversion. Lee's son, Lee Seng-yee, a top executive of the firm and probably, many people believe, a genuine communist, has served Peking so well that a building at China's Amoy University has been named after him. Until recently, at least, he used a friend's "radio shop" to communicate messages to Red agents throughout the region. Another Singapore rubber magnate, Tan Lark-sye, is known to have contributed funds to Malayan and Indonesian communist groups. Other businessmen, with easy profits awaiting them, have needed little persuasion to flood Southeast Asian markets with cheap Chinese goods produced more for political than for economic gain.

Mao has also found ways to deal with some overseas Chinese who are reluctant to support Red China. Since Peking controls many Chinese banks in Southeast Asia, it offers easy-term loans, and demands repayment of them, on the basis of their political attitude. To qualify for a loan, a businessman may have to agree to send his children to communist schools or to "contribute" to communist-front organizations. Occasionally, particularly in Singapore, a Chinese who dares to criticize the Reds openly may find himself the victim of an "accident" in some dark alley.

But not all Red Chinese activities in free Asia are of a subversive nature, for where sweetness and light are feasible, Peking can still be as ingratiating as Moscow. Red China has gone out of its way to promote good will in Burma, Cambodia, Ceylon, Nepal, and Indonesia, which are all receiving Red Chinese economic aid or have concluded profitable trade agreements with Peking. Its relatively warm ties with these countries have helped to counteract adverse Southeast Asian reaction to Chinese instances of aggression while creating an atmosphere conducive to local communist infiltration in their governments, though the overseas Chinese problem recently strained Red China's relations with Indonesia.

CEYLON

But in some countries Red China is having, or is likely to have, a difficult time winning popularity contests with Russia, however friendly it may try to be. In 1959 it cynically bid for the support of neutralist Ceylon, a scenic tropical island just south of India, even while its people, mostly Buddhists, were simmering with rage over Mao's action in Buddhist Tibet and Indian border areas. Mme. Sirimavo Bandaranaike, the world's only woman Prime Minister, extended a barter agreement that has been in effect since 1952, providing for the exchange of Ceylonese rubber for Chinese rice. China's own need to import large quantities of rice to prevent starvation among its people points up the importance Peking attaches to the trade accord, which offers, in addition to the rubber, a convenient tool for infiltration and for counteracting the ill feeling that has resulted from its aggression.

Red China considers this tool particularly important because of Russian plans to move dramatically into Ceylon with programs for a steel mill, though the island has no mining industry to feed it, and a tire and tube factory, both to be built under a credit of \$28.4 million advanced by the Soviet Union in 1958. The loan may be repaid over twelve years in currency or goods—an arrangement likely to increase the currently small Soviet role in Ceylonese trade. Such Russian aid may not only dim Red China's policy of "kindness" toward Ceylon, but may also make American help—mostly foodgrains and technical assistance—look unimpressive.

The Soviet Union has a solid hold on the Ceylon Communist Party, which is legal, has about four thousand members, and constitutes about five percent of the electorate. The party is often supported by two other legal Marxist parties—the Trotskyite Lanka Sama Samaja Party and the independent Lanka Sama Samaja Party—Revolutionary—which together account for another fifteen percent of Ceylonese voters. The extreme left split up in 1940 when the Trotskyites won control of the communist movement and expelled all members sympathetic to Russia. In 1960, however, Trotskyite leaders met with Soviet Ambassador Vladimir G. Yakoviev, reportedly to discuss the possibilities of a new Marxist union of forces which, if ever effected, would presumably be under Moscow's sway. Today these forces have a powerful influence in Ceylon's trade unions, and often throw the economy into chaos by instigating strikes.

NEPAL

The "velvet glove" aspect of Peking's policy has so far proved more successful in countries more directly in its threatening shadow, such as Nepal. The 55,000 square miles of this remote medieval mountain kingdom are sandwiched between the plains of northern India to the south and the Himalayan peaks of Tibet on the north, and were accessible only by donkey expedition from India until air traffic was established between New Delhi and Katmandu, the Nepalese capital, a few years ago. King Mahendra, who has held absolute power since December 1960, when he dissolved the country's first popularly elected parliament—thus creating a sporadically active guerrilla opposition that operates from India—professes a distaste for communism. But with the support of Foreign and Home Minister Dr. Tulsi Giri, who is bitterly anti-American and anti-Indian, he has nevertheless opened the door to heavy Red Chinese infiltration because he wants to remain on good terms with a dangerous neighbor and to balance India's traditionally preponderant influence in Nepal.

Peking has used Nepal, like Burma, as a showcase of Red Chinese reasonableness to compensate for the unfavorable effects in Asia of its Tibetan and Indian policies. It signed an agreement with Nepal in October 1961 that delineated the border between the two countries, dividing Mount Everest, which it had previously claimed all for itself, between them. At the same time, Peking agreed to help Nepal build a highway—which had been surveyed by Soviet experts—from Katmandu to Tibet. The Nepalese claim that the road is intended to permit Katmandu to communicate with isolated northern Nepal and to reduce the nation's economic dependence on India. But Western and Indian observers are not oblivious of the fact that it could also be used as a Chinese invasion highway into Nepal and India. Further, the agreement will admit to Nepal an undisclosed number of Chinese technicians who can be expected to double as spies and agents.

Red China has also granted and promised other aid amounting to $12.6 million, and has indicated it may offer still more. This does not compare with India's $60 million and America's $50 million aid programs, but Peking has made a greater impression because of the "impact" of its more spectacular projects. Its most immediate aim, it appears, is to split India and Nepal, rendering both more vulnerable to Chinese aggression. Chinese intentions are a source of intense worry to the Indian government. When Nepalese officials indicated in February 1962 that Communist China might seek to send troops into northern Nepal to stem a reported anti-Chinese military build-up among Tibetan refugees who had allegedly infiltrated into the area from India and Sikkim, there was even talk in New Delhi of sending Indian troops to Nepal. In 1959, it was recalled, Nehru had warned that any aggression against Nepal "would be considered by us as aggression against India."

Meanwhile the Nepal Communist Party, which was founded in 1949, is strongly supporting the King against his political enemies, who, in their demand for a return to parliamentary rule, have resorted to terrorism, trying on one occasion to assassinate the Sovereign. The party has renounced its label in line with the order that all political parties dissolve themselves, but its estimated 3,500 members have maintained a strong underground network and have deeply infiltrated civic and youth groups. It controls the largest peasant organization in Nepal, thanks to its unrelenting opposition to the present feudal landholding system and its support of measures designed to benefit farmers. It has also capitalized on the "Indian question" and food shortages. The party won only about seven percent of the votes cast in the 1959 elections, but this included twenty percent of the vote in the Katmandu Valley, Nepal's cultural and intellectual center, and fifteen percent in five districts along the Indian border.

In trying to frustrate the communist master plan for the capture of all Asia, the West appears to be at a serious disadvantage. For although all countries in free Asia wish to see the march of communism halted, few are willing to co-operate with the West in seeking fulfillment of this wish. Many Asians not only retain a lingering bitterness toward the West for its colonial history, but feel that the best way to handle the communist tiger is to avoid antagonizing him, and even to feign friendship for him.

Pro-West nations in Asia include South Korea, Taiwan, Japan, Thailand, South Vietnam, the Philippines, Pakistan, and Malaya, which together contain only about fifteen percent of Asia's population and area. Taiwan, the headquarters of Chiang Kai-shek's right-wing Nationalist Chinese government, is, of course, a staunch ally of the United States, if only because it has no choice, and it has one of the largest and best armies in noncommunist Asia. But because of the strategic impossibility of its return to the mainland it can only be of use if Red China tries to take over Taiwan by force, another virtual impossibility because of the presence in the area of the U.S. Seventh Fleet. Moreover, the Nationalist government, despite impressive economic and social reforms it has instituted in Taiwan, is scorned by most Asian countries because of the image it created in China as a corrupt, rightist regime, and is often singled out as an example of America's outdated "reactionary" approach to the Asian situation.

Other United States allies have poor defenses and are hampered in their pro-West policies by public opinion that is neutralist in varying degrees. Japan is forbidden by its postwar constitution to have full-fledged armed forces, nor would the pacifist attitude in that country, or the residual distrust of Japan in other Asian states, permit it to play a role in free Asia's defense. As a result of public opinion, Malaya, too, while closely tied to British policy, must remain at least ostensibly neutralist.

PAKISTAN

Pakistan, which has long been a military ally of the United States in both Asia and the Middle East, has also shown signs of edging toward neutralism, maintaining that the United States is more interested in bolstering the strength of neutralist India than that of Pakistan. In November 1961 M. H. H. Zuberi, Secretary of the Ministry of Power, Fuel, and Natural Resources, said that his country will seek economic aid and technical assistance "from anywhere." The United States and Russia are already competing to assist Pakistan in fighting salinity and waterlogging, which affect 27,000,000 acres of land in West Pakistan. Moscow has also agreed to help explore for oil.

The United States was most sharply criticized when it decided to grant massive military aid to India after the Red Chinese attack in late 1962. Such aid, Pakistan argued, might eventually be used against it. Hoping to profit from this rift, Peking offered, even while its armies were surging into India, to sign a non-aggression treaty with Pakistan. Pakistani officials said this offer would be "seriously examined." Simultaneously, Foreign Minister Mohammed Ali accepted an invitation to visit Peking. At any rate, because of the fear of both India and Pakistan that the other would take advantage of the Chinese invasion to further its own ends in Kashmir, which both claim, the two countries agreed in late 1962 to negotiate the long unsettled dispute.

Aside from the tendency to improve relations with the communist countries, local communists may extend their influence, particularly in East Pakistan. Open Red activity has been illegal in Pakistan since 1954, but communists continued to infiltrate provincial governments through front organizations until 1958, when Field Marshal Mohammed Ayub Khan seized power in a bloodless coup, declared martial law, dissolved parliament, banned political parties, and established a benevolent dictatorship that has greatly reduced corruption and introduced many social and economic reforms. Martial law severely impeded the communist advance as leading communists were either jailed or driven into hiding, and the party's principal propaganda outlets were closed down or taken over by the government. Among the publishing companies seized was one which controlled the Red-line newspapers *Imroze* and *Pakistan Times*. Nevertheless, an underground party with an estimated 3,500 to 5,000 members, mostly in the east, is still operating.

East Pakistan was carved out of a corner of eastern India about 1,000 miles from the main body of Moslem Pakistan to Hindu India's west, when the Indian subcontinent was partitioned in 1947 in accordance with the religious complexion of the various areas. Though one-seventh the size of the western sector, it contains fifty-six percent of the nation's 93,000,000 people. It also possesses all of Pakistan's raw jute—eighty percent of the world supply—which provides about forty percent of the nation's foreign exchange. The communists in this region have exploited the fact that despite the importance of this area to Pakistan it has been getting only a small share of development funds, even with the increased share obtained under Ayub. They have also exploited the feeling among easterners that West Pakistan has been trying to dominate them culturally, though Ayub has met one of their chief grievances by granting the Bengali language of the East equal status with the Urdu language of the West.

A slightly built, chocolate-skinned East Pakistani student dressed in ragged Western clothes sat next to me on the wooden seat of a fourth-class railway coach that was taking us through West Pakistan. Above the shouts and laughter of white-robed, turbaned peasants and the cackling of their chickens in boxes and cages under the seats, he told me: "You see all these people in this car? They're Pakistanis and Moslems just like I am. But I don't understand what they are saying because we don't speak the same language. We don't even think in the same way. Actually, I feel greater affinity to the Hindus in eastern India near my home than to my Pakistani compatriots in the western sector. Our

Bengali culture—art, literature, music—is very similar to that of India."

The Reds in the East have had no less success making hay from political dissatisfaction. Though Ayub can point to East Pakistanis in the cabinet and in other high positions, the easterners want greater autonomy and, at the least, an end to dictatorial rule, however benevolent. When Ayub ordered the arrest of several eastern political leaders in February 1962 for "acting in a manner prejudicial to the security and defense of Pakistan," university students in Dacca, the eastern capital, rioted, reportedly with the help of the communists. The granting of limited democracy in mid-1962 through the election of a national parliament has not appeared to pacify the East Pakistanis.

Ayub Khan warned in a speech delivered in Dacca in July 1960 that communist-led riots that had just taken place in the neighboring Indian states of Assam and West Bengal were intended to lead to the formation of a Red state of Assam, West Bengal, and East Pakistan. Certainly the East Pakistani Reds, who receive aid and encouragement from their Indian counterparts across the border, would like to see the East break away from Pakistan. They might possibly be able to take over this region, which is strategically located between India and Burma and is a short distance from Chinese-held Tibet, if it were independent. Also, an independent East Pakistan would deprive West Pakistan of jute income and result in the reduction of its living standards, offering communists in the West, which is separated from the Soviet Union only by a narrow strip of Afghan territory to the north, new propaganda fuel of their own.

SOUTH KOREA

Even South Korea, one of America's most reliable allies, has not been untouched by the winds of neutralism, though this country is by no means in immediate danger of going communist. The presence of more than 30,000 American troops under the United Nations flag and a powerful 600,000-man South Korean army, the third largest in the noncommunist world, is probably sufficient to discourage new military aggression from communist North Korea. Subversion is difficult in view of the South Korean government's rigid anticommunist policies. Though a small underground, reinforced by North Korean agents, is believed to be operating, no South Korean Communist Party or Red-front organizations exist, and most South Korean Red leaders have been in North Korea since 1948. In that year a National Security Law severely restricted communist activities, and in 1949 the South Korean Labor (Communist) Party was formally dissolved after it had instigated riots and other civil disorders. Since the Korean War, from 1950 to 1954, which ended when Chinese and Korean communist forces and American-led United Nations forces agreed to a cease-fire along the 38th Parallel, the suppression of communism has been even harsher.

Furthermore, most South Koreans are extremely hostile to communism after living under oppressive communist occupation rule during the Korean War. Others are hopeful, if not enthusiastic, about the possibilities that their deplorable living conditions will improve under the military government of slim, granite-faced Major General Pak Chung Hi, which overthrew the corrupt parliamentary regime of Premier John M. Chang in May 1961 several months after Chang's followers had ousted the even more corrupt government of President Syngman Rhee. Pak's regime has done some good work so far, greatly reducing corruption, usury, sloth, and profiteering. It has ended the mass theft of about half the country's electric power by householders and businessmen who syphoned off power from the lines and bribed meter inspectors and electric company officials instead of paying bills, while most towns had to be lit by candlelight at night.

The black market that ate up foreign exchange, paralyzed local industries, and produced a wasteful consumer economy has all but disappeared. A foreign exchange reform no longer permits greedy businessmen to make quick fortunes at the expense of the country. Moneylenders can no longer maintain their hold on debt-burdened peasants and fishermen who often had to pay interest rates up to one hundred and fifty percent a year. Helping the government to build up the faltering South Korean economy is an American aid mission of almost six hundred people, the largest in the world. The United States, which has spent over $4 billion on military and economic aid to South Korea from 1946 to 1961, has helped to build a fertilizer plant that is filling about a third of the country's needs, to modernize coal mines and tungsten factories, to reconstruct railroads and highways, to put up chemical, cement, glass, textile, and other plants, and to prepare Koreans to run their own technical and professional schools and training programs.

But Pak's government is still far from loved by many South Koreans, who sullenly resent its heavy-handed, arrogant, aloof attitude toward the people. Most South Koreans don't put much store in Pak's promises of a free election in 1963. Even the American aid program is attacked by many Koreans, who charge that the Korean economy is gradually becoming "semi-colonial" because the United States holds, they say, what amounts to a right of veto on government expenditures. Many Koreans also bitterly complain that little of the enormous aid poured into the country has sifted down to the people, pointing out that more than two million people out of a total national labor force of eight million are still jobless. A Korean student who worked for me part-time as an interpreter—a brilliant, teen-aged, mop-haired youth who proudly wore the dark brass-buttoned uniform of one of the better high schools in Seoul—lamented: "I'm one of the top students in my class, but what have I got to look forward to when I graduate? There are already too many unemployed top students in South Korea. Perhaps I shall end up digging ditches—if there is an opening."

Generally discouraged, some South Koreans, particularly young intellectuals such as my student friend with no adult experience under communist rule, have begun to wonder if some kind of union with North Korea, whose industrial progress has deeply impressed them, might not facilitate an improvement in southern living standards. Though these South Koreans warmly recognize America's role in liberating Korea from Japanese rule and then supporting South Korea against communist aggression, they are not opposed to initiating a policy that would assert the country's independence from American influence as well. In June 1962 students loudly demonstrated in protest against Washington's refusal to permit the trial of G.I. lawbreakers in Korean courts.

Based on economic and nationalistic factors, a tendency toward neutralism is developing in South Korea as the possible key to reunification. Before General Pak came to power, it had begun to take concrete form through unification clubs like the National Unification League at Seoul National University. Such movements have been skillfully fostered by communist propaganda, especially since 1960. North Korean editorials, speeches, and rallies have concentrated on the unification theme, with Radio Pyongyang quoting for its South Korean audience all pertinent statements. Recent communist proposals have had particular appeal because of their "reasonable" nature, calling for co-operation in postal exchange, trade, cultural exchange, joint physical training, and the establishment of an interlocking railway service. In January 1961, before Pak's coup, even a segment of South Korean politicians approved limited approaches on exchanges with the North, while heated discussion in the teahouses of Seoul and other South Korean towns followed a highly publicized suggestion made by United States Senator Mike Mansfield in October 1960 for the unification and neutralization of the two Koreas.

The Reds have made some propaganda mileage through "guided tours" they have given South Korean fishermen who have been captured or have voluntarily visited the north. The recent voluntary exodus of tens of thousands of Korean residents in Japan to North Korea, the first large-scale refugee movement from the free world to communism, has further stimulated interest in reunification through neutralism. Perhaps the most significant tribute to the effect of communist propaganda can be seen in the results of a public opinion poll conducted in Seoul by the periodical *Hanguk Ilbo* at the end of 1960. Only forty-five percent of the people interviewed favored peaceful unification of the peninsula under free, U.N.-supervised elections, as desired by the West, while twenty-seven percent were undecided. The rest presumably favored some kind of accommodation with communism—a minority perhaps, but one which was virtually nonexistent a few years ago. Pak has since cracked down hard on even mildly leftist activities, but it is not clear whether this suppression has greatly reduced what neutralist sentiment had developed.

Lack of enthusiasm about getting involved in the Cold War even among the pro-West Asian nations is clearly reflected in the absence of any effective defense co-ordination among them. A Southeast Asian Treaty Organization (SEATO) exists, embracing Thailand, the Philippines, and Pakistan, as well as the United States, Britain, France, Australia, and New Zealand. Shortly after the organization was formed in 1954, I attended maneuvers of the member countries in Bangkok, Thailand. During a parade of joint forces through the main streets of the city, an American officer remarked with great enthusiasm: "Those soldiers are marching side by side now, and they'll fight side by side if the communists attack. SEATO has brought these different people together, made them aware that they're all fighting for the same thing."

To the extent that member countries have developed an awareness of common interest and common danger and their representatives have come to know and understand each other, SEATO is perhaps of some value. If its existence has made the Reds think twice about possible plans they may have had, or have, for aggression, it has further served a worthy purpose. Nevertheless, SEATO is a militarily ineffective organization, without joint forces, unified command, or real armed strength. It is committed to fight only for the mutual defense of SEATO members, not to intervene in case of attack on other Asian countries, and certainly not in the event of covert communist subversion.

This was underscored when the organization refrained from entering the Laos conflict. Only Thailand, which is directly threatened by communist aggression in neighboring Laos, pressed for SEATO intervention in that struggle, while the Philippines would have gone along, if half-heartedly. Typical of the response to this idea was the statement of Pakistani President Ayub Khan that SEATO was "slow" and "will always be slow, even if all the members did agree to a certain course of action." The United States, he said, should deal directly with Laos, as well as with Cambodia and Vietnam. France and Britain, preoccupied with European problems, have indicated even stronger resistance to the utilization of SEATO as a military instrument.

For all the difficulties faced by the West in keeping communist aggression from turning into an avalanche, Asia is not yet lost. Only one area in Asia—North Vietnam—has, after all, gone behind the Iron Curtain since China fell to communism, while Red drives for power have failed in Burma, Malaya, the Philippines, South Korea, Taiwan, and Indonesia. And it is possible that new guerrilla techniques now being taught to the South Vietnamese and other United States allies, particularly if coupled with social and economic reforms, may effectively counter present communist moves.

The neutralism that exists today in many Asian countries is in itself not necessarily disadvantageous to the Western cause. In some cases it has actually strengthened this cause. If Burma were openly pro-West, Red China, which borders on the country, might have given active support to Burmese communist guerrillas who have been fighting government forces since 1948. But with friendly relations existing between the two countries, no aid has been granted to the rebels. As a result, they have been all but crushed—and without any need for Western intervention. Furthermore, the granting of aid by the Soviet Union and Red China to the neutralist countries, and also to some pro-West nations, while motivated by obviously political factors, will, in the long run, serve in some measure to raise living standards and thereby reduce the poverty on which communism feeds. Nor does communist economic penetration usually mean a greater disposition on the part of the country helped to turn communist, any more than American aid has induced recipients to embrace the American way of life.

But neutralism will pose a grave danger for the West if the neutralists—or, for that matter, nations that are now pro-West—feel they can no longer depend on the West, particularly the United States, to save them from communism. A minority of neutralists, including India and Indonesia, oppose such military alliances as SEATO largely for emotional reasons. They see in such alliances a latent danger of a return of colonialism to Asia, however ridiculous such a possibility may seem. But most Asian neutralists favor the principle of a Western military guarantee against communist aggression, even though they may choose nonalignment for themselves as long as they are in no imminent danger of being devoured by the Reds. Cambodia has indicated that while it is opposed to SEATO because it includes Thailand, its traditional enemy, it sees nothing wrong with United States intervention in areas attacked by the communists. A high Burmese official frankly told me that the trouble with SEATO is that it is a paper tiger which, while capable of provoking Red aggression, has neither the force nor the will to fight it. In other words, if it were not a paper tiger, SEATO, or some other guarantee of military protection, would be welcomed.

If America does not provide such a guarantee the will of most Asians to resist communism—already weakened by the failure of SEATO to intervene in Laos when the communists first seriously threatened it in 1961—may diminish still further. Asians might move ever closer toward the communist orbit, not only as the result of increasing subversion and infiltration, but in the conviction that only by humoring the Reds have they a chance to survive. The danger would be doubly great if the communists could impose on Asian governments, as the price of "freedom," the condition that local Reds be included in them, as they have done in Laos.

The deep involvement of the United States in South Vietnam appears to indicate that Washington will use force in the future if necessary to defeat communist ends in Asia—until more peaceful means can take effect.

XIII

INDIA:

BURIAL OF A MYTH

The tiny isolated town of Gangtok, capital of the Indian protectorate of Sikkim, is enlivened by the presence of thousands of Tibetan
refugees. Characteristically making the best of a difficult situation,
they lend a strange note of gaiety to the otherwise bleak and solemn
atmosphere of this frontier hamlet as they play with their children
and joke with each other, the men dressed in black trousers and
boots and the women in ankle-length frocks and brightly colored,
striped half-aprons. As I strolled through the teeming market place,
where Tibetan and Sikkimese merchants sell everything from
small, intricately designed rugs woven in Lhasa to fine wood carvings from Kashmir, the Indian official accompanying me looked
toward the great white-tipped Himalayan peaks that cast a shadow
over the town.

"I'm glad you came here," he said. "On the other side of those
peaks are the Communist Chinese. This is about as close as you'll
ever get to them on this side of the Indian frontier. Take a good
look, because then perhaps you'll begin to understand why India is
neutral in the Cold War."

What this official was saying in a roundabout way was that India
had a potential enemy on its borders and had little desire to test its
mood. Unfortunately, despite the most fervent Indian efforts to
remain friendly with Peking, the Communist Chinese have spurned
the role of the good neighbor. In October 1962 Red China cul-

minated three years of border aggression with a full-scale attack. Its troops penetrated, within a month, about 50 miles into Indian territory along the 2,500-mile-long boundary between the two countries before halting. The reasons for its decision to cease fire, at least temporarily, are not clear. Perhaps its aim was simply to take the 50,000 miles of Indian territory China has traditionally claimed and no more. Perhaps it only wanted to discredit India as a competitive Asian leader and to let the smaller Asian neutralists know who is boss in the region. Perhaps it balked in the face of mounting hostility in the Afro-Asian world; significantly, it sent messages trying to justify its aggression to most neutralists before the cease-fire. Perhaps it was wary of overextending its supply lines.

Whatever the reasons, this aggression was probably only an initial step, if a premature one in Moscow's view, in a long-range plan for the eventual absorption of India into the communist empire. India is the ultimate Red target in South Asia. A captive India would place under the control of international communism over 400,000,-000 people, including a highly trained technical, administrative, and commercial elite, huge quantities of waterpower, metals, coal, and other fuel.

By Leninist reckoning, India should be a communist state today. Lenin had predicted that India would be easier to win, and would be captured sooner, than China. A communist India was to facilitate the communization of China. Peking now intends to reverse this calculation. *It* plans to communize India.

The program for doing so becomes clearer every time the communists make an aggressive move in Southeast Asia. The fall of Laos and South Vietnam would presumably open the way for concentrated infiltration and the eventual submission of Cambodia, Thailand, Malaya, and Burma, which adjoins India, in domino fashion. The stage would then be set, with the aid of the Indian Communist Party, for a subversive and possibly a non-stop military assault on the whole of India.

In 1959 Chinese troops started occupying five areas that have traditionally been considered part of India. Some of this territory is in the Northeast Frontier Province, but most is in barren, mountainous Ladakh Province at the northeastern tip of Kashmir, which four hundred years ago was an Asian crossroads where Persians traded fine rugs for the tea and silk of China. Today the precarious mountain passes over which traders and adventurers once threaded their way run parallel to a modern military highway that connects two large Chinese army bases, Rudok and Gartok, in western

Tibet, and links Lhasa, the Tibetan capital, with arsenals and bases in Sinkiang Province. The passes that lead into India are situated only a few thousand feet above the highway, making it militarily feasible for the Chinese to attack India from advantageously high ground. And unlike previous invaders they are backed by operational supply lines.

As Ladakh thus commands communications along the southern ramparts of China, control of this area has probably been Mao's chief objective, and he attained it in his massive attack, capturing almost the whole region. He also overran a large part of the Northeast Frontier Province, but he may have done this for bargaining purposes. He can offer to return the Northeast to India in exchange for permanent retention of Ladakh.

Now that the Chinese have a physical foothold in India, obtained at a calculated but heavy price of good will in most of free Asia, they aren't likely to give it up. To Indian arguments that the boundary has been clearly defined and is supported by treaties, geography, and custom, Peking simply maintains that the border has never been delineated and that no treaty between India and China defining the border exists.

This point of view is probably more Chinese than it is communist. Ladakh was part of Tibet before it won independence in the fifteenth century. And even afterwards this staunchly Buddhist territory continued to recognize the suzerainty of the godly Dalai Lama. In the middle-nineteenth century, British-led Indian soldiers captured Ladakh as well as the rest of Kashmir and negotiated with Tibet a fixed boundary between Kashmir and Tibet. However, China refused to recognize the agreement, claiming then as it does now that both Tibet and Ladakh, which it has always considered a part of Tibet, were Chinese.

In regard to the Northeast Frontier Province, the British reached an agreement with Tibet in 1914, fixing the 850-mile border between this province and Tibet. China was also present at the negotiations but would not formally sign the accord, which established the McMahon Line, named after Sir Arthur Henry McMahon, who represented the British. China subsequently ignored the McMahon Line on its maps, denying its validity long before Red Chinese Premier Chou En-lai, in answer to Indian protests, called the line a "product of British aggression against Tibet."

But now for the first time China is in full military control of Tibet and is therefore in a position to back its claims with force. More ominously, traditional Chinese claims dovetail neatly with the much larger claims of communism and provide an excuse for communist expansion into free areas that can be used as a springboard for more extensive operations in the future.

Peking's aggression against India came as a shocking blow to Indian Prime Minister Nehru who, in the hope of avoiding any clash of interests with Red China, had politically leaned over backwards to win its friendship since the day Mao Tse-tung came to power. India was one of the first countries to recognize the Red regime and has energetically fought for Communist China's entry into the United Nations. During the Korean War, though India contributed ambulance units to the United Nations forces, Nehru pleaded Peking's case, denying that it had committed aggression. Even when Chinese troops invaded Tibet in 1950, threatening the security of India itself, Nehru agreed that Tibet fell within the Chinese sphere of influence. This friendship blossomed into full flower in June 1954, when Nehru and Chou, who was visiting India, proclaimed the five principles of Panchshila: mutual respect, non-aggression, noninterference, recognition of equality, and peaceful coexistence. Here was proof, Nehru told the West, that it was possible to deal with Peking on friendly terms. Five years later Red China, without provocation, violated every one of the five principles.

Nehru banked on Russia to help keep Red China in line. He grasped Moscow's open hand as warmly as he grasped China's in the past. "I doubt," he said before Peking's massive attack, "that there is any country that cares more for peace than the Soviet Union. I doubt that there is any country that cares less for peace than China." But following the all-out assault, Khrushchev, embarrassingly caught between his ideological obligations to China and his professed friendship for India, asked India to agree to Chinese peace terms. In the final analysis, it was impossible for Russia to back a "bourgeois" government against a communist regime, however hostile the latter might be. Not only would such a choice be an ideological heresy, but it could greatly strengthen China's position in the struggle for the support of the world's communist parties. Though Russia hesitantly agreed to open a consular office in the Black Sea port of Odessa to facilitate the shipment of 1.5 million tons of oil to India over a three-year period and even stopped talking about peace on Mao's terms in an effort to keep India from joining the Western bloc, Nehru sorrowfully learned the limitations of Soviet good will.

It should be kept in mind that if Khrushchev was silently displeased by China's action, the reason did not stem from sympathy with Nehru or his regime. He simply saw tottering the whole structure of false friendship he had so meticulously built in the Afro-Asian world, "friendship" intended to create an atmosphere conducive to communist infiltration and subversion. Moreover, even if India itself were militarily defeated by external communist forces—and this could be achieved only at the risk of World War III—it would be difficult, if not impossible, to contain nationalist resistance indefinitely in so huge a country. In Khrushchev's eyes the proper way to proceed in India, at this stage of the Cold War anyway, is to leave the main job of communization to an Indian Communist Party subtly guided by Moscow, not to destroy the party's prestige and power through aggression by a communist country—especially when that country is a hated and feared ideological competitor of Russia. And if China's aim was only to gratify traditional Chinese hunger for certain border areas, it no doubt seemed foolish to the Russians that the long-range communist aim of world domination should be jeopardized by the dictates of narrow, undisciplined nationalism.

Russia started wooing India in about 1954 as part of its post-Stalin program to reverse its bitterly hostile policies toward national bourgeois leaders in underdeveloped countries. It has been particularly anxious to win over Nehru because of the tremendous influence he wields in the Afro-Asian world. If he played along with Russia, most other leaders of this world would also be disposed to do so.

The Soviet press began to portray Nehru as a great nationalist and liberator of his country. For the first time it had words of praise for Mahatma Gandhi, too, despite his despised views on nonviolence that had so effectively throttled the spread of communist class-warfare concepts. Relations between the two countries reached a peak degree of warmth when Khrushchev and Nicolai Bulganin, who was then Soviet Premier, toured the country, discussing crop problems with peasants and drinking milk from coconuts. When a year later Soviet tanks mowed down Hungarian workers on the streets of Budapest, Nehru proved his worth to the Kremlin by waiting three weeks to condemn Soviet action even mildly.

Russia, in turn, has staunchly backed Indian interests. It not only responded with sympathy when China first occupied Indian territory, but promised Nehru that if his troops forcefully took over the Portuguese colonial enclaves of Goa, Daman, and Diu on the west coast of India, it would support him in the United Nations and prevent the institution of sanctions against India. The Indian leader had been trying to get Portugal to turn over these territories to India since the subcontinent became independent. But the Portuguese government refused, maintaining that they were, like all Portuguese overseas possessions, "provinces" of Portugal. In 1955, when twenty Indians were killed in peaceful demonstrations against the colonialists, Nehru broke off relations with Portugal, declaring: "History will remove them."

But with Indian elections scheduled in early 1962, Nehru decided to push history along and thereby enhance his own, as well as his Congress Party's, popularity. Certainly, dynamic action would not hurt the chances of left-leaning Krishna Menon, his Minister of Defense, who appeared to be engaged in a tough struggle for his political life. And with Russian backing, Nehru had little to lose by resorting to force—other than his moral standing. Therefore, in December 1961 Nehru, despite his constant admonition to the world to settle international differences by peaceful means, sent his forces into the enclaves that had been administered by Portugal for over 450 years. While the United States and other Western powers condemned this action as "aggression," Khrushchev cabled Nehru his warmest congratulations.

Several months later, India arranged to manufacture Soviet jet engines for Indian supersonic aircraft and ordered MIG-21 fighters from the USSR.

But Russia's biggest propaganda harvest has come from its foreign assistance program for India. The United States poured about $4 billion into India in the period from 1951 to 1962, but the value of this aid in terms of impressing the Indian people is small compared to the tremendous impression made by Soviet projects totaling less than $1 billion for the same period. The most spectacular of these projects is a steel mill that has been built in the town of Bhilai. Bhilai was a hot, dusty village of mud huts in 1955. Today it is a booming town of 65,000 steelworkers and their families. And to most Indians the mill that is its heart ranks with the Taj Mahal as one of India's proudest achievements. A measure of Russia's success in propagandizing the project, which was completed in 1961, is the fact that while Britain and West Germany have also built steel mills in India, and the United States has expanded the existing Tata steel plant at Jamshedpur, these three countries have received virtually no popular recognition. Yet the Russian mill is by no means a gift. India must pay for the mill—$133 million plus the expenses of the one thousand-odd technicians furnished India and the more than five hundred Indians sent for training in Russia—in twelve annual installments carrying two and a half percent interest.

I met several of the Indian trainees on a plane going from New Delhi to Moscow. "The Russians," one of them told me, "know how to deal with Indians. They're extremely polite and thoughtful, and never order us around, and they give us responsibility as soon as we're ready for it. And if they're trying to brainwash us you'd never know it. They won't discuss politics with us."

The Russians, some of whom are still in Bhilai, have been discreet indeed in their relationship with their Indian colleagues, unlike some Westerners, who often get impatient with inefficiency. They have tried to give the Indians a feeling of importance far beyond the recognition they deserve—insisting, for example, however contrary to reality, that the Soviet Union provided the machines and the technical know-how but that the Indians built the mill themselves. And to help support this myth, the Russians marked each piece of the plant before sending it to Bhilai, so that the Indians would know how to assemble them largely on their own. The lengths to which they went for the sake of making the Indians happy was reflected in the cost, in money and time, of pre-assembling sections of the plant to permit marking of the pieces, and then disassembling for shipment.

To a large extent, Indian technicians trained in the Soviet Union were given greater preparation for the assumption of responsible jobs than those who went to Western schools. After studying steelmaking theory, they were trained in practical work by Russian workers, finally serving as subforemen.

Nor were the Indians unimpressed by the rigid adherence of the Russians to their construction timetable. Delivery of materials from Russia was punctual. If some items were found to be missing, jet planes brought them in without delay. Though construction was started some eighteen months after work on the German plant was underway, the Russian mill was in full operation first, a tremendous accomplishment in Indian eyes, considering the German reputation for efficiency.

Moreover, the simple living habits of the Russians have not gone unnoticed. Unlike the Westerners, they don't hire Indian servants. The women do their own cooking and housework. Since Soviet technicians are paid half their salary in rupees, local stores and market places have happily found them steady customers, though most of the Russians have already returned home. The Indians are also grateful for the free Russian movies shown at an outdoor theater, where Western and Indian pictures are also shown—for an admission charge. The Russians frequently visit Indian homes, shrewdly confining conversation to small talk about family problems.

Another Soviet propaganda bonanza has been the 30,000-acre Suratgarh mechanical farm that has sprung up in the Rajasthan Desert about 150 miles west of New Delhi. The idea for the farm was born during Khrushchev's visit to India in 1955. While touring a 16,000-acre farm at Terai in the Himalayan foothills, he grandly promised an outright gift of all the machinery and equipment necessary to establish a farm twice the size. Three months later, to the utter astonishment of the Indians, Soviet ships unloaded in a single lot equipment worth about $1.8 million—69 tractors, 75 plows, 500 harrows, 50 cultivators, 80 seed drills, 42 couplers, 50 winnowing machines, 60 harvester combines, 3 seed loaders, 2 grain-cleaning machines, 15 trucks, 6 bowzers, 2 passenger cars, 2 jeeps, 6 auto trolleys, 3 motorcycles with sidecars, and 4 auto trailers. Also included was a complete set of equipment for a workshop—lathes, drilling machines, electric welders, 5 mobile workshop trucks, a 15-kilowatt electric generator set, a bulldozer, a scraper, 2 ditchers, 12 excavators, 6 sprinkler irrigators, a complete 100-line automatic telephone exchange, and equipment for setting up an air-conditioned room for calibration of fuel injection parts in Diesel engines. As part of the gift, five Soviet experts came along to train Indians in the assembling, maintenance, and handling of the equipment.

Several years after receipt of this giant shipment twenty-five percent of the equipment is still in storage, either because it is not suitable for use on Indian soil or because the rate of progress on the farm simply has not yet permitted its absorption. Yet, with every necessary machine at hand, progress has been impressive. The farm will be used not only for the growing of crops, but will embrace an animal-breeding and poultry center, an orchard and nursery, and a belt of forest around the perimeter to seal off the cultivated land from the desert.

Needless to say, this dramatic Soviet gift produced headlines of appreciation throughout India.

With Communist China suddenly considered an enemy and the USSR a friend by most Indians, the Indian Communist Party, which boasts 230,000 members and won a respectable 10.5 percent of the vote in the 1962 parliamentary elections, has found itself in a painful dilemma as the result of China's aggression. If it supported Communist Chinese claims on Indian territory it would expose itself as a non-Indian party. If it denied the Chinese claims or expressed even as much sympathy toward the Indian cause as Russia, it would stir the wrath of Peking without necessarily obtaining greater backing from Moscow, which, for the moment, does not want to jeopardize the good will it has won in India by interfering too conspicuously in Indian politics.

As it was, the party had never quite recovered from its decision to approve the Chinese invasion of Tibet in 1950. It has had to struggle against two great handicaps since then: popular animosity in most of the country and deep internal dissension. The majority of members, or at least leaders, have always seemed to regard the Soviet Union as the main guiding influence, but many have looked upon China, whose agrarian and population problems are more closely related to those of India than are the more sophisticated problems of industrialized Russia, as the real leader of Asian communism.

The top party leadership has been deeply split on this issue. One group, led by Reds from West Bengal, which contains the communist stronghold of Calcutta, leans sharply toward Peking, feeling that the national interest must be sacrificed for the overall communist interest, which, in its fanatically ideological view, requires the blind backing of claims made by communist states against bourgeois states. A majority pro-Moscow group is, like the Russians, inclined more toward practicality than ideology and has considered it tactically wise and, in the view of some "national" Reds, "patriotic" to support the Indian government and the McMahon Line.

In 1959, when the Chinese moved across the Indian border, the party took a vague position calling for "peaceful negotiation" of differences between the two countries, charging that "powerful forces" within India and without, including Pakistan and the United States, were interested in keeping the frontier dispute alive and "causing discord and tension." But in 1961, after new Chinese border aggression, the party, eying elections scheduled in early 1962, flatly condemned the incursions. Secretary-General Ajoy Ghosh, a middle-of-the-road communist, was bitterly castigated by Peking for this action. When Ghosh, a clever politician who was largely responsible for keeping the organization together, died in January 1962, the pro-Moscow faction grabbed control of the party, further splitting it.

Shripad Amrit Dange of Bombay, a thin man with a high forehead and a bony face who is known as a friend of Moscow, was selected chairman, though he was defeated for re-election to parliament in early 1962. And as a "concession" to the pro-Peking faction, Elamulam M. S. Namboodiripad, the chief minister of Kerala when the communists were in power there, was named secretary-general, though he too has tended to lean toward Moscow, if less enthusiastically than Dange.

Under the leadership of these men, the party, following the massive Chinese attack on India in late 1962, desperately sought to save itself from the public's wrath by joining the rest of the nation in calling for an all-out struggle against Peking.

If Russia's influence appears to be dominant for the moment, Red China's is nevertheless strong. For example, it has prevented the party from supporting Khrushchev's attacks on the Albanian communists and, by implication, the Chinese Reds. Also, individual communists publicly supported Chinese policies, at least before the full-scale attack was launched. After the Dalai Lama escaped to India during the Tibetan uprising in 1959, an Indian communist leader, at the behest of the Chinese Embassy in New Delhi, actually agreed to serve as Peking's spokesman in the Lok Sobha, India's upper house of parliament, in an incredibly overt display of Chinese interference in the internal affairs of India.

With the pro-Moscow faction of the party at the helm, communist tactics are oriented toward the Kremlin rather than the Peking version of the Yenan Way. Despite opposition from communists who favor sabotaging Nehru's policies through strikes and even violence, in line with Mao's attitude, the party supports the Indian leader. The moderates reason, as Moscow does, that since Nehru's Congress Party, the party of Gandhi and of independence, is still all-powerful, they can win control of the government eventually only if they can subvert the organization, which embraces almost every shade of political opinion from extreme right to extreme left. In April 1961 the Communist Party frankly stated that it and "other advanced and conscious democratic forces" must establish "a united front with the progressive elements in the Congress . . ."

The Reds are attempting to do this in two ways. They are supporting these leftist elements on the parliamentary level and in elections, backing, aside from Nehru, men like ex-Defense Minister Menon, a fervent anti-American, and opposing such "right-wing reactionaries" as Finance Minister Morarji Desai. And they are infiltrating the Congress Party itself in the hope of taking it over. This is not a new Red technique. The communists have been trying to infiltrate the Congress Party since it was established in 1922. But during the Stalin era they had little success because they usually identified themselves as communists and preached communism in direct opposition to Gandhi's teachings. The assassination of Gandhi in 1947 cleared the way for greater success, and so did the death or political demise in the following years of leading conservative Ghandists. With Khrushchev's go-ahead in the early 1950's, the Reds had their work cut out for them.

Recent infiltration, unlike the Stalinist efforts, has been subtle. Thousands of communists have crossed over into the Congress Party and called themselves simply Congressmen. The Madras newspaper, *Hindu,* reported that 2,000 Reds from a single center in the northern state of the Punjab made the switch in June 1961. Once in the Congress Party, the communists support left-wing elements in internal party politics. The Communist Party has admonished them: "It is necessary to recognize that while a large part of the forces of the Right are inside the Congress Party, the bulk of those who are our potential allies are also inside the Congress Party . . . [Links must be forged with] democrats inside the Congress and the mass of Congress members, our friends and potential allies in the struggle for the consolidation of political independence."

The conflict between the pro-Moscow and pro-Peking Reds follows a historical pattern of factionalism and indiscipline within the Indian Communist Party, with the internal stresses probably greater now than they have ever been before. This history of disunity is a microcosmic reflection of the regional, linguistic, cultural, social, and religious divisions that plague the massive Indian subcontinent as a whole. The party has included stubbornly independent men in the tradition of the Indian nationalist movement, one of the first and most skillfully organized in the underdeveloped world. As far back as the Second Communist International Congress in 1921, Indian communist leader M. N. Roy, who at that time led the strongest Red movement in Asia, vigorously opposed Lenin himself on the question of policy in the underdeveloped countries. "Join forces with the national bourgeoisie against the imperialists, feudalists, and monopoly capitalists," cried Lenin. "That would be disastrous," replied Roy. "We must fight all capitalist factions, including the national bourgeoisie."

After Lenin's thesis, the heart of Mao's Yenan Way, was accepted by Stalin's successors, the Indian Communist Party found itself wooing the "progressive" bourgeoisie in the Congress Party. Nevertheless, the more intemperate Indian communists to this day have found it difficult supporting a "progressive" figure such as Nehru, who has often branded them traitors to India. On a number of occasions, factional disagreement on this and other matters has been resolved only by an international communist edict.

The party has embraced radical revolutionaries with a fondness for violence in the spirit of pre-independence anti-British riots and the communal killings of hundreds of thousands of Indians in Hindu-Moslem holy wars that accompanied independence. Communist agitators, for example, were known to have encouraged the rioting at Moslem Aligarh University, about eighty miles southeast of New Delhi, in October 1961. Several students were killed in the fighting, which followed a student election won by the more numerous Moslem sector of the student body. Reds are also believed to have been involved in the same period in other communal rioting in Uttar Pradesh, where nineteen people were killed, and in early 1961 in Jubbulpore in the state of Madhya Pradesh, where at least sixty-five persons died.

The party has also produced moderates and, in a few cases, even supporters of nonviolent resistance tactics in line with Gandhist tradition. Thus, A. K. Gopalan, a communist leader in Kerala, fasted for about two weeks in June 1961 in protest against the eviction of squatters from forest land to make room for a hydroelectric project. The Kerala government, accusing the communists of trying to make political capital of the situation, arrested Gopalan on a charge of attempting suicide, but he maintained that he would fast until the government conceded "the just, human, and minimum demands of the evicted persons"—almost the very language of Gandhi when he was peacefully struggling against British rule.

The party has included peasant factions, worker factions, intellectual factions, and factions based more on regional than national or international interests—all of these groups operating in concentric circles more or less independently of each other, and all of them torn between Indian tradition and communist dogma, between tactical pragmatism and ideological discipline. In the period from 1928 to 1935 the party was wracked by "deviationism" as the result of Moscow's unrealistic order that it attack Gandhi, Nehru, and their "national bourgeois" Congress Party in suicidal defiance of the popular tide. And even after Nazi Germany invaded Russia—the signal for all communists around the world to join in a no-holds-barred anti-Axis war effort—the Indian Communist Party alone displayed conflict and uncertainty. Prior to Russia's entry in the war, this party, like all others in India, described the conflict as an "imperialist war" which did not concern the colonies. The sudden involvement of the USSR caught the Reds flatfooted, particularly because of Gandhi's continued insistence that the war was still "imperialist," and that Indians should not co-operate with the British. Communists who had been imprisoned for long periods and were out of touch with Indian sentiment favored immediate and unconditional compliance with the Soviet call for support and collaborated with their former British jailkeepers. But many other communists who were free to mingle with the people were reluctant to heed the order, though they finally did. As a result, for years after the war the Reds were looked upon as traitors to the cause of national freedom.

This situation reflects the incredibly powerful influence of Gandhism on Indian thinking. It is the central factor in the party's history of disunity and indecisiveness. Gandhi has been a source of constant frustration to the communists because their alien revolutionary doctrine has never been able to compete with his intrinsically indigenous philosophy, which is a denial of the most basic Marxist-Leninist precepts, including the need for class struggle and the violence with which it is supposed to be waged. Because Gandhi was the most formidable barrier they had to face in Asia, he was also the most vilified of all nationalists in that region up to Stalin's death. He was described not simply as a national bourgeois but as a reactionary feudalist. In a book by Roy, *India in Transition,* published in 1922, the Indian communist leader wrote:

> The victory of Indian nationalism will be the victory of the progressive middle classes, which may build a monument to the memory of the Mahatma for the valuable services he rendered them involuntarily, but which will never share his pious indignation against Western civilization, which is after all a certain stage of social development through which every human community has to pass. In itself, capitalist society has many defects, but it is undoubtedly an improvement on patriarchal or feudal civilization for which Gandhi and his kind pine. Indian society is inevitably heading toward capitalist civilization, in spite of the premonitions of Gandhi . . . Gandhism is the acutest and most desperate manifestation of the forces of reaction, trying to hold their own against the objectively revolutionary tendencies contained in the liberal bourgeois nationalism . . .

Thus, according to Roy, Gandhi, like the communists, opposed capitalism, but for a reason exactly contrary to that of the Reds. It was too progressive a system for him. Apparently worried about the effects of this extreme view on Indian public opinion, Roy and his wife Evelyn wrote in another book published a year later, *One Year of Non-Cooperation from Ahmedabad to Gaya,* that perhaps Gandhi had a few progressive tendencies after all, although Gandhism, far from being revolutionary, was a "weak and watery reformism." This appraisal more accurately expressed the root of communist fear and hatred of Gandhi. He not only stole the communists' thunder by calling for reform, but preached that reform be achieved without bloodshed—making all the harder the communist job of persuading the masses to seize power from the bourgeoisie by force in line with Marxist-Leninist dogma. Nor did Red efforts to portray Gandhi's principle of nonviolence as dictated not by humanitarian motives but by the desire to prevent a people's rebellion against the bourgeois exploiters carry much weight with the Indian masses.

The post-Stalin view of Gandhi, whose assassination was a blessing to the Reds, has changed considerably in line with the "right strategy." Namboodiripad, the pro-Moscow Indian communist leader, wrote in *The Mahatma and the Ism,* published in 1958, that while Gandhi held reactionary views on many issues, it was precisely these views that enabled him to form a bridge between the peasants and the modern national democratic movement. A reactionary outlook produced a revolutionary phenomenon. But Namboodiripad repeats the argument that Gandhi's nonviolent tactics in the anti-imperialist struggle were based on his fear that violence would develop into revolutionary action against his own bourgeois class. And it is no surprise that the Reds still support this thesis, for they may not get very far in India unless the people can be persuaded to believe that any means, however immoral, are justifiable in the pursuance of an end—a concept, incidentally, furthered in no small degree by Nehru's use of force to swallow up the Portuguese Indian colonies. The communists are well aware that to the extent that they have joined Gandhi and his followers in common cause, party popularity has increased; while to the extent that they have moved to the left their strength has diminished. Their dilemma is how to praise Gandhi and to tear down his preachings at the same time.

Disunity, fed by Moscow's disregard for Indian public opinion —particularly in regard to Gandhism in the Stalinist years—and by Peking's similar attitude currently, has made the path to power rough going for the Indian communists. If they had gone along with Gandhi, they might have won a leading role in the Indian government when the British granted India independence after the war. Instead, they were frozen out. Unable to infiltrate or win the co-operation of the Congress Party, they desperately began resorting to violence even before Stalin proclaimed in 1948 that Asian parties adhere rigidly to the "left strategy." They concentrated on the region of Telengana, in the eastern part of Hyderabad, where the Nizam of Hyderabad refused to agree to the absorption of his state into the new Republic of India. Armed communist brigades grabbed control of the villages in this area and instigated the impoverished peasants to revolt against local officials and landlords and take over the land for themselves.

Indian troops arrived in September 1948 in reply to the Nizam's stubborn defiance and met mainly the resistance of Red guerrillas, who dreamed they could gradually build up a huge peasant army as Mao had done in China. They were encouraged by the Moscow edict calling for rebellions all over Asia. Guerrilla action soon spread to the neighboring state of Andhra, and the party called for general strikes and peasant uprisings throughout India. But the attempted revolt never got off the ground. The people of Hyderabad were horrified by the Red-instigated murders of more than one thousand people. An Andhra party spokesman reported: "The people did not join us. Our activities proved to be like a battle in the air . . . On the whole there were no struggles or strikes in the entire province." Even more indicative of the communist failure was the decision of two-thirds of the 20,000 "communists" in Andhra to leave the party in their disgust with Red tactics. Strikes and uprisings planned by the communists in other parts of India were also stillborn.

Only when the Reds changed their tactics in the post-Stalin period did they begin to regain ground. With violence no longer their principal weapon, they have discovered that, paradoxically, while the Gandhian concept of peaceful resistance hurts them, it can also be at least a minor source of their strength. For communism, like Gandhism, is a dynamic mass movement offering all the drama and idealism of Gandhi's inspiring example without requiring the emotional restraint that characterizes it. At the same time, the very regionalism that had helped to produce factional division could foster party advances on the provincial levels. For at these levels the Reds can support popular welfare policies and form united fronts with various other parties on strictly regional, non-ideological questions in opposition to Nehru's Congress Party, whereas no parties will co-operate with the communists at the national level where more vital issues are at stake.

Red gains at the provincial level in recent years have been particularly notable in West Bengal, Andhra, and, most important of all, Kerala where, in 1957, the communists actually came to power, the first case in history of a major territory democratically voting into office a communist government. Kerala, which on the map looks like a fingernail on the giant finger of India, is nestled between the Arabian Sea and the High Ranges at the southwestern tip of the subcontinent. It is a bountiful land rich in minerals, rubber, rice, tea, coconuts, and rain forests that shelter great herds of elephants. But Kerala, the smallest of India's fourteen states, can be proudest yet of one other product—its people. More than fifty percent are literate and almost every child goes to school, a record exceeded in Asia only by highly industrialized Japan.

It is, to a considerable extent, because of its more sophisticated population that Kerala has regarded communism more sympathetically than any other area. Of the two million-odd jobless in the state, which has a population density of 1,200 per square mile, the highest in India, many are frustrated revolutionary-prone high school and college graduates who spend the day looking for work and the night sleeping on sidewalks. Workers and peasants, too, better educated and therefore less tradition-bound than their counterparts elsewhere in India, are more receptive to the unorthodox but glowing promises of communism. Nor did these innocents feel they had anything to risk. The Reds pledged to rule by parliamentary means and, in any case, the central government could always step in if constitutional safeguards were violated.

The multireligious structure of Kerala's society also lent itself to communist tactics. The Reds aggravated Hindu prejudice against the highly influential Catholic community and then branded the Congress Party as the "Christian party." More significant was the division among the noncommunist political organizations—the Congress, Praja Socialist, and Moslem League parties. Together, they represented a majority. Divided, each was weaker than the Communist Party.

With these parties divided in the 1957 provincial elections, the communists won thirty-five percent of the vote and sixty seats, plus five garnered by procommunist independents, out of a total of one hundred and twenty-six seats, enough to put them in power. "We now have the opportunity to prove to India that communism is superior to any other system," the Reds cried gleefully. Indian President Rajendra Prasad added, "I am happy that this great experiment . . . is going to serve . . . as an example of coexistence." India—and the world—watchfully waited to see if communism could work within a democratic framework.

The experiment was strange indeed. Unable to exert the kind of dictatorial authority prescribed by Marx and Lenin because of the government's regional nature, the communists, led by Namboodiripad, then the provincial chief, launched confused and uncertain policies. They began with several dramatic gestures—reducing cabinet salaries, raising the salaries of teachers and village administrators, and halting evictions of farm tenants. But hardly had the nation sighed with relief than the communists began to act like communists. Reds convicted of criminal offenses, including murder and robbery, were released from jail. A magistrate who refused to withdraw criminal charges against a communist was demoted. A policeman who tried to prevent a group of Reds from breaking up an anticommunist student demonstration was transferred. Other "nonco-operative" government officials were purged.

"Co-operation" meant, among other things, that the police could not intervene in labor-management disputes unless and until actual violence was committed. Since the communist labor unions were always the aggressive force, this order gave them practically a free hand. Farm laborers on tea and rubber plantations were permitted to keep employers virtual prisoners in their homes after cutting off their telephone, electricity, water, and food supplies as long as they did not resort to violence. Law and order gradually disintegrated as Red mobs stole rice and coconut harvests and attacked anticommunist demonstrators while the police, fearful of punishment, detachedly looked on or, on several occasions, fired into hostile crowds. Criminal cases rose by more than twenty percent.

Corruption on an individual basis was reduced, but was more than made up for by the systematic state corruption designed to fill Communist Party coffers. If a landlord wanted to get rid of a tenant, very well—he had only to offer a small contribution to those who made it possible. If an employer wanted to fire several workers, why not? He had only to pay up, and perhaps hire one or two communist agitators in their place. "Corruption has prevailed in all parties," *Malayala Manorama,* a newspaper in Kottayam editorialized, "but the Communists have nationalized corruption. The Kerala exchequer is not only serving party interests inside the state but also strengthening party men in other sections of India."

The government served party interests in other ways, too. About 1,200 "people's committees" embracing about 10,000 members, almost all communists or procommunists, were appointed to oversee and advise on almost all phases of private and government economic activity, including labor contracts, public works, and price control.

The government also tried to introduce ideological "brainwashing" techniques in the schools. School textbooks "are meant as a device to indoctrinate pupils with communist ideologies and impress them with the excellence of the communist social order," the chairman of Kerala's School Managers Association wrote in an official complaint to the central government. Even children's picture books followed this formula, stressing Russian technological advances. Tact and subtlety were completely ignored. A book on Asia included four pages of glowing praise for Communist China while summing up India in seven lines. A volume of selected biographies embraced the lives of Mao and Marx but ignored Gandhi. Religion, if dealt with at all, was treated in an unfavorable light.

The practice of leaving the choice of textbooks to competent private authorities was scrapped in favor of accepting books written by communist-approved authors. Even teachers hired by private schools, which meant 7,000 out of 9,000 schools, most of them church-run, had to be selected from an approved list. The bulk of the private schools closed in protest.

Such communist measures were not balanced by an improvement in Kerala's economic situation. In fact, unemployment increased, taxes and prices went up, and industrial activity declined as the government devoted itself mainly to building up the communist party.

In July 1959 the explosion came. Hundreds of thousands of workers went on token strikes. Students picketed schools that had not closed. Farmers walked off their fields. When local police started to retaliate, Indian army units moved in. Finally President Prasad, who twenty-eight months earlier had seen Kerala as an "example of coexistence," dismissed the communist government and proclaimed "President's Rule" in Kerala. In a new election held in February 1960 the three anticommunist parties, working together at last, won ninety-four seats, squeezing out the communists this time and putting an end to the great experiment.

But perhaps more significant was the Reds' capture of forty-two percent of the vote, a larger percentage than in 1957, despite their two years of misrule and the reluctance of many communists to support their own country in the frontier conflict with Red China. And they managed to increase their strength still further in the 1962 election, obviously confirming that the people are more concerned with local difficulties than with foreign affairs. Moreover, many believe the communist propaganda that the only reason why the Red regime did not produce better conditions was that "reactionary" opposition forces had sabotaged its program. The communists had offered many Keralans hope, and to admit that their promises had been empty would be to kill that hope. Like a man clinging to a straw until he drowns, these citizens are still clinging to communist promises.

So are many people in other parts of India. In Calcutta, a communist defeated a Congress Party candidate in a parliamentary by-election, though it was held just after the Chinese had moved into Indian territory. Reds also hold forty percent of the seats in the city council. While visiting that city several years ago, I did not have to look far to understand why after my arrival by train. On the floor of the station squatted thousands of Hindu refugees from Moslem East Pakistan. They slept, nursed their babies, cooked over small fires, all within the few square feet of space that was the "home" of each family. Outside the station dozens of beggars assaulted me. Some were grisly, bearded old men, living skeletons covered with skin. They supported themselves with sticks or sat against the wall beckoning feebly. Many were blind from trachoma, and others had deep indentations in their faces instead of noses —lepers.

Worst of all, children, eight or ten, clawed at me pleadingly. Usually a baby was clinging to their backs, held on by a dirty sash. Almost invariably the infant was deformed, deliberately crippled by unscrupulous "beggar kings" who control the beggar trade much as a pimp operates a prostitution racket. Even on the main streets people sleep and keep house on the hard cement, and those lucky enough to find housing space in "residential" areas still sleep on the ground with only the shelter of makeshift mud or tin walls and roofs. Such conditions exist to some degree in all Indian cities, but they are probably more widespread in Calcutta than elsewhere.

It is the people living in railroad stations, on the street, and in dilapidated huts, as well as the disgruntled unemployed intellectual elite and a large segment of labor, who make up the crowds of up to 50,000 that meet frequently in the Maidan, a huge park in the center of town, to cry for a better life under the banner of communism. While enterprising booksellers hawk the writings of Mao and Lenin and a work called *Eight Years of Resistance against United States Aggression in Korea,* communist leaders exhort the cheering audience to campaign for peaceful settlement of the border dispute and continued friendship between India and China. A student, wearing a large hammer-and-sickle button in his lapel, comments, "What difference does it make what China's foreign policy is? They've got the right social system."

Another potential threat to Indian democracy lies in Kashmir, which has a long common border with Red China's Sinkiang Province and with Tibet and is separated from the Soviet Union only by a narrow strip of Afghan territory. If the local communists won control of the state, Indian security, already compromised by Chinese inroads into Ladakh, would be in grave peril. And the Kashmiri Reds are not without propaganda fuel. Great sums of money have been spent on all-weather highways linking the state to India proper and other primarily military projects for defense against Pakistan, which controls the western half of Kashmir and since 1947 has been engaged in a tug of war with India for possession of the whole territory. But little has been spent so far on flood control and other projects closer to the interests of the people.

In the lakeside town of Srinagar, amid the breath-taking splendor of the Himalayas, I sat one day comfortably sprawled, maharajah-style, on a large springy seat in a colorfully canopied gondola, or *shikura,* en route from my palatial houseboat to the exotic Isle of Shalimar nearby. The boatman, standing at the rear of the craft and paddling it through a solid field of water lilies, suddenly broke the spell of the moment: "You Americans are very rich. You come here for a holiday and have a fine time. Kashmir is a wonderful place to visit. But it is not such a wonderful place to live. We are very poor. And we realize how poor we are more than most people do, because we are always with rich tourists like you."

The bitterness in this remark helps to explain why the Communist Party in the area has gained considerable ground in recent years. On the surface, it is still a relatively minor political force in Kashmir. But it is closely allied with the National Democratic Conference, the minority opposition party, which defended Chinese occupation of Tibet and is sharply oriented toward the left. Moreover, since Kashmir is predominantly Moslem, loyalty to Hindu India is a factor that works against the Reds to a lesser degree than in the rest of the country.

Kashmiri Premier Bakshi Ghulam Mohammed is not a man entirely to be trusted, either. He calls himself a democratic socialist but is one of Kashmir's biggest capitalists, sharing ownership of the Bakshi Brothers Corporation, which is involved in all state contracts and purchases. He says he is neutralist in the Cold War, but remarked some years ago, "America relies on its dollar and military strength to further its interests in Asia, little knowing Asia is wide awake and will resist such moves to enslave it." Several members of his cabinet are believed to have been, and to be, far-leftist. In short, Bakshi is an opportunist and eventually could find opportunity in dealing with the Red giants who surround his majestic Himalayan state.

The Indian communists, like their brethren in most underdeveloped countries, are considerably more active than the politicians of any other party. To win over the illiterate peasants, they visit the countryside and harangue them at informal village meetings held in open air. To "brainwash" the workers, they preach frequently at union gatherings, controlling the 500,000-member All-India Trade Union Congress, the largest labor federation in India. To attract the intellectuals, they distribute tons of propaganda literature. Ninety-four locally produced communist periodicals with a combined circulation of about 654,000 were published in five Indian languages and English in 1960. In addition, Russia exports hundreds of thousands of books to India and, in conjunction with a local publisher, turns out English translations of Russian scientific books. Under the arrangement, ten percent of the print runs are distributed in India, and the remaining ninety percent are purchased by the USSR for export outside India. In the last half of 1960 eight titles were published in editions of 10,000 copies each; in 1961 forty-nine scientific works were turned out.

Indians, who are rabid movie-goers (India produces more movies each year than any other country in the world), were treated in 1960 to more than one hundred and fifty films from communist-bloc countries. They visited four Soviet and Red Chinese cultural exhibitions. They were submitted to a barrage of radio propaganda from Moscow and Peking. India and Russia exchanged over fifty delegations between them, and India sent about one hundred and eighty students to communist-bloc schools. About fifty communist-front organizations are doing their best to subvert India, including the All-India Kisan Sabha, a peasants' organization with 570,000 members, and the All-India Students Federation with 80,000 followers.

The Indian central government is desperately trying to reduce the poverty on which communism feeds. Its third Five-Year Plan, extending from 1961 to 1966, calls for the expenditure of $24.3 billion, more than that of the first two combined. The plan seeks to increase per capita income from $70 to $80 a year; to achieve self-sufficiency in food grains; to expand basic industries such as steel, chemicals, fuel and power; to increase exports by one-third; to provide schooling for 64 million youngsters, compared to 43 million in 1961; to speed and expand rural uplift and health programs. The prospects are good that India will achieve, or come near to achieving, most of these goals.

One reason is that the United States is expected to supply a large share of the $4 billion in foreign exchange that India will need under the plan, despite the reluctance of Congress to meet

President Kennedy's aid requests as the result of irritating Indian Cold War attitudes. In addition, the Soviet Union and its satellites, which have everything to gain if the plan fails, will nevertheless contribute to its fulfillment. Moscow will provide a heavy-machinery plant, a factory to produce coal-extraction machinery, two thermal electric power plants, an optical-glass factory, and technical aid in the development of the Korba coal fields. It may also put up pharmaceutical and surgical instrument factories. Czechoslovakia will furnish machinery for a foundry forge and complete a sugar refinery in Assam. Romania has been drilling for oil in the Punjab and helping to finance a state-owned refinery in Assam. East Germany is providing textile machinery, and Poland has been working on a sugar refinery in Madras.

Moscow has no doubt calculated that the communist contribution will win the good will of the Indians without helping to raise living standards to a level high enough to blunt the effectiveness of communist agitation. And to judge by the recent past, this calculation appears to be sound.

India's previous plans produced a miracle of economic expansion in the period from 1951 to 1961. Agricultural production increased forty-one percent, school enrollment eighty-five percent. Malaria was almost wiped out. Roads were built linking villages to marketing centers. The great Bhakra Nangal project in northwestern India opened millions of acres to irrigation and electricity. Steel mills and other new enterprises nearly doubled industrial production.

"In everything but blood-letting, this is a revolution," J. R. Wiggins, editor of the *Washington Post,* wrote after an extensive tour of India in 1960.

> It is a transformation so sweeping that its dimensions can hardly be conveyed to Western minds. England would have been jolted as much if it had leaped from Henry VIII to Elizabeth II. The attendant confusion is greater than this, however, for it is as though Henry VIII and all the succeeding generations were being retained while the second Elizabethan age merged. Modern India is not just rising on the foundations of its ancient discarded cultures, with the archaeological horizons of successive civilizations and the artifacts of former periods safely beneath it. It is rising with the past all about it.

The fruit of this vast revolution can be seen in almost every town and village in India. Fields of wheat and barley shimmer over the graves of millions of Indians who died of starvation in past years. A bicycle-rickshaw boy complained to me in New Delhi that business is falling off "because everybody is buying his own bicycle or car." Everywhere the foreign sightseer goes he will be joined by busloads of middle-class Indian tourists who, for the first time in their lives, have enough money to travel and enjoy life. An interview with a businessman almost inevitably means a visit to a brand-new, air-conditioned office building. And no messenger will be squatting outside his door ready to run messages, as was the custom until recently; the businessman will, instead, reach for one of the several telephones on his desk if he needs to contact somebody. Emanating from an isolated village of mud huts may be the sophisticated strains of "Star Dust" produced by a new community-owned battery-operated radio. An Indian woman with a baby on her back pulls a pail of safe drinking water from a well that didn't exist two years before.

Yet despite all this evidence of progress, the surface of India's poverty has hardly been scratched. If Indians are not starving today, a very large proportion eat barely enough to keep alive, particularly the thousands who pour into the large cities from unproductive rural areas to find themselves living on the sidewalk and snatching food scraps from garbage heaps virtually out of the mouths of sacred cows that freely roam the city streets. And the romantic music of an affluent world flowing from the village radio adds little to the affluence of the villager who may now earn $60 a year instead of the $50 he earned a decade ago. Nor is the jobless intellectual impressed by the air-conditioning in the offices he must haunt looking for work.

The trouble is that economic progress simply cannot keep up with population growth. The Indian population was about 440 million in 1961 and is increasing at the rate of 2.1 percent a year. By 1966 it is expected to be over 490 million; and a decade later, 625 million. This means that the estimated 20 million unemployed and the 40 million who can find only part-time work will inevitably be joined by additional numbers each year. According to the new Five-Year Plan, only 14 million of the 17 million people who are expected to enter the labor market during the five-year span will find jobs.

Expenditure on birth control in the new plan has been budgeted at $50 million, five times the outlay of the second plan. But unless oral contraceptives become generally available, control efforts, according to past experience, will have only limited success. The masses simply have rejected, for the most part, the use of mechanical contraceptives, while hardly more than 20,000 have accepted government offers to sterilize men who have already fathered three or more children. As for abortion, which has kept Japan's birth rate down, Indian public opinion is against it. It is, in fact, wary of population control regardless of the method, due to various complex influences—religious principles, the fear of side effects, the feeling that human dignity is at stake, the unrealistic desire for a larger population in the face of Chinese competition.

Even the rhythm method has met with failure. In one test case a peasant family was given a wire of wooden beads, some red and some blue. Each day, the wife was told, a bead should be moved to one end of the wire. If the bead was red, it would be safe to have sexual relations without danger of pregnancy. But during the "blue-bead," or fertile, days, relations were to be avoided. About a month later the woman became pregnant. "I don't understand it," she explained, "we only had relations when the beads were red." "Never when the beads were blue?" asked the doctor. "How could we?" the woman replied. "I painted them all red."

As if India's economic difficulties were not sufficient, the nation must now divert much of its funds to defense purposes, perhaps one aim of Mao in launching his brutal attack.

There are other than population and economic factors that make for communist optimism. The renewal of communal rioting between Hindus and Moslems offers the Reds excellent fishing grounds. So does the related hostility between India and Pakistan over control of Kashmir. Cultural differences between the various parts of India add further to the chaos that pleases the Reds. India has fourteen major languages and dozens of dialects. In 1960 Nehru agreed to the division of Bombay State into two states, each with its own language, after previously having permitted the establishment of Andhra on a linguistic basis. Other regional disputes are also boiling. Assam has been torn by rioting between the Assamese majority and the Bengali minority. And in Punjab, Tara Singh, a Sikh leader, fasted for several weeks in 1961 until Nehru agreed to consider demands for a new state with a Sikh majority. Still another potential source of communist fuel is the condition of the 60 million casteless "untouchables" who are still treated in most villages as subhuman by members of the four castes and 3,000 subcastes of India, despite the fact that they are now protected by law. Just making available well water to the "untouchables" is enough to produce village riots.

The most remarkable thing about India is that, despite all the conflicts that divide it, the nation has not only survived, but has managed to retain a large degree of unity and register extraordinary economic progress without resort to authoritarian rule. The man largely responsible for this, of course, is Nehru. His over-whelming popularity has permitted him to rule democratically while almost all other underdeveloped nations, neutralist or pro-West, have found it necessary to resort to at least temporary dictatorship to solve problems minuscule in scope compared to those of India.

If Nehru is unpopular and even distrusted in the West, particu-larly in the United States, it is his own fault. While professing neutralism, he is far quicker to deplore such Western "acts of im-perialism" as the 1956 invasion of Suez than the brutal communist colonialism of Hungary. And when the Soviet Union unilaterally ended the moratorium on nuclear testing, he refused to condemn Moscow outright, although he had plenty to say about French tests in the Sahara a short time before. He refused to act with resolution even when Communist China occupied Indian territory, until Mao's massive attack left him with no choice but to call for a fight to the death. Up to then, the only time he appeared willing to speak out courageously, and rattle bayonets if necessary, was when smaller nations like Portugal or Pakistan were involved. And then, when the United States and Britain came to his aid with large arms ship-ments, he gracelessly implied that they were only acting in their own interest.

Still, the combination of Chinese aggression and Soviet fence-sitting, in so brutally exposing the bankruptcy of Nehru's Cold War approach, has profoundly affected his outlook. In one of the most remarkable soul-searching political confessions of our time, he recently told his government information officers: "We are get-ting out of touch with realities in a modern world. We are living in our own creation, and we have been shaken out of it." He then broodingly asked for the Western arms aid he had so often preached was never given without strings attached.

It is not necessarily Nehru's non-aligned foreign policy that has failed India. The disaster has its roots, as Nehru himself hinted, in the national psychology that he helped to cultivate in an effort to justify this policy on false moral and nationalistic grounds. Unlike the leaders of such countries as Burma and Cambodia, who have always been fully aware of the danger represented by international communism and do not try to disguise the fact, at least in their own minds, that their neutralism is simply a tactical maneuver to avoid irritating the dragon, the Indian government has embraced non-alignment as a righteous philosophical aloofness from the petty quarrels of the world around them. India, as a huge, proud nation, could not afford, psychologically, to admit even to itself that it was frightened of its communist neighbors, and so its leaders wove the myth that detachment from military blocs was a kind of modern manifestation of the Gandhian concept of non-violence.

Once the basic myth was born, it was not difficult for the regime to rationalize that, unless unduly provoked, international communism was not really an aggressive force—Nehru, even after the Chinese invasion, insisted that misplaced Chinese nationalism alone, and not communism, fueled the aggression—but fed exclusively on human misery and poverty. Nor did Nehru find it unnatural to curry favor with the communists he subconsciously feared by exhibiting arrogance toward the West, which, despite his lingering anti-colonial bitterness, he realized would come to his aid in an emergency regardless, and could therefore be used as a public scapegoat to further his psychological ends, especially in view of its conveniently imperialistic background.

So thoroughly did the Indians rationalize their non-alignment that they convinced themselves that there was no need for a large defense establishment, a notion encouraged by their intense desire to concentrate on solving their enormous economic problems. Even when the Chinese started infiltrating Indian border areas in 1959, Nehru was able to indulge in his myth to such an absurd extent that he virtually placed India's security in the hands of Russia, which, he persuaded himself, would never permit a massive Chinese move against India. Disillusionment thus came with shattering force to India, and particularly to Nehru, and with an ironic twist, too. For India's fellow neutralists, giving Nehru a taste of his own medicine, have, despite their pro-India sentiment, declined to support his demands that Chinese troops withdraw to their pre-attack positions before peace talks take place.

Nevertheless, considering his long conditioning, Nehru is not likely to foresake neutralism in the Cold War, though he—and certainly Indian public opinion, which began to awaken long before he did—will more clearly realize in the future how dependent India is on the West ultimately for its security, whatever its official view of military blocs. Some Indian leaders and newspapers have, indeed, suggested that the nation join the Western camp despite Nehru's opposition.

Such an eventuality would not necessarily benefit the West more than the maintenance by India of a more realistic neutralist policy. There is at least some value for the West in the embarrassment Moscow has suffered throughout the underdeveloped world as a result of its inability or unwillingness to support actively a non-aligned friend, and also in the new strains imposed by the events in India on the tenuous Russian-Chinese relationship. Conversely, an India formally tied to the West could offer Russia an excuse for militarily supporting China sooner or later, and might actually provoke such an eventuality.

At any rate, however irritating and unfair to the United States Nehru's statements may sometimes be, however blind this country may think he is, however cowardly his policies have been, it is clear that he is one of the few genuinely democratic leaders in the underdeveloped world; and he is in power in a huge, extremely influential country that, by offering an alternative to Chinese communism, may hold the key to the future of Asia. Nehru's profound sense of social duty has attracted him to Marxist theory, as reflected in the quasi-socialist program of his Congress Party. Like most leaders in the underdeveloped world, he has been impressed by the dynamism of communist society. But he deplores the totalitarian regimentation that generates this dynamism. His philosophy is a hybrid of Indian humanist tradition and Western political values absorbed under the British. Unlike neutralists cut from a more opportunistic cloth, such as Indonesia's Sukarno, he has refused in his domestic policies to make a deal with those who repudiate this philosophy, though he may flavor it with arrogance.

Indian communists are constantly under police surveillance. They are restricted in their travel outside India, and even delegations to international communist-front meetings are limited in size and number. Communists who break the law are promptly prosecuted, and those suspected of plotting violence are held in preventive detention. The government and the Congress are constantly campaigning against the Reds, and sometimes Congressmen join communist-front organizations in large numbers in order to prevent communist control, a reverse twist in infiltration.

The threat to Western security is not that Nehru is in power, but that one day he will be out of power. For it is not at all certain that a man of lesser stature—and there appears to be no one in view at the moment with comparable leadership talents—will be able to hold seething India together and solve its problems without resort to totalitarianism, perhaps eventually of the communist variety. Before the massive Chinese attack, a leading contender for Nehru's mantle was Defense Minister Krishna Menon. It is not surprising that he was enthusiastically backed by the communists in the 1962 parliamentary elections—one reason why he won handily —for he has rendered them many services. After having barely brought himself to criticize Red Chinese aggression on Indian territory, he actually tried to paint the United States as the villain in the piece. The United States had tried to pull India into a war with

China, he said during the election campaign, but he, as Defense Minister, would not be a party "to putting Indian troops where they cannot defend themselves." He further claimed, to the delight of the Reds, that Britain and the United States, "tied up with big business" in India, were behind efforts to defeat him.

Menon, who was fired when Mao's assault caught India unprepared, also served the Reds well in other ways. He is believed to have arranged a political deal bringing two procommunists into the Kashmir cabinet. Some of his enemies—many Indians dislike him as much as do most Westerners—have charged in parliament that, as Defense Minister, he was using the army to further his own political ends, promoting officers friendly to him. Some Indians also criticized him for preventing the appointment of Finance Minister Morarji Desai, who is known for his warm attitude toward the United States, as Nehru's chief deputy in parliament, a position that would enhance Desai's own prospects of succeeding Nehru.

Pro-Westerners, however, cannot complain about the choice of Y. B. Chavan, a tough, realistic ex-wrestler, anti-British freedom fighter, and Chief Minister of Bombay, as Menon's successor. A member of the Kshatriya warrior caste, he has warned Indians not to trust either Moscow or Peking again because a "communist country never gives up violence or abjures the use of force."

India's future is dangerously uncertain. Yet the situation is far from hopeless. The Communist Party itself is almost as divided and faction-plagued as the nation it plans to rule, while India's 400,000-man army, though until recently under the control of Menon, appears to be led largely by officers of the Chavan stripe whose respect for democratic institutions up to now has been more Western than Asian in nature. Another source of hope is the great, though often obscured, reservoir of good will toward the traditionally anticolonialist United States that so spontaneously bubbled over in the intensely emotional welcome given President Eisenhower during his visit to India in 1959, a greeting far exceeding in warmth that which Khrushchev received four years earlier. Hope, too, lies in the nonviolent Gandhian tradition that still runs deep in India, and in the awakening of most Indians to the true nature of Communist Chinese ambitions. But most important of all, hope resides in the independent, freedom-loving character of the great majority of Indians, who would not lightly submit to a new colonialism.

XIV

BURMA:

BLOOD AND BUDDHA

The Burmese are a curiously paradoxical people. They are among the most spiritually devout inhabitants of Asia, yet have shaped a history of violence. So gentle are they—most are firm believers in Buddhism, which forbids the killing of any living thing—that they are reluctant to harm even insects. A military junta took over the government in 1958, and in one of its first actions destroyed about 50,000 homeless mongrels that roamed the streets of Rangoon, the Burmese capital, by dropping chunks of meat, most of it poisoned, throughout the city. When Burmese began to react in horror, the government was able to calm the furor only with the ingenious explanation that the dogs had been "free" to choose the unpoisoned pieces of meat, and therefore had not been "killed."

Yet Burmese have been killing each other in extravagant numbers throughout their history, often in the name of religion. In 1885 five hundred Burmese and one hundred foreigners would have been buried alive by Burma's last King, Thibaw, so that their spirits might protect his soul, if British colonial troops had not arrived in the nick of time. When the British were finally ready to leave Burma about sixty years later, violence still reigned. In 1947, a year before this colony was granted independence, three assassins casually walked into the government secretariat and mowed down seven ministers who were to lead free Burma. Within two years, a rickety, makeshift Burmese regime led by a relatively unknown politician named U Nu was fighting armed rebellions by more than half a dozen political, military, and regional groups, including two communist factions. Bloodshed has continued uninterrupted ever since.

Dressed in traditional collarless shirt, long multicolored, wrap-around skirt, or *longyi,* and Aunt Jemima-like head-scarf knotted on one side, which gave his round, serene face an elfish allure, Prime Minister U Nu explained to me some years ago in Rangoon: "We are staunch Buddhists. But we will fight if necessary, not out of hate or greed, but to preserve the very values of Buddhism that make for love and peace." U Nu was deposed in March 1962 for the second time in four years by army commander General Ne Win for running the government "inefficiently." But the General, though keeping him under detention, would undoubtedly agree with him that the combination of force and faith has triumphed. For though the government in the postwar era was up against what appeared to be insurmountable odds, at one time retaining effective control of only Rangoon itself, it has in recent years all but crushed the communist and other insurgent bands. This has been possible, U Nu said, "because the great majority of people have always been on our side."

But while this may be true, the communist danger has by no means been obliterated. Almost 4,000 members of the two rebel communist factions, one internationally controlled and the other Trotskyite, are still holding out in the dense Burmese jungles. Two other Red groups, numbering about 6,000, have legal political status, but they, like all other political parties, have had no real power since Ne Win took over the government. A large Peking-dominated Chinese community constitutes a powerful fifth-column threat, particularly with the presence of a Red Chinese embassy in Rangoon. The ultimate sword of Damocles poised over Burma's head is the ability of China, which shares the nation's northern border, to start actively aiding the Burmese Red insurgents whenever it deems the moment propitious.

Nevertheless, until that moment comes, the communist menace is likely to be contained, especially if General Ne Win remains in power or oversees developments should he unexpectedly decide to give power back to the politicians in accordance with the pattern he set in 1960 after a year and a half of military rule. His second, like his first, experience in office is resulting in economic and social reforms unconducive to communism and in a crackdown on communist subversive activities. This was dramatically highlighted in July 1962 when his soldiers killed fifteen students and wounded dozens more at the University of Rangoon for violating a ban on demonstrations. The students had gathered, according to the General, at the behest of communist agitators. Ne Win has rescinded a ban on cattle slaughter that had sent meat prices skyrocketing and a decree making Buddhism the state religion. He has reduced corruption, streamlined the government bureaucracy, reversed U Nu's tendency to accommodate to the nationalist demands of numerous powerful ethnic minorities, and postponed implementation of a plan for nationalizing the import trade.

Ne Win has banned from Burma the American Ford and Asian Foundations and the Fulbright scholarship program on the grounds that the nation should depend less on foreign assistance. But he has also canceled several Soviet economic projects, leading some observers to believe that the American assistance was sacrificed to permit a reduction of communist aid without making neutralist Burma's Cold War sympathies too obvious. Certainly the increasing leftist and pro-Peking tendencies of the majority faction in U Nu's Union Party was a prime reason why Ne Win assumed power, although he is a socialist like most noncommunist political figures in Burma.

But if U Nu's government was falling more and more under the sway of leftist influences, no Asian leader understands better the meaning of communism than the former Prime Minister, who was Burma's guiding light in its most perilous days. In an anticommunist play U Nu wrote called *The People Win Through*—he is a talented playwright—in which evil Reds shoot the hero at the end, a guerrilla explains: "I'm fighting the communists to prevent the people from being led about on a nose rope like castrated cattle." A civil servant says: "Communists mustn't breathe through their own noses . . . They know perfectly well that white is white, but their bosses tell them that white is black; black it is for them." A refugee reports: "The communists have given us a New Order . . . Break wind and you're hauled off to the people's court . . ."

But if U Nu, as well as General Ne Win and most other Burmese leaders, are staunchly anticommunist, their country is a Cold War neutralist, though not practicing the "positive neutralism" of many other unaligned countries that diplomatically lean toward the Soviet bloc. Nor is the desire to squeeze both sides economically for all their worth a factor in Burma's neutralism. For a period it completely shut off economic aid from both sides. Burma believes in all sincerity that a neutralist group of nations is necessary to keep the Cold War from spreading, and perhaps developing into a hot war. But a consideration closer to home is the need to remain friendly

with Red China to permit Burma to clean up its domestic communist problem. Burma might well be a communist satellite today if it
had joined the Western bloc it silently favors despite a residual distrust of the colonial powers. For Peking would almost certainly
have supplied the Burmese Red rebels with arms and other supplies long ago, engineering the overthrow of the government, if not
producing another Korean or Indochinese war. But U Nu bought
Mao's noninterference with his neutralism, and thus was able to
subdue the local Reds without outside aid.

Burma's neutralist role has also permitted it to reach an advantageous agreement with Red China on the rugged boundaries of the
two countries. Peking's reasonableness was dictated less by love
for Burma than by a desire to counteract the shock of most Asians
over Chinese aggression along India's borders and in Tibet. Burma,
at the same time, has not been encouraged to lean openly toward
the West by the fate of many Vietnamese and Lao who are either
behind the Bamboo Curtain already or may soon be. After North
Vietnam fell to the Reds in 1954, U Kyaw Nyein, a Burmese
leader, commented: "It is criminal, unforgivable that the super-
power upon whom so much depends should be the amateur . . .
the Soviet Union the professional."

But Burma's neutralism does not call for Nehru-style moralistic
preaching to the West, though few national leaders—certainly not
Nehru—are endowed with greater moral sense than the Burmese
chiefs. During the Hungarian revolt, which Nehru mildly condemned only after he had been greatly pressured by public opinion,
U Ba Swe, who was Burmese Prime Minister at the time, stormed,
even while border negotiations with Peking were in the balance:
"For a big power to station its troops without consent of the small
country and, what is worse, to suppress the people and impose on a
helpless government its own puppets and stooges, is the most despi-
cable form of colonialism. Yet that is exactly what has been happening in Hungary . . ."

Under U Nu Burma had a Fabian-type socialist government with
"New Deal" overtones, not unlike that of Israel, which influenced
the Burmese in both the political and economic spheres. It has even
established Israeli-style *kibbutzim,* or communal settlements, in
outlying areas. The close friendship between U Nu and Prime Minister David Ben-Gurion was dramatically demonstrated when the
Israeli leader visited Rangoon in late 1961 and entered a Buddhist
monastery for several days to meditate. However, Ne Win is currently exploring the possibilities of a more authoritarian socialism
tailored to what he considers Burma's needs.

Economically, the Ne Win government has discouraged capitalist contributions, including foreign investment. Some joint ventures, such as the British-Burmese Burma Oil Company, are in operation, but they may not be for very long. The chief exponent of nationalization, as well as of farm collectivization, is the Minister of Agriculture, Brigadier Tin Pe. His doctrinaire zeal has been checked in some degree, however, by the more pragmatic Minister of Commerce, Brigadier Aung Gye.

Politically Burma, though now run by a military government, has democratic roots that reach deeper than in most underdeveloped countries. This was evidenced when General Ne Win voluntarily returned the reins of government to civilian politicians in 1960 after having instituted necessary reforms that would have been difficult to achieve under parliamentary rule. He resumed power a second time, it is true, but only reluctantly. And while he now favors a one-party system, several parties, however weak, still existed in early 1963. Though it may be long indeed before real parliamentary government returns to Burma this time, the people of that country understand democracy better than most Afro-Asian peoples, partly as a result of their fifty-percent literacy rate, one of the highest in Asia. On one municipal election day, I visited several Burmese villages and found in each block-long lines of people waiting their turn to vote at the polls, many of them women daintily dressed in sheer, long-sleeved blouses and tight, gaily colored, ankle-length skirts, and carrying parasols for protection against the relentless tropical sun.

Unlike many socialists in the underdeveloped world, most Burmese leaders reject Marxism, including the noncommunist kind, though Ne Win's new philosophy contains elements of it. "Karl Marx had very limited knowledge," U Nu said in 1958, "which is not equivalent to one-tenth of a particle of dust beneath the feet of Lord Buddha." Nu, Ne Win, and most other Burmese leaders, however, were moderate Marxists in the 1930's and early 1940's, when it was fashionable for all young Burmese intellectuals who dreamed of national independence to be Marxist in some degree. This ideology gave them a tool with which to harness a long-dormant Burmese nationalism.

Many years before the British arrived in 1824, the people strongly felt their Burmese identity, partly as the result of the nation's isolation from countries to the north and east that are sealed off by jagged mountains and steaming jungles. Almost all inhabitants speak Burmese as their first or second language and use phonetic Burmese script, with some educated people speaking fluent English as well. The Burmese were never very happy under British rule, but they made the most of colonialism, eagerly approving British economic development schemes and the establishment of the British school system. But it was not long before schools were turning out more students than there were jobs available for them within the growing economy, producing considerable discontent, especially with the opening of the University of Rangoon in 1920.

Unrest reached a head in 1931 when students bitterly deplored British action in crushing a peasants' revolt in 1931 that followed a drop in rice prices. A group of them at the university, including U Nu, formed the Dohbama Asiayone, or *We Burmans* Society, and defiantly began calling each other *Thakin,* master, a title that had usually been employed only when referring to the British. Yet this group owed a great deal to the British: most important of all, a dedication to British legal and parliamentary institutions. But they needed more. They needed a system for organizing mass support for their independence movement, and in Marxist techniques they found it.

Marxism, they felt, also offered a humanistic philosophy that could be merged with the democracy the British had taught them, though this philosophy was of less importance than the organizational aspect of the ideology. Having learned their lessons well, the Thakins, led by U Nu, a graduate student in philosophy, went on strike and burned the Union Jack before Rangoon's colonial law courts, winning control of the student body. The Thakins, who included a few communists, then took over the labor movement, calling for strikes and demonstrations and holding the first all-Burma Labor Conference in 1939, from which emerged an All-Burma Trade Union Congress and a program for "peaceful, democratic" socialization of the country. The young nationalists also developed an All-Burma Peasants Organization and other mass movements.

When World War II broke out, the Thakins thought they saw a golden opportunity to achieve independence. For a guarantee of freedom, they told the British, they would back the Allied war effort in the Far East. When the British refused, they threw their support to the Japanese, to whom they looked for "liberation"—resulting in the imprisonment by the British of Nu and other Thakin leaders. "When the Japanese bombers came," Nu later said, "the people would not take cover. They tore their shirts, sang, danced, clapped their hands, shouted, and turned somersaults as if they did not care a curse what happened." Disillusionment for

Nu and his fellow Burmese began to set in shortly after the Japanese invaded Burma. On one occasion, a procession led by monks offered gifts of fruit and rice to the Japanese soldiers. A member of the procession afterwards told Nu, "We expected the Japanese commander to be thankful. But all he did was to take his hand from his trousers pocket and give us a hard slap in the face."

The Japanese did establish a nominal Burmese government, in which U Nu was Foreign Minister. But this was hardly the kind of "independence" the Thakins wanted. In 1943 the Thakins broke into two groups, one forming the Socialist Party led by the most influential nationalist, Aung San, and the other the Burma Communist Party, led by Than Tun, a relative by marriage to Aung San. The following year the two organizations joined together in a resistance movement against the Japanese called the Anti-Fascist Peoples Freedom League (AFPFL), with Aung San the president as well as commander of a new Burmese Defense army, and Than Tun secretary-general. The League led an uprising against the Japanese in 1945 as Allied troops attacked through the jungles. It vowed, however, to continue resistance action against the British when they returned if they did not grant Burma immediate independence.

The Japanese surrender found the communists in a powerful position, for, although a smaller group than the socialists within the AFPFL, they were far better organized. Even before liberation they had been able to win control of labor and peasant organizations. They gained strength after the war as discharged soldiers threw them their support and contacts with the strong Indian Communist Party became possible. According to the socialists, the communists from the beginning of the coalition had planned to liquidate them and take over the government when the war ended. The Reds "betrayed the trust of the people again and again," they charged.

The socialists, however, benefited from a split in the Communist Party early in 1946. One faction, led by Thakin Soe, a Trotskyite ex-clerk in the British-controlled Burma Oil Company who had served with Nu in the same prison cell, was against all compromise with the returning British, though most AFPFL members wanted to negotiate for independence. Burma, Soe said, must wage a "People's War" against the British, not negotiate. He and his followers withdrew from the AFPFL and, forming a new so-called Red Flag Communist Party, launched an armed insurrection of its own against the government. Than Tun, on the other hand, refused to break with the AFPFL, hoping to bring about a communist state from within the organization. His larger, Moscow-directed group became known as the White Flag communists.

But Than Tun miscalculated the determination of the socialists to prevent a communist takeover. The socialists, since they greatly outnumbered the Reds, particularly after the communist split, were able to oust Than Tun from the post of secretary-general in July 1946; four months later, on a motion by U Nu, they expelled him from the organization. Than Tun had lost his gamble.

Meanwhile the British, in 1946, offered Burma its independence, and Aung San agreed to head the first cabinet of free Burma—only to be assassinated together with most of his cabinet colleagues in 1947. A small man with a bullet-shaped head, Aung San, though originally a Japanese collaborator like most Burmese leaders, had later helped the British organize a resistance movement, assuming the title of *Bogyok,* or General. As head of the AFPFL, he had risen to power by calling strikes among civil servants, teachers, and the police, and was considered the Burmese George Washington. His violent death cast ominous shadows over Burma when, in January 1948, the country, to the sound of drums beaten with sticks made from lions' bones, became completely independent after one hundred and twenty-four years of British rule, refusing even to join the British Commonwealth as India and all other liberated British colonies chose to do. U Nu, who had been Speaker of the nation's new Constituent Assembly, reluctantly accepted the responsibility of leading the infant nation.

Within a few months Nu found himself buried in chaos, as almost half of Burma's elected members of parliament and their supporters revolted against the government. The Red Flag Trotskyites, about 6,000, left without Britons to fight, transferred their violence against Nu in the hope of taking power. The White Flag communists, numbering 13,000, struck in March, two months after independence, in conformity with Stalin's order that communist parties throughout Southeast Asia attack noncommunist governments whether controlled by colonial or by nationalist forces. In July 8,000 professional soldiers also revolted in support of both communist factions with whom they had fought side by side against the Japanese. The People's Volunteer Organization, an army veterans' group, joined in, largely because of its leaders' personal ambitions.

In August 1948, 12,000 Karens, members of a largely Christian minority group, rebelled when the government refused to grant them an autonomous state on the Thailand border. Missionaries had assured the Karens that under the British law that prevailed before independence they had equal rights with other peoples, thus stimulating zealots to make highly unreasonable demands of U Nu. Added to these many antigovernment forces in 1949 were the undisciplined remnants of Chiang Kai-shek's armies that had been chased into Burma by the Red Chinese. Further adding to Nu's troubles, the Ministerial Services Union went on strike in early 1949, bringing government services almost to a halt.

When the White Flag communists, by far the most powerful of the rebels, were about to revolt, U Nu desperately offered to appease them with a fifteen-point plan for "leftist unity" and the propagation of "Marxist doctrine." If the Reds had accepted this proposal, they might have had the opportunity to seize the government by peaceful means. But the White Flags, under orders from Stalin to use violence, turned a cold shoulder on the offer which U Nu, in a cooler moment, regretted having made. "Give us three years," White Flag leader Than Tun replied defiantly as he attacked, "and Burma will be ours!"

U Nu, determined to meet the assault, dramatically beseeched his people to fight for democracy in a broadcast in April 1948:

> When Stalin, highest of the communist leaders, met a good-will mission dispatched to Russia by the British Labor Party, with Harold Laski as its leader, Stalin said to them, "There are two roads to socialism, the British road and the Soviet road. The British road attains it in slow but steady stages; the Soviet road attains it quickly but involves bloodshed." I remember reading this . . . If the government becomes vicious and you want to remove it, go to the people and ask for power by means of democratic method . . . [Only] when it is made impossible to obtain power from the masses by lawful methods, when democratic remedies are denied and there are no alternatives to seeking power by violence, then seek it by that method . . .
>
> . . . From now onwards the people of the Burma Union will have to mark out two circles on the ground. Let those who like violence enter the circle of those who urge violence. Let those who favor seeking power by the method of democracy enter the circle of democracy . . . For myself, I have already chosen the circle of democracy and in it I shall stand hand-in-hand with others who have chosen the same side, and together we shall exert our utmost efforts to protect this great Union of Burma from the dangerous threat of those who seek violence.

Nu immediately backed his words with action, stopping the White Flags only seven miles from Rangoon with a 12,000-man army and three air-force fighters. In the spring of 1949 his forces recaptured communist-held Mandalay in the north. By 1951 they had won control of the strategic Irrawaddy Plain; and in 1952 the Chinese Nationalists were forced to take refuge behind the steep Salween gorges in the north. U Nu broke the back of the rebels with peaceful overtures as well as with military force. Four thousand communists surrendered when he offered to grant them amnesty following courses in democracy. Almost thirty thousand Reds had surrendered by 1957. The Karen revolt lost its force when he appointed Karen leaders to the cabinet and promised the Karens autonomy, if within a smaller territory than they had demanded. He took the Chinese Nationalist problem to the United Nations, and United States planes flew more than half of the Chinese Nationalists to Taiwan.

The considerable skill and courage of the Burmese army, of course, has been a principal factor in the government's success. But this success can also be attributed to the lack of any common objective among the various rebel forces, who have been bitter rivals for power in some cases, occasionally even fighting each other. Furthermore, no rebel group has been able to win the support of any substantial number of peasants, who are better off than they have ever been, paying reduced taxes and rental fees and, with the government's help, marketing their rice at good prices. All the peasants want is peace and quiet, something which none of the rebels stand for. Communist talk of capitalist exploitation makes no sense at all to most peasants because of the lack of an indigenous capitalist class in Burma.

The communists took their worst drubbing in 1958-59 during the first period of General Ne Win's military dictatorship—established when U Nu's government began to disintegrate under the cumulative pressures of a decade of civil war. The economy had become a shambles. Rice exports, which were the largest in the world before World War II, dropped almost to zero as paddies were turned into battlefields. Burma's rich timberlands and silver, tin, and tungsten mines could not be exploited. The government, eager to put its socialist doctrines into practice even without the resources to do it, squandered funds on unfeasible industrial projects. A pharmaceutical plant was built, but the vitamins it produced could not be sold. A steel mill was also constructed, but there were no raw materials to feed it when wartime supplies of scrap metal ran out. What funds remained to the government either went to the military or into the pockets of corrupt officials.

Most important of all, it looked as though the communists might gain peacefully what they had failed to gain through force. The Reds took full advantage of a government announcement that any communist could win parliamentary respectability by renouncing the use of violence to achieve his ends and withholding aid from his rebel friends. Soon legal Reds dominated an opposition political organization called the National United Front (NUF) that consisted of a number of Marxist groups, including the Burma Workers Party, with a membership of almost 4,000, the People's Comrades Party, made up of some 2,000 former Red insurgents, and the People's Unity Party. As in Malaya, a hard core of Reds continued to harass the authorities, just to let them know that they were not beaten yet, and also to maintain themselves as the nucleus of a potential fighting force in the future when the time is ripe for a new all-out attack. But also as in Malaya, the communists, unable to take over the government by force for the moment, decided to infiltrate it peacefully. (In Malaya, however, they have had to do so by stealthier means because of the illegality of communism in that country.)

While the Reds developed their parliamentary strength, some of U Nu's ambitious subordinates within his Anti-Fascist People's Freedom League, the organization that had been formed during World War II, decided it was time to change leaders. The AFPFL split, with Nu at the head of a so-called *clean* faction and U Ba Swe, a leading politician who had replaced U Nu as Prime Minister for a short time in the mid-1950's, leading a *stable* faction. The bickering and corruption within the AFPFL neatly played into the communists' hands, and the disgusted public gave the National United Front one-third of its votes in the 1956 elections. The Reds now held a virtual balance of power in the government. They glowed as U Nu, with his political life in danger and his opponents within the AFPFL resorting to terrorist tactics against his followers, experienced one of his few periods of panic. Threatening the *stable* faction with civil war, he allied his own group with the National United Front.

As the tide of fortune seemed to be turning in the Reds' favor, the army stepped in to save the day—and the country. There could be neither a civil war between the anticommunists nor agreements with the communists, it bluntly told both AFPFL factions. Nu was apparently relieved by the army's action, for he made a radio broadcast asking General Ne Win to take control of the government temporarily until a national election could be held to determine who should lead the country. Burma, one of the few underdeveloped nations with a democratic government, had finally succumbed to military rule.

Burma's army of officers, however, are primarily middle-class nationalist politicians who became soldiers, rather than militarists hungering for political glory. Hence they see the army's role through civilian eyes despite the uniforms they wear. Ne Win, a post-office worker who joined the nationalist movement in his youth, was subjected to the same socialist yet democratic influences that helped to mold the political thinking of U Nu and most of the other Thakins. The careers of U Nu and Ne Win began to diverge only during World War II, when the former cooperated with the Japanese on a political plane, and the latter went to Japan for training as a military officer in the Burmese militia, used by the Japanese to maintain internal law and order. Many other Burmese army leaders were classmates of U Nu and his civilian colleagues at the University of Rangoon and participated in the same defiant nationalist activities. "The people who rule over us," said Colonel Ba Than, director of the army's Psychological Warfare Division, "must be those we choose from among ourselves . . ."

But the military regime of Ne Win that took over the country in 1958 felt it necessary to use militant methods to keep the government out of communist hands. To create a climate conducive to clean living and clean administration after its first coup, it started out with a campaign to clean up Rangoon in a physical sense. When I visited this town prior to that takeover, I found it to be one of the dirtiest and dreariest capitals in Asia. Starving dogs foraged in garbage heaps on the streets; rats as large as rabbits scurried from gutter to gutter; and odorous slum areas of board and thatch shacks spilled over parks, religious grounds, and even into alleyways, occupied by almost a quarter million peasant refugees, nearly a fourth of the city's population, who had fled from communist terrorism in Red-infested areas. Within a few months after Ne Win came to power, the dogs and rats were gone, the streets had been scrubbed almost spotless by "broom squads" that included even businessmen and politicians, the filthy shacks had been burned to the ground, and the refugees were living in Rangoon's suburbs in neat little houses they built themselves with materials provided by the government. Nor was bathing permitted any longer at public wells or water taps, terminating one of the most interesting sights I had seen in Rangoon. Men and women had been able to bathe without undressing by wrapping a dry skirt over the wet one, which was then dropped in the bath. Men were also forbidden to urinate in public, and pony carts were banished from the streets as a traffic hazard.

An economic cleanup came next. Black marketeers were arrested; price controls forced down the cost of living; rice-marketing machinery was improved, thus resulting in increased exports; and an army-controlled holding company was established that soon dominated private business and fostered many commercial undertakings ranging from shipping to shoe manufacturing. Not only were trains made to run on time, but passengers were required to buy tickets—something which many of them previously had failed to do because of a shortage of tickets available at railroad stations.

Finally, the Army intensified the struggle to liquidate the communist menace. It banned the Red press and cracked down on "legal" communists who were secretly providing Red rebels with supply lines and courier service. So many were thrown into jail that to make room for all of them a new concentration camp was set up in the Andaman Islands in the Bay of Bengal, about three hundred miles south of Rangoon. A special effort was made to purge the University of Rangoon of communist agitators. Leaders of the Red-controlled Students' Union were jailed, and to rid the institution of nonstudying "professional" students, academic requirements were severely tightened. The army also encouraged villagers, who had been forced to pay rebel taxes and were afraid to report on rebel movements to the government, to give information by stationing regular troops in threatened areas. In some cases government soldiers burned down villages whose inhabitants wouldn't talk.

Understandably, Thakin Chit Maung, leader of the Burma Workers Party, wailed: "Ne Win has cut away the pillars of our movement and carefully left a few leaders out in the open to deceive the world into believing the army supports democracy. We are still free to advocate communism, but they have destroyed our means of doing so."

Military attacks, imprisonment, and other harsh measures constituted only one element in the effort to isolate and destroy the communist rebels. An equally important factor was, and still is, a religious campaign against the Reds. This campaign grew out of a great Buddhist revival that began to stir Burma in the early 1950's largely as the result of U Nu's influence. Many governments, including that of the United States, invoke God's name in blessing the cause for which they may be fighting. But in most cases they have in mind simply a political God, a God that will resolve in their favor a materialistic or territorial conflict.

U Nu, however, fought a truly spiritual battle, a battle to gain nothing except an end to the violence which he detests but has been unable to avoid. He believes in peace less because violence results in physical destruction, than because it contradicts the way and will of God. Nu is a genuine Theravada Buddhist who accepts Buddhism as a way of life, not just as a theocratic doctrine. Like few men in modern times, he has inspired in his people, through example and gentle persuasion, a renewal of faith that might have failed them under the pressure of the materialistic forces that have been vying for their souls. While Prime Minister, he authorized civil servants who wished to meditate to leave work a half-hour in advance. He shortened the prison terms of convicts who learned their Buddhism, and asked members of his cabinet to help in the construction of pagodas. He himself prays several hours every morning and eats only vegetables, in line with orthodox Buddhist requirements.

U Nu, whose father was a vendor of religious articles, was not always a pious, godly man. In an autobiographical novel he wrote in 1943 entitled *Man the Wolf of Man,* he said: "In his native town, the nickname of Tate Sanetha, Saturday-born street Arab, was well known to everybody . . . By the age of twelve he was a heavy drinker. Often as a sequel to his drinking bouts, his stupefied little body might be seen carried home on someone's shoulder. His father, deeply ashamed and hopeless of reclaiming him, could only banish him to live as he would in a paddy godown outside the town. The boy brewed his own liquor there."

Then, "something deep down inside him suddenly changed . . . A cool moonlight night, a verdant prospect, pretty women, sweet music began to move him profoundly. Whenever he was moved by beauty, he wanted to be alone with his joy." Moved by the beauty of a society girl whose picture had appeared in a newspaper, the hero clipped it out, and whenever he looked at it, was inspired "to do good deeds, champion the weak, subdue the oppressors."

Such inspiration, projected on the country as a whole, has created a powerful barrier to communism. Even noncommunist Marxism, which had been so closely identified with the nationalist movement before independence, has fallen victim to the religious surge. Not only U Nu but most other Burmese leaders, too, have rejected it for spiritual reasons. Few attempts are now made by any of them to reconcile Marxism with Buddhism, as U Ba Swe tried to do some time ago. Marxism, he had said, does not reject religion but merely the theory of creation, and therefore parallels the Buddhist philosophy. Each concept, he added, occupied a separate sphere of life, which did not conflict with the other. Today, the communists alone are resorting to such rationalizations. And with the government making effective use of religion as a positive means of fighting communism, they have good reason to do so.

Religion first became an anticommunist weapon in 1956, when the government decided that while the communists could promise more material benefits than could the more honest noncommunists, the latter had the spiritual field all to themselves. The Burmese cared more about the love of God than a new pair of shoes. The army, which in most countries is too busy thinking about military tactics to concern itself greatly with religion, took over the religious campaign. Throughout 1956 and 1957 it grilled a large number of the 10,000 communists who had been taken prisoner, seeking concrete evidence of Red aims to destroy Buddhism. But the army was able to collect only hearsay, including one report that Than Tun, the White Flag leader, had said of Rangoon's magnificent gold-encrusted Shwedagon Pagoda: "All that gold all over that pagoda is sheer waste. If I ever come into power I will take it all off the pagoda and use it for the government of the country." What was needed was written evidence, and none of the prisoners would give it.

But in 1957 the army's efforts were rewarded. A notebook fell into its hands containing notes taken in indoctrination classes held by Thakin Soe, the Red Flag leader. The Army Psychological Warfare Division immediately prepared an anticommunist pamphlet based on the notes, entitled *Dhammantaraya*, "Buddhism in Danger." "The Buddha's teachings, beginning, middle and end, are dead wrong," Soe was quoted as saying. Pictures and stories of communist desecration of religious idols were also featured. "Already the Communists of Burma," the pamphlet editorialized,

> are calumniating the Buddha . . . the Buddhist traditions, and traducing the best elements of the Buddha's teaching, hell-bent on the destruction of that gentle influence which is the foundation of our civilization . . . A [terrible] fate awaits Buddhism in Burma sooner or later if her great Buddhist public will not bestir themselves to protect it, defend and safeguard it, but let the Burma communists poison the minds of the young and adolescent against Buddhism as they are doing now.

To make sure the pamphlet would have the maximum effect, the government solicited the comments of a university student, a peasant, a Buddhist fanatic, and even a communist, making changes accordingly. The publishing and distribution job represented one of the most formidable propaganda attempts ever made in Burma, and was handled with all the secrecy and complex planning of a major military operation. The Army, Ministry of Information, and Ministry of Religion were all involved and every brigade and command headquarters was utilized. Once distribution had begun, the public itself was asked to participate in the anticommunist campaign by contributing toward the cost of publication. "You will gain merit in the next world if you help out," they were promised. Popular response exceeded the government's most optimistic predictions, and within a year more than one million copies of the pamphlet, most of them paid for by ordinary Burmese, had found their way into every corner of Burma. "It is," said one official, "the greatest best-seller in Burmese history."

To avoid offering the impression that the government was using religion for its political advantage, the case against the communists was given a national flavor, with emphasis on the dangers that Red atheism poses for Burma as a whole. "This book," a newspaper advertisement read, "is the most valuable contribution to the cause of Buddhism that has been made so far by those in authority; made in absolute sincerity and without regard for glory or power . . . It certainly is not an action to catch votes! It certainly is not a misuse of religion for political gain!" Similar pamphlets have been published by private groups for the benefit of Burma's Moslem and Christian minorities. They demand even stronger action against the communists than does the Buddhist version, which tries not to offend Buddhists who oppose bloodshed regardless of the provocation. The Islamic pamphlet quotes the Koran: "Fight in the way of Allah against those who fight against you . . . Destruction of religion is worse than killing."

The government has also reached the illiterate fifty percent of the population with huge billboards depicting such scenes as an evil-faced communist standing over a dead monk amid the ruins of a shrine. Great mass rallies at which national and local dignitaries denounce communism for its antireligious attitude have drawn audiences totaling over a million in hundreds of villages throughout the country. At one gathering, a Buddhist priest described the communists as "devils and ogres" and called for a crusade against communism like that of Shin Maha Kathapha, a Buddhist saint, against the *deikti,* heretics who had tried to kill Buddha. At most meetings it has been stressed that communism seeks to destroy all religions; that communism, and even noncommunist Marxism, offers an explanation of life in conflict with Buddhist teachings, and that Buddhism fosters individualism and is therefore incompatible with the "cattle" mentality of communism. Occasionally, Christian and Moslem leaders have joined hands with the Buddhists in the anticommunist campaign.

The impact of this campaign on the Burmese population can perhaps best be judged by the great effort the communists have made to discredit it. For years the Reds had tried to convince the public that there was no contradiction between Buddhism and communism. Thakin Soe, whose indoctrination lessons ridiculing Buddhism provided the core of the anticommunist campaign, intensively studied Buddhism during World War II in an effort to substitute Buddhist terms for Marxist phraseology. His analogies, usually quoted out of context, did exert a considerable influence on his pupils. After the war the Reds intensively wooed Buddhist monks with such double-talk and claimed that "Even the honest *Phongyis* (Buddhist monks) love and support the party."

But in the last several years the Reds have found themselves not only suffering military defeat, but watching their carefully laid religious propaganda efforts collapse. The legal communist groups, which had tried to infiltrate the U Nu government, did not dare to attack it for using religion as a weapon against communism; although one pro-Red warily opined in parliament that it was too bad billboard space formerly used to publicize public welfare measures are being devoted to "other purposes," a tendency, he said, that appeared to show the government was becoming less interested in economic problems. General Ne Win's government has been even less disposed to listen to communist complaints.

But the illegal communist rebels, for their part, have bitterly condemned the government for publishing "lies." The title alone of a White Flag communist brochure reads, "Rip Off the Masks to Expose the Real Selves of the Fascist Colonels . . . and a Few Others, the Stooges of the Anglo-American Imperialists . . . Who Attempt to Shield the Establishment of the Fascist Military Dictatorship System in Burma with the Anti-Communist Campaign of Dhamma in Danger." The aims of the anti-Red pamphlet's authors, charges the counter-pamphlet, which was distributed while U Nu was still in power, are:

   1. To shield the biggest danger of the people of Burma, which is to destroy the democratic rights of the people and to establish the Fascist Military Dictatorship System.

2. To create a gap between the Buddhist mass and the communists, who form the bulwark of the people's front in resisting and fighting undauntedly against the oppressors whose purpose is to establish the Fascist Military Dictatorship System.

3. To provoke a quarrel between the *Sanghas* and the communists who have strived to bring about the internal peace through compromise based on the "Give and Take" principle . . .

4. To oppress the democratic forces which oppose the establishment of the Fascist Military Dictatorship System lawfully as above-ground communists.

5. To drag Burma into the anticommunist camp by violating the five Principles of Peaceful Coexistence.

In reality, the Red pamphlet claims, the communists believe in the freedom of religion and wish to protect and preserve all pagodas, shrines, and monastic buildings.

But the communist counterattack does not appear to have greatly blunted the effect of the government campaign—even according to the admissions of captured communist rebels themselves. And if nothing else, the campaign has created a synonym for the word "communism" that is now commonly used throughout Burma—*Dhammantaraya*, "Buddhism in Danger."

When the army voluntarily stepped down in favor of U Nu in April 1960 following a national election in which Nu's new Union Party won an overwhelming majority of votes, the communists had never been in a weaker position. Occasionally some of the 3,000 White Flag communists and the 500 or so Red Flag communists still at large raided villages and police outposts, sabotaged communications and transportation, and made some rural areas dangerous for travel at night, often benefiting from the government's preoccupation with regional minority insurrections, which had spread to the Shan and Kachin peoples. But strong organized attacks had ended. Remarkably, the Burmese army had done alone what whole divisions of British Commonwealth troops were required to do in Malaya.

As for the legal communists, their National United Front suffered a tremendous defeat in the new election and has since been plagued with internal dissension. After U Nu released several communist leaders who had been detained under the Army's rule and permitted resumption of leftist press activities, the Front began cooperating with the Prime Minister in the hope of increasing its influence within the government. For the first time it approved the government's policy of unconditional surrender for the underground insurgents, although it implied that amnesties should be granted to rebels who surrendered. Still, some of the splinter groups within the Front bitterly opposed collaboration with the government. Today, with Ne Win in power again, the Front's activities, like those of all other political parties, are circumscribed though not banned.

The Burma communists are not getting much help, either, from the Soviet Union, some of whose efforts to influence Burma have been disastrous. Russian technicians undertook the construction of a new luxury hotel in Rangoon, but, despite the fact that the temperature in Burma sometimes rises to 100 degrees in the shade, neglected to install air conditioning. When the Burmese government reacted in fury, the Russians had to spend an extra $200,000 to put in an air-conditioning system—obtained, embarrassingly, in the United States. Russia shipped a whole year's supply of cement to Burma immediately before one monsoon season. When the rains started, the cement, still on the docks, hardened into an unbreakable, unusable block.

The Burmese government was also angry with the Soviet Union for purchasing Burmese rice and reselling it on the international market at cut-rate prices, and for going over its head to offer Friendship University scholarships directly to students. It turned down fifty applications for permission to accept them—several Burmese newspapers commenting that the mission of the university was to train cadres for revolutionary movements in Asian countries. Relations with Russia did not improve when an official of the Soviet Embassy, after requesting political asylum in Rangoon, was kidnaped by Russian agents and, before the gaping eyes of the Burmese, forcefully carried aboard a plane headed for the Soviet Union. The Burmese were no less shocked when a new book about Mongolia arrived from Moscow. One of Rangoon's leading newspapers reprinted in full, under the headlined title of the book, *Facts about the Mongolian People's Republic,* a passage that proudly described the killing of 37,000 Buddhist monks.

Russia has not impressed even the Burmese communists greatly. A group of them were probably the first Reds in the Free World to make their stand in the Moscow-Peking controversy unmistakably clear when they burned Khrushchev in effigy and shouted the praises of Mao in late 1961.

Communist China is also more popular, or seemingly so, on the government level, though this popularity has diminished considerably since Mao's all-out attack on neighboring India. But Burma, though deploring the Red Chinese incursions on Indian territory as well as the Tibet massacres, has indirectly benefited from these events. For Peking needed to offer an impressive exhibition of co-operation with at least one free Southeast Asian nation to remove some of the tarnish from the image of an aggressive Communist China devouring foreign territory. In a dramatic show of "reasonableness," it therefore agreed early in 1960 to recognize most of Burma's claims along the disputed Burma-China border.

This frontier problem plagued relations between the two countries long before the communists took over China. The British, on annexing upper Burma in 1885, tried to win the good will of neighboring China, whose influence was thought to be great in Burma, by agreeing to send "decennial missions to present articles of local produce" to that country. In return, China agreed to "permit" Britain "to do whatever she deems fit and proper in Burma." But Britain soon came to realize that it wasn't necessary to bribe China to do what she deemed "fit and proper" in Burma, for the Burmese had never recognized China's claimed suzerainty; and although invading Chinese hordes had won temporary control of Burma during certain periods in history, the Burmese had always managed to chase them out. In precolonial days, Burmese missions bearing gifts and excess daughters to China were sent only in exchange for similar missions from China.

Britain conveniently forgot to send the decennial missions. Instead, she began badgering China for an agreement demarcating the Chinese-Burmese border, though this region had never really been charted. Various tentative accords were reached from 1894 to 1941, including a treaty in 1897 giving the British the Namwan Tract on lease. Until Burma became independent in 1948, the British—and Burmese—simply considered the extension of the McMahon Line from India as Burma's northern frontier. The Chinese, however, never fully accepted this line, and, following World War II, the Nationalist government continued to publish maps of China showing large parts of northern Burma as Chinese. When the communists took over China, frequent clashes took place between Chinese and Burmese troops in the area, with no settlement seeming possible—until the Indian border conflict mushroomed into headlines.

General Ne Win flew to Peking in January 1960, during his first period of power, and came away with an agreement largely confirming the McMahon Line as the Burmese border, though China had rejected this line in the case of the Indian frontier. While Burma agreed to hand over three frontier villages and a pocket of land in the Wa States to China, it retained the heretofore leased Namwan Tract as its own. The three villages—Hpimaw, Gawlam, and Kangfang—are important to China because they command a number of mountain passes leading into that country, and the Namwan Tract is vital to Burma because a highway linking the Shan and Kachin States runs through it.

Burma was overjoyed with the accord. U Nu, having returned to power, went to Peking in October 1960 and signed the border treaty in an atmosphere of unrestrained hospitality and fanfare. Chinese Premier Chou En-lai made a reciprocal visit to Rangoon in January 1961 accompanied by Buddhist, art, cultural, military, film, and journalistic delegations numbering some 420 people, the largest mission ever sent abroad by Peking for any propaganda-diplomatic occasion. It was the most lavishly received group to have visited Burma since independence. Nu conferred on Chou the rank of "Supreme Upholder of the Glory of Great Love," an honor never before bestowed on any foreigner. With a gold and jade metal glittering from his tunic, Chou drank fruit juice and spoke of "coexistence" at sumptuous banquets while the sky lit up with fireworks.

Almost before the final sparks went out, Burma also had an interest-free loan of $84 million, repayable over ten years—a sum greater than the cumulative total of communist-bloc economic assistance to Burma since 1955. Through this credit the Chinese are providing industrial equipment and technical experts and are training Burmese technicians. A new trade agreement signed in October 1960 also provided the basis for considerable expansion of Sino-Burmese trade. Among other things, Peking agreed to purchase about 350,000 tons of Burmese rice at a price exceeding the current market quotation. This rice deal wiped out a two-year trade deficit with China.

The firm status of Communist China in Burma, however, does not mean that Burma is heading toward a procommunist type of neutralism. The attitude of the Burmese toward the Red Chinese is not comparable to that which many wishful Indians held toward them before Peking embarked on aggression in India. The more realistic Burmese are under no illusions as to the purposes or sincerity of Peking. In their study of Burmese history and in their long struggle against the domestic communists, they have become only too well acquainted with Chinese ambitions and Red deceit.

Their silent suspicion is manifest in many ways. Although Peking offered, with Rangoon's approval, five student scholarships in 1958, expecting scores to apply for them, only four did. In 1960 not a single student applied. The need to spend a year learning the Chinese language and the poor living conditions in China have been factors in this reluctance to study in that country. But the principal element, several students told me, is that they do not want indoctrination but the liberal kind of education offered in the West.

While Communist Chinese as well as Soviet books and pamphlets published in English can be sold in Burma and are available in quantity and at extremely low prices, rarely exceeding one dollar a volume, the distribution of Burmese-language material has not been permitted. Significantly, relatively few Burmese can read English.

But if most Burmese recognize the true nature of international communism, they also recognize the unfortunate fact that Burma's future, to a large extent, depends on the behavior of Peking. "China is our next-door neighbor," Nu said to me. "It is therefore in Burma's interest that we remain friendly with her." This view is understandable. For if and when the Chinese decide to furnish the Burmese Reds with massive military aid, as they have been helping the rebels in Laos and South Vietnam, Burma's security would be gravely endangered. And Rangoon is not a little worried that if those two areas fall, the time will be near for Burma to face the same pressure. But meanwhile, it is convinced, it can best serve the nation's interest by taking advantage of Peking's obvious effort to impress the rest of Southeast Asia with its friendly policies toward Burma, even though, paradoxically, a show of friendship between the two countries, however false, cannot help but increase Red China's influence there. It should be noted that Burma, unlike other neutralists in the area, has never issued strong words against SEATO and has privately condemned it mainly because it is so ineffective. For if a showdown with Red China should ever come, the nation will fight bitterly for its freedom, as it has been doing since World War II, and will almost certainly welcome Western aid if it is deemed necessary.

It is precisely because of the danger posed by Red China that the Burmese so feverishly wanted a frontier accord. For presumably the agreement will make it easier for the Burmese to avoid armed conflicts or provocations that the Chinese could use as a pretext for aggression, as well as to control the movement of agents from one country to the other. Burmese communists have found it easy in the past to cross into China's Yünnan province, where they have tried to establish a base for their rebellion against the

Rangoon government. They have failed so far, probably because the Red Chinese have hesitated to arm them heavily for fear of getting prematurely involved in the Burmese civil war. But such a stronghold may well be established at what Peking considers the opportune moment, and then a better-controlled border may significantly benefit Burma.

Until recently at least, Peking smuggled into Burma from 2,000 to 4,000 civilian agents a month. Some of these people, including whole families, have moved from the Yünnan side of the mountainous border to the Burmese side and are thus in a position to hamper Burmese resistance against a possible Chinese invasion. Other agents have traveled thousands of miles from the Canton and Fukien coastal regions of China with the mission of mixing with their Chinese brothers in central and south Burma, most of whom come from the same areas, and spreading the communist influence among them. Over half of these agents have been women, some of them young and pretty, under orders to marry influential members of the Chinese community. Many agents have been discovered being smuggled into Burma in the rear of trucks disguised as military vehicles, while some have posed as peaceful traders, complete with false identity papers.

A Chinese Nationalist guerrilla officer evacuated from northern Burma to Taiwan reported in early 1961 that the Chinese Reds had built a military highway from Yünnan Province into Burma. He said that the communists used the road to move arms to troops concentrated in the border area. Moreover, the wartime supply route built largely by the United States—the famed Burma Road connecting Lashio, Burma, and Kunming, Yünnan—as well as the Stilwell Road to the north, have been reported as restored in part by the Reds.

The overseas Chinese in Burma are, in a sense, a potentially more dangerous fifth column than their counterparts in countries like Indonesia, Malaya, and Thailand, which do not border on China and could not easily be invaded by that country. The great majority of the 300,000 Burmese Chinese are believed rather sympathetic to Communist China and probably would not hesitate to help clear the way for any future Chinese attack. This attitude has been fostered by agents who have been smuggled in to remind them of the advantages of being on the winning side, and also by pressure that Peking exerts on the Chinese community through its large embassy in Rangoon.

Shortly after independence, the communist Chip-Bee Student

Association won control of the Chinese-language schools, while the Chinese Chamber of Commerce and the Hokkien Association fell under communist influence, with the Peking-operated Bank of China and Bank of Communications offering loans on easy, no-interest terms. All the borrower had to do was employ workers approved by the banks, enroll his children in communist schools, donate small sums to communist organizations, and shun friends who were not loyal to Red China. In the mid-1950's the banks began extending loans even to these "disloyal" friends in the hope of winning them over or forcing them into the service of Peking.

Finally, China sprang the trap. It no longer made loans easily, demanding, in fact, immediate payment of those it had made. Funds flowed into the embassy treasury, not only from this source but from forced and voluntary contributions, illegal remittances sent to China, and trade deals with Burma. Although it has not been proved, Burmese officials believe that much of this accumulated money was used to finance the parliamentary campaigns of the legal Burmese communists in 1956 and 1960, and also to strengthen Burmese communist-front organizations. The most important of them are controlled by the Burma Workers Party, the leading communist group in the National United Front, and include the Burma Trade Union Congress, the All-Burma Peasants' Unity Organization, the People's Youth Organization, and the All-Burma Women's Unity League. Peking funds are possibly also being used to help the communist rebels keep their rebellion going.

Actually, the government isn't quite sure which are its worst enemies—those Chinese who support Red China or the pro-Chiang Kai-shek minority that was suspected of helping the Nationalist soldiers who held out in northern Burma until the last ones were shipped to Taiwan in early 1961. The presence of Nationalist soldiers in the country until recently has been the sorest point in Burmese-American relations in recent years, for Burma felt the United States could have brought pressure on Chiang Kai-shek to remove them if it had so desired. The problem arose in 1948 when the Chinese Reds chased about 10,000 Chinese Nationalists into the Burmese jungles. This force then began using Burma as a base for harassing tactics against the communists in Yünnan Province, but was repulsed and, according to the Burmese government, turned to banditry, foraging off the countryside and attacking government forces that were having a hard enough time fighting the domestic communists and other rebellious elements.

But what disturbed the government most of all was that the presence of the Chinese Nationalists on Burmese soil might present Red China with a pretext to invade the country or at least give substantial aid to the communist rebels. In 1955 Burma took the matter to the United Nations. As a result, all but 2,000 of the Nationalists were evacuated to Taiwan, easing Burmese relations with the United States. Having cut off American economic aid in 1954 in a fit of pique over the Nationalist issue, Burma began accepting assistance again, and in quantities far exceeding the aid received from the communist bloc.

Then, early in 1961, the situation suddenly exploded once more when the Burmese captured in northern Burma weapons, ammunition, and other supplies in wooden crates marked with the United States aid handclasp emblem, and shot down an unmarked Nationalist aircraft crammed with supplies. The Burmese did not agree with Taiwan's reaction that they should be grateful for the protection afforded them by the Nationalist soldiers against the Red Chinese. Fear that Peking would tear up the border agreement that had just been reached added fuel to the explosion. While combined Burmese and Red Chinese forces drove the remaining Nationalists into Thailand and Laos, Rangoon students, who had intended to demonstrate peacefully before the American Embassy, were suddenly agitated to violence by a few extremists. In an orgy of shooting, stone-throwing, and club-swinging, two Burmese were killed and fifty injured.

The ill feeling against the United States, however, has since been largely dissipated and may not return now that the Nationalist problem is solved. However wrong Burmese judgment of American responsibility in the matter may have been, at the root of Burmese indignation was not a preference for communism but a fear of it. The Burmese felt that the United States had helped to intensify the threat posed by the Reds—an attitude hardly comparable to that of communist-led mobs in some other underdeveloped nations.

Factors of irritation between the United States and Burma still exist. The Burmese, like most Afro-Asians, are critical of the United States for racial disturbances in this country, which are fully publicized in the local press. But unlike many other Afro-Asians, they often temper this criticism with expressions of respect for the efforts of the American government to solve this problem without trying to minimize its importance. In general, the Burmese recognize that their struggle against the communists almost since independence has paralleled the American struggle against international communism.

"Don't think we don't realize," one Burmese official said, "that if it weren't for the United States, Burma might not be a free country today."

XV

INDONESIA:

NO NEED TO PUSH

The car stopped in a small village deep in the highlands of central Java, the main island of Indonesia. My interpreter and I got out and approached a group of barefoot Indonesian youths dressed in tattered shirts and shorts standing outside a large clay hut. They regarded me coolly and suspiciously as the interpreter, whom I had hired, explained that I was an American correspondent and would like to talk with them. After a short, heavy silence, one of the youths said, his voice reflecting even less warmth than his expression, "We are sorry, but we have nothing to say. We don't know anything about America, but we have been told it is not friendly to us." Who told them? They were silent, but the answer was written on the front wall of the mud hut—a large, red, crudely painted hammer-and-sickle emblem. We left, and as we passed through the village almost every hut, we noted, was decorated with the same emblem.

"You came too late," the interpreter, who was at the wheel, commented. "Those communists have taken over just about every village in Indonesia."

The interpreter was greatly exaggerating, of course. The communists have not yet taken over Indonesia. But they are well on the way toward doing so, and by peaceful means. The Indonesian Communist Party, or PKI, as it is called, today claims more than 1,500,000 members, making it the largest political organization in

Indonesia and one of the largest communist parties this side of the Iron Curtain.

One reason for its success can be found in the issue of West New Guinea, or West Irian, as the Indonesians call this area. The Dutch, while reluctantly granting independence to Indonesia in 1949 after administering its 3,000-odd islands as the East Indies for more than a century, would not yield West New Guinea until August 1962. At that time, as the result of American and United Nations mediation, the Dutch agreed to turn over the territory to United Nations administrators, who are to transfer authority to the Indonesians in mid-1963.

The Dutch are bitter about their defeat, though the region, about the size of California, was a costly burden to them. The Indonesians based their claim to the territory on the fact that it was a part of the East Indian chain that the Netherlands had ruled as a unit. The only alternative to union—an independent West Irian —would be absurd, they said, in view of the small, splinter nature of the area and the primitiveness of its 700,000 people, mostly naked Papuans, many of whom still practice head-hunting and use stone tools in the isolation of almost impenetrable jungle, inaccessible mountain chains, and crocodile-infested swamps.

But the Netherlands demanded that the New Guineans themselves be given the opportunity to determine their own destiny— union with Indonesia or independence. West Irian, the Dutch pointed out, has no real cultural or ethnic connection with Indonesia. Therefore, making it a part of that country without the people's consent would deprive them of a right guaranteed by the United Nations charter. The Dutch, in an effort to prepare the Papuans for self-government, set up a network of village schools, entrusted social legislation to an elected council of sixteen Papuans and twelve Dutch members, and gave natives administrative responsibility for over half the area they controlled. The territory was even given its own national anthem, *My Country, My Papua,* and a red, white, and blue flag, as well as a West Papuan Volunteer Corps to help the Dutch in the area's defense. What do most Papuans think of all this? It's hard to say, because they have never heard of either Indonesia or the Netherlands.

After years of fruitless negotiation over the status of the region, the Indonesian government threatened to take it over by force if necessary, and, in fact, landed small numbers of commandos, most of whom were apparently captured or killed by the Dutch. This situation was made to order for the communists. Their cries of "Western colonialism" blended harmoniously with the cries

of most other Indonesians, giving them a highly attractive nationalist look. And now that Indonesia has won control of the area by
peaceful means, they can claim they had spearheaded the anticolonial campaign and thereby further enhance their status.

Nevertheless, the Reds were probably hoping for a full-fledged
war with the Dutch. As Robert Trumbull, Southeast Asian correspondent for the *New York Times,* wrote in January 1962:

> A conflict could give Moscow, which is already providing Djakarta
> with massive economic and military aid, almost complete control
> of Indonesia's potentially rich economy. A military agreement
> providing for Soviet bases in the strategically situated Indonesian
> islands could be another result of a war . . . In such an eventual-
> ity, the communist bloc could control the vital sea lanes between
> the Indian and Pacific Oceans. The political effect would be felt
> immediately in the wavering countries of Southeast Asia and might
> even be reflected in Australia, where leftists gained heavily in re-
> cent elections.

But whatever role the Soviet Union might have played in a war, if
Indonesia had lost, the chaos and disillusionment in the country
might well have facilitated a Red surge to power.

The West Irian issue, moreover, threatened to remove the most
important barrier to a communist takeover in Indonesia—the
army. Led by National Security Minister and Chief of Staff Abdul
Haris Nasution, an outspoken anticommunist who crushed a Red
revolt in 1948, the army helps run the government, ranking with
the communists and President Sukarno, the popular strong man of
the country, as one of the three major precariously balanced forces
in Indonesia today. Sukarno is a shrewd, if sometimes foolhardy,
politician. By giving the army a large share of power, too, he feels
he is able to cater to communist whims without great danger of the
Reds' taking over completely. Until recently, at least, the army was
doing a good job of keeping them in check, banning communist
newspapers and rallies and preventing Red participation in the
cabinet itself. During his visit to Indonesia in February 1960,
Khrushchev reportedly offered military aid to Indonesia, but the
army apparently refused it, though it had accepted such assistance
in 1958.

Then less than a year later, in January 1961, Nasution himself, in need of arms for a West Irian campaign, journeyed to
Moscow and was given the full red-carpet treatment. At a reception he listened while Soviet Deputy Premier Mikoyan said at an
elaborate reception: "The colonialists believe that they will succeed
in maintaining their domination over an inalienable part of Indo-

nesian soil . . . That is what they in the West, in the so-called
'free world,' are trying to present as justice. But the common people
simply call it robbery . . . The whole world knows that all this is
not done without the approval and sanction of the NATO bloc,
which became a headquarters for the struggle to preserve the
remnants of colonialism and carry out a policy of neocolonialism
in defiance of the unbending will of the peoples . . ." On his departure from Moscow, Nasution, after being promised massive
military aid, responded: "We Indonesians met real friends in
Russia."

"The purpose of Soviet credits to Indonesia can only be political," Dr. Guy J. Pauker, political science professor at the University of California, Berkeley, wrote in the March 1961 issue of the
Asian Survey. "If Soviet aid were on a smaller scale, it would be
reasonable to assume that the purpose may be primarily to balance off Western influences and strengthen Indonesian neutralism.
But, if this were the only Soviet objective, the order of magnitude
of Soviet aid seems disproportionately large. It seems more plausi-
ble to assume that the Soviet Union is preparing a major political 'coup,' by trying to win over the last significant anticommunist
factor in Indonesia, namely the Armed Forces."

This effort is not going unrewarded. When Nasution returned
home from Moscow, he gradually began to give up policies hostile
to the communists, abolishing the National Front for the Liberation of West Irian, which he had created in 1958 mainly to prevent communist infiltration of worker, peasant, youth, religious,
and other organizations. Indonesian Communist Party leader
D. N. Aidit was finally able to say: "The paramount problem in
Indonesian political life now is no longer how to marshal national
unity, but how to consolidate, widen, and strengthen it."

The Reds had found in West Irian a weak spot in the army's
anticommunist armor.

Current communist successes in Indonesia are not a little ironic
considering that of all the communist parties in Asia the Indonesian
party was considered after World War II the least likely to succeed.
Although it could boast 50,000 members and a large share of control over the labor movement within three years after its formal
establishment in 1920, this party was, largely because of Stalin's
utter lack of understanding of local problems, gradually reduced
to near-impotence in the years to follow.

At the Second Comintern Congress the Indonesian party, like
all others represented, was expected to support actively the revolutionary liberation movement led by the national bourgeoisie and to

try to take it over. In Indonesia this meant mainly the Sarekat Raya, a Moslem society. On March 25, 1925, the *Communist International* reported that "other nationalist organizations are progressing, that is, they are being revolutionized and their membership is growing, although not as rapidly as our party and the Sarekat Islam, which is under communist influence." The man who led the communist faction in this organization was Tan Malaka, who became one of the top Comintern agents in the Orient and the most influential Red in Southeast Asia during this period. But Malaka's group failed in Indonesia because, under Stalin's orders, it had to attack the Islamic principles of the Sarekat Islam. As the communists in India severely damaged themselves by condemning Gandhism, so did the Indonesian Reds discredit themselves with their anti-Islam propaganda. Despite a last-ditch "neutral" stand on the religious issue, they were expelled from the organization.

Embittered by their failure and resentful of Moscow for imposing impractical dogma on them, the party boldly decided in 1926 to disregard Comintern policy and to consider the national bourgeoisie as their enemy. They tried to form soviets in villages and factories in Java and Sumatra with the aim of setting up a soviet republic. But this effort was smashed by the police, the Communist Party was banned, and many Reds fled to the wilderness of southeastern New Guinea, where, surrounded by jungle and swamp, they built the settlement of Tanahmerah on the banks of the crocodile-inhabited Digoel River. Unable to make their way to the New Guinea coast, the Reds remained in their jungle isolation for over fifteen years.

Then one day, after the Japanese had occupied Indonesia during World War II, a plane landed nearby, and a Dutch representative from General MacArthur's Headquarters at Canberra, Australia, stepped out. He offered to have the Reds ferried out of their jungle prison in Allied aircraft if they would join the underground against the Japanese. The communists agreed, and for several years they assisted in anti-Japanese guerrilla operations.

With the landing of Allied troops in Indonesia, the Indonesian nationalists led by Sukarno declared the nation's independence in August 1945 and frustrated communist efforts to infiltrate their movement, though the Communist Party did become legal for the first time in eighteen years. Infuriated, the Kremlin actually joined the Dutch in condemning the nationalist leaders as Japanese collaborators and fascists. Some domestic communists even supported the return of Indonesia to Dutch control, convinced that they could more easily win power as an anticolonial than as an antinationalist force. Dutch troops, helped by the British, did their best to please, fighting the nationalists for fourteen months. In November 1946 a compromise settlement was reached, recognizing nationalist authority over about eighty-five percent of Indonesia and calling for a "Netherlands-Indonesian Union" under the Netherlands royal house.

Moscow and the Indonesian Communist Party approved the accord because it limited the power of the nationalists and therefore gave the Reds a better opportunity to edge their way into control than they would have had under a stronger nationalist government. But a few communist leaders, led by Tan Malaka, violently disapproved the agreement and called their fellow-communist chiefs traitors. The Reds must fight, not kowtow to, the imperialists, they insisted. Malaka's orthodox colleagues branded him as a "Trotskyite" and pledged their co-operation to the new government. Malaka, far ahead of his time in terms of communist policy, felt that the Reds would have a better opportunity to come to power as part of a strongly anti-imperialist nationalist movement than in an isolated role weakly linked to it. He almost proved his point early in 1946 when, on the strength of his anti-Dutch stand, he barely missed taking over the nationalist movement—and the government—with the armed forces declaring for Sukarno only after considerable hesitation.

Malaka who, as a uniquely independent-minded Comintern agent in Southeast Asia, led a fantastic life of intrigue and hairbreadth escapes throughout the area—in 1925 he smuggled himself into the Philippines and embarrassed American authorities when they discovered high-placed friends had issued him an American passport—in many ways personified his people, and perhaps symbolized their future. As Willard A. Hanna wrote in the April 6, 1959, issue of *American Universities Field Staff:*

> Tan Malaka's ideology and personality are to a great extent typical in their strengths and their weaknesses of both the Indonesian people as a whole and of their leaders to date. His personal achievement was to charm, to divert, to dramatize, and to inspire. He failed to discipline, to co-operate, to organize, or to plan. His achievements and his shortcomings are typical of Bung Karno [Sukarno] who has managed, nevertheless, by outshining Tan Malaka and all others in personality, to override even graver personal and political hazards. They are typical also of most of Bung Karno's revolutionary colleagues, past and present . . . The story of Tan Malaka, however, like that of Bung Karno him-

self, may indicate that the Indonesian safety valve against the rising pressures of communism is a high-spirited refusal to be bound by anything so unequivocal and exacting as an outright communist program.

Malaka was delighted when fighting broke out again between the Dutch and the nationalists over the implementation of their "joint leadership" accord, and wanted the communists to back the nationalists. Instead, with Moscow's new "left strategy" line in force, the Communist Party was ordered to revolt against the nationalists while they still had their hands full with the Dutch—though Malaka and some other Reds considered such a move suicide. Before differences could be resolved, communist officers stationed in the Javanese town of Madiun who were being removed from the army settled the issue. They resisted efforts to discharge them, setting off a small revolution by all procommunist officers in Madiun. Capture of the town and surrounding region was followed by a general communist rebellion. Three months later, in December 1948, nationalist forces commanded by Abdul Haris Nasution, then a colonel, smashed the revolt. Its leaders were executed and the Communist Party was nearly destroyed as a political force, precisely as Malaka had foreseen.

Its remnants, however, doggedly clung to the possibility of seizing power in the chaos of the anticolonial war that was in progress and continued to oppose the nationalists, preferring temporary Dutch rule to firmly established nationalist leadership. These Red die-hards received what seemed like a *coup de grace* when the Dutch finally agreed to give Indonesia full independence.

Yet within a few years the Communist Party, financed and advised by the country's largely pro-Red Chinese community, had made an incredible recovery. It startled the nation in the 1955 parliamentary elections by winning six million votes, almost twenty percent of the total. Since then, membership has increased by about one-third.

How did the Reds manage to pull off this miracle? One important factor was the party's switch in tactics in the early 1950's in line with the general communist reversal of the Stalinist "left strategy." It suddenly embraced the nationalist leaders as fellow anti-imperialists, and Sukarno himself as a "great Indonesian patriot." The switch paid off almost immediately with the granting of legal status to the outlawed party in 1953. Once enjoying the blessing of Sukarno, who is extraordinarily popular in Indonesia, the Reds were for the first time listened to seriously by the downtrodden masses.

Sukarno, a short, youthful-looking man with an infectious smile and a glowing personality, saw no potential danger in his blessing. In 1957, on his fifty-sixth birthday, he told friends in an appraisal of himself: "I was born under the sign of Gemini, and I am destined to live a double life according to astrologers. I am a Marxist but I love religion. I am a scientist but I am also an artist. Sometimes I'm serious, sometimes I horse around. I can mix with communists and socialists, Moslems and Christians, revolutionary nationalists and compromising nationalists."

One major reason for the communists' success lies in the chaotic condition of the Indonesian economy stemming from inefficiency, large-scale corruption, and the smuggling by local Chinese of enormous wealth out of the country. "I think we'd get along just as well if Indonesia had no government at all," a disgruntled Indonesian student told me in Djakarta as he gazed contemplatively upon the murky brown waters of the broad canal that winds through the city like a slimy serpent. At the canal's edge, women were washing clothes while their children swam and romped in the glossy currents. Nearby, several people squatted on the bank, relieving themselves in the all-purpose waterway. "My heart breaks when I look at scenes like this," the student said. "I know we can't build a clean, new world overnight, but we are not even making a start. The government simply squanders and misuses our tax money without giving us any benefits from it. I'm no communist, but it's little wonder they're so strong here. You can be sure that they would do *something*."

This observation reflects the mood of fatalistic surrender that engulfs most of Indonesia today. In India at least an attempt is being made to overcome the tremendous economic problems that burden that nation. But in Indonesia one has the feeling that nobody really cares. Why try to move a mountain when, after all, nobody is starving or without shelter? Yet the mere chipping of this mountain would probably mean a significant rise in living standards. For after the United States and the Soviet Union, this country may be endowed with the richest natural resources of any nation on earth.

In its bowels lie untapped valleys of petroleum, tin, bauxite, manganese, copper, coal, iron, asphalt, phosphate, nickel, gold, silver, platinum, diamonds, tungsten, sulphur, and iodine. Great rivers and mountains mean an enormous potential of hydro-electric power. It has a huge population of ninety million, the sixth largest in the world, a labor force sufficient to exploit all this wealth. Attesting to the nation's rich soil, the Dutch produced here before the war four-fifths of the world's pepper, one-third of its rubber, palm oil, and coconut products, two-fifths of its kapok, a fifth of its tea, and copious quantities of coffee and sugar.

But Indonesia's economic situation has been deteriorating since World War II. When the Netherlands reluctantly agreed to nationalist demands for independence in 1949, the native government was highly unprepared for such responsibility. There were virtually no trained administrators and only a thousand or so college graduates in the country, which has a seven-percent literacy rate. Yet never in Indonesian history was there greater need for talented, able leaders. As a result of the Japanese invasion early in the war and the struggle against Dutch rule after the war, the Indonesian economy was a shambles. Roads, railroads, and canal systems were all but destroyed. Coffee, tea, and sugar crops rotted in fields taken over by thousands of homeless squatters, and rice yields were so low that the nation had to spend $140 million on rice imports two years after independence. The situation could hardly have been worse. But today it is worse. So great is the inflation and general economic anarchy that sacks of rice have been stored in government offices so that in case starvation does threaten, food handouts can be distributed to the most needy.

Almost as welcome to the communists as economic deterioration has been the nation's lack of unity. It was no simple job even for trained Dutch administrators to control and rule efficiently a necklace of islands stretching over a distance of 2,800 miles, many with a deep sense of individuality, their own traditional culture, and their own language. Nor have the chauvinistic passions of the outer islands been gratified by the fact that Java, whose exports amount to less than twenty percent of the nation's total, consumes over seventy percent of the imports, however abnormally high a population density Java may have. Thus, since independence the government has had to devote much of its energy and income simply to putting down regional revolts—one explanation for Indonesia's economic anemia. For years the government has been struggling to crush an effort by dissidents in the South Moluccas to set up an independent republic. An army revolt in Sumatra started in 1956, and others in the Celebes and Sundas that broke out the next year have still not been completely snuffed out.

Curiously enough, even the predominance of the Moslem religion in most of the Indonesian archipelago has not been a factor for national unity. Moslem fanatics, moderately religious groups, and the nation's near-agnostic leadership are constantly at each other's throats; and the Reds are in the thick of the battle. The communists have by no means lost ground by helping to fight the Darul Islam, which, since independence, has terrorized large areas of West Java, the southern Celebes, and northern Sumatra in an effort to turn Indonesia into a theocratic state. In May 1962 members made an abortive attempt on Sukarno's life. The Reds did not suffer either when Sukarno outlawed the Masjumi Party, a large moderate anti-communist Moslem group, for refusing to co-operate with the communists within a governmental system he calls "guided democracy."

The character of Sukarno has also been a vital factor in the communist surge to national prominence. Sukarno is in a position perhaps unique among the world's leaders. A superb demagogue, he is so popular among the people that he doesn't have to do anything for them to retain their confidence. However bad conditions get, he is the last to be blamed, though he holds almost absolute power in his country. And Sukarno himself rationalizes that he is doing his best for his impoverished people—even as he spends fantastic fortunes on chartered "good-will" trips around the world that are usually highlighted by brief, well-publicized escapades with attractive young ladies.

Sukarno's contempt for hard work and hard thinking has often led him to seek convenient short cuts to his goals. Because of his extraordinary demagogic talents and his disarmingly charming manner, his people do not think the worse of him for this opportunism. Born in eastern Java, the son of a poor Javanese school teacher and a high-caste Balinese mother, Sukarno graduated at the top of his class in civil engineering at a technical college run by the Dutch. Then he turned to underground politics, and at twenty-six became the top nationalist leader in the country. The Dutch jailed him from 1929 to 1931, then exiled him to an outlying island, where he remained until the Japanese landed in Indonesia in 1942.

Sukarno openly collaborated with the Japanese—apparently in the hope of using them as an instrument of eventual liberation from both Dutch and Japanese rule. The new colonialists, unlike the old, permitted him to roam the country and deliver broadcasts, and with good reason. "America we shall iron out, England we shall destroy," he proclaimed. He also asked his people to enlist in Japanese-led defense forces, and even provided his masters with *romushas,* or slave laborers. Yet after the war the bitterly anti-Japanese public wanted him as their leader over nationalists who had risked their lives fighting the Japanese in the Indonesian underground. Today Sukarno is playing up to new forces he thinks can help him—the communists.

The President, a quasi-left-wing socialist with little real understanding of Marxist ideology and none of the discipline required for its implementation, decided to accept communist support unequivocally shortly after the Red show of strength in the 1955 elections because this tactic appeared to be the easiest and surest way of maintaining his authority in the face of threatened anarchy and political opposition from the Masjumi Party, the Socialist Party, and smaller groups. When the Sumatra rebellion broke out in 1957, the marriage was sealed. Faced with the choice of appeasing the anticommunist rebels by breaking with the Reds or joining with the communists to crush the rebels, Sukarno chose the latter course. He concluded, after being exposed on a trip to Peking to the efficiency of Red Chinese totalitarianism, that Red support would be of maximum value if channeled through a system of personal dictatorship sugar-coated, for purposes of moral rationalization and political propaganda, with elements of traditional Indonesian philosophy. Parliamentary democracy—which had, it is true, meant chaos under power-hungry politicians who had been trained only in the negativism of anticolonial revolt—thus gave way to "guided democracy."

"Western democracy," explained Sukarno, "is an import democracy . . . not in harmony with our spirit . . . In this Western democracy . . . we come across the idea of opposition. It is this very idea . . . which has made us go through hardships for . . . years. Because we interpret this idea of opposition in a manner which does not agree with the Indonesian soul. [The aim of the opposition is always the] overthrow of the existing government and its replacement by a government of the opposition itself . . . We should not only pull down all the pillars, the roof, the walls; we should pull down everything—not excluding the foundation—lay a new foundation, erect a totally new building."

Sukarno's "new building," completed in 1959, is an incredibly ornate Oriental edifice with a maze of corridors that seem to lead nowhere. Its foundation is called *Usdek,* a word formed from the initial letters, in Indonesian, of five policy slogans that, in addition to "guided democracy," include "guided economy," "Indonesian socialism," "Indonesian personality," and "return to the 1945 Constitution," which was of an authoritative, emergency nature. In simpler terms, *Usdek* stands for virtual political dictatorship and almost complete socialization of the economy. The monstrous inefficiency and arbitrariness with which these control principles have been applied have served only to compound the confusion of the past. Corruption and bureaucracy are today more rampant than ever.

Sukarno rules a cabinet responsible only to himself, feigning to consider the advice of a potpourri of consultative bodies whose responsibilities have never been clearly defined. One of these is a handpicked *Goton Rojong* parliament comprising functional organizations and members of eight parties that have agreed to support Sukarno. Opposition groups such as the Masjumi and Socialist Parties have been forced to dissolve. The sugar-coating is reflected in the name of the parliament. *Goton Rojong* means "mutual aid" and refers to Indonesia's traditional system of village rule whereby representatives of the village reached a decision only after long deliberation and mutual compromise by all concerned. In practice the *Goton Rojong* parliament simply rubber-stamps Sukarno's wishes which, somehow, seldom conflict with those of the PKI, whose aim is to take full control of the government when Sukarno departs from the scene.

Still another major element in the rise of the communists was the support, until recently, of Indonesia's Chinese community, more than seventy percent of whose members are Peking-oriented, either by choice or by force of circumstance. The 2,500,000 *Hua-Chiao,* although making up only three percent of the population, firmly control the commerce of Indonesia, as have their ancestors for hundreds of years. Since Peking controls most of the Chinese, they have contributed generously to the party's growth, in both a financial and a political sense. Local Chinese Reds were probably responsible for saving the party from complete extinction after the 1948 disaster at Madiun, taking over its administration and rebuilding its foundation. A Chinese was even appointed editor of the *Harian Rakyat (The Daily Masses),* the party organ. When the party finally became legal in 1953, the Chinese discreetly turned over their posts to Indonesians and concentrated their activities in front organizations.

Chinese communist-oriented high schools began springing up even before China fell to Mao, with Djakarta High School turning out trained agitators by the classful. In 1948 leftist Chinese teachers formed the Nan-hwa Educational Association and learned that a good source of material for current events courses was the pro-communist Chinese newspaper *Sin Po,* or *New Post.* Also available for use were, and are, Red Chinese textbooks smuggled into the country on fishing boats, sometimes in rice bags, from Hong Kong or Bangkok, together with gold bars, opium, and other items intended to finance subversive activities. Borneo in particular is a center for pro-Peking activity. Almost 300 of its 400 Chinese-language schools are run by communists or fellow travelers, while communist cultural centers, some of them floorless shacks, draw crowds of Chinese businessmen and workers each night for Marxist discussions, interspersed with folk singing.

As the Nationalist Chinese controlled the Overseas Chinese Association of Indonesia after the war, the Peking-influenced *Hua-Chiao* formed a competitive organization which grew to double the size of the original group. These and other elements of the Chinese community have contributed large sums of money to the PKI, including most of the funds spent by the Reds in the critical 1955 election for subversion and propaganda. The fact that Surabaja, Indonesia's second largest city, voted seventy percent communist can be attributed largely to huge outlays by the *Hua-Chiao,* who constitute twelve percent of the city's population and virtually direct the municipal government through their Red-tinged neighborhood associations.

Overseeing the activities of this highly potent fifth column are the two hundred Chinese Communist diplomats who use their architecturally splendid embassy, which deceptively resembles a traditional Chinese temple of worship, as a headquarters for espionage and agitation. To finance its elaborate conspiratorial network, the Embassy sponsors benefits and cultural events, forces wealthy merchants to kick in if they want a letter of credit from the Bank of China to trade with China, and engages in smuggling operations. The Embassy, in turn, donates heavily to the local party and to its trade-union federation, SOBSI (Sentral Organisasi Buruh Sulurah Indonesia), which closes the circle by intimidating Chinese employers—often the same as those approached by the Embassy—into offering new donations or signing exclusive contracts with the organization.

As I passed through one central Javanese town on a Chinese holiday, almost every store was festively decorated with Communist Chinese and Indonesian flags. I asked the Chinese proprietor of a shop selling locally woven cloth if he was really a supporter of Communist China. Glancing up at Mao's banner as it fluttered in the breeze, he replied with a smile that spoke louder than his words: "Of course. China is China, communist or not. And it has never been more powerful or feared by the world. One day that flag you see there may be flying over the capitol in Djakarta." If it ever does, this merchant and most of the Chinese in Indonesia hope to be on good terms with the new masters.

Red China is not ungrateful for this widespread, if dubious, loyalty among the Indonesian Chinese. So determined is it to maintain this community as a pliable political tool that it risked a near break in diplomatic relations with Indonesia in 1959-60 over their fate. Sukarno, however leftist he may be, is a nationalist first. And one of the deepest nationalist grievances for many years has been the Chinese "stranglehold" on the Indonesian economy. Indonesians have long charged, partly out of envy, that Chinese businessmen have been exploiting the nation for their own profit and the profit of China—a tremendous quantity of goods is smuggled to China from Borneo and other Indonesian islands. Completely ignored are the contributions made by the Chinese to the national economy. This bitterness has not been eased by recollections of the support the Chinese, who suspected what was coming, gave the Dutch in the struggle for independence.

In 1955, following the Afro-Asian Conference in Bandung, Sukarno and Red Chinese Premier Chou En-lai reached an agreement whereby the Indonesian Chinese had to accept Communist Chinese citizenship or apply for Indonesian nationality. No provision was made for a choice of Nationalist Chinese citizenship, although about one-quarter of the Chinese community favored Taiwan. In fact, Sukarno began closing down Nationalist schools and shops when the Sumatra revolt broke out, claiming the Nationalists were supporting the rebels. Peking, to whom about seventy-five percent of the Indonesian Chinese pledged allegiance, was pleased —until Sukarno extended his suppression to some 80,000 rural "foreign" businessmen, worth about $65 million, who were ordered to sell out and move into the cities or out of the country by the end of 1959.

The uprooting of these Chinese, though barely mentioned in the world press, has been one of the tragedies of our time. Wang Chen, who operated a small restaurant he had inherited from his father in the small town of Tjimahi in Western Java, is part of this tragedy. He had to pack up his things and, with his wife, three children, two in-laws, and two nieces, who made up his household, leave the home and restaurant that had been in the family for three generations to live in a refugee barracks in a nearby town. Wang would have liked to move to Djakarta or Bandung instead. But such overcrowded large cities were forbidden to refugees, and anyone who even offered to put the family up was subject to a fine of about $220.

He had thought of simply refusing to move, as officials from the Chinese Embassy urged all Chinese to do; but this would have been useless. He watched how army trucks pulled up in front of friends' homes and literally dragged the occupants out. So he decided to leave peacefully for a town already crowded with refugees and oversupplied with restaurants. How would he make a living? What would happen to his children? Well, there was always Red China. But that was no answer either. He had only just received a letter from a friend who had gone to China. "Don't return to China," read the letter, which had been smuggled out of the country. "The situation here is much worse than in Indonesia." Taiwan didn't seem to offer a future either. It was only a matter of time before it would be swallowed up by the communists.

Thank heaven that he had been able to save up a tidy sum over the years, Wang thought. He had earned over $100 a month, ten times as much as the average Indonesian worker makes, and about equal to President Sukarno's salary. Yes, the Chinese were relatively rich, Wang conceded, but they had worked harder than the Indonesians. And if some Chinese lent money at high rates or speculated in black-market goods, as the Indonesians charged, well, the profit from this was little indeed compared to the vast corruption in the government bureaucracy. But why evaluate the past? It was the future that counted. Yet there seemed to be no future.

If no one else took up Wang Chen's cause, Red China, an expert itself in the art of suppressing, and even massacring, minorities, righteously protested. "Overseas Chinese are now being regarded as nationals of a hostile country and subjected to the most cruel treatment," Foreign Minister Chen Yi bellowed. Sukarno, who had not intended to let his ultranationalism interfere with his friendly policies toward Red China, sent Indonesian Foreign Minister Subandrio to Peking to explain matters. Subandrio returned home blistered with insults.

As relations between the two countries swiftly deteriorated, Indonesia accused Red China, among other things, of using its diplomatic pouch to smuggle anti-Indonesian propaganda material into the country for sale in communist bookstores in violation of the regulation that foreign publications must be cleared through customs. Djakarta was particularly incensed over the illegal import of an issue of *Peiping Review* which said that two Chinese women had been "murdered" in a west Java village. The Indonesians angrily explained that the women were killed accidentally when a group of Chinese rioted. The attorney general ordered seizure of all copies of the publication sent through the mails and banned its sale. The Indonesian government spurned a Peking demand for an apology for the killings.

For the first time Indonesia's Communist Party, under the prodding of the Chinese Embassy, turned against Sukarno. The anti-Chinese law, cried Party Secretary-General Aidit, was "shoddy chauvinism, inspired by racial hatred and a desire for personal gain." But then Aidit went on a trip to Eastern Europe and learned that Khrushchev had arranged to visit Indonesia as Sukarno's guest. The Premier should arrive, Aidit was told, in an atmosphere mellow with friendly coexistence. The Indonesian Red leader was quick to recognize who the top man in the communist world was, whatever changes might come in the future. With the extraordinary flexibility that only the true communist has mastered, Aidit returned home and proclaimed that Sukarno had every right to deal harshly with the local Chinese. After all, weren't they strangling the economy for their own selfish purposes? Actually, he stormed, the whole Chinese community should be deported—the community that was responsible to a considerable degree for the success, and even the very existence, of the Indonesian Communist Party.

Up to that time, Indonesia had been rather reluctant to warm up to the Soviet Union. Diplomatic relations, which had been opposed by the country's Moslem parties, were established only in 1954. Sukarno did not visit Moscow until he had first gone to the United States, which would not support his demands in regard to West New Guinea. When Russia offered him economic aid, the Indonesian parliament stalled before finally agreeing to it. Sukarno had also asked the United States for arms aid—in vain—before he turned to the Soviet Union for it.

But things had changed by the end of 1959. Sukarno invited Khrushchev to Indonesia in the hope of offsetting Red China's hostility within the communist world, from which he needed, as a good neutralist, economic assistance to balance American aid. Khrushchev accepted the invitation in order to cash in on this hostility to strengthen Russia's influence in Asia, just as he had made a special play for Nehru's friendship after Peking's aggression in India. The Soviet Premier wasn't quite ready to turn over Asia to China's sphere of influence. "You must settle your own problems," he told Sukarno on his arrival in February 1960. "And don't worry if anybody complains." Sukarno reveled in this unexpected support. "There are people," he gratefully told a crowd, "who questioned why I have invited Khrushchev, a communist, to Indonesia. I reply: 'Why not, is a communist some sort of a devil?' Khrushchev is just a human; he is not very tall and he is, if I may say so, rather stout."

And at odd moments Khrushchev acted like a human. When Sukarno wrapped a sarong around his ample waist, the Soviet Premier grinningly asked, "Don't you wear pants under these things?" But he also exhibited an arrogance that startled many Indonesians. In Jogjakarta, when asked for his opinion of an exhibition of delicately hand-painted cloth and finely worked Javanese silver, he gruffly commented, "I don't like anything. I don't like anything . . . They represent a bygone day. They cost too much, not only in price but in human life. If we go on like this, there will be no progress. Life will be very expensive. Machines, machines are what you need." Sukarno and other art-loving Indonesians present greeted the outburst with horrified silence.

"That remark," a Western diplomat told me, "may hurt the cause of communism in Indonesia far more than what happened in Hungary or Tibet. No self-respecting Indonesian would sacrifice the joys of beauty and art for a pottage of higher living standards."

But Khrushchev helped to soothe hurt feelings, at least temporarily, by signing an agreement with Sukarno before he left for home granting a credit of $250 million to Indonesia. This credit, extending over a period of seven years and carrying two and a half percent interest, was to help finance, among other projects, a 120,000-kilowatt hydroelectric power station in north Sumatra; two mechanized 40,000-acre rice projects, an iron and steel plant, and more than 400 miles of highway in Borneo; a superphosphate factory in central Java; a steel plant in west Java; a 100,000-capacity sports stadium in Djakarta; and plants producing aluminum and chemicals. Furthermore, Russia had earlier agreed—in 1958—to grant arms credits worth about $200 million dollars for bomber and fighter aircraft, submarines, torpedo boats, and other military equipment. And with the additional $400-million arms aid program obtained by General Nasution on his mission to Moscow in January 1961, the Indonesian army, navy, and air force have become the most powerful in Southeast Asia.

American aid to Indonesia far exceeds the Russian brand, totaling $617 million from independence through 1960. But it is being used largely for far less glamorous and eye-catching projects—the training, for example, of agricultural technicians—in line with the conviction of United States economic experts that Indonesia, like most underdeveloped nations, should concentrate on agricultural rather than industrial development. Thus, the United States again finds itself being outpropagandized by the communists, who, while offering less aid, link each dollar to political gain.

The Soviet Union also maneuvered an edge over the United States in obtaining vital Indonesian raw materials such as rubber as part of the new accord. Moreover, Moscow will be repaid in Indonesian goods or convertible currency, while the United States has agreed to accept repayment partially in Indonesian rupiahs. Nor was Russian assistance offered free of political strings. In the communiqué announcing the new agreement, Indonesia said it "firmly adheres to its active and independent foreign policy, a policy of nonalignment with existing military alliances." Khrushchev's fear that this policy might change in the wake of the bitter quarrel between Indonesia and Red China was allayed. As a final token of friendship, Khrushchev grandly announced that the Soviet Union would build a 200-bed hospital and clinic in Indonesia—absolutely free of charge or strings.

But for all the shine and polish of Soviet-bloc aid, the United States in at least one important case has come out ahead in terms of prestige. In August 1961 the Indonesian army was holding maneuvers near Balikpapan, Borneo, on a twelve-mile completed strip of the highway the Russians are building to link the east, west, and central parts of the island, when the road, together with troops, began sinking into the jungle swamps. Russian equipment being used on the $100-million project, Indonesians complain, is old and unsuited to the terrain. Bulldozers are too small and other earth-moving equipment is inadequate, they say.

On the other hand, Indonesians are marveling at the results of a similar road project that was recently completed by the American Shell Oil Company in East Borneo. American bulldozer operators, working twelve hours a day, seven days a week, pushed the eighty-four-mile highway, which leads to the Shell oil fields in Tanjung, through jungle and swamp at the rate of one and one-fourth miles a day. The Indonesians are little impressed by the Russian argument that the Shell highway was motivated by "capitalistic greed," especially in view of the fact that the Russians pay their workers only twenty-five cents a day, about one third the daily wages of Shell workers. "Frankly, I'd prefer to work for the capitalists," one Indonesian newspaperman who visited both projects said. The Indonesian newspaper, *Berita Indonesia,* complained: "Scores of [Russian] experts are here, but there are still few results."

The same has been said about other Soviet projects, too, even by the government. The super-phosphate plant that was to be built in central Java has been postponed due to the Soviet discovery that the region has little phosphate. On projects financed only in part by Russia, Indonesia has had to pay salaries up to $700 a month to

Soviet technicians and to purchase American machines when Russian equipment has broken down.

Nevertheless Soviet aid, particularly military assistance, has to a considerable extent struck home. On a trip to the Soviet Union in 1961, Sukarno declared at a Kremlin dinner, "We have come to the conclusion that the progress of newly liberated countries is being impeded by capitalism, colonialism, and imperialism. We, that is, the Afro-Asian nations, have to contend with many difficulties, and we carefully study the attitude of other countries toward us. Our eyes are turned, first and foremost, to the Soviet Union because we know that it wants freedom for all nations that have proclaimed independence."

Russian tactics have also affected Red Chinese policy. With both Russia and the Indonesian Communist Party tacitly repudiating Peking's effort to protect local Chinese, and with the relative insignificance of Chinese aid—$27 million from 1953 to 1961—underscored by Soviet generosity, China was in danger of losing all its influence in Indonesia. Its paternalistic interest in the unfortunate refugees thus sharply declined in the latter part of 1960, and Indonesian officials in Peking began to be treated once more like brothers under the skin—leaving true brothers like former restaurant-owner Wang Chen to seek their own way out of the cruel trap in which they were caught.

The Indonesian Communist Party, finding itself in the middle of the Moscow-Peking rivalry in Asia, may in the end suffer as a result. This possibility could be clearly detected in a conversation between Sukarno and Soviet Ambassador Nikolai A. Mikhailov in 1960. The Soviet Union, the Ambassador said, didn't care what became of the Indonesian Communist Party, "but we want to be friends with you." Indonesian communist leaders silently accepted this disavowal of support by those for whom they had made a considerable sacrifice. Having burned their Chinese bridges behind them, though not beyond repair, they now were apparently confronted with a burned Soviet bridge in front of them.

It is perhaps because of such calculated Soviet aloofness, and also because of the need to improve relations with the Chinese in view of China's proximity that the Indonesian Communist Party refrained from supporting Khrushchev's move in late 1961 to expel Albania from the communist camp. At the same time, it did not directly back Mao's position. As Albania is strongly pro-Peking and anti-Moscow, its condemnation would be equivalent to a condemnation of Red China. Aidit shrewdly sat on the fence, declaring that if all Marxist-Leninist parties would observe agreements reached in 1957 and 1960 their unity would become stronger. The Soviet Union and Communist China accuse each other of violating those agreements.

But the difficulty of keeping a balance has by no means diminished the energy with which the Communist Party is pursuing power in Indonesia. One source of this energy lies in the dynamism of Secretary-General Aidit, a Moscow-trained tactician with a tense face and gleaming eyes, who, as the switch on the overseas Chinese issue showed, learned his lessons well. Still in his thirties, Aidit can boast of achievements unexcelled by any other communist leader in noncommunist Asia. A member of the communist-front youth underground during the Japanese occupation, he was briefly imprisoned by the Dutch after the war and elected, on his release, to the PKI central committee as head of the party's propaganda machinery. In 1954, after spending about a year in Red China and Vietnam, he was selected secretary-general of the withered party.

Aidit has done a masterful job of converting the Communist Party from a weak elite group into a mass-membership organization—with the aid of local and Peking Chinese. He has also had the unique opportunity—for a communist leader not in power—of "conferring" with an American President. As a member of the Indonesian United Nations delegation in October 1960, he accompanied Sukarno to the White House when the Indonesian leader was invited to have a chat with President Eisenhower. "President Sukarno introduced me to the American President," Aidit recounted later, "which created some shock on the latter person. President Sukarno sought to ease the shock by saying, 'These are good people.' After having calmed down, President Eisenhower said while addressing me, 'Oh, a democratic communist?' This question I answered with, 'Of course, our party is always democratic. But our democracy is guided democracy.' "

Aidit was also disturbed by evidences of cultural "decadence" in the United States. Before leaving on the trip, he had excitedly asked, "Where is the Statue of Liberty located? . . . Going to the United States is a dream come true. As a youngster I read about your heroes—Washington, Jefferson, and Lincoln. Lenin once said that communism is a 'socialist democracy plus American efficiency.' " But on his return to Indonesia he reported that, quite unlike the situation in the Soviet Union, in visits to more than fifteen New York bookstores clerks, when asked if they had Indonesian history books, "answered 'no,' and some of them even

laughed at me as though I were looking for something odd . . .
What did I see that I wanted to see? During my stay in America I
did not get an opportunity to see the conditions in industries and
agriculture. I could only see the rooms of the U.N. headquarters,
warehouses, bookshops, restaurants, and hotels, skyscrapers and
many cars. There was efficiency at my hotel [the Waldorf-Astoria],
but efficiency ended when you forgot or did not give a sufficient tip."

Aidit rules a vast network of communist cells covering almost
every industry, including the huge tin fields and rubber plantations of Indonesia. Through the PKI, he also oversees a large
number of affiliated organizations for labor, youth, students, peasants, veterans, and women. Labor union membership is two million, of which about half are members of SOBSI. SOBSI's affiliates
in every trade enable it to dominate the Indonesian labor movement, while affiliations among the civil servants provide the PKI
with an important means of penetrating government departments.
Gerwani is the largest and most active women's organization in the
country. Barisan Tani is the biggest and most powerful peasants'
group. Pemuda Rakia, or People's Youth, with a membership of
200,000, is the party's principal youth front and an effective instrument of agitation.

The only well-organized cultural group is communist-sponsored
LEKRA. Also part of the party's cultural program is the publication of five propaganda journals and many books and pamphlets
through a publishing house called Jajasan Pembaruan. A People's
University has been opened in Djakarta with branches in the provincial capitals, catering to over 1,000 students in all, while over
300 more are studying in Sino-Soviet bloc countries, the largest
number from Southeast Asia. Other effective propaganda instruments include friendship societies that sponsor large programs,
cultural exhibitions and receptions for visiting communist dignitaries, and Sino-Soviet radio programs totaling thirty-six hours
weekly.

Even the exotic island of Bali, just east of Java, has not been
immune to the indelicate, culturally leveling influence of communism. This magnificent Hindu island, with its purple mountains,
softly flowing streams lined with palm, coconut, and banana trees,
its thick monkey forests, its terraced rice paddies, its quaint
thatched villages, and its spectacularly colorful religious festivals,
has often been likened to a Garden of Eden. Even more entranc-
ing than the landscape and color are the two million Balinese
people—the lovely bare-breasted women and the rice farmers who

in their spare time turn artist, sculptor, dancer, or musician, using bamboo to make flutes and instruments that resemble the xylophone and the clarinet.

In recent years, however, the Balinese love and artistry of living have been giving way to material worries. As education has increased, young men no longer wish to work in the rice fields with their fathers. They want jobs in offices and factories. But in Bali there are few such jobs available, for there is no real industry. The Reds have taken full advantage of this deepening frustration. They publish one of the two Balinese newspapers and work through Red-dominated unions at the few small printing, canning, textile, and cigarette establishments operating on the island. There must be an end to the old way of living, they say. Too much music and dancing and festivity will not lead to industrialization. Nor is it proper for a proletarian Balinese girl to wear nothing but a sarong and a rose in her hair.

"It's a great tragedy that so-called civilization is finally catching up with Bali," a European artist living on the island told me in his secluded village home as long ago as 1955. "In the towns, one can now find cheap, Western-style houses that are alien to the Balinese setting. And intellectuals, especially the communists, are trying to pressure the women into covering themselves. As a result, you see many women dressed in ugly, misfitting jackets that are completely unsuited to their beauty. Is there no room left on earth for even one small island of paradise?"

A clue to the success of communism in penetrating the remotest mud hut lies in Aidit's belief that communist strategy in Indonesia must be guided less by foreign communist example than by the specific conditions existing in that country. If these conditions had not been ignored in the Stalin postwar era, he feels, the party might never have spun into eclipse. In a speech explaining why he revised Red Chinese infiltration tactics as applied in Indonesia, he said: "One of the basic mistakes of the party was that it tried only to find the similarities between the Chinese revolution and the Indonesian revolution, but it did not try to discover the differences." This country, he said, lacks China's natural suitability to guerrilla warfare and the presence in its rear of a powerful ally like Russia. He made it clear, however, that he favored the application of Peking's Yenan Way in Indonesia as the best method of peacefully infiltrating government organs. In applying the Yenan Way, the Reds, he indicated, should keep in mind that "of the classes in society the peasants are the firmest and most reliable ally of the working class, the [petty] bourgeoisie is an ally, and the [wealthy] bourgeoisie is an ally in certain circumstances and within certain limits."

The party must "develop the progressive forces, unite with the middle-of-the-roaders and isolate the die-hards," Aidit wrote recently. "This means implementing the slogan: 'Improve national front activities. Further isolate the die-hard forces!' Improving these activities means . . . establishing unity between the progressives and all the middle-of-the-roaders, not confining it to their left wing as is the case now."

But an equally important task, Aidit added, was to win over more peasants:

> Party work among the peasants, although we have made some progress, leaves much to be desired. The party holds that there cannot possibly be a genuine national front and "it is impossible to talk of the leading role of the Communist Party in this front unless we organize and lead the masses of the peasants." The party has organized what we have called the "going down" movement with the implementation of the "three togethers" by the party leaders [to work, live, and eat with the peasants]. This movement has given us a clearer picture of agrarian relations and the still deeply rooted feudal survivals in the villages. It has made clear also that the revolutionary peasant movement must be based on the agricultural laborers and the poor peasants, and that with the leadership of the communists they can become the close ally of the working class in the struggle against all enemies of the working people.

The communists have concentrated indeed on the "going down" and "three togethers" movement—one reason why so many huts in so many villages, particularly in Java, are smeared with communist symbols. Not even the fact that Islam is deeply rooted in most villages has stemmed the Red tide. In most Arab countries the communists have made considerable inroads into intellectual and urban ranks because of a diminishing interest in Islam among these groups. But penetration of the still intensely religious peasantry has been more difficult. In Indonesia the peasants have responded to communism without, in most cases, relinquishing their spiritual fervor. For the Reds, completely ignoring the atheistic aspects of communism, have been able to convince a large proportion of them that Marxism is actually little more than an extension of Islam. "You can be a good communist and a good Mohammedan at the same time," the peasants are told, much as their ancestors were told by the early communists that Islam was evil. "We support *Pantjasila*."

Pantjasila means the five principles first proclaimed by Sukarno in 1945, shortly before Indonesia's declaration of independence. The philosophy of *Goton Rojong* that characterizes Sukarno's "guided democracy" is supposedly rooted in these five principles—nationalism, humanitarianism, representative government, social justice, and belief in one god.

The wide acceptance of communist claims by the peasantry is consistent with the uniquely flexible and dynamic nature of Islam in Indonesia, which is flavored with centuries-old religious beliefs, as well as with later Hindu and Buddhist influences. Never disciplined by a central national church or subject to governmental regulation, Indonesian Islam has always been open to change and new ideas. For example, in the early 1900's its leaders adopted many elements of the modernist Islamic movement that was growing in Egypt, which incorporated into Moslem teachings the need for social and political reform. With the communists appearing to preach the very same thing, the peasant sees little contradiction between his faith and communism.

In fact, many have been led to believe that communism has much in common with the primitive kind of collectivist system under which almost the entire rural population of Indonesia lived until a few decades ago. At one time, all land belonged to the community. The system was modified in the last century to permit peasant families to hold a kind of permanent lease on their land, but *adat* law, or custom, provided that such land could be sold only with the consent of the village. If a family moved away without obtaining such consent, the land was taken over by the community after a certain period. Not much communally owned land remains today, but the principle is still part of Indonesian tradition—dovetailing, at least in communist propaganda, with the Red conception of social collectivism.

The communists have been slick not only in their "going down" movement, but in frustrating efforts by opponents to use similar propaganda methods. An American official of the United States Information Administration, William Otto McClarrin, told me in his office in Jogjakarta, the heart of central Java's communist belt: "We can't reach these people with our literature, because they can't read. All they know about America is what the communists tell them. There's only one answer. We've got to go among them, talk with them, be kind to them, like helping them fix a bicycle or showing the women faster ways of doing their housework. We've got to show them movies not about how well off Americans are—that only makes them envious—but maybe documentaries teaching them how to grow more corn per square acre. And we should entertain them, too—God knows, they don't have the opportunity to have much fun. In other words, we've got to show these people that we're decent and warm and that we care about them. Only when they believe this will they take communist propaganda with a grain of salt."

McClarrin, a tall, powerfully built Negro and former official at Howard University in Washington, whose example other USIA officials might do well to emulate, began putting some of his ideas into practice. A one-man Peace Corps, he went out to the villages with an interpreter and talked to the people. He showed them Mickey Mouse films and films about crop growing. He staged free USO-type shows in the town whenever any talented Americans came through, particularly artists sponsored by the State Department who ordinarily performed only in the large cities. McClarrin made so many friends that he soon became known throughout the area as "Uncle Bill." At one open-air show starring an American Indian who did rope tricks and war dances, the crowd of thousands, when the show was over, chanted deliriously, "Uncle Bill, Uncle Bill," demanding that McClarrin, who had introduced the performer, come out and take a final bow. Then hundreds followed him to his hotel, asking for his autograph or wanting to chat with him.

"You see what I mean?" McClarrin said. "We can win over these people if we give them our hearts."

The local communists apparently realized this, too. Searching for some way to get rid of Uncle Bill, who single-handedly was threatening the whole communist propaganda program in the area, they finally discovered that the USIA had not received formal permission to establish an office in Jogjakarta. Taking advantage of a technical administrative error, they demanded that the office be closed. Sufficient pressure was exerted on the central Indonesian government to prevent its coming to USIA's aid. Uncle Bill thus had to shut down the office and leave—"and just when we're beginning to make headway."

If communist infiltration techniques in Indonesia have proved highly successful, a number of barriers still block the Red path to power. National disunity has given the communists an opportunity to tighten their hold on Sukarno and increase their influence in the national government, but it has also weakened their chances of imposing their control on the whole archipelago should they come to power. If they were to take over the central government today, the chances are they could maintain effective authority only in Java and a few other islands. Certainly their rule would not be accepted in most of Sumatra, the Celebes, and many other regions which are reluctant to obey even Sukarno, whose tremendous national prestige is largely responsible for keeping the nation from disintegrating completely.

Most peasants in Sumatra and in some of the other territories, more isolated from new international currents and therefore habituated to a more orthodox Islam than the Javanese, have shown far less inclination to swallow communist propaganda. Moreover, as the communists are so strongly entrenched in Java, many other regions fear that that island, which is already being favored by the government economically, would receive an even greater share of the national income if the Reds were in power. This view is particularly prevalent among army officers who come from the various outlying islands, but is also widespread among the people in these places.

During a trip I made through the jungles of central Sumatra, the native bus in which I was riding made a brief stopover in one village, giving me an opportunity to meet some grass-roots Sumatrans. As soon as I stepped off the bus, I was surrounded by about twenty fierce-looking youths dressed in ragged Western clothing. Most of them were armed with rusty rifles and I was a bit apprehensive about their intentions—until one of them explained that they had just returned from an unsuccessful hunt for a man-eating tiger that had dragged away and devoured a village child the night before.

"You're American?" one of them said in passable English. "There haven't been Americans through here for many years. So happy to see you."

They had learned English in school, I was told. They had also learned some American history.

"We like Americans," the spokesman declared with a grin. "You throw out British imperialists just like we throw out Dutch."

And what about the communists? I asked. "They no good," came the reply. "We very good Moslems. No good Moslems like communists. Americans very nice though. Please stay here few days so we can practice English. You can stay my home."

He pointed to a clay house half hidden behind a wall of thick tropical growth. It was an attractive structure with a concave-shaped thatched roof of graceful Sumatran design, with the two ends swooping sharply upward. I turned down the invitation and continued on my bus tour, but not without a sense of deep gratitude, particularly after having experienced rather cool welcomes in the communist-influenced Javanese villages I had passed through.

Only much later did I fully realize how great an impression an American—or any foreigner—can make in a remote, isolated village unaccustomed to receiving strangers from a far-off country, and what such an impression could mean in terms of influencing judgment about the country from which the stranger came. Igor Oganesoff, correspondent for the *Wall Street Journal,* wrote me from Indonesia about a year after my visit there: "There I was in the middle of the Sumatran jungle when suddenly a youth ran toward me screaming, 'Don Koortzman! Don Koortzman! You are American like him? Do you know him?' You could have knocked me over with a palm leaf."

National disunity is not the only double-edged sword as far as the communists are concerned. So is the concept of guided democracy that they have so enthusiastically embraced. On the one hand, this system has eliminated all anticommunist political parties from the scene, at least in a legal sense. But on the other, the communists' potential influence may have been curtailed through the reduction of the number of parliamentary seats that are open to political parties under the current set-up; for the Reds could probably outpoll other parties in any election and win a greater share of the seats in a legitimate parliament.

A further disadvantage is the fact that the army, though it may be collaborating to some extent with the communists in the common effort to grab West New Guinea, is still basically anticommunist and probably wouldn't stand idly by while the Reds took over the government. Significantly, when the communist newspaper, *Harian Rakjat,* published Aidit's speech announcing, shortly after Nasution's return from Moscow, that national unity had finally been achieved, the army suspended the publication. While the army has only fifteen members in the parliament, as compared to about seventy for the communists and their followers, the army command helps to select candidates to represent functional groups in the body. The Reds wield considerable influence, too, in the President's Supreme Advisory Council, the principal policy-making body in the country, but have only two members in the cabinet, in which army leaders can veto the execution of Red-sponsored measures.

Sukarno has wanted the army as a kind of backstop should the communists get out of hand. But to the President's regret, it has turned out to be more than that. Before General Nasution's trip to

Moscow in January 1961, the army actively tried to suppress communist activities and, despite Sukarno's intervention, succeeded to a considerable degree—thanks largely to the forceful personality of Nasution. The General helped to lead the post-World War II struggle against the Dutch, crushed the Red revolt at Madiun in 1948, and then became army chief of staff. But he was removed from this position in 1952 for joining a group of colonels who tried to force Sukarno—unsuccessfully—to dissolve parliament and become a dictator as the only alternative to political chaos. But when trouble started brewing in Sumatra in 1955, Sukarno called Nasution back in order to counter the rebellious elements—Nasution being an influential Sumatran. The General pledged that no religious, military, or political group would take over the government by force while he ran the army. His anticommunist attitude is rooted to some extent in his deep belief in Islam. Sometimes he calls a break in a staff meeting if it is time to turn toward Mecca and pray.

Wisely, Nasution has taken some positive steps to win over the peasants from communism, ordering his soldiers to help improve life in the villages. Officers and sergeants, trying to overcome a reputation for corruption and arrogance, are teaching peasants to read and write, dig irrigation ditches, purify water, and build bamboo fish traps.

Under Nasution the army, before the West Irian issue led to greater military tolerance of the communists, issued orders banning the painting of slogans on walls and the display of non-Indonesian flags at celebrations or demonstrations; forbidding delegations to present protests directly to foreign embassies such as those which visited the United States Embassy in 1958 to denounce American "intervention" in Indonesia's civil strife; prohibiting interference "by whatever quarter" in the operations of the country's fuel installations after Secretary-General Aidit had told the United States Ambassador that "unless the United States stopped giving aid to the rebels," the communists would call for action against American economic interests in Indonesia, including the oil field installations of Caltex Pacific Oil Company and Standard-Vacuum; and stipulating that only Latin and Arabic characters can be used in publications, thus barring the printing and distribution of Chinese-language publications and the import of Red Chinese propaganda.

When the communists, frozen for a while out of cabinet positions, publicly criticized the cabinet, the army retorted that behind the communists' "words and tactics is concealed a strategy that is not in conformance with our national aspirations." The communists are attempting to play the army off against the President in a bid to destroy stability, the army said, "because the existence of stability would mean a loss of the group's breeding ground." It would constitute high treason if the Reds sought to exploit the sufferings of the Indonesian people for its own advantage. The nation, added the army, should not be hoodwinked by "cheap mottoes" and "cheap agitations." It then suspended publication of several communist newspapers, sponsored mass anticommunist rallies in Borneo and Sumatra, repossessed Dutch properties from SOBSI labor squads that had seized them, arrested hundreds of Red-led rubber workers in northern Sumatra for striking in violation of a martial law decree, and jailed communists in a central Javan village for possessing arms illegally.

Sukarno, decrying those "inflicted with the disease of communist phobia," has tried to come to the rescue of the communists in many of these cases in order to restore the balance of power between the two forces. The odd relationship between Sukarno, the army, and the communists was demonstrated at the PKI Sixth National Congress held in September 1959. The army had agreed to the meeting only after several cancellations, but even so, placards were banned and the party had to submit detailed session-by-session reports to the army on all speeches made. The guest speaker? Sukarno. Standing under enormous pictures of Lenin, Mao, and himself, he told the cheering audience:

> In the beginning, Aidit came to me in my palace and asked me, "Bung (Brother) Karno, there's a ban on political activities, but could the PKI within a short time hold a Congress?" I said, "Yes, have your Congress. But after August first" . . . And now that Congress has taken place and Aidit has asked me to attend this reception. And here I am in your midst, welcomed with love as a comrade for which I express my gratitude . . . I may be the only President in the world, the only President of a nonsocialist state attending a communist congress.

Sukarno's effort to balance his two co-governing forces appears to have paid off to a large extent as a result of the storm over West Irian. He would not in any case oppose the army too openly for fear of a coup. On the other hand the army, which is as administratively inefficient and probably as corrupt as most other government organs, has displayed little inclination to burden itself with complete power—particularly in view of Sukarno's overwhelming popularity.

The Reds, too, have been afraid to defy the army, fearing a repetition of the 1948 Madiun disaster. As the nation's strongest political force, possessed of the desire but not the means to achieve power at the moment, they feel they are too far ahead to take any unnecessary risks. Aidit has been under pressure from some of his lieutenants, especially Deputy Secretary-General Mohammad Lukman, to toughen the party's stand toward its enemies, including the army when necessary, and become more militantly revolutionary. But nobody favors a showdown, particularly now that the army is co-operating with the Reds. In any event, the communists feel, they can afford to bide their time. They are gradually infiltrating sectors of the army and local village guards. They have already won the support of some air force leaders. The navy, while still uncommitted, might also back them. Most important of all, in the long run, they are winning new peasant adherents daily. Why rush things when time is on their side?

XVI

THE PHILIPPINES:

ANATOMY OF A MIRACLE

The Philippines today are probably less vulnerable to communism than any other country in Southeast Asia. Yet, after World War II no nation in the region seemed riper for absorption by the communist bloc. The explanation for this remarkable political recovery could hold at least a partial key to the salvation of other threatened Afro-Asian states.

The communists in the Philippines, as in many Southeast Asian nations, emerged from World War II as a popular force because of their heroic guerrilla struggle against the Japanese armies that occupied the country early in the conflict. But they enjoyed even greater immediate advantages than their counterparts in other Asian states. Whereas the French returned to Vietnam after the war and held off the communist offensive for several years, American liberation forces were evacuating the Philippines within months after V-J Day—with the granting of independence to that country, which the United States had controlled since the turn of the century. And whereas the Reds who tried to take over Burma by force in the postwar years were fatally split, the Philippine communists were united and well organized and had plenty of arms obtained from American surplus stockpiles. These communists benefited most of all from the hatred of millions of landless, impoverished people for their weak, corrupt government and the demoralized national army that often intimidated and brutalized them.

But the Reds, who expected to rule the Philippines by 1949, when they had reached a peak of strength, began their swift decline in that same year. For this they have one man to blame, a simple peasant who developed into one of the greatest leaders in modern Asian history—President Ramón Magsaysay. When Magsaysay died in 1957, the communist threat had been eliminated, and the Philippines were well on the way toward political maturity and economic reform.

"Magsaysay was our Abraham Lincoln," a taxi driver told me in Manila, the sprawling, sun-baked Philippine capital, shortly after the President's death. "He was one of us. He understood us. He ruled with his heart." A young leftist student I met in a village coffeehouse offered an even greater tribute: "It's Magsaysay's fault that the communists are not running the country today. He used all kinds of devious tactics to win the people over."

What were Magsaysay's "devious tactics?" He brought honesty to the government, gave land to the landless, instilled self-respect in the army, and converted thousands of pro-Reds into useful, democratic citizens. He deprived the communists of the food that had nourished them. Never in any country has this process been carried out as successfully as in the Philippines, though social and economic evils that have returned to some extent since his death have fostered a certain amount of communist infiltration in political, labor, and cultural organizations in the last few years.

Communism got its start in the Philippines in 1924 when an American far-leftist labor leader, William Janequette, invited the blossoming Philippine labor unions to participate in the first Congress of Oriental Transportation Workers, a communist-organized meeting to be held in Canton, China. Five Philippine delegates attended. Their leader, Domingo Ponce, was so impressed by communist arguments that when he returned to Manila he set up, with the help of a few supporters, a Philippine secretariat which he placed under the direction of the Communist Third International. Members infiltrated labor unions and peasant groups in the next few years and finally, in 1928, organized a communist-oriented Workers Party, with a fiery, rugged labor leader named Crisanto Evangelista, who had been indoctrinated in Moscow, at its head. Two years later, as party ranks swelled, Evangelista saw no need to disguise his organization's true nature any longer and launched the Philippine Communist Party.

The party had an explosive birth. Mass meetings and rallies were immediately called, protesting against the poverty of worker and peasant. Propaganda leaflets were showered over the country.

Matters came to a head on May Day 1931, seven months after the party's inauguration. The government had at first granted the party a permit to hold a parade on Manila's outskirts and then had revoked it when it appeared that violence might break out. But when a huge crowd had gathered anyway, Evangelista suggested to the police officer in charge that he address the people and explain to them that the parade could not be held. The officer agreed.

Then Evangelista, raising his fist in the communist salute while the people shouted *"Mabuhay!"*—a cheer of approval—cried: "Comrades, or brethren, the municipal president, Mr. Aquino, has allowed us to hold the parade, but for reasons unknown to me, the permit has been revoked. This shows that the big ones are persecuting and oppressing us, who are small, which they have no right to do." Someone in the audience shouted, "Let's fight them until death." As Evangelista began again, "My heart bleeds . . ." policemen grabbed him and other agitators and arrested them, turning a hose on the crowd when it tried to intervene.

Evangelista and twenty-six other communist leaders were charged with sedition and incitement to revolt, and twenty, including Evangelista, were convicted and sent to prison. The Communist Party was outlawed and the Supreme Court confirmed the ban in 1932. The Reds went underground, but they were not without friends above ground. With the communists out of the legal picture, the small left-wing Socialist Party, under a lawyer and intellectual named Pedro Abad Santos, expanded enormously. Santos and his assistants, including Luis Taruc and Casto Alejandrino, denied they were communists. The Socialist Party, unlike the Communist Party, was a mass, and not an elite, organization, they pointed out. Furthermore, they said, they believed in parliamentary government.

The communists themselves exhibited disdain for them—not because they were too much to the right, but because they were "leftist deviationists." The "socialists" were far more violent in their methods than the communists ever had been. They murdered landlords, burned rice and sugar-cane fields, killed work animals, and forced people to join their organization. Violence, the Reds thought, had to be controlled and directed according to international communist rules to be effective. The unplanned, premature class war provoked by the socialists, they pointed out, had led landlords to establish their own organizations which set up uniform practices in payments to tenants, agreed to accept only tenants who could show reasonable cause for having left their previous landlord, and mustered votes for landlord candidates in elections.

But the socialists were clever. When they were forbidden to hold rallies of their own, they "infiltrated" other large gatherings, including church meetings. After services, one of them would stand and ask questions of the presiding clergyman about why the people were so impoverished, and then launch into a propaganda harangue.

After the United States had granted a considerable degree of autonomy to the Philippines in 1934, the government's policy on communism softened. James Allen, an American communist, persuaded President Manuel Quezon, the country's first chief executive, to free the Reds who had been imprisoned in 1931. The last to be pardoned, Evangelista, emerged from prison in 1938. With Allen acting as a catalyst, the communist and socialist leaders met and, despite some dissent from democratic elements among the socialists, agreed to merge their parties into an expanded Communist Party, with Evangelista president and Santos vice-president.

These two men by no means dominated the party. Other younger men also made their influence felt. One was Dr. Vicente Lava, an aristocratic chemistry professor at the University of the Philippines and a graduate of New York's Columbia University where he spent much of his time reading Marx and Lenin. Another was his pupil, Luis Taruc, also a man of great charm and intelligence. The two men helped to recruit cadres by organizing parties at the homes of literary figures in Manila to which members of the intelligentsia were invited for discussions on literature. Politics were never brought up. The idea was to permit Lava and Taruc to observe which young men would be easiest to win over to the communist movement. Taruc, who came from a poor farm family, won many peasant followers as well.

From 1938 to 1941 the Reds avoided violence and concentrated on political infiltration. They wooed all groups left of center and became the kernel of a Popular Front Party under whose label they were able to run candidates in elections held in 1938 and 1940, despite the fact that the party was technically outlawed. One American-educated communist who had worked in a Chicago post office actually became a mayor. But the party confined its activities almost entirely to the province of Pampanga on the main island of Luzon, where absentee landlords owned much of the land and their tenants were greatly oppressed, some burdened with perpetual and growing debts originally incurred generations back.

The outbreak of World War II gave the communists their first real chance to weld their ranks into a powerful national force. Lava, who had become party secretary-general, had ready, by the

time the Japanese entered Manila, a plan for a Barrio (Village)
United Defense Corps that would maintain order, prevent looting,
deprive the Japanese of the local harvests, and supply communist
guerrilla forces. Such forces, the Reds decided, would not be used,
however, to support Filipino-American efforts to resist the Japanese invasion, which they considered could not be prevented. Although Supreme Allied Commander General Douglas MacArthur
had refused a request by Santos that the United States supply the
Red guerrillas with arms, a communist-controlled fighting force
was established in central Luzon.

On March 29, 1942, deep in the steamy forest of this area, the
communist leaders and their supporters, dressed in tattered civilian
clothing, some without even shoes, met to establish formally a
People's Army against the Japanese, or Hukbong Magpalayang
Bayan—whose members were to become known simply as the
Huks. The two top Red leaders, Evangelista and Santos, were absent; they had been captured by the Japanese. Taruc thus became
the Supremo, the Huk leader. His second in command was Casto
Alejandrino, who came from a middle-class, landowning family.
Lava was at the jungle meeting, too, as an adviser, while another
participant was Lino Dizon, a gaunt, one-eyed old peasant organizer who wrote impressive poetry when he wasn't writing propaganda.

Some of those present were not communists, but simply wanted
to fight the Japanese. Such a man was Bernardo Poblette, a moderate socialist who had come with his own band of fighters. And such
a woman was Filipa Culala, alias Dayang-Dayang, about whom
Taruc wrote, "Most men were afraid of her. She feared nothing."
She had come to the meeting also with her own unit of guerrillas;
about one hundred, who, a few hours before, had killed in an
ambush almost an equal number of Japanese soldiers. Little did
she realize that the organization she was helping to form would,
within a few months, liquidate her for refusing to follow party
discipline. She was shot by a Huk firing squad.

As the war progressed, the Huks grew stronger. Short of arms at
first, they retrieved a large supply from the smoldering battlefields
of Bataan and other regions. A Chinese colonel from the Red
Chinese army trained the guerrillas, using as a training manual Ed-
gar Snow's *Red Star Over China*. The Huks actually controlled
many areas, and refined and extended the blueprint for civilian
authority drawn up by Lava at the beginning of the war. They collected taxes, administered justice, and conducted Marxist classes.
As courageous Filipa Culala had learned, supporters who would

not obey party orders were branded as "traitors" and shot. The Huks themselves claimed after the war that they had killed 25,000 people—of whom only 5,000 were Japanese.

The Huks would very seldom co-operate with other noncommunist guerrilla forces that might dilute their own glory. They represented only a small element in the total Philippine resistance movement—one of the most important guerrilla armies was led by a man named Magsaysay—but they were convinced that if they remained militant and maintained their separate identity they could take control of the country when the war was over.

As soon as American troops landed in the Philippines to liberate the country they had lost at the start of the war, the Huks appointed civilian officials in the areas which they controlled, hoping to keep them in their positions once peace was established and thus pave the way for a communist takeover of the nation. But with the Japanese surrender and the accession to the presidency of Sergio Osmeña—President Quezon had died in exile during the war— the central government refused to recognize Huk political claims and appointed its own provincial and local officials. Meanwhile, American authorities arrested Taruc, Alejandrino, and other Huk leaders for murdering unco-operative Filipinos. The communist conspiracy was momentarily frustrated.

But not for long. For the Reds were given every opportunity to forge ahead with their plans by the failure of both American and Filipino officials to take the Huk threat seriously. Instead of eliminating this threat before leaving the Philippines on their own, the United States decided to grant independence to that country on July 4, 1946, less than a year after V-J Day. The situation was made to order for the Huks. The economy was in chaos. Public buildings and schools had been reduced to ruins. Roads had been destroyed. Many of the country's resources had vanished. Money was scarce. The people, impoverished and miserable, were ready to listen to anybody who promised them a new and better life.

The Americans, before they departed, unwittingly encouraged the Huks to get on with their conspiracy. First, they released the imprisoned communist leaders, then provided them with the means to overcome virtually all resistance by leaving behind without proper controls a tremendous store of arms, food, construction materials, and other military supplies that had been intended for use in an invasion of Japan if it had been necessary. These supplies were to be turned over to the Philippine government for sale to private purchasers, the proceeds to be used for reconstruction purposes. But most of this surplus material disappeared almost overnight in an orgy of graft and outright thievery that lined the pockets of government officials and their friends and filled the jungle armories of the Huks. Items which finally trickled into government hands were in most cases useless, for they had been stripped of removable fixtures and materials.

The Huks benefited from a double advantage: the people, already demoralized from the effects of war, began to despise their government for its uninhibited greed and corruption, while the Huks now had enough arms and supplies to carry on a major military campaign against the government.

The communists profited from other American mistakes, too. The United States had pulled out before making sure that Filipino soldiers were given their back pay. As a result, usually only those men who agreed to pay off finance officers and other corrupt army officials, or promised to work for the election of certain military figures with political ambitions, received the money coming to them. To many soldiers who had spent years living and fighting like animals in the forest so that their country might be free this treatment came as a bitter blow. Vowing vengeance against the government, many joined, or at least supported, the Huks.

The army was further demoralized by the granting of promotions on the basis of political favoritism, and was rendered nearly useless when only 37,000 out of 132,000 men were retained after the war, with 24,000 of this number given the status of military policemen under the Interior rather than the Defense Department. It was their job to deal with the Huk danger, though the Huks themselves constituted a full-fledged guerrilla army. Nor did the Huks have a difficult time turning the people against the national army and police. Many of the policemen, in particular, had collaborated with the Japanese, while others were known for their opposition to peasant movements in Luzon and often mistreated the people, even shelling villages that shielded Huks.

Not only the military but civilian administrators as well bled and abused the people. A peasant who might ask the government for some medicine for his sick child or for some other minor favor would be sent from official to petty official, having to pay off each with his meager funds before reaching the person who could help him. Then he was helped reluctantly or gruffly told that no aid could be given. But the Huks would learn about his trouble and give him the medicine he needed, and even pay for the funeral if the sick child died, for the father's money was most likely all spent on the bribes demanded by dishonest bureaucrats.

The Huks adroitly exploited popular dissatisfaction through a communist organization ponderously called the Political, Economic, Intelligence, and Research Association (PEIRA), which flooded the islands with copies of a mimeographed newspaper *Titis* (*Flame*), a magazine *Kalayaan* (*Freedom*), and inflammatory pamphlets.

It wasn't difficult to stir up a spirit of revolt, particularly since rebellion has long been a Philippine tradition. Filipinos have engaged in uprisings against injustice since the seventeenth century. They revolted against the old feudal Jesuit clergy, against greedy landlords, and against Spanish rule, which finally ended when Spain chose to surrender the country to the United States as the only alternative to defeat at the hands of the native Philippine army. All revolts invariably failed, but never before had there been a revolutionary movement with the purposefulness and organization of the Huks.

Not all Huk supporters were the resentful victims of government wrongdoing. The Reds also found many backers among people who saw them as courageous war heroes, and among youths who had become so dependent on the law of the jungle during the war that they found it difficult to take their place as responsible citizens in a peaceful society. They had forgotten the meaning of the traditional strong Philippine sense of obligation to one's neighbors, and they were attracted to Huk promises of adventure, power, and loot. Outright criminals, too, were drawn to the Huks, who gave them protection and expedited their banditry. Some Filipinos became Huks because they or their families were threatened if they refused, others because of a sense of loyalty to Huk friends.

Significantly, few people joining the Huks developed hostility toward the United States despite all the anti-American propaganda to which they were subjected. Most Filipinos well realized the United States had begun preparing them for self-government from the beginning of their rule, giving them suffrage and other civil rights, education, and political stability, however corrupt some politicians were. America's role in liberating the Philippines from the Japanese and its granting of independence to the country immediately after the war further added to Philippine regard for the United States. Even charges that the United States was economically imperialistic made little impression on the people, though the Payne-Aldrich Tariff Law which was in effect until after independence permitted the United States to flood the Philippines with duty-free consumer products, preventing that country from developing an important industrial economy of its own.

Few Filipinos joined the Huks for ideological reasons. Taking a leaf out of Mao Tse-tung's book, the Huk leaders proclaimed themselves simply "agrarian reformers" and champions of the oppressed. To avoid offending nationalist feelings their links with Moscow were ignored, and in deference to the strong hold of Catholicism on most Filipinos, the atheistic aspect of Marxism was likewise ignored. The time for serious indoctrination would come, the chiefs believed, when they controlled the country. And the only way they could achieve such control was to win over the people through any means possible—lies, deceit, threats, or kindness. Nevertheless many peasants, particularly young people, in the villages controlled by Huks were submitted to considerable brain washing. The Huk educational program offered the following subjects:

Primary schools: resolutions of Communist Party central committee conferences, the Communist Party, recruitment and organization of the liberation movement, intelligence network.

Intermediate schools: history of the Communist Party, present economic system, present state of the government, history of the peasant and labor movement, new democracy, bookkeeping and accounting.

High schools: dialectical materialism, political economy, imperialism, the state and revolution, importance of the Communist Party, political strategy and tactics, military strategy and tactics, proletarian morals, principles and techniques of teaching, new documents.

Advanced school: dialectical materialism, national problems, agrarian problem, women problems, evading tactics.

The Huks even operated "Stalin Universities" for the training of cadres.

The Communist Party itself was an elite organization to which only the ideologically dedicated Huks belonged. All party members were organized in cells of three to five members. Like Red cells throughout the world, these little groups met frequently for ideological discussions and harrowing sessions of self- and mutual criticism. Despite the effort to indoctrinate some, the situation was not yet propitious to force all Huks to be good communists. But all were, as during the war, subject to iron discipline. One captured Huk document bluntly warned: "Those who surrender but do not betray the Huks will be caught and tried by court-martial. If they are not guilty of betrayal, they will be sentenced to hard labor. If they refuse to rejoin the Huks and refuse to comply with orders, they will be killed. Any who betray the Huks will be killed immediately."

The Huks split the Philippines into ten military zones, called *recos,* each of which operated an independent supply and intelligence system and was commanded by several party leaders, who were divided among a number of one hundred-man squadrons. Through their puppet National Peasants Union, the regional leaders organized peasants in supply sections to facilitate the collection of part of the regional rice harvest, as Mao had done in China. They trained men in administrative duties and put them in authority in areas under their control. They collected taxes, thus supplementing income contributed by supporters and obtained through train robberies, bank raids, and confiscation. An American communist, William Pomeroy, who helped to organize the Huks' education and propaganda program, described in an unpublished book the headquarters village of one *reco:*

> Here was centered the National Educational Department of the Communist Party, under Peregrino Taruc, brother of Huk Supremo Luis Taruc. Here was the headquarters of the Communist Party's regional committee Number Four, which embraced the region covered by the provinces of Laguna, Quezon, Batangas, and Cavite. Half an hour's walking distance away was the headquarters of Casto Alejandrino, head of the party's military department. Also in that camp a large force of organizers and soldiers was assembling under Mariano Balgos, number three Filipino communist, in preparation for the long expansion march south into the Bicol Provinces.

> A *reco* school was in progress and at night, in the still air, the students could be heard singing and declaiming in regular cultural programs. A mimeograph machine in the office building clicked away all day long and into the night, turning out leaflets, documents, and newspapers. There was no shortage of supplies: a "dugout" was stacked to the roof with paper, stencils, and ink, and more kept arriving steadily from the towns, slung on the backs of Huk soldiers in the burlap cargo sacks that were the most distinguishing feature in the mountains. It could be said, in fact, that the ordinary Huk soldier literally carried the revolutionary movement on his back, uncomplainingly, in the worst of weather, over the worst of terrain.

> Couriers, mostly young girls and boys chosen for their inconspicuousness, came and went in a steady stream, from the city, from the party district committees and section committees in the provinces, from the field commands of the Huk army. At times, they bore with them, in the woven *bayongs* (palm leaf sacks) of the ordinary marketer, as much "mail" as a letter carrier would haul about in the city. Each time the couriers or the soldiers went

out, on missions or supply trips, it meant anywhere from one day to one week of walking each way, through steep and often treacherous mountain trails.

The Huk leadership, before setting out on a serious military campaign, experimented to see how far it could get through legal methods. Hardly was Taruc released from prison by the Americans than he and other Reds announced their candidacy in the 1946 national elections. Taruc was the only communist candidate to win a seat in the lower house. But in view of Huk terrorist activities and the prewar ban on communist political activity, which had never been lifted, house members voted to deprive Taruc of his seat. The wily Huk leader headed for the mountains. The matter was settled. The Huks, now formally called the People's Liberation Army, would come to power through civil war.

The Huk guerrillas, operating mainly in central Luzon, grew bolder day by day, assassinating many local officials in broad daylight. President Manuel Roxas, who had succeeded Osmeña, thundered that his forces would wipe out the Huks in two months. His soldiers, poorly trained, underpaid, and demoralized, were sent to do the job—and went on a rampage. They terrorized villagers in their search for Huks, beat them, bombed their communities. Soon the Huks had the sympathy, if not the outright support, of almost the whole Luzon countryside.

Failing to root out the communists by force, the government switched tactics and appealed for a peaceful solution to the Huk problem. The Huk leaders agreed to a three-months' truce, and representatives of both sides began touring villages together to see that the truce was kept. But the Huk representatives used this opportunity for communist demagogy, and one of them disappeared, bringing communist accusations against the government of kidnap and murder. Fighting broke out again, more vicious than ever.

With the death of Roxas in early 1948, Elpidio Quirino came to power and reverted to a policy of conciliation. The government contacted the Huk leaders through the offices of the *Manila Chronicle,* and negotiations were conducted by Taruc and the President's brother, Antonio Quirino, who agreed to a general amnesty for all Huks if they would disarm. Taruc, after some hesitation, approved the arrangement and accepted an invitation to return to Manila, where he was greeted by the President in regal manner. He was even given back his seat in congress. But when the government asked the Huks to disarm now that peace had been established, Taruc replied that they would not do so until reforms had been carried out. He was not impressed by the President's argument that such reforms might take years to complete. Taruc, with his back congressional pay in his pocket, vanished into the hills again, and battle was resumed.

The Huks, already exhilarated by the communist takeover in China in 1948, enjoyed their biggest boost during the 1949 elections in which Quirino and his Liberal Party beat José Laurel and the Nationalist Party—not because Quirino won, but because the election was so crooked. Hundreds were killed by goon squads hired by each side as they came out to vote, and thousands more were intimidated and remained away from the polls rather than risk their lives. Ballot boxes were stuffed, and in two provinces more votes were counted than there were registered voters. Flowers, birds, and dead people had somehow cast ballots. The election travesty, moreover, was followed by corruption unprecedented even in the immediate postwar years. Politicians and their friends and relatives of high government officials made fortunes overnight selling political favors, import licenses, and American property. Meanwhile, many government workers, including teachers, went unpaid for months.

As the people's faith in democratic government plummeted and the economy tottered on the brink of collapse, the Huks intensified their military campaign, certain they would be in the saddle by 1951 at the latest. They extended their hold even to the remotest of the Philippine Islands. Sensing the government's desperation, the Huks, in their wild fling to grab power, abandoned all pretense at kindness toward the people. Gangster elements came to the fore. They burned down unco-operative villages, murdered, raped, kidnaped. In one particularly horrifying atrocity, a band of Huks attacked a hospital in the capital city of Tarlac Province and slaughtered more than fifty patients and nurses, gouging out the eyes of some of them while they were still alive. "Nothing the Japanese had done to us was as senselessly cruel," Carlos P. Romulo, former Philippine Ambassador to the United States, wrote of Huk terror. As panic spread, thousands of peasants fled into the towns, leaving their unharvested crops behind.

Fortunately for the Huks, their brutality was often matched by that of the government forces who sought to destroy them. After soldiers had killed many innocent civilians, an army major was moved to write in a newspaper: "The increase in the number of dissident elements and their sympathizers in central Luzon during the past few years may largely be attributed to the misconduct of officers and men who have been entrusted with enforcement of law and order." Quirino himself threatened to court-martial any soldiers guilty of such misconduct.

The Huks set up a secret headquarters in Manila, the "Polit-bureau-in," complementing their "Politbureau-out," which directed the rebellion in the field. Its job was to prepare for the takeover of the administration of the country. Stand-by governments were also formed in all other important towns in Luzon ready to assume local power: these included mayors, local councils, communications technicians, and police forces. Red optimism appeared justified. It looked as though communism would inevitably engulf the Philippines, just as it had China.

By 1950 it had become clear that unless the armed forces were reorganized, cleansed of corruption, and instilled with a will to win, the country could not be saved. Quirino shopped around for a new Secretary of Defense who could do the job, and settled on a little-known forty-three-year-old congressman named Ramón Magsaysay. He was less cultured than most other government leaders, and intellectually he was by no means a giant, but as a guerrilla leader during the war he had proved himself tough as nails. And he had a reputation for honesty. In any case, few qualified people wanted the job, for it looked hopeless.

Magsaysay was a strange addition indeed to the government roster of polished, largely aristocratic political veterans. The son of a peasant who taught carpentry in the local school, he spent most of his youth working with his seven brothers and sisters on his father's farm in the mountains of Zambales. He was brought up in an atmosphere so rigorously moral that his father lost his teacher's job for refusing to pass the son of the superintendent of schools. Ramón walked about twenty miles each day to attend high school, where he was only an average student. He was admitted to the University of the Philippines but dropped out when he couldn't make the grade, and enrolled in a less demanding college. He later got a job with a transportation firm and within a few years had become a branch manager.

When the Japanese attacked the Philippines, he turned over his fleet of cars to the American army and fought with the Philippine forces until the fall of Bataan. He then helped to organize, and led, a western Luzon guerrilla force of 10,000 men. Though the Japanese put a price on his head, his half-starved men continued to harass the enemy throughout the war, finally winning control of the Zambales coast and thus enabling MacArthur's soldiers to land without resistance.

A month after the landings, MacArthur appointed him Military

Governor of the Zambales. A year later he left the army and entered the political arena, and in the 1946 elections was elected a congressman for Zambales by the largest majority in provincial history. He devoted much of his time to the chairmanship of the congressional committee on national defense, and was therefore uniquely familiar with the Huk problem.

Magsaysay's first day in office as Defense Secretary set the tone of his approach. No sooner had he sat down at his desk than he received a mysterious telephone call from a man who asked him to appear that midnight, alone and unarmed, at a nipa hut in Manila's slum sector. The man, a known Huk, said he had some interesting information to offer. Despite the warnings of his advisers that he might be walking into a trap, Magsaysay made his way as directed through a labyrinth of narrow, dirty alleys to the designated palm-frond hut. A thin, nervous little man greeted him and told him that some friends were to meet them there. While they waited, the minister tried to talk his host into joining the government forces.

The Huk refused, but as Magsaysay was about to leave—the other expected guests had not shown up—the man suggested that they meet again the following night. They met several times, and at one meeting the man asked Magsaysay for money to buy a car. The Minister immediately gave him the money. The Huk, now trusting him completely, told him that the men who were supposed to have attended the first rendezvous but didn't appear had planned to kill him. He then advised Magsaysay to have the police follow a certain twelve-year-old girl who posed as a vendor of fruits and vegetables. The police did so and she led them to the hiding places of the top dozen Huks in "Politbureau-in," which was planning to take over the central government. All were captured or killed. As a result of Magsaysay's courage and foresight as exhibited from almost the first minute he took office, the Huks suffered a blow from which they never recovered.

Simultaneously with this dramatic coup, Magsaysay, with $10 million in aid from the United States, reorganized and strengthened the armed forces. He placed the ineffectual constabulary under the army's control and reduced it to about 7,000 officers and men, integrating the rest into the army. He raised salaries and allowances, promoted worthy individuals, and dismissed incompetent officers, despite warnings by some high officers that he was demoralizing the army. He rooted out communist infiltrators who had informed the Huks of every contemplated move against them. He countered guerrilla tactics with guerrilla tactics, sometimes dressing his soldiers in women's clothing. He opened espionage schools. He visited his men in battle areas, and showed personal concern for every casualty. Almost overnight he turned a demoralized, inefficient army into an effective fighting organization.

But Magsaysay did more than that. He turned it into a people's army—though the people had only shortly before despised the government forces even more than the Huks. He severely punished those who mistreated civilians and ordered civil affairs officers to take part in community activities. He told his men, "We must help the people, not fight them." The miraculous change in atmosphere could be seen in the reaction of the people to a plan of Magsaysay to station garrisons in areas where the Huks were strongest and attack Huk regional commands individually until all were destroyed. Thousands of refugee peasants streamed back to their villages in these areas, displaying complete faith in the will and ability of the army to protect them from the Huks.

The man who led Magsaysay to some of the top communist leaders was only one of many Huks who threw their support to the Minister. Magsaysay had originally planned to destroy or bring to justice every last Huk, but after his experience with the midnight informer, he decided to apply this policy only to the rebel leadership. Most Huks were not communists, he knew, but bitter, frustrated people who would follow any false messiah who promised to do away with corruption and virtual serfdom. He interviewed hundreds of captured Huks, listened to their deep-rooted grievances, sympathized with them, promised to try to improve conditions. His magic worked again and again. Many even agreed to rejoin their Huk units as government agents. Others formed anti-Huk brigades, one of which attacked and captured a formidable Huk stronghold on the island of Panay, killing its commander, Guillermo Capadocia, a top Red leader. Magsaysay persuaded other Huks to surrender by pledging to grant them amnesty, restore their citizenship, and give them jobs.

Even when Huk leaders, enraged by Magsaysay's successes, attacked his home town and murdered many of its inhabitants, he did not lose his compassion for the enemy or his faith in their capacity for salvation. After talking with one of the perpetrators of the crime who had been captured, he shocked his associates by telling him, "I think you can become a good citizen, and I'm going to give you a chance to prove it." The chance Magsaysay gave this man, and hundreds of other Filipinos like him, may well have been the straw that broke the Huks' back.

Magsaysay, having come from a peasant family, realized that the central factor in popular discontent was the land problem.

The people of central Luzon, in particular, where the Huks were strongest, could hardly be expected to support a democracy that permitted their exploitation through the absentee landlord system. "Communism is an idea you cannot kill with a sword or gun," Magsaysay said. "When a man with an empty belly works in a rice paddy on land which is not his, always in debt and with his children hungry—when a man in that position hears someone say, 'Land belongs to the man who works it, come to us and we will give it to you,' then something happens to that man. It is as if a cool wind blew through a hell on earth."

Magsaysay decided not to wait for complicated land reform schemes under study by the government to be put into effect. He would start distributing land to the landless immediately—government-owned land that had never been cultivated. In this way, he would undercut the extravagant promises of the Huks.

After the war top army officers had planned to develop a homestead settlement for retired soldiers on unoccupied public lands on the island of Mindanao, but nothing had come of the idea. Magsaysay now threw his weight behind this dormant plan. Most of the settlers would be landless Huks, with carefully selected ex-military and non-Huk peasant families scattered within the new communities to provide a stabilizing influence. The army would protect the settlers and help them plant their first crops, further tightening its bond with the people. The Economic Development Corps (EDCOR), one of the most imaginative and effective schemes to fight communism ever devised, was born.

Soldiers, with the voluntary help of civilians from miles around, began clearing jungle areas in Mindanao. Within a year the first of several EDCOR settlements had been established, complete with rows of thatched cottages, schools, civic center, hospitals, church, tennis court, playground, library, officers' club, communications facilities, plant nursery, and water purifying system. Each family was given free twenty-five acres of land. Schooling, transportation, farm supervision, protection, medical care, water, and electricity were also provided without charge. Residents had to pay only for their houses, tools, work animals, and food—on a long-term credit basis. To qualify for a farm the settler had simply to promise not to be absent from his land for more than thirty days a year, to do his own farm work, and to obey the laws of the community.

By the time the EDCOR communities were ready to receive settlers, the Huks had already begun to disintegrate. Hundreds of them, fed up with the hardships of life in the mountains and demoralized by the increasing number of Huk military defeats, had surrendered. Now that the government offered them land and a home, the very things they had hoped to obtain by supporting the Huks, the rate of surrender accelerated. The Huk leaders grew desperate. They distributed pamphlets describing the EDCOR settlements as barbed-wire-enclosed concentration camps where prisoners in chains slaved away under the watchful eyes of armed sentries who were not shy about using their bayonets. Some party lecturers warned their men that the settlements were actually extermination camps, adding that anyone who indicated an intention to surrender would be liquidated by the Huks first. Huk guerrillas, at the same time, assassinated a number of EDCOR officers.

But nothing the Huk leaders could do was able to stop the surrenders. And no eligible ex-Huk was ever refused the opportunity to start a new life. True, the whole program embraced only several hundred ex-Huks, for many, while desiring land of their own, did not want to move to areas far from their traditional homes. But the scheme offered proof to the people that the government was interested in helping them and that democracy was worth another try.

"Why is it that a foreign power has been able to trick some of our simple Filipino peasants into serving it?" Magsaysay asked in a speech shortly after the EDCOR program was launched:

> Let us be frank. It is because we have for too long turned our backs upon them while we satisfied our own selfish desires. However, when a persevering governmental program has been able to bridge the gap of misunderstanding and has succeeded in inspiring their confidence, and when they have become convinced that governmental authorities exercise their power as a means for their liberation, then they respond with unfailing enthusiasm and loyalty. Left to themselves, they were easy victims for the clever international swindlers who are buying men's souls with empty promises.
>
> Today, through EDCOR, your armed forces are proving this fact. They have said to the Huks, "As guardians of our nation's safety, it is our duty to hunt you down and kill you if you do not surrender. But, as fellow Filipinos, we would rather help you return to a happy Filipino way of life." Many former Huks have accepted this offer of help and today are carving out a new and good life for themselves in the lands of Mindanao.
>
> In this same project another great lesson in democracy is being taught the little people of our land. Working with the new settlement in friendly co-operation are members of the armed forces, demonstrating by actual deed that a democratic army is a people's army—not a club to be held over their cowering heads, but a force dedicated to the protection and welfare of every decent citizen of

our republic. By this policy of all-out force and all-out fellowship
we are making good progress; we are fighting a winning war.

By early 1954 the war had been won. With only a handful of
disorganized Huks still holding out, government forces often did
not even shoot at Huks unless shot at. Instead, they chased the
rebels and tried to capture them without employing violence. These
tactics impressed the people all the more. Finally, in May 1954,
Luis Taruc, the Huk chief, gave himself up. There is some question whether he did so because his capture appeared inevitable or
because other Red leaders had decided to liquidate him. In any
case, his surrender symbolized the end of the Huk rebellion as an
organized movement, with only a few hard-core communists and
wanted criminals left to wither in the mountains and jungles.

Magsaysay had become the idol of the people. Ironically, because of this the government he had saved turned against him. His
demands for large-scale reforms threatened the influential political
and business interests who cared only for themselves, while President Quirino saw him as a prospective competitor for his office. As
relations between the two men cooled, Magsaysay resigned his
post, bolted Quirino's Liberal Party, and agreed to run as the opposition Nationalist Party presidential candidate in the 1954 elections.

Magsaysay, usually wearing a sport shirt, went among the people he loved and who loved him. He visited outlying villages to
which no candidate for high office had ever gone before. He joked
with the villagers, told them about his own experiences as a farm
boy, and how reluctant he had been even to step on the beautiful
rugs the first time he entered a government building. He was not a
good speaker, but that made him seem all the more sincere. He had
not been a good student in school—the opposition had made that
clear—but that further humanized him. Despite strong-arm efforts
by ruling-party supporters to intimidate those who campaigned for
him, Magsaysay defeated Quirino by a landslide.

On taking office, he immediately launched an intensive campaign to wipe out the remaining Huks, both with bullets and kindness, and inaugurated a program which provided for land reform,
new schools, and public works, including an artesian well, to make
water drinkable, in hundreds of villages. He also fought communism on the international front, helping in the creation of the Southeast Asian Treaty Organization (SEATO) proposed by the United
States. Magsaysay, many people thought, would eventually become
a powerful influence throughout free Asia, for he had provided

Asians with a dynamic Asian-designed alternative to communism. But tragically he died in a plane crash in 1957.

Vice-President Carlos García, a veteran politician, took over the presidency and promised to continue Magsaysay's anticommunist and progressive policies. One of his first moves was to sign an Anti-Subversion Act which now formally outlawed the Communist Party and Huk movement—the party having previously been declared illegal in 1932. The first case tried under this act, which established specific penalties for communist activities, was thrown out of court for lack of evidence against the accused, Agaton Bulaong.

Unfortunately, García did little of a constructive nature to guarantee against a revival of the communist threat. Under his rule, the general condition of the Philippine economy improved, with the gross national product climbing to a peak of about $6 billion, or about half that figure by free market standards. But since García was not strong enough to withstand the pressure of crooked politicians and absentee landlords, as Magsaysay had done, few measures were taken to promote a substantial rise in living standards among the masses, even though corruption never reached the level achieved during Quirino's rule.

In Manila and its environs, where much of the nation's wealth is concentrated, beautiful homes and shiny new American automobiles offer the impression of Western-style prosperity. But only a few blocks away clusters of squatters' shacks, many of whose occupants are among the nation's two million unemployed, stand pitifully in the shadow of luxury. In the villages many peasants still dream of the day when they will own their own land. The government has reported that "three out of ten barrio people have a cash earning of 100 pesos (about $24) a year . . . The average income of the rest ranges from 200 to 300 pesos a year. But sixteen percent of all those interviewed reported no cash income at all for the year." Yet the cost of living has skyrocketed. Rice prices soared to such heights in the autumn of 1961 that the government had to declare a state of emergency and fix a maximum price on that staple item. Sugar prices spiraled to a new record.

The people reacted to this situation by voting into power in November 1961 García's Vice-President, Diosdado Macapagal, a handsome ex-lawyer with a winning smile who reminds many people of Magsaysay. Like him he is known for his uncompromising honesty and respected for his humble beginnings. His father was an impoverished poet and playwright, and his mother raised pigs and took in boarders to see him through high school. He had to drop out of college for a while because of the lack of funds, but eventually graduated from the University of Santo Tomás and scored the highest grades of any candidate taking the bar examinations. During the war, he quit as professor of law at Santo Tomás to work with the anti-Japanese underground. After the conflict he was elected to the House of Representatives and finally became Vice-President.

In his campaign for the presidency Macapagal, who once produced and acted in native operettas, made a point of going among the people, as Magsaysay had done, and talking to them in frank, homely terms. He promised them higher living standards and an end to corruption. Since assuming office, he has vigorously fought corruption, among other things, terminating restrictions on the use of foreign exchange and freeing the peso of controls. Under these control laws businessmen had resorted to bribery to get foreign exchange licenses and the bureaucrats thus had tremendous power. The country has also registered economic progress under Macapagal.

It is fortunate that the country is advancing once again, for there is a danger of a communist revival—though most likely of a nonviolent type. The Philippine Reds have completely switched tactics since the failure of the Huk movement, a not unforeseen development. While Magsaysay was still in power, Major-General Jesús Vargas, army chief of staff, warned in a Manila address:

> We would be far from wise if we thought . . . that our communist problem here had ended with the surrender of Taruc or will end with the capture, death, or surrender of the other communist leaders. Communists are communists. They have a way of shifting with ease from surface activities to underground movement, depending on the exigencies of the situation they are in. There is such a thing as a bloodless revolution, and this is exactly what the communists always pull on innocent democracies whenever they are not in a position to overthrow an enemy government militarily.
>
> With the return of the communist leaders to peace, that kind of revolution is what they will seek to wage. They will seek to associate with worthy causes. They will adopt misleading party names and alliances. They will maintain the "hard core" of membership. They will enhance hatred and promote strikes and violence. They will resort to sabotage. They will seek to divide us. Above all, they will infiltrate into the government, universities, civic organizations, even churches. That is the usual communist pattern. With the communist leaders back with us and the masses, that is the problem we are up against.

General Vargas was right. Although the stage of violence and sabotage has yet not been reached, there has been serious infiltration of educational institutions, labor unions, and the intellectual class. The Reds, for example, have won control of such organizations as the so-called Labor Unity Movement (KMP), the National Progress Movement (KMB), and the Manila Leftist Intellectual Circle. The main objectives of their propaganda have been to loosen Philippine ties with the United States, weaken SEATO, encourage a neutralist foreign policy, and promote relations with Communist China, the Soviet Union, and other Red nations which the Philippines today do not recognize. To accomplish these aims the Philippine communists have appealed to nationalist emotions, urged abandonment of American bases, and fueled worker and peasant discontent. In particular, they have made the most of the American Congress's ill-considered original decision not to repay debts accumulated in the Philippines during World War II, though this decision was reversed in mid-1962.

The overseas Chinese community in the Philippines constitutes another latent communist danger. Representing less than two percent of the Philippine population, the Chinese are nevertheless believed to control almost twenty-five percent of the total commercial investment of the Philippines. It is hard to determine the political sentiments of most Chinese, for as communism is outlawed in the Philippines, anyone who expressed sympathy for Red China would risk considerable trouble. But the great majority of Philippine Chinese appear at the moment to be either pro-Nationalist or to harbor an indifferent attitude best characterized in the expression, "a plague on both your houses." The Chinese community in the Philippines, as in other Southeast Asian nations, nevertheless represents a potential Peking fifth column. A clandestine branch of the Chinese Communist Party probably embraces no more than 2,000 members today, but this figure could easily shoot up to 30,000; and most Chinese, opportunistic like their overseas brothers elsewhere, would probably support Red China if the Philippines established diplomatic relations with it—one reason why President García said in 1958 that his government would not recognize Peking even if the United States did.

The local Chinese Communist Party was founded in 1930, but had little success before the war, for most Chinese workers were relatives of their employers and were little impressed by slogans against capitalist exploitation. During the war, however, the party developed close relations with the Huk guerrillas and picked up strength. In 1952 it was reported that the party had received about

$200,000 in funds from Peking. Several million dollars worth of goods are also smuggled in from Red China every year, while millions more are transmitted to China, directly or indirectly, by Philippine Chinese. Some of this money is sent as the result of Red Chinese threats to harm relatives on the mainland if it is not forthcoming. One high Filipino officer told a congressional committee: ". . . There are Chinese associations in Manila, like the Music Associations, Athletic Associations, that are being used as fronts by the Chinese Communists . . ." When the Director of the National Bureau of Investigation was asked by a congressman whether the Chinese Chamber of Commerce is communist-inclined, he replied, "Yes. As a matter of fact, there are Chinese businessmen here in the Philippines who are given the facilities by the Chinese banks without any guaranty, provided that the guaranty be done by the Chinese Communists and their desire is to entice them. The situation is serious."

Philippine intelligence sources have also charged that some teachers in Chinese schools in Manila support the communists, despite the screening of all teachers by the Philippine army. A number of Chinese principals and teachers have been deported for subversive activities, while a communist cell was discovered in a Chinese school in Cebu.

To an even greater degree than in other Southeast Asian nations, the Chinese in the Philippines look upon themselves as residents of a foreign country. In places like Thailand, Burma, and Indonesia, the Chinese at least feel a common Asian bond with the indigenous people. But this bond is largely lacking in the Philippines. For while the Chinese strongly feel their Asian identity, many Filipinos have so thoroughly absorbed Western culture—first under the Spaniards, who converted most of them to Catholicism, and then under the Americans—that they have all but forgotten their Asian inheritance.

Philippine discrimination against the Chinese has further reduced understanding between the two peoples. Chinese are not permitted to own land, exploit natural resources, or operate public utilities. They are excluded from many professions and find it difficult to obtain import licenses and government contracts. The books of all businesses in the Philippines must be kept in English, Spanish, or a local dialect—a regulation that forces Chinese merchants to employ Filipino clerks. Most important of all, a Retail Trade Nationalization Law prohibits Chinese from starting new retail ventures and transferring those already owned to their heirs, a measure which, if enforced, will eventually eliminate Chinese from the retail field altogether.

Furthermore, constant police raids on Chinese business establishments for the announced purpose of uncovering illegal business connections with Red China has instilled fear even in the most anticommunist Chinese businessmen. Some of these raids have been justified. According to one official report:

> Banned articles are packed in Hong Kong and either addressed to the commuters or prominent citizens, including a former senator. The packages are described and listed as "personal effects" . . . and within the 5,000 pesos [$2,500] quota exempt from customs duties. Because of alleged connivance of certain customs personnel [they] . . . easily pass through customs agents . . . In instances where the "luggage" containing banned items from Hong Kong is intercepted by police agencies, influential citizens, mostly politicians, exert pressure for release of the articles . . .

In one case, "a two-gallon tin can" of counterfeit coins and counterfeiting tools was found in a Manila home, leading officials to charge that the raid had "struck into the heart of an organized counterfeit ring which . . . was being financed by the same alien syndicate behind the illegal traffic of goods from Red China." There was an "organized communist plot to 'sabotage' the Philippine economy."

But some Filipinos consider the police raids as undemocratic as the communism they are supposed to uncover. Mayor Arsenio H. Lacson of Manila deplored the fact that sometimes police entered establishments without warrants. Even when warrants were obtained, he said, the raiders had often "gone beyond the terms of the search warrant itself and have even illegally confiscated goods from Chinese establishments merely on suspicion . . ." The *Manila Times* reported that the Cebu City police had found "what is believed to be a well-knit gang who extort from Chinese businessmen under investigation for alleged trafficking in narcotics and dollars . . . The gang, it is said, has been raking in thousands of pesos."

Sometimes the Nationalist Chinese Embassy in Manila encourages the government to take action against Chinese whom they describe as "communists," though the only crime these Chinese may have committed was to question the policies of the Chiang Kai-shek regime.

Anti-Chinese bitterness in the Philippines has already tended to play into the hands of the communists. Even Chinese opposed to Peking are reluctant to co-operate with the police in uncovering Red activities, for they fear that trouble will result for the whole Chinese community in the name of anticommunism. But despite the potential threat of a communist revival, the Philippines, which in 1950 seemed to be going the way of China, appears to be in less danger today than any other Southeast Asian nation. The government fought the communists on their own guerrilla terms—and won. For it gained the support of the people. Other free governments in Southeast Asia, as well as in other areas of the underdeveloped world, would do well to study the Philippine answer to communism. Yet, if all might derive some profit from this answer, it should be borne in mind that the Philippines have been blessed with certain advantages in the struggle against communism that most underdeveloped countries do not enjoy.

First, the Philippines, being a cluster of islands, cannot offer the communists a rear base of operations or an easily defended sanctuary, from which attacks can be launched and guerrillas supplied, as in Laos and South Vietnam. The Huks had to move from base to base until almost all of them were destroyed. Second, it isn't often that a leader of Magsaysay's caliber happens along. Third, not many underdeveloped nations are imbued with the democratic traditions of the Philippines. Peasants in countries like Laos and South Vietnam, with Confucian or other authoritarian traditions, are less likely to resist communism. To them it is simply one more form of dictatorship, and that is the only kind of government they know. In addition, the communists in such countries find it easy to exploit anticolonial bitterness, something which does not exist to an appreciable degree in the Philippines, where candidates for office vie with each other in promising closer ties with the United States.

Still, there is much such lands could learn from the Philippine experience in their struggle to solve their own communist problems.

XVII

JAPAN:

COMMUNISTS AREN'T

GENTLEMEN

The wild demonstrations by Japanese leftists which blocked President Eisenhower's scheduled visit to Japan in June 1960 gave the impression that Japanese public opinion is dangerously Marxist and anti-American. Actually, the great silent majority of Japanese are probably among the most conservative people in the world and favor close relations with the United States. This has been clearly indicated by the many overwhelming electoral victories of the conservative Liberal-Democratic Party.

Equally significant, most of the leftists themselves, while neutralist, do not harbor the bitterness toward the United States commonly found among Red-tinged groups in other countries. Some—between rounds of stone-throwing at such targets as President Eisenhower's press secretary, James Hagerty—even apologized to Americans in the crowd. They had nothing against the United States, they said. They were only angry at the "reactionary" Japanese government for maintaining military ties with it.

This rather confusing attitude reflects the unorthodoxy of the Japanese leftist movement. In few countries of the free world is the influence of Marxism, particularly among intellectuals, more pronounced than in Japan. But leftist tendencies there have been spawned not so much by communist propaganda as by a search for new values to replace the Emperor worship that disintegrated in the horrifying glare of Hiroshima. Moreover, leftists are embracing only those elements of Marxism they consider adjustable to the Japanese environment. Few of them follow the stereotyped communist line. Though most are by no means reluctant to collaborate with communism, on either the international or the domestic level, they consider the communist way of doing things crude and "un-Japanese."

This unusual attitude is consistent with Japan's traditional methods of cultural selection. Throughout its history, Japan has proved its capacity to devour foreign civilizations almost at a bite and adapt them to its own purposes. Every country has to some degree borrowed aspects of its culture from other nations, but Japan is often singled out for doing so because it has borrowed in concentrated spurts, between long periods of utter isolation. It imported Chinese culture wholesale from the seventh to the ninth centuries, then after a thousand years of medieval insulation swallowed Western technology just as avidly in the nineteenth century. Massive importations of a cultural nature flowed in from the West after defeat in World War II. But if this history of "catching-up" has given Japan a reputation as a nation of copiers, the country is probably purer culturally than most states, as evidenced by the many unique aspects of its religion, literature, art, and architecture.

The current phase of Japan's "Westernization," in which the absorption of some Marxist principles is one element, contrasts sharply in many ways with previous borrowing efforts. In the past, revolution resulted from the sudden realization that Japan was behind other parts of the world culturally or technically. The Japanese feared that the armies of the more advanced nations might overrun their country, while their pride was stung by the revelation that other states, particularly China, appeared to have a more advanced culture. Thus, fear and pride combined to produce an inflexible determination, nursed by an aggressive Shinto religious doctrine that proclaimed the Japanese superior to all other peoples, to prove this conviction correct. Paradoxically, to do so the Japanese had to master the secrets of power of the "inferior" countries.

In the cultural revolution that began after World War II, militarism for the first time was not a factor. And even the pride propelling it is a more refined brand, no longer based on the egoism and arrogance born of the concept that an inflexible hierarchy modeled after the domestic social structure, with Japan at the top, is the natural order of international society. Rather, the new pride was conceived in the need for reconstruction, peace, and higher living standards. Still, the present transformation has confirmed the constancy of Japan's genius to fit great alien innovations to its purposes without destroying the basic threads of indigenous culture.

Many of the changes that have taken place in Japan since the war are superficial. Tokyo, for example, strikes many visitors at first glance as simply a Western city transplanted in the Orient. Yet a second look reveals that the city is still very much Japanese. The huge department stores tower over small shops which display goods on the street. The modern factories arrange to have many parts made in primitive workshops, where the workers are sometimes children. Cabaret hostesses wear beautiful Western-style evening gowns and often rubber bosoms, but they treat their male customers with the deference and gentility of the geisha, who customarily binds her chest. The main streets are broad and jammed with traffic, but to visit almost any Japanese home you have to wind through a maze of unnamed twisting alleys. Christmas is exuberantly celebrated with gift-giving, carols, and Santa Claus, but less than one percent of the population is Christian.

A far more profound change has come about in Japanese social standards. Hierarchy has traditionally characterized the nation's social structure, hierarchy so rigid that the behavior of every individual—from the manner of bowing to one's role in preparing tea—is governed by rules according to sex, occupation, family position, age, and class. This complex hierarchal structure is held together by a net of obligations called *on*. The Japanese is constantly repaying *on* to his parents, relatives, friends, and acquaintances, and at least before the war, owed his very life to the Emperor. This formal repayment of debts—the slightest favor or gift must be returned or the slacker is treated as an outcast from his community—is called *giri* (*ko* in the case of the parents, *chu* in reference to the Emperor), a word that has always meant near-slavery to the Japanese, who have never known the relative casualness and informality of Western social relations.

Perhaps the hardest burden to bear is the repayment of *giri* to one's name. The nation's history has been shaped by the fact that a Japanese cannot ignore personal insults because they reflect on his family name, and therefore on all the ancestral ghosts he eternally honors. He must clear or purify his name whether through legal means, vengeance, or suicide. Nor is it easy for the Japanese to suppress all outward evidences of "human feeling," or *ninjo,* which he must channel into such specified means of expression as poetry writing, other artistic accomplishments, and lovemaking, usually with a mistress or prostitute.

Though *giri* is still an important ingredient in the Japanese social composition, it has lost its edge since the war, and people are less prone to view their social debts as inflexibly binding. For to the Japanese, the very fact that their country lost the war proved that its values were far from perfect, and indeed that they could learn something more than industrial techniques from the West. Women have been emancipated to a large degree and often divorce their husbands for neglecting them. Workers are no longer factory serfs. Most important of all, the Emperor is no longer regarded as a symbol of God. Instead of bowing to the ground in his presence, the Japanese, when they see him—he greets them on the grounds of his palace in Tokyo every New Year's Day—wave and scramble to take pictures. As a human being, the Sovereign is far closer to the people than he was when an object of worship.

But the sudden breakdown of traditional values has left a moral and spiritual void that has not yet been filled. Many Japanese have been seeking to fill it with democratic values. Others have found democracy a much less positive ideology than Marxism, which spells out in detail how they should think, as the militarists and Shintoists did in the past. In both cases, alien concepts are being fitted into an indigenous cultural mold.

It is understandable, therefore, that the Japan Communist Party is a peripheral force in Japanese political life, drawing only about 50,000 members from intellectual, white-collar, and labor groups. Its failure to win mass support among the workers is one of its major weaknesses; and the party has no peasant backing at all. It won only 2.9 percent of the total popular vote and only three seats out of 467 in national parliamentary elections held in November 1960.

In prewar days the party was about as weak as, or weaker than, it is today. Established in 1922 during a period of severe economic recession when discontented Japanese workers began joining labor unions on a large scale for the first time, the party expected to make swift and important gains. But oddly enough, most unions—as well as intellectual groups—sought an answer to their economic and social grievances not in extremist doctrines but in democracy, a tendency fostered in the 1920's by the increasingly liberal policies of the Japanese government. In the 1930's, with the militarists growing in power, the communist influence was even feebler, as a result of both governmental suppression and a popular surge, even among labor unions, toward fascistic totalitarianism. By the end of the decade most Reds were in jail, where they remained until World War II was over.

When peace came, the Japanese Reds were in one of the most advantageous positions of any communist group in Asia. With militarism and fascism utterly discredited, the communists, who had been among the few Japanese who had opposed Japan's aggressive policies from the first—though less out of a desire for peace than in deference to Soviet interests—poured out of imperial jails and returned from exile abroad to be hailed as near-heroes by a people desperately searching for an alternative to their fallen gods and the values they represented.

One of those who returned from exile was Japan's communist leader, Sanzo Nozaka, a little man with a stern face and sleepy eyes. Nozaka was first attracted to communism in the 1920's as a student in London. He made two visits to Moscow, remaining there throughout most of the 1930's, and was appointed to the Comintern's Presidium. Then he went to Yenan in 1940 and took graduate lessons in subversion from Mao until the end of World War II. The United States Air Force flew him to Tokyo in 1945, and he set about putting his years of study abroad to practical advantage—particularly what he had learned in China. The Yenan Way, he was convinced, could eventually bring communism to Japan. True, the revolutionary reforms that the American Occupation authorities were pushing through deprived the communists of considerable propaganda bait, but most of the Japanese politicians working with the Americans were conservative and opposed many of the reforms, offering the Reds excellent targets. The Americans couldn't stay forever, Nozaka reasoned, and when they left, the communists could probably step into power—in co-operation perhaps with other "progressive" elements—by simply arguing that they would extend the reforms, whereas the conservatives would cancel them.

While pressing for a united front among all leftist elements, the communists, under Nozaka, won control of Japan's new labor unions. They infiltrated parliament. They subtly propagandized against the Emperor system itself with some success. On May Day 1946 tens of thousands of people carrying red flags invaded the Imperial Palace grounds to protest against a food shortage. General Douglas MacArthur did little to frustrate communist activity, having promised the Japanese freedom of speech and assembly. The communists took full advantage of this tolerance, while many Japanese, ironically, interpreted this tolerance as American approval of Red aims, and were all the more ready to follow the communist path in order to "please" the conquering Americans. After all, they reasoned, both the communists and the Americans claimed that they wanted "democratic" reforms, such as elimination of the

Zaibatsu trusts and redistribution of the land to the peasants. Only in February 1947, when the Reds planned to stage a general strike which might have resulted in a communist seizure of the government, did MacArthur finally crack down, forbidding the strike.

Still, the communist movement grew. For it fed on more than American tolerance and the hunger and misery that prevailed in the early postwar years. Red dynamism and dedication appealed to the people. So did Red promises and flag-waving. The communists were profiting from the same demagogic tactics that had been used by the militarists to turn soldiers into suicide attackers. The bitter, hungry, disillusioned Japanese appeared ripe for a new revolutionary adventure—a fanatical reaction to the one that had failed.

The collectivism preached by the communists, moreover, was easier for the highly regulated Japanese society to understand than was the unorderly individualism of the Americans. Liberals, revisionist by nature, were attracted by the communist theory of collectivism, which promised to eliminate all social distinctions between people through the establishment of a classless society. Some conservatives were attracted by the communist system as it was actually practiced with the emphasis on a hierarchical leadership similar to that which characterized the Japanese political and social structure. A few traditionalists even thought that it might be possible to fit communism into the framework of the Imperial system.

In the elections of January 1949 the Communist Party won an impressive ten percent of the vote. At the same time, the Yenan Way produced considerable support from the large left wing of the Socialist Party, which appealed to Japanese who backed many communist policies but could not accept the revolutionary and un-Japanese tactics of the Communist Party itself. This socialist faction seemed to promise a less alien means of obtaining revolutionary results.

But though Nozaka's tactics appeared to be paying heavy dividends, Stalin was not happy. In 1948 he had ordered that all Asian communist parties take a militant stand against the governments in their countries; he urged that they use violence and even resort to rebellion where possible. But Nozaka was playing the understanding friend to noncommunists. It was clear even to Stalin that the Japanese Reds could not oust the American Occupation administration but could step up their anti-American propaganda and create as much chaos as possible. Warned to change his ways, Nozaka apologized, publicly criticized himself, and shifted to more revolutionary tactics. The Reds tactlessly used Japanese prisoners returning from the Soviet Union for their propaganda purposes, corralling them as they disembarked from repatriation ships and forcing them to participate in Red rallies without even giving them a chance to be welcomed back by their long-suffering families. The Japanese were shocked. What sort of people were these communists? Did they have no respect for the parents of the returning soldiers? Could real Japanese be so crude and impolite and insensitive? It was disturbing enough that they seldom bowed correctly or tried to disguise sadness with a smile. But this was going too far. The communists were obviously not gentlemen. Public feeling against the Reds rose as arrogance developed into violence in labor disputes. The last straw was the communist-led rioting at the Imperial Plaza in Tokyo on May Day 1952, which resulted in injury to many innocent people. Memories of prewar rightist terror were revived. The people were horrified. Communist popularity slid swiftly to its present hard-core level.

Even the party's reversion in 1955 to the "right strategy" has failed to win back many adherents who were burned once and do not intend to be again. Nevertheless the party, still under Nozaka, is not without importance. For its influence has been magnified by the success of its infiltration tactics. Japanese security officials estimate that 15,000 party members have infiltrated government offices and key industries. The Reds have also spread the party line through more than one hundred front organizations in almost every field of political, scientific, cultural, and academic endeavor, finding the job relatively simple in view of the utter lack of awareness by many Japanese that they are pulling the strings. The party has been particularly successful in manipulating organizations that support "peace," increased trade with Communist China, and closer relations with the communist bloc in general, and that oppose rearmament, nuclear testing, and Cold War alignment with the United States—themes popularly identified with the national interest. Not surprisingly, one of the most successful fronts has been the Japan Council against Atomic and Hydrogen Bombs (GENSUIKO), though it lost considerable face—and support— when the Russians broke the moratorium on nuclear testing.

The party has not made it clear whether it favors the Moscow or Peking ideological line, but it has adopted a "go-slow" revolutionary policy, calling for a two-stage revolution that may be oriented more closely toward the Kremlin's views. The first is to be directed primarily at "American imperialism," the second at "Japanese monopoly capital." In other words, the party is now concentrating on a "democratic revolution" designed to end the Mutual Security Treaty which permits the United States to maintain bases in Japan, and to wipe out American influence in general. Once this goal is accomplished, a "socialist revolution" would follow. Communists opposed to this view, those who feel that since Japan is a sovereign and highly industrialized nation there should be only one revolution that would achieve both goals simultaneously, have been thrown out of the party as being too extreme.

In line with the party's policy of concentrating initially on the condemnation of American "imperialism," its main propaganda efforts have been directed toward the neutralization of Japan. With the elimination of the Mutual Security Treaty as its tactical goal, the party constantly seeks to co-operate and identify itself with other "progressive" groups, such as the Socialist Party and left-wing labor unions. Although its efforts to form a united front with the Socialist Party have been formally rebuffed, the Communist Party is one of the most active groups in the anti-Security Treaty movement to which almost all other leftists belong.

Unlike the orthodox communists, these leftists, most of whom back the Socialist Party, which is supported by about one third of the electorate, are highly undisciplined, ranging from neo-Trotskyite to British-style Laborite. But though each sees the integration of Marxist principles in the Japanese cultural pattern differently, almost all have in common an extreme tendency toward pacifism born of the shock and disillusionment of the war. This is a major reason why most of them favor what they call "peaceful revolution" and denounce the communist theory of "violent revolution." They favor neutralism and demand the withdrawal of all American forces from Japan, as do the communists, of course; they would even strip the nation of Japan's own defense forces, which, they say, should be turned into a nonmilitary "engineering and disaster relief corps." The defense of Japan would be left to the United Nations supported by an agreement between Japan, the United States, the Soviet Union, and Communist China.

The fact that many conservatives tend also to harbor a "peace-at-any-price" attitude helps to explain the size of some of the demonstrations that have been held in Japan and the ability of the Socialist Party to win as much as one-third of the national vote.

This widespread pacifism has prevented any change in the constitution drawn up during the American Occupation which specifically bans the development of armed forces. It accounts for the establishment of technically legal "Self-Defense Forces" rather than an "army." The effort to get around the ban has produced some ludicrous incidents. On one occasion a Dutch liner saluted a Japanese naval vessel on the high seas, but the latter did not return the salute. A Japanese naval official later explained that "lingering doubts about the status of the Self-Defense Forces" left it unclear whether the Japanese vessel was actually a "warship." It is almost impossible to see a Japanese soldier wearing a uniform when he is off duty, for to wear one is simply to invite insults by passers-by.

The most extreme of the leftists, those responsible for spear-heading almost all demonstrations, belong to a fringe leadership faction of the 280,000-member student organization Zengakuren, or All-Japan Federation of Student Autonomy Councils. For all the stormy publicity they have had, students who have taken part in violence represent only a fringe sector of the leftist movement and also of the Zengakuren. Only about 2,000 members are communists, and another 3,000, supporting elements, it is estimated. Even those listed as communists are largely opposed to the policies of the Communist Party—because, incredibly enough, the party is too moderate. The leaders, who are Trotskyite-oriented, are contemptuous of the orthodox Reds for their soft "coexistence" policies.

Before the Communist Party switched in 1955 from Stalin's policy of violence to a policy of co-operation with all possible anti-government groups, these leaders worked largely through the party. But they refused to go along with the new party line and were therefore thrown out of the party in 1958. However, these few extremists are not the great menace headlines have made them out to be. True, rank-and-file Zengakuren members, most of whom join the organization automatically upon enrolling in a university, are generally leftist-inclined, but, as many informal polls have indicated, most of them are opposed to violence.

The antics of the Zengakuren are a manifestation of the longing of Japanese youth for something in which to believe. In their near-desperation, many are reaching for an ideological illusion and resorting to unreasoned, emotional extremism, quite contrary to the calculated logic of the genuine communists, to achieve their impossible goals. They are, moreover, fighting themselves as well as the police and society as a whole. For they are torn between the lingering traditionalism of home life and the tormenting desire to destroy every reminder of the past. Adding to the new burden of emptiness is an old one that Japanese students have borne for centuries: the savage nature of the competition into which they are drawn. Competition for admittance into the universities, competition to remain in school, competition for the best marks, competition for appropriate jobs after graduation. To fail in any of these respects means an agonizing loss of face to the Japanese, a violation of *giri* to one's family name, and therefore, in some cases, a compulsion to suicide.

The radicalism of the youth is nurtured early in the secondary schools, about ninety percent of whose teachers belong to the far leftist Japan Teachers' Union. Only about five percent of the membership are estimated to be pro-communist, but even the remainder still feel bound in some degree by the deeply embedded tradition of conformity and group discipline. And the group is told by its leaders to preach the destruction of capitalism and the building of socialism. The United States, the leaders say, should be condemned in the classroom for trying to revive militarism, while the communist countries should be praised for trying to help the people.

Fortunately, most students, on entering the rigid world of *giri* after graduation from secondary school or university, soon give up their radicalism and fit themselves into Japan's generally conservative society. A more genuine danger is the General Council of Japan Labor Unions, or Sohyo, Japan's leading labor federation with some three and a half million members. Formed originally in 1950 as an anti-communist organization after a mother federation had slipped under communist control, it soon was infiltrated by Reds, too. Today perhaps ten percent of the leadership are communist while the rest are willing to do business with the Reds.

The top chiefs deny they are communists and occasionally accuse the Reds of using pacifist and cultural movements for their own ends. Some have even said that to be a communist is to be "un-Japanese." They appear to have an utterly confused philosophy reminiscent of the wild-eyed European radicalism of the 1920's— understandable considering that organized free unionism was crushed by the militarists in the early 1930's and that new unions unoriented to modern trends and needs were superficially created by the Occupation regime after the war.

"We support parliamentary politics and the policy of establishing a socialist society by peaceful means," Sohyo said in a statement of policy. But the statement also declared that "we are opposed to the theory of two large parties, each making concessions to the other." From this it would appear that Sohyo wants a one-party parliament similar to the communist type. But how it expects to get rid of opposition parties by peaceful means is a mystery. Indeed, as long as the Socialist Party, which is simply the political arm of Sohyo, hews to a strictly class line, it is almost impossible to imagine the socialists coming to power except through the violent means it claims to reject. Therefore, when frustration reaches the boiling point, the danger of an attempted coup or revolution cannot be discounted.

Yet Sohyo's leaders are highly intelligent men. Secretary-General Iwai, a tough, square-jawed ex-railroad worker, is more politician than ideologist. That he has had no little success is indicated by the hold Sohyo has on the Socialist Party. Another Sohyo top official, President Kaoru Ohta, is believed to look more favorably on the prospect of dictatorship—if the dictatorship is of the "proletariat." A chemical engineer who immediately after the war represented management at the bargaining table, Ohta is essentially a Marxist ideologist and crowd-pleasing speaker, though it is not clear to what extent he is Moscow or Peking oriented, if he is either.

Some labor officials, unable to stomach the confused, extremist views of Sohyo, split the federation a few years ago, re-enacting Sohyo's own revolt against its parent organization for veering too far toward communism. They formed the All-Japan Trade Union Congress, or Zenro, which today has slightly less than one million members. Its leader, Secretary-General Haruo Wada, an ex-seaman, told me that his federation's interest is not primarily political, as is Sohyo's, but economic—to win increased benefits from management. There should be no class war, he said, but "co-operation between the bosses and the workers." While opposing the Mutual Security Treaty, mainly because of the uncompromisingly neutralist attitude of the workers, he favors close relations with the Free World. The greatest obstacle to Zenro's progress is its rational approach. Sohyo appeals more to the worker's emotional need for a strong, militant cause. Many Japanese, while despising militarism, still have to be militant about something. Sohyo and other leftist groups give them the chance to be militant about pacifism, no contradiction in terms in postwar Japan.

The Socialist Party is to a large extent the creature of Sohyo, depending on it for financial support and an important bloc of votes. Individual socialists are deeply divided, reflecting the innate chaos of Japanese leftism. Some agree with Sohyo that their party should be a strictly "class" party, while others favor the establishment of a "national" party in some measure, at least until the socialists can take over power. One right-wing group, led by Suehiro Nishio, broke away from the Socialist Party some time ago to form a moderate Democratic Socialist Party with a program similar to that of Zenro, which has become the labor affiliate of this party.

However, it is having troubles similar to those of Zenro. Most Japanese leftists prefer the stronger, more exhilarating taste of the militant group.

But conservative ex-Premier Nobusuke Kishi, who resigned from office after he had had to cancel President Eisenhower's visit to Japan because of leftist demonstrations, observed to me shortly before he resigned: "Although the Democratic Socialist Party may eventually threaten my own party's power, I consider its establishment one of the most hopeful political developments to have occurred since the war." He meant that if this organization can eventually develop mass appeal, Japan will have achieved what its fledgling democracy needs most today—a two-party system under which each party has a reasonable chance of coming to power. The Socialist Party, because of its present class nature, has almost no chance of winning a majority in the foreseeable future, creating pressures conducive to violence.

The widespread pacifism in Japan and the leftist and neutralist tendencies that have grown out of it cannot be fully understood without consideration of Japan's geographical and strategic position. Situated just across the Sea of Japan from this country are the two communist giants, the Soviet Union and Communist China, to whom Japan, the only highly industrialized country in Asia (other than Soviet Asia itself), is one of the most coveted of all potential victims. The two countries, directly and through the Japan Communist Party, have done all in their power to fight the Mutual Security Treaty and to encourage the spread of neutralism in the hope of softening up Japan for the ultimate kill.

Russia's principal tactic has been to hurl thunderbolts of dire threat at the Japanese, warning them that they will be among the first to perish in the event of war, if they retain their alliance with the United States. Sometimes the thunder is mixed with tempting promises of sunshine. In 1961 Khrushchev said he would hand back to Japan Habomai and Shikotan, two of the four Kurile Islands the Soviet Union occupied at the end of the war, except for the fact that they would "fall into the hands of the United States." He followed up this bait by cynically offering not to harass the 60,000 Japanese fishermen who ply their trade in the Northwest Pacific at the risk of arrest by the Soviets—from fifty to one hundred Japanese fishing boats are seized a year—if only Japan would scrap the Security Treaty. There would be other benefits, too, the Soviets have said, such as Japanese participation in the development of Siberia. When the Japanese would not swallow the bait, Russia served notice that it would never return the Kurile Islands.

It has also dumped important quantities of low-priced textiles on the Singapore market in direct competition with Japanese products. In late 1961 Soviet Deputy Premier Mikoyan visited Japan and, while touching upon trade and cultural exchange in his talks with Japanese officials, made it clear that his real message was that Japan was following a "suicidal" Cold War policy.

Nevertheless, trade between the two countries has increased, owing in part to their joint fear of being shut out of Western European commerce by the Common Market, but also to the Soviet policy of keep a foot in every door. In September 1962 Moscow contracted to purchase 45 vessels from Japan, totaling $96,000,-000, and indicated it might also buy steel products, mining equipment, and—in a sideswipe at American import quotas—cotton goods.

Neither the carrot nor the stick, however, has served to enhance Soviet standing in Japanese eyes. Russia, an imperial competitor in the Far East for more than half a century, has never been popular in Japan, and seldom less popular than now, even among many leftists. But its threats no doubt have had some effect among people who are still suffering from the effects—psychological and physical —of the atomic bomb.

Japan's relations with Communist China have hardly been better, but that country has had more political leverage in Japan for two reasons. First, the Japanese feel an emotional attachment to China, whatever the complexion of its government, stronger than to any other nation, because of its proximity, and because Japans' culture is largely an outgrowth of China's. Second, Japan, which exported almost twenty percent of its products to China in prewar days, dreams of opening new markets in that country, and some people are willing to make political concessions in return for such trade.

To understand the intensity of this dream, one need understand only a few simple economic facts about Japan. The meager natural wealth of the country, which has adequate quantities of rainfall and second-grade coal, little more, is insufficient to maintain the growing population. The four main islands of Japan together constitute an area smaller than California, with only sixteen percent arable because of mountainous terrain. Yet these islands are bursting with almost 95,000,000 people, considerably over half the population of the rich, sprawling United States. The population will reach a peak of 105,000,000 by 1985 before present birth control measures—mainly abortions, which are legal in Japan—take effect.

If Japan is simply to maintain its present living standards in the future, its economy will have to expand continually and with unusual speed in order to absorb the increasing populace. In the last several years Japan has succeeded in this endeavor, managing in fact to double the industrial production and triple the national income registered in peak prewar years. With Japan possessing few resources of its own, this incredible economic growth has been made possible largely by the expanding export of Japanese manufactured products. Japan, more than most countries, must export to live.

This abnormal dependence on trade for national livelihood has cultivated in Japan a massive undercurrent of insecurity and fear lest one day this single pipeline to prosperity be cut off. Every suggestion in the United States of new restrictions on Japanese imports creates something approaching hysteria in Japan. On the other hand, China, an enormous country next door with an unbounded market potential, looks most inviting to the Japanese—and all the more so each time the distant American market appears threatened, even in the slightest.

From 1952 to 1957 Japan maintained limited commercial ties with Red China, primarily through private channels. But in 1958 China abruptly cut off this trade, supposedly because an anti-communist youth tore down a Communist Chinese flag at a trade fair in Nagasaki. But Peking actually wanted to test the effect of economic pressure on Japanese political policies, hoping that Japan, under the prodding of domestic leftists, would loosen its ties with the United States, and possibly even break its current bonds with Taiwan and recognize Peking.

But Red China discovered that the Japanese government was not ready to pay a political price for Chinese trade and good will, however desirable. Even so, Chairman Inejiro Asanuma of the Socialist Party—who was later stabbed to death at a public meeting in Tokyo by a fanatical Japanese ultrarightist student—visited Peking in 1959 and, to the embarrassment of his own party, publicly stated that the United States is the "enemy of both Japan and Communist China." This statement has since been repeated by other socialist visitors to China.

When Prime Minister Kishi, a bitter foe of Red China, was replaced in 1960 by Hayato Ikeda, a less belligerent conservative, relations between Peking and Tokyo began to improve slightly. Japanese businessmen were invited to a trade fair in Canton and came away with $12.5 million worth of contracts. Some iron and steel companies, in their enthusiasm for Chinese trade, even agreed to pay a price higher than the world level for Chinese coal. But the coal they received through Japanese trading firms was inferior to that which they had been promised. The trading firms were thus stuck with most of the coal, which the iron and steel companies refused to accept.

Experiences like this have considerably cooled Japanese hopes of developing any important trade contacts with China. But the desire is still there. It would be irresistible if Japan were struck by a serious recession, produced perhaps by heavy American restrictions on Japanese merchandise. The Japanese, understandably, would struggle for every crumb of Red Chinese trade, possibly even if each were attached to a political condition, such as neutralism. And Red China, it can be safely said, would not hesitate to offer a whole loaf—at whatever economic cost to itself—if it could profit politically.

What many Japanese often tend to forget, or perhaps wish to forget, is that trade with China, other than that resulting from political concession, will always be limited. In the coming years, though China might need Japanese manufactured products, it is not likely to import them in bulk simply because communist governments, particularly at China's stage of development, are not interested in creating a nation of happy consumers at the expense of capital investment. In the more distant future China itself will be industrialized and will turn out its own products. When that time comes, not only may Japan have a harder time than ever selling to China, but it could have trouble competing with China for markets in Southeast Asia. Except for India, this area is likely to retain its predominantly agrarian character and become, when it has the purchasing power, an extremely large importer of manufactured goods.

In recent years Red China, though few of its own people even have shoes, has offered previews of what to expect. It has exported to Southeast Asia through Hong Kong small quantities of everything from synthetic camphor to radio-controlled toys at cutthroat prices, though such exports have virtually halted since about 1960 due to deteriorating economic conditions in China. The Japanese are already worrying about their commercial future in Southeast Asia—and Peking no doubt calculates that as worry gradually develops into desperation it will be able to bargain favorably over the availability not only of the Chinese market but of the Southeast Asian market as well.

Whatever direction Japan may take in the distant future, it is firmly hewing to the path of democracy today as carved out of

Japan's totalitarian jungle by the American Occupation forces after the war. The people have a freely elected parliament and all the basic human liberties. But to a considerable extent Japan is more democratic in form than in substance. The feudalistic tendency of the Japanese to follow traditional patterns of behavior rooted in hierarchy rather than act as individuals is still strong. As I explained in my book, *Kishi and Japan: The Search for the Sun:*

> "After their bitter experience with totalitarianism, they have turned to the alternative—democracy. But they are trying to build this new way of life, in large measure, on a foundation of decayed values. They are treating democracy as a new kind of ideological structure, hopelessly seeking their places within it. They do not completely understand that democracy denies such a structure as restrictive of individual liberty, that it actually represents freedom from systematization, with rules kept to a bare minimum."

But the fact that genuine democracy has not yet flowered in Japan does not mean that communism or some other variety of extreme leftism is likely to take over the country in the foreseeable future. Superficially, it may appear that the main obstacle on the democratic path—the remnants of feudalism—is proving beneficial to the leftist cause. For the rank and file of such organizations as Zengakuren, Sohyo, and the Japan Teachers Union blindly follow their extremist leaders.

Nevertheless, it is significant that the great majority of members of these and other leftist organizations follow only reluctantly, lacking the tradition of democracy and individualism necessary to produce a spirit of rebellion, and are not likely to follow beyond a reasonable point. Many who belong to the Teachers Union, even while obeying orders to strike against the government or teach a certain curriculum, are extremely conservative; a large number of country instructors are also small landowners. Further, teachers cannot completely ignore the feelings of parents, most of whom are conservative. In one village parents were so angered by the leftist propaganda fed their children that they boarded up the homes of the teachers to prevent them from going to class.

In the case of the *Zengakuren,* the extremists are almost the only students who are willing to sacrifice their study time to devote themselves completely to the organization. Also, with their future careers at stake, few moderates are willing to risk being labeled "communist" through association with the leadership. A leftist student friend revealingly told me that after graduation he hoped to get a job with a "name" company and eventually work his way up to the top. "I am a social idealist," he said, "and I oppose capitalism. But as long as it exists, it's best to master its techniques. I'm realistic enough to know that my idealism will gradually wither away under the inescapable pressure of tradition and leave my soul empty."

As for Sohyo, it is severely handicapped by the traditional attitude of the workers. Many of them do not feel that they owe greater loyalty to their union than to their bosses, who have always been their protectors and providers under Japan's feudal-like paternalistic industrial system. Not all are convinced either that collective bargaining will win for them greater benefits than they might already be receiving in the form of free lunches, free vacations, free transportation, and other such fringe allowances. Even fewer workers think in terms of political or ideological gains. Most political strikes, unless enforced with strong-arm methods, are doomed to failure for lack of widespread compliance, while strikes for legitimate economic reasons usually fizzle out before management is greatly pressed.

Another important safeguard against extreme leftism is the wave of prosperity that is raising living standards at an extraordinary rate. It is hard to believe that only a few years ago Japan, in defeat, was like a graveyard, with most industry destroyed, most cities in ashes, and the people dazed and desperate. Though many of the hundreds of thousands of migrants flooding into Tokyo each year may be impoverished, more than half the city's inhabitants have television sets and washing machines. And housewives, traditionally slaves to the kitchen, now have new electrical appliances that permit them to spend considerable time at the beauty parlor or in the park playing with their children.

The unskilled laborer earns only about $45 a month, but staple commodities are twice as cheap as in the United States. The basic needs of most Japanese are much simpler than Western needs. They require little or no furniture for their homes, and their diet consists mainly of rice, fish, and vegetables, items of nominal expense in Japan. Extensive fringe benefits further ease financial pressures.

As a result, many workers in Japan today are able to buy a TV set and washing machine and still save more than ten percent of their income, though workers in smaller household factories live less satisfactorily. What is more, most purchases are made in cash, for installment buying is still an embryonic concept among the Japanese. "I never thought we'd be able to live comfortably and have enough money to send the children to college," a factory worker named Shigenori Shimizu said when I visited him in his small wood-and-paper home provided by his company. "What else could I ask for?"

Japan's agrarian prosperity is even more conspicuous. Most peasants were tenant farmers before the war—like Eisaku Yamaguchi. Yamaguchi had to give more than fifty percent of the crop he cultivated to his absentee landlord, leaving him and his family hungry most years. But during the American Occupation the landlord was required to turn over all but three acres of his land to Yamaguchi and his other tenants in return for a twenty-year government bond, and Yamaguchi had twenty-four years in which to reimburse the government for his 1.5 acres of farmland. Actually, as the result of inflation the value of the bond dropped to almost nothing and Yamaguchi was able to cancel his debt in a few years. Today he earns a net annual income of about $1,000 from the sale of his rice, wheat, barley, and poultry, of which he is able to save thirty percent.

He lives with his wife—who, like most peasant women, wears black knicker-like trousers and a long-sleeved white apron—and three children in an old three-room house that his great-grandfather had built. Only two pieces of furniture decorate the mat-floored house: an ancient round teakwood table one-foot high around which the family kneels at mealtime and—a brand-new 19-inch TV set. Soon, Yamaguchi intends to start building a new house, complete with water-paintings on the paper walls.

Shimizu and Yamaguchi, who have never had it so good, are not easy targets for the revolutionaries, peaceful or otherwise. Whatever shortcomings workers like Shimizu may see in free enterprise, it has been kind to them. As for the Yamaguchis, they need only read—ninety-nine percent of the Japanese people are literate—about the miserable failure of Red China's communal farms to realize how lucky they are. A leftist student summed it all up when he told me despairingly: "The government is guilty of bribing the people with a lot of luxuries—buying their support."

But even if Japan does not veer toward Marxism, the pacifism of the Marxists is shared by most Japanese. Hence, a neutralist government may yet come to power and force the evacuation of American bases in Japan. This would not signify, however, that Japan was lost to the West. Even the Socialist Party, once burdened with responsibility, would probably be more rational in its Cold War approach. In any event, the key to future relations between the United States and Japan lies more in the economic than in the ideological realm. As the Japanese showed with their switch from totalitarianism to democracy after World War II, they are not a dogmatically consistent people. They are not above changing their policies again in what they might consider the best interests of Japan—particularly if the nation were hit by a severe depression.

Since Japanese democracy is still in its infancy, hardly more than economic bonds link the two countries. Culturally they have little in common despite Japan's wholesale importation of American fads, from strip-teasers to the dating system, from hamburgers to falsies. A Japanese may wear Western clothes to work, eat Western food in a restaurant, and dance the Twist with a geisha or night-club hostess, but when he goes home he is likely to put on a kimono, savor *tempura* or *suchi* with rice while sitting on the matted floor, and keep his wife in the kitchen when he has guests, among whom there will never be a Westerner. He would not be comfortable with a foreigner around, and he is certain that the foreigner would be equally uncomfortable, particularly if he had to use the Japanese-style toilet, simply a hole in a porcelain floor. Even many clubs and bars deny entry to Westerners. "Japanese buy drink for many host-esses like in geisha house, American wants sit only with one girl," one Japanese cabaret-owner explained to me. "Very cheap for us." A bar manager indicated Americans made his waiters lose face by demanding an itemized bill, something no Japanese would request. Even many prostitutes discriminate against Westerners, fearful of being boycotted by Japanese if they cater to them.

Unable to cope with people who do not know the complex rules of their tight, insulated society, the Japanese—though prepared to borrow from these people the surface values of their alien culture in order to fit them into the traditional Japanese way of life—feel no real sense of communication with them. The close relations that exist between Japan and the United States today are based strictly on mutual interest and will continue to be until the Japanese develop a true democratic tradition that will lend a more permanent fiber to the ties.

With Japan's ideological future in the balance, it is a political necessity for the United States to make sure that the country maintains and strengthens its economic muscles, even if this policy proves economically disadvantageous to a small number of American manufacturers.

XVIII

MALAYA AND SINGAPORE:

THE DRAGON'S BROOD

In the dense green jungles of the Federation of Malaya a strange war was recently fought. For twelve years, from 1948 to 1960, communist guerrillas and British-led troops in this former British colony engaged in a relentlessly waged contest of guns, knives, bows and arrows, wits, endurance, and patience. The anticommunists won the war, whittling down the communist Malayan Races Liberation Army (MRLA) from about 11,000 to 500. But to do it they had to use tens of thousands of Commonwealth and local troops, hundreds of thousands of home guards, and spend more than half a billion dollars.

They had to fire almost two million shells from land batteries and naval ships and drop hundreds of millions of propaganda leaflets into the jungle. One infantry battalion wore out 15,000 pairs of jungle boots, about 20 pairs per man and over 130 miles to a pair. A cavalry regiment covered 3,500,000 miles in armored cars in three years. Casualties among the anticommunist fighters—Malays, Chinese, Indians, British, Australians, New Zealanders, Fijians, and Africans—totaled about 2,500 dead and 800 missing, significant figures considering that only 6,700 communists were killed and 1,300 captured despite the overwhelming discrepancy in the size of the opposing forces and the quality and quantity of their equipment. (The word "Malay" refers to racial origin, the word "Malayan" to nationality.)

"There's never been a war like this," a gray-templed British officer with an understandably harried air told me at military headquarters in the steaming Malayan capital of Kuala Lumpur, as the fighting neared an end. "It's like chasing shadows at night—now you see them, now you don't. There's nothing to shoot at like there was in Korea. Not even once in a while like in Indochina. You just shoot when you see something move, hoping you'll hit the right target. Imagine having to use whole armies to flush out a few thousand fanatics armed only with rifles and knives. Yet I'd rather take my chances against tanks any day."

A young Australian lieutenant sitting beside his British superior in the dingy office added, "Excuse me if I sound like I'm moralizing, but as far as I am concerned, the worst thing about this war is its complete defiance of moral law, insofar as such law can apply to war. A terrorist can kill one of us in an ambush, then surrender and give information about the whereabouts of his buddies and he'll be treated like a king. But if that same man did not surrender but was caught, he would be treated like a cold-blooded murderer. Expediency has replaced moral law in this goddam war."

The Australian made a significant point. The communists were largely beaten not in battle, despite the fact that a big percentage of them were killed. The war was won by bribing the rank-and-file Reds to give up—about 3,000 did—with promises of amnesty, money, and food, which government measures sealing off most supply sources succeeded in keeping from them.

But however costly victory was in terms of time, money, men, and morality, it brought in its wake a political and economic stability rare in Southeast Asia, thanks in considerable degree to the enlightened leadership of portly, round-faced Prime Minister Tunku Abdul Rahman. The Malayan economy, based largely on rubber and tin, is booming. And there is no explosive nationalist movement in the Federation, which consists of nine states plus the two former British settlements of Penang and Malacca. For the population, about 6,500,000, is heterogeneous, being fifty percent Malay, forty percent Chinese, and ten percent Indian. Malaya remains strongly anticommunist at home and, while nominally unaligned in the Cold War, inclines sharply to the West. The Communist Party, outlawed when the Emergency, as the jungle war was called, broke out, is still illegal and is likely to be so for some time.

This seemingly optimistic picture, however, does not mean that the Red threat has been crushed. About 500 hard-core survivors, including Secretary-General Chen Ping and several other members of the Communist Party politbureau, are still entrenched in the jungle-covered mountains of northern Malaya and southern Thailand, north of Malaya, where, despite Malayan and Thai efforts to flush them out, they remain a constant potential danger. More important, communists who surrendered and other Reds who didn't participate in the fighting—the Communist Party proper has about 5,000 members today—have simply switched tactics, resorting to subversion rather than to violence to achieve their ends.

Despite harsh security measures retained from the Emergency, such as preventive detention of suspects, these Reds, who receive their orders directly from Peking or from its agents in Singapore, are penetrating labor unions, youth and student groups, and political parties. They are being helped by an underground communist auxiliary civilian organization called Min Yuen, which, during the Emergency, provided guerrillas with food, money, and information. Min Yuen, like the parent Communist Party and the now depleted Red military force, consists almost entirely of Chinese and may number anywhere from 10,000 to 100,000.

Prime Minister Rahman, who has headed Malaya's parliamentary government since Britain granted the country independence in 1957, has warned that communist subversion and "underground efforts to overthrow us" will be intensified now that the shooting war is over. "The communists," he said, "have never experienced defeat in other countries. So they will be nursing a real feeling of revenge. Therefore, they will intensify their subversive and underground efforts to overthrow us. We have banned the Bank of China as well as any trading operation which has the aim of spreading the communist government here." He promised new anticommunist laws.

Rahman has not exaggerated the new communist menace. Few Malayans of Malay stock are sympathetic toward communism, but Chinese Malayans bombarded with propaganda from Peking lean in large degree toward support of Communist China, though most may not be communists themselves. And the danger of communist subversion may increase when plans to absorb the island of Singapore, now an autonomous British territory at the southern tip of the Malayan Peninsula, into an expanded Malaysian Federation materialize. For Singapore has a population of 1,500,000, of which seventy-five percent are Chinese, most of them inclined toward the far left.

The Malayan Reds are not novices in the business of subversion despite their concentration on armed violence in recent years. If

Stalin had played his cards right, Malaya might today be a communist state. In early 1948 the Malayan Communist Party was the largest and strongest political organization in the country. It had infiltrated the schools and community organizations. Its members were the most powerful element in Malaya's new postwar labor unions, and fully controlled the largest—the Pan-Malayan Federation of Labor. Moreover, the party was legal and had managed to win the co-operation and confidence of other Malayan parties.

Much of this postwar success stemmed from the dominating role of the communists in the 7,000-man Malayan guerrilla army that constantly harassed the Japanese occupation forces from 1942 to 1945. This army, in fact, took orders from the Communist Party. When Malaya was liberated, the communists were idolized by most of the people. Most Malayans even tolerated the mass murder of Japanese soldiers and collaborators by communists who stormed into the towns following the Japanese surrender. But when the Reds started killing people just because they were anticommunist, looting their homes and confiscating their property, most Malayans began to see for the first time what their heroes were really made of. Nevertheless, the Reds' wartime activities permitted the Communist Party to emerge as a highly respectable organization.

"If the communists had bided their time," a British administrator, twirling his large mustache, told me in his small wooden headquarters at the edge of a jungle village, "Malaya would probably have fallen into their hands."

But Stalin was impatient. The Malayan party, like most other Asian communist organizations, was ordered in 1948 to revolt openly against the government and all other forces opposed to Red rule. In June of that year 11,000 communists, hoping to win quick control of Malaya from a Britain that had shown little inclination to use force to stay on in such places as India and Burma, began terrorizing the British and their local collaborators in much the same manner as they had the Japanese, often killing innocent Malayans in indiscriminate bombing, machine gun, and grenade attacks on trains and road vehicles, as well as on villages harboring anticommunists. Automatically they relinquished the tremendous gains they had made through peaceful infiltration. Communism was outlawed, and the Reds, many of whom had doubted the practicality of Stalin's order even while obeying it, soon discovered that their apprehensions had been justified. The British and their Malayan and Commonwealth allies were determined to put down the revolt regardless of cost.

How were the guerrillas able to last as long as they did against enormously superior numbers? One answer lay in the rugged jungles which were almost impenetrable in many areas. Often government troops passed within a few feet of rebels hidden in the brush without seeing them, making easy targets for rebel attacks. But an equally important factor in the Reds' staying power, at least in the first few years of the war, was the co-operation given them by 400,000 Malayan peasants, mostly Chinese, who, after the Japanese surrender, squatted and cultivated on the fringe of the jungle. Such co-operation at the start of the fighting was often won through brutality and threats, particularly in the case of reluctant Malays—the kind of treatment the Reds had reserved for collaborators during World War II. Thus they were able to keep themselves well supplied with information on enemy movements and the identity of informers, who were promptly tortured and killed, as well as with food which did not grow in the jungle. Eventually, the terrorists learned that persuasion and civility often worked as well, if not better, than violence and arrogance in winning such co-operation. In many cases jungle dwellers willingly helped the communists, and some even joined the Red bands.

But this new moderation was based not only on the communist need for the military co-operation of the villagers. It also derived from a reappraisal by the Reds of their military position. By 1951 they realized they could not hope for an armed victory. Yet there was no way they could end the war without abject surrender, a solution they would not consider. So three years after the war started, they decided to shift some of their energies, as a communist directive put it, toward "repenetration of all strata of civilian life," particularly Chinese community organizations. Since they lacked the resources to engage with maximum effect in subversion and violence simultaneously, they started concentrating on the former, a major factor in the surrender of many rebels once they were promised they would be set free. But to compensate for their immediate loss in striking power the Reds began giving intensified jungle training to elite groups, who, even if they could not beat the government forces, could probably hold out indefinitely and become the cadre of a future army when conditions were more militarily favorable to the communist cause.

To create a popular climate suitable for subversion and to gain the military co-operation of the people, Red leaders ordered their men to restrict their terrorist attacks to purely military objectives. No more villages were to be burned, no more civilian trains derailed, and no more indiscriminate attacks made in the towns—

whether to force people to collaborate or to get rid of anticommunists and informers. Such tactics would disrupt efforts to launch the Yenan Way once again. Though these orders were often disobeyed and appeared to be lifted during certain periods to let the enemy know it still had a fight on its hands—some of the worst terroristic acts were committed in a fit of contempt after the government offered unconditional amnesty to those who surrendered before February 1956—terrorism generally diminished in the early and middle 1950's.

The communists' decision to de-emphasize the military phase of its program was well-timed. For in 1951 the British-led forces started taking what was probably the decisive measure in sealing the fate of the rebels. They moved almost one-third of the Malayan Chinese—all those living in jungle isolation—into New Villages heavily guarded and surrounded by barbed wire. The terrorists were deprived of their principal source of food and intelligence. This drastic step, conceived by British High Commissioner Sir Henry Gurney and largely put into effect by General Sir Gerald Templer after Gurney was killed in an ambush in 1951, gradually starved many rebels out of the jungle and weakened the fighting ability of others. Such conditions accelerated the communist effort to revert to subversive tactics, and after 1954 violence sharply tapered off, though the Reds never permitted the authorities to relax for long.

But if the resettlement program broke the back of the terrorists, it also—ironically—planted the seeds of future communist gains. For the thoughtless and often cruel execution of this program gave rise to a resentment of the British and their allies and a corresponding sympathy for the communists, who were regarded with some friendliness by many Chinese even before they were moved out of the jungle. In many cases the British gave peasants only four or five hours' notice of their removal. A truck or jeep would pull up before a thatch-roofed mud hut resting on four thick bamboo poles, and the farmer and his family with their meager cloth-wrapped belongings would be whisked away from home and livelihood against a backdrop of burning corn, potato, and vegetable crops that might have fed the rebels.

Even rubber tappers working on rubber plantations in the jungle had to move to the New Villages. On a visit to one plantation in northern Malaya I met a tapper who was preparing to leave. A forlorn figure in shorts and ripped undershirt as he stood in the midst of a forest of green rubber trees, he said in halting English, "I've been tapping here for more than ten years. Now I've got to move. What will I do? This is the only work I know. Do you know what it's like being lifted up by the roots?" He spat on the earth.

Life was difficult in the New Villages. Farmers had to clear new fields for new crops, and in many cases they were situated so far from the main towns that they were unable to transport their produce to market. Worst of all was the psychological blow: the Chinese could not own the land they worked under old Malayan land tenure laws framed to favor the indigenous Malays, who traditionally feared Chinese domination. The British were able to grant only leases extending up to thirty-three years. Also, the hard-working Chinese were permitted to keep little of the food they grew for themselves, for a strict rationing system was imposed to make sure that excess food did not get into the hands of the communists. Those Chinese who had been terrorized by the rebels, and they numbered not a few, accepted this new hard life with resignation, almost enjoying the sense of security they had lacked while at the mercy of jungle bands. But many others, even while unenthusiastic about communism, might well have welcomed "liberation" by the communists, who, they noted, had largely given up their aggressive, arrogant attitude toward the population. And after all, the Reds were Chinese.

Actually, most Chinese in Malaya—about four-fifths—are urban dwellers, not farmers. Outside of some competition from the Indian community, they firmly control Malayan commerce—a fact that deeply irks their Malay countrymen, the great majority of whom are peasants. Most Malays, like the indigenous populations of other Southeast Asian nations, consider the Chinese as aliens however long they may have been settled on their land. And the British, viewing the Malay community as a valuable ally during their rule, largely catered to its demands. The Chinese, though constituting almost half of the country's population, have been, and are still, deprived of such basic civil rights as ownership of land and, in most cases, the vote.

Independence has aggravated this deep-rooted internal discord. The Chinese now demand more loudly than ever equal civil rights with the Malays. The Malays, though many are repulsed by the very thought of hard work in Malaya's lazy, tropical climate, insist on a greater share in the economic benefits of independence, a share that must be taken from the beaver-like Chinese. Independence has also underscored the most touchy question of all— national loyalty. While all persons born in this multiracial state after independence are automatically citizens, the Malays doubt that the Chinese will or can be loyal to Malaya. Malay extremists demand that the Chinese be denied all political as well as civil rights. Others would give them most civil and political rights, but on the condition that they vowed loyalty only to Malaya and not to China.

"If the Chinese were a small minority," a Malay official in Kuala Lumpur told me over a lunch of lamb and curry, "the question of loyalty would not be of such great importance. But they make up almost half of Malaya and must become an integral, one hundred percent loyal part of the country, or it is no country. We will not become a branch of China, communist or otherwise."

But that is, of course, the precise aim of Communist China. To help achieve it, Radio Peking saturates the Chinese community with a constant flow of propaganda encouraging bonds of loyalty to the mainland and pride in Red China's accomplishments. As elsewhere in Southeast Asia, such propaganda seldom fails to touch a chord. In one degree or another, a huge part of the population still consider China their motherland and Malaya merely their place of residence.

Politically, the struggle between the Malays and the overseas Chinese, curiously enough, is being waged largely within one massive organization, the Alliance Party. This party won 74 out of 104 seats in the lower house of parliament in the 1959 elections. The Alliance is made up of the United Malays National Association, the Malayan Chinese Association, and the Malayan Indian Congress, each representing most members of their respective racial groups. This coalition was formed during the Emergency under British urging to unify the nation against the communist threat. But as long ago as 1955 the communists were infiltrating the Malayan Chinese Association, and they are believed to be making their influence felt in the organization today, feeding on the contradictory demands of the Malays and Chinese.

While such subversion is the most immediate danger facing Malaya today, the Red military threat, though suppressed for the moment, still lingers in the jungle thickets of the peninsula. The 500 or so guerrillas continuing to hold out have firmly established themselves in a strip of no-man's-land straddling the Malayan-Thai border. This could easily become the base of another violent effort to overthrow the government after subversion has sufficiently softened it up. Malaya would probably be doomed if the Reds captured Thailand. Nor is this an impossibility should communist Vietnamese forces take over South Vietnam or "neutralized" Laos, both of which border on that country.

The no-man's-land cuts across the winding waist of the Malayan Peninsula for over three hundred miles and is about fifteen miles wide, extending from the Malayan customs post of Changloon, six miles south of the border, to the Thai customs post of Sadao, nine miles north of the frontier. At some points, however, the communists operate up to thirty miles inside Thailand. The fact that both countries maintain their checkpoints so far from the border is a tribute to the firmness of the communist hold on the hilly bushland in between. The Reds first infiltrated Thai territory in 1951 when they decided to reduce their terrorist assaults in favor of increased subversion. The Thai jungles, they felt, offered them just the base they needed for the development of a small, elite, permanent force that could one day form the nucleus of a new and massive guerrilla army. This plan was in accordance with the Mao doctrine that attacks on urban areas, to be effective, had to be launched from a strong, stable, rural base. On the one hand, Malayan troops could not cross the border to fight the rebels, and on the other, the Thai government, though anticommunist, appeared to lack the will and the means to launch a serious military campaign against them.

The guerrilla army's operational headquarters for northern Malaya started directing the war from Thailand in 1954, and the Malayan Communist Party moved its headquarters there shortly afterwards. Soon the Reds were running the whole border area like an independent Soviet territory. In the Thai zone villagers, most of whom are Chinese, have had to pay taxes to both the Thai government and the Malayan rebels, who, equipped with neatly mimeographed tax rolls, sometimes go from hut to stilted hut demanding payment. Extortion? Not at all, say the communists. The taxes go, they point out, to maintain such public services as health clinics—some of the very few in the area—and the training of militia "to keep order." And after all, do not the local Red rulers hold free Marxist classes in the villages?

The most remarkable thing about the "Red regime" in the Malayan-Thai border area has been its invisibility. On a train trip from Singapore to Bangkok through one of the lushest, most richly vegetated areas in the world, I crossed the frontier zone without seeing any evidence of the communist "presence"—except several torn posters plastered on the walls of some Thai village shops asking the population in the Thai and Chinese languages to turn in to the police any information they might have on the whereabouts of guerrillas.

At the Malayan customs station near the border, hardly more

than a clearing in the middle of a thick wood, a uniformed Malayan official said while examining my passport: "The communists are all around here. They might be hiding in those bushes about thirty yards away at this very minute ready to attack the train. They're everywhere and they're nowhere . . . Have a nice trip."

But despite the potential threats of subversion and renewed guerrilla activity, the West can look with some satisfaction on a number of factors that are likely to make the going difficult for the communists. One such factor is the intelligence and moderation of Prime Minister Rahman. While maintaining a rigid anti-communist posture, he has managed to create at least a façade of national unity. Rahman, the Malay leader of the Alliance Party, became Prime Minister under the British regime after the election of Malaya's first federal legislative council, or parliament, in July 1955.

He was born in 1903, one of many sons of the Sultan of Kedah, a jungle principality in north Malaya. The family dynasty was founded by a Mongol chieftain who was shipwrecked on the Malayan coast, and has continued unbroken through nine Hindu rajahs and twenty Moslem sultans. A brother of the Prime Minister is the current Sultan of Kedah. Never anti-British, Rahman began to think of an independent Malaya while studying at Cambridge University, where he also played soccer. The British themselves planted the nationalist seed in his mind. One of them told him when he tried to find a room on the campus, "This college is built for Englishmen." University authorities intervened, but he refused to accept the accommodations. "I was offended at the time," he said recently, "but that soon passed. I was a good mixer and popular, so it did not matter. Nevertheless, the incident made me decide for the first time that I must help make my country my own."

On returning to Malaya, he held a series of administrative posts in Kedah, working in harmony with the British until the Japanese invasion of Malaya during World War II. When the British began moving the elderly Sultan of Kedah, his father, to Penang to prevent his capture by the Japanese, Rahman, who felt the Sultan should remain among his people, ambushed the British cavalcade and returned him to his palace. After the war Rahman entered local politics and joined forces with the Malayan Chinese Association in municipal elections held in 1952 to form the nucleus of the Alliance Party that swept the national elections of 1955. To stress his profound desire for strong multiracial ties, he and his wife adopted two Chinese children.

One of his first acts as Premier was to accept Chinese suggestions that unconditional amnesty be granted to all terrorists who surrendered before February 1956, regardless of their crimes. He then agreed to a communist proposal, strongly backed by his Chinese colleagues, that he meet with Red Secretary-General Chen Ping in a northern Malayan village to explore the possibility of peace.

But Rahman would go only so far in appeasing the communists. He refused to accept the demands of young, boyish-looking Chin, who had come to the meeting from his refuge in Thailand, that captured terrorists be freed and permitted to pursue civilian activities of their choice, and that the Communist Party be legalized. At the same time he cracked down hard on subversion, particularly among the youth. In 1956 he forbade group visits to Malaya by Singapore Chinese students after some of them had tried to set up Red cells in Malayan Chinese-language schools. In 1957 he ordered that overage professional students be expelled from such schools, despite violent student strikes against the measure. In 1958, in the face of renewed strikes and rioting, he pushed through regulations requiring Chinese students to take special examinations in the Malay and English languages and in advanced mathematics to qualify for admission to senior high schools. It is likely, in the light of this record, that he meant what he said when he promised after the Emergency was declared officially over that many new measures to frustrate subversion could be expected.

Rahman's carrot-and-stick policies are, moreover, being conducted in an economic atmosphere conducive to political stability. Since the Emergency, which devoured about two-thirds of the national budget, Malaya has experienced the greatest boom of any country in Southeast Asia. Exports reached almost $1 billion in 1960, a twenty percent increase over 1959, and the figure is steadily rising. The root of this prosperity is the world's increasing demand for Malaya's rubber and tin, which amounts to eighty-five percent of its exports. But an important contributing factor has been the government's devotion to free enterprise, an extremely unusual attitude among the underdeveloped nations, most of which view socialism as the only possible answer to their economic problems. While this discrepancy is partially explained by the advanced stage of development of Malayan industry in contrast to the situation in most former colonial or semicolonial states, which have little or no available capital to start with, it also reflects Rahman's basic economic philosophy.

"There is no need for government in industry," he said. "It is our policy to encourage private enterprise. We have set up small banks, government agencies, and private corporations to grant loans to private business."

Impressed by the government's economic policies, a remarkable number of foreign companies have moved into Malaya recently despite the potential danger of a new communist threat—among them such American firms as the Colgate Palmolive Co., Caltex Oil Ltd., Standard-Vacuum Oil Co., Singer Sewing Machine Co., the Bank of America, the First National City Bank of New York, and Beatrice Foods Co.

To permit the smooth functioning of the Malayan economy, Rahman has not, as have more emotional Afro-Asian nationalist leaders, prematurely thrown colonial administrators out of the country. The Permanent Secretary of Defense and the head of the Public Works Department are English, and the Governor of the central bank is Australian. They will remain until Malayans are trained sufficiently to take over these jobs. With the completion of Malaya's first five-year plan, which was almost entirely fulfilled even though it coincided with the Emergency, a second five-year plan with a $700 million budget, more than twice the last one, got underway in 1960 and is expected to mean an inportant rise in living standards—hardly a prospect to stimulate glee in the communist camp.

Malaya's political fate in the long run may be determined by the nature of the Malaysian Federation now being planned. This federation will embrace Malaya, Singapore, and the three British-controlled areas of Brunei, Sarawak, and North Borneo, which, together with Indonesian Borneo, form the huge island of Borneo to the east of the Malayan Peninsula. The idea of such an expanded state was conceived by Rahman in 1961 as a means of making Singapore's annexation feasible. Rahman and his fellow Malays were caught in a peculiar dilemma after independence. They wanted to absorb Singapore for its strategic and economic advantages. But they had to oppose such a merger because the overseas Chinese, composing forty percent of the Malayan and seventy-five percent of the Singapore population, would outnumber the Malays in their own country. Of even greater immediate importance, the government of such a state would probably be leftist in line with majority Chinese sentiment.

The solution, Rahman decided, lay in the larger five-territory federation, which would leave the Chinese a minority. There was much in common among all the areas, he pointed out, including the

Malay language and a long history of British rule. Further, such a state, spanning an area of 129,000 square miles and possessing one-third of the world's tin, one-fourth of its rubber, and—in Brunei—one of its richest oil fields, would be a major power in Southeast Asia.

Nor do many people in Singapore, to which the British granted internal autonomy in 1959, take issue with the desirability of a merger with Malaya. Over seventy percent approved the idea in a referendum conducted in September 1962. Chinese socialist Prime Minister Lee Kwan Yew, a moderate politician who once championed the far left, is one of the strongest proponents of the union and has been doing his best to foster the feeling among Singaporeans, whether of Chinese, Indian, or any other descent, that they are first of all Malayans. He has appointed a Malay as head of state and proclaimed Malay the national language.

Many natural economic and historical factors bind the two territories. Separated from Malaya only by the mile-wide Strait of Johore, which is spanned by a causeway, Singapore has served for almost a century as Malaya's main port and commercial capital for its rubber and tin interests. But if union is believed desirable to guarantee Singapore's long-range commercial health, it is considered indispensable as a means of giving the overcrowded island an outlet for its excess population. Singapore is also influenced by its traditional political ties with Malaya under British rule. Before World War II, both areas were treated as parts of a single colonial unit called the Straits Settlements. Even after World War II, when the mainland became the Federation of Malaya and the island city a separate crown colony, the two territories shared postal and telecommunication services, broadcasting facilities, a common income-tax system, and the University of Malaya.

But a more immediate consideration, at least in the minds of the Singapore government, was summed up by Prime Minister Lee when he recently said, "Independent Singapore means communist Singapore." Precisely because it does, the Reds, almost alone among Singaporeans, favor an independent Singapore, and have threatened to use force if necessary to prevent the city's absorption into a larger territorial union.

The merger project poses a delicate question for the British, who still control Singapore's defense and foreign affairs. The city, though only 224 square miles in area, is Britain's most important Far Eastern base, headquarters of its Asian service commands, and the co-ordinating center for all of its regional diplomatic and intelligence activities. The island's inclusion in a Malaysian Federation will mean that Britain will be completely dependent on the Malayan government for its rights in this vitally strategic city, and at a time when the communists are strongly entrenched there. On the other hand, inclusion may be the only way to reduce the tremendous influence of the Singaporean Reds.

Although the great majority of people are not communist—the vote for a Malaysian union underscored this—the communist influence is powerful in this restless, bawdy, prudish, energetic, materialistic, fun-loving, fear-ridden, brooding, picturesque, multi-racial metropolis. This influence does not stem primarily from poverty, discontent, or extreme nationalism as it does in most underdeveloped countries. Per capita income, $400 a year, however low by Western standards, is from eight to ten times larger than in most other territories in Southeast Asia, despite increasing unemployment. Modern air-conditioned apartment buildings are mushrooming in areas previously occupied by dingy cubicle shacks that served as shop and home. Neat new bungalows are going up as fast as the jungle can be cleared. Boys and girls, mostly Chinese, joyfully throng the city's two amusement parks, the Great World and the Happy World, while their elders never tire of a great gaudy outdoor wax museum in which seemingly live wild animals frighteningly abound and human figures can hardly be told apart from the visitors. The city's heartbeat is perhaps reflected most aptly of all in the sight of scores of ocean-going vessels and hundreds of *tongkangs* and *proas* crammed with Malayan rubber, Indonesian spices, and the products of many other nations speckling the noisy, bustling harbor, fifth busiest in the world.

This portrait of Singapore hardly bespeaks the usual conditions that foster communism. Instead, a kind of moral emptiness and rootlessness have spurred its growth. "Singapore is a place with little community feeling," an Indian shopkeeper said as he stood outside his haberdashery trying to entice me in. "Most people are here because it's a good place to make money. We are homeless people dreaming of home. The Chinese still consider themselves Chinese living abroad. And the same is true of the Indians and the British. As for the Malays, there are very few of them here. This is a city without a soul of its own. Just a conglomeration of scared, insecure people thinking only of themselves . . . Would you be interested in a cashmere sweater? Very inexpensive."

This lack of nationalist or civic consciousness, while prevalent among overseas Chinese everywhere in Southeast Asia, gives Singapore a singularly unpatriotic character because of the great Chinese majority. The people reserve their pride for their countries of origin, which are to them anchors of security and spiritual comfort. Nowhere is Red China exploiting these needs more than in Singapore, well aware that this island is the one territory in Southeast Asia where the Chinese, because of their superior numbers, can aggressively promote Peking's interest without inviting undue suppression.

British-controlled Hong Kong, of course, is an all-Chinese city, but subversion isn't really necessary there for the Red Chinese could physically take it over at any time they chose. Also, the presence of hundreds of thousands of refugees in Hong Kong offers living testimony to the other inhabitants that Mao's China is anything but a paradise, and renders most Red propaganda valueless. By contrast Singapore, being fairly distant from China, could not be taken, in the foreseeable future at least, by military means, and at the same time is not overly aware of life under the communist regime. It is, furthermore, in an excellent position to contaminate neighboring Malaya. Not surprisingly, this lusty port metropolis has become one of Peking's chief centers of subversion in Asia.

The Singapore Communist Party was banned simultaneously with its Malayan counterpart, with which it maintains vague organizational ties, in 1948 when the Emergency began. It is still outlawed today. But it operates a vast underground network that has deeply infiltrated schools, labor unions, and political parties. Only about 300 Reds are known to the police and even they have managed so far to escape the grasp of the law, so concealed are their activities. Communist undercover agents, including noncommunists being used for Red ends, operate at several removes from the real leaders. Although Red books and other literature have been banned from the city together with the party itself, material is published clandestinely. Radio Peking is an important source of influence and a means whereby Communist China communicates the party line to its cadres.

Peking is making its biggest play for Singapore's Chinese youth, and with considerable reason. Half the city's population is under twenty-one years of age, and as time goes on they will find ever greater difficulty in getting jobs. At the present rate of population growth, the school-age group will increase by more than fifty percent in the next decade. Just to educate the youth in about 1970 will require the equivalent of the total 1960 budget. Currently, about half of Singapore's 250,000 students are enrolled in Chinese-language institutions, a highly favorable situation for Peking propagandists.

Red China's influence was first openly manifested in 1954, when Chinese high school students demonstrated against a military conscription law that was to take effect when Singapore became autonomous. Though students were exempt under the bill, professional "students" spread the word that they would be sent to fight the communists in Malaya and Vietnam. When police charged demonstrators at Chung Cheng High School, which was known for its far-left tendencies, the students withdrew behind the fence of the school compound and conducted classes among themselves. They finally agreed to end their siege when the police threatened drastic action.

But this incident had an explosive effect on the Chinese community. Those who disagreed with the students' tactics were branded by demagogues as traitors to their race, and most Chinese, wanting to live in peace, either kept their mouths shut or approved the student action. Even a leading Chinese-language newspaper, *Nanyang Siang Pau* (*South Seas Commercial Post*), after receiving threats and losing circulation, suddenly substituted praise for condemnation of the students in its editorials. Within a few months the communist students controlled all the Chinese-language schools, and in 1955, when Communist Party leaders were arrested, they ran the party itself, supported by Red-dominated secret societies whose members murdered a number of anticommunists in the streets.

A police investigation of one institution, Hua-Chiao High School, yielded this report: "This school has long been a veritable Marxist academy in Singapore and as such it has been an inexhaustible source of supply of recruits for the Malayan Communist Party and the Chinese Communist Party . . . Teachers have practically no control over the students and this state of affairs is partly due to the apathetic state of the former." Teachers or principals who have tried to throw agitators out of the schools or even to defy their will have found their lives in danger. And students themselves have been under tremendous pressure to co-operate with the Reds. They have had to join communist-led school committees to protest government policies and support Red projects. They have had to attend discussion sessions at which the Reds have done all the talking. They have had to sing songs extolling the new life in the motherland, often at compulsory picnics. Many have gone to China for advanced study.

Communist student leaders have worked—and rioted—together with the labor-union representatives, particularly members of the Red-controlled Factory and Shopworkers Union, which was finally broken up after Prime Minister Lee's government came to power in 1959. In 1955, after many workers were dismissed during a strike, students and workers instigated riots in which a number of people were killed, including an American correspondent, Gene Symonds of the United Press. The Prime Minister then in power, David Saul Marshall, an anticommunist Asian Jew and flamboyant criminal lawyer, closed the Chinese-language schools, but when new demonstrations threatened, meekly reopened them. The upshot was that the Reds became stronger than ever in both the schools and the labor unions.

Finally, in 1956, Prime Minister Lim Yew Hock, a moderate labor organizer who succeeded Marshall in the post, decided to take drastic action against the Reds. He ordered that such communist-front organizations as the Singapore Women's Federation and the Brass Gong Musical Society be shut down. He arrested a number of local Reds and deported several alien agitators, including teachers and union leaders. A concert sponsored by a front group was banned because songs entitled "The People of China and Russia are Firmly United" and "The Great Mao Tse-tung" were scheduled. Most important of all, Lim struck at the heart of the communist menace—the students. He ordered the dissolution of the Singapore Chinese Middle School Students Union, and tried to close the Chinese-language schools again until they could be rid of communists.

When several thousand students barricaded themselves in the Chung Cheng and Hua-Chiao High Schools, the police attacked after an ultimatum was spurned and cleared them out. But riots spread throughout the city as more than 25,000 students and unionists burned buses, stoned cars, and hurled bombs. When the disorder ended four days later after British and Gurkha troops had taken command, thirteen people were dead, almost four hundred wounded, and over one thousand under arrest. With even most Chinese shocked and disgusted by communist-instigated excesses, the underground suffered an important defeat. But it was not discouraged. Those Chinese it could not hold with propaganda, it cowed with back-street terrorism. Its secret societies killed, kidnaped, and extorted. One student was murdered simply because he listened to "yellow," or decadent, American rock-and-roll music. His classmates were afraid even to attend his funeral, and witnesses remained silent, as they did in almost every case. But since such individual acts of terror could not win for the Reds and their supporters the power they coveted, they simultaneously intensified their political activities, throwing their weight behind an emerging young leftist politician named Lee Kuan Yew.

Before he came to power in 1959, Prime Minister Lee, known to his friends as Harry Lee, appeared to incline far to the left. A third-generation Singapore Chinese, Lee, born to wealthy parents in 1920, graduated in law from Cambridge University with the highest grades in his class and returned to Singapore a radical socialist. After successfully negotiating industrial disputes for several Singapore unions, he entered politics, joining forces with Marshall and Lim Yew Hock to defeat British-backed conservative candidates in Singapore's 1955 elections.

But far more radical than either Marshall or Lim, Lee broke away to form the People's Action Party (PAP) and welcomed the support of the communists, who were not permitted to form a party of their own. In the 1959 elections to choose Singapore's first autonomous government, Lee, campaigning in his shirt sleeves, promised to "restore the dignity" of the Asians, "fight against the white man," and "be as far to the left as it is possible for a democratic party to be." Frightened investors transferred their capital out of Singapore, British expatriates took flight, and even Southeast Asia's oldest newspaper, *The Straits Times*, moved its head offices to Kuala Lumpur to avoid communist intimidation.

But hardly had his party swept into office with an overwhelming majority of parliamentary seats than Lee, who can speak English with greater fluency than he can speak Chinese, began to show a more conservative strain in keeping with his thoroughly British upbringing. As a sop for his far-leftist supporters, who represented almost half the party, he gave them important, if secondary, positions in his administration, had portraits of Queen Elizabeth II torn down from government office walls, cut the salaries of British civil servants, and banned such manifestations of the West's "yellow culture" as jukebox saloons, pinball machines, "cheesecake" publications, and comic books. Nevertheless, Lee soon made it clear that his party would fight the communists uncompromisingly unless they accepted democratic procedures. He ordered tighter police vigilance aganst Red terrorist activities, and introduced a national education system designed to cleanse the Chinese school curriculum of Peking influences.

Economically, too, Lee, a youthful-looking man with narrow, intelligent eyes and a strong, broad face, has proved to be anything but a radical socialist—the reason lying partly in the fact that Singapore has no major industries to nationalize and insufficient funds for large-scale welfare projects. Announcing that he would "teach the capitalists how to run their system," he has offered attractive terms to potential foreign investors, and has landed several big companies, including Shell Oil Co., which is building an $18,000,000 refinery. Lee has also forced changes in trade-union leadership and has established an arbitration court to reduce strikes. To guard against communist infiltration into positions of executive power within the PAP, Lee is using a cadre system borrowed from the communists themselves. He is also employing communist techniques to keep the Reds from winning recruits among the unemployed, who number in this overpopulated city about 50,000 out of a working force of 500,000. He has organized work brigades complete with uniforms, salutes, and barracks life.

Moreover Lee, despite his strong anticolonial and professedly neutralist sentiments, has rejected communist demands that the British be forced to relinquish their place on the special Internal Security Council, formed when Singapore became an autonomous area. The purpose of the council, which also includes representatives of the island city and Malaya, is to take all necessary steps to prevent subversion. Nor does Lee want the British to give up their control of Singapore's foreign affairs and external defense, which permits them to retain bases in the area, before a merger is consummated. Even then, he has stated, it may be feasible to eliminate the British base only in "five, ten, fifteen, or twenty years."

Lee realizes that the British base is almost indispensable to Singapore's economy. Britain is spending $100 million a year on it, permitting the employment of 40,000 workers directly and many additional thousands indirectly. But Lee also sees the base as a guarantee against a communist takeover until Singapore can be put under the protection of the Malayan government.

"Any challenge to ultimate authority," Lee warned the Reds in a parliamentary speech, "will be made not to the Singapore government, whose force is not supreme, but to the British. To stand in front of British armed forces when a collision is taking place with forces of violent revolution would be foolhardy."

Lee struck his hardest blow at the communists when, in July 1961, he dismissed eight allegedly Red government officials—five parliamentary secretaries and three political secretaries—for opposing his policies. One of the political secretaries was Lim Chin Siong, described in a document produced in parliament as the leading overt communist in Singapore. A young, affable ex-assemblyman and an effective trade-union organizer, Lim was arrested for his role in a 1956 riot, only to be given a high government position—secretary to the Finance Minister—by Lee in payment for his support in the 1959 election. The two other political secretaries dismissed, Fong Swee-swan and S. Woodhull, had been arrested and freed with Lim. They were assigned by Lee to the Labor and Health Ministries respectively. After their dismissal, the eight procommunist officials issued a manifesto declaring that "the struggle in the PAP is one between socialists and progressives representing the rank and file and a reactionary right-wing group which has not only betrayed the trust of the people but has resorted to open hostility to the people."

The left wing of the PAP thereupon deserted Lee, leaving the party with a precarious one-vote majority in parliament. If his government falls and a new election is held, it is possible that the extreme left may win political control of this strategic area. Fully aware of this, Lee has tried to reduce the pressure on himself by reverting in some degree to anti-West or neutralist demagogy. He has threatened to mobilize what he termed the "xenophobia" in Singapore to pressure Britain into refraining from the use of its base there for SEATO purposes. Western officials were worried by this threat, for Singapore plays an important logistical role in the joint deployment of Allied forces in the Southeast Asia area. But they have been assured by Rahman that when the projected British-supported Malaysian Federation is realized in late 1963 the British will enjoy continued use of the base, presumably including its employment for SEATO purposes.

Actually, Lee's political courage in standing up to the communists despite grave political risks is largely based on the gamble, which he has apparently won, that Singapore's problems will soon be in the hands of the Malayan government. No doubt, too, he has calculated that strong resistance to communism was necessary, as indeed it was, to encourage that government to take Singapore under its wing.

Realizing that they cannot buck the tide, the communists and other far leftists, while favoring independence, have tentatively approved the idea of a merger, but are demanding conditions they know will not be accepted. Rahman has already agreed to leave Singapore autonomous in the fields of education and labor— in which leftist Chinese are strong. But the procommunists demand also a guarantee of full Malayan citizenship for all Singapore inhabitants and proportional representation in the Malayan parliament, measures which would give leftist Chinese a powerful foothold in the central government.

Under British pressure, the native leaders of Sarawak, North Borneo, and Brunei have agreed to join the proposed federation. But the procommunists in Singapore are receiving considerable support in their struggle to sabotage the project from leftists, and even many traditionalists, in the three tiny territories.

In Sarawak, which was ruled for a century by the "white rajahs" descended from Sir James Brooke before the last one ceded the area to the British Crown in 1946, the United People's Party, led by Stephen Yong, a far-leftist Chinese, strongly opposes the merger, even though the only alternative for the time being would be continued British rule in view of the extremely primitive condition of the 50,000-square-mile colony. Communist Chinese sources in Singapore are supplying the party with substantial funds to purchase the support of the indigenous, backward Dyaks—Polynesians who compose almost half of the 750,000 people in this rubber, timber, and spice center. Among the Chinese, who represent about one-third of the population, most conservatives are also wary of the merger, fearing that the Chinese, being largely educated, would have to play too prominent a role in running the community, risking conflict with the more numerous Dyaks. Only the Malays, who make up less than twenty percent of the population, strongly favor union with Malaya.

Majority sentiment in the neighboring colony of North Borneo, which was ruled by a private British company until the British government took over in 1946, also appears to oppose a union, at least for the time being, but not for the same reasons that the communists are against it. On the contrary, most of the inhabitants regard the British and the West as their friends and protectors. The 100,000 conservative Chinese here, about one-fourth of the population, not only fear that federation would introduce leftist influences into the colony, but want the British to promulgate an immigration law that would keep out their Singapore Chinese brothers.

North Borneo's native tribes, many of which are descended from head-hunters and still use blowpipes to kill game in the jungle or occasionally members of hostile tribes, are also unenthusiastic about union with Malaya. The Dusuns and Muruts, who are either Christian or animist, are afraid that the Moslem Malays may try to interfere with their religion and customs. They, as well as the Bajaus, a Moslem tribe, and the Chinese want English, not Malay, to be the official state language. The tribesmen spend most of their time farming and fishing, selling their produce on Sunday mornings in nearby village market places where, in colorful native dress, they gather on horseback amidst a sea of fruit, fish, spices, cloth, and manufactured items imported by Chinese merchants.

Content with their easy-going lives, they are happy under British rule. The British, tribal leaders say, should remain in North Borneo until the backward territory is capable of self-government. Later, it could be merged with Sarawak and Brunei, the third British Borneo colony that Malaya wants in its expanded state. A loose confederation with Malaya would be the final step, say the tribesmen, maintaining that "the departure of the British too soon would be abandonment and a betrayal of trust." Reflecting an unusual attitude toward colonialism among Asians, many people, at least those who are politically conscious, indicate that one reason why they do not favor immediate federation is that SEATO, whose armed forces often maneuver here, would no longer be permitted to "protect North Borneo from communism."

Brunei, too, is not overly anxious to join a Malaysian Federation, for it is a wealthy territory. A stanchly Moslem enclave of only 2,000 square miles, it has the world's twelfth richest oil field at Seria. Royalties of $40,000,000 have provided the 85,000 people of this sultanate with a yearly per capita income of $450, exceeding even that of Singapore. The people, moreover, get free schooling, free medical care, old-age pensions, and other special benefits almost unknown elsewhere in Asia. Nevertheless, much of the royalty money is going for such luxuries as a great golden-domed $2,500,000 mosque equipped with the first prayer-tower elevator in all Islam, and German electronic equipment to amplify the call to prayer of the *muezzin,* the traditional Moslem announcer of prayer time. Its monumental splendor, enhanced by multicolored marble mosaics installed by Italian artisans and four enormous cut-glass chandeliers made in England, looms like a glittering mirage over the poor fishing village of Kampong Ayer—Water Town in Malay—a community which, like Venice, lives on the water, but in shacks built on wood pilings driven into the mud of the Brunei River bed and connected by board streets.

A British colony governed through a resident minister from 1906 to 1959, Brunei today enjoys internal autonomy under a sultan with absolute power. The sultan has promised, however, to hold limited local elections soon as a first step toward representative government. In any event, most people in Brunei, though sharing a common religion with the Malays, see little reason why they should share their immense wealth with them. This sentiment was violently expressed in December 1962 when Brunei rebels led by a Moslem nationalist, Sheik A. M. Azahari, revolted against the

British in an effort to form an independent state comprising all three British dependencies. This rebellion, crushed by the British, at least temporarily, may have been instigated by Indonesia, which controls most of Borneo and would like, no doubt, to control all of it, an ambition that fits in neatly with communist designs.

But whatever the attitudes of the peoples of Sarawak, British Borneo, and Brunei, they have little choice but to accept Britain's decision on the federation issue.

The merger will probably reduce the present grave communist threat in Singapore. Yet there is also a possibility that this threat might spread to the expanded state as a whole if the procommunists in the turbulent island city succeed in linking their subversive activities more effectively with those of their Malayan and Borneo counterparts. Therefore, the future of Malaya and Singapore is likely to remain uncertain for many years.

XIX

THAILAND:

HAPPINESS DISTURBED

"There are probably fewer ulcers per capita in Thailand than in any other country in the world," a United States Embassy official told me in the exotic Thai capital of Bangkok, where Thai charm and friendliness vie with jewel-studded temples as a tourist attraction. "You never see a scowl. The world could be coming to an end and they would still be their happy selves."

To a large extent, this observation was valid. But at least among government leaders today scowls are by no means uncommon. For the traditional Thai world, a generally contented world untarnished by hunger or hatred, is gravely threatened. The virtual communist takeover of Laos, which shares a 1,000-mile border with northeastern Thailand, has made the latter a priority communist target in Asia. Washington's recognition of this fact was underscored in May 1962 when about 5,000 American troops were dispatched to this ancient kingdom after Red forces in Laos reached the Mekong River that separates the two countries. Two months later, after a coalition government was set up in Laos, less than half of the Americans were removed.

Though Thailand may be safe from communist domination as long as the G.I.'s remain, subversion and infiltration are likely to increase. The Reds appear to be confident that it's just a matter of time before the Americans leave and give them the green light to launch a Laos-like guerrilla operation. Vietnamese and Lao agents of North Vietnam dictator Ho Chi Minh are soliciting recruits along the northeastern frontier. And in southern Thailand near the Malayan border, Malayan communist holdovers from the recent war in Malaya, which the Reds lost, are entrenched in the jungle and wooing the inhabitants of that area.

With or without the Americans, according to Premier Field Marshal Sarit Thanarat, Thailand will fight the Reds if necessary. "We know full well that if Thailand falls under the power of the communists," he said recently, "our national independence would be lost, our religion could not be maintained, our king and throne would be destroyed . . . If the situation in Laos or elsewhere develops to the point where it is obvious that it will inevitably become a danger to the nation, I shall have to fight in defense of it."

Sarit spoke for one of the few countries in Southeast Asia that has consistently taken an uncompromising stand against communism. Its full grasp of the Red danger has been demonstrated by its immediate dispatch of troops to Korea when war broke out there, by its unswerving support of American Cold War policies in the United Nations, by its pleas for a stronger SEATO that will act, not just talk, when any Southeast Asian nation is threatened by communist aggression. Thailand, more than the United States, has wanted to take the communist bull by the horns. With the bull charging almost without interference through neighboring areas, no American ally felt more let down by its "protector" before the G.I.'s landed, a disillusionment that started to lead to neutralism.

The Thai leaders were stricken with fear when in August 1960 a young leftist Lao paratroop commander, Captain Kong Le, seized the Lao capital of Vientiane. Laos was immediately split three ways politically. Captain Kong, supported by the communist Pathet Lao movement, represented one force. Prince Souvanna Phouma, a neutralist who became Premier under Kong, headed another. And General Phoumi Nosavan, ousted Minister of Defense, controlled an anticommunist army with headquarters at Savannakhet, near the Thai border in southern Laos.

Britain and France threw their support behind neutralist Souvanna as a compromise between left and right, despite the fact that leftist Kong also backed him. The United States wavered between Souvanna and rightist General Phoumi, realizing that Phoumi had little public support, however ideologically acceptable his position was, and definitely decided on the General only when he appeared to be getting the upper hand militarily and Souvanna fled to Cambodia. But Thailand did not hesitate. It backed Phoumi immediately, deploring what it considered Washington's flabby indecisiveness.

Then, when the Red Pathet Lao forces, reinforced by equipment flown in from Communist China in Russian planes, began winning the Lao war, Thailand pressed SEATO to move militarily against the Reds if necessary. Again the United States vacillated. "Thailand's faith in SEATO has been shaken a lot," mourned a Thai delegate at a meeting of the organization in Bangkok. And by "SEATO," he made it clear that he meant its leader, the United States.

Added to their injury, from Thailand's point of view, has been insult from all sides. The communist powers have condemned the nation as an "imperialist agent" and the neutralists have called it a "Cold War pawn." Rigid anticommunist policies hadn't even yielded them economic advantages, the Thais argued. Neutralist Laos and Cambodia are granted more American aid per capita, they said, and other neutralist countries such as India, Afghanistan, and Burma are prime beneficiaries. Besides, all these nations receive considerable communist aid in addition.

Furthermore, the Thais haven't forgotten what was to them perhaps the most emotionally upsetting American action of all. In early 1960 the Thai Ambassador in New Delhi was negotiating for the sale of surplus rice in India when Washington announced a gift of six million tons of wheat and one million tons of rice to India. Foreign Minister Thanat Khoman was so shocked that he offered to resign for "failure to protect my country's interest," but Premier Sarit refused to accept the resignation. Thailand eventually had to dispose of its excess rice at a lower price than in previous years.

As long as Thailand felt it could rely on American military support it was willing to accept the disadvantages of living almost hermit-like in a largely neutralist world. But when Washington's Laos policy put even such military backing in doubt, many Thais suggested changes in their country's Cold War orientation. Luang Vichit Vadakarn, who is often referred to as the "gray eminence" behind Premier Sarit, urged that Thailand accept aid from, and increase its trade with, the Soviet Union. Foreign Minister Khoman said in a newspaper article published in Bangkok that Thailand should "cultivate better understanding and relationship with other nations who do not share our views on many world issues . . . The above proposition may even be extended to those who do not share our social system." Premier Sarit himself met several times with the Soviet Ambassador to discuss an expansion of Thai-Soviet trade, the establishment of closer cultural relations, the feasibility of exchanging students and technicians, and matters related to possible Soviet aid.

Many Americans did not take such signs of a trend toward neutralism seriously, considering them simply maneuvers to pressure the United States into taking a stronger military stand in Southeast Asia, and perhaps to win a few extra aid dollars in the bargain. They pointed to the fact that Thailand, far from swinging away from SEATO, had been asking for tighter co-operation among the Asian members of the alliance who, aside from Thailand, include the Philippines and Pakistan. These cynics may have been right. But if the Thais should ever become convinced that only neutralism can stave off the day of doom, even temporarily, they are not beyond switching to such a policy in line with the traditional Thai axiom that a "reed must bend with the wind." The Thais feared Japanese domination before World War II, but they didn't resist a Japanese invasion. Characteristically, most Thai leaders collaborated with the Japanese—until it looked as if the invaders might lose the war. Then the Thais began supporting the underground Free Thai movement.

Still, Sarit is an unusually sturdy reed. A plump, unpretentious man who is fond of dressing simply in unpressed khaki trousers and an open-neck khaki shirt, the Premier, son of an army major, worked his way into politics from the army, as have most Thai leaders. He attended Thailand's military academy after studying at a Buddhist temple school and rose steadily in rank until, as a regimental commander in 1947, he played a prominent role in a coup that installed Field Marshal Pibul Songgram, a veteran politician, as Prime Minister. In appreciation, Pibul appointed him army commander within a ruling triumvirate made up of the Premier, Sarit, and General Phao Sriyanond, the head of police and Minister of Interior. Pibul, to maintain himself in power, played off his two colleagues—classmates at the military academy—against each other. But he made the mistake of getting both men angry simultaneously by ordering them in 1957 to give up their extensive business interests. Both resigned in protest. Sarit, however, sprang a coup that ousted Pibul and replaced him with Lieutenant-General Thanom Kittikachorn as Prime Minister. But unsatisfied with the new Premier's government, he made another coup a year later, in October 1958. Declaring martial law, he banned all political parties, dissolved parliament, and scrapped the Constitution, taking over the premiership himself even while protesting that he was suited only to support a cabinet, not to head it.

Most people believed him. He had always seemed more dedicated to the operation of a national lottery, the entertainment of young ladies, and hard drinking than efficient government. Western diplomats still recall an embassy dinner party at which Sarit, complaining about the quality of the liquor served, guzzled down in the course of the evening a full bottle of cognac he had brought with him. But suddenly burdened with the responsibility of the nation's highest office, as well as with cirrhosis of the liver, Sarit gave up liquor, went on a diet of oranges and nuts, and began working through the night to establish what, by Thai standards, might be called good government.

In doing so, however, the Premier has, in his own words, taken "one step backward in order to take one hundred steps forward." He has established a military dictatorship, if a benevolent one, with powers no Thai government has wielded since 1932, when the absolute monarchy that had ruled Thailand for seven hundred years was overthrown in a bloodless coup and replaced with constitutional government offering at least a semblance of parliamentarianism. When Sarit took over, the legislature was half appointed and half elected. Now, under a new temporary constitution, it is all appointed. Strict press censorship has been imposed, and courts, which previously gave Thai citizens some legal protection, now take orders from Sarit.

The Premier, who, lacking Western education, is less influenced by Western concepts than his European-educated predecessors, often plays the role of judge, jury, and prosecutor personally, particularly in cases involving communist terrorism. In 1958, after a brief investigation, he condemned one Supachai Srisati, the leader of an allegedly procommunist group, to death. Another time he ordered four Chinese merchants—he considers all overseas Chinese potential agents of Peking—shot when a personal investigation convinced him that they had burned down their shops to collect insurance, a long-established custom among Thai Chinese in need of money for expensive Chinese New Year celebrations. Sarit explained to the public: "Whether this act is appropriate or inappropriate, I would not consider. I only hold in high consideration the happiness of my Thai brethren. I alone take all the blame for this act, if there is any wrong."

But Sarit is having his hands full trying to suppress communist activities—at least in the northeastern region that borders on Laos. The northeastern provinces, comprising fifteen provinces, make up one-fourth of Thailand's total area. About eight million of the nation's twenty-six million people, mostly peasants, live in this sector—a high, dry jungle-rimmed plateau sloping eastward to the Mekong River. Yet this land of crusty brown earth and dusty winds is the most economically backward part of Thailand, lacking fertile soil found elsewhere in the country, and alternating between floods and droughts. Jute and corn, its main products, are usually in adequate supply, but barely enough rice, Thailand's staple food, is available to feed the population. Communications are also poor. Two rail lines touch only the fringes of the area, and rutted dirt roads connecting small isolated villages are often washed out.

Feeding on two vital advantages—freedom to move across the border and the economic difficulties—communism has made some headway. A Red guerrilla movement is believed in the process of being formed and the possibility is increasing that this area may soon be plagued with the equivalent of Laos's Pathet Lao or South Vietnam's Vietcong. Sporadic clashes between government and anti-Sarit bands, usually as the result of Red ambushes and robberies, indicate that these bands are receiving military support from the outside. The Thai police have found material showing command ties with the Pathet Lao and political ties with the Neo Lao Hak Xat, the political arm of the Pathet Lao. Notebooks have been discovered containing the name of Prince Souphanouvong, the Lao communist leader, in the possession of some agents.

The immediate aim of the Reds appears to be to impress the peasants with the inability of the government to enforce its authority. Their ultimate goal, of course, is to overthrow the Thai monarchy and clear the way for the establishment of a communist Thailand.

Thai recruits in groups of seven to nine, according to the police, cross into Laos and follow fifteen-day training courses in political indoctrination, sabotage, and the use of firearms and explosives at a special camp near the Thai border. Then they return to their villages in Thailand and establish communist cells. The indoctrinated Reds employ the usual methods of threat and coercion mixed with conditional kindness and propaganda to get peasants to supply manpower, food, and intelligence. The killing of a farmer's water buffalo is a common kind of coercion used. Propagandists tell the peasants that they are really Laotians and not Thais, basing this assertion on the fact that the dialect spoken in the region is more closely related to the Lao than to the Thai language—aside from the common ethnic origin of the two peoples. Therefore, the Reds say, the northeastern provinces should secede from Thailand and merge with the communist-dominated section of Laos. Then they would receive agricultural equipment and become prosperous.

Since May 1961, about the time the Lao Reds established themselves along the Thai border, Thai police have arrested hundreds of agitators, including some Thai government officials. Two Thai politicians were among those accused of such treasonous activity, and were executed by firing squads in their home towns as an example to other plotters.

The gravity of the rebel threat has been emphasizd not only by the movement of American forces to the northeastern area, but previously by the Thai government's decision to send its own troops to the frontier zone for the first time since an agreement demilitarizing this strip was reached after a border war in 1941 with French colonialists who then controlled Indochina. The Thai leaders hope that these military moves will strengthen the morale of the local inhabitants and prevent their intimidation and indoctrination by the Reds. At the same time, the government plans to build up a volunteer home guard to be trained in guerrilla warfare, which will help patrol the long border with Laos. At present, frontier posts along the banks of the Mekong are often separated by ten to twenty miles. From the long-term point of view, this region will receive priority in economic and social development.

Though the influx of Pathet Lao infiltrators has greatly increased the communist menace in the northeast in recent months, the seeds of subversion were planted during World War II when about 50,000 rebels against French rule in Indochina took refuge there. While some of these refugees were from Laos and Cambodia, the bulk came from Vietnam, swelling the number of established Vietnamese residents to about 40,000. After the war, most of the Vietnamese in the area joined the Vietminh communist movement of Ho Chi Minh, and have been operating an extensive underground movement in the region ever since. Its effectiveness has for some time been reflected in the high percentage of left-wing candidates who win elections in the northeast. The Thai government has concluded an agreement with Ho's government for the repatriation of most Vietnamese refugees to North Vietnam, but few Thais think the Red dictator will ever implement the accord, particularly with Thailand likely to become a prime communist target. Perhaps the most ominous aspect of subversion in the northeast is the belief in many Thai quarters that former Premier Pridi Phanomyong, popular leader of the wartime Free Thai movement who has been in Red China since 1954, is connected with the rebel activity.

Even the Cambodian frontier, south of the Lao border, is a refuge for communist agents. A typical Red-infested frontier village is the bustling little dirty-street hamlet of Ubon, which bounds on

Cambodia. While passing through this friendly, one-donkey town, which almost never sees Americans, though brightly colored American-style soda-pop signs featuring thirsty Oriental girls wearing Bikinis hang from store fronts), I met one of these agents in a coffee shop. Speaking in broken French, he readily admitted he hoped Ho would one day become the "protector" of Thailand, and that he was trying to persuade the people here that this would be beneficial to them.

Phya, as this smiling stranger with big cauliflower ears called himself, explained that he was a Cambodian of Thai racial origin. He didn't hate Westerners, as do the Vietnamese Reds. Indeed, he even treated me to a board-seat loge at the local theater where Thai dancers in colorful costumes and intricately designed cone-shaped metal headpieces entertained an audience that applauded and stamped their approval.

Where did he live? On the Cambodian side of the border. But he was at home on either side, he said, as both sides are Thai-populated. After the show, he simply walked across the frontier, as do hundreds of other regularly shuttling Cambodians, Laotians, and Vietnamese each day.

A less immediate threat lies along Thailand's narrow southern border with Malaya, where the several hundred Malayan Reds have entrenched themselves in the jungle, devoting themselves to the subversion of the Thais along the southern border, most of whom are Chinese like the Malayan Reds. Thai police and soldiers, including paratroops, periodically hunt the rebels in the dense jungle, but usually in vain. It may take a day for a patrol to hack a single-file path through three hundred yards of bamboo thicket. The rebels themselves, though they have been living in the forest for years, are familiar only with the particular areas that they frequent. Government forces once stormed a communist camp and took prisoner Malayans who knew nothing about the remains of an American bomber that had crashed about fifty yards from the camp site in World War II. The bomber would have yielded them considerable ammunition as well as medical supplies.

The Thai Chinese in this border zone are a relatively easy mark for the Reds in view of the fact that many of Thailand's three million Chinese, one-sixth of the population, are sympathetic to Red China, though not necessarily to communism. Until the end of World War II, the Thai Chinese were well on the way toward assimilation in Thai society, mainly because Chinese education had been banned—in contrast to the policies followed in other Asian territories under colonial control. Many had started to speak Thai, eat Thai food, dress in Thai clothing. Intermarriage was common. Only in 1945, when the Japanese were forced out of China, did the Thai government, in deference to the victorious Nationalist Chinese regime, permit the opening of Chinese schools. Almost immediately about half the Chinese students who had been attending Thai schools switched to the Chinese institutions. When the communists took over China, the Bangkok government clamped down again and allowed Chinese education only through the fourth grade.

But the tide away from assimilation was strong, and by 1955 over 3,000 students, to get a "Chinese education," went to Red China to study. Since such emigration was prohibited by the Thai government in 1956, hundreds of youths a year are believed to have entered China illegally.

Other students discovered that they could get the training they wanted right in Thailand—from procommunist Chinese teachers fired from their jobs. They have received clandestine instruction based on communist textbooks smuggled in from China, Hong Kong, or Singapore. Under Pibul's rule, every indication of Chinese orientation toward communism was countered with new discriminatory pressure on the Chinese, who had become a problem, in the Premier's eyes, almost indistinguishable from that of communism. The Chinese, for their part, reacted to each increase in pressure by orienting themselves more closely toward communism. Wisely, Sarit has substantially reduced the pressure on them, even though mistrusting them.

Stoking Chinese resentment is a Chinese Communist Party that serves the Chinese community alone and is tied closely to Peking. The party, which has up to 5,000 members, operates through Chinese labor unions, Chinese schools and newspapers, Chinese social and cultural associations, and some commercial enterprises, centering in Bangkok, inland towns, and the Malaya border area, where it co-operates with the Malayan Reds.

The Thai government's identification of the Chinese community as a whole with communism stems in part from the fact that, except for the Vietnamese, only the Chinese among the inhabitants of Thailand have been attracted to this ideology in more than minimal measure. Though Red propaganda has yielded some results among the Thais in the northeastern region, in general communism can boast few supporters among the indigenous people of this country. This failure to win over many Thais is reflected in the insignificance of the Thai Communist Party, one of the weakest such parties in the world. With most of the leaders either in jail or in China, it consists of a hard core of only about two hundred members, who are so closely watched and ideologically undependable that Peking agents among the Chinese and Vietnamese are reluctant to work with them.

Red China, before Sarit came to power and banned all political groups, worked mainly through noncommunist Thai organizations with anti-West axes to grind. Such organizations were heard most loudly from 1955 to 1958, one of the few periods in Thai history when Thais were free to form political parties—Pibul had decided to experiment with genuine democracy—and scream their creeds, all except communism. By 1957 more than twenty parties had mushroomed, some of them led by left-wing intellectuals. Five of these leftist organizations, the Socialist, Economist, Hyde Park Movement, Social Democrat, and Free Democrat Parties consolidated their forces in a Socialist United Front under the Economist Party leader, Thep Chotinuchit, who had just come from Red China, where he had received advice on the virtues of neutralism and anti-Westernism.

In line with this advice, the Front condemned American "imperialist" policies and urged the government to adopt neutralist policies like its neighbors. It performed the function of a communist party without subjecting itself to anticommunist measures. Yet this organization's policies were motivated less by ideology than by anti-Western sentiment. Though it described itself as socialist, it was denied admission to the Asian Socialist Conference because, conference leaders concluded after an investigation, it did not know what socialism meant. Peking even got an orthodox Buddhist party to serve the communist cause. Called the Sri Ariya Metrai, which refers to the next incarnation of Buddha and the utopia that would follow, the party bellowed its opposition to SEATO and other Western manifestations of "imperialism." It demanded formation of a coalition government of workers, peasants, petty bourgeoisie, and national capitalists. Not surprisingly, the head of the party, Chiab Chaison, had also enjoyed a long sojourn in Red China.

The rasping demands of such Red dupes were not entirely ineffectual. Pibul began sliding toward closer relations with Peking, granting China permission to appoint a Thai bank as its trading agency in Bangkok, lifting an embargo on the export of nonstrategic materials, including rice, to China, and taking a neutral stance toward the Taiwan problem, which, he said, was, atfer all, a "family problem." This tendency quickened Sarit's decision to overthrow Pibul and ban all political parties in 1957.

But despite this brief period of leftist and neutral activity, communism has made relatively little progress in Thailand so far, and even anti-Westernism is a strictly minority phenomenon. This resistance to Marxist penetration is largely explained by the unique social, political, and economic character of the country. Thailand is the only nation in Southeast Asia that has never known Western colonialism. While Britain and France were colonizing neighboring areas, they jointly and formally recognized the independence of Thailand in 1898 in order to maintain it as a neutral buffer between their respective possessions. Its long history of independence has provided the country with a double insulation against the effects of communist propaganda.

On the one hand, the slogan, "down with Western imperialism," has little real meaning in Thailand, certainly not enough to stimulate a revolutionary atmosphere as in many underdeveloped nations. Most Thais, lacking complexes vis-à-vis Westerners, are warm and friendly toward them and perfectly at ease in their company. "We like you Americans," a Thai taxi driver who tried to talk me into witnessing a "very cheap" sexual orgy ("A fine show—three women, two men, a boy, and a dog"), told me with great enthusiasm. "You have such unusual ways."

On the other hand, independence has fostered among the Thais the growth of indigenous social and economic values. Western influences have for many decades been felt in Thailand, but have been incorporated into the Thai ethos only after they have been sifted for compatibility with traditional Thai custom and philosophy. The resultant values are firm and deeply rooted, and not easily dissolved in the alien communist ideology. By contrast, most colonial territories have had imposed on them Western cultures, which, to a considerable extent, have replaced indigenous thought and practice or left them in a state of disintegration. And since little effort was made at selectivity in Western innovations, severe maladjustments have resulted, rendering these countries highly susceptible to the penetration of the foreign Marxian influence that promises a perfect blend of modernism and traditionalism.

Aside from the effects of political independence, the Thais are endowed with a remarkably individualistic nature that is hard to gear to any mass movement. No Thai government, however authoritarian the leaders, has ever been closely identified with the masses. Traditionally, the people and their leaders have lived in almost completely detached worlds of their own, with little liaison between them. A Thai "dictator," in a sense, is dictatorial only in his relationship with other potential leaders, whom he fears, usually with considerable justification, are out to take his job. Sarit is trying to change this concept of Thai politics, as evidenced by his personal inspection tours around the country to see that people obey even minor statutes regulating garbage disposal; but so far it appears that most Thais do not take him much more seriously than his predecessors.

In any event, governing to Thai politicians has always been simply a matter of perpetuating oneself in power as long as possible without—if it could be avoided—doing bodily harm to one's foes, who, after all, might some day be in a position to reciprocate. Comic-opera coups, accompanied by rewriting of the constitution, have thus been the accepted manner of changing government, with each change taking place without reference to the people, most of whom could hardly care less who their leaders are as long as they are able to enjoy without interference their lazy, untroubled lives on their ricelands and in their sampans, which picturesquely crowd the winding canals of Bangkok.

This odd political game began with the birth of the present constitutional monarchy in 1932. On that occasion a joint movement of about one hundred idealistic, European-educated students and ambitious young graduates of France's St. Cyr Military Academy overthrew the absolute monarchy of King Prajadhipok without firing a shot. On the surface the coup seemed to represent a victory for democracy. But though its promoters called their movement the People's Party, the people, illiterate and uninterested in politics after centuries of "absolute" government, took no part in the "revolution." It is estimated that fewer than one-fourth even knew that a political change had taken place.

The period between this first coup and that of Sarit in 1957 was largely dominated by a bitter struggle between two of the chief instigators of the initial conspiracy: Pibul Songgram, one of the military leaders, and Pridi Phanomyong, the civilian chief behind that coup. Pibul openly collaborated with the Japanese during World War II (though he co-operated with the underground Free Thai movement after he realized the Allies might win), and gained the trust of the West only several years—and coups—after the war. Pridi, who worked closely with the Allies during the war as head of the Free Thai movement and was Premier for a time after the war, was long considered by his many occidental friends an idealistic pro-West democratic socialist. One of them even offered him the use of his motor launch to make good his escape from Thailand in 1947 after Pibul tried to have him arrested. It was ironic, therefore, when Pridi turned up in Communist China in 1954 and, apparently "brainwashed," urged his countrymen to resist "American imperialism" and its Thai "puppet," Pibul.

The present young monarch, King Bhumiphon, who ascended the throne in 1946 after his brother, King Ananda, was mysteriously shot in bed, wields no power at all, though he is popular among his people. Nor is Bhumiphon, the great-grandson of King Mongkut, who was the principal subject of *The King and I,* the Broadway musical comedy, interested in politics, preferring to write popular songs and listen to jazz. At the same time, political parties have never had a broadly popular base. The real power has always been in the hands of military men able to win the support of the army. The army's sole important opposition comes once in a while from one of the other services—the navy, air force, or police.

A typically dramatic coup occurred one sunny day in June 1951. Premier Pibul, smartly dressed in formal beribboned uniform, stepped out of a limousine on the bank of the Chowphya Menam River in Bangkok and jauntily strode up the gangplank of the American dredge *Manhattan.* On deck, a squad of Thai marines stood at attention as he clambered aboard to be greeted by representatives of Thailand's diplomatic society, headed by the American Ambassador. Pibul was to accept this ship, a gift from the United States, on behalf of his government. Suddenly, just as the ceremony got underway, the marines drew their revolvers and surrounded the Premier. A few Americans started to intervene, but he waved them off melodramatically: "No, please don't. Perhaps it is better this way." He was then taken prisoner aboard a nearby navy vessel. But before the day was out, dive-bombers of the air force, siding with the Premier and the army against the navy, miraculously hit the vessel (at the risk of Pibul's life), which caught fire and began to sink. In the confusion, Pibul swam to shore and hid for several shivering hours until rescued. The following day he was back in power again, just as if nothing had happened. Few people knew that anything did happen, and fewer cared. Public reaction was no stronger when Pibul was finally overthrown by Sarit's coup in 1957.

If the people are not very particular about who their leaders are, they are equally uninterested in their efficiency, policies, or degree of honesty. The fact that they are exploited by a tax system that collects the greater part of their rice profits doesn't seem to bother them. There is still enough left over for themselves. It doesn't irk them either that their leaders are directors of Thailand's biggest corporations, whose monetary fortunes rise and fall in relation to political fortunes. The mass of poor Thais are not concerned with how money is made within a money economy they shun for the headaches it holds, and the educated and semi-educated, who hope to get government jobs themselves, have even less desire to destroy a system from which they, too, might one day profit. Bad government? Not at all, one Thai official told me after consuming his third martini at a diplomatic reception. How could good men be induced to seek high office in government without the bait of ample financial compensation?

A teacher I met during a visit to a school in Bangkok earnestly pointed out with curious Siamese logic, "Our political system represents a kind of democracy, because the great majority of us are satisfied with it—in the sense that we're not against any of our rulers. They probably all mean well. Let them have their fun, and we'll have ours."

This statement reflected the Thai's basic philosophy, so at odds with communist militancy and regimentation. In fact, "fun" is sometimes given as the English translation for the Thai word, *sanuk,* which Thais believe should be the essence of all experiences in life. Closely related to *sanuk* is *choei,* an escapist doctrine which teaches that unhappiness can be avoided through coolness of mind and control of emotions. These complementary concepts have made for an attitude of aloofness toward all problems not of an immediately personal nature, and this attitude in turn has led the Thais to avoid social responsibility, scorn political discipline, and tolerate class differences. In other words, to think and act as individuals.

The individualism of the Thai is also rooted to some degree in his devotion to Buddhism, which, like *sanuk* and *choei,* discourages social conflict, materialistic thinking, and violence while emphasizing the importance of individual merit rather than class birth in the fulfillment of a person's destiny. Few Thais have not been influenced by the Buddhist proclamation that "by oneself is evil done; by oneself one suffers; by oneself evil is left undone; by oneself one is purified."

The favorable economic conditions prevalent in most of Thailand also militate against the spread of communism. They permit the Thais to live comfortably—by their standards—without having to resort to economic collectivism. If the people of most relatively prosperous countries, including those with far less individualistic natures than the Thais, are fairly immune to communism—which, of course, thrives on poverty and discontent—the Thais are all the more resistant to it because of their deep sense of self-reliance. Not surprisingly, the area in Thailand most susceptible to the Red influence—the northeast—is the one area that is in poor economic shape.

Hunger does not exist anywhere in Thailand, and in most sectors of this underpopulated, land-rich nation, any enterprising peasant has up to now been able to clear himself a patch of wild forest and grow rice. True, in recent years the land brought under cultivation has been increasingly marginal, and considerable investment will be needed in the future to enlarge the rice output and devote some land to other food crops in order to feed an expanding population adequately and permit balanced economic development. But the problem of land is by no means serious yet. Almost anybody today can be a landlord, and about seventy percent of the people do own land, eighty-five percent of which they operate themselves.

Thus the communists are faced not only with the obstacle of full stomachs, but with the lack of class friction, or even class identification. Those who prefer to live on a subsistence level, persuaded that a mud hut, plenty to eat, and plenty of time to sleep offers greater happiness than the worries and responsibilities that come with improved living standards, feel no resentment toward those with greater ambitions.

In the cities the expanding Thai economy is able to absorb the small available working force, depriving the Reds of an "unemployment" peg. Moreover, unions, on which the communists are concentrating, are split up according to ethnic groups, with each group controlling different sectors of labor, weakening whatever possibilities there might be for a unified proletarian front with class feelings. Further, many workers are employed in small family workshops in which they are virtually social equals with their employers.

As for the intellectuals, they traditionally go into the government, and there is plenty of room in this field for all of them—unlike the situation in India and Cambodia, where frustrated intellectuals are unable to find jobs and are willing to listen to communist promises of important positions under a Red regime. If educated Thais should change their attitude toward the "materialistic" business world they consider beneath them, they would find little trouble establishing themselves. Almost all sizable business is at present in the hands of either the government or the overseas Chinese and other alien groups.

While most Thais are satisfied with the way things are, they are being treated to an egg in their beer in the form of large-scale American aid, however much the Thai leaders protest that some neutralists are getting more. The United States poured more than

$240 million into the Thai economy in the decade starting in 1951, in addition to $300 million to build up a 100,000-man army and a hard-hitting air force. The United States projects include 500 bridges, 800 hospitals and clinics, 4 principal highways and a $14-million power plant that Vice-President Lyndon Johnson inaugurated himself in May 1961. To get the most out of American aid, Sarit has tried to promote private enterprise by abolishing all monopolies maintained by private and government corporations. He has offered highly attractive terms to foreign investors. That Sarit, with United States aid, is succeeding in his economic program is indicated by a current yearly export figure of $400 million and a five-percent annual growth in national production.

Wisely, Sarit is giving priority to plans for putting the communist-endangered northeast back on its feet. In the next five years about $300 million will be spent on communications, health facilities, education, and land development in this area. The Premier is convinced that communist influence will diminish in relation to betterment of conditions.

Sarit is playing a strong personal role in pushing his policies, as none of his predecessors had ever done, or tried to do. To convert the traditional indifference of the people into active support of his government, he dramatically cut the price of pork and rice, school fees, and bus fares. When Bangkok butchers demonstrated reluctance to reduce the pork price, he simply told the people over the radio that the next day the price would be cut by twenty-five percent. The butchers didn't dare make a liar out of him.

The Premier has also instituted many social reforms, including a municipal cleanup campaign. He often inspects the streets of Bangkok himself, and if he sees anyone throwing refuse on the pavement, he lectures the startled offender and orders him fined. He has also told housewives to dry their linen out of sight, banned pedicabs and pushcarts from the streets, and purchased sixty new garbage trucks for Bangkok. He has extended compulsory education from four to seven years and had started replacing slum areas with government housing projects. Like his predecessor, Pibul, he is encouraging the emancipation of women, though there is no longer in effect a wartime decree that required husbands to kiss their wives good-bye before leaving for the office as a means of raising the status of the ladies in their men's eyes.

Sarit, it seems, has reduced the amount of corruption, at least in the most obvious cases, that has always been a hallmark of Thai politics. American officials are as amazed as they are delighted that most United States aid can be fully accounted for, a highly unusual situation in Asia. Nevertheless, corruption reaches far too deeply to have been done away with to any great extent. It is not even clear whether Sarit himself has relinquished control of the vast economic interests he accumulated on the way up the political ladder. If he has, he has undergone a remarkable transformation, for one of his reasons for overthrowing Pibul is believed to have been an order by the latter that he give up these interests. In any event, the matter of a little corruption would hardly influence public sentiment one way or the other toward the Thai leaders.

The widespread indifference of the carefree, individualistic Thais to politics makes them, with the exception of some of the economically distressed inhabitants of the northeast, poor candidates for conversion to the collectivism, regimentation, and fanaticism of communism. Red propaganda runs up against the same wall of apathy as all other political matters. The people are cool to communism and tend to regard lightly its danger, however concerned their leaders may be about it. Even most of those who do appreciate the threat are not easily stirred to defensive action, any more than they were when they accepted Japanese rule during the war. Paradoxically, the very contentment and complacency that constitute a barrier to communism could one day clear the path for a Red takeover.

An overseas Chinese businessman who treated me to a sumptuous meal at a Chinese restaurant in Bangkok, opined with a cynical smile: "If the communists invaded Thailand, there'd immediately be a pitched battle between the services to see who would lead our defenses. If they ever got together, they would fight only as long as it appeared they might win. If they started losing, they would probably give up. Thais are not idealistic enough to fight for a losing cause. And they love life too much to die for one."

As the situation is now developing in Southeast Asia, the Thais may yet get the chance to test this view of their will to fight.

XX

CAMBODIA:

PHILOSOPHY OF THE ANT

Neutralist Cambodia is among the least subverted, yet among the most seriously menaced of the noncommunist Asian nations. Few Cambodians have been attracted to communism, but the country may nevertheless be swallowed up should Laos and South Vietnam —or either of these two countries, which form a buffer between Cambodia and communist North Vietnam—fall under Red domination.

Realizing this, the communists, external and domestic, find it more appropriate at this time to humor than to threaten the government, as long as it remains neutralist. The apple, they are confident, will fall of its own weight when it is ripe. Nor does Cambodia's youthful, plumpish, sleepy-eyed leader, Chief of State Prince Norodom Sihanouk, who has just turned forty, dispute this possibility in his more fatalistic moments. Though not a man to let life pass him by—he plays the saxophone, composes jazz, delights in his dozens of concubines, drives fast cars, keeps a stable of race horses, and has even produced and acted in his own movies—Sihanouk sadly told a closed session of his political party: "I know the communists are going to cut my throat, but I am ready to die for my country."

But whatever the future holds, the communists have little influence in Cambodia today. There is no evidence that a Cambodian Communist Party as such even exists. What communist apparatus there is operates covertly, through the Pracheachon Party, which it dominates. And this party has only about 1,000 members, plus about 30,000 sympathizers, not all of whom are communist. Most supporters of this party are among the intelligentsia, particularly teachers and students, and include very few peasants. The Communist Party of Vietnam, and also of France, may have enlisted some Cambodians, but only a handful; and Chinese Communists living in Cambodia confine their activities largely to matters concerning their racial group.

This remarkable aloofness from communism achieved virtually on the borders of the communist world is a tribute to the ultraconservative nature of the Cambodian people. No people in Asia are more traditionalist, or savor national independence with greater joy. Most of the new countries today are truly new, with no national history or traditions to offer them guidance. Before the Dutch ruled the East Indies, the islands of Indonesia were never unified under one flag; and prior to British imperialism in India, that subcontinent was a patchwork of individual kingdoms. In tribalistic Africa, national boundaries were unknown before the white man came. The struggle of these territories for independence, which in some cases began after World War II, was fueled more by a negative anticolonial hostility than by a clear concept of national independence. Thus, when colonialism was defeated, and they found themselves free, many floundered uncertainly in the power vacuum that was left, as some are doing today, leaving ample opportunity for communist infiltration in most cases.

Cambodia, on the other hand, is not a new nation, though it received its independence from France in 1953. It is a country with a history reaching back about 2,000 years, and with a people, the Khmers, who comprise almost ninety percent of the population, as homogeneous and racially pure as they were in ancient days. For centuries they struggled against Siamese and Vietnamese domination, and then against French rule. The French found Cambodia the most difficult of the three Indochinese states—the other two were Vietnam and Laos—to control, and had, in fact, to issue all orders in the name of the Cambodian king to make the people obey. The Cambodians were never bitter against the French, nor for that matter against the Siamese, though hostility has been deeper to the Vietnamese. Their hearts were too full of dreams to harbor rancor. Dreams of a resurrection of the Khmer empire which, five hundred years ago, extended from Annam (present-day Vietnam) to the Gulf of Siam and contributed to the world some of the most extraordinary art ever produced, namely, the temples of Angkor Wat with their exquisite stone carvings. To the Cambodians, the achievement of independence in 1953 fulfilled these dreams, signifying a return to the days of national greatness.

Hardly a public pronouncement is made without some reference to the glorious past. When Sihanouk returned from the Geneva Conference on Laos in July 1961, after having contributed almost nothing to a solution of the crisis, he proudly told his people, "Our nation is justly proud of its role and of a prestige which we have not savored since the fourteenth century." At the dedication of a hospital in Cambodia, Sihanouk quoted an inscription dating from the reign of Jayavarman VII, who founded over one hundred hospitals, gave rice to the needy, and provided rest houses for travelers on the great pilgrim routes: "The pain of their subjects, and not their own pain, is the sadness of kings."

A Cambodian guide who was conducting me on a tour of the magnificent ruins of Angkor Wat, which was the capital of Jayavarman's empire, asked me, as if ignorant of an answer he must have received from dozens of tourists, "What year was America discovered?" When I replied, "1492," his eyes widened theatrically, and he said, "1492? Why, this temple was built one hundred years before that. I wonder if our kings ever sent assistance to you underdeveloped Americans."

The close association of Cambodians with the past has not proved conducive to the introduction of revolutionary communist doctrine in Cambodia. The people are not anticommunist, but they are unable to see a link between Khmer tradition and Red promises of paradise. Enthusiasm for communism has not been stimulated either by the fact that North Vietnam is communist and evidently has every intention of dominating a Red Indochinese empire. Cambodia has mistrusted Vietnam ever since the days prior to French rule when Annamese conquerors vied with the Siamese for control of the country. The North Vietnam government has tried to ease Cambodian anxiety by expressing its peaceful intentions and even promising to give favorable consideration to the status of the Cambodian minority in South Vietnam when it eventually wins control of that area. And to some extent these promises have made an impression, especially in view of the present South Vietnam government's unfriendly policy toward this minority. But the Cambodians realize that whereas domination of Cambodia by South Vietnam is a remote possibility indeed, domination by North Vietnam would be inevitable if Cambodia turned communist, as was indicated during the Indochinese War against the French when the Cambodian Communist Party existing at that time was directly responsible to the Vietnamese Red authorities.

Further insulating most Cambodians from the communist influence is their religious devotion. Their faith is Theravada Buddhism, which had replaced Hindu Brahmanism—the inspiration for the Angkor Wat temples—by the fifteenth century. Religious tradition has had an important effect on Cambodian political orientation, with the king regarded as guardian and protector of the church and the divine leader of the nation. Significantly, when Sihanouk returned from a visit to Red China in February 1956, he reported in a broadcast: "In a communist country the people work without respite day and night in factories and on construction sites; teams of workers succeed each other one after another. Women and old people cannot remain inactive. Over there human life is of little importance . . . Cambodia is faithful to the worship of Buddhism; it is thus impossible for it to accept such a regime. You can thus be entirely assured on this point. Let us content ourselves with the present regime of our country." Sihanouk could not have condemned communism more effectively. Aside from the fact that the Cambodians are not overly fond of work in general, much less hard, compulsory work, and consider it barbaric to deprive the elderly of well-earned leisure, the revelation that "human life is of little importance" under a Red regime sharply contradicted the Buddhist view that all life, even that of insects, is indeed important.

Sihanouk, who, though a member of the Khmer dynasty that supposedly extends back beyond recorded history, was not actually in the direct line of royal descent in 1941 when the French stretched legitimacy to crown him, fully understands the natural resistance of Khmer tradition and culture to communist infiltration and has taken some wise moves to strengthen this bulwark. As a constitutional monarch when his country achieved independence, he had little legal power. This power was left almost entirely in the hands of the politicians, some of whom were inclined to the far left. The King decided that he would have to exert his influence to maintain political stability, guarantee social reform, and prevent the leftists from gaining a substantial foothold. He could have done this by simply disregarding constitutional restrictions, and the majority of people, who saw no reason anyway why the King's traditional prerogatives should be throttled, would have supported him. But he chose instead a legal route. He abdicated his throne in favor of his father, became a full-fledged politician, and established the Sangkum Reastr Niyum (People's Social Community) Party, which inevitably, in view of the Prince's unapproachable prestige, won every seat in the parliamentary election of March 1958. He thus used the power of tradition, in a democratic way, to further his political ends. His own party included some far leftist, but, the Prince concluded, they were far more harmless under his direct control than if they were in the opposition. At the same time Sihanouk, who was premier several times before settling for his present title of chief of state, has condemned the opposition Pracheachon Party to obscurity by treating it as a subversive group secretly under orders from North Vietnam.

The communists are also handicapped by the lack of social conflict to exploit. There are few big landlords to pose a problem as in most underdeveloped countries. And with all adult Buddhist males required by religious tradition to spend some time as monks, living and worshiping together in lonely monasteries, no great social gap between ruler and ruled exists, despite the ancient belief that the king is of divine origin. This spirit of social democracy permeates even Cambodian legend.

According to one legend, an old peasant named Ta-Chey offered samples of the sweet cucumbers he grew in his kitchen garden to the King, who found them so tasty that he gave Ta-Chey a lance and told him to protect his garden. To test the old man's alertness, the King one night stole into the garden and Ta-Chey slew him in the dark. "Whereupon all the . . . dignitaries of the realm, seeing that Ta-Chey was an upright, just, and meritorious man, called him to the throne and crowned him King of Cambodia."

No great poverty on which communism might feed plagues Cambodia, either. Exports have suffered as the result of border trouble with South Vietnam and several crop failures, and the transport and communications systems, which were destroyed in the Indochinese War, have still not been completely repaired, though American and Red Chinese technicians have been hard at work on them. All this, plus the traditional reluctance of Cambodians to overexert themselves, has put a heavy strain on the economy, and many people are in debt to Chinese moneylenders. Nevertheless, everyone has enough rice to eat, disease is under control, and anyone who really wants a job can probably find one, for this country, with only five million people, is one of the most underpopulated in Asia. Only twenty-five percent of the arable land is now under cultivation, and important deposits of iron ore, limestone, phosphate, jet, copper, manganese, and gold have never been exploited.

With so many factors militating against the growth of communism, Cambodia would probably be considered one of the "safest" underdeveloped countries—if it were located farther away from the communist heartland. But its proximity to this heartland puts it on the danger list, and may soon place it on the critical list. At present Cambodia is geographically separated from the communist world by a precarious buffer area—Laos to the northeast, South Vietnam to the east and south, Thailand to the north, and the Gulf of Siam to the southwest. But with Laos in danger of being communized in the near future, and with South Vietnam under attack from North Vietnam-led guerrillas, Cambodia may very well border on a communist state before long. Even today bands of Vietcong guerrillas—communists operating in South Vietnam—frequently infiltrate across Cambodia's jungle frontiers, as do Thai and South Vietnamese raiders on occasion.

If the buffer zone around Cambodia collapsed, Red infiltrators would find it easy to co-ordinate activities with communists living in Cambodia—Khmer, Chinese, and Vietnamese. Among the Vietnamese residents, who comprise about five percent of the population, even many noncommunists would probably be only too glad to help bring Cambodia under Vietnam's control, regardless of their mother country's politics. Most Vietnamese consider Cambodia a rather savage country that was never meant to be anything but a vassal of Vietnam. In particular, the government fears that perhaps 4,000 Vietnamese communists who operated in Cambodia against the French during the Indochinese War have submerged themselves in the Vietnamese population in this country, and are simply waiting for the propitious moment to rise again. Nor is it at all certain that present Khmer resistance to communism would remain unshaken in the face of concentrated subversion by communists with a base on the country's border. The Pracheachon Party could form the nucleus of a popular communist movement, although today it consists largely of frustrated students and intellectuals who find themselves frozen out of important government jobs—government is still the only "prestige" field in Cambodia—by traditionalist leaders who are afraid of the radical changes that might be instituted by younger people.

Communist operations in Cambodia before and during the Indochinese War offer some indication of what could be expected if the buffer zone now protecting this country should be cracked. Ho Chi Minh's forces, called the Vietminh before they formed the state of North Vietnam, began to infiltrate Cambodia in 1947 when the Khmer Issarak, or Free Cambodia nationalist movement, based in Bangkok, received arms and financial aid from them. When this movement refused, however, to place itself under the Vietminh's command, Ho sponsored a rival Cambodian nationalist movement. This caused a split in the Khmer Issarak, with part of the group joining the communist-controlled organization, and part breaking off relations with the Vietminh completely. Thus, two guerrilla groups roamed the Cambodian countryside sniping at French forces, one nationalist and one communist.

In addition, the Vietminh organized special Vietnamese armed units known as Vietnam Troops to Help Cambodia, which laid the groundwork for the transfer of the whole Vietminh command in southern Vietnam to Cambodian territory. In 1950 the Vietminh divided Cambodia into three zones and a number of regional and local units, setting up a Cadre Committee in each zone made up almost entirely of Vietnamese—due to the lack of experienced Cambodians. To make up for this deficiency, however, the Vietminh established in "liberated areas" of Cambodia a political school for 140 pupils and an army school for about 100. Other schools were set up to train Cambodians in the art of governing a communist state, offering courses in propaganda, police duty, education, and economics. Special classes were held for monks gullible enough to attend, and the few who did were used as showpieces at all public meetings.

Shortly after the creation of a formal Vietnam Communist Party in 1951, the Vietnam Reds set up a puppet Revolutionary Cambodian People's Party, and then a pseudo-Cambodian revolutionary government. Finally, in 1954, with the Vietminh making diversionary offenses against the French in Cambodia, the Cambodian and Vietnamese communist rebel forces merged into a Khmer People's Liberation Army, with Vietminh units supposedly serving only as attached groups. But efforts to fool the people into believing that this army was truly Cambodian-controlled met with little success.

I went on patrol with a French platoon searching for communist guerrillas and learned something of the attitude of the Cambodian peasant toward them. We stopped in one village to eat our paper-wrapped lunches and began talking with a young peasant woman. At least we thought she was a woman. Her hair was closely cropped, and she was dressed in the traditional *sampot* worn by both sexes, a loosely fitting garment wrapped around the waist and under the legs. Yes, she said, guerrillas had been in the village—just the day before. They had demanded rice from the villagers, but most had found some excuse not to furnish it. Some of the guerrillas were Cambodians, she added, but she also recognized some Vietnamese and she wouldn't share her food with Vietnamese if they were starving to death. Were they communists? She didn't know. She only knew that some were Vietnamese, and she simply didn't trust those people.

With the conclusion of the Geneva agreement in 1954 calling for the partition of Vietnam into two parts, the Cambodian communist movement all but evaporated. About 2,500 Communist Vietnamese troops in Cambodia were forced to withdraw to North Vietnam under the cease-fire accord, and many Cambodian communists accompanied them, planning to return when the time was ripe for Cambodia's capture. But more dangerous are the many Vietnamese and the few Cambodian communists who remained in this country, and who today constitute a fifth column.

The work of this fifth column has, ironically, been facilitated to an important degree by the neutralist Cold War policies of the very symbol of Cambodian conservatism and tradition—Prince Sihanouk. Yet neutralism itself, or variations of it, are part of the Khmer tradition, as adopted from Indian culture. It is not unnatural that the advice of Indian Prime Minister Nehru was an important element in Sihanouk's decision to follow the neutralist path, as the Indians have always exerted a great influence on Cambodia. Cambodian school children even today are taught the legendary origin of Indian civilization in Cambodia. The prince of a "southern province" (India), they learn, dreamed that a spirit gave him a bow and arrows and told him to conquer the sea. In the effort, he arrived in Fu-Nan (the Chinese name for Cambodia), where a queen ruled. The queen's troops tried to defend the country, but when a magic arrow killed one of them, the queen surrendered. The prince married the queen, and taught the people to wear clothes and make cloth.

In a temple called Banteai Srey, or Women's Citadel, northeast of Angkor Wat, I saw a masterful sculpture that illustrated an Indian myth pertinent to current Cambodian policies. It seems that the gods created a beautiful woman, Apsara Tilottama, and sent her down to earth to destroy the demons. When the demons gazed upon her beauty, they fought over her until all were killed. "And in this way," the fable goes, "the world was saved." And in this way, Sihanouk wishfully hopes, Cambodia might, in Cold War terms, be able to survive the battle of big-power demons.

But to Sihanouk neutralism is not simply a matter of the ant stepping aside when two elephants are fighting, as he once described his neutralist philosophy. It is also a matter of protecting

Cambodia against other ants—namely, South Vietnam and Thailand. Possible aggression by these two small, traditionally hostile neighbors right on Cambodia's borders is far more real to Sihanouk than an invasion from communist areas, though South Vietnam would undoubtedly be feared even more if it should become Red. Neutralism has permitted Cambodia to exact a promise of aid from Red China should Thailand or South Vietnam attack, without binding the nation to the communist bloc. "Be sure of one thing," Sihanouk has said. "In spite of all the disapproval of the West, I will never abandon my friendship with the Chinese and the Russians. I will never give them up. It isn't that I like them more than the Americans, but without them the partisans of the other bloc (i.e., Thailand and South Vietnam) would sit on us till the seams burst." Chinese Premier Chou En-lai has obligingly assured Sihanouk that China would support Cambodia and "put itself by her side" in case of menace "from whatever source."

The possibility that active communist aid might actually be requested was enhanced in October 1961, when Cambodia broke off diplomatic relations with Thailand after Sihanouk charged that the Thais planned to invade the country. "If the free world permits Thailand to attack Cambodia it will be the end for the free world in Cambodia," the Prince told parliament. He added ominously, "Cambodia will be able to defend itself with the aid of friends who oppose aggression." The Thais, for their part, accused Cambodia of permitting its territory to be used as a base for communist infiltration in Thailand, though agreeing with bitter reluctance in mid-1962 to return a disputed border temple to Cambodia after the World Court at the Hague ruled in Cambodia's favor.

There are also constant flare-ups with South Vietnam. In May 1960 Cambodian troops supported by five aircraft attacked a band of 100 armed Vietnamese on the Cambodian side of the Vietnamese frontier, killing thirty-one and capturing two. And in April 1960 a fight between Cambodian and South Vietnamese gunboats was narrowly averted after Saigon laid claim to a chain of small islands off the southern Cambodian coast that have been under Cambodian control since 1939. On several occasions, the Cambodians have attacked North Vietnamese infiltrators using Cambodia as a base for guerrilla assaults in South Vietnam, though Saigon charges that Sihanouk is permitting their presence.

Conflict between Cambodia on the one hand and Thailand and Vietnam on the other extends back for centuries. Thailand claimed suzerainty over Cambodia in the fifteenth century and struggled to enforce its claim until 1603 when it enthroned a Cambodian king completely under its wing. For the next 260 years Thailand and Annam competed for control of the country, with the former winning lands in the north and the latter, territories in the south, that to this day are in dispute. The Cambodian kings, masterfully pursuing the "elephants and the ant" game, managed in considerable degree to play the two conquerors off against each other until 1846, when Thailand and Annam jointly crowned King Ang Duong, thereby subjecting Cambodia to dual vassalage.

But the king then shrewdly placed Cambodia under the protection of the French, who were fighting the Annamese at the time, after ceding two western provinces to Thailand as payment for its acquiescence to the arrangement. (France forced Thailand to return the provinces after World War II.) It is therefore not without significance that the Cambodians, who voluntarily became French colonial subjects as the better of two distasteful alternatives, are today threatening to seek Red Chinese "protection" against their traditional foes—though the United States countered this threat to some degree in the autumn of 1962 by increasing military aid to Cambodia in reply to a request by Sihanouk that both blocs guarantee his country's security. Yet the Cambodian leader's incredible reiteration of this warning at the very moment Red Chinese troops were thrusting into India—an attack deplored in private by Cambodian diplomats abroad—suggests that a fear-inspired desire to cultivate the dragon's good will is at least one motive for the threat.

Still another factor in Cambodia's neutralist stand has been the attraction of Communist Chinese and Russian economic and technical aid. Sihanouk launched a two-year development plan in 1956, but needed more new investment and credit facilities than were being provided by the United States and France. The Reds promised him almost anything he wanted.

After leaning westward for about three years following independence, Sihanouk, influenced by a talk with Nehru and a visit to Red China in early 1956, decided that Cambodia would become neutralist. The mood of the country suddenly changed. The Chinese community, which makes up about five percent of the population and controls the nation's commerce, veered overnight from a pro-Nationalist to a pro-Peking position. The Chinese newspaper *Mekong Yat Pao* (*Mekong Daily*) became the *Jen Minh Jih Pao* (*People's Daily*), complete with Radio Peking program schedules. Chinese businessmen imported Red Chinese films for local showing. A Chinese communist lending library was set up in the capital of Pnompenh. The Vietnamese communists in Cambodia also became more active, as did the Pracheachon Party, spouting the Red line in their newspapers. All Cambodian newspapers carried only the Red Chinese version of the rape of Tibet despite the persecution of fellow Buddhists in that territory.

Since then, and particularly since Cambodia recognized Communist China in 1959, subversive activities have greatly increased. Books and other literature extolling the Soviet revolution and promising monks that a communist Cambodia would be under their spiritual guidance have been widely distributed. Radio Peking broadcasts totaled 21 hours a week by 1960, in addition to 10½ hours from the Soviet Union. Products from China, including cigarettes, are sold in Cambodian stores with anti-American slogans on the wrappings. Finally, Communist China has poured in over $60 million in aid from 1953 to 1962, almost two-thirds since 1960, while Russia has contributed another $6 million. With this assistance have come streams of Chinese technicians and advisers.

Communist money, most of it offered on a loan basis, but with a few gifts thrown in, is going for such "impact" projects as cement, plywood and paper factories, a foundry with an annual output of 40,000 tons of cast iron, 20,000 tons of steel, and 15,000 tons of rolled iron, a mechanical-engineering workshop, technical aid in the organization of state-owned co-operatives and agricultural projects, and a joint Chinese-Cambodian shipping line. While in Moscow in December 1960, Sihanouk received lavish offers of Russian aid in the form of a technological institute, a geological survey, and dams.

But perhaps the most effective offer of all in propaganda terms is a Red Chinese plan for the construction of a railway from Pnompenh to the port of Sihanouk. For this railway would run parallel to the Cambodian-American Friendship Road which, when completed in 1959, was billed as "the most conspicuous impact project" of all those financed by the United States with the $300 million granted Cambodia from 1955 to 1961. It has certainly had impact —as one of America's biggest white elephants in Asia. The highway is in such bad shape that Sihanouk on one occasion, after being bounced from pothole to pothole, had to turn back and fly to his destination by helicopter. American engineers will now rebuild about forty miles of the road at a cost of about $3 million, but they can hardly repair the damage already done to United States prestige. Nor have American capitalistic principles been glorified by a House investigating subcommittee report that described "the performance of [contractor A. L. Dougherty Overseas, Inc. of Hammond, Indiana] as unsatisfactory in that the contractor tried continuously to employ substandard materials and techniques . . . resisted [engineering supervision], showed an excessive interest in obtaining an increased fee, and permitted over-all costs to rise out of proportion through inefficiency and indifference." Furthermore, the investigators reported, the engineering services of Michael Baker, Jr., Inc., of Rochester, Pa., were also inadequate. "Its field staff lacked co-ordination—its inspection force was unable or unwilling to enforce reasonable compliance with specifications, and failed to substantiate, by adequate testing prior to approval, the base course formula . . ." Also reprehensible, the investigators added, was the failure of United States foreign aid officials to require reports from which it could be determined that the road was being built according to specifications.

American stock in Cambodia has suffered in other ways, too. Still unforgotten by many people is the American exhibit at an international fair in Pnompenh in late 1955 which was dedicated to "peace, freedom, and progress." As the communists were quick to point out, alongside exhibits of television, modern home furnishings, and kitchen gadgets was a display of rifles, mortars, light machine guns, and land mines. Sihanouk has, moreover, linked the United States with a plot allegedly hatched in 1959 by pro-West members of a resurgent Khmer Issarak movement and Thai and South Vietnam leaders to remove him from power by coup. "I cannot name those who informed me of the conspiracy," he said, "but I can say who abstained from doing so." He then referred to a "great Western power." The Prince has since claimed many times that the Khmer Issarak is preparing a coup to force Cambodia into the Western bloc, though the United States is helping to train his own 25,000-man army.

The fact that there has been guerrilla activity in Cambodia on behalf of pro-Westernism is significant, however small the dissident forces. Such activity has indicated a growing fear of the communist danger. Even Sihanouk himself has been showing increasing signs of uneasiness. In 1960 he suspended four procommunist newspapers and took measures to reduce the possibility of a Red takeover of Chinese schools in Cambodia. He has expressed alarm over the communist influence among Khmer students in Paris, as well as over Soviet attempts to attract students to Moscow's Friendship University through nongovernmental channels. In early 1962 he had fourteen known communists arrested on charges of conspiring to overthrow the government. Most important of all, he told a press conference in October 1961, "I think it would be possible for the United States to interfere militarily in South Vietnam because North Vietnam is interfering in South Vietnam." Not surprisingly, he added, "But I advised my American friends not to send troops to Laos because you can be sure the Chinese would intervene, too. And you know the Chinese are very numerous. The Americans would surely be defeated. There would be a serious conflict and we would be its victims."

In other words, he did not oppose American military action if it was likely to be effective. But he did oppose such action if victory was dubious, on the grounds that it would only provoke the communists without holding them in check. His pleas that SEATO be dissolved are not inconsistent with this attitude. While SEATO, Sihanouk feels, is too weak and indecisive to constitute a genuine defense against communist aggression, it could be directed by Thailand and South Vietnam, who support it, against Cambodia, possibly on the pretext that such operations were necessary to keep Cambodia out of the Red camp. But the use of American troops outside the framework of SEATO could, if they were sent under favorable conditions and in sufficient strength, halt the communist march without threatening his own country.

Sihanouk was no doubt sincere when he signed a joint communiqué with Chinese President Liu Shao-chi in December 1960 condemning "the acts of certain countries designed to create tension in Southeast Asia and to interfere in other countries' internal affairs," meaning SEATO. But the motives of the two men could hardly have been in sharper contradiction. One signed as an elephant, and the other as an ant.

XXI

LAOS:

THE RELUCTANT WARRIORS

Captain Kong Le is not a man of imposing appearance. He is only five feet tall, and even the small mustache he wears does not make him look much older or tougher than a Boy Scout. Yet this brooding American-trained Lao paratroop commander unleashed forces one fateful dawn in August 1960 that are still shaking the world. In a lightning coup, he overthrew the anticommunist government that was ruling Laos, and thereby:

Plunged Laos into a full-scale civil war between rightists and leftists which, though terminated, set the stage for a possible communist takeover of the country.

Made it possible for the communist forces of neighboring North Vietnam to step up their aggression in South Vietnam through the use of Laos as a base and transit zone.

Generated a severe threat to the security of all Southeast Asia by destroying the illusion of a SEATO defense barrier.

Set off a Cold War explosion that has sent tremors of nuclear fear shivering around the world.

Ironically, Captain Kong's Laos is the same country that, until a few years ago, was among the most happily isolated lands in the world. A necklace of jagged mountain ranges physically insulated it from widespread contact with other countries, and the carefree, placid nature of the Lao people stimulated little curiosity about what life was like on the other side of the mountains.

Lao serenity, tolerance, and detachment from worldly reality, summed up in the favorite Lao expression, *bo mi,* the equivalent of "too bad" or "so what," survived even French colonialism. While neighboring Vietnam and Cambodia—which until 1954 formed, together with Laos, the French territory of Indochina—strongly opposed French rule for many decades, Laos cheerfully accepted it—at least until World War II. And even since the country was granted freedom—internal autonomy in 1949, complete independence in 1954—many Lao have retained a kindly feeling toward the French.

Yet the French did little of a positive nature to earn Lao affection. They spent virtually nothing on the development of the country. Few Lao outside the nobility are literate—the eighty-five percent illiteracy rate is the highest in Asia—and most live on a subsistence level in stilted bamboo and thatch huts amid their swampy rice paddies. But as long as they were free to sleep, fish, worship in their curly-roofed Buddhist pagodas, and, in some areas, grow opium, the word "progress" did not stir the Lao. The best thing about the French, in their view, was that they left them alone most of the time. Western influences were limited even in the capital of Vientiane, which was little more than a large village. The French colonialists' principal diversion was to watch lovely, oval-faced Lao girls, their long hair bunched into a high chignon slightly to the side of the head, bathe in the Mekong River—fully dressed, but with their darkly hued cotton calf-length sarongs daintily pulled up and clamped under their arms while they washed themselves.

Today, however, Laos is no longer sealed off from alien influences. It has, indeed, become one of the chief focal points of the great international power conflict. For when the French departed, they left behind a political vacuum in the center of one of the most strategic areas in Southeast Asia. Although embracing only about two million people and less than 100,000 square miles of sparsely productive territory, Laos is bordered by five nations—China to the north, Vietnam to the east and southeast, Thailand to the west, Cambodia to the southwest, and Burma to the northwest.

Inevitably, into this vacuum, a natural base for Red aggression throughout the region, were drawn the United States on the one hand, and the Soviet Union, Communist China, and North Vietnam on the other. The peaceful little kingdom of Laos has become a tragic pawn in the Cold War, and the local Reds, after defeating government troops with outside communist military support, are playing a major role in a precarious coalition cabinet formed in July 1962 that also includes "neutralists" and anticommunists, but might well give way to an all-Red government in the face of subversion and infiltration.

Probably no war has ever resulted in fewer casualties than the recent civil war in Laos. When one side attacked, and usually it was the procommunists under the ruthless prodding of dedicated North Vietnamese cadres, the other often retreated with the sound of the first shot. On one occasion, Royal Lao paratroopers, about to attack a leftist stronghold, demanded that they be dropped near their target, refusing to march through the jungle like common infantrymen. Not only the easy-going, noncompulsive Lao nature, but a lack of nationalist fervor has produced this comic-opera brand of war. In Vietnam, the communists have been able to interlink Marxism with deeply rooted nationalism and thereby win over a large sector of the people. In Laos, appeals to nationalism cannot easily arouse popular emotions; even French imperialism was not particularly resented.

For Laos was never really a national state before the French departed. Most of the territory now comprising the country was originally named Lan Xang, or the Kingdom of the Million Elephants. Fa Ngoum, its founder, was the son of a Lao chief who in the early fourteenth century had fled to Khmer. He was brought up by a Buddhist monk and married the Khmer king's daughter. In midfourteenth century he organized an army and reconquered some of his father's former lands. Though he himself was deposed by his ministers and exiled in 1373, the country he had established lasted until 1698, when it was split into the petty kingdoms of Champassak, Vientiane, and Luang Prabang. When the French arrived in these territories and in a fourth neighboring kingdom, Xieng Khouang—all of which are today Lao provinces—they had begun to disintegrate under pressure from Siamese and Chinese marauders. The French, therefore, were greeted more as protectors than as conquerors—one explanation for the lack of anti-French feeling, particularly among the nobility, even today.

Only Luang Prabang, with a five-hundred-year ruling dynasty, one of the oldest in the world, continues to function, if in greatly modified form, as a unit today. Its importance was recognized by the designation of its ruler, King Sisavang Vong, as the first King of Laos when France granted the united four kingdoms autonomy in 1949. Sisavang's son, Savang Vatthana, has reigned since the former's death in 1959. So uninspired are the Lao by their national status that, in a survey conducted in the late 1950's, only three percent of the rural Lao and six percent of the urbanites interviewed even knew who their king was.

Laos lacks, in addition to a history of political unity, a homogeneous people. Less than half the population is composed of ethnic Lao, or persons of Tibeto-Burman stock, who live mainly in the valleys. The rest, Lao only by nationality, consists of dozens of minority ethnic groups, mostly mountain tribes, including the Meo, Yao, Musso, Kha, Kho, Lu, P'hunoi, Black Thai, and White Thai. The Lao, while having traditionally ruled over these people, make no claims to being the aborigines in this region. According to Lao legend, the dark-skinned mountaineering Khas were the first people to inhabit Laos. An envoy of the King of Heaven thrust a red-hot iron into a great pumpkin, and the Khas fell out, somewhat darkened by the ashes. The Lao then followed, emerging with lighter skin because most of the ashes had fallen on the Khas. Actually, the Khas, who usually wear long hair and G-strings, nothing else, are of Indonesian stock.

The people of Laos are divided along social and economic, as well as ethnic, lines. In the main, the valley Lao have imported their hierarchical, semi-caste system, as well as their religious and political structure from India, while the mountain tribes have taken their social organization, trade, and family systems from China. The importance of the social hierarchy among the ruling Lao helps to explain why most politics in Laos today, even in the name of the "proletariat," is conducted by royal personages, who have traditionally been the only active leaders in the community. Even slavery and serfdom once existed—certain Kha tribes, for example, were placed under the patronage of the king, the princes, or the chief representatives of the nobility. Lao laws reflect the rigid hierarchical principle. For the hand of a princess, a bridegroom must make *kha khum phi,* or payment, to the girl's royal parents of 1,500 piastres in honor of the household spirit; the daughter of a *tiao krom,* or judge, commands 500 piastres; and the daughter of a common man brings in only 100 piastres. Nor, under the French, was anyone not of noble birth given the opportunity to advance in government or attend a university in preparation for national leadership. Thus, the struggle in Laos, at least on the surface, has mainly revolved around three royal princes: rightist Boun Oum, neutralist Souvanna Phouma, and leftist Souphanouvong.

Prince Boun Oum, a stocky man with bushy gray hair, is the last surviving member of the royal family of the Kingdom of Champassak. His selection as Premier in 1960, a job he held until his withdrawal from politics following the formation of a neutralist coalition government in mid-1962, can be attributed more to his prestigious social rank than to his ability. Before becoming Premier, he was Inspector-General of Laos and had a ceremonial position at all state occasions. The honors bestowed upon him have apparently been intended to offset to some degree the discontent in his own kingdom stemming from the accession of the King of Luang Prabang to the Lao throne. Actually Boun Oum, who is far more at home in a night club or on the back of an elephant hunting tigers than at the political conference table, lives like a king, maintaining lavish residences in both his home region and in the capital of Vientiane, complete with his own retinue and a large staff of servants. If Laos has got to be ruled by some foreign power, he once said, France was certainly preferable to China or Vietnam. The French at least permitted the country to live in the old medieval hierarchical way in which the relationship of the nobility and the people was conducive to order, peace, and happiness.

In his anticommunist government, Boun Oum was actually little more than a front man for his Deputy Premier, General Phoumi Nosavan, who retains his title in the new cabinet. Born in 1920, Phoumi began his career with the Lao police, then joined the French-led army in 1950 in the war against the procommunist Vietminh. He soon became a regional commander and, in 1960, Minister of Defense. When Captain Kong made his coup, Phoumi took charge of the rightist forces and became Deputy Premier when Boun Oum was named Premier. A well-meaning man of forceful personality, he has often proclaimed himself the champion of social and economic reform. But his followers, who are extremely close to the feudalistic power structures in Lao society, have somehow managed to grow richer even while crying for reform.

One of the biggest of the few advantages enjoyed by the anticommunists has been the support they receive from King Savang Vatthana. For though he is a weak ruler, the tradition of monarchy in Laos is strong enough to make even the communists think twice before attacking the throne. The King took over many of the functions of the throne even before his father died in 1959. He is mild-mannered and steeped in French culture; many Lao complain that whereas he has a fluent knowledge of French, he cannot read and write his own native language well. Nor does he visit among his people, one reason why he is virtually unknown by most of them. Nevertheless, he does represent a national symbol to Lao capable of grasping the concept of the modern national state. In any event, it simply isn't customary for the Lao to defy the will of a king, whoever he may be.

Standing in the political middle is short, paunchy Souvanna Phouma, Premier and Minister of Defense in the coalition government, who has served as Premier a half-dozen times since 1953. A son of the viceroy of the Kingdom of Luang Prabang, Souvanna, an idealistic neutralist, has appeared to lean leftward in his neutralism since he took over as Premier for a short while after Captain Kong's coup in August 1960. Certainly the United States did not win his affection when it threw its military weight behind the ousted rightists instead of supporting him, especially in the light of the communist backing he received. Yet, ironically, Souvanna had previously tended to favor Western policy even while cloaking himself in neutralism, and had distrusted the Reds, though often appeasing them. With the rightists all but beaten on the battlefield, the Kennedy Administration has backed Souvanna as the only alternative, feeble as it may be, to outright communist control of Laos. But it is gambling on a man who has plenty of reason to be more grateful to the communists than to the West.

The Pathet Lao, as the communist forces are called, was founded and is still led by Souvanna's half-brother, Prince Souphanouvong, a bony-faced man with a large mustache, a fanatical look in his eye, and a strong, biting personality that contrasts sharply with that of gentle, mystical Souvanna. Souphanouvong, who, like General Phoumi, is a Deputy Premier in the neutralist cabinet, probably introduced communism into politically unsophisticated Laos, where, before World War II, this ideology was virtually unknown. Born in 1912, the Red Prince studied engineering in France. Then, after graduating in 1937, according to a communist source,

he worked on the docks of Bordeaux and Le Havre. Here he met a very different type of Frenchman compared to the colonialists he had known in Laos. He contacted progressive intellectuals and members of the working class. He was strongly influenced by French revolutionary and humanist culture in such stark contrast to all he had observed of colonialist comportment. He studied classics of the French Revolution and was caught up in the spirit of the great days of the popular front.

After France he went to Vietnam and worked at his trade, building many bridges and roads in many parts of the country. He saw life on rubber plantations, at the railways, construction camps and mines, and was appalled by the misery and exploitation of the workers. He saw more clearly the savagery of the colonialists. When the Japanese invaded Indochina, Souphanouvong was in Vietnam. He contacted the revolutionary movement there and was impressed not only by their ardor and self-sacrificing spirit but also by their organization, the practical way in which they were planning eventual seizure of power. Once he met Ho Chi Minh [leader of the communist-led Vietminh nationalist movement in Vietnam at the time] and asked him for advice: "Seize power from the colonialists," was the reply.

Souphanouvong began organizing in a similar way. First of all he contacted young Lao in Vietnam, then he returned to Laos and formed revolutionary groups, mostly from young intellectuals and other patriotic elements. It was he who prepared the ground and organized the seizure of power . . .

The prince started to implement his plans in 1944, when he joined the Lao Issara, or nationalist Free Lao movement, during the Japanese occupation of Laos. He soon became Minister of Foreign Affairs in the Lao government in exile, which was formed in Bangkok. After the war, he served as commander in chief of the Lao Issara troops who briefly fought returning French forces, and was wounded in battle. His anti-West attitude hardened when the United States and Britain spurned his appeal for help in expelling the French. In 1948, when the French offered Laos internal autonomy within the French Union, most members of the Lao Issara happily returned home from exile in Bangkok. But one faction, led by Souphanouvong, vowed to continue fighting the French until they granted Laos complete independence. Collaborating closely with Ho Chi Minh's Vietminh movement, Souphanouvong, in 1950, converted his faction into a similar resistance organization, the Pathet Lao, which means the Lao Nation. Like the Vietminh, it posed primarily as a nationalist rather than as a communist group to attract the widest possible following.

Souphanouvong initially concentrated on establishing a revolutionary base area as Mao had done in Yenan before capturing all of China. Such a base was intended to give the Reds a strong military foothold in the country, convince the Lao that the communists were the "true" nationalist liberators who would inevitably take over power and force the government to make political concessions to them. The Red Prince received considerable help in this endeavor from the Vietminh, which, with Communist China, masterminded the plan for the capture of Laos. Ho Chi Minh's troops twice violated Laos's frontiers in force, fighting government units and recruiting Lao for the Pathet Lao with both threat and persuasion. Within several months the organization grew from about 100 to 2,000 men, armed with weapons provided by the Vietminh, and in many cases trained in special camps and re-education centers set up in Vietnamese territory.

The ability of the Pathet Lao to win followers despite its close ties with the Vietnamese has been one of the best measures of its success. For the Lao have traditionally distrusted the Vietnamese, whatever their politics. They remember bitterly Vietnamese efforts to rule them in the past, and the employment of Vietnamese by the French in supervisory posts in Laos when both countries were part of Indochina. Nor have the two peoples much in common culturally or linguistically. Yet Souphanouvong openly deals with the Vietnamese, has used them in his armies, and even married a Vietnamese girl—a fact that the rightists have been trying to exploit, but without success.

In 1953 Thao Nou Hak, a Lao communist leader, reported:

> . . . We have not always had an extended operation base with which to support our long-term resistance. During April this year . . . [we] liberated nearly 40,000 square kilometers of territory which included the entire province of Sam Neua, a large part of Xieng Khouang, and part of Luang Prabang and Phong Saly province . . . This victory gives us a vast, wide operational base full of obstacles, a base where paddy, forest products, and soil resources are abundant, a base which borders on the free zone of the friendly country of Vietnam. In this place we will build up our armed forces, establish our authority, and reinforce our front.

By the time of the Geneva Conference to determine the fate of Indochina in 1954, the Reds claimed "liberation" of 100,000 square kilometers of territory with a population of more than a million.

Although these claims were probably exaggerated, the Pathet Lao was in a powerful position when the conference met, having won control of a large area contiguous with Red China and North Vietnam and converted it into a pseudo-communist zone complete with youth movements, "peace" groups, and rice requisitioning powers. The conference had little choice but to permit Souphanouvong to keep his 2,000-man army and its weapons, though he agreed to maintain his armed strength at the existing level and to confine his forces to the two provinces of Phong Saly and Sam Neua exclusively—until they could be integrated into the regular Royal Lao Army.

With its control of part of Laos internationally recognized, the

Pathet Lao switched tactics and demanded the establishment of a coalition government that would include the communists. This switch represented an important deviation from the tactics the Chinese communists had used in their own drive for power. After Mao and his forces, in 1927, had been thrown out of a coalition government headed by Chiang Kai-shek, the Chinese Reds steered clear of all new coalitions, meeting the government head-on instead. But the Pathet Lao and its foreign masters were apparently convinced that it could more easily take over the government from the inside—as Mao had failed to do—than from the outside. This confidence was probably based largely on the fact that the Lao government leaders were far weaker and less anticommunist than Chiang Kai-shek had been; but also on the likelihood that a coalition government would result in the neutralization of Laos before the United States could pour arms and economic aid into the country, and might also serve as a pattern for the neutralization of all Southeast Asia. If the communists, even under such favorable conditions, were unable to take over Laos through subversion, they could eventually resort to violence again, and this time fight from a revolutionary base that had been greatly strengthened during the peaceful interim.

But the government, which was then pro-West, refused to form a coalition. So Souphanouvong, scorning the Geneva accord, began recruiting new soldiers and accelerating the flow of arms from North Vietnam for what now appeared to be, in communist eyes, an inevitably violent showdown. He also organized clandestinely in 1956, with North Vietnamese help, the Neo Lao Hak Xat Party (NLHX), or Lao Patriotic Front, the political counterpart of the military Pathet Lao.

Eventually, neutralist-minded Souvanna Phouma took over as Premier, and the government attitude toward communism softened. Souvanna went to Peking in the summer of 1956 and told the Chinese Reds, "Laos is a small country, but it is aware of the duties deriving from its geographical position, and it would not do anything that could be regarded as a threat by its neighbors." Premier Chou En-lai assured Souvanna that China would respect Lao sovereignty. "China and Laos are just like relatives," he said. The two men then signed an accord providing for Lao neutralism, "peaceful coexistence," promotion of friendly relations between local authorities on both sides of the frontier, and the development of Lao-Chinese economic and cultural relations.

With significant infiltration of the Lao government possible at last, Souphanouvong agreed to open discussions with his half-brother. In August 1956 a preliminary accord was reached calling for a Cold War policy of neutralism and integration of the Pathet Lao into the national community. In November 1956 an armistice agreement was concluded ending hostilities in the northern provinces under Pathet Lao domination, but the two leaders continued to dicker over political details. Finally an accord was reached, only to be rejected by the National Assembly for making too many concessions to the communists. Souvanna resigned, but agreed to form a new government that would "try to meet the Pathet Lao halfway," even while conceding that it was making unreasonable demands. He told the National Assembly in May 1957:

> An analysis of the situation shows clearly that our Pathet Lao partner is behaving at all times as if its chief concern were to assure itself, through the Neo Lao Hak Xat Party, of a special position in the state. It conceives of its political activity as of that of the "party" par excellence, with a monopoly on orthodoxy, in matters of domestic and foreign policy, of the champion of the defense of democracy and national independence with the duty, and consequently the right, of steering government policy in the sole direction which is orthodox: its own!
>
> The corollary of this attitude is the tendency, manifested in every instance by our partner, to tax government policy with being reactionary, to accuse it of being in the tow of the "imperialists," the moment that cabinet action is not in strict conformity with the Pathet Lao's ideas on the matter in question . . . I express the hope that the present declaration may lead the Pathet Lao to understand that it does not have the monopoly on civic feeling and that, consequently, it has not the right to entrench itself in the negative attitude which it tends to adopt. These difficulties, these differences of basic ideas, the impossibility of surmounting them—there is what is at the root of the present situation.

Nevertheless, Souvanna appeased the Reds. A final agreement in November 1957 provided for the integration of the Pathet Lao into the national community. Six thousand rebel soldiers were to be demobilized and the remaining fifteen hundred absorbed into the Royal Lao Army. The area under communist control was to be turned over to officials designated by the government, but specified key positions were reserved for Pathet Lao members. In addition, a coalition government was called for, with Souphanouvong as Minister of Planning and Urbanization, a job that included, ironically, responsibility for negotiating the American aid program. Another communist, Phoumi Vong Vichit, was selected, no less curiously, as Minister of Religion and Culture. He was a leader of the Neo Lao Hak Xat Party, which now became legal. Souvanna also agreed to his half-brother's demands for the exchange of diplomatic missions with Communist China and North Vietnam.

The communists thus for the first time had a foothold in the Lao government. The Red ministers planted communist civil servants in responsible administrative posts in all sectors of the central government and in the provinces. Now the Neo Lao Hak Xat was free to parrot the Moscow-Peking-Hanoi line in a legal party newspaper. The party, whose charter was almost an exact duplicate of that of North Vietnam's Lao Dong, or Communist Party, posed, however, as an all-embracing nationalist organization, despite the fact that about eighty percent of its membership was communist.

But the granting of full legal rights to the Reds, of course, did not appease their appetite for power. They continued to operate clandestinely no less actively than above ground, as confirmed by the discovery of secret Red stores of arms and ammunition and even radio transmitters. Furthermore, the communists would not permit genuine integration of the Pathet Lao into the Royal Lao Army, demanding that its forces remain intact as military units so that they could continue to be used for communist purposes even within that army. The six thousand demobilized soldiers, on the other hand, simply went home and formed propaganda cells in their villages, remaining under communist discipline. Moreover, retention by the Reds of key political posts in the two northern provinces they had supposedly turned over to the national government permitted them to maintain control of these areas despite the presence of Royal Government officials. In any event, due in various degrees to their brainwashing efforts, intimidation, exposures of rightist corruption, and the splintering of noncommunist political parties into many competing units, communist and other leftist candidates won thirteen out of twenty-one seats contested in parliamentary elections held in 1958. Prince Souphanouvong himself, running as a candidate from Vientiane province, won the largest number of votes received by any candidate in all of Laos.

Awakened to the danger of communist infiltration by these evidences of subversion and increasing popular support for the Reds, and pressured by anticommunist military leaders and bureaucrats, the National Assembly dissolved the coalition government in August 1958. A purely nationalist cabinet came to power. The communists retired to the northern provinces they still controlled. Their effort to take over the government from within had failed, just as Mao's had failed in China. But the Pathet Lao was in a far more powerful position now in Laos than Mao's forces had been in China in 1927. It had not only a forward base within Laos from which to operate, but a rear base comprising all of China and North Vietnam. It could strike either way—through coalition or, with the help of its neighbors, through naked force.

Moscow and Peking were reluctant, however, to approve immediate military action, apparently fearing American intervention and a new Korean-type war at a moment when the Russians were frantically peddling their "peaceful coexistence" propaganda, and the Chinese were faced with great internal problems, stemming in particular from the agricultural commune system. At any rate, the Reds reacted to their ouster from the government with unending demands for another coalition, and resorted to only minor fighting in 1959, hoping to convince the government that it could never maintain peace without co-operating with the communists.

But the government ignored the warning. It hindered the access of the Neo Lao Hak Xat Party to Hanoi. It tried by force, if unsuccessfully, to put under its command again Pathet Lao troops who had broken away from the Royal Lao Army when the political break came. It swung toward the West, precluding relations with communist states. During much of 1959 it held Prince Souphanouvong under house arrest or confined him to Vientiane—where on one occasion he attended an American Embassy reception, charming the guests with his fascinating chit-chat. Yet the Lao government, with traditional Lao tolerance, would not try him for treason, and subsequently even permitted him and several associates to "escape" custody.

The communists concluded that only large-scale violence could prevent a rollback of the strength they had accumulated during the period of coalition. They awaited the propitious moment to strike with full force.

It came shortly after Captain Kong sprang his dawn coup on August 9, 1960, overthrowing the anticommunist government of Premier Tiao Samsonith. Kong appointed neutralist Souvanna Phouma as premier for the sixth time and asked him to set up a genuinely neutralist government including both rightists and leftists. Whether Kong had acted under communist direction was not clear. But at any rate the Pathet Lao supported him and the United States did not, although hesitating over the decision for some time. While all United States officials agreed that a procommunist government could not be permitted to emerge from the confusion, they were divided on the best way to prevent such a development. The American diplomats in Laos favored reconciling the rightists and neutralists, while the military and Central Intelligence Agency called for a rightist military victory over the neutralists.

The rightists themselves helped to determine the decision. General Phoumi, who had been Minister of Defense in the ousted cabinet, was offered the post of Deputy Premier in the new Souvanna government but turned it down. Instead, with Prince Boun Oum he formed a revolutionary committee and prepared to attack Kong Le's forces. The United States swung to his side and American supplies and equipment cascaded into his camp. At the same time, the United States and its SEATO ally, Thailand, cut off all aid and supplies to the neutralist government in Vientiane. Washington, however, opposed Thai and Philippine proposals for the intervention of SEATO troops if necessary.

The communist powers decided the time was ripe to move. With Souvanna furious at the United States, they did not have much trouble persuading him to accept Soviet military aid to offset American arms shipments to Phoumi. Nor did they feel that this action would provoke a Korean-type war, for it had become obvious that SEATO troops would not be brought into the conflict, particularly as the time drew near for presidential elections in the United States. Before Kong Le's men could be fully equipped with Russian weapons or trained to use them, however, the rightists struck in December 1960 and captured Vientiane after a four-day battle which sent Souvanna fleeing to neighboring Cambodia.

King Savang Vatthan then declared Prince Boun Oum Premier; General Phoumi Nosavan, who was the real leader but used the Prince as a front because of his royal prestige, became Deputy Premier. With the United States basking in the apparent wisdom of its decision, Captain Kong's troops suddenly showed up in the strategic Plaine des Jarres to the northeast of Vientiane. Aided by a diversionary action staged on the North Vietnamese border, they took control of the provincial capital with its airport and direct road links with North Vietnam.

Meanwhile, Soviet transport planes continued to pour arms and supplies from North Vietnam and Red China into the battle areas of Laos. Some of the goods were made in Russia and China, but most were American-manufactured, having been captured by the North Vietnamese from the French during the Indochina war. Technicians, advisers, gunners, and political and military leaders accompanied the supplies. Soon Captain Kong's forces, which had set off the Lao powder keg in the first place, were swallowed up by a Pathet Lao bolstered with small but crack North Vietnamese units, and the Captain himself became a General and has been serving as a showcase figure in communist propaganda efforts to sell "positive neutralism" to the Lao people.

General Phoumi's troops made gradual progress along the road leading north from Vientiane until March 1961. Then the full weight of the communist build-up began to tell, and the rebels devoured territory almost as fast as Royal Lao troops fled before them. Royal troops sometimes did not even wait for the bullets to fly before retreating, having been completely demoralized in advance by panicky radio reports from their own government that great hordes of North Vietnamese were striking from across the border—fabricated stories intended to squeeze more aid out of the United States. Within two months the Pathet Lao commanded the corridor leading to South Vietnam and Cambodia, and was threatening most of Laos's major towns, all located along the strategic Mekong River.

Realizing the hopelessness of the situation, the Boun Oum government and the Western powers sought a cease-fire. But the communists, while approving the idea, continued to seize territory until the danger of direct Western military intervention became apparent. A truce was finally called in April 1961, and indecisive peace talks involving the Western and communist powers were held in Geneva. The three princes, Souvanna, Boun Oum, and Souphanouvong, then met numerous times trying to agree on the composition of a neutralist government headed by Souvanna. But with Boun Oum, on the "advice" of General Phoumi, holding out for the key ministries of Defense and Interior, which Souvanna maintained should be under neutralist control, the Pathet Lao forces, after a year of deadlock, resumed their military advance in May 1962, causing the United States to rush 5,000 troops to the Lao border in Thailand in a show of strength.

Even before the renewal of hostilities, Washington, persuaded that Phoumi had no real intention of ever agreeing to the establishment of a government including communists, and that the alternative to such a government would be either the military loss of Laos or a war involving American forces, decided to withhold economic and military aid from the rightist government until it displayed willingness to compromise. Shortly after United States troops arrived in Thailand, the rightists, reeling under the short-lived but severe pounding delivered by the Reds, gave in, permitting neutralists to take over control of the two disputed ministries. A neutralist coalition government was thus formed after thirteen months of negotiation.

At the time of agreement, Royal Lao Army troops numbered

approximately 70,000, double the estimated size of the enemy forces, but 10,000 procommunist soldiers were imported Vietnamese, about half of whom were organized in ten combat battalions, and the other half consisting of advisers, technicians, mechanics, and cadres. Ninety percent of the Pathet Lao itself were members of Lao minority groups, who are far better soldiers than the ethnic Lao who made up most of the government forces. Only General Kong's 3,000 to 4,000 "neutralist" troops, who allied themselves with the Pathet Lao, could match the ineptitude of Phoumi's units. It is not clear how, or if, the integration of the two enemy forces will take place under the coalition government. Nor is it clear how the Vietnamese, who, together with all other foreign military personnel, are supposed to leave the country under the peace accord, can be forced to depart. Most are known to have remained, disguised as Lao peasants.

Though the deterioration of the anticommunist position in Laos may have been inevitable regardless of American action, the Eisenhower Administration could perhaps have stemmed the Red offensive at birth if it had not resorted to indecisive, halfway policies. When Captain Kong accomplished his coup and named Souvanna Phouma as Premier, three choices were open to the United States: support of a Souvanna government including rightists and leftists; full-scale backing of the rightists with SEATO forces, including Americans if necessary; limited backing of the rightists, ruling out the use of non-Lao forces.

The first alternative, favored by American diplomats on the spot, might have denied Russia the excuse for flying into Laos the planeloads of arms that helped to make the Pathet Lao the powerful organization it has become. As a result, a neutralist government at that time may well have been weighted in favor of the rightists, who were stronger militarily. Today, when the United States is only too willing to support a neutralist government, the Pathet Lao is the dominant force.

The second possibility, unlimited support of the rightists, might have produced a speedy communist defeat. Thailand, the cultural mother of Laos, whose borders are threatened by the Pathet Lao advance, strongly favored SEATO intervention and was prepared to send a Thai contingent into battle. The Philippines also would have contributed to a SEATO force. The United States was influenced in its decision not to go all the way by its British and French allies, and even by its own military, which wanted to back the rightists, but without risking American military involvement in view of the difficult combat conditions in the mountains and forests of Laos. Perhaps the principal argument against all-out aid was the possibility of provoking Red Chinese military intervention. Yet the willingness to use SEATO troops was, for all the risks, the only real alternative to acceptance of neutralism; for the third path—limited aid to the rightists—which the United States conveniently settled for, offered assurances to the communists that they could not lose if they applied sufficient military pressure, as indeed they have done.

The reason for communist military success thus lies partly in massive Russian arms shipments, which largely canceled the value of American arms to the anticommunist forces, and in the use of tough, indoctrinated North Vietnamese troops, who are infinitely better soldiers than the Lao fighting on either side, and have more than compensated for the numerical superiority of the entirely Lao rightist army.

But another vital factor has been the ability of the Pathet Lao to win the sympathy of a large part of the Lao population. Communist organizational activities in the areas under Red control, patterned after those in Red China and North Vietnam, have been skillfully applied to this end. In almost every town and village the Neo Lao Hak Xat Party has established army and party cells operating under the supervision of the party's central committee to train cadres for the dissemination of propaganda. The Lao Reds, however, appeal more to family groups than do the Chinese and Vietnamese communists. A "mass organization" is based not so much on individuals as on families, with five to ten families headed by a party official comprising such an organization. Cells and larger groups, it is believed, meet about every five days for ideological discussions and self-criticism.

Discipline is harshly applied, and those who do not hew to the party line are often given secret trials, expelled from the party, and isolated from their families until they realize their error. Others are sent to re-education centers. Organizations for peasants, youth, and women exert pressure on members to refuse to take orders from village chiefs not in sympathy with communists and circulate petitions demanding the removal of such officials.

But the Reds balance and sugar-coat their intimidation with techniques of friendly persuasion that often convince the victim that what he does is voluntary and not done under pressure. Even the Royal Lao government marveled in a report in 1957: "The Pathet Lao propagandist knows how to present himself as a friend who helps and advises and works with his own hands. He acts disinterestedly, shows honesty and enthusiasm, and knows how to get along with a minimum of comfort. The success of his work lies in those qualities and in the fact that he is always there . . ."

Outside the communist-controlled zones, propaganda, which is mainly delivered via the Peking and Hanoi radios—the Chinese have built Laos's most powerful radio station in Pathet Lao-held territory—almost never touches on Marxism. Nationalist themes are often used, despite the lack of any deep nationalist feeling in Laos. Homage is paid to such traditional symbols as Motherland, Constitution, Religion, and King, and even when the pro-West King embarrassingly takes measures or issues orders in conflict with communist interests, he is never criticized personally but is simply ignored. By posing as the true upholders of tradition, the Reds hope in particular to win the sympathy of royalist troops loyal to the throne. The Pathet Lao's objective, one communist broadcast announced, was to "liberate the King and Luang Prabang from the rebels' [*sic*] grip."

Another major traditionalist target of the communists is the Buddhist monk. Buddhism—of the Hinayana sect—runs deep among the ethnic Lao, if not among the minority groups, having been introduced about a thousand years ago. It is the state religion, and under the Lao constitution the king himself must be a practicing Buddhist. Homage is paid to monks on state occasions, and the most venerated figure in most villages is the abbot of the *wat,* or Buddhist pagoda. The clergy is not confined to a small group of mystics. Until a few years ago most Lao youths became, or studied to be, monks for periods ranging from a few months to a lifetime. They did so to pay their spiritual debt to their parents and to achieve status in the community, but also because studying to be a monk in a pagoda was an inexpensive means of getting free board in town and a basic education, which could later be used to obtain good jobs in government. To make headway among the people, the Reds have well realized, it is necessary to win the sympathy of the clergy. And so far they have done an excellent job, despite the suppression of religious activities in the areas under communist control.

They feed on the resentment of most monks that few youths have recently entered the clergy—with so much money to be made in the American-sponsored police or army. This resentment is aggravated by discussions with members of the Pathet Lao, who invariably seek out monks when they pass through villages. They represent the poor, the communists claim, in the struggle against those who would replace spiritual with materialist values. As the monk sacrifices himself for humanity so did the Pathet Lao practice self-sacrifice in the jungles for the same cause. The monk is usually impressed with such ascetic talk and quite ready to believe that American imperialism and its "followers" are destroying the Lao's spiritual values. Some monks are persuaded to broadcast anti-American propaganda for the Reds.

At the same time, the Pathet Lao received considerable help in its campaign to win clerical sympathy from the recent rightist government itself, which made virtually no effort, as the Burmese government has done in Burma, to appeal for the support of monks by exposing communist treatment of their brothers in Red-held areas or by other means. On the contrary, the Boun Oum government, while proclaiming its loyalty to Buddhist ideas, reacted to the Pathet Lao's infiltration of the clergy by trying to impose greater control on the monks.

The Pathet Lao made its greatest inroads into clerical ranks in February 1960, when a group of monks in Vientiane held an anti-government demonstration in protest against the transfer of a Buddhist teacher who had apparently opposed the government. A traditionalist newspaper, *L'Independent,* sharply criticized the participating monks for carrying banners which "for the first time in the history of the kingdom, vigorously called for the complete autonomy of the clergy in all fields." Such a demonstration, said the paper, was worthy only of the working class, desecrated Buddhist tradition, and furthermore was led by communist infiltrators.

The Pathet Lao saw its opportunity. The monks "have always been fervent believers," said the Pathet Lao newspaper, *Lao Hak Xat.*

They are also patriots and peace-loving people anxious to see the country in peace so that Buddhism, the national religion, may flourish, and Buddhists may worship freely. The customs and constitution of Laos have always considered Buddhism as the national religion and the Buddhist monks as virtuous, patriotic, and peace-loving people who care for the moral life of the people. In the history of Laos the Buddhist community has always kept its own internal organization managed by monks. Never have we seen such arbitrary measures as arresting and dismissing monks and setting up special "courts" run by the administration to try monks.

Almost all Buddhist monks have seen that the United States interventionists and their followers are actually those who have provoked the civil war, massacred the people, arrested and detained thousands of innocent people, and sown mourning and poverty everywhere, at complete variance with Buddha's preachings for fraternity, peace, and patriotism. That is why Buddhist monks in

Laos have resolutely opposed the United States imperialists and their followers in order to defend the splendid morality of Buddhism, the independence of the motherland, and the peaceful life of the people. They are joining in the struggle for peace, neutrality, and independence, unity, and prosperity of the country which they consider as fully corresponding to the teachings of Buddha and the supreme interests of the country and people.

American propagandists have been doing their best to counter both the Pathet Lao line and traditionalist blunders with regard to the monks. The United States Information Service in Vientiane has distributed literature, shown films, and held exhibits dealing with Buddhism. One special issue of its native-language magazine, *Free World,* described how Buddhism is practiced in the United States and contained pictures of Southeast Asian Buddhist shrines. Monks have been learning English under American-sponsored language programs, and some have taken advanced courses in the United States. Private American organizations have subsidized the publication of books on Buddhism and have helped in the reconstruction of pagodas.

But all this apparent interest in a flourishing Buddhism does not seem to have impressed the clergy greatly. Booklets, movies, and the like, they have noted, have not stemmed the materialistic tide that has been given impetus by United States economic and military activities. A young man under the rightist regime was still more likely to join the army than the clergy. But the Pathet Lao, many monks believe after absorbing its propaganda, is trying to save the very moral values threatened by the Americans. "Here, take one," a monk told a visitor outside his pagoda, handing him a USIS pamphlet on Buddhism. "It's been put out by those Americans who are corrupting this country."

Pathet Lao propagandists have also concentrated on the minority ethnic groups who make up more than half the nation's population. The results so far have been far from negative, but less gratifying than the success registered among the Buddhist monks, whose influence is confined to the valley Lao. For one thing, these tribes are even less nationalistically inclined than the ethnic Lao. They have never had an important role in government and have seldom, in fact, submitted to the government's authority, each tribe having traditionally ruled itself almost autonomously. The only important revolts ever carried out in Laos against the French occurred among these people, usually when tax collectors were sent around. But when the French didn't bother them, they were not overly concerned about their presence in Laos.

By the same token, the communist rallying cry of "American imperialism" has had little effect, for no Americans have tried to disturb their way of life. Also, many tribesmen—most of whom are animists, not Buddhists like the ethnic Lao—have been converted to Christianity and therefore regard the West with a kind of primitive respect.

Furthermore, the minorities have not been happy about the iron-handed rule imposed in areas under communist control, which are mainly inhabited by these people. The only major military resistance to the Pathet Lao has been put up by units of Meo tribesmen, who represent the largest minority group. They felt little loyalty to the rightist government, which unfortunately paid scant heed to the minorities, except to refer to them as "foreign groups" who "do not speak Lao nor eat glutenous rice." The rightist leaders failed even to mention the ethnic origin of Meo politician Toubi Lyfong when he became a cabinet member, one of the few minority chiefs ever to attain such high office. The Meos have fought on the side of the traditionalists simply in defense of their group identity. The traditionalists have left them alone, and the communists have not.

Nevertheless, the Pathet Lao is hammering away at the minorities and making some headway. The hammering began in 1950 when the organization was born. Minority leaders sympathetic to communism were included from the beginning. Soon minority guerrilla units and women's and youth groups were in operation. Prince Souphanouvong has actually concentrated more on capturing the minorities than the valley Lao—not unnaturally, considering that the part of Laos originally occupied by Pathet Lao forces was almost exclusively a minority area, and that most Pathet Lao troops are, in fact, members of minority groups.

The top Pathet Lao minority puppets are Phay Dang, a Meo chieftain who led revolts against the French in northern Laos, and Sithon Kommadam, a Kha, whose father led similar uprisings against the French in the south. Both men are vice-chairmen of the Neo Lao Hak Xat central committee and would probably be cabinet members in a communist government. The Pathet Lao would put an end to the discrimination of the Lao traditionalists against the minorities, they claim. Why should the tribesmen have even fewer schools and hospitals than the valley Lao? Why are there so few tribesmen in the government? If the minorities united under Pathet Lao leadership, such discrimination would end. Furthermore, the Red minority leaders point out, many of the tribal people are ethnically related to the Vietnamese, who are hated and feared by most valley Lao, and therefore should make common cause with the Vietnamese communists. The fact that North Vietnam is having a difficult time keeping its own mountain people in line is, of course, ignored.

Propaganda is often disseminated in broadcasts delivered by members of the various tribal groups, and is sometimes diffused in person by party workers traveling from village to village. Occasionally the visitors pose as supernatural magicians, threatening to convert themselves into tigers at night if the tribesmen do not support the procommunists. At other times, the Reds use an ancient Lao art form to bring across their message. Three-man teams of troubadours, called the *Mohlam,* take to the air waves or the road—when they appear in person they usually wear gay traditional costumes—telling illiterate villagers in ballad and verse as they sit around the village fire at night of the glory of the Pathet Lao and the evil of the "imperialists."

These propaganda efforts, however, have so far proved of limited value, partly because the USIS sponsored under the rightist government a counterpropaganda program also utilizing the *Mohlam.* Three *Mohlam* teams, each paid a total of $300 a month in American aid funds, made the village rounds, singing tunes far lighter and brighter than the heavy communist political messages.

In one song, the troubadours compared the Pathet Lao to a man who has lost his arm:

> *The man is unhappy,*
> *But he goes around saying how happy he is*
> *Because he doesn't have to work hard.*
> *"To be happy like me, cut off your arm,*
> *And we'll all be armless and happy together," he says.*

Another ballad goes:

> *A communist is like a man*
> *Who cannot love.*
> *He wants all men to be like him.*
> *But women, they know he's unhappy.*

The singers also recounted the story of a young man who married a beautiful girl, but was forever unhappy because his sister-in-law was a nagging old maid who told him where to work and how to live. The sister-in-law was supposed to symbolize the Pathet Lao. The villagers were also urged to build the new well that is probably being financed with United States funds, for then pretty girls will come to drink and love. According to some American officials, such songs proved more effective in building up a resistance to communism than all the king's armies.

Because many Meos have been particularly resistant to their advances, the Reds have directed much of their propaganda toward them. But most of the 50,000 to 100,000 Meos in Laos are rugged, independent-minded mountaineers who are reluctant to take orders from anybody. They fought the French colonialists; they fought Japanese invaders during World War II; and many have been fighting the communists. The men wear dark pajama-like clothes, silk mandarin skull caps, and silver neckpieces that resemble dog collars. The women usually work bare-breasted despite the chilliness of the mountain air, with their long hair painstakingly woven into a huge bun. Their work is mainly the cultivation of opium in the rocky soil. Many Meo rebellions against the French flowed from the latter's efforts to tax their opium profits. Income from the government opium monopoly paid for about two-thirds of the cost of administering the Lao protectorate.

The independent Meo attitude is rooted deeply in history. The Meos once had a powerful kingdom of their own that fiercely fought incursions by the Chinese. The last Meo king was killed in a losing battle against the Chinese, in which the Meos were scattered as far south as Thailand. But the Meos have never ceased to believe that one day a Meo king will appear again somewhere, and, like a Messiah, unite and rule them as an independent people once more. "As soon as the arrival of a *phoa thay* [liberating king] is reported somewhere," it has been written, "the Meo army . . . will start on its way to put itself at his disposal."

Several tribal revolts and near-revolts against the French as well as the independent Lao government have stemmed from the belief that a supernatural king had reappeared to lead them to freedom. Even converted Christians have not lost their faith in the coming of their royal Messiah. One Meo was arrested in 1959 for trying to incite his people to rebellion by predicting that Jesus Christ himself would soon appear, riding in a jeep and dressed like an American. All the Meos would then unite and rule all of Laos. Meanwhile, he told villagers, they should rise up against local officials.

On an earlier occasion, the French wrote this official account of one Meo revolt:

> In July 1919 [a rebel leader] . . . called Batchay sent out emissaries whose mission it was to devote themselves to secret propaganda efforts among the Meo groupings of upper Laos in favor of a king who, "accomplishing the will of heaven, was to bring them happiness, peace, and prosperity." The rumor circu-

lated rapidly among these credulous tribes that a prophet who had fallen from the sky was summoning all Meos to revolt and form a great independent kingdom . . . To the accompaniment of incantations and magic formulas, the able-bodied population was called to march against the Lao, Khas, and Annamites and to build the palace of the awaited sovereign.

In vain did the King of Luang Prabang send messages to the Meo leaders in protest against these absurd rumors. Within a few weeks armed bands were formed which began to pillage the villages of Trans-Ninh [Xieng Khouang], Luang Prabang, and Sam Neua. Our militia attacked and Batchay was killed . . . in October 1922. They returned in peace to their agricultural labors . . . A special administrative statute gave them the canton and village autonomy they desired . . .

The communists, well aware of the strength of the Meos' faith in the coming of their Messiah, have tried to steal Batchay's thunder by promoting a pan-Meo movement themselves that would embrace—under leftist leadership, of course—the Meos of Laos, Vietnam, and Thailand, but without much success so far. Meanwhile, they hope to influence the Meos by making it appear that past Meo revolts have been motivated entirely by imperialistic exploitation. Thus, the Pathet Lao has offered this version of the 1919 uprising against the French described above:

> The revolt was against the opium tax and the corvée system and started in Sam Neua, in the village of Muong Son where Chao Pha Pachay [the French spelled the name Batchay] was the chief. The French had named another chief, but Pachay was chief as far as our people were concerned. The French wanted to collect two kilograms of opium from everyone whether they grew it or not . . . Pachay refused and the people supported him . . . Next time the agents came with French troops he ambushed them . . . and sent messengers to other tribes telling them to resist also. Everywhere our tribespeople, led by Pachay, rose up against the French . . . We didn't know how to organize in those days. We had no program. We hated the enemy and wanted to wipe him out. That was all . . .

The leader of the Meo struggle against French, and now American, "imperialism," the Pathet Lao says, is Phay Dang, the Meo communist leader. "Phay Dang was chief of a village atop a thousand-meter peak near Nong Et, in Xieng Khouang Province, not far from the Vietnamese border," one communist broadcast reported. "And he was a chief in the truest sense of the word. He was elected to lead his people in war and peace . . . 'It was in our area where the repression was the most severe . . . Soldiers were sent all the time to pillage our people . . .' Phay Dang sent word back to his village as to where he was and what was happening. The whole village moved over to him, and after that two neighboring villages."

Phay Dang is quoted as saying after talking with his master, Prince Souphanouvong, in the late 1940's: "I visited village after village throughout our mountains and talked with the chiefs and the people. Everyone hated the French and were glad to know our plans to fight. Every village appointed organizers and formed scouts and defense corps." Phay Dang claims to have created a Lao Xung (Meo) Resistance League embracing almost every Meo village in Xieng Khouang Province. "They created such strong inter-village organizations and set up such formidable defenses, that the French and their agents—including the tax collectors—scarcely set forth in [Meo] areas . . ." Observers agree that the communist organization has produced many Meo followers, but consider Phay Dang's estimate of his success highly exaggerated.

The communist leader of the Kha tribe, Sithon Kommadam, the other important minority Red chief, is also built up as a traditional opponent of colonialism. Sithon's father, Voloven Kommadam, led a Kha revolt against the French in the early 1900's after the French puppet Lao government forbade the Khas to kidnap Vietnamese on the other side of the border and sell them as slaves for gongs, cloth, metal, and buffalo. Thousands of Khas attacked the French after being told that French bullets would turn into frangipani flowers. The bullets didn't, and 150 people were killed in Savannakhet. The revolt was finally suppressed, but Voloven Kommadam escaped capture.

The Pathet Lao claims that the Khas revolted against the French because of colonial cruelties, and pictures Kommadam as something of an early communist:

> Komadome [another spelling for Kommadam] was a remarkable figure, and developed into one of the great leaders of the Laotian people. He began gathering the threads linking all the [Kha] tribes together, sending his agents from mountain-top to mountain-top . . . It was a long and painful process. Contact could only be established by personal couriers on foot. Komadome with his wider contacts and network of allies, however, could keep changing his bases.
>
> He developed also something of a political program, urging the people to oppose the colonialists by all means: to refuse to pay

taxes, refuse to be conscripted into the army or labor service. In order better to propagate his ideas and co-ordinate the activities of the widely spread tribes, Komadome developed a written language for the [Kha] people and established study classes among his own and allied tribes. He made alliances with other racial groups . . . At one period, the French mobilized a major portion of their forces in Indochina against Komadome, massing everything from elephants to fighter and bomber planes against him . . . The . . . revolt . . . continued without a break until 1937. Komadome was sixty years old when he was killed . . . Sithon (his son) became one of the leaders of the Pathet Lao forces . . .

In the effort to win over the people of Laos, the communists' trump card has been its anti-American campaign. When General Phoumi's forces chased Captain Kong's troops out of Vientiane in December 1960, Prince Souphanouvong appealed: "I would like to propose to compatriots throughout the country that December 13, 1960, be made a 'Hate and Bitterness Day' against the nation's enemies—the United States imperialists, the reactionary aggressors . . . who have brought such great damage to the lives and property of the people in the capital."

The Reds had little difficulty making their point that the rightist government was a United States puppet, for quite obviously it was. That in itself, however, probably did not have an overly important effect on most Lao, who have never particularly objected to being ruled by outsiders. Nor did the rightist government's neglect to mention the expression "democracy" in defining its aims greatly upset the Lao, who have traditionally lived under a rigid hierarchical system and do not even know what democracy means. But many Lao are sensitive to the growing gap between their living standards and those of their rulers, particularly now that subsistence-level peasants are entering the money economy in increasing numbers. And they are blaming the United States for this situation.

American aid has not helped to balance communist propaganda, as it has in many countries, but rather to enhance its effectiveness. The poor remain poor, the communists have only to charge, while the rich are growing richer as the result of bribes paid to the ruling class by the United States for its lackey services. In no country in the world is such propaganda easier to believe. Since 1954 the United States has poured over $350 million into a nation with an annual consumptive capacity of about $24 million—more aid per capita than has been granted any other recipient state. No greater proportion of such funds has gone to waste in any other country, either.

Most of this American assistance has been used to create a 25,000-man Lao army that, with all its soldiers and arms, cannot and will not fight. For one thing, the rightist army has been very poorly trained. Under the 1954 Geneva agreement, only the French had the right to train Lao troops, though the United States could provide arms and ammunition. While the French, preoccupied in Algeria, reduced their training mission to a few hundred men, the United States flooded the country with weapons, many of which the Lao soldiers have never learned to use. Moreover, what little training the French did offer was of a conventional nature and did not prepare the army for the guerrilla-type war that the communists were fighting. The United States, for its part, equipped the troops for conventional war, building up a ponderous motorized army in a country with less than 500 miles of highway.

No less regrettably, the creation of a large army, financed down to the last private's salary by the United States, has contributed to the moral corruption of many thousands of people, lending substance to a statement of the late Prince Phetsarath: "Our young men now value money more than honor." Traditionally, many youths joined the Buddhist priesthood in the belief that it was one of the most prestigious careers a young man could choose. But a few years ago they began joining the army instead, not in most cases because they believed in the rightist government's cause, but because of the unusual opportunity the military offered for making money. Not only were salaries good and the uniforms attractive, but it was relatively easy for soldiers to steal supplies and indulge in graft. In any event, young officers found ways of obtaining cars and other luxuries. Some officers, as well as teachers, sent abroad under a United States training program, used for such purposes the money they were given for travel and study.

The dollars directed into civilian channels have also had a disturbing effect on the community. The United States has met almost the whole civil service payroll, and has paid the salaries of many rural school teachers as well. Yet while the Lao government contends it is too poor to make such payments itself, important government officials have multiplied their originally substantial wealth since American aid started flooding in, widening the gap between the living standards of the rulers and the ruled.

Few high government officials, for example, would be seen dead without a Mercedes-Benz. As one American observer pointed out, this luxury car, obtained through currency manipulations and other questionable methods, has replaced the elephant as the symbol of authority. But whereas the elephant is a beloved animal in Laos and is a source of great public joy, particularly when it participates in traditional festivals colorfully decorated—a Lao woman feels complimented when she is told that she walks like an elephant—the Mercedes-Benz simply means to the average Lao government corruption.

Many officials have come to feel that the United States owes them a living. The late Deputy Premier Katay Don Sasorith publicly took the United States to task in 1959 for its tardiness in paying Lao police salaries. The French, he angrily pointed out, had been far more prompt. Nor do some officials see anything wrong in openly squandering American money. On one occasion an American aid official was invited by a provincial governor to a special meeting of regional officials. The governor warmly welcomed him, then handed him a formal government request together with the mail-order catalogue of a Chicago firm. The picture of a pool table was encircled. "Would it be possible for it to be sent by air freight?" the governor asked before the startled United States official could choke out an explanation of what American aid was all about.

Although Laos is almost entirely an agricultural nation, the capital of Vientiane appears to have benefited most from the aid program, if to a large extent indirectly. Hardly more than a village a few years ago, it is today something of a minor metropolis, complete with cinemascope theaters, fancy restaurants, cabarets featuring hostesses brought in from Hong Kong and Saigon, and streets crowded with automobiles. The rich live in new homes and hotels, work in new office buildings, buy imported items in new stores—including Western clothes, which urban men now wear instead of the traditional sarong. And all of these structures are serviced by a new Diesel-operated power plant contributed by the United States aid mission. Some American aid has sifted down to the average Lao, if only by virtue of its sheer weight. For example, many schools and hospitals have blossomed in the capital. But as far as most Lao are concerned, they can hardly be seen for the blur of bright lights that burn for the rich.

Barely more than $500,000 in United States aid reached the villages in 1960, and this small sum had little effect, either materially or psychologically. Some time ago an American-supported Civic Action program was inaugurated under which young men, particularly soldiers, were given six-weeks' training in agricultural methods, education, health, and propaganda. and then dispatched to villages, loaded down with agricultural equipment, medicine, and films, to help raise living standards. But it soon became apparent that the Lao trainees, with the little schooling they themselves had, were hardly prepared for so difficult a task, made all the harder by the unreasonable demands of the villagers who expected to become rich overnight. The program was quietly discarded.

The corruption and inefficiency of the traditionalist administration has been recognized by some of the younger traditionalists themselves. In 1958 a group of them, supported by army officers, including General Phoumi, formed a Committee for the Defense of National Interests (CDNI). In 1960 it was converted into a political party. The CDNI called not only for a strong stand against communism but for better administration, decentralization of government authority, revision of the judicial system, increased education, currency reform, price control, and campaigns against corruption, gambling, and alcoholism. But party members did not go into the villages to spread their message of reform, nor did they cultivate the priesthood or minority groups, as the communists have made it a point to do. Instead, they appeared to concentrate on gathering in most of the spoils of the American windfall for themselves. "They meant well," one Lao observer said. "But the old ways were just too ingrained in them. They are still living in a world that has disappeared."

Prince Boun Oum himself has confirmed this state of mind. "I desire," he once told the people, "that Laos remain as it was, with its pagodas and *bonzes* [monks], and I am determined to fight, hand in hand with you, against those who want to destroy our age-old customs and who cause harm to our country." Among the weapons the traditionalists used in this fight was the stuffed ballot box. The rightists won few friends and, indeed, set the stage for Captain Kong's coup when in the elections of April 1960 they blatantly fixed the results, destroying the effectiveness of their argument that a communist government would not tolerate opposition.

The tragedy of American aid in Laos, aid funneled with little discretion, discrimination, or control through a corrupt feudal system that has left only a minimum residue for the benefit of the people as a whole, could not have provided the communists with more pungent propaganda fuel. Though corruption and misgovernment existed in Laos long before the Americans arrived, the United States, by helping to accentuate these conditions, however unintentionally, has permitted itself to become a scapegoat for all that is distasteful about traditionalist Lao rule. This factor has counted far more than that of ideology in the growing popular support for the Pathet Lao, as dramatically suggested by the words of Captain Kong Le when he briefly took over power in late 1960:

> What leads us to carry out this revolution is our desire to stop the bloody civil war, eliminate grasping public servants, carry out inquiries on military commanders and officials whose property amounts to much more than their monthly salaries can afford, and chase away foreign armed forces as soon as possible . . . It is the Americans who have bought government officials and army commanders, and caused civil war and dissension in our country.
>
> The government officials have massacred, arrested, and imprisoned patriotic Laotians and have appropriated United States dollars. Patriotic and peace-loving Laotians must understand that as long as the above government officials assume leadership of the country, there cannot be peace, but endless war; our race will perhaps degenerate, and the people will perhaps die instead of these officials. For this reason, all Lao must remain wide awake and not allow themselves to be led like ignoramuses. We must help each other drive these sellers of the fatherland out of the country as soon as possible. Only then can our country live in peace.

Were these the words of a communist? Not according to Captain Kong. "The time has come," he said, ". . . to declare that Laos will remain neutral, that is, it will become neither procommunist nor procapitalist . . . I support the throne, but I oppose corruption and persons who live on the sweat of others." Yet if he wasn't a communist, he was soon swallowed up by the pro-Red Pathet Lao, as have been thousands of well-meaning, frustrated Lao who long only for reform and find nowhere else to go.

XXII

SOUTH VIETNAM:
DAM AGAINST THE FLOOD

"HO CHI MINH," the huge block letters read. They were burned into the steep, weedy hillside overlooking a small, isolated French outpost in northern Vietnam during the Vietnamese struggle for independence from French colonial rule. A French lieutenant, his hands on his hips, contemplated the crude inscription for a moment and said: "They must have done that during the night. It scares you. Like a ghost leaving behind its signature after it haunts you."

But Ho Chi Minh, who had headed the "nationalist" movement during that war, and then took over the communist North Vietnam government that was established in 1954 when Vietnam was divided into independent communist and noncommunist sectors, is no ghost. He is very much alive, a vital, ruthlessly efficient human machine—under the push-button control of Peking and, to a slightly lesser extent, Moscow. Yet he has always operated like a phantom. He is almost never seen. He speaks out only rarely. At various times during his cloak-and-sickle career he has worked so silently and secretly behind the scenes that he has been taken for dead. Then suddenly this gaunt, Fu Manchu-like figure with a high-domed forehead and wisp of straggly beard would appear again at the opportune moment, like a specter out of the grave.

Currently he is haunting the United States—with the possibility of a Korean-style war, or even a world war. For the outcome of the struggle between Ho's North Vietnam, backed by the communist powers, and Ngo Dinh Diem's South Vietnam, supported by the United States, may well determine the fate of all free Asia. And if full-scale war is necessary to save this region, Washington is apparently prepared to accept that eventuality, however reluctantly.

When Vietnam was partitioned, Ho Chi Minh never imagined he would have so much trouble absorbing the south. Nor did most observers. Just before the partition, a French officer told me in the depressing town of Hanoi, now Ho's capital: "If Vietnam is divided in two, the communists will control the whole country within a year." And he had logic on his side. The free south was a collection of hostile political groups under the over-all rule of Emperor Bao Dai, a man despised by the people for his corruption and collaboration with the French. Several semipolitical, religious, and purely gangster secret societies, with their own private armies, demanded a role in the new government. The southern economy had been wrecked by war and found itself hopelessly burdened with almost a million homeless refugees from the north. By contrast, the communist zone was politically unified under a Red government, whose leaders had gloriously directed the battle against the French, and embraced the only substantial industrial complex in the country. It looked as if South Vietnam would inevitably fall, and probably without a shot being fired.

But as the years ticked off, the inevitable didn't happen. Premier Diem, who took over the southern government after having refused to collaborate with the French previously, consolidated his regime, crushed the secret societies, threw out Bao Dai, settled the refugees, instituted a land reform program, expanded education, built up light industry, and stopped the spread of disease.

By 1958 it was clear to both the Western pessimists and the communist optimists that they had miscalculated. South Vietnam would never fall—that is, unless a good many shots were fired. The communists therefore turned to force as a means of extending their power to the south, and by 1962 were killing about 800 people a month and exerting their control over about one-fourth of the southern villages. If they should take over the rest of the country, Laos, which borders on both North and South Vietnam and is already partially controlled by the Reds, would have an even harder time staying out of the Red orbit, if it isn't already in it when and if South Vietnam collapses. Neutralist Cambodia, which shares its eastern border with South Vietnam, might well be subject to irresistible communist pressure. Thailand, which also borders on South Vietnam, Malaya, and Burma, would be greatly endangered as well. But if South Vietnam is able to remain free, the Reds will have received a tremendous setback in Southeast Asia. Certainly the stakes are frighteningly high in South Vietnam.

The Vietnamese peasants have been easier to impress with the Reds' mixed brew of propaganda and terror than any other rural people in Southeast Asia—a discovery first made when Vietnam communists alone among the communists of this region succeeded in winning control of a nationalist movement and using it to ride into power. Similar efforts since World War II by Reds in Malaya, Burma, Indonesia, and the Philippines all have failed miserably, with only the Indonesians making a comeback—through peaceful means—and threatening once again.

The Vietnamese have proved relatively easy targets, partly as a result of the same Confucian thinking that helped pave the way for Mao in China. Under direct Chinese domination for a thousand years and strongly influenced by its huge neighbor to the north for another thousand, despite the nominal independence it was granted in 931, Vietnam is to a large degree a product of Chinese culture. Like China, it was governed according to rigid Confucian hierarchical principles, with all political and religious power vested in an emperor assisted by mandarin bureaucrats, who wandered about their assigned regions collecting taxes and settling numerous local problems in the name of the government. The Soviet system of rule, calling for an absolute ruler and a tightly drawn administrative hierarchy, has appeared to many Vietnamese as a modern extension of the Confucianism with which they are familiar.

At the same time communism, supported secretly and at great risk, contains many of the conspiratorial and pseudo-religious elements of the secret societies to which Vietnamese, like Chinese, are addicted; though, paradoxically, such organizations originally developed as a means of plotting against the authoritarianism of the Confucian system, and were themselves organized along totalitarian hierarchical lines. It was not too difficult to substitute the fantasy of the great communist promise for the mysticism of animism and ancestor worship—most Vietnamese are Buddhist as well—that have lent a fanatical flavor to the traditional societies.

Another factor that has eased the way for communism has been the leading role the communists have played in the nationalist movement. The Reds have profited from a long Vietnamese nationalist history. The people of Annam, as the Chinese called the area they dominated, never relented in their struggle to free themselves from China. Even the killing or imprisonment of all male leaders did not pacify them. The women simply took over. When the husband of Trung Trac was beheaded by the Chinese governor in 40 A.D., she rounded up an army of her own, captured the governor's fort, and crowned herself queen. She was, however, overthrown by the Chinese two years later in a battle that saw one of her army commanders give birth to a baby on the battlefield.

After winning nominal independence from the Chinese, the Annamese devoted much of their energy to fighting renewed imperialistic efforts by these old conquerors and trying their own hand at imperialism in Cambodia and Laos, two weaker neighboring states. Modern Vietnamese nationalism was born soon after the French took control of Vietnam in 1885. In breaking up the traditional Confucian patterns of rule, the French made it easier for the people to defy authority than it had been under their own rulers. Moreover, exposure to foreign influences nourished their dreams of freedom. One of the principal influences was Marxism, which offered them an organizational structure through which to channel these dreams.

Socialist ideas began to spread early in the century when some Vietnamese youths went to Japan to study and made contact with Japanese students who had begun to be interested in Marxism as their country underwent the birth pains of industrial revolution. But it was during World War I that Marxism made its greatest advance in Vietnam. About 100,000 Vietnamese were sent to France to serve in the armed forces and industry, and many of them were influenced by French Marxists who emphasized the equality of all races and called for an end to the war and the beginning of class struggle. The 1917 Bolshevik Revolution in Russia impressed on the Vietnamese the fact that Marxist theory could be put into practice, and they became all the more enthusiastic when the French leftists promised to support their nationalist movement.

One of the most enthusiastic of them was a young man who called himself Nguyen Ai Quoc, or Nguyen the Patriot, who was later to take the name of Ho Chi Minh. Born in 1894 in a small village in the northern Vietnam province of Vinh, Ho visited the United States as a sailor when he was only in his teens. He later worked in London as a dishwasher and in Paris as a photo retoucher. These hungry, impoverished years amid people who were relatively well off sharpened his searing bitterness toward the West that had been nurtured since boyhood by France's humiliating colonial policies in Indochina. He was thus an easy mark for the gilded social promises of Marxism, with which he became familiar in Paris while educating himself in his spare time. The pattern of his life was set.

He entered politics in 1920 as an Indochinese delegate to the French Socialist Party Congress, in which communists participated. A split occurred over a motion for affiliation with the Third International, and the communists formed their own party. Ho immediately joined this group. In addition to his party activities, he started in 1922 an "anti-imperialist" newspaper, *Le Paria,* which he edited and hawked on the streets himself. A year later he went to Soviet Russia as a delegate to the Communist International Peasants' Congress and stayed three years to study the Soviet system.

Ho was sent in 1926 to Canton as assistant to Comintern agent Michael Borodin, Russia's "Gray Eminence" in south China, and became as well chief adviser to the Kuomintang Party, which then included both Chiang Kai-shek's group and the communists. But his real task was to found in Canton the Vietnam Revolutionary Youth League, ostensibly a nationalist organization but secretly intended to foster communist ideas. The creation of an Indochinese Communist Party, Ho explained to friends, was unfeasible, for "no one as yet understood the significance of the word *communism.*" However, it was "possible to constitute an Indochinese nationalist, socialist, and revolutionary party whose leaders would be responsible for bringing all its members step by step to orthodox Marxism."

In 1927, after the break between Chiang and the communists, Borodin returned to Russia and Ho was jailed. On his release, he embarked on missions of Comintern intrigue throughout Southeast Asia, winning fame—and more jail sentences—as the mysterious Nguyen Ai Quoc. Meanwhile, impatient members of the Vietnam Revolutionary Youth League that Ho had formed resigned in 1929 and established an Indochina Communist Party despite Ho's disapproval. A third group, calling itself the Indochina Communist Alliance, also came into being. Ho then went along with his less subtle comrades and fused all three organizations into a Vietnam Communist Party, which, together with the Communist Parties of Malaya and Thailand, came under the direction of the Comintern's Southern Bureau he administered in Shanghai. By 1930 Ho's party had gained control of the Vietnamese peasant movement.

Until then, the Reds had sponsored peaceful rallies and demonstrations demanding land reform and improvement of the peasants' condition. But as discontent spread, the communists, despite Moscow's cautious policy at this time, openly rebelled against the French. They looted local government offices, burned tax rolls and land registers, and killed and robbed officials and landlords. They actually created soviets in the Nghe An and Ha Tinh provinces, and started distributing land to the peasants. The French army brutally crushed the insurrection, suppressed the Communist Party, and tried its leaders as common criminals.

Party leaders, including Ho, received no sympathy from the Kremlin, which was deeply angered by their impetuosity. Shortly afterwards, Ho's whole Comintern apparatus in Southeast Asia crumbled as he and other top Reds were arrested in Hong Kong and Singapore by the British. Ho was released after thirteen months and clandestinely began the arduous job of rebuilding his shattered party.

In 1940, with the defeat of France by the Nazis, Ho led another insurrection in the western provinces in the hope of toppling the isolated French forces in Indochina; but the French smashed this revolt, too. Ho, exiled, had to regroup his forces in southern China as the Japanese moved into his homeland and ruled in collaboration with the Vichy French. But he was not beaten yet. He founded the Vietnam Independence League, or Vietminh, which embraced all Vietnamese fighting for freedom but was led by the communists.

The air of mystery shrouding Ho was one of his most important political assets. To many thousands of illiterate, long-exploited Indochinese peasants he was not just flesh and blood, but a sort of guiding national spirit. A Communist? What is that? they asked, as many South Vietnamese peasants are asking today. All they knew was that Ho had promised to chase the foreigner from their land, whether Japanese or French. They understood the meaning of "foreigner." There was no mystery about that. The great communist deception, the Yenan Way, had begun.

Slipping into North Vietnam, Ho propagandized against the "fascist occupiers" and tried to get the Vietminh accepted as the legitimate Indochinese representative of the Allies. To win them over, he co-operated for a while with the United States Office of Strategic Services. On September 2, 1945, the day the Japanese surrendered, the Vietminh, by now in full control of the nationalist movement, declared Vietnam's independence and formed a new government headed by Ho, with all key positions in the hands of the communist minority. The French, however, returned, and Ho, unprepared to throw them out by force, tentatively agreed to autonomy within the French Union. As dismay spread among the nationalists, he told the nation dramatically: "I, Ho Chi Minh, have always led you on the road to liberty. I have fought all my life for the independence of our country. You know that I would prefer death rather than to betray our country. I swear to you that I have not betrayed you."

What Ho could not frankly say was that his agreement with the French was simply intended as a stall until the Vietminh forces were strong enough to fight them. They soon were. Within months Ho's forces were at war with the French and the puppet government of Emperor Bao Dai. In the early 1950's the struggle grew in intensity, and each day that passed brought the inevitable outcome into clearer focus.

The blueprint for that war, and the current one, was drawn up by communist commander General Vo Nguyen Giap, and represented a refinement of the guerrilla tactics that won all of China for Mao Tse-tung. Born in 1909, Giap began his political life while still a college student in Hue, in central Vietnam. He became a communist journalist, and in 1944 was given the task by the Vietnam Communist Party of organizing the first units to take up arms against the French when they tried to restore their authority after World War II. Giap's guerrillas withdrew from the towns and villages and forced the French to fight in the rice fields and jungles of Vietnam, a kind of war for which the colonialists, with their tanks, artillery, and bombers, were not prepared. Eventually, the French could do little more than hold the main lines of communications by means of forts and blockhouses.

They dominated some regions simply because of their numbers, but in the countryside the Red guerrillas honored the Mao doctrine: "You are fish in the water, and the water is the people." While covering that struggle I took a jeep ride with a French officer through a communist-infested region in northern Vietnam. Peasants in ragged clothing and broad, cone-shaped straw hats were working in their flooded rice fields under a mournfully cloudy sky. "You want to see the enemy?" asked the officer. "Just look around you. Those peaceful peasants you see—they're not so peaceful at night, when they remove their rifles from haystacks and start attacking us. How can you fight an entire people?"

France couldn't. After making a last and unsuccessful stand at the strategic fort of Dienbienphu, the French threw in the sponge. They agreed at the Geneva Conference of 1954 to evacuate Vietnam, which would be divided in two, with Ho Chi Minh in control of the north and anticommunist Ngo Dinh Diem heading the southern sector.

Actually, these two men reflect a similar Confucian mentality, however divergent their ideological views. Each has simply adapted the ancient Annamese concept of hierarchical bureaucratic authority to his own modern brand of dictatorial rule. The governmental systems of North and South Vietnam are in reality very much alike, if the fact that there is no major government-operated sector in the southern economy is discounted. Both leaders have the absolute power of ancient emperors, and are as personally aloof from the people as the emperors were. Both run highly centralized administrations under which their local "mandarins" are never out of Big Brother's view. Both operate one-party systems, though permitting as window-dressing the existence of small puppet parties, provided they don't get out of line. Both ruthlessly stamp out all political opposition, sending "guilty" persons to "political re-education" centers. Both cling to ideologies—Ho to communism, and Diem to a government philosophy called *nhan-vi,* or "personalism," a vague blend of authoritarianism, mysticism, and drastically modified Western liberalism.

If Ho was influenced to some degree by his father, who was a mandarin, Diem himself was one. The son of an important imperial adviser, Ngo Dinh Kha, Diem showed early signs of unbudging stubbornness. When he was only four years old, the story goes, he took up horseback riding in defiance of his father's orders, forcing a junior cavalry officer to give him secret lessons. He is also said to have bullied his parents into giving him his own bedroom, though this was contrary to Vietnamese family tradition. Diem, whose ancestors were converted to Catholicism in the seventeenth century, entered the novitiate in his youth, determined to become a priest after a girl he loved had entered a convent. But he soon withdrew—he is still a bachelor—and, after passing civil service examinations at the head of his class, became a mandarin.

He rose quickly from district administrator to provincial governor, and finally to Chief Minister in young Emperor Bao Dai's cabinet. But characteristically, when it became clear to him that Bao Dai was simply a puppet of the French, he resigned. Having become strongly anticommunist when, as a mandarin in the field, he had had the opportunity to learn something of communist subversive tactics, he now became, with equal bitterness, anti-French. Even Ho Chi Minh was impressed with Diem's uncompromising anticolonial stand and, on establishing a republic after World War II, offered him a cabinet position. Ho knew Diem well, having arrested him several months before. "I don't believe you understand the kind of man I am," the young mandarin had told his captor. "Look me in the face. Am I a man that fears?" He was released, but his elder brother Khoi, a provincial leader who had, like himself, fought the communists, was murdered. Reminding Ho of this crime, Diem, a stubby man with a round, deceptively effeminate face, contemptuously rejected his offer.

He exiled himself to the United States in 1950 as Ho tightened his grip on the nationalist movement, hoping for a miracle that would dispose of both the French and the communists. In 1954, with Vietnam about to be partitioned, he returned to take charge of the south on the theory that half a miracle was better than none. "I know what is best for South Vietnam," he said. And in true mandarin tradition, he has been saying it ever since.

The communists, in agreeing to partition, were convinced that they would soon have the whole country under their wing. At first they thought this could be done peacefully. The Geneva agreement had called for nation-wide elections in 1956. Therefore, they figured, it would be easy winning enough votes in the north where they could control the balloting, while they would only have to make a moderately good showing in the south, whose population was about equal to that of the north, to take the election by a substantial majority. The Reds thus concentrated on verbal propaganda against the Diem government in the immediate post-Geneva years, and with Diem swamped in political and economic problems they had plenty of grist for their mill.

Communist calculations, however, proved to be wishful thinking. Diem refused to hold an election, arguing that no provision had been made for effective supervision of the balloting, and that voters in the north would not be free to express their true choice. Nor was he bound to hold an election, as he had cleverly refused to sign the Geneva agreement in the first place. At the same time, Diem consolidated his political power. He sent into exile his army chief of staff who was planning a *coup d'etat*. He then crushed the private armies of the secret societies: the Cao Dai and Hoa Hao, pseudo-Buddhist sects, and the Binh Xuyen, which had paid Emperor Bao Dai a million dollars a year to control vice and the police. Finally, he held a national referendum which resulted in the transformation of South Vietnam into a republic with himself as President. Bao Dai, the hated French "puppet" who had been the Reds' most important propaganda peg, was sent ignominiously into exile.

With the corrupt secret societies and their patron Emperor went the vice. When the French were still in control of Vietnam, the first place I was taken to by an American official showing me around Saigon was an opium den where I was to get a feel of "local color." He knocked three times on a door in an alleyway, and an elderly Vietnamese woman let us in. We were led into a dimly lit carpeted room filled with the sickening sweet odor of opium, and told to remove our clothes and put on cotton sarongs that were supplied us so that we could "enjoy our experience in perfect comfort." A grisly old man with a small beard entered and, as we lounged on the carpet, started heating a ball of opium held between two metal sticks over a small lantern flame, then depositing the glowing narcotic in a long opium pipe.

"Opium won't have any effect on you unless you smoke it often," my American friend said. "You wouldn't believe it, but half the diplomatic corps takes a puff once in a while. After all, it's part of life in Saigon."

Another "part of life" in what was known as the "Paris of the Orient" was a house of prostitution that Vietnamese proudly claimed was the largest such institution in the world. It consisted of about 500 rooms, and even more girls—or so I was told. There were two entranceways: one for poorer customers who purchased the favors of the less attractive young ladies in a bedroom with strictly second-hand furniture, and another for bigger spenders, who were first entertained by a bevy of Saigon's "most beautiful women" in a lavishly plush reception room, and then led into a suite resembling something out of the Versailles museum.

Despite the current violence in South Vietnam and the passage of a "purification" law that prohibits, among other activities, dancing, even at private parties, Saigon is still one of the gayest, most lively cities in the Orient, particularly since the arrival of several thousand American officials, advisers, technicians, and soldiers. Probably more bars than ever are doing business, more lovely hostesses dressed in stunning evening gowns are available, and even the juke-box music is louder, playing largely hillbilly tunes now instead of the low-key nostalgic French ballads that used to make Frenchmen dream of home. And it is Americans now rather than Frenchmen who relax at sidewalk cafés watching the delicate-featured Vietnamese girls strolling seductively by in their exquisitely feminine long-sleeved, high-collared dresses split from the waist down over a pair of filmy, ankle-length pantaloons. Nevertheless, under Diem, a Catholic ascetic, the lurid shades of "local color" have been blacked out. As a result, the communists have had greater difficulty in effectively bleating about "bourgeois decadence" in South Vietnam, though many people, including the Americans, consider the "purification" law absurdly extreme.

Socially and economically, too, the communists were faced with nothing but bad news. Diem resettled the nearly one million refugees from the north. He reconstructed and extended war-damaged roads and railroads. He expanded light industries and constructed power plants. He built schools everywhere, resulting in an enrollment of 1,500,000 elementary school children in 1960 as compared to 400,000 in 1956. He established clinics in about half of South Vietnam's 6,000 villages and hamlets, and had doctors and nurses trained to operate them. He launched a malaria eradication program that reached into every region. But probably the most aggravating news of all for Ho Chi Minh was the south's successful agricultural program. Land was redistributed to 300,000 tenant farmers, and loans were made to peasant families under an agricultural credit program that liberated the farmers from exploitation by usurers. Partly as a result of such policies, agricultural production soared, with rice exports having quadrupled since 1954.

Meanwhile the north, which had always depended on the south, particularly the rice-rich Mekong delta, for most of its food, was beset with peasant revolts as Ho first redistributed land to tenant farmers, then cruelly took it back from them in a drastic effort to increase production through overnight collectivization. Finally, the communist dictator was forced to take a "step backward," and move more slowly toward this goal. But by 1960 about 40,000 cooperatives, including almost all farmers, had been established.

Production, however, instead of increasing, nose-dived as the result of such natural handicaps as unresponsive soil, droughts, and floods, and also because of man-made difficulties like poor management and, most important of all, the lack of peasant cooperation. "A great number of peasant families have tried to hide paddy, to waste paddy, and not to sell paddy to the state stock, and so forth," charged *Nhan Dan* (*The People*), a party organ, in January 1961. "This is becoming quite popular." In July the same newspaper despaired: "A number of peasants, dazzled by immediate returns, have given up production to engage in trade." Another party journal, *Hoc Tap,* queried with remarkable frankness: "Why is life worse today than it was before the revolution?" Whatever the answer, it was clear that communism could not make up for bad climate and geography, nor for the stubbornness of human nature. North Vietnam had coal, iron, and Marx, but it needed, most of all, the rice of the south.

Ho has had only one, if dubious, propaganda theme to exploit among the southerners. He has tried to keep alive the powerful spirit of nationalism that had swept the French from Vietnam, while sealing off news of northern discontent. He has charged over and over that Diem is nothing more than a puppet of the United States, which is really running South Vietnam, and has even suggested that the south will be autonomous under his rule. To some extent, this effort has succeeded. Many southern peasants refer to their government today as *My Diem,* meaning in communist ter-

minology, "U.S.-Diem." But this propaganda has been countered
to an important degree by several factors. With a relatively small,
if increasing, number of Americans in Vietnam, it has been hard
to convince most peasants that Americans are controlling the country in the sense that the French did. Also, unlike the situation during the Indochinese War, the element of nationalism has been
diluted by at least a partial realization that Ho's primary aim is to
communize all of Vietnam. While most Vietnamese would probably accept communism with docility if it came, few have been
sufficiently indoctrinated to fight for, or even desire, it.

Ho has apparently taken cognizance of this handicap, for he refers to the present war as a struggle for "liberation" rather than for
communism. He has set up an organization called the Front for
Liberation of the South, embracing "liberation" groups for youth,
peasants, workers, women, intellectuals, and various other segments of South Vietnamese society. Largely unpublicized is the role
of the south's illegal Communist, or Lao Dong (Workers) Party.
Part of and controlled by Ho's northern Lao Dong Party, this party
plays a leading part in the Front as well as in the Vietcong, the
name given to the rebel movement as a whole, political and military. In January 1962 North Vietnam announced the formation of
a new organization in South Vietnam called the Vietnam People's
Revolutionary Party, which Hanoi radio said would be in the
vanguard of the "national liberation" movement. This "new" group
may simply be the old Lao Dong Party in fresher revolutionary
dress.

By 1956 or 1957 it had become evident to Ho that the longer
the Diem government remained in power, the harder it would be
to win over the southern peasants, whose living standards were
gradually rising; and the hungrier would be the northerners, deprived of the south's ricelands. Force, therefore, was required, and
it would have to be exerted, to promote an atmosphere of chaos
that would cause the peasants to lose confidence in, and even
despise, their anticommunist rulers. The peasants themselves had
to be wooed, but also terrorized to "prove" that Diem was helpless
to protect them. Then, in their desire for security, they would fall
in with the "more powerful" Reds.

This cynical plan, Ho doubtless calculated, would have the
further virtue of provoking Diem's forces to take harsh counter-
measures against peasants who, in their state of terror, would not
co-operate with them. Thus, peasant resentment of communist violence would be largely offset by at least equal resentment of anticommunist violence. The ultimate outcome of the present struggle

is, in fact, likely to hinge on whether the South Vietnam regime, with the help of the United States, can give the peasants the security on which their lives and livelihoods depend.

The seeds of this war were planted at the time of partition. For though Ho Chi Minh transferred most of the military units loyal to him to North Vietnam, several thousand of his best-trained guerrillas secretly remained in the south, settling mainly in the jungles of the southern delta or in the remote mountainous regions along the Lao and Cambodian borders, where they would not easily be discovered. Agents were also left behind in almost every southern village. Many Reds who had gone north married southern women before they left—some women were forced into such marriages—and the wives were ordered to provide intelligence to northern agents and let them use their homes as bases and way stations. Also, tons of arms and ammunitions were cached throughout the country.

The original assignment of this vast fifth column was to propagandize against the Diem government and pave the way for a peaceful northern takeover through the elections that were to be held in 1956. But when Diem refused to hold them, Vietcong morale was severely shaken, and many agents defected on the practical grounds that the South Vietnam government, which was rapidly gaining strength, would probably be around for quite a while. Certainly, some judged, its overthrow was not worth another bloody war.

Ho decided differently. Between 1956 and 1958 he rebuilt and strengthened the Vietcong forces, infusing them with highly indoctrinated agents and guerrillas trained in the north and supplying them with more arms and equipment. Terror was confined to a few individual cases until 1958, when it began to spread throughout South Vietnam. Personnel from the north infiltrated at an increasing rate, and local inhabitants were either terrorized or propagandized into joining, or at least collaborating with, Ho's agents. A massive effort was made to get members of the southern government and army to defect. South Vietnam found itself entering a new era of violence and bloodshed.

The Vietcong guerrilla army consists of about 20,000 men, two-thirds of whom are believed to be natives of the south, including many who have been trained and indoctrinated in the north and then sent back to their southern homes. The Vietcong represents a triple threat. One is the village guard, the peasant, laborer, or fisherman who works for himself during the day and for the communists at night or in emergencies, receiving no pay for his extracurricular duties. Five to ten agents of this type live in most villages, a full squad of ten to sixteen in those largely under Vietcong control. These villagers, who devote seventy percent of their training time to ideology and only thirty percent to military tactics, are likely to be equipped with several rifles or submachine guns and a large arsenal of such native weapons as machetes, knives, bows and arrows, and spears.

A second kind of Vietcong guerrilla is the half-time soldier who is a member of an irregular force organized in each district, with several companies of fifty or more such fighters operating in each. This guerrilla, who receives half-pay and must enhance his income with odd jobs he can find while not on the attack or in training, is better equipped than the village guard and undergoes a training program that is half political and half military.

Finally, there is the full-time regular guerrilla, the backbone of the Vietcong, who belongs to a provincial or regional unit—spending, because he is already highly indoctrinated, only one-third of his training time on ideology and the rest on military tactics. Probably a veteran of the war against the French, he is a member of a battalion of 300-400 men or of one of three provincial companies, each comprising 100-150 men. Leaders of this guerrilla group have all been trained in the north, many in specialized schools run by the Red Chinese, while some units as a whole have come from the north.

The part-time or regular guerrilla is not permitted to go on combat missions, or even carry a weapon, until he is fully trained. He starts out by transporting supplies and collecting weapons from the dead after a battle, and then becomes a member of the auto-defense forces that guard the bases or do scouting and intelligence work. Eventually he is issued an old rifle and given intensive "dry-run" training; then he is sent along on a minor combat mission, usually an ambush, as an "observer," before finally being assigned to full-fledged combat duty.

Military personnel and espionage agents make their way from the north in a steady stream, often traveling, together with supplies, in junks, posing as fishermen. Others enter the south along secret trails leading across a heavily wooded, mountainous region into the western part of the country, while some come via the jungles of Cambodia. Since part of Laos fell under communist control in late 1960, even greater numbers have been crossing into the south via the so-called Ho Chi Minh Trail. This route actually

consists of a series of elephant trails, forests, and valleys which
originate in North Vietnam, along the Lao side of the border, and
enter Kontum Province in South Vietnam.

Soviet transport planes based in North Vietnam have been air-
lifting supplies into Tchepone, only twenty miles from the Vietnam border in east central Laos. The supplies are intended for
North Vietnam guerrillas headed south. So far, however, there
have been few Soviet or Red Chinese arms—in line with Ho's effort, dictated by nationalist considerations, to de-emphasize the role
of the two Red giants in the Vietnam war. The guerrillas have
been using French and American weapons almost exclusively,
many of them captured in raids on the South Vietnamese forces.

The tactics being used by the communists closely parallel those
that expelled the French from Vietnam and the Nationalists from
China. Mao, and also General Giap in his new handbook entitled
People's War—People's Army, lays down these general conditions
for winning a guerrilla war, which are being followed today: 1.
The rebels must firmly control a base on the border of the area under attack, as they do, of course, with North Vietnam. 2. Communists must educate, mobilize, organize, and arm the whole people
against the enemy. 3. Guerrillas must get along largely with weapons and food captured from the enemy so as not to overtax supply
lines from the rear base. 4. Rebels should attack only when they
are sure of outnumbering the enemy by about ten to one. 5. It is
necessary to grasp firmly the strategy of long-term resistance and
infinite patience. "Thousands of small victories accumulate into a
great success, and carry off the final victory."

So far, the Vietcong has scored many "small victories." They
have attacked numerous undermanned police stations, self-defense
corp units, civil guard outposts, and small units of the South Vietnam Army. By striking with suddenness and superior force they
are usually able to capture supplies of arms and ammunition, reducing their dependence on the long supply line from the north.
The remote medical clinic is another favorite Vietcong target, not
only because it is an easy source of medical supplies, but because
the Reds want to destroy all constructive social projects of the
Diem government which might ease the conditions of the peasants
and generate kind feelings toward Saigon. For the same reason,
schools have been destroyed and hundreds of teachers murdered.
Additional hundreds of village chiefs and other local officials have
been killed to underscore to the peasants the futility of trying to
depend on the Diem regime for security. Torture is common and
even the children of the enemy are murdered. The chief of the

Cau Ke district, Le Van Nghia, together with his wife and two other persons, were killed when their car hit a mine. The chief's two children, aged one and three, miraculously survived the blast, only to be shot on the spot by Vietcong who had laid the ambush.

The communists often use means other than terror to discredit and harass the government. Sometimes groups of them, posing as official mosquito sprayers, have entered villages and simply confiscated farm equipment, canceling whatever psychological advantage the government's antimalarial campaign might have had in that village. On one occasion the Reds distributed a shipment of rice it had stolen from a junk to the peasants of a nearby village, earning their gratitude. Then the Reds informed the southern military where the stolen rice could be found. Soldiers swooped on the village and confiscated the rice, making the communists look all the more kindly.

The peasant is the focal point of the Vietcong campaign, as prescribed by Mao and Giap; and as evidence of this, political officers—not military leaders—assigned to all units down to the platoon decide how the guerrillas will be used. The peasant is won over through a skillful psychological blend of indoctrination and terror, a brainwashing effort that is largely the job of a special unit of nonfighting "activists" trained in propaganda techniques and sabotage. Almost any night a platoon of these men may appear in a remote hamlet of several huts that have walls made of woven palm leaves and peaked roofs thatched with palm fronds. The peasants are likely to be bombarded with assurances that South Vietnam is an American colony, and that only Ho Chi Minh can offer them true independence and social justice. Outright ideological propaganda, however, is seldom used. When the speeches are over, the terror begins. Usually not physical terror—that is reserved, as indicated above, for government representatives, landlords, and other openly anticommunist targets against whom many peasants have grudges anyway.

Terror, however, is applied subtly. Anyone who does not cooperate with his "liberators" or co-operates with the Saigon government, the peasant is told, might be liquidated. In some cases, the parents or children of a farmer are kidnaped and held for ransom, the ransom being his agreement to join the Army of Liberation. A captured seventeen-year-old Vietcong "volunteer," when asked by Peter Kalischer of the Columbia Broadcasting System why he joined up, replied: "Because they took my father away for ten days and tried to force him to join their organization. But my father refused. Then they took me and forced me to co-operate. They threatened to kill my father if I refused. That is why I joined them."

Once the peasant joins—some, of course, are genuine volunteers—he is treated well and the indoctrination may produce a fanatic. Those who fail to "volunteer" may nevertheless be sympathetic to the Vietcong, and even those who are not probably won't co-operate with the government since their lives are at stake. A great many are, in any event, likely to be fed up with the Diem regime, which, they feel, must be as weak and corrupt as the communists say, if only because it can do nothing to prevent the "liberators" from intimidating people like themselves.

In theory, at least, a guerrilla can be punished even for taking a peasant's food without paying for it. However, it is considered legitimate to extort "taxes" from the peasants to help pay the costs of guerrilla operations, as well as the salaries of regular and semi-regular soldiers. Other sources of income are larger landowners and plantation owners who must contribute to the Vietcong to stay alive or be "protected" from the devastation of their land. Officials and businessmen are kidnaped for ransom. Transportation companies must ante up or have their buses or boats sabotaged. Sometimes guerrillas stop buses, divest the passengers of their money and valuables, and then deliver a lecture on "communist justice."

Cynical as such behavior may seem, hard-core members of the Vietcong believe every word of propaganda they may dispense in the interest of the "unenlightened." They are utterly dedicated, and willing to make any sacrifice for the cause. They are political men primarily, military men only because they can best serve communism in that capacity. Consequently, though they are among the most disciplined soldiers on earth when it comes to taking orders, their discipline flows more from political fanaticism than from military conditioning. Their preoccupation with the "deeper meaning" of the war is reflected in their usually sullen, aggressive personalities, in their contempt for periphery parade-ground rules. Their hair is long, their faces unshaven, their bodies unwashed and pocked with jungle sores, their "uniform"—a peasant's black pajama-like pants and shirt with a colored band around the sleeve —stiff with sweat and mud. Some insight into their undiluted devotion to an ideal which they tragically associate with the extravagant promises of communism can be induced from a number of personal diaries that have come into the possession of the South Vietnam government.

"The most precious thing for a man is his life, because one has

only one life," philosophized Mai Xuan Phong, a Vietcong medical
officer who left his diary behind when his camp was attacked by
government troops:

> One must, then, live in such a way that one does not have to
> regret the wasted years and months, that one does not have to be
> ashamed of a pitiful past, that one is able to say before passing
> away: my whole life, my whole strength have been devoted to
> the most elevated and the most beautiful cause—the struggle for
> the liberation of mankind . . . And one has to live in a hurry. A
> stupid accident, disease, or any tragic hazard may suddenly put
> an end to one's life . . .
>
> April 20, 1961—Departure for a new mission to which I have
> been assigned. There are so many happy memories which will en-
> courage me to fulfill my duty . . .
>
> May 14, 1961— . . . We arrived at the post of Muong Phin
> [Muong Phine] which has just been liberated. We slept at Muong
> Phine and, next day, we cross Highway No. 9 . . . We stop here
> and help build a road to allow trucks to bring in rice supplies. For
> two days we have been short of food and had only glutenous rice.
> This portion of our route is really hard. The sun is burning hot.
> We do not have enough drinking water . . . but our patriotism
> and our determination to liberate the native land will help us
> overcome all the difficulties and accomplish our duty . . .
>
> September 21—At 5:30 our forces launched a massive attack
> on the land development center of Quang Nhieu, Ba Moi Thuoc
> [Ban Me Thuot], and we proceeded to armed propaganda. We
> gathered together about 400 people and propagandized on the
> policy of the Front for Liberation of the south . . . We have
> secured good results. We have awakened these people after the
> dark years they lived under *My Diem*. We seized many documents
> and much military equipment . . .

Another diary that pitifully explores the success of communist
deception in capturing the human soul was found on the body of
Do Luc, who was killed in September 1961 at Daktrum. A brief
introductory note appears on the first page, written by Do Luc,
who apparently pretended it was a message from his loved one,
Nguyen Thi Minh Chau, in the north:

> We are in love and we have talked about that many times. Even
> though mountains and rivers will separate us, I shall wait until
> the revolution succeeds! My heart aches when I look toward the
> south, my darling! Is it not true that in the south there is still boil-
> ing oil, burning fire, and many painful and mournful situations,
> my darling?

Do Luc made his first entry in his diary on May 4, 1961:

Leaving temporarily the beloved north to return to my native south to liberate my compatriots from the yoke of misery imposed by *My Diem*. This has been my ideal for a long time . . . Here is the Vietnam-Laos border. I will always remember the international love which is engraved deep in my heart.

On August 6, Do Luc wrote after entering South Vietnam:

A few lines to remind me of this remote place! Not enough rice; meals tasteless because there is not enough salt; clothing is not warm enough for this very high peak. Nevertheless, in his determined heart, the fighter for liberation of the south remains faithful to the party, to the people of the south, and he remains faithful to his only love.

On August 14, Do Luc started reviewing his part:

Memory! One afternoon which is turning into evening. I am sitting on the peak of a high mountain. This is a famous scenic place. This is the highest peak of the whole chain of mountains, and it is all covered with mist. All this scenery arouses nostalgia in my heart! I try to recall my life since I was a young boy.

I answered the call of the party when I was very young, and what did I do for the people of my village? I devoted myself to the people. I took part in propaganda and aroused the people to carry out the policy of the party and the government and helped organize village defense and fighting forces. On March 25, 1954, I began my fighting career and I contributed my part in fighting the French Expeditionary Force. With the army of Interzone 5, I saw the end of the war on July 20, 1954, and then on April 26, 1955, I left my native place and all the ties with my family and friends to go north as a victorious fighter.

Since that day, my spirit has matured together with that of the regular army. We have built up a beautiful and prosperous and strong north; the construction sites and factories spring up quickly everywhere under a bright sky and under the superior socialist regime. Close to me there was a unique source of consolation in my life. My life was beautiful, my happiness immeasurable. Enough to eat; warm clothing in my daily life; earning a living was fairly easy; often I enjoyed songs and dances which deal with the healthy life of all the people in the north and with the maturity of the army . . .

After relating how he had participated on the rebel side in the Laotian civil war, Do Luc continued:

Our friends' war has stopped and the guns are silent. On the call of the party, I returned to my beloved Fatherland! My life returned to normal. I enjoyed again the peaceful atmosphere and my happiness. I continued training daily for the defense of the territory of the north and for the continuation of the liberation of the south. But I was back with my only love. Hurrah! How happy and how sweet. But my life could not continue that way!

For the third time my life turned to war again. For the liberation of our compatriots in the south, a situation of boiling oil and burning fire is necessary! A situation in which husband is separated from wife, father from son, brother from brother is necessary. I joined the ranks of the liberation army in answer to the call of the front for liberation of the south.

Now my life is full of hardship—not enough rice to eat nor enough salt to give a taste to my tongue, not enough clothing to keep myself warm! But in my heart I keep loyal to the party and to the people. I am proud and happy.

I am writing down this story for my sons and my grandsons of the future to know of my life and activities during the revolution when the best medicine available was the root of the wild banana tree and the best bandage was the leaf of *rau lui,* where there was no salt to give a taste to our meals, where there was no such food as meat or fish like we enjoy in a time of peace and happiness such as I have known and left behind. But that day will not take long to return to my life.

Toward the end of his diary, Do Luc listed "10 disciplinary rules for military security":

1. Do not disclose army secrets. Do not be curious about your own responsibilities and duties.

2. Do not discuss the duties you must carry out.

3. You must respect absolutely the regulations which protect documents during your activities. Do not carry with you those things that regulations prohibit you from carrying. If you are captured by the enemy, be determined not to give in. Slogans:—absolute loyalty to the revolution, death is preferable to slavery.

4. Keep secret our method of hiding weapons.

5. Do not take the liberty of listening to enemy broadcasts or of reading their newspapers or documents. Do not spread false rumors.

6. Do not have any relations with any organization with evil segments of the population which are harmful to the revolution.

7. Do not take your family or relatives or friends to military camp sites.

8. Keep order and security among the population as well as among yourselves.

9. Do not cease to carry out self-criticism or being vigilant, and continue your training.

10. Implement seriously these ten rules, mentally as well as in deeds.

Ironically, Do Luc himself failed to obey these rules. For in keeping a diary, he violated his own regulation on documents.

Still another revealing diary was kept by Captain Nguyen Dinh Kieu, who in July 1961 entered South Vietnam with sixty soldiers. "From this day on, I am in the Fatherland again," he wrote . . . "What is more thrilling than to stand here on my beloved Fatherland looking at the beautiful Truong Son mountain range?" Captain Kieu added in the same entry: "The capacity of the population here for understanding politics seems higher . . ." But ten days later he conceded disappointedly, "The people are kind but show no understanding of politics . . ." Nevertheless, firmly supporting the strategy outlined by Mao and General Giap, he wrote: "Be extremely friendly with local comrades and very parsimonious with the food supply they give us . . . Respect the local population and never touch their property . . ." And deploring the fact that some of his men lacked the killer instinct, he maintained: "This can be remedied only by intense political activity during rest periods."

Like Do Luc, Captain Kieu disobeyed one of his own rules: "Only attack when victory is certain." He was killed in September 1961 in an action won by southern forces.

To counter the fanatical aggressiveness of the Vietcong, President Kennedy has irrevocably committed the United States to help Diem win the struggle—without the use of American combat troops if possible, but, quite evidently, with their use if necessary. He established in February 1962 a new United States Military Assistance Command in Vietnam under General Paul D. Harkins, Deputy Chief of Staff of the United States Army in the Pacific and former commander of the 45th and 24th Infantry Divisions in Korea. The command consisted of approximately 12,000 men by the end of 1962—military advisers, helicopter pilots, and other noncombat personnel. These Americans are engaged in an operation completely new in Western military annals—guerrilla warfare. They are teaching South Vietnamese Ranger units to fight the communists on their own terms, the terms of Mao and Giap.

Previously, South Vietnam's 170,000-man army, while well-trained and disciplined under American supervision, knew how to fight only positional warfare, the kind of combat that, as the French discovered several years ago, is futile against a guerrilla enemy. The conversion of many of these soldiers into guerrillas has not been easy, for it has meant getting them to readjust deeply rooted military concepts, to forget what they had learned in the past. The new training plan calls for better mobility and communications rather than for more manpower or firepower. So far, the results have been gratifying. In one notable case Rangers ambushed a Vietcong force of 500 in the marshy Plain of Reeds west of Saigon in July 1961, killing about 170 and wounding dozens more. American-piloted helicopter raids in Vietcong territory have also been effective, if only in impressing the peasants that Diem's forces are on the offensive.

American advisers and instructors are also working with South Vietnam's grass-roots Self-Defense Corps, a people's militia made up principally of peasants. United States money and arms, too, are going to this force of about 60,000, which, through 1961, was poorly trained and armed, poorly paid, sometimes infiltrated by Vietcong guerrillas, and living under the constant threat of death. In 1961 over 1,600 were killed and 2,000 wounded. But as they are strengthened, these militiamen, who live in the areas they are assigned to protect, will be able to afford not only themselves, but their fellow villagers, better protection against the Vietcong. The Civil Guard, an armed police auxiliary, is also being expanded and trained so that it can take over some of the "positional" jobs now done by soldiers who should be operating as guerrillas.

United States technicians are teaching women how to shoot. They are superintending the construction of jungle roads and airstrips, and operating radio installations. They are arming and organizing thousands of mountaineer tribesmen in the region bordering Laos. They have directed forays into Laos itself, with southern troops reported to have patrolled the Ho Chi Minh Trail and taken up strategic positions along some of its rocky prongs in an effort to "plug" the trail to some degree. They have planned parachute jumps into North Vietnam, though the United States is reluctant to promote such tactics for fear of provoking Red Chinese troop intervention in the war. An undisclosed number of South Vietnamese paratroopers dressed as North Vietnamese peasants have parachuted out of unmarked C-47's and destroyed such installations as a Soviet-built power plant in the provincial capital of Vinh and a communist military school in Sonla, and set fires in mines, factories, and construction sites. The main area of operations has been in North Vietnam's vast mountain areas inhabited by fiercely independent-minded Meos, Black Thais, and other tribal groups opposed to communist rule.

Newly designed American equipment for use in guerrilla warfare will eventually represent another contribution to South Vietnam's fighting power. Such devices will include a wire gun capable of shooting about 500 feet of saw-toothed steel bands to "lasso" the enemy, a starlight-amplifying instrument to permit troops to see at night, radios that can "squirt" messages too swiftly for detection. (United States military officials have denied persistent reports that a new concussion bomb will soon be used for the purpose of breaking the eardrums of enemy guerrillas and thereby rendering them militarily useless.) Already special radio sets distributed in villages have permitted Vietnamese planes responding to an S O S to strafe targets in a matter of minutes, encouraging peasant defenders to put up a fight.

The most drastic of all American schemes is the Delta Plan, which is modeled on the New Villages program that crushed the communist rebellion in Malaya, and has in fact been designed by Robert G. K. Thompson, the former Defense Minister of Malaya. Of larger scope than the Malayan concept, the Delta Plan, like its predecessor, calls for the resettlement of peasants, forcibly if necessary, in new Strategic Villages surrounded by moats containing bamboo spears and nail-studded planks in order to isolate the Vietcong from the population. Government troops carry out the resettlement without warning for fear that villagers might bolt for the woods if they know they are to be moved. Once they are loaded on trucks with belongings they are able to carry, the abandoned villages are burned to deprive the Reds of shelter and food, according to the Malayan pattern. But unlike the British in Malaya, Diem's government does not pay peasants on the spot for anything they leave behind, compensating them only when they have indicated they will not try to run away.

To reduce the hostility aroused by the abrupt relocation—most of the peasants have to be removed forcefully—the Strategic Villages in most cases offer many social benefits, including schools, Buddhist temples, clinics, orphanages, and community halls where they are subjected to intense anticommunist propaganda. The peasants are also given a plot of land, food, and seed until their first crops are cultivated, but must return from their fields at the sound of a curfew bell or risk being shot by night patrols. Such villages are first being established in the Mekong Delta and, if successful, will be extended throughout the country, permitting the Self-Defense Corps of each to relieve regular army units for service in offensive movements.

Though this program could be the key to victory, as in Malaya, its possible failure could do irreparable harm to Diem's cause. In mid-1962 it was not yet working with great success. Many peasants, when they have an opportunity, slip off into the jungle to join the communists, who promise to give them back their land. Diem experimented with a similar Prosperity Center, or *agroville,* scheme in 1959-60, but abandoned the idea when it seemed to turn more peasants against the government than it won over. One reason was that the program was far less organized than Malaya's, or for that matter, the Delta Plan. Police and government officials were more brutal and militant in their approach, rounding up thousands of peasants, sometimes in the midst of the rice-harvesting season, and putting them to work building *agrovilles* without pay, a situation that holds true in some areas under the Delta Plan, too. Many had to walk a dozen miles or more to the site of construction each day. Then, when the new village was completed, there was only room enough, in some cases, for less than half the peasants who had been forced to build it.

But other factors also entered into the failure, and are likely to present similar difficulties for the present plan—factors that the British did not have to contend with in Malaya. Whereas most of the peasants gathered in the Malayan New Villages were Chinese rubber plantation and tin mine workers who had simply squatted on their jungle lands after World War II, the Vietnamese peasants have worked the land of their honored ancestors, and to be torn from it is to be torn from their sacred heritage. The British felt, moreover, that they could afford to antagonize the Chinese minority in Malaya in view of the support the government received from the anti-Chinese Malay majority. But Diem is dealing with the whole indigenous people, and may not be able to afford antagonizing them at the very moment the communists are appealing for their support. Also, since Malaya does not border on a communist territory, there was no way of adequately supplying the rebels with food once the New Villages were set up. But South Vietnam, of course, does border on a communist area, and therefore the Reds could always depend on a supply line from the north, reducing the value of the Strategic Villages.

Aside from the Delta Plan, Diem government officials, under American prodding, are taking other measures to thwart Vietcong tactics. To cut down on assassinations, some provincial governments no longer appoint hamlet chiefs, but let the hamlets elect their own. As the communists don't want to antagonize the peasants unnecessarily, they are far more reluctant to kill elected than government-appointed officials. The government in such areas no longer forces the chief to give information concerning the Vietcong, permitting him to tell the communists honestly that he has offered only minimum administrative co-operation to the government. In the end, it is hoped, such humanistic handling of the Vietcong problem may win over many peasant friends. This leniency is based on the theory that if the government is not yet able to protect the hamlets from intimidation, the hamlets should be permitted to protect themselves as best they can. Some Vietnamese authorities, however, think that this attitude on the part of the government may be interpreted as weakness by the peasants and encourage them to co-operate all the more with the Reds.

The United States military role in South Vietnam has been limited to the training and organization of Diem's forces. No American fighting troops have yet been dispatched to the country, and with good reason. First, the use of Americans in a combat capacity would inevitably stir memories among many Vietnamese of the days when they were fighting the French and would buttress communist propaganda that the Americans are no less imperialistic than the French. Second, American soldiers would be severely handicapped in a guerrilla war, even if they were trained for it. For as Mao himself said, an effective guerrilla must be a "fish in the water," and an American would be a strange fish in the Vietnamee water. Third, the introduction of United States troops could bring in Red Chinese forces and perhaps result in a much larger Asian war. Nevertheless, American combat units, if sent to South Vietnam as a last resort, could probably hold the towns at least, and perhaps save the nation simply through forcing a Korea-like stalemate.

While the United States has poured into South Vietnam military aid totaling some $500 million from 1954 to 1962, it has also been helping to fight the Vietcong on the economic and social fronts. Such assistance has not always been rendered with great, or even adequate, efficacy. Careless contracting methods have quadrupled the cost of highway projects and unreasonably delayed the construction of a radio network begun in 1953. Until recently one-third of American officials in Saigon lived in houses costing the government $400 monthly, far in excess of such expenses in most other countries, while receiving hardship pay as well as enjoying commissary privileges. Some officials have accepted free homes or cars from the Vietnamese government and foreign aid contractors. An excessively low evaluation of aid money by the Vietnam government for some time deprived the United States of control of over half the funds and resulted in unreasonable profits for importers and the local government. Considerable United States aid is stolen and resold by local government officials.

But despite these wasteful shortcomings, American aid alone

has made possible the impressive progress in these fields registered in the first few years of South Vietnam's existence as a sovereign state. A new program announced in January 1961 has intensified the effort to raise living standards in the country. This program has undertaken to support attempts to train village officials in local administration, expand rural health, education, and agricultural credit systems, develop communications to enable villages to summon emergency military or medical aid, link rural communities with main highways to help ferret out Red guerrillas, launch an extensive pest control campaign, reconstruct flood-stricken areas, inaugurate public works to relieve unemployment, speed up industrial development, and facilitate the resettlement of peasants living in some isolated regions.

The difficulties in carrying out this program and using it as a weapon against the communists are enormous. More schools and clinics, the reconstruction of flooded areas, and other such projects would undoubtedly have an impact on the population. But the Reds control much of the rural area, as seen in their concentrated attacks on this kind of project. And with the Vietcong bent on destruction, efforts at construction cannot be very fruitful until the security situation is vastly improved.

Americans are no less worried about Diem's apparent lack of widespread popularity. Many of the peasants oppose the Delta Plan and resent the corruption of local government officials, who even steal and sell U.S.-contributed food. Businessmen are exasperated by rigid economic controls. Many Buddhists complain that, as a Catholic, Diem discriminates against them: they point, for example, to the government's ban on the use of fireworks on Buddhist holidays. The Chinese community is bitter about discriminatory laws—particularly one excluding foreigners from eleven professions—and sometimes retaliates with economic sabotage. In 1956 the Chinese blocked rice exports, which they control.

But most important of all in the view of many Americans is the resentment harbored toward Diem by opposition politicians, intellectuals, and many military officials who condemn his autocratic rule, even while agreeing that he is the only southerner with enough stature and popularity to head the government. "The president's authoritarian attitude has kept him apart from the people," one United States official told me. "The people hold him responsible for the lack of freedom in South Vietnam, and that's one reason why many are willing to listen to the communists."

The truth in this statement was dramatically indicated in November 1960, when three battalions of paratroopers surrounded his yellow stucco Freedom Palace while its leaders forced him to announce his intention to institute political reforms. Within thirty-six hours, however, troops loyal to the President crushed the revolt and Diem's promises were immediately discarded. "The government continues to serve the nation," he said, though the rebels had never intended to overthrow him in the first place, but just to make him loosen his reins. About a year later, Diem barely escaped death when two of his air force officers dropped bombs on his palace.

True to the Confucian spirit, Diem holds the reins of government tightly indeed. "A sacred respect is due the person of the sovereign," he once wrote. "He is the mediator between the people and heaven as he celebrates the national cult." Working up to fifteen hours a day, he deals personally with the smallest details of government. Until recently at least, he determined who could receive a passport, who could study abroad, and even the distance between roadside trees. Field officers, down to company commanders, have had to wait for his approval before attacking, often losing military advantages as a result. When one oppositionist managed to win an election despite Diem's tight control of the balloting, he was denied his seat because he made "false" campaign promises. Such tactics have given birth to a new South Vietnamese word—"Diemocracy."

Diem trusts no one—no one, that is, except his family. One brother, Archbishop Ngo Dinh Thuc, heads the Roman Catholic hierarchy. Another, Ngo Dinh Can, runs central Vietnam with the help of a private secret police organization. A third, Ngo Dinh Luyen, is Ambassador to London. Still another, Ngo Dinh Nhu, is Diem's chief political adviser, while Nhu's beautiful wife is a member of the national assembly and heads all important women's organizations. Mme. Nhu's father, Tran Van Chuong, is Ambassador to the United States, and her mother is an observer at the United Nations.

Brother Nhu, who openly states that "freedom must not prevent the march of progress," has helped to sell Diem on the government philosophy of "personalism." In line with Vietnamese tradition, he thrives on semisecret political activity, running a clandestine movement called the Can Lao Nhan Vi, or the Revolutionary Labor Party, which, in a sense, is the southern counterpart of the northern Communist Party. Organized along communist administrative lines, which dovetail closely with the Confucian hierarchical lines of the orthodox secret society, 70,000 members have infiltrated into the government, army, villages, press, and schools, and are believed to hold all significant civil and military appointments. For her part, Mme. Nhu is doing her best to uphold the gospel of "personalism." Aside from her domination of women's groups, she is the sponsor of the "purification" law and a Family Law that would not even permit Vietnamese to divorce without Diem's personal approval.

Diem has further suffered in the public eye, some observers say, from the widespread belief, perhaps stemming from the secrecy of their activities, that Nhu and his wife are guilty of gross corruption, involving in particular the illegal transfer of private funds abroad. But no proof has yet been offered to back such charges. There is plenty of proof, however, of corruption among lower-echelon local officials who, picked more for their loyalty than their ability, often extort money from the peasants —one reason why the Vietcong can kill them without arousing much popular protest.

Diem, who has never been personally accused of dishonesty, violently defends his family and claims that the great majority of Vietnamese are opposed neither to his "family system" of rule nor to his authoritarianism. "I know my people," he says. Democracy is a good thing, perhaps, in times of peace and calm, but not during a military emergency, when even established democracies often forgo the luxury of political liberties. Moreover, he claims, the people can hardly resent the slowness of democratic reforms when they have no democratic traditions by which to judge their value. What the people want at this critical time is security, and all else is secondary. "I know my people."

And Diem, the mandarin, may be right—as far as most peasants are concerned. As for the politicians, intellectuals, and military officers, to whom liberalization of his regime is not a secondary matter, he believes they have little choice but to support him however much they may complain—he being the only apparent alternative to communism. These groups, unlike the peasants, he reasons, are not likely to throw their weight to Ho Chi Minh if they haven't done so by now. Diem's logic may be sound—though a new noncommunist military attempt to overthrow him is not impossible—but he ignores the importance of the morale factor among these groups, whose help he badly needs in the common battle for survival. Some of Diem's best officers and men are fighting only half-heartedly, and some of his most capable political colleagues will not work with, or for, him because of his totalitarian ways.

Still, it is likely that the great majority of people, victimized by years of war and terror, will follow the government that can guarantee them peace, whatever its political philosophy. Nor should it be overlooked that Diem's government is probably more honest than most Afro-Asian regimes, and that its authoritarianism is about par for the course. Be that as it may, if the United States permits South Vietnam to fall, even through the latter's own weaknesses—and as a last resort the United States may have to dispatch fighting troops to prevent such a disaster—it might just as well abandon all Southeast Asia to the communists.

XXIII

THE CASE FOR HOPE

Communism has registered important gains in the Afro-Asian world in recent years with the extension of the Yenan Way throughout the area, though these gains have been diluted to some degree by Communist China's overt aggression in India and Russia's refusal to side with India when the ideological chips were down.

Generally speaking, the Soviet Union, under Khrushchev, has won the friendship of the national bourgeoisie, who rule most of the countries, through economic aid and lip service support of their interests, even while periodically reminding these "friends" of Russian nuclear capability. Communist China, under Mao, has won the respect, if not the affection, of the Afro-Asian people for its spectacular effort to achieve social and industrial revolution overnight, and simply for the brutal power that it wields in the implementation of both its domestic and foreign policies, negating in part the value for the West of Peking's diminishing popularity.

Under the Yenan Way, whether the Moscow or the Peking brand, the inflexibility of Stalin's tactics has given way to a pliancy adjustable to conditions in each individual state. Subversion and infiltration are practiced in accordance with the history, traditions, economic level, and political sophistication of the country in question. The Reds operate one way in Ghana, another way in Egypt, and still other ways in Afghanistan, India, Indonesia,

Laos, and South Vietnam. Depending on the nation, economic aid, diplomatic support, ideological propaganda, atomic threats, and military action are used in appropriate combinations almost scientifically determined.

Nevertheless, for all the gains the communists have made, they are still a long way from victory. One measure of the difficulties facing them is the composition of their parties and organizations. With a few exceptions, most conspicuously the Indonesian Communist Party, these groups are made up largely of frustrated intellectual elites—lawyers, teachers, students, doctors. Though every party naturally calls for a government founded on the proletariat, the underdeveloped countries still have very few industrial workers, and most of them are too unsophisticated to be politically inclined or to find much in common with the communist intellectuals who are so aggressively bidding for their support.

The great majority of peasants have also proved exasperatingly elusive, for like peasants all over the world they tend toward conservatism. Indonesian peasants have been attracted to communism partly because of the unusual communal customs of their ancestors, and many Chinese and Vietnamese peasants have been lured into the Red trap by propaganda wrapped in nationalist slogans, as well as by Confucian traditions that lend themselves to communist-style conspiracy. But the bulk of peasants in the Afro-Asian nations feel a deep sense of loyalty to their landlord, king, or tribal chief; while in most Moslem countries Islam is still a deterrent to revolutionary action among them, if not among the more educated urban groups.

Communist gains in recent years have been inevitable. In Africa and the Middle East the Reds began to make a serious attempt at infiltration only in the years following Stalin's death. Starting from near zero, therefore, they could not help but increase their influence. But not a single African or Middle Eastern country has gone communist or actively supports Moscow's or Peking's foreign policy. Even Guinea, which in some respects resembles a communist state, has steadfastly opposed attempts by Moscow to turn it into a puppet nation; while in the Congo communism suffered a humiliating defeat after Lumumba's death. The great majority of African states have demonstrated through the formation of the Monrovia bloc that while they wish to follow a neutralist Cold War path, they lean toward the West. In the Middle East, the communists failed to take over Iraq when victory seemed within their grasp. The Soviet Union, it is true, may have cautioned against a premature direct takeover, but it isn't likely it wanted Iraqi communists to be thrown out of every influential position, as they were.

In Asia, where communism had made considerable inroads even before the war, the popularity of this doctrine has actually decreased in postwar years. Communist influence reached a low point in the late 1940's and early 1950's as the result of Stalin's crude employment of his "left strategy"—armed rebellion against the government in power, whether under colonial or nationalist control. Today the communist danger in free Asia lies to some extent in Russia's radical switch to the post-Stalin "right strategy" and Red China's extension of its more conditional Yenan Way, which have facilitated Red economic and "cultural" infiltration, and enhanced the status of domestic communists. The most immediate threat, however, is not from peaceful infiltration but from the use of force backed by Peking and, less enthusiastically, by Moscow. Only Indonesia has a Communist Party with a widespread popular support not induced by force and intimidation.

To safeguard the region and give it the sense of security it needs to resist communism effectively, the United States cannot avoid taking certain military risks, as it is now doing in South Vietnam. Indeed, if the communist guerrilla offensive in Vietnam can be broken with the counterguerrilla techniques American instructors are teaching the South Vietnamese forces, there is a good possibility that all of free Asia can be saved from the Red grasp— though Laos may continue to totter precariously. For once the communist military machine is neutralized, the Reds will have to rely on peaceful means of infiltration and subversion to achieve power, and the record shows that this technique has never proved of decisive value in the Afro-Asian world, but has produced only powerful counterreactions against communism.

The more the Communists resort to this technique the greater are such counterreactions likely to be in the long run—in those countries not forcibly devoured. Though Mao may be more aggressive than Khrushchev, the Soviet leader is, like him, using terror, mainly atom rattling, as an instrument of foreign policy. This may be an effective instrument—temporarily. But there is considerable significance for the future in the private shock experienced by many neutralists, who may have been silent in public, as the result of the Soviet Union's arrogant decision to violate the nuclear testing moratorium, and on the very eve of the Belgrade conference of neutralists. Some, like Ghana's Nkrumah and Ethiopia's Haile Selassie, even sent notes of protest to Moscow, while a Cairo newspaper bitingly reported that the Soviet people were being kept in ignorance of the bomb explosions in their country. The installation of missile bases in Cuba was also condemned by most neutralists.

Countries drawn to a powerful nation by fear are not dependable. For while fear, in a negative sense, can keep people and nations in line, it tends to have a corrosive effect on the positive attractions of the feared, leaving as a residue only antipathy and distrust.

The United States, meanwhile, was at the peak of its prestige at the end of 1962 as the result of the Cuban and Indian crises. It had come out ahead in neutralist eyes on all counts: its tough stand on the presence of nuclear missiles in Cuba, which proved that the United States could be pushed only so far; its refusal to gloat over Russia's humiliation in that crisis; and its promptly favorable and unconditional response to India's call for arms aid.

It is difficult to predict whether the Soviet Union will be easier to deal with in the future, though that power is trying to give the impression that genuine "peaceful coexistence" is now quite possible. A sign that Moscow might be more reasonable in the future could perhaps be perceived in Khrushchev's moderate response to American toughness over Cuba. Few great powers in peacetime history have so willingly submitted to such abasement as the Kremlin agreed to when American naval personnel boarded Soviet ships to verify that missiles were being removed from Cuba.

The possibility of new Soviet trickery—it is conceivable, for example, that the inspected missiles were dummies or that some missiles remain hidden in Cuba—cannot be dismissed. But considering Russia's deteriorating relations with Red China, Khrushchev may not want another risky confrontation with the West soon, though the danger exists that the split with China may actually force the USSR to hew to an increasingly hard line just to retain the support of its allies.

At any rate, Washington's clear demonstration of its willingness to risk nuclear war if necessary to defend American interest may well have a significant effect on the trend of the Cold War, one way or another. But whatever the trend, certainly this country must not let down its guard, or fritter away the advantages it now enjoys.

If the United States must be prepared to use military means—indirect as in South Vietnam if possible, direct if necessary—to counter communist force wherever employed, it must also, of course, use peaceful means to win friends, or at least to keep from making enemies. One of the soundest ways to do this is through example, particularly with regard to the treatment of nonwhites in America, including diplomats and visitors from abroad. If people of their race, and particularly of their nationality, are humiliated by segregation and other discriminatory policies, it is only human that the Afro-Asian peoples should feel resentment toward the country where the humiliation occurs, however few individuals may actually be responsible.

Afro-Asians can accept, and perhaps even favor in some cases, political dictatorships, communist or otherwise, for they find no affront to their personal dignity in such a regime, whatever Western philosophers may preach about the dignity of the individual. But they do find an affront in racial discrimination. Therefore many, if given the choice between communism and the "American way of life," might well choose the former—that is, unless they have had the opportunity to experience racial bias in the communist countries. Nevertheless, efforts by the United States government in the last several years to do away with segregation have made an impression on many Afro-Asians, and even Guinea's Sékou Touré remarked after a trip to the United States that he was pleasantly surprised by the improving racial situation in this country. Further improvement is necessary, however, if the bitter taste of discrimination is not to continue to strengthen the communist position.

The United States cannot afford, either, to neglect informing the Afro-Asians about the more positive aspects of life in this country, particularly since the communist powers are displaying no modesty about the joys of Marxist life. There cannot be too many cultural exhibitions—art, music, quality films—all of which should be geared for the masses as well as for the elite, though little should be said about American affluence, which usually fosters envy rather than good will. As for literature, the United States Information Service libraries are among the biggest thorns in the communist side, for while books and magazines to be found in these libraries present almost every point of view on almost every political and economic problem, communist reading rooms offer little more than Marxist propaganda. In some countries, the USIS has become the leading cultural center. The vigor of the United States propaganda services has increased under the direction of Edward R. Murrow, the former radio and television commentator.

But perhaps the most important thing the United States can do to keep the Afro-Asian countries out of the communist orbit is to reinforce their strong tendency to seek answers to their economic and political problems within the framework of national independence and their own indigenous cultures. For the stronger this tendency grows, the less chance there will be for an alien, monolithic doctrine like communism to make significant headway.

By continuing and strengthening its economic and technical aid program for the Afro-Asian states, the United States can help them to find answers other than communism, which professes to offer a dynamic, ready-made solution to all their problems. To strengthen this aid program signifies more than expansion. It means closer supervision and making sure that every dollar and technician yield the maximum economic and social benefit for the recipient nation.

One brilliantly imaginative step in the technical sphere is the Peace Corps program introduced by the Kennedy Administration, which is sending idealistic, dedicated young American technicians —teachers, agricultural experts, engineers, and others—to underdeveloped countries to work in the field under local conditions to help the people learn how to live a more rewarding life. This scheme has been criticized in various quarters. The communists, who view the Peace Corps as the first Western competition with their own village cells, understandably claim it represents simply "grass-roots imperialism." Some Americans, including former President Eisenhower, have complained they see little sense in sending at considerable cost a bunch of "inexperienced youngsters" abroad to do a job that even the most experienced technicians would find difficult. In any case, with so many countries needing help, what good, they ask, can a few thousand technicians do scattered over the world like pebbles on a beach?

But little criticism has been heard from the beneficiaries of the Peace Corps plan, because they realize that every pebble counts and is to be coveted like a diamond. The people of the underdeveloped world are hungering for education and technical knowledge today, even more than for food. In the Congo, for example, swindlers have found easy prey among the youth, dozens of whom have turned over their life savings to them in return for "admission papers" to African and European universities, "vaccination certificates," and passage to the countries in which they are to "study."

Yet despite this thirst for knowledge, there are simply not enough teachers or schools to cater to more than a fraction of the young people in most such countries. Teachers who are available are, in general, conspicuously unqualified for their jobs. Deep in the bush of southern Sudan, I saw the tall, stark-naked men of the Dinka tribe, standing storklike on one foot as is their custom, watch in befuddlement as their children, dressed in white robes and seated on logs under a tree, wrote their names on soiled paper with charcoal pencils. The teacher, sent by the Sudanese government, was a fourth-grade graduate.

In Mogadishu, capital of Somalia, as I strolled one evening through the teeming native quarter, a patchwork collection of crowded restaurants, board and corrugated iron houses, and market booths, I observed a number of people, from about seven to thirty years of age, filing out of a rickety little shack, all carrying notebooks. This was a private night school operated by an enterprising secondary school graduate with an excellent knowledge of pigeon English. "I teach them mainly English," he said. "I have thirty students, they paying very little. I don't profit much, but my country needs teachers. And besides I have government job in daytime. Many people want me teach them but I can't take them all. If they have money only for spaghetti (a dish they learned to enjoy in Italian colonial days) or books, they take books. Our country have very little resources. We need good minds to get rich on so little."

In an Ethiopian village, a little man with rotting teeth leaned on the bar of the dingy, oil-lit local tavern sipping *tej,* a sickeningly sweet native wine. Above the exotically tinny strains of the *masinko,* a one-string, sheepskin kind of mandolin played by a village minstrel, he tried to sell me the "services" of a lovely young fourteen-year-old girl. The man was the village teacher, and the girl, whose fragile melancholy face was framed like some Biblical countenance by a long cotton scarf wound around her head, was one of his pupils.

According to a survey prepared by Dr. Gerald F. Winfield of the Agency for International Development, about five million more primary schoolteachers are needed in Africa, Asia, and the Middle East. He estimated that about two-thirds of the teachers now available in these areas have less than a high school education, with the majority limited to six years of school. The Peace Corps alone, of course, cannot overcome this situation. Yet every American technician who makes his way into a remote village means to that village—though some of the older people might resent the tampering with their traditional way of life—a chance to broaden its medieval horizons.

The Kennedy Administration is also displaying considerable wisdom with regard to economic aid, a fortunate thing considering that communism makes its greatest headway in countries in which living standards do not keep pace with educational advancement, spawning discontented intellectuals. In the past the United States has thought too much in terms of direct political benefits from its aid. An American diplomat who had served in Laos told me that one of the main troubles with the United States aid program in that country has been that "we have taken too long to pay the salaries of the civil servants. We only anger our friends in the government by requiring a lot of paper work and checking before we hand out our aid. The Russians and Red Chinese never do that. When they give aid, they simply give it with no questions asked, and so those who receive it are very happy. Frankly, I feel that we should think in those terms, too."

What this diplomat ignored is that Russia and Red China grant aid to pave the way for infiltration and subversion. Squandering and corruption are actually desirable from the communist point of view, for other than the few expensive showcase projects which benefit the Reds in terms of propaganda, the communists are not anxious to help build up the economies of noncommunist countries, thereby reducing the poverty and misery on which they feed and building up potential new consumer markets for the West.

American aid, however, is geared to the very goal the Reds do not want to attain—the alleviation of poverty and misery, not only as a matter of simple humanitarianism, but as the only realistic method of countering the popularity of communism. With this purpose in mind, it is hardly sensible for the United States to pattern its aid program after that of the communists. On the contrary, the United States should stop worrying about "angering" our "friends in the government" and devote more thought to seeing that its aid is used to meet its purpose. Once this purpose is accomplished, political gains will follow automatically, for people with full stomachs make poor targets for communism. Conversely, people with empty stomachs who see their leaders growing fatter make the best Red targets.

Happily, the Kennedy Administration has to some degree begun worrying more about these hungry people than about the sensitivities of their governments. The President pushed through Congress in 1962 the most staggering aid program in American peacetime history. Almost $4 billion was appropriated for the 1962-63 fiscal year as part of a program of $22 billion over a five-year period that began in 1961-62. Instead of grants, which have helped to corrupt and whittle away the dignity of some countries, the stress is on long-range development goals financed through easy-term loans repayable in dollars. Increased participation of American private capital through more liberal investment guarantees totaling about $1 billion is anticipated.

But more important for the health of the program—and of the recipient nations—the Administration pledged that "recipient governments will be expected to accept the necessity for hard political decisions and sometimes politically unpopular actions to insure that the benefits of development programs reach their entire population as rapidly as practicable." This is an "invitation" to leaders of the underdeveloped world to institute land, tax, and other reforms if they expect to enjoy a slice of the American pie.

Peasants cannot be expected to shout the praises of American generosity when funds used for irrigation projects swell the wealth of absentee landlords while giving the peasants more work to do but virtually nothing more in income. Certainly Laos is a good example of how uncontrolled aid can actually defeat United States purposes—both economic and political—by widening the gap between the living standards of the rulers and the ruled. In any event, the United States should maintain a far more rigid control system than it has in the past to keep governments, or individual officials, from misusing aid, regardless of the extra "paper work" required.

Such a policy is what the people for whom the aid is intended want. In my travels through the Afro-Asian world, scores of people have asked me why the United States gives aid to their often corrupt governments without making sure that it reaches those who need it. Many Afro-Asian leaders disapprove of the idea, charging that controls are bound to compromise their country's freedom and independence. Some have threatened—in cases in which the United States has attached conditions to its aid—to accept assistance only from the communist bloc. But the United States need not submit to political blackmail.

Since France withdrew all economic support from Guinea in 1958 after that country voted to become completely independent, and the United States failed to respond quickly to Guinea's needs, President Sékou Touré has run the Guinean economy almost exclusively with communist-bloc aid. Yet Guinea is on cool terms with the Soviet Union today and showing signs of warming up to the United States. And while Egypt's Nasser is receiving most of his help from Russia, his jails have not been emptied of communists. If a country, as a result of communist economic infiltration, should enter the Red camp, the chances are it would have done so one day anyway, regardless of how much assistance the United States pumped into the country. At any rate, the demand by the United States for guarantees that its aid will not go down the drain will in the end win far more friends than a policy of leaving it to immature, often unpopular governments to distribute American funds without adequate supervision. This does not mean that the United States should insist on the establishment of political democracy, which, it is only realistic to recognize, cannot work in some countries at their present stage of development. We can, however, exert pressure on the dictator, if there is one, to promote the economic and social welfare of his people.

If the United States must attach social and economic strings to its aid for the good of the people of the recipient countries, it should also be open in its diplomatic dealings with them. Attorney General Robert Kennedy set a hopeful tone to his trip to the Far East in early 1962. When Indonesian students castigated the United States for not throwing its weight behind Djakarta's demands that Dutch-controlled West New Guinea be incorporated in Indonesia, Kennedy stated flatly that the United States had no intention of deviating from its neutral stand on this issue. Such direct talk, coupled with sincere professions of friendship, won the respect of many Indonesians who had thought of the United States as devious and hypocritical.

The United States can also ill afford to play diplomatic "politics" in the United Nations, whose 110 members include 55 Afro-Asian countries. For whatever its shortcomings, the United Nations is a vital instrument for marshaling world public opinion in the service of peace, constituting a permanent organ of negotiation and discussion, the only alternatives to war. Though United Nations majority opinion may sometimes be contrary to that of the United States, and even appear immoral, as in its approval of India's use of violence to grab neighboring Portuguese colonies, its decisions in most cases reflect the stubborn determination of the underdeveloped world to remain independent. Few countries outside the communist bloc agreed to go along with the Soviet Union's demand that the United Nations get out of the Congo, a demand obviously intended to permit the communists to get in. Even fewer have expressed enthusiasm for the Soviet "troika" plan to paralyze the operation of the United Nations by dividing its leadership into Western, communist, and neutralist sectors, each of which could veto the decisions of the others. And confirming the need for a strong United Nations in Afro-Asian eyes was the decision of both the United States and the Soviet Union to seek the organization's mediation in the Cuban crisis when the world teetered on the brink of nuclear war.

The United States cannot buy Afro-Asian support by backing such projects as the United Nations armed attacks on Katanga, which weakened the moral foundations of the organization even more than did the Indian assaults on the Portuguese colonies, because United Nations soldiers themselves broke the peace. If the Afro-Asian countries continue to steer clear of communism, it won't be because of anything the United States does or does not do. It will be because they so dearly cherish their newly won independence. America, therefore, can best frustrate communist designs by convincing these nations that we genuinely desire to strengthen their independence—an effort that will pay increasing dividends as communism gradually, but inevitably, bares its thinly disguised imperialistic nature to the millions of political innocents interested not in ideology but in a better life.

BIBLIOGRAPHY

The following are among the books, periodicals, and newspapers consulted in the preparation of this book:

BOOKS

ACTON, HARRY B., *The Illusion of the Epoch: Marxism-Leninism as a Philosophical Creed*, New York, British Book Center, 1955

ADORATSKY, V., *Dialectical Materialism*, New York, International Publishers, 1934

ALLEN, JAMES S., *World Monopoly and Peace*, New York, International Publishers, 1946

ALMOND, GABRIEL A., *The Appeals of Communism*, Princeton, Princeton University Press, 1954

ARCIN, ANDRÉ, *La Guinée Française*, Paris, A. Challamel, 1907

ARTIQUE, PIERRE, *Qui Sont les Leaders Congolais?*, Brussels, Editions Europe Afrique, 1961

BENEDICT, RUTH, *The Chrysanthemum and the Sword*, Boston, Houghton, Mifflin, 1946

BORTON, HUGH, *Japan's Modern Century*, New York, Ronald, 1955

BRIMMELL, J., *Communism in South East Asia*, London, New York, Oxford University Press, 1959

BURCHETT, WILFRED G., *Mekong Upstream*, Berlin, Seven Seas Publishers, 1959

CAMPBELL, ALEXANDER, *The Heart of Africa*, New York, Knopf, 1954

CHAMPASSAK, SISOUK NA, *Storm Over Laos*, New York, F. A. Praeger, 1961

COAST, JOHN, *Some Aspects of Siamese Politics*, New York, International Secretariat, Institute of Pacific Relations, 1953

DENNEN, LEON, *Trouble Zone*, New York, Chicago, Ziff-Davis Publishing Co., 1945

EBON, MARTIN, *World Communism Today*, New York, McGraw-Hill, 1948

EGERTON, F. CLEMENT C., *Angola in Perspective*, London, Routledge & Kegan Paul, 1957

ELEGANT, ROBERT, *The Dragon's Seed*, New York, St. Martin's Press, 1959

FISCHER, LOUIS, *The Story of Indonesia*, New York, Harper, 1959

FOSTER, WILLIAM Z., *History of the Three Internationals*, New York, International Publishers, 1955

GHOSH, MONOMOHAN, *A History of Cambodia*, Saigon, J. K. Gupta, 1960

GIBNEY, FRANK, *Five Gentlemen of Japan*, New York, Farrar, Straus & Young, 1953

———, *The Khrushchev Pattern*, New York, Duell, Sloan & Pearce

HALL, DANIEL GEORGE EDWARD, *Burma,* London, New York, Hutchinson's University Library, 1950

HALPERN, ABRAHAM MEYER, AND FREDMAN, H. B., *Communist Strategy in Laos,* Santa Monica, Calif., RAND Corporation, 1960

HALPERN, JOEL MARTIN, *The Lao Elite,* Santa Monica, Calif., RAND Corporation, 1960

——, *Laos Profiles,* Santa Monica, Calif., RAND Corporation, 1961

——, *Government, Politics and Social Structure of Laos,* Santa Monica, Calif., RAND Corporation, 1961

HANRAHAN, GENE Z., *The Communist Struggle in Malaya,* New York, International Secretariat, Institute of Pacific Relations, 1954

HARRISON, SELIG S., *India: the Most Dangerous Decades,* Princeton, New Jersey, Princeton University Press, 1960

HERZ, MARTIN FLORIAN, *A Short History of Cambodia,* New York, F. A. Praeger, 1958

HOSKINS, HALFORD L., *The Middle East,* New York, Macmillan, 1954

HOUART, PIERRE, *La Penetration Communiste au Congo,* Brussels, Centre-de-Documentation Internationale, 1960

HUMBARACI, ARSLAN, *Middle East Indictment,* London, R. Hale, 1958

KENNEDY, MALCOLM DUNCAN, *A History of Communism in East Asia,* New York, F. A. Praeger, 1957

KINGSBURY, PATRICIA AND ROBERT C., *Afghanistan and the Himalayan States,* Garden City, New York, Doubleday, 1960

KIRKPATRICK, E. M., *Target the World: Communist Propaganda Activities in 1955,* New York, Macmillan, 1956

KURZMAN, DAN, *Kishi and Japan: The Search for the Sun,* New York, Ivan Obolensky, 1960

LAQUEUR, WALTER ZE'EV, *Communism and Nationalism in the Middle East,* New York, F. A. Praeger, 1956

——, *Nasser's Egypt,* London, Weidenfeld and Nicolson, 1957

——, *The Soviet Union and the Middle East,* New York, F. A. Praeger, 1959

LENIN, V. I., *Selected Works,* New York, International Publishers, 1943

MAHAN, JACK WILLIAM GRACE, *Spearhead in Malaya,* London, P. Davies, 1959

MAO TSE-TUNG, *Selected Works,* New York, International Publishers, 1954

MARX, KARL, *Selected Works,* ed. V. Adoratsky, New York, International Publishers

MEEKER, ODEN, *The Little World of Laos,* New York, Scribner, 1959

MITRANY, DAVID, *Marx and the Peasants,* Chapel Hill, University of North Carolina Press, 1951

MOREL, EDMUND D., *King Leopold's Rule in Africa,* London, William Heinemann, Ltd., 1904

MURDOCH, JAMES, *History of Japan,* London, Paul, Trench, Trubner, 1925-26

NASSER, GAMAL ABDEL, *The Philosophy of the Revolution,* Buffalo, Smith, Keynes & Marshall, 1959

NKRUMAH, KWAME, *Ghana; the Autobiography of Kwame Nkrumah,* New York, Nelson, 1957

NU, U, *The People Win Through* (a play), New York, Taplinger Publishing Co., 1957

OVERSTREET, GENE D., AND WINDMILLER, MARSHALL, *Communism in India,* Berkeley, University of California Press, 1959

OVERSTREET, HARRY AND BONARO, *What We Must Know About Communism,* New York, W. W. Norton, 1958

PAUKER, GUY J., *Current Communist Tactics in Indonesia,* Santa Monica, Calif., Rand Corporation, 1961

PYE, LUCIAN W., *Guerrilla Communism in Malaya,* Princeton, New Jersey, Princeton University Press, 1956

RAVINES, EUDOCIO, *The Yenan Way,* New York, Scribner, 1951

REISCHAUER, EDWIN OLDFATHER, *Japan, Past and Present,* New York, Knopf, 1946

———, *The United States and Japan,* Cambridge, Harvard University Press, 1957

ROMULO, CARLOS PENA, *Crusade in Asia; Philippine Victory,* New York, John Day Co., 1955

———, AND GRAY, MARVIN M., *The Magsaysay Story,* New York, John Day Co., 1956

SAMPSON, ANTHONY, *The Treason Cage,* London, William Heinemann, Ltd., 1958

SCAFF, ALVIN H., *The Philippine Answer to Communism,* Stanford, Calif., Stanford University Press, 1955

SETON-WATSON, HUGH, *From Lenin to Malenkov: The History of World Communism,* New York, Praeger, 1953

STALIN, J. V., *Works,* Moscow, Foreign Languages Publishing House, 1949, 1952, 1953, 1954, 1955

STEINBERG, DAVID J., *Cambodia,* New Haven, Conn., HRAF Press, 1959

STEINER, H. ARTHUR (ed.), *Maoism; a Sourcebook,* Los Angeles, University of California at Los Angeles, 1952

STERLING, THOMAS L., *Stanley's Way,* New York, Atheneum, 1960

ST. JOHN, ROBERT, *The Boss; the Story of Gamal Abdel Nasser,* New York, McGraw-Hill, 1960

TANHAM, GEORGE K., *Communist Revolutionary Warfare; the Vietminh in Indochina,* New York, F. A. Praeger, 1961

THOMPSON, VIRGINIA, AND ADLOFF, RICHARD, *The Left-Wing in Southeast Asia,* New York, Sloane, 1950

TRAGER, FRANK N. (ed.), *Marxism in Southeast Asia,* Stanford, Calif., Stanford University Press, 1959

TRUMBULL, ROBERT, *As I See India,* New York, W. Sloane Associates, 1956

TURNBULL, COLIN M., *The Lonely African,* New York, Simon & Schuster, 1962

VIRAVONG, MAHA SILA, *History of Laos,* New York, U.S. Joint Publications Research Service, 1958

WALKER, RICHARD L., *China Under Communism: The First Five Years,* New Haven, Yale University Press, 1955

WAR, WILLIAM ERNEST FRANK, *A Short History of Ghana,* London, New York, Longmans, Green, 1957

ZIADEH, N. A., *Syria and Lebanon,* London, Ernest Benn, 1957

PERIODICALS

The Reporter, Newsweek, Atlantic Monthly, Pacific Affairs, Asian Survey (University of California), *Far Eastern Survey, New Republic, Commonweal, Saturday Evening Post, Time, Spectator* (London), *New Statesman* (London), *Encounter* (London), *Commentary, New York Times Magazine,*

New Leader, World Marxist Review, New Times (Moscow), International Affairs (Moscow), Drum (Africa), African Communist (London), Communism and Africa (London), Africa Opinion (London), Washington University Magazine (St. Louis), U.S. News & World Report, Foreign Affairs, American Universities Field Staff Reports, Problems of Communism (Washington, D.C.), Problems of Peace and Socialism (Prague), Current History, Nation's Business, Africa Report, The Economist (London), America, U.S. Department of State Bulletin

NEWSPAPERS & WIRE AGENCIES

Washington Post, New York Herald Tribune, New York Times, Washington Star, Chicago Daily News, Wall Street Journal, Christian Science Monitor, Sunday Telegraph (London), Times (London), Pravda, Izvestia, Rude Pravo (Prague), People's Daily (Peking), Associated Press, United Press International, North American Newspaper Alliance, Le Monde (Paris), Le Figaro (Paris)

SPECIAL REPORTS

U.S. Department of State documents: Soviet World Outlook; The Sino-Soviet Economic Offensive in the Less Developed Countries; Communist Economic Policy in the Less Developed Areas; World Strength of the Communist Party Organizations; A Threat to Peace (and supplement); North Korea: A Case Study in the Techniques of Takeover

U.S. Information Agency: Communist Propaganda Activities in South Asia, in Korea and Japan, in the Arab States and Israel, in the Aegean Area, in Africa; Twelve Years of Communist Broadcasting, 1948-1959; Growth of Book Publishing in the Sino-Soviet Bloc; World Wide Distribution of Radio Receiver Sets

Congressional reports: United States Foreign Policy—prepared for the Committee on Foreign Relations, U.S. Senate, August 1959 and March 1961; Foreign Assistance Activities of the Communist Bloc and their Implications for the United States—prepared for the Special Committee to Study the Foreign Aid Program, U.S. Senate, March 1957

Business reports: The Communist World as Customer and Competitor to the U.S. Businessman (Business International)

Labor reports: Free Trade Unions in the Fight for African Freedom (International Confederation of Free Trade Unions)

INDEX

568 /

USSR *see* Union of Soviet Socialist
Republics (USSR)
Uwaidi, Mohammed Hassan al, 240

Vargas, Jesús, 412–13
Vichit Vadakarn, Luang, 461
Vietnam, North, 4, 10, 518–26,
528–37, 539
Vietnam, South, 518–46
Virius, Joseph, 142
Vo Nguyen Giap, 524, 532
Voloven Kommadam, 512

Wada, Haruo, 427
Wakamba (tribe), 56
Wang Chen, 376–77, 381
Weizsacker, Baron Ernst von, 172
Welensky, Sir Roy, 58
Winfield, Gerald F., 553
Woodhull, S., 455

World Federation of Democratic
Youth (WFDY), 30
World Federation of Trade Unions
(WFTU), 139, 146

Xerxes, 257

Yakoviev, Vladimir G., 298
Yamaguchi, Eisaku, 434
Yannakis, Georges, 143
Yemen, 176–82
Yenan Way, 7–11, 13, 14, 216, 547,
549
Yong, Stephen, 456

Zahir Shah, King Mohammed (Af-
ghanistan), 273, 282
Zhdanov, Andrei, 35
Zuberi, M. H. H., 301

ABOUT THE AUTHOR

DAN KURZMAN has been a foreign correspondent for about fifteen years, and during that time has written or broadcast from almost every major country in Europe, the Middle East, Africa, and Asia. At present, although based in Washington, he is traveling extensively in Latin America as a staff correspondent for the *Washington Post.*

Mr. Kurzman's first assignment was as correspondent for the Paris Bureau of International News Service, and he later became feature editor of the Marshall Plan Information Division in Paris. From 1950 to 1952 he served as Middle East correspondent for the National Broadcasting Company, covering such events as the assassination of Jordan's King Abdullah, the Iranian oil crisis, the Black Saturday anti-British riots in Cairo, the first nationalist riots in Tunis, and the Arab-Israeli border disputes.

In 1953 he made a year-long, village-to-village tour of North Africa, the Middle East, and Asia—from Casablanca to Tokyo. His articles appeared in several major newspapers and magazines.

In 1954 he returned to Tokyo as Far East bureau chief of the Mc-Graw-Hill World News Service. In 1958 he visited Russia, entering by an unusual route—from Kabul, Afghanistan, across the Hindukush Mountains to Tashkent. Later in 1958 he went back to the Middle East to cover the landing of American Marines in Beirut, Lebanon, for the *Washington Post,* following up this assignment with a six-month overland tour of Black Africa, also for the *Post.*

Early in 1959 Mr. Kurzman returned to the United States to work on *Kishi and Japan* (published in 1960), but soon went back to Africa to cover the Congo crisis for various publications, as well as to report on nationalist uprisings in other African countries.